FIFTY WHO MADE THE DIFFERENCE

FIFTY WHO MADE THE DIFFERENCE

Preface by Lee Eisenberg
Foreword by Phillip Moffitt

AN ESQUIRE PRESS BOOK

VILLARD BOOKS
NEW YORK
1984

Preface and Foreword Copyright © 1984 by Esquire Press

All rights reserved under International and Pan-American Copyright Conventions. Published in the United States by Villard Books, a division of Random House, Inc., New York, and simultaneously in Canada by Random House of Canada Limited, Toronto.

The text was previously published in the December 1983 issue of *Esquire*. Copyright © 1983 by Esquire Associates.

Library of Congress Cataloging in Publication Data
Main entry under title:

Fifty who made the difference.
"An Esquire Press Book."
1. United States—Biography—Addresses, essays,
lectures. I. Eisenberg, Lee, 1946–
CT220.F54 1984   920'.073   84-40176
ISBN 0-394-53912-5

Manufactured in the United States of America

9 8 7 6 5 4 3 2

First Edition

CONTENTS

CHAMPIONS
SETTING THE STANDARDS

EPILOGUES
THE NAMELESS, THE FACELESS, THE MILLIONS

FOREWORD:
THE POWER OF THE INDIVIDUAL

IN THESE DAYS OF LARGE, IMPERSONAL INSTITUTIONS WHERE ALL BEHAVIOR CAN BE classified through statistical projection and scientific analysis, we sometimes forget that, at the core, all that comprises any society is a network of individual action.

The individuals profiled in this book have not been chosen because they were perfect models of human potential, or even because their actions were admirable in all respects, but because in the final analysis they made a *positive* difference. I am mindful that their deeds may sometimes assume heroic proportions. But the writers of the profiles are critically minded journalists, not toastmasters; their presentation of these individuals is not a wartless reconstruction of achievements; it is a measured, hard-eyed accounting of specific contributions as they were.

You will not be familiar with every one of these people; in some instances, you may not even agree that what they did was important. Nor will you always like what is said about them. You will, however, find yourself drawn into a process that every healthy society must experience—a continuing debate about its ongoing history to discern which events mattered and how they occurred. This is an organic process of redefining values and exploring new interpretations of the recent and not-so-recent past. And this is the only way for a society to reach a consensus from which a vision of and for the future can emerge.

As you read about these people and their accomplishments one common characteristic will be clear: for some time each was able to humanize the institutions mankind uses to regulate twentieth-century civilization.

It is this attempt—to change our institutions and the common tenets of how we govern ourselves, construct buildings, allocate resources, regard race and ethnic background, run our businesses—that engages us in a constant struggle for a better civilization. And so it should be. Institutions by definition become entrenched and, in self-absorption, lose their underlying common sense, their human origins. All too often we feel overwhelmed by the system in place and lose the impetus to act from our personal convictions. We forget that things can change for the better by the power of individual initiative. The men and women portrayed here, for all their human faults, were able, at least temporarily, to act out of their beliefs and feelings.

It is incumbent on each of us to live our lives by this same dictate and never to forget, even in the midst of hero worship, that no one is infallible and that no one deserves our blind or uncritical allegiance. This is the balancing, the ebb and flow between individuals and institutions that makes for a healthy society. It is a difficult balance to achieve. On the one hand, our society can be justly criticized for relying on individual initiative to solve problems best handled collectively and for depending excessively on the image of the hero. On the other hand, if we feel helpless we never attempt to make a difference. Similarly, to be suspicious of those who *would* try is to prevent others from having a chance to matter.

What gives our society its life and breadth is the communal and often unspoken effort by certain members to make it a just and enlightened one. A successful society is built on individual effort that dares to go against convention, to think big, to believe that all is possible, to persevere without reinforcement, to create spontaneously. The individuals profiled here made that effort, and I think you will find their collective story a celebration of the best in American life.

—Phillip Moffitt
Editor-in-Chief
Esquire

PREFACE

THE WRITING THAT COMPRISES FIFTY WHO MADE THE DIFFERENCE WAS COMMISSIONED
to celebrate *Esquire* magazine's Fiftieth Anniversary. The enterprise, which
lasted nearly two years, was to select fifty subjects who made critical contributions to a wide range of American activities. This in itself was no small task.
The editors of *Esquire* and members of its family of contributors, along with academics and other observers of the American scene, were invited to suggest
those men and women who were the principal shapers of our politics, society,
and culture over the past half century. From a list of more than six hundred
nominees, the editors of the project culled the final fifty.

Completing the puzzle by matching each of the subjects to a notable contemporary author was just as intriguing. To find the best fit, we chose among
journalists and fiction writers, historians and essayists, literary lions and literary
upstarts. These were the craftspeople whose mosaic would depict the color and
meaning of the American experience from 1933 to 1983.

The result is neither a portfolio of formal portraits nor a collection of life
drawings. The pieces are not, strictly speaking, biographies. But, collectively,
they are a chorus of voices on a variety of provocative themes. They are explo-
rations of ideas as occasioned by the lives of the men and women whose efforts
defined, or redefined, our national legacy.

True to their diversity, the contributors to this book present themselves in a multitude of styles. Saul Bellow's tribute to Franklin D. Roosevelt is in the form of a literary memoir. Tom Wolfe's reflections on the computer age is a work of contemporary reporting that will stand as enduring social history. Norman Mailer uses his subject, Jacqueline Kennedy Onassis, to deliver a hard-edged commentary on America's obsession with celebrity. Still, they and the other contributors made certain to bring to life the characters who are the focus of this book, and they do so by bringing them forward into the sure light cast by the writer's intellect.

Rarely, if ever, have so many eminent writers contributed original essays on a single theme. In appreciation of their efforts, and in admiration for their work, we dedicate this book to them.

—LEE EISENBERG
Editor
Esquire

TRAILBLAZERS

Extending Our Horizons

THEY WERE THE PIONEERS WHO LED US TO THE FRINGE OF DISCOVERIES. THE Trailblazers guided us through what were hitherto blind alleys. When they reached their destinations, when they planted their flags, miracles and surprises were loosed. The Trailblazers led us to new and sometimes unthinkable realizations. They got there first.

Before Jonas Salk, American cities, their citizens and nightmares, were visited by fear of a dread disease. Poliomyelitis mostly afflicted children; it seemingly came in the night, beginning as a petty ache and ending a crippled lifetime later. After Salk, the haunting was lifted.

Before Neil Armstrong, and before the millions of man-hours that went into the planning, no human had ever planted foot on ground beyond this planet. Then, on the (earthly) evening of July 21, 1969, as this world watched on television, Armstrong's boots touched the surface of the moon. And he spoke the words that will be forever among mankind's most enthralling.

Before George Gallup, Americans made their fortunes, elected their leaders, and decided just about everything else on the basis of good, old-fashioned instinct. We acted on the *hunch*. After Gallup, after his queries, his samples, his endless supply of sharpened pencils and answer forms, the hunch had been quantified nearly out of existence. Today we know our profit and loss before we set up shop, and we know the election night victor before the polling places open. We have come to believe that if we can't measure it, we probably don't need it.

So it went with the Trailblazers. Before Jackie Robinson, major league baseball, along with other sports and other activities of life, was a white man's game. Then, as fast as you could say his name, all that changed.

Before Oswald Avery, the living cell was a distant mystery—as remote as the moon. We probed, but its meaning was sealed. After Avery, the cell's complex secrets came pouring out—genetic research would come to be recognized as one of this century's great contributions to understanding.

The Trailblazers got there first. Alfred Kinsey opened the door to let sex out into the sunlight. Jack Kerouac traveled a thousand highways, always a mile or two ahead of the countless other seekers of alternative ways. John Rock, along with fellow researchers, perfected a pill that profoundly affected our manners and morals. Richard Nixon led us to renewed relations with one of the world's largest and most mysterious powers. Today snapshots are taken by American tourists who stand on the Great Wall as if they were on a horizon no more lost than Disneyland.

The Trailblazers danced on pivot points. We met up with them at the fork in the road. And it was there, as most of us waited, they studied, schemed, tested, and figured things out—until it became fully clear that it was this way, not that, and off we went.

—L. E.

The Summer Before Salk

CHARLES L. MEE JR.

THE FIRST SYMPTOM WAS THE ACHE AND THE STIFFNESS IN THE LOWER BACK AND neck. Then general fatigue. A vaguely upset stomach. A sense of dissociation. Fog closing in. A ringing in the ears. Dull, persistent aching in the legs. By then the doctor would have been called, the car backed out of the garage for the trip to the hospital; by then the symptoms would be vivid: fierce pain, as though the nerves in every part of the body were being probed by a dentist's device without Novocain. All this took a day, twenty-four hours.

At the hospital, nurses would command the wheelchair—crowds in the hallway backing against the walls as the group panic made its way down the hall to the examining room, where, amid a turmoil of interns, orderlies, and nurses, the head nurse would step up and pronounce instantly, with authority, "This boy has polio," and the others would draw back, no longer eager to examine the boy, as he was laid out on a cart and wheeled off to the isolation ward while all who had touched him washed their hands.

Poliomyelitis is a disease caused by a viral agent that invades the body by way of the gastrointestinal tract, where it multiplies and, on rare occasions, travels via blood and/or nervous pathways to the central nervous system, where it attacks the motor neurons of the spinal cord and part of the brain. Motor neurons are destroyed. Muscle groups are weakened or destroyed. A healthy fifteen-year-old boy of 160 pounds might lose seventy or eighty pounds in a week.

As long ago as the turn of the century doctors agreed that it was a virus, but not everyone believed that the doctors knew. One magazine article had said it was related to diet. Another article said it was related to the color of your eyes. Kids at summer camp got it, and when a boy at a camp in upstate New York got it in the summer of 1953, a health officer said no one would be let out of the camp till the polio season was over. Someone said that public gatherings had been banned altogether in the Yukon. In Montgomery, Alabama, that summer the whole city broke out; more than eighty-five people caught it. An emergency was declared; and in Tampa, Florida, a twenty-month-old boy named Gregory died of it. Five days later, his eight-year-old sister, Sandra, died of it while their mother was in the delivery room giving birth to a new baby.

The newspapers published statistics every week. As of the Fourth of July, newspapers said there were 4,680 cases in 1953—more than there had been to that date in 1952, reckoned to be the worst epidemic year in medical history, in which the final tally had been 57,628 cases. But none of the numbers were reliable; odd illnesses were added to the total, and mild cases went unreported. Nonetheless, the totals were not the most terrifying thing about polio. What was terrifying was that, like any plague, you never knew where or when it might strike. It was more random than roulette—only it did seem to strike children disproportionately, and so it was called infantile paralysis—and it made parents crazy with anguish.

The rules were: Don't play with new friends, stick with your old friends whose germs you already have; stay away from crowded beaches and pools, especially in August; wash hands before eating; never use another person's eating utensils or toothbrush or drink out of the same Coke bottle or glass; don't bite another person's hands or fingers while playing or (for small children) put another child's toys in your mouth; don't pick up anything from the ground, especially around a beach or pool; don't have any tooth extractions during the summer; don't get overtired or strained; if you get a headache, tell your mother.

Nevertheless, kids caught it. In the big city hospitals, kids were stacked like cordwood in the corridors. Carts and wheelchairs congested the aisles. The dominant odor was of disinfectant. The dominant taste was of alcohol-disinfected thermometers. In the Catholic hospitals, holy medals and scapulars covered the motionless arms and hands of the children. On the South Side of Chicago, a mother cried just to see the name above the door of the place where her child was taken: the Home for Destitute Crippled Children. In some places, parents were allowed to visit their children only once a week—not because of any special fact about polio, only because that was how children's wards were run in 1953. A child in bed with polio never forgot the sound made in the corridor by his mother's high-heeled shoes.

Injections of gamma globulin were prescribed for those who had not yet caught it. Certain insurance against measles, gamma globulin did not prevent catching polio, but it did seem to minimize the crippling effects. It was in short supply. Injections were given only to pregnant women and those under the age of thirty who had had a case of polio in the immediate family—or to prevent the spread of an epidemic. The precious supplies were placed under the administration of the incorruptible Office of Defense Mobilization.

In Illinois, rumors spread of bootleg gamma globulin. If you were lucky enough to qualify for a shot, you had to endure the humiliation that went with it: you had to pull down your pants and say which buttock would take the inch-long needle. To buy off your pride, the doctor gave you a free lollipop.

When the epidemic broke out in Montgomery, Alabama, the story was that 620 volunteer doctors, nurses, housewives, and military personnel administered sixty-seven gallons of gamma globulin (worth $625,000), thirty-three thousand inch-long needles, and thirty-three thousand lollipops. In New York, parents picketed the health department for twenty-seven hours to get it for their children. In some places people said that parents were bribing local officials for vials of gamma globulin. At the same time, an article in the June issue of *Scientific American* reported there was doubt that the stuff was worth a damn. *The New York Times* reported that one little girl came down with polio within forty-eight hours of getting a gamma globulin shot.

In the hospitals, meanwhile, children—shrouded in white gowns and white sheets, nursed by women in white surgical masks, white dresses starched to the smooth brittleness of communion wafers—lay in dreadful silence, listening to the faint whispers of medical conversations on the far side of drawn white curtains, the quiet shush of soft-soled nurses' shoes, and the ever-present sound of water in a basin, the ceaseless washing of hands.

Parents stood at a distance—six feet from the bed—wearing white gowns and white masks.

One boy's uncle gave him a black plastic Hopalong Cassidy bank when he was in the isolation ward. After the customary two-to-three-week stay there, after the fevers passed, he was moved into the regular children's ward. On the way, the nurses discarded the contaminated bank along with its savings.

Some children were not told what they had (lest it be too dangerous a shock to them), and so they discovered for themselves. One boy acquired from his visitors the biggest collection of comic books he had ever had. When he dropped one, he jumped out of bed to pick it up, crumpled in a heap, and found he couldn't get up off the floor again.

Some would recover almost entirely. Some would die. Some would come through unable to move their legs, or unable to move arms and legs; some could move nothing but an arm, or nothing but a few fingers and their eyes. Some would leave the hospital with a cane, some with crutches, crutches and steel leg braces, or in wheelchairs—white-faced, shrunken, with frightened eyes, light blankets over their legs. Some would remain in an iron lung—a great, eighteen-hundred-pound, casketlike contraption, like the one in which the woman in the magic show (her head and feet sticking out of either end) is sawed in half. The iron lung hissed and sighed rhythmically, performing artificial respiration by way of air pressure.

Some moaned. Some cried. Some nurtured cynicism. Some grew detached. Some were swept away by ungovernable cheerfulness. Rarely did anyone scream in rage, however common the feeling. All were overpowered, all were taught respect—for the unseen powers of nature, the smallness of human aspiration, the capacity for sudden and irrevocable change, the potential of chance.

As it happened, in the spring of 1953, Dr. Jonas Salk, an insignificant-seeming fellow with big ears, a receding hairline, and a pale complexion, had published a paper in a scholarly journal, reporting that he had induced the formation of antibodies against three types of polio viruses. He hadn't quite fully tested it, he hastened to say, but he had tried it on 161 children and adults with no ill effects. When newspapers got hold of the story, parents phoned their family doctors. Those with medical connections tried to find a way to get to Salk. Salk became famous in an instant—and from the moment of his first announcement, such an outpouring of hope and gratitude attached to him that he came to stand, at once, as the doctor-benefactor of our times.

During the summer of 1953, reporters called him weekly for news of progress. His vaccine, he explained, was a dead-virus vaccine. He devastated the virus with formaldehyde and then whipped it up into an emulsion with mineral oil to fortify it, and in this way he thought he had something that, when it was injected into a person, would stimulate a person's natural defense mechanisms to produce antibodies. However, he was not able to hurry the testing process along. In May 1953, he expanded the test to include more than seven hundred children. And not until the spring of 1954 were more than a million children inoculated in a large field trial financed by the March of Dimes, and, as the papers said, the "total conquest of polio" was in sight. Within the next half dozen years, the Salk vaccine reduced the incidence of polio by perhaps 95 percent, preventing maybe as many as three hundred thousand cases of polio in the United States.

Yet Salk's triumph did not last for long. The March of Dimes, in its own need for publicity and contributions, lionized Salk mercilessly—and his fellow doctors soon got tired of his fame. He was not—and never has been since—invited to join the National Academy of Sciences. And soon enough, Salk's colleagues began to point out that Salk, after all, had made no basic scientific discovery. Many people had been working on a preventive for polio. The basic discovery had been made by three fellows at Harvard—Doctors Enders, Weller, and Robbins—who had shown that a polio virus could be grown in certain tissue cultures of primate cells. Before the Harvard finding no one had been able to make a vaccine because no one had been able to cultivate the virus in test-tube cultures. After the Harvard finding, Salk's vaccine was mere applied science. (The Harvard doctors got the Nobel; Salk did not.) Salk had just pulled together the work of others. And some of the others thought Salk had been premature in publishing his paper, that he was rushing his vaccine into the world incautiously. Then, in 1955, a batch of live virus slipped out, and 260 children came down with polio from having taken the Salk vaccine or having contact with persons who had taken it.

Meanwhile, even as Salk's vaccine was eliminating polio in the United States, it was already obsolescent. Dr. Albert Sabin, a researcher who told interviewers that work was his recreation, was coming up with a new vaccine. His vaccine used an attenuated (that is to say, live) virus with special properties to stimulate the production of antibodies, and it seemed to offer immunity for much longer than Salk's vaccine, possibly for many years. This virus retained the capacity to multiply in the intestinal tract, thus passing from someone who had received the vaccine to someone who hadn't and inoculating them as well. The Sabin vaccine could be stored indefinitely in deep-freeze units; it could be taken orally and produced cheaply. It was given extensive tests in 1958 and 1959. By 1962 it had replaced the Salk vaccine almost entirely in the United States and most of the rest of the industrialized world. Although Sabin never got the Nobel either, in the next two decades his vaccine prevented perhaps two to three million cases of polio.

But Sabin's happiness was not uncomplicated, either. Though no one likes to mention it—and it does not diminish the good of the vaccine, since the odds are only "one in six or seven million"—sometimes a Sabin inoculation would be, as one specialist in polio has said, "associated with" a case of polio: the attenuated vaccine can never be as absolutely safe as the dead-virus vaccine.

Moreover, while the Sabin vaccine has eliminated polio in most of the temperate-climate countries where it's been used, it has not done so well elsewhere: in the Third World, it turns out, polio has not been ended at all. There, uncertain conditions of refrigeration cause the Sabin vaccine to break down. For some reason, too—perhaps because people in parts of the Third World carry other viruses in their systems that interfere with the polio vaccine—some inoculations don't take. The Sabin vaccine does not work with just one dose but requires several doses, which involves massive vaccination of a community. This has been accomplished in Cuba and Brazil but the logistics are staggering in many Third World countries. Despite the inoculation programs of the past two decades, about 375,000 people come down with polio every year in the Third World: seven and a half million in the past twenty years.

Some highly refined ironies: At the moment, conditions of sanitation and hygiene are so bad in the Third World that many children come down with polio before the age of two. Fortunately, however, at that age polio comes and goes often without leaving a trace of paralysis. As physical standards of living improve, children will not get polio at such early ages: they will get it instead when they are teenagers, when the paralytic rate is higher. So as health conditions improve in the Third World polio may well increase, increasing the need for vaccination.

Some say now that the Salk vaccine will make a comeback, that it will work where the Sabin vaccine has not worked—that the Salk vaccine will hold up better under the conditions of Third World refrigeration, that there is even some indication that a more potent Salk-type vaccine might require only one or two inoculations. Recent tests by the Israeli government in the Gaza Strip seem to make a case for the Salk vaccine. A French pharmaceutical company is manufacturing a Salk-type vaccine that also vaccinates against diphtheria, tetanus, and whooping cough. It may be that Salk will become famous again.

These days, as polio continues to occur in the Third World, most of those who gather at the special conferences on the disease feel that the old Salk vaccine—which has continued to be used in some of the smaller European countries—ought to be brought back on a large scale. Most of them feel not that the Salk should replace the Sabin but rather, given everyone's doubts, that both vaccines are needed, in different circumstances, or perhaps in combination.

But when the two grand old men of the fight against polio, Salk and Sabin themselves, appear at these conferences, they disagree. Each man—as modest and thoughtful and impressive as he is in private—takes on a missionary zeal in public, strutting and scrapping for preeminence, each arguing for the ultimate superiority of his own vaccine. Sabin argues politics: the administration of his vaccine must be improved. Salk argues effectiveness is possible with fewer doses with his vaccine and warns of live-virus–vaccine-associated polio. At one such recent encounter, Salk tried everything, even charm and banter, to win over the audience; he and Sabin agreed on only one thing, he said with a skilled debater's smile, "that only one vaccine is necessary."

And so the two renowned old doctors go on grappling with each other and with themselves, speaking not only of the progress of science and the triumph of reason but also—like those of us who got polio in the summer of 1953 and have toted around a couple of canes ever since—of the equivocalness of greatness, the elusiveness of justice, the complexity of success, the persistence of chance.

JONAS SALK *was born on October 28, 1914, in New York City, the oldest of three brothers. His father worked in the Garment District, and the family lived in a tenement at 106th Street and Madison Avenue.*

His first words were "Dirt, dirt."

To his schoolmates Salk was a person of little importance. A thin, small-boned child, untalented at games and not gifted in class, he was tolerated but not sought after.

His mother expected great things of him. As for Salk himself: "I knew I was competent. I knew I had proved it by achieving that which I was supposed to achieve, time and time again." He recalled feeling that "someday I shall grow up and do something in my own way, without anyone telling me how." Thus his childhood became "a period of patient waiting."

For many years he assumed he would become a lawyer.

Although he went to medical school, he had no intention of practicing medicine. He was interested in biology, chemistry, and lab work; he wanted to do research.

He served his internship at New York's Mount Sinai Hospital. Out of 250 who applied to the Mt. Sinai program, only a dozen were accepted. Salk, a doctor in charge remembered, turned out to be "the most stable young man in the place. With all the tensions and pressures . . . the excitement about war and politics, and the need to put the patients' interests ahead of everything else, not many were able to remain calm at all times. Yet nobody ever saw Jonas ruffled. . . . You told him to do something and he got it done. It got done and so did a dozen things you hadn't thought of."

Mt. Sinai's residents and interns elected Salk president of the house staff because, said a superior, "he was the best damn talker in the bunch, had the most common sense and the most charm."

He met his wife, Donna Lindsay, at Woods Hole, Massachusetts. She was on vacation; he was working in a laboratory. She found him a fascinating conversationalist, not at all the stereotype of the introverted scientist. "There was no shell in evidence," she recalled.

Mrs. Salk, a Phi Beta Kappa from Smith, came from a background considerably more refined than her husband's—a discrepancy that caused comment in both families.

In their third year of marriage the Salks moved to a farmhouse on the outskirts of Ann Arbor, Michigan, where they cooked on a wood-burning stove and cultivated a garden. They had three sons, Peter, Darrell, and Jonathan.

When working with children, he would smile into their eyes until they smiled back. He refused to inoculate any child who cried at the sight of a needle; he inoculated his own children while they were asleep.

While developing his polio vaccine he worked seven days a week, often for twenty-four hours at a stretch. At home, when his wife was talking to him about family matters, she could tell that his mind was back in the lab. "Why, Jonas," she would say, "you're not listening to me at all." Salk smiled: "My dear, I'm giving you my undevoted attention."

Before mass inoculations with his polio vaccine began, he tested the drug on his wife and children and on himself. In 1953 he gave his assurance that he would be "personally responsible" for the safe outcome of widespread vaccination.

He received no royalties from the sale of his vaccine. He was nominated for a Nobel Prize but didn't win it.

Salk saw calamity in his research triumph because he knew that his colleagues in the biological sciences were offended by publicity and would hold him accountable for it. "The worst tragedy that could have befallen me was my success," he said later. "I knew right away that I was through—cast out."

In 1963 Salk founded the Salk Institute for Biological Sciences in La Jolla,

California, of which he is director and a fellow. "I couldn't possibly have become a member of this institute if I hadn't founded it myself," he said.

Much of his later work has involved cancer research. His new book, Anatomy of Reality: Merging of Intuition and Reason, *discusses man's evolution as a problem solver. According to a friend, Salk "hasn't changed. He still hates to be told what to do . . . and can't stand being wrong. He still hates to antagonize people. He still hates to face unpleasantness head on. He still believes everything will turn out his way—the right way—in the end, and he still ducks, swerves, and does Immelmann turns while waiting for opposition to expend itself. His susceptibility to pain remains limitless, but so does his ability to endure and outlive it."*

Alfred Kinsey: The Patron Saint of Sex

STANLEY ELKIN

NOTHING HUMAN WAS ALIEN TO HIM. ON THE OTHER HAND, NOTHING *ALIEN* WAS ALIEN to him. And he looked, in his brush cut, bow tie, and baggy suits, savvy as a high school coach in a small town, like a man with liquor on his breath. Though he didn't drink. Only to impress what he persisted in calling the "lower levels," only to put them at their ease, only for science, for the sake of the "sample." As, already in his late forties, he took instruction in cigarette smoking for the same reasons, as he altered his diction to suit the circumstances, all over you with argot or expertise, depending. But a little compromised, as out of sync as a white man's slam dunk or the razzle-dazzle chorea of a brother's salute—all hip handshake's fancy footwork. Patronizing, our patron saint of sex, obsessed, finally, as a scientist in Hawthorne—Chillingworth, Rappaccini's daughter's old man.

Yet, bother his methods, or sample either, that less than scientific, catch-as-catch-can collection of the impositioned, came back with the news—our sexual Founder. And this morning, on Donahue, Christians with books. Flogging biblical liberty on national TV, scriptural passion, positions, oral stuff, God's blessings on the marriage bed, on all the humpty kinky dumpty hymeneal frictions, his go-for-it opinions. Because it wasn't always as it is today, singles' bars uninvented, consenting adults, the Pill. Sexual dark age, lust's hairy palms. When one sat home nights or paid for it in bad neighborhoods. (Me, for example. An old boy from the old school. Driven to the whores. Sure. In 1948, on Labor Day, Sluggo drove Butch and me in Sluggo's uncle's Olds the fifty-odd miles from Chicago to Kankakee to nurse three beers and not one entire courage between us in the Railroad Tavern near the Illinois Central tracks until the bartender himself pressed the buzzer and sent us through the secret door. Surprised, once one became used to the railroad men in their bedticking overalls, that there were actually whores in whorehouses, girls in open shifts, casual as the loitering switchmen, firemen, and engineers, the girls old, most of them, as our mothers, and politely hustling sex like a box of candy, a bowl of fruit, as if, as if—as if there *were* no bad neighborhoods. So surprised and relieved and a little moved, too, by the gentle daguerreotype civilities there, the railroaders browsing newspapers, magazines. It could have been a barbershop.) When sex was a big deal and Petty's and Vargas's slim art-deco girls food for thoughts.

Queen Victoria dead forty-seven years when Alfred Charles Kinsey published *Sexual Behavior in the Human Male* in 1948, fifty-two years and still spinning when *Sexual Behavior in the Human Female* came out in 1953, and though the real effects wouldn't be felt for years, he'd pulled the shades and opened the closets, he'd cleared the cobwebs and aired the attics. He dusted, did windows, and it was the greatest, noisiest spring-cleaning sexuality ever had. But it's a Columbus notion finally, for-want-of-a-nail reasoning, the idea that a single man alters history. Rome wasn't built in a day and Kinsey never got anybody laid. History happens piecemeal, in add-ons, in incremental software integers and suffixions and adjunctives. By frill and circumstance and fringe benefit. It's this all-the-trimmings life we live, our starter-set condition, the world continually trading up. (Because only bad men change the world single-handed.) Yet if there'd never been a Kinsey, I'd never have seen Jacqueline Bisset's breasts, Jane Fonda's, Julie Andrews's, for God's sake. If there'd never been a Kinsey, there'd have been no personals in the classified columns of *The New York Review of Books.* MWM would have never found SWM, and most of us would have gone to our graves believing only models or show girls were these lovely flowers of meat under their clothes. (Because what he did, what he did *really*, once we took it all in—and it's still hard to take in—was to democratize flesh, return us to innocence by showing us guilt—Freud did the same but didn't have the numbers—transporting us back to the Garden itself perhaps, hitting us where we lived and breathed, our mutualized lust like a kind of cloud cover and parting our scandalous needs like a Red Sea.)

And if Kinsey himself seems to have been uninterested in sex except as a subject that could be measured (*his* subject, as communism was Joe McCarthy's, just that jealous; he even repudiated Freud, was out of sorts with Krafft-Ebing), it was only because he was a taxonomist, a measurer, a sexual census taker, trained as a biologist at Bowdoin and at Harvard's Bussey Institute where he began to collect the American Cynipidae—the gall wasp—a parasite whose larvae lived and fed in a bruised oak tissue it irritated into being—rather like a pearl growing an oyster—taking on twenty-eight different measurements, a collection to which he devoted almost twenty-five years of his life and that ran to over four million specimens before it was finally donated to the American Museum of Natural History after his death. But more sociologist than scientist and, finally, more evangel than either. (Because maybe it's different for people with data, maybe the data permits, even obliges them to fight back, maybe you question their data you question their honor. Maybe it wasn't thin skin or self-righteousness that made him impatient with his critics, that deflected his science and lent him the aspect of someone besieged or gave him this ancient-mariner mentality. It was almost like outrage, like someone trying to clear his name. He was certainly good enough at it, a real sweet talker. A friend of mine, Dr. Lee Robins, professor of sociology in psychiatry at Washington University, heard him at a round-table dinner at the annual meeting of the American Psychiatric Association in 1954. The subject was "Psychiatric Implications of Surveys on Sexual Behavior" and the famed psychiatrist, Karl Menninger, was one of the speakers. Hell, they were *all* famed psychiatrists: Kinsey's report had infuriated them; they questioned the reliability of a sample in which 75 percent of the 5,940 women represented had attended college and only 3 percent hadn't gone beyond grade school; they wanted to know, as Lionel Trilling and Margaret Mead and Reinhold Niebuhr did, where love had gone—and Kinsey told them. Lee remembers his speech—Kinsey never prepared a talk, he didn't even refer to notes—as a sermon, a barn burner, Kinsey, the avenging evangel, the John Brown of sexuality.) The studies that would become Kinsey's famous reports actually began as a noncredit, interdisciplinary marriage course offered by Indiana University in the late 1930s. (This was the age of Emily Post, of etiquette columns in the daily papers, of marriage manuals and all the soft instructions.) Asked by the university to coordinate the course and by the students to counsel them, he found that no formal statistical studies of human sexual activity existed, and he began to take data—histories—from the students themselves, to conduct extensive interviews about what people actually did, to themselves and each other, and gradually to codify his questions. Ultimately, each history would include between 350 and 521 items in face-to-face interviews and would take anywhere from an hour and a half to three hours to administer, longer if necessary. His goal, never achieved, was to collect the sexual histories of one hundred thousand people. When he died, in 1956, there were eighteen thousand such histories in his files, eight thousand of which he had personally taken.

Which makes him a kind of intellectual Casanova, a scientific Don Juan, whatever the boozy, set-'em-up-Joe, torch song and torch singsong equivalencies are for the ear's voyeurism, all the scandals of the heart and head, all the gossip of the imagination. Because this wasn't even psychiatry, you see. It wasn't, that is, passive. Kinsey came on like a prosecuting attorney. Not did you, but *when* did you; not have you, but how *often* have you—all the D.A.'s bad cop/bad cop ploys and insinuations. That he got these people to talk at all—this was 1938, this was 1939, this was 1940 and all the 1940s; this was when men wore hats and women looked like telephone operators, their flower styles and print arrangements like those dumb sexual displays in nature, the bandings and colorful clutter on birds, say, who do not even know that what they are wearing is instinct and evolution, *that* innocent, *that* naive, up to their thighs in silk stocking, sitting on underwear, a buried treasure of corset and garter belt, all the comfy, invisible bondages of flesh, their curly hair submissively tucked under in pageboys like a sort of wimple—was largely a matter of flourishing his seventy-six-trombones science like the metallic glint of a flashed badge, using science, always *Science*, capitalized and italicized too, like a cop pounced from a speed trap, pulling them over to the side, badgering, hectoring, demanding —he was famous now, famous enough to be invited to talk to all sorts of groups, to chambers of commerce and Rotaries and Lions, to Sunday school classes, to cons in the pen, faggot Rush Street's boon companion, the guest of honor on Times Square (who cruised on the weekends: "I am Dr. Kinsey from Indiana University and I'm making a study of sex behavior. Can I buy you a drink?")— cooperation in the project, shooting for a 100 percent sample, turning the heat on, having *them* sing for *his* supper—Kinsey didn't accept fees for those talks he didn't prepare anyway, was paid off in low-down intimacies, other people's sex lives like the open stacks in the IU library, assuring them of perfect confidentiality, on his scientific honor like a high horse, offering his objectivity, pledging all his scientific, nonjudgmental markers and swearing he would never betray them. Which he never did. Talking in code to his Bloomington associates. Wardell Pomeroy, who assisted him and took almost as many histories as Kinsey, has described their cryptic shoptalk: "I might say to Kinsey, 'My last history liked Z better than Cm, although Go in Cx made him very er.' Translated: 'My last history liked intercourse with animals better than with his wife, but mouth-genital contact with an extramarital partner was very arousing.'" Talking in tongues, parlor-car stories like the periodic table of the elements, all the tender confidences of the nuclear age.

And the reports themselves as aseptic, as bland, the hot stuff cooled down into charts, graphs, the point something something decimals of neutrality, Masters and Johnson undreamed of yet, all *their* wired protocols of flesh, the special lenses uninvented, the down-and-dirty genitalia like locations, sets, special effects, the body's steamy skirmishes and star wars. (Dr. Masters himself the first to admit that if it weren't for Kinsey and Indiana University, Washington University would never have permitted Virginia Johnson and himself to have begun their astonishing investigations and observations of the physiology of sex—the timid Alphonse and Gaston of research, the *politics* of science, progress waiting on convention, red tape, green light and go-ahead while all that gets tested are the waters.) Published by the W. B. Saunders Company of Philadelphia, medical textbooks to the trade. And the trade had never seen anything like it, two hundred thousand copies in hardbound the first two months after the publication of *Sexual Behavior in the Human Male*, in January 1948, and a roughly equivalent number for the female volume almost six years later. (To date, 300,000 copies of the male volume have been sold, 227,000 of the female.) All this a blow for the First Amendment, free speech good for business, freedom of the press climbing, with a bullet. And maybe what he did for academic freedom and the First Amendment even more important than ever it was for love, the times easier now, more churlish but easier, less polite but easier, etiquette disappeared from the columns, and the streets too, I guess, and marriage-manual mentality all gone, sex by the numbers, but redress of grievance thriving, blooming, anger, outrage, and protest on the big board now and euphemism out of the portfolio altogether—it's a judgment call, this business of influence—and though this was barely perceived during Kinsey's lifetime, it *was* perceived, because that's what all the shouting was about, wasn't it, all that resistance. No in thunder just another weather forecast about your barbarians at the gate. So, it is to the everlasting glory of Indiana University and its president, Herman B. Wells, and its conservative trustees that they not only permitted Kinsey his research but stood foursquare behind it, continuing to pick up what it could of the Institute's expenses after controversy and criticism forced the Rockefeller Foundation to withdraw its support, the university hanging in there as a friend of the court in a suit brought by the Institute—the Institute for Sex Research was incorporated in 1947, Kinsey transferring the ownership of his files and assigning all royalties from the publication of his books to the new corporation—against the government to reclaim "pornographic materials" meant for the Institute's library (which has what are probably the largest holdings of erotica in the world) but seized in 1953 by Customs. The suit, settled after Kinsey's death in favor of the Institute, had a dynamite impact, all landmark and precedent, on the freedom of scientific research.

But what did he do for love?

Well, that's harder, because love had been doing okay. It just hadn't known it, is all, until Kinsey's flawed sample and scientific nonjudgmentals dropped by to reassure it.

For one, he discovered, if not homosexuality, then an incidence that until the publication of his books had been grossly underestimated. Kinsey had devised a "0–6 heterosexual to homosexual rating scale," which indicated that 13 percent of the male population was predominantly homosexual, with an additional 20 percent sitting on homosexual tendencies; the figures for women were lower but still high enough to suggest that putting people in prison for what had been regarded as deviant behavior was not only impractical but unfair.

Genius is something in the air. It makes waves. Its waves are principles, all the connected dots and applied mathematics of being, some what's-good-for-the-goose-is-good-for-the-gander cosmology, and every good lesson democratic. In a peculiar and even farfetched way, then, the waves that Kinsey made go beyond the bedroom to, well, death row. When the Supreme Court ruled that the death penalty was unconstitutional not because it was cruel and unusual punishment but because it was a punishment unequally applied, it was using exactly the argument Kinsey had used when he questioned the rationale for treating homosexuals as sex offenders. Justice as quantity, liberty returned to its nineteenth-century, utilitarian underpinnings.

Because in Kinsey's book sexuality was not so much a physiological phenomenon as a sociological one. (He never heard of G-spots but knew vaginas like the back of his hand and showed—something else the fuss was all about—that women were lusty as sailors, as capable of orgasm, bringing the spilled beans of their fevers and kindling points.) He knew this, I think, all his "science" notwithstanding, that S. D. Harvard had given him and that had fooled him into thinking that those four million gall wasps in his collection, like all the pressed and faded roses of love, represented something more than they did. Because it's as if Kinsey had studied not two sexes but four—upper and lower level males, upper and lower level females. People were stacked in these categories on the basis of their education; grade and high school were lower level, college upper level. (He interviewed blacks but left them, in those separate-but-equal days, to be considered in future studies. In a related way, though he was no bigot, he wouldn't hire an interviewer who had a hyphenated or Jewish name. He wouldn't hire foreigners or women or bachelors or people whose handwriting was not up to snuff, or anyone whose politics could be regarded as radical. He thought he was protecting the project, judgmental only here, at the base of things, assuming not *his* convictions but others', presuming their prejudices.) And his argument, generalized and oversimplified, goes, approximately, like this: The lower levels screw, the upper levels sublimate. Though Kinsey regarded all orgasms—which he called "total outlet"—as created equal whether brought on by intercourse, nocturnal emissions, masturbation, petting— fellatio was only a sort of heavy petting—getting it on with animals, or any other of the assorted sodomies, and admitted the vast differences between the preferences and practices of individuals within a social group, he seemed to imply that blondes didn't have more fun—only more total outlet—than the sweating and swarthy of earth did, your huddled masses yearning to breathe heavily.

Petting, for example. Nowhere, he claimed, were the social levels farther apart: "The lower educational levels see no sense in [petting]. They have nothing like this strong taboo against premarital intercourse and . . . accept it as natural and inevitable and a desirable thing. Lower level taboos are more often turned against an avoidance of intercourse . . . against any substitution for simple and direct coitus. It is just because petting . . . substitutes for actual intercourse, that it is considered a perversion by the lower level."

Forty-eight percent of the boys and 18 percent of the girls who wouldn't go on to college had had premarital intercourse before they were fifteen years old. Only 10 percent of the boys who would go to college had had sex. The figures for older teenagers were 98 percent for those who went only to grade school, 85 percent for those who went only to high school, and 66 percent for the college boys. "Between 16 and 20, the grade school group has 7 times as much premarital coitus as the college group" and "the college group derives 4 to 21 per cent of its premarital outlet from intercourse . . . the high school group derives 26 to 54 per cent . . . the grade school group derives . . . 40 to 70 per cent . . ."

They seem, Kinsey's LLMs and LLFs, to have been sexual snobs, put off, rather, by anything not the old in-and-out, not the old one-two, not the old biff-bam, thank-you-ma'am. Even the erotic stimulation provided by books or pictures did not, it would seem, sing to them. "The upper level male," Kinsey wrote in *Sexual Behavior in the Human Male*, "is aroused by a considerable variety of sexual stimuli," and then, in what itself may be one of the strangest and most frankly snobbish passages in the book, suggests that "the higher degree of eroticism in the upper level male may also be consequent on his greater capacity to visualize situations which are not immediately at hand." (A queer and clubby elitism here, a colorless—blacks were to come later—racism from the old freedom fighter.) But even the attitudes toward nudity along Kinsey's great chain of being were, well, revealing. About 90 percent of ULMs in his sample of 5,300 had sex nude, 66 percent of the men who went only through high school (MLMs?), but only 43 percent of those who didn't go past grade school. Kinsey's LLMs regarded nudity as "obscene," "deep kissing" as "dirty, filthy . . . a source of disease," "mouth-breast contacts . . . perversions." Only 4 percent of the males who went no further than grade school and 15 percent of those who did not go beyond high school ever had "mouth contacts with female genitalia" inside marriage, though 45 percent of those who went on to college did. "Lower social levels," Kinsey said, "rationalize their patterns of sexual behavior on the basis of what is natural or unnatural. Premarital intercourse is natural, and it is, in consequence, acceptable. Masturbation [though between 92 and 97 percent of the total sample had masturbated] is not natural, nor is petting as a substitute for intercourse, nor even petting as a preliminary to intercourse." Maybe they knew where it had been, yet it's odd, a contradiction, that Kinsey's natural man should have been the squeamish one, hung up on fastidy and reserve. (But, come to think of it, it's true, that Railroad Tavern Kankakee whore wouldn't kiss me. It wasn't extra, it was out of the question.) In the case of extramarital affairs the ULM had to play catch-up.

Among Kinsey's lower groups the extramarital experience was, at least in the first years of marriage, much higher than for the upper group. Forty-five percent of LLMs married before the age of twenty had affairs; by the time they were forty the percentage declines to 27 percent, by fifty to 19 percent. ULMs followed a different pattern, the lowest incidences being found in the youngest groups—between 15 and 20 percent. This figure increases steadily till, by the time they were fifty, 27 percent reported having affairs outside marriage. Clearly, I think, lower level males did not go out of town much.

Perhaps because 75 percent of the sample in *Sexual Behavior in the Human Female* had gone to college—the national average was only 13 percent at the time—the second book had much less the notion of the upstairs/downstairs dichotomies about it and seemed to offer a story of progressive sexual liberation, not leaps and bounds but a sense of the steady-state evolutionary. Since many of the histories were taken from women born in the last decade of the nineteenth century—the oldest of these women would not even have qualified for Social Security when the book was published in 1953—the statistics reinforce this. Less than half as many women born before 1900 had premarital intercourse as those born in the early 1900s; up to four times as many women born in the last century, compared with those born in the twentieth, were not naked when having sex. Tellingly, kiss and tellingly, of the 2,480 married women represented in the book, about a quarter of them had had extramarital affairs by the time they were forty, but the figure begins at 6 percent in the women's teens, rises to 9 percent in their twenties, and jumps to 26 percent by their thirties and early forties. One third of the women who'd had premarital sex had had it with from two to five partners. In a recent *Playboy* survey the mean number of partners for women was now 16.1, the median 7.8. Do you know where your children are?

This concern with classification, while scrupulous, lends to the books, and even to their abstracts, an almost infuriating quality of chart, distracting as the proper conjugation of verbs, the correct alignments between articles and endings. One wants, that is, to speak the language, suddenly, all at once, simply to discover one's human place. And if Kinsey did not make that possible, then at least he created the conditions; he cleared the throat, say, and permitted the first halting conversations to begin. It wasn't enough, of course. It could never have been enough. We shall not ever, locked in flesh, discover the wavelengths and frequencies or learn the sexual forks or know what is expected of us. One wants the answer to one question—How'm I doin'? One wants, that is, to measure dick. Because nothing alien is alien to *any* of us and sex is only the interesting fluids of the ego, the strange and lovely magnetism of the skin. It is that compulsive pushing of the centrifugals along the tumbling, degraded orbits of our lives.

———

ALFRED CHARLES KINSEY *was born on June 23, 1894, in Hoboken, New Jersey.*

When he was a boy, his strict Methodist father sent him to buy cigarettes. After the transaction had been completed, his father notified the authorities that the shopkeeper had sold cigarettes to a minor. Kinsey always resented having been used as an informer.

He was an Eagle Scout. Later he criticized the Boy Scout Handbook's *condemnation of masturbation and its assertion that sex was harmful to athletes.*

At South Orange High School in New Jersey, he was known as the boy who never had a girl. His yearbook quote: "Man delights not me; no, nor woman neither."

He began college as an engineering student at Stevens Institute; later he transferred to Bowdoin to study biology.

He joined the Zeta Psi fraternity because he wanted access to their piano and phonograph records and because they served pie for breakfast.

With *"his soulful expressions and his artistry at the piano," a college classmate observed of Kinsey, "he was indeed a magnificent figure."*

He had round shoulders from childhood rickets. His arms were longer than average, and he swung them palms outward. His crew cut was once compared to Kansas wheat.

Working at Indiana University in the 1920s, he became the world's foremost authority on the gall wasp.

Herbert Huncke, an intimate of Jack Kerouac's, once described how, when he was living as a Times Square hustler, a "college girl" approached him in a cafeteria and "explained that there was someone that was very anxious to meet me, and that he would give me some money . . . and that I didn't have to [have any] personal contact with him. . . ." At first Huncke was "a little hesitant . . . I didn't know just how freaky he might be. . . ." Shortly thereafter he met the man, who turned out to be Kinsey, and found him "very likeable, very warm." Huncke became, as he saw it, the professor's "pimp," soliciting subjects for Kinsey to interview.

Eventually Kinsey was kicked out of his hotel after being visited by too many people of questionable character. The Salvation Army then let him work out of its Men's Employment Bureau.

In 1950 he met Tennessee Williams. He saw A Streetcar Named Desire several times and then, with his associates, studied the actors' sexual backgrounds. In his lifetime he took down 7,985 sex histories, including those of writers Cornelia Otis Skinner and Katherine Anne Porter.

For two years Kinsey financed his investigations with his own savings. Finally, in 1940, he requested and received aid from the National Research Council. By 1954, however, the Rockefeller Foundation had cancelled its aid of $100,000 a year. Kinsey complained that some religious groups were pressuring his sponsors to withdraw their support.

After his Sexual Behavior in the Human Male *was published, a Hollywood agent sought to obtain the movie rights from him.*

Although he rarely went to movies, he repeatedly saw Quartet—*a film anthology of Somerset Maugham short stories.*

When he was twenty-seven, he married Clara Bracken McMillen. They spent their honeymoon camping.

His nickname was Prok, short for Professor K.

One summer he designed a lightweight knapsack, which was advertised as "The Kinsey Pack" in the 1928 Sears Roebuck catalog.

He was proud of his aged Buick, which had traveled over one hundred thousand miles.

He owned many knives, including a Finnish hunting knife, a Spanish bayonet, a Japanese short sword, and a Bulgarian cane sword.

He collected recipes for sweet rum drinks. His favorites were the Charleston Cup and the Junior Zombie.

He loved to eat at ethnic restaurants, especially Turkish, Syrian, Greek, Armenian, and Hindu places.

He held very serious record recitals on Sunday nights. When the wife of one guest suggested playing boogie-woogie music at one such gathering, the couple was not invited back.

He always wore a bow tie, and he alternated every other day between identical pairs of moccasins.

He liked to work in the garden, wearing only his bathing trunks. His neighbors were aghast.

He loved flowers—especially the iris, of which at one time he had over 250 varieties.

His extensive collection of erotic art included graffiti from the walls of ladies' rooms. Some of his acquisitions were impounded in New York under the obscenity clause of the Customs Act and were not released until after his death.

He began each day with a cold shower.

He died on August 25, 1956, in Bloomington, Indiana, of a heart ailment and pneumonia.

Is There
Any End to
Kerouac Highway?

KEN KESEY

AHHH I HATE WRITING ABOUT A WRITER. ESPECIALLY ABOUT JACK KEROUAC WHAT WITH all these other tepid tomes being cranked out about the poor man year after prying year. But damnitall it's time somebody spoke up for the man's work and the impact it had on us young book-reading swains a quarter of a century ago (the impact of the work, not the man; all these intimate-insights-about-the-man biographies are primarily pornographic and oughta be taken as such).

On the Road. Good ol' nation-shaking feet-stirring *On the Road.* What can we call to mind that was like unto it, impactwise? I can't recall its equal in politics, or art . . . not even in music. Wait. I got one. Here's a fair parallel:

Remember coming up the aisle outta the captured black-and-white murk of the Rialto after your first seeing of *The Wild One* with Marlon Brando? and going into the Men's to sideways scope, notice, that all your familiar teenage contemporaries are standing in front of the mirrors or at the urinals in a *totally unfamiliar new stance?* a kind of slouching cool indolence, yet alert, like tom-cats might slouch amid the trash-can shadows, indolent on the surface, only with secret danger cocked in their alleywise eyes. And how none of the boys ever stood quite the same again, after seeing Brando in that historic flick?

Well, for the questing book readers of us, stumbling out of the midcentury murk of Hemingway's sad suicide and Dylan Thomas's sodden demise, *On the Road* was equally stance-changing. We all tried to imitate it. Yet, even then, no

one considered it the work of a Truly Great Writer. I recall my initial interpretation of the phenomenon, that, yeah, it was a pretty groovy book, but not because this guy Ker-oh-wak was such hot potatoes; that what it was actually was
one of those little serendipitous accidents of fate, that's all—just the lucky
catch of a once-a-generation wave by a bush league surfer who just happened
to be paddling in the right waters at the right time when that season's ninth
ninth came rolling by.

And like most readers I contented myself with that view of Kerouac and his
work through the bulk of the Sixties. *Doctor Sax?* Second-rate Ray Bradbury
spooky kid fantasy. *The Subterraneans?* Third-rate Aldous Huxley. *The Dharma
Bums?* Really nothin' more'n a kinda jazzed-up remake of Kellogg Albran's *The
Profit.* In fact I didn't really begin to appreciate the slouching genius of Jack's
great sprawling vision until the Seventies, when Allen Ginsberg towed me into
a Boulder bookstore, berating:

"You haven't read *Tristessa* or *Maggie Cassidy,* Jack's tenderest love novels?
Tsk. And you haven't read *Desolation Angels* or *Lonesome Traveler?* Or *Satori
in Paris,* which is just your cup of Mystical Christian tea? Fie, Kenneth; that's
scandalous. Especially for one who thinks he knows the heart and spine of
Jack's work. Tsk and fie and shame. . . !"

—as he piled on me a collection about seven times the size of my meager
work, which happened to be next on the K shelf.

"You'll love this one—published you'll notice abroad because hardhearted
houses in this country wouldn't touch it—and this, about Jack's little angel
brother Gerard who died in his youth, and especially this, the *Vanity of
Duluoz,* which happens to not only be Jack's best retrospective of America's
Golden Disillusionment but is as well probably some of the best football stuff
ever written. It's the final installment in the huge Kerouakian drama, without
which none of the rest can be hindsightedly understood. I mean, just look at all
these pages, the incredible scope of it all. Faulkner's Yoknapatawpha saga is
the only domain remotely close. The sorry difference is Faulkner's territory has
been secured. But there haven't been any kindly old critics come forth to rescue poor Jack the way Malcolm Cowley did for Faulkner."

I had to admit it was a considerable heft of work. I started to go for my wallet.
Ginsberg put a soft hand on my sleeve:

"These are on me. If you'll promise to read them all. I want you to see Jack
was a lot more than merely the gold boy bard of one so-called Beat Generation.
He was the Sammy Pepys, the Rudy Kipling, the Charlie Dickens of at least
three American generations. And on top of that, a saint, I'll be hanged if he
aint. What we've called him here at the Jack Kerouac School of Disembodied
Poetics, corny as it sounds, is Saint Jack. O, you've an eye-opener in store, cal-
low quester Kenny. . . ."

How right he was. At first I was mainly reimpressed with the fluid grace of
the prose and the integrity achieved by that famous fastashandscantype
method of writing it. There's a sort of promise implied by this method that
makes one think of the Fool card in the tarot, the singing jester blithely

stepping over the edge of a cliff, with rucksack over shoulder and eyes to the sky and no safety net below—the rough yipes and yodels spieled out during the Fool's fall, occurring under conditions too urgent for the convenience of careful composition, too late for the luxury of revision.

Next I noticed the continual current of gentleness running beneath that raw spiel of rough words, the mercy with which he described the vast and varied flock summoned from his memory—the tootsies and floozies, fags and wimps and dope fiends, killers and convicts and bullying sailors, hustlers and losers and phonies of the first water—yet, in all his long considering, he never puts a soul of them down.

Finally, as I wound toward the culmination of his long work, I began to feel surrounding me that rare warm glory that shines out of only the best efforts of the greatest artists. It is the light that uplifts and exhorts, that reveals us to each other as the glorious marvels we are, no matter the plugged crapper and the athlete's foot, and it shines on us at the expense of the artist's personal reserve of lamp oil.

No wonder he burned out—all those years illuminating and glorifying all the dim little scenes of our daily mundanities. No wonder he expired in a cloud of acrid smoke.

So in spite of biographers who want to brand him a boozy right-wing bigot, and ex-wifeys and girlfriends trying to label him a cad or a mama's baby, I have come to realize that, corny as it sounds, I have to go along with Ginsberg: sweet sad Jack has every right to be, in the most traditional Catholic sense, considered a candidate for canonization. He not only manifested Grace, and Mercy, and Glory, he also in some beatific way died for our scenes.

Aint that what it takes to be a saint?

———————

JACK KEROUAC *was born on March 12, 1922, the third and last child of Leo and Gabrielle Kerouac, French Canadians who lived in Lowell, Massachusetts. He was nicknamed Ti Jean, or "Little Jack."*

For a while the family lived next to a funeral parlor. Kerouac's father, who owned a printshop, was a big, strong, anti-intellectual, reactionary man. He rarely spoke to his son except when playing sports.

When Kerouac was five, his older brother Gerard died of rheumatic fever. Though Jack and his mother had a relationship that bordered on the incestuous, she once said to him, "You should have died, not Gerard."

His childhood hero was the Shadow, who, Kerouac wrote, spoke "to the bottom of my boy problems [which] could all be solved if only I could fathom his speech."

Arrested as a material witness when his friend Lucien Carr committed a mur-

der, he called his father to ask for $100 bail. His father replied, "No Kerouac ever got involved in a murder. . . . I'm not going to lend you no hundred dollars and you can go to hell. . . ." Reflecting on the incident, Jack acknowledged, "Something's happened to me! . . . I ought to be a real son. Why does it always have to be ought?"

He went to Columbia University on a football scholarship but dropped out to join the Navy. After two months in the service he was given a psychiatric discharge.

He typed one hundred words per minute and, as literary legend holds, knocked off the 175,000 words of On the Road *in twenty days—feeding a 120-foot roll of teletype paper into his typewriter. But by the time Viking finally published the book, in 1957, he had revised it considerably.*

He wanted Montgomery Clift to play the Kerouac character in a screen version of the book. Warner Bros. offered $100,000 for the movie rights, but his agent declined. Later a small production company picked up the option, intending to cast Mort Sahl as Kerouac's pal Neal Cassady. The movie has never been made. Francis Coppola now holds the rights.

He regularly slept with Neal Cassady's wife, Carolyn. He also occasionally slept with men.

Around the time he was exploring Zen Buddhism he also became a fan of Senator Joseph McCarthy. "McCarthy's got the real dope on the Jews and the fairies," said Kerouac, who nevertheless remained largely uninterested in politics and close to his Jewish and homosexual friends.

Violence, as a rule, disgusted him. When he was hit, he often would not hit back.

He was, throughout his life, a compulsive masturbator; he wrote that his first onanistic experience was interrupted by the news that Beauty, his dog, had been hit by a car.

Kerouac suffered from phlebitis, and he once maintained, in a paternity suit, that the ailment prevented him from working regularly.

He once hired a woman in Portugal to stare into his eyes for an hour.

He loved cats and said that "God gives us kittens to teach us how to pity."

On the Road *stayed on the best-seller lists for five weeks. Two years later his mother had finished only thirty-four pages of it.*

After his initial bout of fame, he told a friend, "I'm always thinking, What am I doing here? Is this the way I'm supposed to feel?"

He took part in the early psychedelic experiments of Timothy Leary, whom he called "Coach." Later Kerouac renounced Leary.

When he was older, kids would show up at his door and invite him on joyrides. He would crouch in fear beneath the dashboard.

Years after Neal Cassady's death, he insisted, "Neal's not dead, you know. . . . Naw, he's hiding out somewhere. . . . He can't be dead."

"I wasn't trying to create any kind of new consciousness or anything like that," he told an interviewer late in his life. "We didn't have a whole lot of heavy abstract thoughts. We were just a bunch of guys who were out trying to get laid."

In the late Sixties, he was a supporter of the Vietnam War and an avid reader of William F. Buckley Jr. His last novel railed against the hippies.

By the time he was forty-seven, he was despondent, bloated, and alcoholic, living with his third wife and his mother in a St. Petersburg retirement community. As he sat one morning with a drink, his stomach hemorrhaged. He had been watching The Galloping Gourmet. *A few hours later he died.*

Nixon
Without Knives

GORE VIDAL

OF ALL MY LITERARY INVENTIONS, RICHARD NIXON IS THE MOST NEARLY AUTONOMOUS. Like all great literary creations—Beowulf, Gargantua, Little Nell—one does not know what on earth he might do next. When I first invented him as a character called Joe Cantwell in the play and later the movie *The Best Man*, I thought to myself, There! I have done it. For at least a generation I have fixed on the page—or, in this case, on the stage and upon some strips of celluloid—a splendid twentieth-century archetype. But little did I suspect that my invention would suddenly take on a life of its own and that I would be forced to return again and again to this astonishing protean creature whose genius it is to be always the same.

My last major effort was in 1972, when *An Evening with Richard Nixon* was produced on Broadway. But this time my invention did an end run around me, as he would put it in his jock jargon. When the play opened, most of the press had decided to support Nixon's Committee to Re-Elect the President (the acronym was CREEP—remember?), and my revelations about shoe boxes filled with money and break-ins and illegal spying and other high capers were not only premature but they were the one thing that no American journalist can abide—bad taste. In fact, so bad was my taste that an apostle of good taste at *The New York Times* (a paper that is good taste incarnate—and utter refinement, too) said that I had said "mean and nasty things about our President."

The apostle was English and did not know that although the sovereign of his native islands is called Our Queen, the emperor of the West is known to us aficionados as The Goddamned President.

Needless to say, I cannot stop following the adventures of my invention . . . *my* invention! He is ours in a way that the queen is not England's, because she was invented by history, while Nixon made himself up, with a lot of help from all of us. As individuals, the Presidents are accidental; but as types, they are inevitable and represent, God help us, us. We are Nixon; he is us.

Although hypocrisy has been the name of the American game for most of this century, Nixon's occasional odd bursts of candor are often stunning. Of General Eisenhower, whose despised (by Ike) Vice-President he was, Nixon wrote in *Six Crises:* "Eisenhower was a far more complex and devious man than most people realized"—a truth not generally known even now. Then comes the inimitable Nixon gloss: Eisenhower was complex and devious "in the best sense of those words."

The Machiavelli of Whittier, California, often says what he means when he means to say something quite different, and that is why one cannot stop listening to him. In Nixon we are able to observe our faults larger than life. But we can also, if we try, see in this huge, dusty mirror our virtues as well. So the time has now come for us to regard the thirty-seventh President in the light, if not of eternity, of the twentieth century, now drawing to its unmourned close.

Currently, in a series of books signed with Nixon's name, he himself is trying to rearrange his place in that long cavalcade of mediocrity—and worse—that has characterized the American presidency since the death of Franklin Roosevelt.

Nixon's chroniclers have their work cut out for them, because he is simply too gorgeous and outsize an American figure for any contemporary to put into a clear perspective. To understand Nixon's career you would have to understand the United States in the twentieth century, and that is something that our educational, political, and media establishments are not about to help us do. After all: No myth, no nation. They have a vested interest in maintaining our ignorance, and that is why we are currently stuck with the peculiar notion that Nixon just happened to be the one bad apple in a splendid barrel. The fact that there has not been a good or serious President since Franklin Roosevelt is ignored, while the fact that Nixon was corrupt some of the time, and complex and devious all of the time, is constantly emphasized in order to make him appear uniquely sleazy—and the rest of us just grand. Yet Nixon is hardly atypical. Certainly his predecessor, Lyndon Johnson, far surpassed Nixon when it came to mendacity and corruption. But the national myth requires, periodically, a scapegoat; hence Nixon's turn in the barrel.

Actually, corruption has been more the rule than the exception in our political life. When Lincoln was obliged to appoint a known crook as Secretary of War, he asked a congressman from the appointee's state if he thought that the new Cabinet minister would actually steal in office. "Well," said the congressman thoughtfully, "I don't think he'd steal a red-hot stove."

Neither personally nor auctorially did I feel sorry for Nixon during the days of Watergate and his resignation. After all, he was simply acting out his Big Loser nature, and, in the process, he turned being a Big Loser into a perfect triumph by managing to lose the presidency in a way bigger and more original than anyone else had ever lost it before. That takes gumption. No, I only began to feel sorry for him when the late, much-dreaded Fawn M. Brodie, a certifiable fool (of the dead only the truth), wrote one of her pseudo-psychobiographies of him and plowed him under as if he were a mere Thomas Jefferson (a previous victim of her somber art) in pursuit of mulatto nymphets. Enough is enough, I said to myself; do not inflict this Freudian horseshit on Nixon—*my* Nixon.

So let us now praise an infamous man who has done great deeds for his country. The clatter you just heard is that of knives falling on the floor of the American pantheon, where now, with slow and mechanical and ever-so-slightly-out-of-sync tread, the only great President of the last half of the twentieth century moves toward his rightful niche. Future historians—and with some thanks to Nixon, there may even be future historians—will look to Nixon as the first President who acted upon the not exactly arcane notion that the United States is just one country among many countries and that the communism is an economic and political system without much to recommend it at the moment and with few voluntary adherents.

Simultaneously Nixon realized that coexistence with the Soviet Union is the only game that we can safely play. Nixon also saw the value of exploiting the rift between Russia and China.

In a book called *Leaders*, Nixon praises de Gaulle, from whom he learned two lessons. First, power accrues to the ruler whose actions are unpredictable. Although this tactic might work at a local level for the leader of a minor country, such a system of unexpectedness on the part of the emperor of the West could send what is known euphemistically as the Wrong Signal to the emperor of the East, in which case there would never be enough shovels to protect us from the subsequent nuclear rain. The second—more practical—lesson was in de Gaulle's view that nations are nations, and while political systems come and go, national interests continue for millennia. Like every good and bad American, Nixon knows almost no history of any kind. But he was quick to pick up on the fact that the Russians and the Chinese each have a world view that has nothing at all to do with communism, or whatever happens to be the current official name for Heaven's Mandate.

Nixon proceeded to do the unexpected. He buried the hatchet with the Son of Heaven, Mao, by going to see him—as is proper for the Barbarian from beyond the Four Seas if he wishes to enjoy the patronage of the Lord of the Middle Kingdom. Then, from this position of strength, Nixon paid a call on the Czar of all the Russias, whose mouth, to say the least, was somewhat ajar at what Nixon had done in China. With one stroke, Nixon brought the world's three great powers (all nuclear) into the same plane of communication. There was no precedent for what he had done. Kennedy worshipers point to Kennedy's celebrated we-are-all-in-this-together speech at American University;

but Kennedy was a genuine war lover in a way that Nixon was not, despite his locker-room macho imitation of what he took to be Kennedy's genuine locker-room macho. Actually, neither one ever qualified for the team; they were just a standard pair of weaklings.

Although Nixon is the one who will be remembered for ending, four years too late, the Vietnam War, he is currently obliged to share some of the glory with a curious little man called Henry Kissinger. In the war of the books now going on between Nixon and Kissinger, Kissinger is trying hard to close the fame gap. The Kissinger books give the impression that while Nixon was holed up in the Executive Office Building, listening to the emetic strains of Richard Rodgers's score for *Victory at Sea*, the American Metternich was leading the free world out of the Valley of the Shadow. But, ultimately, a Kissinger is just a Kissinger, something the burglar uses to jimmy a lock. While Nixon allowed the Vietnam War to drag on for four years, hoping that something would turn up, Kissinger did as he was told.

Even so, if the Kissinger books are to be believed, he was a lot tougher than Nixon when it came to dealing with Hanoi. After the election of '72, Kissinger tells us, "basically, [Nixon] now wanted the war over on almost any terms. . . . He had a horror of appearing on television to announce that he was beginning his new mandate by once again expanding the war." But Kissinger was made of sterner stuff. Although he praised (to Nixon's face) the Christmas bombing of North Vietnam, he was taking a tougher line than Nixon in negotiations despite "Nixon's brooding disquietude with my new-found celebrity. . . ." Also, Kissinger, being Kissinger, did not want the press to think that he had concurred in the brutal bombing. "I did not indicate to any journalist that I had opposed the decision to use B-52s," he tells us firmly, then adds, "but I also did little to dampen the speculation, partly in reaction to the harassment of the previous weeks, partly out of a not very heroic desire to deflect the assault from my person."

Meanwhile, Nixon quotes from his diary at the time the decision to bomb was made: "Henry talked rather emotionally about the fact that this was a very courageous decision. . . ." Later, when the war ran out of gas, the diarist reports: ". . . I told [Kissinger] that the country was indebted to him for what he had done. It is not really a comfortable thing for me to praise people so openly. . . . On the other hand, Henry expects it. . . . He, in turn, responded that without my having the, as he puts it, courage to make the difficult decision of December 18th, we would not be where we are today."

The unsatisfactory end to the most unsatisfactory and pointless war in American history will be, like Kissinger himself, a footnote to a presidency that will be remembered for the bold initiative to China combined with a degree of détente with the Soviet Union.

Today we are all of us in Nixon's debt for seizing an opportunity (*ignore his motives: the world is governed by deeds, not motives*) in order to make sense of close to one third of a century of dangerous nonsense.

Finally, I am happy to say that the ever-restless householder of Saddle River,

New Jersey, continues to surprise. In the spring of last year he addressed a fundraising event at the Disneyland Hotel, in Orange County, California. For the right-wingers present, he was obliged to do a bit of the-Russians-are-coming; then he made absolute sense.

"The Soviet Union needs a deal," Nixon said. "And we should give them one. But for a price." Noting that the West has a five-to-one edge in economic power over the Soviets, Nixon said that this advantage should be used as an "economic lever." Because "simply to have a program that would lead to a balance of nuclear terror is not enough. We must try to add to that a new dimension of the use of America's and the free world's economic power as both a carrot and a stick." Predictably, the press did not pick up on any of this, but history will; and since we are all of us Nixon and he is us, the fact that he went to Peking and Moscow in order to demonstrate to all the world the absolute necessity of coexistence proves that there is not only good in him but in us as well—hope, too.

RICHARD MILHOUS NIXON *was born on January 9, 1913, in a small wooden house next to his father's lemon grove in Yorba Linda, California. He was named after King Richard the Lion-Heart.*

When he was three, he nearly died after falling from a carriage and splitting open his head. At four he almost died of pneumonia. Tuberculosis and meningitis took two of his four brothers when they were boys. His mother surmised: "I think that Richard may have felt a kind of guilt that Harold and Arthur were dead and he was alive." Ten years old, he signed a letter: "You good dog, RICHARD."

He was a polite, earnest boy. "He wasn't a little boy that you wanted to pick up and hug," a relative said. "It didn't strike me that he wanted to be hugged."

"He was the best potato masher one could wish for," his mother said later in life. "Even in these days, when I am visiting Richard and Pat in Washington . . . he will take over the potato mashing. My feeling is that he actually enjoys it."

In his first year at Duke law school he stood up to a fearsome professor. In his second year he broke into the dean's office to find out his class standing. He graduated third in his class, but the FBI never responded to his job application.

His Quaker religion would have exempted him from military service, but the thought of being a conscientious objector, he said, "never crossed my mind." Stationed in the Pacific, Lieutenant Nixon built airstrips and ran a ramshackle gambling resort. He dispensed booze and learned poker; he left the wartime card game up ten thousand dollars.

The first time he met Pat Ryan he asked her to marry him. "I thought he was nuts," she said later. He pursued her. Even when she went out on other dates, she recalled, he "would drive me to meet other beaux and wait around to take me home." After two years of courtship, they married.

As Vice-President he was often merely an observer at Cabinet meetings. But once he surprised his colleagues by pulling out of his pocket a mechanical drummer. Winding the toy up, he let it march down the long table while America's leaders watched in silence. Finally Nixon revealed his point: "We've got to drum up support for Republican candidates."

Prior to 1960 he was a patient of Dr. Arnold A. Hutschnecker's, a New York internist who treated successful men and women for emotional and psychological problems. (In 1972, when a history of psychiatric treatment forced Senator Thomas Eagleton off the Democratic ticket, Nixon wrote Eagleton's young son a kind note affirming that "the political man can always come back to fight again.")

As President he dreaded meeting strangers and insisted that an aide sit in on every Oval Office meeting with an outsider. At night he would bowl in the basement of the Executive Office Building. Frequently he would leave his wife in Washington to spend the weekend with Florida banker Bebe Rebozo, with whom he would sit for hours in silent communion.

He found it nearly impossible to fire someone face-to-face. "Well, people make mistakes," he said before dismissing H. R. Haldeman, "but you don't fire a guy for a mistake, do you?" He had his secretary, Rose Mary Woods, tell his family that he would resign from the presidency.

He left the White House in 1974, on August 8. (On the same date in 1815, Napoleon Bonaparte sailed to St. Helena to spend his last years in exile.) "I let the American people down," Nixon later said, "and I have to carry that burden with me for the rest of my life."

He now lives in Saddle River, New Jersey, in a fifteen-room house that has a thousand-bottle wine cellar. He holds occasional stag dinners. He likes to walk in the rain without an umbrella.

Oswald Avery
and the Cascade
of Surprises

LEWIS THOMAS

ONE OF THE LIVELIEST PROBLEMS IN CANCER RESEARCH THESE DAYS IS THE BEHAVIOR of oncogenes, strings of nucleic acid that were originally found in several of the viruses responsible for cancer in laboratory animals, later discovered to exist in all normal cells. By itself, an oncogene appears to be a harmless bit of DNA, maybe even a useful one, but when it is moved from its normal spot to a new one on another chromosome, it switches the cell into the unrestrained growth of cancer. It is not yet known how it does this, but no one doubts that an answer is within reach. Some of the protein products of oncogenes have already been isolated and identified, and the site of their action within the cell, probably just beneath the cell membrane, is now being worked on. The work is moving so fast that most recent issues of *Science* and *Nature* contain several papers on oncogenes and their products.

But cancer is only one among dozens of new problems for the scientists who work on DNA. The intimate details of genetically determined diseases of childhood are coming under close scrutiny, and the precise nature of the error in the DNA molecule has been observed in several, sickle-cell disease, for example, with more to come. The immunologists, embryologists, cell biologists, and, recently, even the endocrinologists have observed the ways in which small modifications of DNA affect the behavior of the systems that they study. *Observed* is exactly the right word here: the DNA molecule can be inspected visually, purified absolutely, analyzed chemically, cut into whatever lengths you like, transferred from one cell to another or into a test tube for the manufacture of specific proteins. The techniques and instruments now available for studying DNA have become so sophisticated that I recently heard a young colleague, one of the new breed of molecular geneticists, complain that "even a dumb researcher can do a perfectly beautiful experiment."

It is indeed a biological revolution, unquestionably the greatest upheaval in biology and medicine ever.

It began just fifty years ago in a small laboratory on the sixth floor of the Hospital of the Rockefeller Institute for Medical Research, overlooking the East River at Sixty-sixth Street in New York. Professor Oswald T. Avery, a small, vanishingly thin man with a constantly startled expression and a very large and agile brain, had been working on the pneumococcus—the bacterium causing lobar pneumonia—since the early years of World War I.

Avery and his colleagues had discovered that the virulence of pneumococci was determined by the polysaccharides (complex sugars) combined in the capsules of the organisms and that different strains of pneumococci possessed different types of polysaccharide, which were readily distinguished from one another by specific antibodies. It was not clear at that time that the type of polysaccharide was a genetic property of the bacterial cells—it was not even clear that genes *existed* in bacteria—but it was known that the organisms bred true; all generations of progeny from a pneumococcus of one type were always of that same type. This was a solid rule, and like a good many rules in biology there was an exception.

An English bacteriologist, Fred Griffith, had discovered in 1923 that pneumococci could be induced to lose their polysaccharides and then to switch types under special circumstances. When mice were injected with a mixture of live bacteria that had lost their capsules (and were therefore avirulent), together with heat-killed pneumococci of a different type, the animals died of the infection, and the bacteria recovered from their blood were now the same type as the heat-killed foreign organisms.

Avery became interested in the phenomenon and went to work on it. By the early 1930s it had become the main preoccupation of his laboratory. Ten years later, with his colleagues Colin M. MacLeod and Maclyn McCarty, the work was completed, and in 1944 the now-classic paper was published in the *Journal of Experimental Medicine,* formidably entitled "Studies on the Chemical Nature of the Substance Inducing Transformation of Pneumococcal Types: Induction of Transformation by a Desoxyribonucleic Acid Fraction Isolated from Pneumococcus Type III."

The work meant that the genes of pneumococci are made of DNA, and this came as a stunning surprise to everyone—not just the bacteriologists but all biologists. Up until the announcement, the concept of the gene was a sort of abstraction. It was known that genes existed, but nobody had the faintest idea what they were made of or how they worked. Here, at last, was chemical evidence for their identity and, more importantly, a working model for examining their functions.

Several years later a new working model was devised in other laboratories, involving viruses as the source of DNA, and in 1953 the famous paper by James Watson and Francis Crick was published, delineating the double-helix structure of DNA. Many biologists track the biological revolution back to the Watson-Crick discovery, but Watson himself wrote, "Given the fact that DNA was known to occur in the chromosomes of all cells, Avery's experiments strongly suggested that future experiments would show that all genes were composed of DNA."

Looking back, whether back to the Watson-Crick paper or all the way back to Avery, the progress of science can be made to seem an orderly succession of logical steps, a discovery in one laboratory leading to a new hypothesis and a new experiment elsewhere, one thing leading neatly to another.

It was not really like that, not at all. Almost every important experiment that moved the field forward, from Avery's "transforming principle" to today's "jumping genes" and cancer biology, has come as a total surprise, most of all surprising to the investigators doing the work. Moreover, the occasions have been exceedingly rare when the scientists working on one line of research have been able to predict, with any accuracy, what was going to happen next. A few years ago certain enzymes were discovered that will cut DNA into neat sections, selectively and precisely, but it could not have been predicted then that this work would lead directly, within just a few more years, to the capacity to insert individual genes from one creature into the genetic apparatus of another—even though this is essentially what Avery accomplished, more crudely, to be sure, a half century ago.

Good basic science is impossible to predict. By its very nature, it must rely on surprise, and when it is going very well, as is the case for molecular genetics today, it is a cascade of surprises.

And there is another sort of surprise that is essential for good basic science, not so exhilarating, enough to drive many student investigators clean out of science. This is the surprise of being wrong, which is a workaday part of every scientist's life. Avery endured ten years of it, one experiment gone wrong after another, variables in the system that frequently made it impossible to move from one question to the next. Reading the accounts of those ten years in René Dubos's book *The Professor, The Institute, and DNA*, one wonders how Avery, MacLeod, and McCarty had the patience and stubbornness to keep at it.

Being wrong, guessing wrong, setting up an elegant experiment intended to ask one kind of question and getting back an answer to another unrelated, irrelevant, unasked question, can be frustrating and dispiriting, but it can, with luck, also be the way the work moves ahead. Avery was especially good at capitalizing on mistaken ideas and miscast experiments in his laboratory. He is quoted by some of his associates as having said, more than once, "Whenever you fall, pick something up."

This is the way good science is done: not by looking around for gleaming negotiable bits of truth and picking them up and pocketing them like game birds, nor by any gift of infallible hunch of where to look and what to find. Good science is done by being curious *in general,* by asking questions all around, by acknowledging the likelihood of being wrong and taking this for granted in good humor, by having a deep fondness for nature, and by being made nervous and jumpy by ignorance. Avery was like this, a familiar figure, fallible but beyond question a *good* man, the kind of man you would wish to have in the family. Accident-prone, error-prone, but right on the mark at the end, when it counted.

One thing for a good basic scientist to have on his mind, and worry about, is how his work will be viewed by his peers. If the work is very good, very new, and looks as if it's opening up brand-new territory, he can be quite sure that he will be criticized down to his socks. If he is onto something revolutionary, never thought of before, contradicting fixed notions within the community of science involved, he tends to keep his head down. When he writes, he writes as Avery wrote, a cautious paper, as noncommittal as possible, avoiding big extrapolations to other fields.

Not all scientists with great discoveries to their credit receive the Nobel Prize, and Avery did not. This spectacular omission continues to mystify the scientific community and has never been explained. René Dubos thinks that the Nobel committee was not convinced that Avery knew the significance of his own work, perhaps because of the low-key restraint with which the manuscript was written; the paper did not lay out claims for opening the gate into a new epoch in biology, although this is certainly what it did accomplish.

I doubt very much that Oswald Avery was ever troubled by the absence of a Nobel Prize or even thought much about it. He was not in any sense a disappointed man. He understood clearly, while the work was going on, what its implications were, and when it was finished he was deeply pleased and satisfied by what it meant for the future. He had set the stage for the new biology, and he knew that.

Contrary to the general view, not all scientists do their best work in their thirties, peak in their forties, and then subside. Avery was sixty-seven years old when his DNA paper was published. He retired four years later and died of cancer at the age of seventy-seven, at peace with the world.

OSWALD THEODORE AVERY *was born in Halifax, Nova Scotia, on October 21, 1877, four years after his parents emigrated from England. His father started out as a papermaker; but discontented with that trade and possessed of a mystical nature, he became a Baptist minister.*

When his father established his ministry in New York, the Baptist community helped the family live on a meager salary. After a fire destroyed the Avery home in December 1890, Mrs. John D. Rockefeller sent a check for one hundred dollars.

In 1892 both his father and his older brother, Ernest, died, and Oswald became the man of the family. His mother went to work for the Baptist City Mission Society. Her work allowed her to mingle with the Rockefellers, Vanderbilts, and Sloans, who took an interest in her sons and invited them to their estates; and Avery acquired sophisticated tastes unusual for his background.

As an undergraduate at Colgate, he earned excellent grades. His yearbook said that only the accident of his being born in Canada prevented him from fulfilling "his aspirations for the presidency." He majored in the humanities and took only those science courses that were required. Nevertheless he went on to Columbia University's medical school.

At Columbia he was called Babe, because of his small size and youthful demeanor. One classmate said he had an "aristocratic daintiness."

After receiving his medical degree in 1904, he practiced general surgery in New York for about three years. But he found it upsetting to deal with patients suffering from chronic pulmonary diseases and intractable asthma, for whom he could do nothing useful. Although he was successful in his relations with patients, clinical practice did not satisfy him intellectually or emotionally.

His favorite haunt was Deer Isle, Maine. He never missed a chance to go sailing. He also walked through the Maine woods collecting wild flowers.

He left clinical medicine when, in 1907, the Hoagland Laboratory in Brooklyn appointed him associate director at a salary of $1,200 a year.

His next important move—to the Rockefeller Institute in 1913—almost didn't occur because, in keeping with his neglectful attitude toward correspondence, he failed to answer two letters offering him the job.

He walked to work every day and, from 1913 to 1948, occupied the same small, immaculate office.

He ate very little—he probably never weighed more than one hundred pounds—but was fastidious about the food he did eat. He was immensely popular and received many dinner invitations, but seldom did he accept.

After joining the Institute, he shunned large gatherings and gave up public speaking. But his office door was always open to people needing advice, and he was an effective lecturer. In college his best grades had been in public speaking, and decades later he still enjoyed declaiming the graceful phrases of a speech on Chinese civilization, one of his early oratorical triumphs.

His shirts, shoes, suits, and ties were always impeccable and always subdued. His voice was soft and his manner retiring, but his handwriting displayed a daring, enthusiastic flourish.

He traveled little, outside of his trips to Maine. When he won the Paul Ehrlich Gold Medal in 1933, he did not go to Germany to receive it; nor did he go to Sweden to receive the Pasteur Gold Medal awarded him in 1950.

He wouldn't hurry; he used to quote an old black patient who, upon watching *the doctors rush by, said, "What's your hurry, Doc? By rushing that way you passes by much more than you catches up with."*

On rare moments when he was alone in the lab, he was prone to move slowly, whistling the lonely shepherd's song from Tristan und Isolde.

In 1948 he moved to a stone house in Nashville, near the home of his brother, Roy. Six years later, while at Deer Isle, he felt pain that was eventually diagnosed as cancer of the liver. His terminal illness was painful; he bore it with characteristic patience. He died at the age of seventy-seven on February 20, 1955, at Vanderbilt Hospital.

And Playing Second Base for Brooklyn ... Jackie Robinson

WILFRID SHEED

IT HAD TO HAPPEN, AND SOMEBODY HAD TO GET HURT. BY 1946 THE NORTHERN CITIES were crammed to bursting with black munitions workers, returned veterans, and the flotsam of war, and they were in no mood for lily-white baseball. Since these newcomers still had some mad money to throw around and since the sophisticated Negro leagues had already groomed a mouth-watering pool of talent, there was clearly a killing to be made by whoever had the guts to break the color bar.

The man with the guts was Branch Rickey of Brooklyn, and he received his reward. Besides well-deserved canonization, he found himself with an instant baseball dynasty: one of the most exciting teams ever, which played to full houses whenever blacks and liberals were gathered together. The victim was Jackie Robinson, and his rewards were more elusive.

It is hardly too much to say that Jackie gave his life for Mr. Rickey's breakthrough. Enjoined to silence during his rookie years, this articulate UCLA football star had to endure enough guttersnipe humiliation, from registration clerk to redneck rookie, to shatter the strongest psyche. Boycotted, stepped on, pelted and spat upon by the surliest rearguard movement since Reconstruction, Jackie bore the whole burden of the black athlete with Christ-like patience; for two years and more he suffered that a hundred Hank Aarons might bloom; indeed, for those years he *was* the civil rights movement to most of us.

When time, and Rickey, removed the lid, Robinson came out snarling. By 1950 or so his teammates had either been won round by his sheer usefulness (he could play any infield position except short and had helped drag a half-built team to two pennants in three years) or been released to pinker pastures, while his opponents had learned that, meek or no, it didn't pay to get him what the Marxists might call "objectively" mad: he was a murderous clutch hitter, particularly and fittingly so when there were two strikes against him. So outside of a few innkeepers down south, nobody in his right mind picked on Jackie the Black anymore. (Jackie the Man was something else.)

By then he also had plenty of black company, and a milder man might have licked his wounds and decided to enjoy a little baseball. But Robinson had bent his nature too far in the direction of saintliness, and now he was going to get even, not with anyone in particular—there were too many scores outstanding—but with the world at large. "He was the most difficult player I ever had to deal with," said umpire Jocko Conlan. "He wore you out." Umpires were white, and the new Robinson lived in a world of black and white, where even called third strikes had racist overtones. In fact, he seemed to become more Negro every year, and he reputedly accused his black teammate Roy Campanella of being an Uncle Tom, not realizing that his own prickly independence had knocked the category practically out of baseball. Thanks to Jackie Robinson, blacks were even free to be nice without shame.

Robinson's smoldering rancor made him perhaps an even more electric ballplayer than nature intended. He ran the bases like a kid with a switchblade, so that when he got caught in a rundown, one felt sorry for the infielders and when he was on third one feared for the pitcher (I secretly felt that his real sport was soccer). But he always seemed to give a little more fun than he was getting. When the infield dust had settled over his career, he claimed that the Hall of Fame would never accept him because he was a black. In fact, they did accept him right away—because he was a black. He didn't understand his own revolution.

For a while after that, Jackie dabbled at being a black spokesman, pioneering for a much more mixed breed of cat. For seven bathetic years he was director of personnel at Chock Full O'Nuts, and it's my purely subjective impression that the personnel became almost as feisty as Robinson as they slapped down the sandwiches. But his own fire seemed to die out gracefully, and when I met him toward the end he seemed as gentle as a Pullman porter, white-haired and prematurely old. He died of a heart attack brought on by diabetes at the age of fifty-three. From the moment he had first stepped on a white man's diamond he had turned his whole sensibility up to high and left it there until it finally proved (in Cole Porter's words) too hot not to cool down. God knows what would have happened if Rickey hadn't chosen this man expressly for his maturity and balance.

As soon as it was chronologically possible, a black man (Aaron) had broken the unbreakable record, Babe Ruth's 714 lifetime home runs, and another (Lou Brock) had scampered past Ty Cobb in stolen bases. Perhaps the most inconsequential by-product of all was the conversion of so many intellectuals to base-ball, as Ali later converted them to boxing. Every little bit helps. But baseball wasn't the half of it. Under cover of helmets and Tweedledee padding, blacks sneaked into pro football quite quietly (who can remember the first one?), at least as far as the public was concerned. But the battle of the locker room was won for every sport by Robinson: dressing, showering, celebrating together—suddenly, what was the big deal about that? Seldom has such a big problem dwindled so quickly, although ugly pockets of resistance remained.

By the time pro basketball—a game that practically looks and smells like a locker room—got really big, black players were already so much a part of the scenery that a white guy who once wouldn't have shared a hotel with a black now thought little of having one stand on his feet breathing fire, pouring sweat—and stealing his job.

The acceptance of physicality was the real breakthrough. Joe Louis and Jesse Owens had long since proved that Negroes were good athletes; and in the 1948 Olympics someone computed the final medal tally as something like: Black America 1, Sweden 2, White America 3. But the blacks ran and jumped alone. And when they boxed, it was from segregated bastions, to which they immediately withdrew. Team sports were the sticking point. An irrational dread of proximity kept the uniracial locker room the last redoubt of sporting segregation.

The white southerners who made life hell for Robinson have mostly died or apologized, wondering perhaps what all the fuss had been about. Once the physical distaste had dissipated, the racist arguments based on Scripture and cranial capacity looked mighty frail. One hesitates to claim too much for sports: civil rights after Robinson still had a long, bloody way to go. But Americans do spend a lot of growing-up time in gyms and such, bashing and hugging one another, and this has to flow over into real life. So the civil rights legislation of the Fifties and Sixties may owe at least a little something to the relaxation of ancient terrors on the playing field.

And then there is the figure of Robinson himself. Branch Rickey was an incomparable talent scout, and he never chose more wisely. Back in St. Louis in the Twenties, Rickey had invented the farm system, which involved, among other things, screening hundreds of country boys for character as well as skill, weighing such will-o'-the-wisps as homesickness potential, bright-lights resistance, and lobby-sitting stamina. So it was only right that Rickey should take on the new dimension, blackness, and succeed so definitively with it.

By first proving himself a gentleman, and then a proud gentleman, Robinson saved years of aborted experiments. His explosive period was almost like a time release designed by Rickey so that his prodigy could prove not one but two points and relieve two symptoms. All in all, what Robinson did could simply not have been done better. And when his hazing was over, one of his teammates gave him the accolade of complaining about some "nigger" who was trying to take away Jackie's job.

By present lights that may not sound like much of an ending—"honorary white" status was the last thing Robinson wanted—but in the temper of the times, which one has to strain to remember, it was a great leap forward. If one man could, by hitting .300, cease being a nigger, so could the next one and the one after, until .250 would do. The trick, of course, was how to hit .300 while turning the other cheek. Robinson knew he had to get a hearing within the language of his profession. A stoic who can't hit the curve might as well give up on the spot and scream with pain.

Robinson proved, overproved, under repeated pressure, that he could break your concentration before you could break his, that he could run the bases with a bucket of water on each shoulder if necessary. He was not so much a great ballplayer as a great athlete playing baseball, with a wheeling, roundhouse swing, evidently self-taught, and a fielding style best described as eager. But with these modest gifts he chinned himself to greatness, so that his final message to his own gang was: Be first-rate, then you can argue.

Ironically, Robinson wound up as a Rockefeller Republican, to the bafflement of his liberal spear carriers. But it was they, and not he, who had reduced him to a children's-book character, a Mrs. Roosevelt in spikes; and he wasn't going to dance to their tune any more than to Jim Crow's. Being his own man was his lifework. And you didn't have to be black to be fortified by it.

JACKIE ROBINSON *was the son of a sharecropper and the grandson of a slave. He was born in Cairo, Georgia, on January 31, during the Spanish flu epidemic of 1919. Six months after his birth, his father left town with a neighbor's wife.*

When Jackie was fourteen, a sheriff caught him wading in a municipal pool that was closed to blacks. "Looka here," said the sheriff, holding a .38. "Niggers in my drinking water."

At eighteen, Jackie entered UCLA; he was soon one of the best all-around athletes in the country, winning twenty-four letters. He was a star forward in basketball, leading the Pacific Conference in scoring for two years; a leading running back in football, averaging twelve yards a carry; and a record-breaking broad jumper. He also played baseball.

For all of that time, he was pigeon-toed and had ankle problems.

Serving as an infantry lieutenant at Camp Hood, Texas, he faced a court-martial after he refused to leave his seat beside a white woman and move to the back of a bus. An Army court later dismissed all charges against him.

By the end of his first season with the Brooklyn Dodgers, he had stolen twice as many bases as anyone else in the National League. He was named Rookie of the Year by The Sporting News.

Early in his career the Ku Klux Klan threatened to shoot him if he played in

Atlanta. During warm-ups his teammate Pee Wee Reese joked, "Jack, don't stand so close to me today." Robinson smiled.

When the Chase Hotel in St. Louis refused to let him stay with the other Dodgers, Robinson maintained that he preferred rooming with other blacks at the Hotel Adams. "I get treated like a hero at the Adams," he said. Two years later the Chase agreed to accept blacks, provided they ate in their rooms. Certain blacks declined the offer. Robinson accepted.

After a few years, the slurs from teammates cooled down. "They hadn't changed because they liked me any better," Robinson said in retrospect. "They had changed because I could help fill their wallets."

In a 1947 poll he was voted the second most popular American, behind Bing Crosby.

In arguments his voice became shrill. "Robinson," a teammate told him after one locker-room discussion, "not only are you wrong, you're loud wrong."

In 1949 he told the House Committee on Un-American Activities that he rejected singer Paul Robeson's contention that American blacks would not fight in a war against the Soviet Union. Twenty years later Robinson said his opinion hadn't changed but that he regretted having allowed himself "to be pitted against another black man."

He knew he angered some fans by suddenly retiring in 1956, after the Dodgers traded him. But as Robinson saw it, ". . . I had outsmarted baseball before baseball had outsmarted me."

In 1960 John Kennedy implored Robinson to campaign for him. Instead, he supported Nixon, explaining, "I was fighting a last-ditch battle to keep the Republicans from becoming completely white." By 1968, however, Robinson had soured on Nixon and Agnew and threw his support to Democratic candidate Hubert Humphrey.

Upon resigning from the board of the NAACP, he charged that the "Old Guard leadership" seemed to reflect a " 'Yassuh-Mr.-Charlie' point of view."

He opposed Malcolm X and black separatists, but was a qualified supporter of Martin Luther King Jr. "My reflexes aren't conditioned to accept nonviolence," he said. "My immediate instinct under the threat of physical attack . . . is instant defense and total retaliation."

His wife once said that she could tell when things had gone badly: he would carry a bucket of golf balls out on his lawn and hit them, one after another, into a nearby reservoir. "The golf balls," Robinson pointed out, "were white."

Throughout his life he neither smoked nor drank. Nevertheless he suffered from high blood pressure and diabetes.

His son Jackie Jr., returned from Vietnam a heroin addict. He was cured in 1967, after being convicted for possession of the drug; but four years later, at age twenty-four, he died when his car crashed near his family's home. "You don't know what it's like," his father said at the time, "to lose a son, find him, and lose him again."

At fifty-three, Robinson was blind in one eye and going blind in the other. Ten days after being honored at the 1972 World Series, he died of a heart attack.

George Gallup's Nation of Numbers

RICHARD REEVES

IN THE SUMMER OF 1932 IOWA DEMOCRATS NOMINATED A SIXTY-YEAR-OLD WIDOW NAMED Ola Babcock Miller as the party's candidate for secretary of state. It was no big deal. No Democrat had carried the state since the Civil War. But it was a nice thing to do, a gesture of respect for her late husband, a small-town newspaper publisher who had spent his life trying, vainly, to bring down Iowa Republicanism.

Mrs. Miller called in the family for help. Her son-in-law, a college professor who had just joined a New York advertising agency, had some ideas. Why not have some people go door to door, using this "scientific" plan he had, and ask voters what they wanted?

The son-in-law's name was George H. Gallup. Mrs. Miller won.

Young George—he was born in 1901—was a go-getter. His father had been a dreamer, a country schoolteacher who tried to develop what he called "a new logic of lateral thinking" and built an eight-sided house on the theory that it would offer better protection against plains windstorms. But George left the octagonal house and the hometown, Jefferson, as soon as he could find his way in a bigger world. The first stop was Iowa City and the State University of Iowa. Then in 1922, between his junior and senior years, he answered an advertisement for summer employment in St. Louis. The *Post-Dispatch* hired fifty students to survey the city, questioning readers about what they liked and didn't like in the paper.

Each and every reader. The students were hired to go to every door in St. Louis—there were fifty-five thousand homes in the city then—and ask the same questions. Gallup, one hot day, knocked on one door too many, got the same answers one time too many, and decided: There's got to be a better way.

"A New Technique for Objective Methods for Measuring Reader Interest in Newspapers" was the way, and the title of Gallup's Ph.D. thesis at Iowa. Working with the Des Moines *Register* and *Tribune* and the two-hundred-year-old statistical theory probabilities of the Swiss mathematician Jakob Bernoulli, Gallup developed "sampling" techniques. You didn't have to talk to everybody, he said, as long as you randomly selected interviews according to a sampling plan that took into account whatever diversity was relevant in the universe of potential respondents—geographic, ethnic, economic.

Although not everybody understood or believed then—or now—this intellectual invention was a big deal. GUESSWORK ELIMINATED IN NEW METHOD FOR DETERMINING READER INTEREST was the lead headline of the February 8, 1930, issue of the newspaper industry's trade journal, *Editor & Publisher*. There was a photograph of a big, stolid midwesterner above the caption: GEORGE H. GALLUP, INSTRUCTOR, U. OF IOWA.

The instructor tried to explain what he was talking about and doing. "Suppose there are seven thousand white beans and three thousand black beans well churned in a barrel," he said then, and again more than fifty-two years later as we walked together near his office in Princeton, New Jersey. "If you scoop out one hundred of them, you'll get approximately seventy white beans and thirty black in your hand, and the range of your possible error can be computed mathematically. As long as the barrel contains many more beans than your handful, the proportion will remain within that margin of error nine hundred ninety-seven times out of one thousand."

Well, it seemed to work for newspapers, and George Gallup, instructor, was in great demand around the country. He became head of the journalism department at Drake University and then switched to a professorship at Northwestern—all the while doing readership surveys for papers in Chicago, Cleveland, Buffalo, and points east and west. He was hot, and in that summer of '32 a new advertising agency, Young & Rubicam, invited him to New York to create a research department and procedures for evaluating the effectiveness of advertising. He did that too. One of his first Y & R surveys, based on newspaper experience, indicated that the number of readers of advertisements was proportional to the length of the paragraphs in a piece of copy.

And, of course, by the end of that year, 1932, with his mother-in-law's election, Gallup was confident that his methodology was valid not only for beans and newspaper readers but for voters too. As long as you understood the sampling universe—white, black, male, female, rich, poor, urban, rural, Republican, Democrat—you could predict elections or calculate public attitudes on public questions by interviewing a relatively small number of people.

So Gallup went out and formed the grandly titled American Institute of Public Opinion. Keeping his job at Young & Rubicam, he began syndicating surveys to newspapers under the title: "America Speaks: The National Weekly Poll of Public Opinion." The first Gallup Poll, released in October 1935, focused on the question, asked of three thousand Americans: "Do you think expenditures by the government for relief and recovery are: Too Little? Too Great? About Right?" Three out of five respondents said, "Too Great."

Gallup was onto an idea whose time had almost come. Only forty newspapers took his feature. At the same time, two other market researchers were beginning to establish their own sampling operations—Elmo Roper for *Fortune* magazine and Archibald Crossley for the Hearst newspapers. But the bean counters were small potatoes compared with the straw voters. Political surveying then was dominated by one giant, *The Literary Digest*. Since 1916 the magazine had forecast the results of every presidential election by sending out millions of postcards—straw vote ballots—to names on mailing lists gathered from telephone directories and automobile registration records. In 1932 *The Literary Digest* mailed out twenty million ballots and collected three million returns; the magazine predicted the outcome of the Franklin D. Roosevelt–Herbert Hoover election almost exactly.

"Magic," reported the press.

Luck, knew George Gallup. On July 12, 1936, months before *The Literary Digest* sent out its first straw ballots for the 1936 presidential election, Gallup wrote a column for The *New York Herald Tribune* predicting that the *Digest* poll would show Alf Landon defeating Roosevelt 56 percent to 44 percent—and that it would be wrong!

The *Digest's* luck had run out. Using his own sampling techniques, Gallup was certain that Roosevelt would win easily but that Landon would do well among people rich enough to own telephones and cars. The Great Depression and the politics of the New Deal had polarized Americans economically—and survey samples had to reflect that, or else.

Gallup was ridiculed. *The Literary Digest* did predict a Landon victory, with 57 percent of the vote. The Republican actually got 37 percent. And the Gallup Poll became a national institution.

George Gallup, the go-getter from Jefferson, Iowa, had quantified public opinion. He had bottled the air of democracy—the stuff that a British prime minister, Sir Robert Peel, had called "that great compound of folly, weakness, prejudice, wrong feeling, right feeling, obstinacy, and newspaper paragraphs, which is called public opinion." What Montaigne had called "unmeasurable." What Alexis de Tocqueville had called "the dominant power."

Gallup, the go-getter who started out figuring ways to sell more newspapers, ended up permanently changing democracy. They, some of the better political thinkers, said it couldn't be done. Lord James Bryce, who ranks with Tocqueville as the most perceptive of the nineteenth-century visitors to America, seemed relieved when he wrote in 1894, more than three hundred years after Montaigne: "The obvious weakness of government by public opinion is the difficulty of ascertaining it."

But what if some kid from Iowa trying to make a buck could ascertain, reliably and quickly, what most of the people are thinking most of the time? That, Bryce said, would take democracy to a new level, what he called the fourth stage.

"A fourth stage," he wrote in *The American Commonwealth*, "would be reached if the will of the majority of the citizens were to become ascertainable at all times, and without the need of its passing through a body of representatives . . . public opinion would not only reign but govern. . . . It is to this kind of government that democratic nations seem to be tending."

Gallup, then, was the principal inventor of a surrogate for decision-making. He killed the "hunch." The mortality of instinct became apparent, first not in government or politics but in commerce. Gallup's sampling techniques became part of the framework of a new kind of commercial contemplation: market research. In the old days, for instance, Cecil B. de Mille or someone else might have had a hunch about a movie title. No more. Gallup was commissioned—once to research possible new titles for a *Saturday Evening Post* story called "Glory for Me." He tested thirty-two titles. The sampled public preferred and the world got "The Best Years of Our Lives." And it wasn't long before surveys were being used to pick not only the titles but also the subjects and story lines of films—and the names of products, the colors of boxes, and the popularity of newscasters.

But the Iowa go-getter and the other pioneers of survey research could also claim some credit for substantial contributions to the human condition, particularly in medical science. "Many of the discoveries of the relationship between disease and environmental factors were the products of simple surveys," Gallup said. "The relationship between cigarettes and lung cancer should have been discovered in the 1920s, but the survey techniques that revealed the connections weren't in common use until the 1950s."

Even though Gallup provided political leaders with private polling data in the 1940s—he says Franklin D. Roosevelt asked for and got private surveys before proposing Lend-Lease military aid to Great Britain in 1940, and the draft in 1941—the business of politics, as usual, lagged behind the business of business in adapting new techniques. So far behind that Gallup and others still take time to deny—disingenuously—that polls have any effect on elections. They do, of course. All information does. In politics, the amount of money a candidate can raise is almost always directly proportional to one of two things: how much money his father or grandfather made or his standing in public or private polls. Rich people give money to themselves; other Americans prefer to back winners.

So, eventually, the ministers and legislators of Bryce's musings—and the candidates of our time and reality—began to play with, then use, then depend on that machinery for weighing or measuring the popular will. They were doubly blessed, because the gears worked with a swiftness Bryce could not have imagined. Or were they doubly cursed? The gears and wheels have been refined now so that the weighing and measuring can be done from day to day, rather than week to week or month to month. Now the minister or legislator, seeing, at the same time as the public, televised images of slaughter in an Arab ghetto or a nun's body crumpled beneath a palm tree, need wait only overnight to learn the impact of such visions on the American will. Soon enough it will be hour to hour. Then minute to minute, perhaps, as the legislators debate the issue of the moment on television before a mass audience of citizens, randomly or self-selected, who will hold bits of machinery enabling them to beam their opinions electronically through computers to the desk at which each legislator sits and deliberates.

The manifestations of current popular opinion, then, will be incessantly on display. That is the kind of government to which this democratic nation seems to be tending. It seems to have been fated to that tendency. George Gallup gave leaders what they have always wanted, perhaps: a guide to leadership. "What I want to get done is what the people desire to have done, and the question for me is how to find that out exactly," said one leader, Abraham Lincoln.

George Gallup, who provided an answer to that question, also happened to believe it was the right answer. In retirement of sorts on his five-hundred-acre farm outside Princeton—he was still going to the office to work on books when we talked at the end of 1982—he thought he had found the better way that didn't exist when he had begun knocking on doors sixty years before in St. Louis. "If government is supposed to be based on the will of the people," he said, "then somebody ought to go out and find what that will is."

Gallup was the only one who did that. "More and more people will be voting on more and more things, officially, and unofficially in polls, on issues as well as candidates," he said. "And that's a pretty good thing. Anything's good that makes us realize that government is not 'them.' We are the government. You either believe in democracy or you don't."

———

GEORGE GALLUP *was born on November 18, 1901, in Jefferson, Iowa.*

He got his nickname, Ted, because his father disliked Teddy Roosevelt. His father was a logician and a speculator in farm and ranch lands.

By age ten George was running a small dairy farm (eight cows). He made more money than any of his schoolmates, and he bought the uniforms for the high school basketball and football teams he played on. He coached the football team during his senior year, after the coach was drafted.

In 1936 he founded the British Institute of Public Opinion. By 1941 the Institute exercised enough influence for Prime Minister Winston Churchill to caution the House of Commons: "Nothing is more dangerous in wartime than to live in the temperamental atmosphere of a Gallup Poll, always feeling one's pulse and taking one's temperature."

After he wrongly predicted the outcome of the 1948 presidential election, letters addressed simply to "Dr. Wrong, Princeton, New Jersey," were delivered to him.

A poll he took in the Fifties revealed that only 55 percent of recent college graduates could name any recently published book that they would like to read. His study of international reading habits prompted him to declare, ". . . fewer people read books in the U.S. than in any other major democracy."

He said in a 1953 speech that "one of the real threats to America's future place in the world is a citizenry which daily elects to be entertained and not informed . . . [we] may kill ourselves laughing."

As a result of his investigations, advertisers began using comics for their ads and Look *magazine was published.*

He was a vice-president of the Young & Rubicam advertising agency for ten years. He is an associate member of the American Psychological Association, the Council on Foreign Relations, and the National Press Club of Washington, D.C. He founded Quill and Scroll, an international society for high school journalists. In the course of ten years he has taught eighteen courses at various universities.

Switzerland is his favorite country, because, he says, it is the "oldest and purest democracy in the world and virtually run by polls; the Swiss vote on all important issues almost every Sunday in the spring and fall."

He thinks the most important poll is of the public's opinion about having a woman as President. In 1937, 37 percent of the populace was in favor of this; recently that figure has risen to 80 percent. He thinks that the United States will soon have a woman President.

He stands six feet tall. He watches his weight but loves banana cream pie. He is frequently described as courteous, affable, and imperturbable. He is absent-minded, and when out on the road frequently runs out of gas or money or gets lost.

He routinely gets calls from drunks asking whom they should bet on in elections.

He does not vote along party lines. He thinks politics is "a dirty business."

His favorite pastime is reading, mostly nonfiction. Every day he reads The New York Times, The Washington Post, The Christian Science Monitor, *and* The Wall Street Journal.

His suit pockets are usually full of newspaper clippings.

He believes in self-education. He watches only the news on TV. His heroes are Presidents Franklin Roosevelt and Dwight Eisenhower, both of whom used polls extensively.

He gets up at nine A.M. *and works until midnight or later. He calls himself an "old fuddy-duddy."*

He likes to say, "I'll give you ten to one you die of cancer, twenty to one you die of heart disease."

He tests many of his polling ideas on his secretary.

He gets ideas by talking with his wife three times a week for an hour at breakfast. His wife is a former French teacher. They met on a blind date.

After an argument with his son George over whether there were more pet cats or dogs, father and son took a pet census. Results: 24.50 million dogs, 20.06 million cats.

He lives on a five-hundred-acre farm near Princeton, New Jersey. Parts of his house date back to the American Revolution.

He loves chow chow dogs and horses and horseback riding. He has owned horses practically all his life.

He thinks presidential elections should be financed by the government. He thinks prisons should be run as factories, not "warehouses."

He says that he has learned three significant things about Americans: "The judgment of the American people is extraordinarily sound. The public is almost always ahead of its leaders. The electorate is better educated and more sophisticated."

Dr. Rock's
Magic Pill

SARA DAVIDSON

"I WAS NOT INTERESTED IN LIBERATING WOMEN," DR. JOHN ROCK SAYS. "THAT'S NOT why I was interested in the Pill. Women ought to stay at home and take care of their men and babies." Dr. Rock is now ninety-three, and as he sits beside the fire in his rustic farmhouse in Temple, New Hampshire, with light snow falling outside, his hearing aid begins to squeak.

"You need new batteries, Doc," says Mike DeLargey, the companion with whom Rock has lived for the last twelve years.

The doctor points to his head. "The trouble isn't with the battery, it's further in." He turns to me with a hint of merriment. "I don't cerebrate anymore. My brain has stopped working, so I just settle down as a nonentity."

"Why were you interested in the Pill?" I say, ignoring the disclaimer.

He stares at the fire. "I wanted to accomplish a pill that would allow my patients free sexual expression without the burden of childbirth. Before the Pill, I fitted diaphragms, although it was against the law in Massachusetts. A group of Catholic doctors tried to get me excommunicated. At least I think they did." He looks at me wistfully. "I wouldn't know my way around the uterus now. The practice of medicine is a distant dream."

It is humbling to meet a person of extraordinary accomplishments at an age when he can no longer remember much about them. John Rock has forgotten all but the most general details of the years he spent working on the birth con-

trol pill. Rock is one of a group of people—with Gregory Pincus at the helm—
who brought the Pill to the world. Little is known about these people: Pincus,
Rock, Min Chueh Chang, Carl Djerassi, Frank Colton, Margaret Sanger, Katherine McCormick, Celso-Ramón García. They did not all know one another,
yet each played a role. Few articles or books have been written about them.
Three have died without telling their stories, and others are unable to remember, which leaves us with a confusing tangle of facts and myths. It is as if they
came together briefly, set a bomb in place, and, shortly after its release, disappeared in smoke.

I did not know this when I began looking into the story of the Pill. It was 1983,
and the Pill was out of favor among the women I knew, who mistrusted the
drug and, in any case, seemed more intent on trying to conceive babies.

In 1983 the very concept of the Pill seemed bizarre: taking a powerful drug
every day, disturbing the body's monthly cycle, and altering the balance of hormones in order to live in a state of permanent false pregnancy.

Yet in 1960, when the Pill came on the market, it was welcomed as a miracle.
We were under the sway of different ideas: a belief in science, in American
technology, and in drugs as keys to the golden future. One of the researchers
who worked on the Pill said, "It was readily accepted because the Western
world was geared to swallowing pills." Aldous Huxley had predicted the Pill in
Brave New World Revisited in 1958.

Two years later, the Pill was available at any drugstore by prescription. It shot
us straight from the era of condoms and diaphragms to the era of physiological,
or internal, birth control. It was the first time in history that medicine was used
for a social purpose, that medicine was given to masses of healthy people.

Listen to the names of the first Pills: Enovid, Ortho-Novum. They ring of innovation and the new. I remember in the early Sixties, when I was a student at
Berkeley, young women who went on the Pill were looked upon as "advanced."
We saw the Pill in much the same way that we saw the new diet soft drinks—as
a boon of the modern age.

The Pill gave us the electrifying sense that there were no consequences. Sex
could be enjoyed without risk, at any moment, without stopping in the middle
or fumbling with messy devices. And this new, worry-free, recreational sex was
available to women as well as men.

Had there been no Pill, the dramatic changes in sexual behavior of the Sixties might have come about anyway, but, as John Rock told me, "the Pill made
things easier and safer."

The Pill told women—whether they took it or not—that it was possible, with
100 percent certainty, to delay having children, to pursue a career, to travel, to
sleep and live with different men.

And women bought it, with a naiveté that, in retrospect, seems astonishing.
Almost no one questioned the safety of the Pill; the only opposition was on reli-
gious and moral grounds. Two of the drug companies refused to market the
Pill, fearing a flood of hate mail and a boycott of all their products by Catholics.

G. D. Searle, the first company to make the Pill, was expecting trouble, but to everyone's surprise, it never came.

Eight years after it was introduced, the Pill was being swallowed by eleven million women in the world. All other drugs were called by their names—aspirin, Valium, tetracycline—but birth control tablets were, in every country, "the Pill."

"Who invented the Pill?" I was asked repeatedly. Gregory Pincus, the biochemist who cofounded the Worcester Foundation for Experimental Biology, was the linchpin: he orchestrated the program to develop the Pill. But Carl Djerassi, the chemist who developed the steroid that would be the basis of the Pill, says there was no "father of the Pill—it was at least a ménage à trois." In the development of any drug, he says, "you need a chemist, a biologist, and a clinician. The chemist synthesizes the drug, the biologist tests it with animals, and the clinician tests it with people."

Djerassi, like many in the field, speaks in reproductive images. "The chemist is the mother who produces the egg. The biologist is the father who supplies the sperm, and the clinician, who brings it to the public, is the obstetrician." In his scheme, Djerassi is the mother of the Pill, Gregory Pincus the father, and John Rock the obstetrician.

There is an opposing view, though, that the mothers of the Pill were two feminists from a previous era, Margaret Sanger and Katherine Dexter McCormick, who in 1951 actually commissioned Pincus to make them an oral contraceptive.

The women were a striking contrast. Margaret Sanger was only five feet tall, a charismatic redhead who, in her early years, was a socialist. She invented the phrase "birth control" in 1914, founded the magazine *Woman Rebel*, and was arrested many times while campaigning for birth control and sexual freedom.

Katherine Dexter was a foot taller than Sanger. She was one of the first women to graduate from MIT, and in 1904 she married Stanley McCormick, son of the founder of International Harvester. Shortly after their marriage, Stanley McCormick suffered a schizophrenic breakdown and never recovered. The couple withdrew from society, and for the rest of her life Katherine McCormick, like a latter-day Miss Havisham, continued to dress in the ankle-length skirts of 1904, her bridal year.

McCormick was so wealthy, her attorney once said, she "could not spend the interest on her interest." She was obsessed with the "population crisis" and the need for effective birth control and developed a friendship with Sanger.

In 1951 Sanger and McCormick went to see Gregory Pincus because of his eminence in mammalian reproduction. No record was made of their meeting, and all three died in the mid-sixties. But a legend has evolved, and the following version was told to me by Pincus's wife, Lizzie.

The two feminists asked Pincus if he could create a contraceptive that women could take "like an aspirin," a pill that would be safe and cheap and that anyone could use, even the illiterate. Was this a fantasy or was it possible?

Pincus said he thought it was possible, but he wasn't certain.

"How much money do you need?" McCormick asked.

Pincus dodged. "Research is expensive; I'd have to hire new people and build a new animal room. . . ."

"Look here," McCormick said. "I'm close to eighty and I want it done in my lifetime. Pull a figure out of your head."

"One hundred twenty-five thousand dollars."

McCormick wrote him a check for forty thousand dollars and said she would send the rest shortly. In the following years, McCormick gave Pincus more than two million dollars for his project, and before the decade was up, she and Sanger had their pill.

Gregory Goodwin Pincus, known to his friends as Goody, was said to be a great scientific entrepreneur: able to mobilize the talents of many and speed them ahead toward a goal.

Pincus had to think of a way in which a drug could actually stop pregnancy. He remembered reading a relatively obscure scientific article in 1937 about an experiment in which injections of the female hormone progesterone prevented ovulation in rabbits. If it worked in humans, and there was no ovulation, there could be no pregnancy. This was the simplest method Pincus could imagine, and he never pursued another tack.

Progesterone is a hormone released in the body after ovulation and during pregnancy and acts to suppress ovulation to avoid overlapping pregnancies. The problem facing Pincus was that progesterone was expensive and had to be injected in large doses to work. He wrote to drug companies around the world, asking if they had developed a synthetic progesterone that was stronger than the natural hormone and would work by mouth.

He received hundreds of compounds, and in April 1951 Pincus directed his colleague, the biologist Min Chueh Chang, to begin testing the drugs on rabbits. Among the compounds sent to Pincus was a steroid, norethindrone, created by Carl Djerassi at the Syntex Corporation in Mexico. Djerassi says the drug was developed to treat menstrual disorders and fertility problems. "Not in our wildest dreams did we imagine that eventually this substance would become the active ingredient" in the birth control pill. The same was true of the compound norethynodrel, developed by Frank Colton at G. D. Searle.

Chang tested more than three hundred drugs on rabbits and rats and found that the products made by Syntex and Searle were the strongest. For Chang it was a pure-research question. "I wanted to see how the drugs would work on eggs and sperm. I didn't know if the animal was happy or not. I left that to Pincus."

Chang is a wiry, cheerful man whose English is difficult to unscramble. He has retired but still comes to the Worcester Foundation to do experiments. He shows me the animal room, where he is observing two white rabbits on whom he recently operated. It is chilling: the rabbits are immobile in their cages and their fur is riddled with scars.

I ask Chang if his wife or daughters ever took the Pill. "I never discussed it with my daughters." If they came to you, I say, would you recommend the Pill? He fidgets. "My personal attitude is, if you can help it, don't take any pill, even aspirin."

At the same time Chang was giving progesterone to rabbits, John Rock, forty miles away, in Brookline, was giving progesterone to his infertile patients. There is a flip-flop relationship between helping women conceive and helping them avoid pregnancy. Rock told his students, "If you reverse the treatment for one, you may achieve the opposite result."

Rock was giving progesterone to women who he thought had immature reproductive systems. Rock was aware that during treatment, which lasted three to five months, the women would not ovulate. It was a "rest" for their systems, and after treatment stopped, about 15 percent quickly became pregnant in what was later called the "Rock rebound" effect.

Rock and Pincus met at a conference in 1952 and, when they learned of each other's work, agreed to collaborate. Rock's participation was fortuitous. He possessed charm, humor, and great powers of persuasion. He was a devout Catholic who went to mass every day, and he was *the* Dr. Rock to generations of Harvard medical students, whom he had been teaching since 1922.

When Rock had started practicing medicine, gynecology was only fifty years old and relatively little was known about reproduction. The hormones that regulate a woman's cycle had not been isolated, and there was no laboratory test for pregnancy.

Rock wanted to pursue research; every day he left his house at six A.M. to work in the laboratory before starting his rounds. In 1944 he achieved, with Miriam Menkin, the first fertilization of a human egg in a test tube. He succeeded in freezing sperm for a year without loss of potency, and he confirmed that ovulation takes place fourteen days before menstruation.

Rock's major interest was infertility, and he founded one of the first infertility clinics. He was meticulous in the way he treated his patients. Ann Jane (A.J.) Levinson, Rock's daughter, who worked in his office, says, "He never gave a woman anything he hadn't tried first on himself. I remember once he injected a new compound into his hip and it formed a large lump that couldn't be absorbed and had to be removed surgically."

Rock was formal and courtly; he rarely used first names. He opened doors for his patients and offered them his arm, and if one dropped a handkerchief, he swooped to pick it up. His patients adored him, and Rock took pride in the fact that few were kept waiting in his office, although he might see thirty in an afternoon.

A.J. says Rock was excited by the prospect of helping women control reproduction. He had been touched by the plight of women who had ten children, women who looked old and used up at thirty, but he never intended the Pill for the unmarried. "We had many arguments late into the night," A.J. says. "He thought the appropriate use of the Pill was for women who'd already had children, who'd already done their job on this earth. I told him young people need time to enjoy each other and work through their problems before being strapped with children. He said, 'Your ideas are interesting, but it's not my job to provide a playground. The purpose of marriage is children.' "

Rock and his wife, Nan, had four daughters and a son in the eight years after they were married. A.J. says, "He was a complicated man. He admired enormously the achievements of women. My mother drove an ambulance in World War I, but Daddy admired her because she also was a good wife and mother. I understand he was one of the people who kept women out of Harvard medical school. He believed, and he ingrained in us, that women weren't capable of being physicians."

His views were not unusual for the time, 1952. Contraception was illegal in Massachusetts and Connecticut, and, as one of Rock's colleagues said, "If we were sleeping around, we weren't talking about it." The baby boom was at its peak, and the majority of Rock's patients were desperate to have children.

Pincus sent Rock batches of the synthetic progesterone that had worked with rabbits. Rock tried it on a group of thirty women and monitored them carefully to verify that ovulation had stopped. The results were gratifying: not one woman ovulated while taking the drug, and the treatment led, as before, to 15 percent becoming pregnant on the rebound.

Pincus now believed he had the Pill in his grasp. What remained was the most risky part: testing it on a large scale. Pincus and Rock decided to use the Searle compound, norethynodrel, and selected Puerto Rico as the site. They chose Puerto Rico because it had a severe overpopulation problem, the government was eager to cooperate, and the subjects, living on an island, would be easy to keep track of.

Pincus enlisted the help of Celso-Ramón García, who had set up the department of obstetrics and gynecology at the University of Puerto Rico medical school. Rock, García, and a team from the Worcester Foundation devised a program to give the drug to volunteers in a large housing project, Rio Piedras.

Anne Merrill, a scientist who had worked closely with Pincus and went with the team to Puerto Rico, says, "We were confident the Pill would work to prevent pregnancy, but there were many things we didn't know: Would there be any birth defects in babies born to women after they stopped taking the Pill? Would there be the proper ratio of boys and girls born? Would cancers develop? Would there be any permanent loss of fertility?"

The fact that thousands were given the Pill when such serious questions were unanswered raised an ethical dilemma that, ten years later, would haunt the team. Feminists accused them of "genocide" and "using Third World women as guinea pigs for American drug companies."

García becomes angry at the charges. "No one forced those women to come into the program, and they were free to drop out anytime. We had tested the drug in Massachusetts and had a very good idea what to expect. We discussed the risks carefully with the women, and all—from the most intelligent to the simplest people—said, 'Of course we want to try it.' "

Anne Merrill says, "We all felt we were doing something good. In biological research, you have to weigh the risks against the benefits. If the end is worthwhile and if it's important for humanity, you conduct the experiments. You learn to look at the test subjects the way a general looks upon his soldiers."

Rock personally checked the medical records of volunteers, and by 1959, after five years of testing, Rock and Pincus were satisfied the drug was safe. Searle applied to the FDA to license the Pill but was rejected. Searle asked for a hearing, and Rock flew to Washington to plead the case.

The doctor assigned to rule on the Pill, Pasquale DeFelice, was young, thirty-five, trained in obstetrics and gynecology but not yet board-certified. DeFelice recalls, "Standing before me was John Rock, *the light of the obstetrical world!* . . . Anything he said had to be listened to." Rock said that he was angry that such an inexperienced doctor was charged with making this ruling. Rock kept referring to him as "Young Man" and at the end of the hearing grabbed DeFelice by the lapels and told him to make a speedy decision. Several months later, in May 1960, Searle was formally notified that the Pill had been approved.

Rock then set out to persuade the Catholic Church. He gave lectures and wrote a book, *The Time Has Come: A Catholic Doctor's Proposal to End the Battle for Birth Control.* The book was attacked by conservatives, but that did not disturb him. Rock had always told his daughters, "Follow your conscience, nothing else."

At the end of the Sixties, when Pincus had died and Rock was nearing eighty, Americans reacted against the Pill with the wrath of people who were once naively trusting. Reports were published linking the Pill with potentially fatal side effects: blood clots, strokes, heart attacks, gallbladder disease, and malignant tumors. In 1970 the Senate called hearings on the safety of the Pill; although no conclusions could be drawn from testimony, the FDA began requiring drug companies to insert warning labels in all packets of the Pill.

Not surprisingly, use of the Pill fell off among American women, from about twelve million women in the mid-Seventies to about six million in the early Eighties. In the rest of the world, however, the Pill became the most popular method of contraception, with an estimated sixty million now using it.

The dosage has been reduced, which has lowered the risk of side effects, especially for nonsmokers under thirty-five. In addition, studies released in 1983 by the Center for Disease Control in Atlanta suggest that the Pill prevents cancer of the ovaries and uterus. American women continue to be wary of the Pill, though, and the crucial issue—whether it is harmful in any respect in the long run—has yet to be resolved.

It is late morning in Temple, New Hampshire, and John Rock is sitting by the fire. He looks dapper, wearing a crisp white shirt and tie under a navy jump suit, and his cheeks have a pink, strangely youthful glow. Irving Stone's *The Origin*, about the life of Darwin, lies on his lap. "I'm reading it for the second time," he says. "Since I forget what I read, I can start right over again."

Mike DeLargey throws a log on the fire. A tall, lanky man, now thirty-five, he came to live with Rock during a shaky period in his own life and never left.

Rock encouraged DeLargey to finish his studies. Now DeLargey works full-time and plays in a country-and-western band, and because he is away frequently, they have an eighteen-year-old boy living in.

"This is a male habitat," DeLargey says.

"I had enough of women," Rock says. He turns to me. "Why the devil did *Esquire* pick me for this group?"

"Because of the Pill." He gives me a skeptical look. I ask what he thinks of attacks on the safety of the Pill.

"I think the Pill is perfectly harmless. But this business of remembering, take a pill, take a pill. . . ." His eyes wander. "If I were young, I think I'd depend on the Pill and use the rhythm method as a safeguard."

"How could you use the rhythm method with the Pill?"

He looks confused. "Don't expect me to make intelligible answers. I'm half asleep."

He makes his way, with a cane, to the sofa, where he lies down on his back and closes his eyes. "Just enjoy yourself," he says. "You're no trouble to me."

I ask what the most gratifying part of his life was.

"Right now. It frequently occurs to me, gosh, what a lucky guy I am. I have no responsibilities, and I have everything I want. I take a dose of equanimity every twenty minutes. I will not be disturbed about things."

Rock says he did not expect to be ninety-three; he has suffered six coronaries, yet he has outlived his wife and two of his five children. "Paul Dudley White says I'll probably die in my sleep."

I move my chair closer to the sofa. "Do you believe in an afterlife?"

"Of course I don't. Heaven and Hell, Rome, all that church stuff—that's for the solace of the multitude." He begins breathing rhythmically. Then he starts. "I was an ardent practicing Catholic for a long time, and I really believed it all then, you see."

"What made you stop?"

His mouth drops open; he is snoring.

I have the fleeting impulse to curl up in a chair beside him, escape from my own responsibilities. The room is peaceful, with its worn, comfortable furniture and antique maps of Boston. The fire crackles and birds are feeding by the window. The impulse passes, and I let myself out and drive to the airport.

———

JOHN ROCK *was born twenty minutes ahead of his twin sister, Ellen, on March 24, 1890, in Marlborough, Massachusetts. The Rocks were Irish Catholics; his father, Frank Sylvester Rock, owned a saloon, a theater, and a racetrack.*

While his brothers roughhoused with other boys, John preferred to skip rope, perform skits, and play dolls with his twin sister. Other boys called him Sissy Rock.

When he was fourteen a talk with a parish curate made a lasting impression on him. Rock recalls the priest telling him, "John, always stick to your conscience. Never let anyone keep it for you. And I mean anyone."

He was on the swimming and running teams in high school, and in his senior year won an essay contest that sent him to South America. Afterward, he worked for nine months on a Guatemalan banana farm. It was after returning from the farm, Rock remembers, that he had his first "spontaneous erection"—"while working on some audit books."

As an undergraduate at Harvard he went out for track and joined the Hasty Pudding Club. He graduated in three years. At Harvard medical school he was interested in psychiatry and gynecology—"the two major functions of humans, cerebration and reproduction," he noted. He actually preferred psychiatry but was put off by the longer residency requirement.

In 1925 he married six-foot-tall Anna Thorndike; it was one of the most publicized Boston society weddings of the decade. William Cardinal O'Connell insisted on marrying the couple—an honor previously accorded only to Rose and Joseph Kennedy. The wedding almost didn't take place. The day before the ceremony Rock performed a cesarean section, an operation then forbidden by the Catholic Church. When he went to confession, a local priest refused to forgive this trespass, thus making it technically impossible for Rock to receive the sacrament of marriage. The day was saved when Cardinal O'Connell overruled the priest. Rock, although absolved, was greatly disturbed by his church's arbitrary rule-making.

He and his wife had five children in eight years—four girls and a son who died at age nineteen in an auto accident.

Rock stood just over six feet one inch tall. In his prime he was a tireless perfectionist. Gracious with patients rich and poor, he would personally call them cabs after their visits. A great storyteller, he enjoyed parties, dancing, and martinis.

In 1938 he and Dr. Arthur Hertig isolated the first complete fertilized human egg; it was taken from the uterus of a woman who had just undergone a hysterectomy. Their research helped usher in the study of test-tube fertilization.

He tried to involve men in birth control. Operating with the knowledge that sperm cannot be produced if the scrotum is heated beyond its optimal temperature, he invented a warming oilcloth underwear-liner for men. It was nicknamed the Rock-strap. It never caught on.

In 1963 Rock's bishop, Richard Cardinal Cushing, reviewed his book The Time Has Come: A Catholic Doctor's Proposal to End the Battle for Birth Control. Cushing observed that Rock had shortcomings as a theologian but that "in his book there is much that is good." An associate of Cushing's described the cardinal's review as "a slap on the wrist—and two pats on the back."

In 1965 Rock wrote a report rebutting the contention that women derived sexual pleasure from using tampons.

"The Pill, in time, will usher in the golden age of womanhood," affirmed Dr.

Andrew Elia, chairman of Boston University's obstetrics and gynecology department, in 1965. "It will set them free as nothing before in history has. It will enable them to plan not just for their pregnancies, but their lives. . . . Women will be able to pursue higher education. . . . They will also be free to spend more time with the few babies they do have. [It] will also set their husbands free. They will not be crushed under the burden of supporting large families, locked into jobs they hate but can't afford to leave. . . . More than all that, the Pill will do something absolutely transcendent for the world. It will usher in the age of the wanted child."

Some of his research has been called unethical. He has been criticized for conducting early tests of the Pill on mental patients without their consent, and for encouraging hysterectomy candidates to have intercourse before the operation without fully explaining that their excised organs would be searched for fertilized eggs.

His colleagues Dr. Min Chueh Chang and Dr. Gregory Pincus developed a "morning after" birth control pill, made of diethylstilbestrol (DES). Rock refused to join this research, because he viewed this pill as an abortion agent.

Neil Armstrong's Famous First Words

GEORGE PLIMPTON

THAT NEIL ARMSTRONG SHOULD BE THE "SPACE AGE" REPRESENTATIVE IS A MATTER of evidence: a shy hero, in the Lindbergh tradition, self-effacing, and graced with a glamorous-sounding name—*Armstrong*—that a novelist wouldn't dream of giving a fictionalized astronaut. Best of all, he turned out to be a man with a great flair for producing the right phrase at the appropriate moment—"That's one small step for a man, one giant leap for mankind"—an amazing set of words that will be remembered from one's schoolboy years and thence quoted for years to come. Indeed, the genesis of those remarkable words struck me as the key to the assignment.

I thought it would be reasonably easy: a short trip out to Lebanon, Ohio, where I'd meet the great man—recently professor of engineering at the University of Cincinnati, he is now a consultant—and perhaps he'd invite me out to his home, where we'd sit with our boots up on the porch fence; he'd reminisce about that great week in July 1969, and eventually he'd give the "gen"—as your old contributor, Ernest Hemingway, used to say—about the famous lines . . . how they came to mind, who made them up (that is, if he didn't himself), had he rehearsed them, what would he have said had he sunk to his waist in moon dust, and so forth.

The trouble, of course—which I didn't know at the time—is that not only does Armstrong not grant interviews, but he doesn't think of himself as a shaper of history, or even worthy of representing U.S. space efforts. When I requested a meeting, he wrote a pleasant, self-deprecatory letter suggesting that I concentrate on the contributions of Dr. Wernher von Braun, a perplexing choice since Braun was not American-born, was dead to boot, and would be remembered as much for the Nazis' V-2 military rocket as for his contribution to the American space program.

So, given Neil Armstrong's reluctance to talk, I shifted plans and spoke to a number of his peers in the space program to get their opinions and impressions about his famous words, promising myself at the end that I would call Armstrong himself, willy-nilly, and hope for the best.

Curiously, the general public does not think Armstrong made up these lines himself. First, the words themselves are almost too good to be true; surely a wordsmith somewhere in Houston's Mission Control, or perhaps a public relations firm, had come up with the phrase, one of many offered, picked after heated discussion around a conference table and then delivered to the proper authorities at NASA in an envelope to be handed to the appropriate astronaut. Second, on the moon Armstrong supposedly made a mistake in his delivery of the line itself—he left the "a" out before "man"—which would not be a likely error with a line of one's own composition. Third, shortly after the line was said, a blackboard in the Houston press bullpen had the lines written on it correctly, which would suggest that someone there was in the know. And fourth, NASA would hardly have left an occasion so incredibly momentous to the speechifying abilities of an engineer–test pilot.

I started out by talking to the two astronauts who had been with him— "Buzz" Aldrin, the second man on the moon, and Mike Collins. Aldrin produced an interesting analogy. He said he was the "understudy . . . an actor without lines listening to the star recite the Gettysburg Address without knowing that it would turn out to be the Gettysburg Address."

I asked if he knew Armstrong was going to pronounce "the lines."

"No."

"I mean it wasn't discussed at all on the way up?"

"No."

I asked what Aldrin would have said in a similar situation, and he said he wouldn't have said anything. He said, "Preoccupation with utterances like that is an overemphasis on rhetoric."

Aldrin, however, did mention a description of the moon he'd come up with himself of which he was quite proud—an oxymoron, of all things—namely: "magnificent desolation."

But he seemed snippy about Armstrong. He referred to the missing "a"—the indefinite article was supposed to precede "man" in "one small step for a man"; he pointed out that Armstrong was thus only barely comprehensible to the *Japanese* (of all people) sitting in myriads in front of their Sonys, since the word in their language for man and mankind is the same . . . thus effecting a curious redundancy in the sentence.

Sour grapes? Perhaps. In some of the early checklists for the landing of the

Eagle, the lunar module, Aldrin was selected to be the first to step on the moon. Armstrong ignored this; acting on his authority as commander he designated himself to be the first out—which in April, three months before the launch, became official policy. From that point on there was a definite change in Aldrin's disposition—his mood became gloomy and introspective . . . leading eventually, a couple of years after the moon flight, to his well-publicized breakdown.

It might be worth mentioning that the crew of *Apollo 11* are not an especially close trio. One might think that an enormous camaraderie might have been built up over the months of preparations and the flight itself, the bond that so often exists between those who have gone through great stress together—military men, athletes, adventurers—but such is not the case. There have been one or two official reunions—the tenth was quite a blast—but the astronauts rarely communicate. Mike Collins found a nice phrase to describe the group: "amiable strangers."

As for Collins, who was in the *Columbia* circling the moon during the landing, he never heard "the lines." He was on the far side of the moon when they were said—out of communication for forty-eight minutes back there; indeed, only in touch with the pair on the surface when his spacecraft entered a vector above them, which gave him thirteen minutes to listen to what was going on. The first words he was privy to from the moon's surface were some palaver about how pretty the American flag looked, sticking stiffly out above the lunar landscape.

Collins told me he was sure there was no official apparatus set up by NASA to provide astronauts with appropriate remarks. Somebody might have whispered the famous phrase in Armstrong's ear as a suggestion, but it would have had no official sanction.

"Actually, I thought Neil would come up with something pretty good," Collins went on. "He probably composed it right at the end. He tends to be a procrastinator—the kind of pilot who lands with ten seconds of fuel left."

Peter Conrad, the next astronaut I talked to, told me an interesting story that would seem to support the contention that the astronauts were given free rein to say whatever they wished. In August 1969, several months before Conrad himself was to go up in *Apollo 12* on the second expedition to the moon's surface, Oriana Fallaci, who didn't seem to like Neil Armstrong very much (my guess would be that he had turned her down for an exclusive interview), refused to believe that those sacred words had not been supplied him by NASA. Everyone followed orders, she said.

Conrad finally made her a bet that the two of them would agree upon a phrase that he would subsequently deliver, whatever it was, when he got to the moon. The words decided upon—rather self-mocking, since Conrad was the smallest of the astronauts in the program—were as follows: "It may be a small step for Neil, but it's a big step for a little fellow like me." Fallaci simply wouldn't believe it. NASA would never let such an irreverency pass. The bet was agreed upon. Five hundred dollars.

Sure enough, the astronaut imparted those sprightly words on the *Apollo 12* flight when he had the chance. Fallaci, incidentally, never paid up—which Conrad told me did not surprise him, since he felt that this kind of default was typical of all "rich writers."

The people I talked to at NASA were all very insistent that the astronauts had never been prompted. John McLeaish, who is at present the chief of the public information branch of NASA's Johnson Space Center in Houston, said, "Not only that, but we've never censored anything they've said. The transcripts of the air–ground transmissions have always been published verbatim—even the swearing. We are not in the expletive-deleted business."

Blithely he gave me a couple of examples. On the *Apollo 10* flight, which was the first to skim the moon's surface, Tom Stafford, remarking on a landmark crater, announced, "Here comes Censorinus, it's bigger than shit!" And then, according to McLeaish (and presumably the transcripts), John Young on the *Apollo 16* flight suddenly informed Mission Control: "I've got the fucking farts again."

Nonetheless, the NASA people, while they agreed there was no prompting of Armstrong, were surprised the words were spoken, startled by their quality, and especially that Armstrong, of all people, had produced them.

Eugene Kranz was the flight director of the LM. He is one of those aeronautics people who says "That's affirmative" rather than "Yes."

"What did you think he was going to say?" I asked.

"Once he had egressed?"

"Well, er . . . yes."

"Neil was *supposed* to be giving Houston verbal confirmation of the moon's surface, its consistency and various features, so that the LM's position could be plotted exactly. So I thought he was going to say something like 'We have no problem here. The surface is a relatively light powdery dust.' "

According to Kranz, the "small step" words didn't sound like Armstrong— whom Kranz described as "very matter-of-fact, businesslike, unemotional." At Mission Control, a lot of people looked at each other as if to say, "What was that?" and Kranz remembers that there was a certain amount of snickering at the "small step" part, since the distance between the bottom rung of the LM's ladder and the moon's surface was a "pretty good-sized hop."

Julian Scheer, who was assistant administrator for public affairs at NASA, and, as McLeaish suggested, would have been the obvious person to prep Armstrong, heard the words just when the rest of the world did; at first he, too, was surprised.

"I shouldn't have been," he admitted. "Later, when I asked Neil about what he'd said, and how startled and pleased I'd been, he grinned at me, shrugged his shoulders, and he said, 'You're not the *only* person who can speak the English language.' No, I shouldn't have been surprised. For all that reticence, Neil's a remarkable guy. When I was with the *Apollo 11* astronauts on a world tour after their flight, I had a speech writer along. But Neil would always stuff the material in the back of his pocket and he'd speak extemporaneously. At 10 Downing

65

Street I heard him give a speech off the top of his head about how the British were responsible for the development of the chronometer—he gave a whole history, a litany on how extraordinary this contribution was, and essential, and that therefore the British could rightly feel proud and share credit for what had been done. It was a great performance. You know how the English tap the top of the dinner table to applaud? What Neil said raised a storm of sound. If the British people had heard that talk, he would have been the prime minister the next day.

"He's the kind of man who says what's on his mind," Scheer went on to say. He remembered Walter Cronkite interviewing the three astronauts just before the *Apollo 11* launch and asking them what they did to keep in shape. Collins told Cronkite he jogged—about five miles a day. Buzz Aldrin said, "I not only run, but I do an hour of isometric exercise." When Armstrong's turn came, he said—in that flat, unemotional midwestern accent—"Well, Walter, I believe that the good Lord gave us a finite number of heartbeats and I'm damned if I'm going to use up mine running up and down a street!"

I asked Scheer if in his capacity as a public affairs administrator it had ever crossed his mind to advise the astronauts on what might be said. Well, he'd considered it, he admitted. He had done some research. On the Pacific shore, either Lewis or Clark, he couldn't recall which, had written, "There's a beautiful blue ocean out there . . . I'm tired and I'm going to rest." But then he decided it would be very crass to make recommendations of any sort to the astronauts. Indeed, when Frank Borman came to him to ask if he had any ideas about what might be said for television on the *Apollo 10* flight with the spacecraft emerging from behind the moon on Christmas Day, Scheer said, "Frank, I cannot and will not suggest anything." On that flight the astronauts took up a Bible and in turn read verses from Genesis—which came as a great relief at Mission Control, where a rumor was circulating that the astronauts had planned a rousing chorus of "Santa Claus is comin' to town . . ."

I finally put in my phone call to Neil Armstrong. It started off clumsily; he said he thought he'd made it clear that he was not to be the subject of any piece about space-age contributions. I explained that I had been writing about *Apollo 11*, its crew, and that it would have been odd to leave him out completely—it would have turned him into a kind of phantom commander. Besides, I was concentrating on what he had *said*, rather than the astronaut himself.

That seemed to placate him. I asked him about the sentence. He quietly told me that he had produced the lines on his own ("I'm afraid I'll have to take the full blame") and the words were composed not on the long trip up there, as had been supposed by most of his colleagues, nor beforehand, but *after* the actual landing of *Eagle* on the moon's surface.

When I expressed astonishment that he had waited until then, he produced a most practical reason: "I always knew there was a good chance of being able to return to Earth," he said, "but I thought the chances of a successful touchdown on the moon's surface were about even money—fifty-fifty. An awful lot of the puzzle had not been filled in; so much had not even been tried. Most people don't realize how difficult the mission was. So it didn't seem to me there was much point in thinking up something to say if we'd have to abort the landing."

"NASA had nothing to do with what you said," I asked, "not even suggesting you ought to say something?"

"So many peoople had mentioned it, letters, the press, and so forth," Armstrong said, "that obviously something had to be done. But NASA always maintained the position that they would never tell us what to say."

I asked about the missing "a." Armstrong, replying that he had not misquoted his lines, felt that the "a" had been lost in the transmission, which was through a voice-activated system called VOX. "VOX can lose you a syllable every so often," Armstrong explained. Certainly he had said the sentence as it appears in the history books.

I even asked him the crazy question about sinking to his waist in lunar dust— would he have still blurted out "the lines"?

He laughed and said he probably would have produced something more appropriate to the situation—"something hilarious, I guess, or maybe awful."

I asked him how much "the lines" meant to him now—did he look back on them with satisfaction . . . a sense of accomplishment?

"I don't really think about it," he said quickly.

Charles Lindbergh is supposed to have said, "Well, I made it!" when he touched down at Le Bourget. What he actually said, leaning out, with the crowd surging around his plane, was: "Are there any mechanics here?" And then, "Does anyone here speak English?" So it is apparent that however self-deprecatory Armstrong is about his own contributions, he is certainly a giant leap ahead of Lindbergh in the immortal-words department.

———

NEIL ALDEN ARMSTRONG *was born on August 5, 1930, on a farm near Wapakoneta, Ohio. As a child he had the recurring dream that, by holding his breath, he could hover over the ground.*

He took his first plane ride in 1936; eight years later he began taking flying lessons, which he paid for by working at the local pharmacy and hardware store for forty cents an hour. (The flying lessons cost nine dollars an hour.) On his sixteenth birthday, he earned his pilot's license. He hadn't yet learned to drive.

He worked for a while in a bakery—getting the job because he was small enough to fit into the mixing vats to clean them at night. Each night he helped turn out 110 dozen doughnuts.

In high school, he played baritone horn in a jazz combo called the Mississippi Moonshiners. He can also play the piano, trombone, and bass.

When he told his mother that he had won a Navy scholarship to college, she dropped a quart jar of preserves on her right foot and broke her big toe.

A Boy Scout for most of his youth, he finally completed his Eagle Scout requirements when he was a freshman at Purdue University.

After spending three years admiring his future wife, Janet, he finally asked her out on a date. "He is not one to rush into anything," said Janet.

By the time he was twenty-one he was flying Panther jets in the Korean War. He once guided a badly damaged plane back to the aircraft carrier Essex. He was shot down behind enemy lines. Though he came home with three Air Medals, he has said of his seventy-eight combat missions, "I'd be lying if I said they'd done me any good."

"I loathe danger," he once said. Asked if he would go to the moon if he thought he might not come back, he replied, "Nonsense. Die on the moon! To get a look at the moon! If it were a matter of staying there for a year or two . . . maybe. . . . No, no, it would still be too high a price to pay: because it's senseless."

Armstrong was the only one of the Apollo 11 astronauts to have no religious affiliation.

Describing the moon, he said, "Since the sky is black, the impression is of being on a sandy athletic field at night where it is well illuminated by floodlights."

"Becoming an astronaut must have given you great joy," Oriana Fallaci once said to him. "I wouldn't know," he replied. "Let me think. . . . Well, yes, I suppose I was pleased. It's always nice to gain in status. But I don't have any personal ambition. My one ambition is to contribute to the success of this program. I'm no romantic."

After the moonwalk the Ohio Dairymen's Association had Armstrong's likeness sculpted in nine hundred pounds of butter at the Ohio State Fair. The Wapakoneta Airport was renamed Neil Armstrong Airport.

Visiting the town of his ancestors in Scotland, he learned that his sixteenth-century relatives were a clan of thieves and rogues. His kinsman Johnnie Armstrong wreaked havoc throughout the countryside before he was finally captured and hanged. Neil Armstrong, better behaved, was sworn in as an honorary Scot.

"As the traveling and speaking wore on," fellow Apollo 11 astronaut Buzz Aldrin observed, "Neil became more and more withdrawn." Aldrin remembered that soon after returning to Earth, "Neil told me he had been offered the presidency of an important university. He later declined, evidently feeling he had insufficient experience for the job."

Armstrong stands five feet eleven and has blue eyes, rounded shoulders, and blond hair. He wears size 11 shoes. He and his wife do not care for parties.

"I smoke one cigar a month," said Armstrong. "But sometimes I forget to."

Persistent rumor once linked him romantically with singer Connie Stevens. A colleague remarked that it would have been "completely out of character" for Armstrong.

"He is capable," Life reported in 1969, "of cold, tight-lipped rage, triggered

most often by what he considers either dishonesty or subterfuge." His parents and wife have called him "a very easy man to live with."

"Silence is a Neil Armstrong answer," says his wife. "The word no is an argument."

He is fond of Japan, which he visited during the Korean War. At his home in El Lago, Texas, he had a Japanese garden outside and a large green Buddha in the living room.

Armstrong left NASA in 1971 to become professor of aerospace engineering at the University of Cincinnati. The Armstrongs have a 185-acre farm in Lebanon, Ohio.

LEGENDS

The Real
and the Mythic

THOUGH MYTHIC, THEY WERE MORTAL, CREATED PARTLY BY THEMSELVES AND partly by us. Jack and Jackie Kennedy, Muhammad Ali, Lyndon Baines Johnson, Elvis, and Walt Disney were divergent souls. And yet they are of a kind: imbued with heroism, equipped with their own folktales. They were intrinsically gifted; still, their notoriety and achievement took on a special aura because, simply enough, we needed their greatness.

As for JFK, history has been stubbornly romantic. It chooses to look past details of policies and personal peccadilloes. Instead, it continues to shine on Kennedy's knighthood, his gallantry, his charm. We remember him as our last duly elected Young Man. When he died, he took our innocence with him. We continue to look back, back through his fallibility, only to see clear images of glamour—our own, really.

Jacqueline Kennedy Onassis, too, was divined by our own longings. When first we met her she was our American sweetheart: stylish, alluring, composed. In her grief we saw her differently. She was our widow: pale, courageous, composed. As the years passed she became a wisp in the clouds, tolerating (it appears) our intrusive stares. From our lookout she hangs suspended beyond the ordinary world: timeless, gracious, composed.

Then there was Elvis. He became another kind of legend. He started out as a good-looking kid who drove a truck and sang okay. He was hardly of royalty born. But he was touched by fantastic timing. We were young, restless, and ready to move. It matters not whether Elvis knew that. He just opened his mouth and glory came out.

The Legends took root in our imagination. We sent our photographers and our notetakers to cover their movements. We kept informed. Muhammad Ali was not much of a poet. But his rhymes captured our attention, as he backed them up with his dancing feet and flying fists. No opponent—Joe Frazier, the U.S. Army, our fundamental dislike of the show-off—could whip him. When he said he was the greatest, we agreed.

LBJ was a master politician. His life as a legend began at thirty-five thousand feet, when he raised his right hand and recited the oath of office. With mournful yet fervent emotion, his and ours, the Great Society was enacted. And as the months passed, this imposing Texan, escalating a war, exposing his scar, grew to gigantic proportions. The man was now bigger than his office—and the presidency has been a fishbowl ever since.

Walt Disney *created* legends. His craft and his creatures are etched in our imagination: they are a part of our consciousness. Generations of children are visited with dreams and daydreams inspired by Disney's enterprises. His was the modern American mythology.

The Legends are not who they really were. They were drawn, colored, and animated by us.

—L. E.

The Short, Classy Voyage of JFK

WILLIAM STYRON

THE HARBOR:
Edgartown, Massachusetts.
August 1963.

THE WRITER IS EXCEPTIONALLY NERVOUS. HE WOULD BE NERVOUS ENOUGH MEETING the President of the United States in any case. But this day his distraction is compounded by the fact that he is in the throes of a struggle—so far successful—to stop smoking cigarettes. Sitting this summer morning on the porch of his rented harborside house on Martha's Vineyard, he wonders if his hard-fought battle (not a puff in three weeks) will come to naught, lost through such an ultimately insignificant (in the eye of eternity) event as a meeting with the President and his ravishing wife, both creatures beyond legend. The Writer in his extremity has become knowledgeable about all aspects of smoking (he has even recently finished a review-essay on the matter for *The New York Review of Books,* complete with a droll David Levine cartoon showing haggard-looking addicts sprouting cigarettes from mouths, noses, and ears) and is aware of how readily an emotional crisis may cause a quick lapse and a return to the habit. In short, the Writer is sick with worry that this imminent encounter might make him at last light up one of those Winstons he has kept in a pack on his bedroom dresser, awaiting just such an eventuality.

At bottom, the Writer is aware of the extreme foolishness of a palpitation like this. He knows he should not be so jittery, even when the event in the offing is no large-scale affair, where he might melt into the background, but a small nautical get-together—one might even call it intimate—in which he will doubtless have to remain wittily on the qui vive. The Writer gives a sound that emanates partly from discomfort, partly from mirth. By chance he has only the day before been rereading a book of Mencken's essays, one of which hilariously anatomizes the historical negligibility of most American Presidents, "like a roll call of forgotten Sumerian Kings"—James K. Polk, Chester A. Arthur, Millard Fillmore—and for an instant he finds it bracing to reflect that John F. Kennedy might one day rest in that forlorn Ozymandian company. But soon the apprehension returns. Let's face it: In the year 1963, after these many months into his office, JFK is no ordinary chief magistrate, like all those frock-coated and muttonchop-whiskered nonentities from bygone days, but the glamorous and gorgeous avatar of American power at the magic moment of its absolute twentieth-century ascendancy. The entire world, including even the Russians, has gone a little gaga over this youthful demigod and his bewitching consort, and the Writer has to confess that he is perhaps a touch gaga himself. Though not in the truest sense a starfucker (this term is not then current but is apt), the Writer in the early years of the star-mad Sixties is scarcely less vulnerable to the Kennedy charisma than the next American citizen fatigued with the Fifties and their baggy style and the Eisenhower drone. To be sure, there is space in both the Writer's heart and mind that might be more satisfactorily filled had Adlai Stevenson won the prize. Not as magnetic as Kennedy, and about one-tenth as sexy, he nonetheless possessed a judiciousness that would have let him avoid some of the mistakes that are already proving to be troubling signs of Kennedy's immaturity (Would Adlai have committed an imbecilic blunder like the Bay of Pigs?), but given any other alternative, the Republic certainly could have done worse.

The Writer is rehearsing a few of the matters that he feels he might wish to broach with the President (should he be given the chance)—when the telephone rings. It is the ingratiating voice of agent Clint Hill of the Secret Service. If this were not a true but a fictional tale, the Writer—writing from a vantage point of twenty years later—might wish to halt the narrative and utter a somber and premonitory word, known in the profession as "foreshadowing"; or if perchance this were a film of, say, Luis Buñuel's, we might have an extremely brief scene, only seconds long, of phantasmagoria: the limousine in Dallas, blood everywhere, blood staining Jackie's skirt as she attempts to leap backward over the trunk, a male figure at the same time leaping forward to push her back, to push her down into the seat of the car, the athletic body protecting her. The figure is agent Clint Hill of the Secret Service, his voice now inquiring politely if the Writer and his wife and their two friends would be so kind as to be at the Edgartown town dock at eleven-thirty. He will meet them in a launch and take them out into the harbor to rendezvous with President and Mrs. Kennedy on their boat, which has just cruised across Nantucket Sound from Hyannis Port.

This day is sloppy and gray. There is no rain, yet an augury of it is in the air, damp, like the faintest aerosol mist. It is also chilly, much too cold to swim. On the spray-swept launch, standing next to his two friends (a married couple who are friends of the Kennedys and responsible for the invitation to this outing), the Writer fights off the need for a cigarette and broods, a little glumly, at the cheerless seascape, the oily chops of the waves and, beyond these, the shore-line of the island of Chappaquiddick. (Our narrator forgoes here another grue-some "foreshadowing.") The Writer is, with some trepidation, approaching the dread year of forty. Domestically and financially secure, he nonetheless feels somewhat unfulfilled in his craft, and unrecognized; were it not for a certain fictional project upon which he has been embarked for a year, he knows he would sense being much on the downward track. The thought of the proj-ect—a long and complex novel that keeps him cheerfully and doggedly at his desk—boosts his spirits a little, although he is perfectly aware that President Kennedy has never heard of him or any of his work. The Writer catches scraps of the banter of his two friends, who have seen the Kennedys infrequently since their occupancy of the White House. "I know it's wrong to call him 'Jack,' " says the wife, "but I just can't bring myself to say 'Mr. President' after knowing him for so long." Her husband is humorously didactic: "You are paying respect not to the man, Sue, but to the office. *Please* say 'Mr. President.' Hearing you address him as 'Jack' sets my teeth on edge."

Out of the haze looms the presidential yacht. It is not the *Honey Fitz,* cele-brated in the media and almost a household word, but a lesser craft, a forty-five-foot cabin cruiser named the *Patrick J.* There is nothing particularly distin-guished about this vessel—a standard "cocktail boat," as the canvas sailors of the Edgartown Yacht Club would disparagingly describe it—but it has unusual company: a Coast Guard cutter protectively standing off at a discreet three hundred yards or so. Drawing near in the launch, the Writer and his friends dis-cern two male figures moving slowly about on the yacht's forward deck; the Writer involuntarily and rather deliciously draws in his breath as the taller of the two shapes loses its blurred indistinctness and becomes the President of the United States, in khaki pants and Navy flight jacket, waving and greeting. The launch comes alongside, and there is a lot of spray and bumping about, a good deal of shouted palaver between the President and his friends that to the Writer sounds delightfully chummy and familiar. On board Jackie appears in sweater and white slacks. There are introductions all around; the President's smile is broad, honest, and Irish, his handshake firm, and he plainly relishes his embrace with Sue, who is a looker and who calls him, yes, "Jack."

Aided by one or two Bloody Marys, the Writer sheds much of his nervous-ness at brunch, which is set for seven people (the only other person present being the President's brother-in-law, Stephen Smith) on the open afterdeck. In the background, from a portable record player and mercifully not too loud, comes the sound of the Twist, the musical craze of those years. While the Writer talks with Jackie he is aware of the President's voice chatting to the others of something that seems disappointingly parochial and inconsequential:

Massachusetts politics. Why, the Writer wonders, does the President continually refer to the commonwealth as "that state," as if it were Kansas or Texas, instead of the state they were in? A minor mystery of the grammar of politics. In the back of his mind the Writer is also wondering if he will have the nerve, the courage, the chutzpah to bring up a subject that for quite some time has been troubling his mind and heart. This is the matter of Cuba in particular, and Latin America in general.

Almost from birth the Writer has entertained the imperious view of Latin America shared by most of his countrymen, if thought is ever given to that vast part of the hemisphere at all: a region of malaria, bananas, oleaginous women, and marimba music, a jungle of no culture and corrupt, devious people. But through the good fortune he has had, in the past two years, to travel and meet Latin American artists and writers, he has been able to alter his vision of the place and, with a sense of residual shame for his past arrogance, to come both to appreciate the richness and variety of that part of the world and to be appalled at the United States' role, past and present, in affairs below the border. One did not have to be pro-Communist to feel that Kennedy's dealings with Castro were disastrous and that even the Alliance for Progress—with its phony-sounding Orwellian Newspeak of a name—was doomed to failure, merely promoting more violent coups and sleazy interventions. But how might one find the polite way—the politic way, that is—to express these animadversions to JFK without sounding stuffy or impertinent or, worse, like a dangerous radical? The Writer rather quickly realizes that he'd better leave the subject alone, and feels a twinge of guilt for his failure of initiative.

He also realizes that the President is now talking about—of all people—the literary critic Alfred Kazin, and that a question is being addressed to him. Has the Writer read the piece by Kazin in *The American Scholar?* The Writer has, and says so, though making sure that the tone in his voice commits himself to no viewpoint. The article in question had been tough, canny, caustic: it made, in the Writer's opinion, a fairly good case for the fact that the President, while enchanting and certainly anything but a dumbbell, was scarcely charged with the intellectual high voltage ascribed to him by some admirers. What did the Writer think of the piece? the President inquires. The Writer flushes, feeling as if he were being forced to catch a smoking, red-hot cinder. But he is saved immediately by another question, spoken in a kind of angry petulance and so naive, really, as to validate rather strongly Kazin's judgment: What qualifies a critic to make an assessment of a work if he himself has never created one? Boy, thinks the Writer, Alfred's really got Kennedy's goat. But then he tries to explain, in as discreet a way as possible, how the critical faculty and the creative faculty were of two different orders of talent, not necessarily interdependent, and so on and so on, for about forty-five seconds.

Here intervene a few passages from the Writer's notebook entry for that day:

> In the Marines we were supposed to envy the Navy for its superior chow, but the food on the good ship *Patrick J.* has to be eaten to be believed. Ice

cold hot dogs in buns so soggy from some steam bath that the bread sinks like paste beneath thumb and fingers. An attempt at *oeufs engelée,* but the yolks either hard as a rock or running out in a horrible goo. The Filipino mess steward all aquiver with nervousness and dropping spoons in everyone's lap, including Numero Uno. Worst moment comes when the beer is served. It is meant to be chilled but arrives frozen in tall tapered glasses which fall over with each roll of the boat. The party in good humor about this, though, especially Jackie.

A background noise of static and voices as the Secret Service keeps up heavy traffic on the radio. The code word for the President is "Lancer," and I wonder how intentional is this double-entendre. Lord knows he does not have to work too hard for his reputation in the sack since when all is said and done he is lethally glamorous and even a heterosexual male has to be aware of that. Odd that with all this power and beauty which is like that of some super matinee idol one does not sense the preening vanity of the movie star. He has a beguiling and self-effacing modesty which comes out in the really funny little remarks he makes about himself, and that is one of his nice charms.

Mildly awkward moment comes when, in parody of Chubby Checker's "Let's twist again, etc." I suggest a nuclear variation: "Let's test again, like we did last summer." Jackie thinks this is very funny and repeats it to JFK, who does not seem overwhelmingly amused. The frozen Budweisers work their squalid magic.

At the end of the lunch, the President passes out to his male guests Partagas cigars, made in Havana. The Writer, reflecting that these are contraband items under an embargo against Cuban goods instituted by the President himself, tucks a cigar in his pocket for a souvenir. Again he has a small but keen spasm of discontent, thinking of the hateful but irreconcilable differences, the ferocious animosity that separates Castro and Kennedy. The Writer has never met Castro but, fascinated by his career, has learned a great deal about him, enough to perceive that of all the world's leaders the Harvard man and the Marxist from Havana are temperamentally and intellectually most alike; they probably would have taken warmly to each other had not the storm of twentieth-century history and its bizarre determinism made them into unshakable enemies.

Then there is the pleasant moment when the President, chewing at the end of his Partagas, asks the Writer: "What are you writing?" The Writer does not yet know it, and Kennedy never will, but the racial revolution in the U.S.A.— the terrible and cleansing holocaust—is some years in the offing; yet already the warning signals are flying. Martin Luther King Jr., has become a mighty presence, James Baldwin has just raised his voice in *The Fire Next Time,* and even today the President has murmured of the upheaval the previous fall at Oxford, Mississippi—an episode that once and for all has engaged Kennedy in the fight for equality. So it seems to coincide smoothly with the President's mood of mild worry and perplexity when the Writer replies that he has been working on a novel with both a racial and a historical theme: a slave revolt in Virginia in the early years of the nineteenth century. The President is fascinated. "Tell me about it," he says. It does not surprise the Writer that Kennedy has never heard of Nat Turner; outside of a few historians specializing in American slavery, no one is aware of this rebel Negro, and that includes most Negroes. Afraid to bore, wary of becoming too wound up in his own obsessions, the Writer tries to abbreviate his account, but the President is plainly captivated and probes for more detail, more information. His questions are searching and pertinent, as if he shares—or at least wants to share—the Writer's involvement with that mysterious and catastrophic event. Flattered by this close attention, and very much impressed by the bright and persistent nature of the interrogation, the Writer cannot help feeling that Kazin's misgivings about the President's brainpower are misplaced. Time disappears. Only the commencement of a soft drizzling rain puts an end to the conversation. It is past midafternoon and the *Patrick J.* heads back to Edgartown.

A contretemps of moderately serious proportions is avoided just as the yacht is about to dock at the Edgartown Yacht Club. Recognizing the place at the last moment—a stronghold of Boston and New York bankers and stockbrokers— Kennedy barks out an order to the skipper to reverse engines and put into the public pier. "My God, they'd have my hide if they learned I'd just barged in there without permission. *The Wall Street Journal* would have a field day." He runs his hand through his hair and adds: "I'll bet there's not a Democrat within five miles of here."

Before the party disembarks, Kennedy says once again to the Writer: "I'll really be waiting to read that book of yours."

It is difficult at this writing, twenty years after his death, to assess John F. Kennedy and his presidency. Both the die-hard idolaters and the sour revisionists have been busily at work, so that if one merely consults one's favorite historian one is likely to be left with the judgment of one's choice (always making allowances for his brief tenure): that he was a dazzling and gifted leader or a hollow calamity. Somewhere between these extremes, it seems to me, lies a just appraisal. Certainly Kennedy's faults and defects now appear more striking in the perspective of the years that followed his presidency. Much of what Kennedy did early in his administration, especially in foreign affairs, he was forced to do because of the Cold War legacy of the Eisenhower years; the demonology of communism taught by those Protestant missionaries John Foster Dulles and Henry Luce was (and still is) a doctrine nearly impossible for Americans to forswear, and Kennedy had little choice but to become a Cold Warrior himself. Yet it is plain that Kennedy was afflicted by feverish manifestations of machismo and could respond to the faintest ripple of a "Communist threat," when he felt the need, with the unseemly zeal of any right-winger. His failure almost at the outset to strive for any reasonable accommodation with Castro is one example of this Bourbon intransigence. More desperate to contemplate, though, is that itchy and trigger-happy lust to get the United States and its swollen military apparatus into places we had no business being. It was Kennedy's will that first led the nation to flex its muscles and show its colors in Southeast Asia. Since the consequences were unspeakable, we need not dwell on them, except to allow the observation that if Kennedy cannot be held entirely responsible for the war in Vietnam, it was nonetheless he who drew up the first blueprint for disaster.

It is a major irony of the Kennedy presidency that in so many respects he must be judged on what he might (or probably would) have achieved. After a sluggish beginning on civil rights, Kennedy gained a respectable momentum. The violent events at Ole Miss had indeed shaken him up, and on the day of our boat ride I could not fail to be impressed by the commitment and passion he brought to the idea of the struggle for equality. The civil rights legislation he proposed was eventually adopted and passed by Congress during the Johnson administration, and doubtless the same would have come to fruition had Kennedy lived. This has to be considered an achievement. As for Kennedy's cojones, he must have felt they were in good shape again after the Cuban missile crisis; aside from offsetting the humiliation of the Bay of Pigs, the showdown gave the President the opportunity to demonstrate that he could hang tough, face down an adversary as powerful as Khrushchev and emerge the glorious, undisputed winner. Had he lived long enough, it might have proved to be his psychological salvation, permitting him an inner security that in turn would have eliminated the need for so much strong-arm and clandestine activity around the globe.

And this brings us to the most entertaining riddle of all. If Kennedy had lived, and if he had been reelected, would his conscience have let him face the Vietnam horror with courage—enough to cause him to do a virtual turnabout and begin to extricate America from the morass, even though it would mean a certain personal loss of face and pride? Some of his more faithful admirers, including members of his inner circle, have said that they are almost certain he would have brought an end to the war. I would think that this is merely wish fulfillment. Tom Wicker, whose study of the political careers of Kennedy and Johnson remains a brilliant tour de force, risks only the observation that Kennedy would have at least had the option to stop the war, while Johnson was committed to continuing the conflict almost from his first day in office. Perhaps, with his macho instincts gratified after the Cuban missile crisis, Kennedy would have felt that he could honorably close the books on another misbegotten adventure. But there is another possibility that may not be as farfetched as it sounds. I do not endorse it wholeheartedly, but it is worth pondering. It is that Kennedy—who, after all, was such a different breed of cat from Johnson or Nixon, and a thoroughbred at that—would not only have suffered agonies of conscience to which the other two men were impervious (and proved it by their actions), but would have been unable easily, if at all, to endure the scorn and loathing of those for whom he had, deep down, the highest regard. It is ludicrous to think of Johnson giving a good goddamn about what Alfred Kazin thought of his intellect, just as he could without a qualm turn his back on Robert Lowell and Norman Mailer when they marched on the Pentagon. But there was a delicacy and grace in Kennedy that would have found, I think, the pure hatred poured out upon him by such men and others close to him intolerable.

Nor could I imagine him for long being able to bear the awful rhyme of the jingle that LBJ shrugged off: "Hey! Hey! JFK! How many kids did you kill today?"

UPPER FIFTH AVENUE.
New York City.
November 1963.

This is a big black-tie affair, to which the Writer and his wife have been invited after dinner. "We'll probably get a glimpse of him anyway," she remarks on the way over, "even if he's surrounded by people."

It is a duplex apartment and one descends to the festivities by way of a staircase leading from the upper floor. As they go down the stairs the Writer sees a throng of people standing and sitting and (marvelous to relate) the President of the United States leaning with his foot propped up against the bottom step, quite alone and looking abandoned. When he catches sight of the couple he greets them with a grand smile creasing the Palm Beach suntan, and squeezes them like long-lost loved ones. "How did they get *you* to come here?" he says. "They had a hard enough time getting me." Spoken like a true politician, thinks the Writer, but a magic bit nonetheless. For long minutes the three stand talking. The race issue is again uppermost in Kennedy's mind; he is in an amiable mood, but there is an undercurrent of seriousness, almost an agitation. Does the Writer know James Baldwin, Ralph Ellison? It is important that Negro writers know what steps the White House is taking. Does he think, if they were invited, they would come down to Washington? That book of his, how is it coming? A fascinating story. Does he know any Negro historians? There is so little known about Negro history, slave revolts. "What a great idea for a novel, I hope it's done soon."

Utter charm. The Writer senses his ego expanding like a big balloon and is overtaken by a grand effervescence, as if he were being bathed in sparkling water. Then the President is distracted by someone and turns away, and that is the last the Writer ever sees of him. Exactly two weeks later, on another Friday, he lies dead.

JOHN FITZGERALD KENNEDY *was born on May 29, 1917, in the Boston suburb of Brookline, Massachusetts. The second of nine children, he strove against his older, bigger brother, Joe. Once the two boys had a bicycle race in which each went around the block in opposite directions. Approaching the finish line head-on, each refused to give way. Joe was unhurt, but the collision cost Jack twenty-eight stitches.*

As a Navy ensign, he shared an apartment with Inga Arvad, a former Miss Denmark who had been an intimate of Joseph Goebbels and Adolf Hitler. The FBI, suspecting Arvad of being a Nazi spy, once bugged her hotel room when she visited Kennedy in Charleston, South Carolina. J. Edgar Hoover, who listened to the hotel tapes, sent the information to Richard Nixon to use in the 1960 presidential race. Nixon never used the information.

In 1947 he was diagnosed as suffering from Addison's disease, an adrenal disorder that at the time was frequently fatal. All his life Kennedy tried to cover up the disease, which contributed to his spending several days near death in 1954. But he once confided that because of his "slow-motion leukemia," he didn't expect to live past forty-five.

The first Nixon-Kennedy debate took place in 1947, when the two freshman congressmen argued the Taft-Hartley bill before an audience in McKeesport, Pennsylvania. Nixon recalls that on the train back to Washington, they "drew straws for the lower berth, and—this time—I won. . . . [We] were too different . . . to become close friends, but . . . we shared one quality which distinguished us from most of our fellow congressmen: neither of us was a backslapper, and we were both uncomfortable with boisterous displays of superficial camaraderie. He was shy, and that sometimes made him appear aloof. But it was shyness born of an instinct that guarded privacy and concealed emotions. I understood these qualities because I shared them."

He was a sore loser. During one game of checkers with Navy undersecretary "Red" Fay, an old friend, JFK deliberately upset the board when it became clear that Fay was winning. "One of those unfortunate incidents of life, Redhead," he grinned. "We'll never really know if the undersecretary was going to outmaneuver the Commander in Chief. . . ."

He had a keen taste for gossip. He went to Frank Sinatra for Hollywood tattle. Over lunch in the White House he and J. Edgar Hoover would look at photos of call girls. "Boy, the dirt [Hoover] has on those senators," Kennedy told a friend. "You wouldn't believe it."

He was linked romantically with Gene Tierney, Jayne Mansfield, Angie Dickinson, and Marilyn Monroe. Monroe called JFK's lovemaking "very democratic" and "very penetrating." She told a friend, "I think I make his back feel better."

He hated being left alone in the White House at night. When Jackie was away, he would summon his old friend and counselor Dave Powers. He and Powers would eat dinner, watch TV, or read. Around eleven o'clock, Powers would look on as the President slipped into his short-length sleeping jacket, knelt beside his bed to say his prayers, and got under the covers. "Good night, pal," JFK would say. "Will you please put out the light?" Only then would Powers head home.

An aide recalls Kennedy saying in the spring of 1963 that he would completely withdraw U.S. troops from Vietnam in 1965: "In 1965 I'll become one of the most unpopular Presidents in history. I'll be damned everywhere as a Communist appeaser. But I don't care. If I tried to pull out completely now from Vietnam, we would have another Joe McCarthy red scare on our hands, but I can do it after I'm reelected. So we had better make damned sure that I am reelected."

He was not prone to displays of emotion, but he cried after the death of his baby son Patrick, during a conversation with Richard Cardinal Cushing about the Bay of Pigs prisoners, and after saying good-bye to his paralyzed, mute father at Hyannis Port—a month before his own death in Dallas.

On November 22, 1963, at Parkland Hospital in Dallas, the First Lady slipped her wedding ring on her slain husband's finger.

Muhammad Ali
Is the Most Famous
Man in the World

BOB GREENE

It was the voice that was shocking.

"How much you going to pay me?"

The voice was slurry, blurred, almost a whisper. Coming over the long-distance line, the words seemed to be filled with effort.

I said that as far as I knew, *Esquire* did not pay people who were written about in the magazine. In any event, this was a special sort of issue; fifty men and women from the past fifty years had been selected as the most influential of their time. He was one of them. The magazine wanted to include him in the issue.

"You're just using me to sell magazines," Muhammad Ali said. The voice was fading. "You just want to put me on the cover."

No, I said, Ali would not be on the cover. But he would be in very good company.

"I'm the most famous man in the world," the voice said.

I said that there would be other famous people in the issue; people, perhaps, as famous as he.

"Who?" Ali said.

I said that some of the others were John F. Kennedy, Franklin D. Roosevelt, Martin Luther King Jr.

"They're all dead," Ali said.

84

• • •

I waited for American Airlines' Flight 184 from Los Angeles to arrive at Chicago's O'Hare International Airport. Ali's manager, Herbert Muhammad, had told me that Ali would be on board, and then would be switching to another flight to Washington, D.C. Ali would be addressing a rally of Muslims in Washington.

Herbert Muhammad had said he could not guarantee that Ali would speak with me; it would be up to him. He said that if I wanted to take a chance I should pack a bag, buy a ticket to Washington, and be at the gate when Ali's plane arrived.

So I sat on a chair directly next to where the jetway opened into the terminal. The plane was a few minutes early. About a dozen passengers disembarked, and then came Ali. He was wearing a gray suit; he wore no belt with the pants. The suit was expensive, but his brown shoes were worn and scuffed.

I walked up to him and introduced myself. He did not look at me, but he said: "Where's Herbert?" The voice was as soft and fuzzy as it had been on the phone.

I said I didn't know; I said the Washington flight would be leaving in forty-five minutes from a gate just down the corridor.

Ali removed his suit jacket. Even though it was a frigid winter day, he was wearing a short-sleeve blue shirt. He began to walk toward the next gate.

The scene in the airport was like one of those brokerage commercials in which everyone freezes in place. I have traveled with celebrities before; I had never seen anything like this. Everyone—everyone—stopped in their tracks when they caught sight of Ali. He was considerably heavier than in the days when he had been fighting; now, in 1983, he had just turned forty-one, and his hair was flecked with gray. But there was no question about his recognition factor; each pair of eyes stared at him, each mouth silently formed the word "Ali."

"Champ, you're the greatest there ever was," a man cried. Ali walked past him, not looking.

"Where's Herbert?" his voice said again.

I said again that I didn't know. A woman—she was middle-aged, well dressed, not eccentric looking in the least—caught sight of Ali and dropped to her knees in front of him, as if praying. He stepped around her.

I led him to the proper gate. We took seats in the boarding area. He was carrying a briefcase; actually, it was bigger than that, more like a salesman's sample case. He opened it and took out a book called *The Spectre of Death, Including Glimpses of Life Beyond the Grave.*

He opened the book. He leaned over to me and began reading aloud from it, but so softly that I could barely make out the words:

"Life will soon come to an end, and we will part with the comforts. Whenever you see a dead man being led to the grave, remind yourself that one day you will also meet your end. . . ."

I asked him what else he had in the salesman's case. He began to rummage through it; the contents looked like something in a bag lady's sack. Pamphlets, old photographs, receipts, scraps of paper—the case was chock-full. He pulled out a copy of the Bible and opened the cover. There was an autograph I could not quite make out.

"Oral Roberts," he whispered.

A woman was standing in front of us. Her young daughter—she said that the girl's name was Clarice, and that she was six—was with her. The woman shoved the girl gently in Ali's direction. The girl kissed Ali on the cheek.

"She's not real, real friendly," the mother said. Ali, saying nothing, stood up and kissed the mother on the cheek, too.

"See," the mother said to her daughter, "now you met somebody great."

A man named Joseph Loughry, manager of international banking programs for General Electric Information Services in Rockville, Maryland, stopped in front of Ali. "I have a little guy named James," Loughry said. Ali, not looking up, not saying anything, accepted a piece of paper from Loughry, and wrote on it: "To James from Muhammad Ali."

Loughry said some words of thanks to Ali, but Ali neither spoke to him nor looked at him. When he had walked away, Ali said to me: "The least little thing we do, God marks it down. Each little atom, He sees. On the day of judgment, all the good and all the bad will be weighed. Every leaf that falls from a tree, God sees. Think of all the trees."

A man was sitting behind us, in a chair facing the other way. "Watch me do this," Ali said. He rubbed his thumb and first two fingers together in a way that resulted in a cricket sound. He turned around, placed his fingers next to the man's ear, rubbed the fingers together and made the sound. By the time the man turned around, Ali was looking away, as if nothing had happened. But then he did it to the man again. The man jerked his head to the side. He rubbed his ear. When he had gone back to his newspaper, Ali reached back again, made the cricket sound with his fingers again.

The man stood up and looked around. But Ali was talking to me again, as if nothing had happened. I said something about him being treated as a "super figure."

"Super nigger?" Ali said.

"Figure," I said. "Super figure."

"I know," he said. "I heard you the first time. I was just joking. I don't know about 'super figures.' But I do know that I am the most famous person in the world."

"Are you sure?" I said.

"Who's more famous?" Ali said.

"What about Reagan?" I said.

"Be serious," Ali said. "If Reagan were to go to Morocco or Persia, he could walk down the street and no one would bother him. If I go there, they have to call out soldiers to guard me. I can't go outside."

"Why?" I said.

"What do you mean 'why'?" Ali said.

"Why you?" I said. "You were a great boxer. But all of this other stuff . . . why you?"

"I don't know," he said. "I'm not smart. I'm dumber than you are. I can't spell as good as you. I can't read as good as you. But people don't care. Because that shows I'm a common person, just like they are."

At that moment a woman named Pam Lontos interrupted us. She handed Ali a business card; the card indicated that she was the president of a sales motivation firm based in Dallas, and that she made motivational speeches.

"Have you ever done any motivational talks about how to believe in yourself?" she said to Ali.

He did not speak, did not look at her.

"I'd like to talk to you about making public speeches," she said. "Are you with any booking agency? I think you'd be amazed at how much money you can make for just forty-five minutes' work. You can make just a ton of money."

Ali still did not look up at her.

"The booking agency I'm with handles David Brinkley and Norman Vincent Peale," she said. "Wouldn't you like to make a lot of money just by getting up and talking?"

"I talk for free," Ali said. "For God."

Just then Herbert Muhammad arrived. Ali's manager was a rotund man wearing a fur cap. "Ali, where have you been?" he said. "I've been looking all over the terminal for you."

The gate agent announced that the flight was boarding; Pam Lontos walked away, and we got in line to get on the plane. There was a businessman in front of us. Ali reached forward, put his fingers next to the man's ears, and made the cricket noise. When the man turned around, Ali was looking in another direction.

We sat in the first row of first class on the right side of the plane. Ali was by the window; I was on the aisle. Other passengers were filing on. Ali didn't seem to be paying any attention to them, but then he said to me, "I have to do something."

He climbed over me. He reached for a man who was heading back into the coach section. He tapped the man on the shoulder.

"*Psst*," Ali said.

The man turned around. His face froze at the sight of Ali. Ali pointed to the floor of the plane, where a ticket envelope lay.

"You dropped something," Ali said.

"Why . . . why, thank you," the man said.

But Ali had already turned away. He walked up to the cockpit. He bent over slightly and ducked inside. He tapped the pilot on the shoulder.

The pilot and the first officer and the flight engineer looked up in wonder. Ali nodded at them. Then he turned and came back toward his seat by the window. Before he could get there, though, a flight attendant who was struggling to lift a carton onto the overhead rack said to him: "Would you like to put that up there? You have more muscles than me."

Silently Ali put the box away. He slid past me. Another flight attendant leaned over and said: "Would you like a cocktail or a soft drink after we take off?"

"Milk," Ali said, so softly that the woman could not hear.

"I beg your pardon?" she said.

"Milk," Ali said, looking straight forward.

We taxied out onto the runway. As we picked up speed and then lifted off, Ali said to me: "You never know when your time to die will come."

About five minutes into the flight, he turned to me and said, "I'm not going to say anything to you for a while. It's time for me to pray." He held up his wrist; he was wearing a fancy watch with a floating arrow inside.

"This is a Muslim prayer watch," Ali said. "We have to pray at different times during the day. An alarm goes off every time I have to pray. The arrow is always pointing toward Mecca."

"Where'd you get it?" I asked.

"The king of Saudi Arabia gave it to me," he said. "He was wearing it on his arm and he took it off and gave it to me. I was wearing a Timex before." He closed his eyes, as if in prayer.

When he opened his eyes, he said to me: "My desire, my main goal now, is to prepare myself for the hereafter. That should be all men's goal."

"But what about life right now?" I said.

"This life is not real," Ali said. "I conquered the world, and it didn't give me satisfaction. The boxing, the fame, the publicity, the attention—it didn't satisfy my soul.

"Who could be more popular? Who could achieve greater heights? It's all nothing unless you go to heaven. You can have pleasure, but it means nothing unless you please God."

A man who had been sitting across the aisle unbuckled his seat belt and came over to us. He was William Doré, the president of Global Divers & Contractors, Inc., in Lafayette, Louisiana.

"Ali," he said, "I want to shake your hand. I made twelve dollars on you when you fought against Sonny Liston."

"Is that all?" Ali said.

"I only bet three," Doré said.

Ali was looking away by now.

"It's been a pleasure to watch you over the years," Doré said. "You've done a lot for the game."

When Doré had returned to his seat, Ali said to me: "Boxing was nothing. It wasn't important at all. Boxing was just meant as a way to introduce me to the world."

But he was interrupted in mid-thought. Pam Lontos, the motivational speaker, had come up from the coach section; she was kneeling in the aisle, and she was pushing a brochure at Ali. The brochure began: "The basics of broadcast selling help you find your true potential, to turn that potential into profit . . ."

A flight attendant put both hands on Lontos's shoulders. "Ma'am," the flight attendant said, "if you want an autograph, we'll be happy to bring you one back."

"But I don't want an autograph," Lontos said as she was led back into coach.

Ali was sniffling. He seemed to be getting the beginnings of a cold. He took the small pillow from behind my head, tore a piece from its paper casing, and blew his nose. In a moment he was sleeping.

We were approaching Washington. Ali tapped me on the shoulder. He pointed out the window. The lights of the monuments and government buildings were below.

"What do you think of that?" he said.

"It's pretty," I said.

"Look at all those lights on all those houses," he said. "Those are all my fans. Do you know I could walk up to any one of those houses, and knock on the door, and they would know me?

"It's a funny feeling to look down on the world and know that every person knows me. Sometimes I think about hitchhiking around the world, with no money, and just knocking on a different door every time I needed a meal or a place to sleep. I could do it."

We walked into Washington's National Airport. A group of Muslims were waiting in the concourse for Ali; they were sponsoring the rally he had come to address.

We walked toward the baggage claim area. There was an immediate difference in Ali. On the airplane, even though his voice had still been slurred and vague, his mind and his attention had appeared to be fairly sharp. In here, though—with every person calling to him and stopping to gaze at him—he seemed to put himself back into the same sort of trance he had apparently been under back at O'Hare. His eyes glazed over; he looked at no one; his face took on a blank, numb expression. As the voices spoke his name, this grew more marked.

All I could think of was: He's not punch-drunk in the traditional sense. He's not woozy from being hit too many times. Rather, he is suffering from a different kind of continual beating. For twenty years and more, he has been assaulted with constant attention, constant badgering, constant touching, every time he has ventured out in public. That is what he has had too much of—not the fists, but the nonstop contact from strangers. Clearly it had done something to him; and what it had done was most noticeable when he was in the midst of more onslaughts.

He moved through the crowds. His eyes stayed unfocused. Only once did he speak. A man stepped right in front of him. The man talked not to Ali, but me. He said: "Hey, ask Ali if he can still fly like a butterfly and sting like a bee."

"Float," Ali whispered, not looking at the man. "Float like a butterfly."

There was screaming and shouting as Ali was led to a car waiting outside. We were driven by one of the Muslims to a Holiday Inn downtown. It was not one of Washington's fancier hotels. Ali's suite was on the far end of the seventh floor.

The manager of the hotel, Thomas Buckley, was waiting for Ali in the living room of the suite. "Is there anything I can do for you?" Buckley said.

Ali's cold seemed to be getting worse. "How do you make it hotter in here?" Ali said.

Buckley went to the thermostat and adjusted its lever. "I'm in the service business," Buckley said.

Ali's eyes still seemed to be somewhere else. His voice was barely decipherable.

"Service to others is the rent you pay for your room in heaven," he said.

In the morning, Ali sat in the hotel's coffee shop with Herbert Muhammad and several of the Washington-based Muslims. He wore the same suit he had been wearing the day before. His address at the Muslim rally was not for another day; today he had been scheduled to appear at several inner city schools.

"Herbert," Ali said, his voice as soft as it had been the day before, "what does Allah give you credit for?"

"What do you mean?" Herbert Muhammad said.

"Well," Ali said, "if you help an old lady across the street, does Allah give you credit for that?"

"I'm sure He does," Herbert said. Ali nodded; Herbert turned to me and said, "Ali has a good heart."

Ali had ordered some wheat toast; it was slow in arriving. He reached across the table and took a piece of toast from one of the Muslims' plates. When Ali's toast came, he took the top piece and handed it back to the Muslim.

The woman at the coffee shop's cash register picked up the ringing telephone. She listened for a second, and then came over. "Mr. Ali," she said, "it's for you."

"Who is it?" Ali said, looking at his wheat toast.

"The person said he was Eddie Cantor," the woman said.

Ali stood up and walked to the phone.

"Ali," Herbert called to him before he got there, "who are you going to talk to?"

"Eddie Cantor," Ali said in an emotionless tone.

"Ali," said Herbert, laughing, "Eddie Cantor's dead. If he's calling you I want to hear about it."

Ali picked up the telephone and started talking. As he did, he used his fingers to make the cricket sound next to the ear of the cashier. She looked around, then rubbed her ear furiously. Ali did it again. She rubbed her ear again.

He came back to the table. I asked him who had been on the phone.

"Eddie Kendricks," he said. "He used to sing with the Temptations."

"How did he know to find you here?" I said.

Ali shrugged. He looked at his Muslim prayer watch, then gave me a signal to be silent. As the others in the coffee shop worked on their breakfasts, he closed his eyes and prayed.

We drove through the streets. At the Sister Clara Muhammad Elementary School, up a flight of stairs in a run-down section of town, Ali stood in front of a class of seventy-five students. He crossed his arms while the children sang to him. Once in a while he motioned back and forth with a finger, as if conducting an orchestra.

"I'm so happy to see all you children," he whispered to them. They were very young; it was obvious that they knew he was an important man, but unclear if they knew precisely who he was.

At Shaw Junior High School, in a modern, low-slung building, faculty members and students ran toward him and pawed at him as he was led to the school auditorium. Lipstick smeared his cheeks from where the female teachers had kissed him.

We were shoved back and forth in a sea of bodies as we tried to get to the stage. The school band was playing; the auditorium was alive with shrieks and shouts.

"This is the whole world," he said to me. "This is what my whole life is like."

He made it to the stage. While the band played the theme from *Rocky* he took a blue comb from his pocket and ran it through his hair.

"Boys and girls," the principal said into the microphone, "being here on this stage with this man is probably the greatest moment of my life. And it should be the greatest moment of your life."

Ali, whose cold had seemed worse all morning, took out a handkerchief. A cook from the school's kitchen yelled, "Muhammad Ali, I love you." Ali blew his nose.

The principal called Ali to the lectern. He said that he wanted the students to ask questions of Ali, but that he wanted to ask the first one himself.

"Muhammad," he said, "would you say your toughest fight was with Frazier?"

"My toughest fight was with my first wife," Ali said.

He talked with the students for about fifteen minutes. On the way out he stopped in front of a couple of boys. Ali began to shadowbox with them, moving his feet back and forth in the famous Ali Shuffle. The boys held up their hands and backed off. A woman teacher who had not been at the assembly caught sight of him and began to tremble. "Oh, Lord," she said, her eyes wide.

At Cardozo High School, in one of Washington's toughest neighborhoods, police officers stood guard at the front door. The students were gathered in an assembly, but had not been told that Ali was scheduled to come.

So they were listening to another speaker when, unannounced, Ali walked in a back door of the auditorium. First a few of them caught sight of him, then a few more. A buzz moved through the room as he walked, sniffling, down the aisle toward the stage.

By the time he was halfway there the chants had begun: "Ali! Ali! Ali! Ali!"

When he started to speak, though, his voice was so soft and slurred that no one could hear him. They began to call out for him to speak louder; but he didn't seem to notice, he just kept calling them "boys and girls" in that whispered tone.

He asked if there were any questions. A pretty young woman in the front row, who had been visibly puzzled by his slow, quiet, faltering speech pattern, raised her hand, and he pointed at her.

"Are you really Muhammad Ali?" she said.

Ali stared at her. "I'll see you after school," he said. "And tell your boyfriend that if he don't like it, I'll see him after school, too."

A fellow who apparently was her boyfriend stood up. "Fool," Ali said, "I'll see you after school." But beyond the first five or six rows, no one could hear him.

Ali turned to the principal and, with his fists raised, again went into the boxing routine and the Ali Shuffle. The principal shook his head and backed away.

Ali was coughing badly as we arrived at Dunbar High School. He followed wherever the local Muslims led him; in this case, into an administration office.

Ali stood there coughing and wiping his nose, waiting to be instructed where to go next. A female administrator looked up at him and said, "This man is sick. Has anyone called a doctor for him?"

But he was already being taken to a classroom. In the hallway a young mother who was visiting the school ran up to him and handed her baby to him. Ali reached out for the child, but Herbert Muhammad said, "Ali, you have too bad a cold to be handling that baby." Ali handed the infant back.

We moved through the corridors. Children moved to the doors of their classrooms. Ali leaned close to me and said, "They're all mine. This is what Allah has given me. This is heaven in the world." We moved past an elderly man who for some reason was at the school. Ali made the cricket sound with his fingers next to the old man's ear, but the man, apparently hard of hearing, did not react.

We went into the school library. Everyone in the room stopped what they were doing. One boy, though, had his back to us; he was reading at a table, and was immersed in his book.

Ali approached him. He put his hand on the boy's shoulder. The boy looked up and his mouth fell open. He started to say something, but Ali held a finger up to his own mouth, as if to silence the boy.

On the way out of the room, Ali passed by a tall, muscular young man. Ali stopped.

They looked at each other. Then Ali held up his fists. He went into the Ali Shuffle and began to leap about in front of the young man.

The young man did not back off. He held up his own fists. He did not attempt to strike Ali, but neither did he give an inch. He moved with Ali, making it clear that he was not afraid. Ali began to perspire. The young man moved closer. The young man had a confident smile on his face. He started to push Ali, establishing command of the situation.

No one in the room stirred. Ali coughed. The young man brought his punches closer and closer to Ali's face. Their arms began to make contact. The sound of their forearms slapping against each other echoed off the walls, and suddenly there was a clattering sound, and everything stopped.

There, on the yellow carpeting, was Ali's Muslim prayer watch. Ali slowly leaned over. He picked up the watch and fastened it back onto his wrist.

"Come on, Ali," Herbert Muhammad said. "We're running late." They moved toward the door of the school library. Ali's eyes met the eyes of the tall young man for just a moment. Then they clouded over, and once again he seemed to be somewhere else.

———————

MUHAMMAD ALI *was born Cassius Marcellus Clay, Jr., on January 18, 1942, in Louisville, Kentucky. Cassius Marcellus Clay, Sr., according to his son, was "the fanciest dancer in Louisville." For a living, the elder Clay painted signs.*

His delivery was a difficult one, because, said his father, "his head was too big to come out." In the hospital, his mother discovered that a nurse had put the wrong baby in her bed. She knew it wasn't Cassius, she said, "because the other baby was a quiet, nice baby."

According to some genealogical accounts, Clay's maternal grandfather was a white Irish American and his paternal great-great-grandfather a freed slave who took the name of his former master, an abolitionist and relative of statesman Henry Clay. Of his aunt's assertion that Henry Clay himself was an ancestor, he has said, ". . . if slaveholder Clay's blood came into our veins along with the name, it came by rape and defilement."

He stands six feet three inches tall and weighs—in peak condition—220 pounds. He enjoys being naked.

He "prayerfully resolved" to avoid sex as a youth. But when he was sixteen, competing in the Golden Gloves trials in Chicago, Clay and a friend hired two prostitutes. Despite his befuddlement at one's offer of a "trip around the world," he took the trip, and was "miserable" afterward.

His sexual appetite has not been entirely satisfied by his three wives.

When he lived in Louisville, he and a friend would sometimes dress up in African costumes and speak in made-up languages to get themselves admitted to whites-only establishments.

He threw the gold medal he won in the 1960 Olympics into the Ohio River after getting into a fight with a white motorcycle–gang leader who wanted the medal as a "souvenir." He won the fight, but discarded the medal in disgust.

Trying to goad Sonny Liston into fighting him, he flew to Las Vegas, found Liston at a gambling table, and screamed: "Come on, you big ugly bear! I'll whip you right now!" Liston pulled out a pistol and shot at him. Clay ducked and ran. He later discovered the bullets were blanks.

After his first victory over Liston, Cassius Clay ate ice cream with Malcolm X.

The next day he announced that he had become a Black Muslim and changed his name to Muhammad Ali.

In 1967 he was sentenced to five years in jail and stripped of his heavyweight title after he refused induction into the Army. "I ain't got no quarrel with those Vietcong," he explained. "They never called me nigger." His refusal brought numerous death threats and a letter from philosopher Bertrand Russell, who wrote: "They will try to break you because you are a symbol of a force they are unable to destroy, namely, the aroused consciousness of a whole people determined no longer to be butchered and debased with fear and oppression. You have my whole-hearted support. . . ."

In 1970 the Supreme Court reversed his conviction. He went on to become the only man ever to win the heavyweight crown three times.

He says that when he was delirious from punches in the ring he used to envision a "Near Room" where alligators played trombones and snakes screamed.

He reports that Egyptian president Gamal Abdel Nasser once offered him his daughter in marriage but that Muslim leader Elijah Muhammad frowned upon the idea.

He performs magic tricks. He can turn pennies into dimes and make a handkerchief and a candle disappear.

He loves horror movies, particularly The Mummy *and* The Invasion of the Body Snatchers.

Critics raved about his performance—as himself—in the 1977 movie The Greatest; *they panned him in the 1979 TV movie* Freedom Road.

He likes to talk on the telephone. A Philadelphia home of his had twenty-two phones—at least two in every room. He sometimes carries a briefcase equipped with a phone.

He has had several chauffeurs but prefers to do the driving himself; the chauffeurs sit in the back. He likes driving at night best—cruising through the Pocono Mountains and chatting with truckers on his citizens-band radio. His CB handle is The Big Bopper.

President Jimmy Carter sent him on an unsuccessful diplomatic mission to Africa to find allies for the U.S. boycott of the 1980 Moscow Olympics. The President, Ali reflected afterward, "sent me around the world to take the whipping."

He graduated near the bottom of his high school class and has trouble reading.

He was nominated for a Chair of Poetry at Oxford University. "Cassius has an ear," wrote poet Marianne Moore, "and a liking for balance . . . comic, poetic drama, it is poetry."

"Hey, Hey, LBJ ..."

TOM WICKER

THE FIRST TIME I HEARD IT I COULD HARDLY BELIEVE MY EARS—A LINE OF PICKETERS behind police barricades shouting: "Hey! Hey! LBJ! How many kids did you kill today?"

That was late 1965 or maybe early 1966, outside the Waldorf in New York, where President Lyndon Baines Johnson had come to speak. In the tortured years that followed, outcries against American participation in the Vietnam War—hatred for the man so many held responsible for it—became as familiar as body counts. Eventually he could travel only to military bases without the chants and jeers of picketers greeting him; and by then it was his own political judgment that he could not be renominated without tearing his party apart or be reelected without further dividing a country already rent by the passions and costs of a war he could not win, end, or justify.

By March 1968, when he announced his withdrawal from that year's presidential campaign, Lyndon Johnson may well have been the most despised President in history—an ironic fate for a politician who had been elected four years earlier by the biggest popular majority ever, to wield briefly perhaps more power than any other President. And such a giant's downfall was even more cruel for a man who had believed that power as he understood it could win him what he wanted most and never really had—the love and approval of the American people.

But Johnson's decline was still in the almost unimaginable future the first time I heard the vicious "Hey! Hey!" chant. As the Washington correspondent of *The New York Times*, I was not then accustomed to such anger and hostility in American politics. Green in the memories of all in the Washington press corps, too, was the magisterial succession Lyndon Johnson had managed in the dangerous weeks after the terrible national shock of John Kennedy's murder on November 22, 1963.

Emerging from the obscurity of the vice-presidency, Johnson had quickly reassured the nation and the world with the credo, "Let us continue." Thereafter, moving into the White House as if born to it—he may have believed he was—the new President had demonstrated an eerie instinct for where the power lay, a classic sense of political timing, deep knowledge of Washington ways, awesome powers of persuasion.

He pushed through Congress the major civil rights and tax reduction bills that had been bogged down in Kennedy's time; he overcame the tangled religious deadlock that had prevented federal aid to education; and he achieved, after more than a decade of efforts by liberals, a program of medical care for the aged. After his landslide election and the proclamation of his program for what he called the Great Society, I was not alone in the expectation that Lyndon Johnson might earn a place equal to Franklin Roosevelt's in the transformation of modern American life.

But these were not the only reasons the picketers outside the Waldorf surprised and offended me in the mid-Sixties. Even had Johnson been less impressive, the man was *President of the United States*; and it is difficult today to remember, much less for people under thirty-five to understand, the extent to which "the President"—any President—was then revered, respected, feared. The tragic irony of Lyndon Johnson is that the lowering of the presidency, not the Great Society of which he dreamed, is his most obvious legacy.

Exaltation of "the President" into an elevated national symbol—combining great military and political power with moral leadership and an aura of monarchy—began, I believe, with Franklin Roosevelt, who in the era of modern communications first took the full role of commander in chief in wartime. FDR, conferring with Stalin and Churchill in the newsreels, touring the World War II battle theaters with black cape flying, was the first President to be *seen* as a man of worldwide power. As the Depression and the New Deal had made FDR the nation's symbol of hope, World War II made him a symbol of its power—still the heart of the presidency when Lyndon Johnson took office.

Harry S Truman had the dubious but profoundly important distinction of being the first President with the added power—atomic power—to blow up the world; by contrast, the scandals of his administration seemed minor. And Truman's Main Street demeanor contributed to the growing belief—then held by serious people—that the presidency somehow could confer greatness on its most ordinary incumbent; didn't plain old Harry Truman rise to the occasion of firing magnificent General Douglas MacArthur?

Dwight D. Eisenhower, himself a father figure to an infatuated people, made "the President" a sort of universal national parent; and in the placid Fifties that meant that public affairs could safely be left to Father while the rest of us made money and enjoyed Togetherness. John F. Kennedy effected the transition of this symbolic, monarchical presidency from the old to a new generation "born in this century, tempered by war, disciplined by a hard and bitter peace"; and his and his wife's beauty and wit brought to the White House a new, contemporary glamour that enthralled a middle-class society.

All these Presidents held office in a time when what had been an inward nation had moved out into global prominence and into a long and edgy two-power race, deeply tinged with fear of and antagonism toward the Soviet Union, for global preeminence. "The President" naturally became the nation's champion in this contest that sometimes seemed a moral crusade.

Eisenhower and Kennedy held office, too, just as television began to transfix the national consciousness (and transform national politics). Television made "the President" more familiar to the public than any other American; television made him a *star*, climaxing a process in which he had come to occupy the central, commanding place in American life.

Men of the postwar leadership as eminent as Dean Acheson and Averell Harriman used to speak of "the President" in voices hushed with respect. When Eisenhower came home from the Paris summit in 1960, after being berated and derided by Khrushchev over the U-2 incident, the people stood by the thousands in the streets of Washington to cheer "the President" as he rode beneath banners and crossed fire ladders, a homecoming hero instead of a humiliated old man.

James Reston once stopped a story on Kennedy with the comment that he would not have *the Times* "muckraking the President" (not Kennedy but "the President," as if they were somehow separable). And when I first put a news conference question to President Eisenhower in 1957, I went home walking on air—a young reporter for an obscure newspaper who thought he had joined, somehow, the select circle of illimitable power the monarch commanded. Later, frequently questioning Kennedy for *the Times*, I learned from the mail that the public did not like reporters to "insult the President" with what television viewers thought were disrespectful questions.

Power was at the root of such reverence—the power "the President" represented, that he actually had, that men thought he had; the power to commit armies and topple nations, to order the world and sway its populace, even to destroy the race. In the presence of so much power—the *assumption* of so much power—who could believe that "the President" entrusted with it could possibly be "one of us," a mere man "of few days and full of trouble"?

Twenty years after John Kennedy's death, I believe it was in his thousand days that reverence for the President reached its apogee. He was the last symbolic monarch to occupy an unbloodied throne, the last President in whom the American people perceived a pure symbol of power and purpose, the last leader to whom they gave their full trust.

97

Not, of course, that Kennedy had no political opposition or detractors; not even Eisenhower reached that elevated state. But to the day of his death Kennedy could have commanded the virtually unanimous support—even fealty—of the nation in a foreign crisis, a summit setback, a missile confrontation. In the jargon of the time, "bipartisanship" would have seen to it that the people "rallied around the President" while "politics stopped at the water's edge." In crisis, people would have *trusted*—even expected—him not only to do the right thing, but to *know* the right thing.

Now it may well take another Pearl Harbor to unify, in that instinctive sense, a nation that no longer sees in "the President" an unquestioned symbol. The reverence, the childlike dependence, the willingness to follow where the President leads, the *trust*, are long gone—gone, surely, with Watergate, but gone before that, as Richard Nixon learned when he tried to hide himself within the idea of "the President," in the old monarchical style. After Lyndon Johnson, after the ugly war that consumed him, trust in "the President" was tarnished forever.

Even had there been no war, it would not have been hard to distrust Lyndon Johnson. Hadn't he been elected to the Senate by only eighty-seven votes, widely believed to have been stolen in Texas's notorious Duval County? Hadn't he managed, in 1960, the slippery feat of getting himself elected Vice-President and U.S. senator at the same time?

A veteran of more than thirty years in Washington, he seemed all too evidently a man of politics, in the least admirable sense of the word. With no national reputation except for having been an effective but tricky Senate majority leader, not certifiably a liberal or a conservative, a westerner and a southerner (still a political liability in the Sixties), LBJ looked and sounded like a Texas wheeler-dealer stained with oil and gas, a usurper who had no real right to the young emperor's throne.

Kennedy had even been killed in Texas, giving rise to dark mutterings from the most paranoid Americans. Despite a lifetime in low-paid public office, the new President was soon known to have accumulated a fortune, mostly from radio and television stations he insisted were his wife's properties. And just as he succeeded to the presidency, his once close lieutenant, Robert G. "Bobby" Baker, was under investigation for suspicious-looking business entanglements—some involving gifts to Johnson.

The new President had another handicap. He had realized as soon as he took office that no matter what he *did*, he would suffer a severe disadvantage from how he *looked* in comparison with the glamorous Kennedy—a smash hit on television, handsome, witty, composed, a cool man in a cool medium. It was weeks before Johnson would hold a televised news conference, the forum in which Kennedy had been at his best; even when Johnson finally did so, he rarely used the State Department auditorium, where Kennedy had staged his successful meetings with the press.

LBJ was at his most effective in small groups—with congressional leaders, or a clutch of businessmen or labor leaders in his office, or reporters standing around his desk, or working over a few senators whose votes he craved. In such gatherings Johnson was beyond comparison the most dominant personality I have ever encountered—funny, crude, overpowering, brilliant, mercurial, persuasive, with a vivid gift for imagery. Of Robert McNamara, for example, Johnson said after the first Kennedy Cabinet meeting: "That man with the Stay-Comb in his hair is the best of the lot."

A talented mimic, he turned on and off at will cruel imitations of people he didn't like (Adlai Stevenson, for example) or did hilarious takeoffs on House speaker John McCormack or almost anyone else. Johnson may have been the best—certainly the most prolific—presidential storyteller since Lincoln, drawing on an endless collection of yarns such as the one about Magnus Johnson, a Swedish congressman who'd risen in the House to declaim: "The only thing to do is grab the bull by the tail and look the situation in the face."

That was mild; Johnsonian discourse was peppered with such colorful crudities as his classic description of why he wouldn't force J. Edgar Hoover to retire at age sixty-five: "Because I'd rather have him inside the tent pissing out than outside pissing in."

Charlie Mohr, who covered the White House for *the Times* in early 1965, at the peak of Johnson's power, tells one of the classic stories of his powerfully direct style. Mohr, a tough questioner, asked Johnson about a report that he had raised his staff's salaries after winning the 1964 election.

"Well, here you are," Johnson drawled, "alone with the President of the United States, the leader of the free world, and you ask a chickenshit question like that."

This sort of thing could hardly be transferred to television; and in any case, Johnson preferred to present himself to the public in an almost transparently false manner, as sober, responsible, dignified—his notion of what the public expected of a President. Perhaps in trying to create an image that so little suited him, Johnson seemed on television to lose entirely the vivid personality with which he dominated private meetings, as well as the colorful stump orator's manner with which he had campaigned so effectively in 1964.

The result was that this dominant, fascinating—I would say unique—man, with his repertoire of stories and his mimic's talent and his gift of phrase, appeared on television, an instrument more powerful than his armies, primarily as a bore; secondarily, with the grim face he put on and the grimmer message he often delivered, as a menace. Particularly when talking about the Indochina war, as he more and more frequently had to do, Johnson never approached his remarkable private persuasiveness; quite the opposite. Showing him unconvincing and dour, his television appearances, if anything, contributed to his inability to maintain the kind of public support he needed to sustain the war.

After his first few months in office, moreover, Johnson became disenchanted with a press—print and broadcast alike—that would not present to the world the picture of him and his policies that he wanted. Back to his long career on Capitol Hill he had always believed that reporters wrote what publishers or some other controlling figure told them to. To counter, he believed he had to "buy" the press with interviews, inside information, flattery, invitations—even, on occasion, a supply of deer-meat sausage from the LBJ Ranch. In return, of course, he expected a favorable press. When he didn't get it, the flow of invitations and access began to slow, finally coming virtually to a halt.

Johnson seemed to me to regard the public much as he viewed the press. Neither, he feared, would sufficiently love, admire, and praise him merely for what he *was* or did. As the press needed to be bought with favors, so did the public; and as the public was showered with better schools, improved medical care, voting rights for blacks, facilities of all kinds, surely it would love the man responsible. With all his unsurpassed cunning, shrewdness, and craft, with the profound knowledge of the corridors of power given him by three decades of politics and government at all levels, Lyndon Johnson, I believe, set to work on these premises, to give the public what he thought it wanted—and to wring from it what *he* needed.

Something of Johnson's personal power and guile is suggested by a story that grew out of his decision soon after Kennedy's death to set up a commission to investigate that Dallas assassination. He still didn't know, he told me at the time, "if this is a worldwide conspiracy involving Cuba or Russia." Taking the investigation that seriously, he wanted Chief Justice Earl Warren to chair it; but Warren refused Johnson's first overture, on grounds that a Chief Justice should not accept executive-branch assignments.

Here are the notes I made after a conversation with Johnson at the LBJ Ranch, January 14, 1964, when he described how he pursued Warren:

> J. said, "Well, tell him to come down here to the White House and say it to me face to face." Told Warren he was first lt. in WW I. Knew he would walk across Atlantic ocean to save the lives of 3 Americans—said possibly 100 million lives at stake here. So "I'm putting you back in that uniform." Never mind what "some puny-faced assoc. justice might say."

Put on the spot that way, Warren gave in. By then Johnson had persuaded Senator Richard Russell, of Georgia, to serve on the commission, thus satisfying the keen LBJ eye for a balanced ticket. But when Russell was told that Earl Warren would be chairman, the Georgian exploded, telling Johnson: "I wouldn't sit in the same room with him!"

Johnson appointed Russell anyway, knowing his man—knowing that the senator, on such grounds, would not publicly back away from a job "the President" wanted him to do.

Johnson achieved much by such dexterity; but he paid a high price for it, too. It may have been the root cause of his downfall, because it led people to believe that he could not be entirely honest—that his remarkable achievements must result from trickery and deceit. His hooded eyes, his devious and secretive ways, his capacity to be warm and generous in one moment, cruel and ruthless in another, as his purpose might require, created the impression—perhaps correct—that he trusted no one and manipulated everyone, believed everyone *could* be manipulated. Inevitably, that made people think they couldn't trust *him.*

In everything he did, good and bad, Johnson also was a man of excess—excessive energy, determination, and ability; excessive vanity, pettiness, and greed; excessive ambition, vision, and drive (the Great Society was surely the most visionary program ever put forward by a President). Excess would later mark his conduct of a war that in 1964 and early 1965 was little more than a small cloud on his seemingly unlimited horizon; but perhaps the most significant of his excesses was the Texas-born and Texas-size sense of inferiority that gave him at once a smoldering resentment of easterners and intellectuals—"Ivy Leaguers" and "Harvards," he would call them contemptuously—and a desperate yearning for their approval.

Born, no doubt, of his Southwest Texas State Teachers College education, his acute awareness of a background limited almost entirely to Texas and Washington politics, and his westerner's sense of eastern social advantages, Johnson's fears and needs were observable—and the more obvious in a man otherwise so impressive—in almost any conversation or encounter with him.

It was a curious contradiction to observe, that this man of power and accomplishment, as he was in 1965, when he had won a landslide election and had an approval rating of 69 percent in the Harris Poll—that this apparent colossus was beset by unadmitted fears of his own inadequacies; by resentment of people he thought belittled him and schemed against him; by a hungry need to be loved and admired, to have his virtues confirmed as if by some cosmic election victory.

Johnson could not let his deeds speak for themselves. He thought the press, if left alone, would not give *him* the plaudits it had lavished on Kennedy; so he was constantly figuring out new publicity angles, seeking more television exposure and ways to improve his image. No stone could be left unturned in the ceaseless quest for approval; and a memory of LBJ that persists in my mind is of the President of the United States, for the edification of reporters, pulling from his pocket and spreading on his desk a sheaf of newspaper clippings—editorials praising his achievements, polls proving his popularity.

He could insist, as if it proved something, that *his* staff was smarter than Kennedy's, and he once told me pointedly that two foreign leaders had asked him for advice on poverty and medical care programs—"and these are *sophisticated* people with *real style.*" To John Pomfret, a *Times* White House correspondent in 1965, Johnson said he planned to set up higher-education centers so excellent that "McGeorge Bundy wouldn't have the IQ to get in." In a speech at Princeton he listed all the college professors in his Cabinet; and he often spoke privately about how he'd put "all the intellectuals' favorite bills" through Congress when "a Harvard man"—Kennedy—couldn't do it.

But when he opened the White House to a festival of artists and intellectuals, they responded with attacks on his foreign policy and snickers at the cultural effort. Johnson, resenting such people even as he angled for their support, thought the trouble was his western manners and heritage; and some of it may have been. But I think he never understood that his passion to persuade his critics, his yearning to be the leader of them *all*, repelled most intellectuals— whose common denominator was not a Harvard degree but an inclination to think for themselves. Nor did he see that his devious tactics caused them to fear that he really only wanted to *use* them—which in a political sense was largely true. Moreover, as a man of power and politics, Johnson constantly kept his eye on the *ends* he sought; intellectuals were more choosy about the means he employed.

Johnson held strong, Fifties-style anti-Communist views. He didn't believe "fat Communists" were better than lean and hungry Communists, he told me; Communists were all alike and "the more trouble they have the better for us." He was of the World War II generation, too, and did not doubt its primary lesson—"the lesson of Munich"—that aggression unchecked is aggression unleashed, continuing, expanding. And he had lived through the Democratic party's trauma of the early Fifties, when Republicans had campaigned on the premise that Democrats, perhaps of doubtful loyalty, had "lost" China to the Communists.

Even so, Lyndon Johnson was inhibited about situations that he did not fully understand, that were beyond his immediate power to control; and I think it arguable that he would not have entered upon so hazardous an enterprise as the war in Vietnam had he not been surrounded by "Harvards" who told him he was doing what Kennedy would have done—had he not, therefore, believed that *he* would be criticized for *not* doing it.

What was about to unfold in Southeast Asia, at the time I heard those picketers outside the Waldorf, already had had a preview in Johnson's first major foreign policy crisis. On April 28, 1965, while rushing ahead with the Great Society, he staged the first U.S. military intervention in Latin America since Coolidge sent Marines to Nicaragua in 1925. Even so, Johnson's order sending Marines into the Dominican Republic was generally accepted by North Americans (polls later showed) as a necessary act of presidential power in pursuit of national security. In those days, "the President" still knew best.

It's not clear whether Johnson acted only to protect American lives in a civil war, as he first said, or whether his real motive was to prevent in the Dominican Republic the possible establishment of another Castroite Communist island in the Caribbean, as he later contended. (Probably both, in no known order of priority.) But his frenetic performance in the following days foreshadowed his long, stubborn, convulsive efforts to justify and sustain the much larger intervention in Vietnam.

The Dominican crisis brought Johnson the most significant criticism he had suffered in seventeen hugely successful months in the White House: he was denounced as trigger-happy, militaristic, panicky, and untrue to Kennedy's Alliance for Progress. He reacted like a man who could not tolerate dissent *or* lack of the approval he had enjoyed up to then. He indulged in repeated harangues to congressional leaders, long walks around the White House driveway with panting reporters, hours on the telephone with any influential person he could reach; most important, he made three television appearances in four days, including one sudden invasion of the networks' evening news broadcasts.

All this probably made more of a minor crisis than the public otherwise would have. But instead of convincing his critics, Johnson played into their hands with what seemed his bent for trickery—alternating between the claim that he had acted to save American lives and the contention that he had sent the Marines because "a popular democratic revolution" had been "taken over and really seized and placed into the hands of a band of Communist conspirators."

This assertion proved to be a vast Johnsonian overstatement, like his colorful description of Ambassador W. Tapley Bennett having to write cables under his desk while the Dominicans shot up the U.S. embassy in Santo Domingo. Such overkill was soon reported in a press at which Johnson became outraged.

In fact, he had been precipitated into a foreign crisis he did not understand as he understood Congress, a crisis that he had no immediate power—even with the Marines and the 82nd Airborne Division—to control. He could not establish in Santo Domingo the mastery he displayed in Washington; and many who resented anyway the ease with which he had taken Kennedy's place and surpassed Kennedy's achievement first found in the Dominican intervention an opportunity to strike back at him.

Then Johnson's resentment of criticism and his need for approval—the one unprovoked, the other unsated, in his first months in office—produced a blustery reaction in which he tried too frantically to justify his use of force. Predictably, he only damaged both his credibility and his presidential stature. He even sounded an ominous note of self-pity (What could be less characteristic of "the President," as Americans had come to think of him?) in a speech to the AFL-CIO Building Trades Council: "Now I am the most denounced man in the world. . . ."

But what awaited him—what already had been set in motion—was infinitely worse.

On September 25, 1964, in Eufaula, Oklahoma, campaigning against Barry Goldwater, Lyndon Johnson poured it on:

"We don't want our American boys to do the fighting for Asian boys. We don't want to get involved in a nation with seven hundred million people and get tied down in a land war in Asia. . . ."

And three days later, in Manchester, New Hampshire, he was even more explicit: "What I have been trying to do with the situation that I found was to get the boys in Vietnam to do their own fighting with our advice and with our equipment. . . . So we are not going south and run out. . . . We are going to continue to try to get them to save their own freedom with their own men."

Then Johnson won his landslide, the triumphant peace candidate demolishing Barry Goldwater, who was pictured as too belligerent to have his "finger on the button." But LBJ had been sworn in for his own term less than three weeks when, on February 7, 1965, a vicious Viet Cong mortar attack came down on the American advisers' camp at Pleiku while infiltrators breached the South Vietnamese security perimeter to blow up several American aircraft. Eight Americans died and 108 were injured—a small battle but one of the most consequential in American history.

Within hours Lyndon Johnson had sent forty-nine American carrier planes to attack staging areas and base camps in North Vietnam. A second wave of bombers went north on February 8. Both attacks, the White House said, were "in response to provocations ordered and directed by the Hanoi regime."

Operation Rolling Thunder had begun, and with it the long decline of Lyndon Johnson and the presidency. It was not just that the attacks were on North Vietnam, when thoughtful people knew that the real problem was in the South; if South Vietnamese forces were not strong enough to protect American planes, could the war be won by bombing the North? Neither Johnson nor events ever demonstrated that it could be. But beyond everything else Rolling Thunder appeared to be exactly what Johnson in his campaign had warned against and pledged not to do—had even excoriated Goldwater for advocating.

Here seemed guile and trickery indeed, for eventually even the authority on which Johnson ordered the bombing—the so-called Tonkin Gulf resolution—came to be seen as one of his slippery moves. Six months before, in August 1964, when North Vietnamese torpedo boats had attacked American destroyers in the Gulf of Tonkin, Johnson not only had ordered a one-shot air strike in retaliation (neatly countering Goldwater's tough campaign talk) but had asked Congress for a resolution that empowered him "to take all necessary measures to repel any armed attack against the forces of the United States and to prevent future aggression."

In the wake of the Tonkin Gulf attacks, Congress had little choice but to pass a resolution authorizing the President to protect American boys; but as the months passed and the war intensified, Johnson repeatedly cited the resolution as authority for bombing in the North, for ground combat in the South, and for the buildup of a vast military machine in Southeast Asia. Thus, many members of Congress and the public they represented believed themselves typically deceived and manipulated by the trickster in the White House. In 1967 Under Secretary of State Nicholas de B. Katzenbach defended the resolution as "the functional equivalent of declaring war," which had not been what most members had thought they were voting for. A high White House official told me that Johnson had been carrying the text around "in his pocket" long before the Tonkin Gulf episode gave him the opportunity to make sure of its passage.

Similarly, Rolling Thunder had been under active consideration during the "warmonger" campaign against Goldwater. Johnson may not have been certainly resolved upon it then, but he surely knew that he *might* undertake a bombing campaign when he spoke with such seeming firmness in Eufaula and Manchester. Once started, moreover, the bombing could not be stopped unless Johnson conceded its inefficacy; after all, it was supposed to be protecting Americans. Nor could he long continue the pretense of retaliation, since it gave the Viet Cong and Hanoi the initiative; under that rationale, only when they attacked could the U.S. bomb.

Inevitably, the bombing of the North took on a life of its own, became an end in itself, discrediting the original claim of mere "retaliation" and striking another blow at Lyndon Johnson's fading credibility.

Rolling Thunder, moreover, drew in more American forces to protect air bases and personnel in the South; thus, although the bombing failed to improve the war situation significantly, the campaign eased the way for Johnson ultimately to take the more fateful step of bringing in American ground troops to fight the Viet Cong and the North Vietnamese. Some critics thought that was *why* he undertook Rolling Thunder in the first place; they believed Johnson, as John Randolph said of Martin Van Buren, "rowed to his object with muffled oars."

In any case, on July 28, 1965, Johnson announced that he was sending fifty thousand fighting men (in addition to the seventy-five thousand Americans already in Vietnam) to do what he'd said only ten months before he didn't want Americans to do: "the job that Asian boys should do." Insiders knew that this decision, too, bore characteristic Johnson markings; for weeks he'd orchestrated a public debate about sending far *more* ground troops to Vietnam, so that his announced decision to send fifty thousand would seem "moderate"— even though he knew hundreds of thousands more were bound to follow.

This sleight of hand did not long appease those who opposed escalation of the war. And that same July 28 Johnson added a fatal new justification for his policy: "If we are driven from the field in Vietnam, then no nation can ever again have the same confidence in an American promise, or in American protection."

To many, this seemed just one more twist-and-turn in LBJ's never-ending effort to justify "his" war and a claim that contradicted the narrower view of the Indochinese conflict that Johnson had so clearly expressed in 1964. Nor was it persuasive to anyone who thought American combat forces had no business in "the field" of Vietnam to begin with. And it effectively painted Johnson into a corner from which not even he could escape; for if such dire consequences awaited failure, nothing was possible but to keep striving for what LBJ, with his ear for an effective phrase, more than a year later called "that coonskin on the wall."

Johnson's finely honed political instinct may for once have led him to a profoundly ironic miscalculation in committing ground troops to a war on the Asian mainland. He was pushing hard, that summer, for his Great Society legislation; and some students of the period believe he feared he would not have the political clout to pass this ambitious program if he "lost" Vietnam, as the Democrats had been accused of losing China only fifteen years earlier. Thus, it may be that he escalated the war to *save* the Great Society—and only assured its demise in the costly struggle that he brought on himself and the nation.

But if he remembered the dismal China episode, Johnson forgot or ignored the clear warnings left him by Dwight Eisenhower, who knew something about armies and wars. As President in 1954, Eisenhower had successfully resisted immense pressures (not least from liberal Democrats like Senator Hubert Humphrey) to intervene in Indochina to help the French stave off defeat by the Viet Minh.

Eisenhower repeatedly expressed a soldier's aversion to pitting American troops "against the teeming millions of Asia," and he quickly saw the problems created by the history of colonialism in the region. "The jungles of Indochina . . . would have swallowed up division after division of United States troops, who, unaccustomed to this kind of warfare, would have sustained heavy casualties. . ." he wrote in a passage ultimately deleted from his memoirs.* "Furthermore the presence of ever more numbers of white men in uniform would have aggravated rather than assuaged Asiatic resentments."

And as if in specific warning to the LBJ of a decade later, Eisenhower told a news conference questioner on March 10, 1954: "There is going to be no involvement of America in war unless it is a result of the constitutional process that is placed upon Congress to declare it. Now let us have that clear. . . ."

Better and more-prescient advice has seldom been available from a President to one of his successors. Johnson turned his back on every aspect of it— perhaps to save the Great Society, no doubt in the belief that Kennedy's legacy and the lessons of Munich and China left him little choice, but surely in an excess of confidence in his own and the nation's power.

The consequences were immediate. After July 1965 the costs of the war mounted ever more steeply—in American and Asian lives, dollars, destruction, national unity, international amity. American boys by the thousands went to Canada or Sweden or jail to avoid the draft and a war LBJ gave them no convincing reason to fight; some were aided by fathers who were World War II veterans.

Television, covering its first big war, brought directly into the American living room the terrible images that scarred a generation: burning villages, burning children, a land and a people being destroyed so that—Lyndon Johnson kept insisting—they could be saved from communism, and American promises could be vindicated. Perhaps no war less enthusiastically supported than, say, World War II could have survived the appalling disclosures of the television screen.

The man of excess seemed to wage a war of excess—all the industrial might and technological ingenuity of the world's most powerful nation thrown against a backward and impoverished Asian people. Vast fleets of helicopters, B-52s thundering from Guam, the immense supply base at Cam Ranh Bay, ultimately more U.S. bombs dropped on North Vietnam than on Germany in World War II, even the defoliation of the Indochinese jungles. Could any end justify such profligacy of power? Perhaps victory, but that never came. And

*This quotation is from *Eisenhower the President: Crucial Days, 1951–1960*, by William B. Ewald Jr. (Prentice-Hall, 1981), page 119. Mr. Ewald was research director for both volumes of the Eisenhower memoirs.

what conceivable purpose could be served that was worth such a costly endeavor? The solemn and lugubrious President who appeared on television screens offered many answers, but none that convinced enough people.

Predictably, despite centuries of enmity between China and Indochina, the war eventually was pictured as one to halt the advance of "Asian communism with its headquarters in Peking." But no more evidence supported this thesis of a massive Chinese threat to all of Southeast Asia than had shown the Dominican revolution to have been "taken over and really seized" by Communists. The new theme appeared to be still another Johnsonian scam to make the war palatable.

Even when the administration disclosed, in late 1966, that the third-biggest war in American history was costing twice its budgeted figure—$20 billion a year instead of $10 billion—Johnson never publicly wavered in his commitment to it. He had proclaimed and probably believed, in his grandiose style, that the country was rich enough to have guns and butter, too; yet he finally had to call for an income tax surcharge to pay for the war that was sapping the life from his Great Society. Some economists believe that the early funding of the war without additional taxes was the root of the inflation that persisted through the Seventies and into the Eighties. Certainly the public confession of the higher costs further shook what remained of the nation's trust in Lyndon Johnson.

The man of excess appeared not only to wage a war of excess; his belief in it seemed excessive, too. As casualty lists lengthened and costs mounted, the intensity and dedication of the antiwar movement seemed not to affect Johnson; and to the usual charges that he had deceived the people and was waging an unjustified war was added the indictment of "unresponsive government." He was not listening, critics said, and did not care what the people thought.

That was not true: Lyndon Johnson, with his need for approval, cared intensely. He repeatedly sought to placate critics (though he called them "nervous Nellies") with bombing halts, negotiating offers, "peace offensives"— even a typically overblown Johnsonian offer to develop Indochina's Mekong River into a sort of Asian TVA, if only Hanoi would listen to reason. Notably, these efforts were invariably aimed at winning over the antiwar movement— critics from the Left, the "Ivy Leaguers" whose favor LBJ had always sought even as he appeared to scorn it.

Johnson's practical political fear, however, was of *the Right*—of hawks like Goldwater who advocated widening the war beyond the limits Johnson carefully maintained (it was Nixon who later expanded the fighting into Cambodia and Laos) and who he thought would risk what he dreaded most, war with Communist China—"a nation with seven hundred million people." To avoid any possibility of such a war, Johnson tightly controlled the military (contrary to popular opinion). "I won't let those Air Force generals bomb the smallest outhouse north of the seventeenth parallel without checking with me," he said; and whatever his detractors may have thought, that was true.

Perpetually torn, as he put it, between giving "the hawks more war" and "the doves more peace," Johnson did a little of both and not enough of either. This cautious middle course (however savage critics considered it) played into the hands of the determined men in Hanoi who were willing to fight for as many decades as necessary. It failed either to win the war or to silence its critics; and since it satisfied neither hawks nor doves, it succeeded only in strengthening the opposition of both, as well as the widespread belief that Lyndon Johnson, the President of the United States, was not to be trusted.

As in the Dominican crisis—that prelude to disaster—Johnson the master manipulator, the man of power and guile and excess, had plunged into a situation he could not master as he had mastered Washington and Texas, even with five hundred thousand troops and five thousand sorties a month. He could not win without committing more resources than was politically possible, without risking war with China (he believed), without shattering a divided society. He could not negotiate because Hanoi would negotiate nothing but the withdrawal of American forces and the unification of Indochina. And he could not justify to enough of the public the only course that was left—to keep on fighting for that unreachable "coonskin on the wall."

"We've got a bear by the tail," Johnson remarked not long after he launched Rolling Thunder. Every day that passed made good that judgment; and by 1967 even his own administration was torn by dissent. "McNamara's gone dove on me," he had to tell Clark Clifford. Still he could not let go of the bear.

And that, finally, ruined him and cracked the American people's deepest faith in "the President." That faith might have survived one man's loss of credibility, even his excesses; but it could not survive the cruel revelation that *he did not have the power after all.* "The President" was one of us—not superhuman, just human. He could deceive, as any man could, and he could be deceived. He could make bad judgments and find no way to redeem them. He could send armies, wreak havoc, uproot societies—not to make the world safe for democracy or for any large purpose, indeed for no reason he could explain to the people, but because he did not want to be a President who lost a war.

He had not even understood the power he did have. "Among all the powerful nations of the world the United States is the only one with a tradition of anti-colonialism. . . ," Eisenhower wrote in that passage dropped from his memoirs. "The standing of the United States as the most powerful of the anti-colonial powers is an asset of incalculable value to the Free World. . . . It is essential to our position of leadership in a world wherein the majority of the nations have at some time or another felt the yoke of colonialism. Thus it is that *the moral position of the United States was more to be guarded than the Tonkin Delta, indeed than all of Indochina.*" (Emphasis added.)

But that was not the kind of power Lyndon Johnson understood or knew how to wield. So in his time "the President" turned out to be no longer an emperor, if he ever had been; he was just Lyndon Johnson with a bear by the tail.

So he withdrew and returned to the LBJ Ranch, that moment of power for which he once said he had waited all his life gone in the dust of Vietnam and the tides of excess. Richard Nixon followed, vainly trying to maintain the emperor's throne after it had been lowered to human levels; "the President" has not meant quite the same to us since.

That may not be unalloyed loss; I believe disillusionment is enlightenment. And if the revered presidencies of Eisenhower and Kennedy yielded a high degree of national unity, purpose, and pride, if the less-exalted presidencies of Carter and Reagan and the foreseeable future reflect a shaken national confidence, we may nevertheless live today more nearly in a world of reality. Surely we have a better sense of limits. Having less power, or less than we once assumed, we set less store by it.

But Johnson's fall, though it bordered on tragedy, holds for me no cathartic value. He was the nearest to a giant among the leaders of my time, the one in whom I sensed the most potential for good. But Shakespeare cautions us: "Oh, it is excellent to have the strength of a giant; but it is tyrannous to use it like a giant."

Tyranny was not Johnson's purpose, whatever some "Harvards" may have thought. I believe he only wanted power, and to use it to benefit people, thus fulfilling his own deepest needs. But power *is* a sort of tyranny that those who wield it too eagerly may not even know they inflict; and when Lyndon Johnson, the man of excess, tried to extend his power beyond its limits, waging a war that a democratic people would not support, enough of them ultimately rebuffed the tyranny implicit in the effort.

But I do not celebrate his downfall. We shall never know what we lost: what, with his giant's strength, he might have achieved—had he not in his need and his excess used it like a giant.

Lyndon Baines Johnson was born on August 27, 1908, near Johnson City, Texas. His parents had trouble agreeing on a name for him. One morning, three months after his birth, his mother, Rebekah Baines Johnson, refused to get up and make breakfast until her baby had a name. His father, Sam Ealy Johnson, suggested Clarence, then Dayton—both names of lawyer friends. When Rebekah rejected them, he offered another lawyer's name. "Would you call him Linden?" "Yes," she said, but insisted they spell it Lyndon. *"Spell it as you please," said Mr. Johnson. She got up and made the biscuits.*

In high school he began reading the Congressional Record. *Later his reading dropped off. According to an unauthorized biography, he probably did not finish reading more than six books after leaving college.*

After college he taught Chicano children in Cotulla, Texas. Each morning he had them stand up and sing:

> How do you do, Mr. Johnson,
> How do you do?
> Is there anything that we can do for you?
> We will do it if we can,
> We'll stand by you to a man.
> How do you do, Mr. Johnson?
> How do you do, do, do?

Lady Bird's first impression of him: "He was tall and gangling, and he talked quite incessantly. At first I thought he was quite a repulsive young man. Then I realized he was handsome and charming and extremely bright."

In World War II Johnson spent seven months as a U.S. emissary in Australia and New Zealand, during which he accompanied other GIs on missions in the Pacific as an observer. He won a Silver Star for a mission on which his plane was attacked and forced to turn back. Doubtful of his heroism, he considered returning the medal, but changed his mind and wore it almost daily for the rest of his life.

As JFK's Vice-President he was so invisible that Candid Camera did a show in which people were asked, "Who is Lyndon B. Johnson?"

By all accounts, he was an enormously physical man. "When Johnson wanted to persuade you of something," said Ben Bradlee, "you really felt as if a St. Bernard had licked your face for an hour. . . ."

Hubert Humphrey had scars on his shins from LBJ's surefooted encouragement to work harder on Senate business.

He liked to pressure serious, intellectual people into swimming naked with him in his swimming pool.

A close associate observed, "He had been told that he was ugly enough times that he believed it." He considered the left side of his face taboo to photographers. He sometimes pressured editors to kill bad photos.

He loved to go deer hunting on his ranch near Johnson City. A friend explained: "Lyndon's idea of a hunting trip, however, was a mechanized safari in a fleet of air-conditioned cars equipped with intercommunications systems."

His favorite car was an immense Lincoln convertible, which he would race around the ranch. When passengers complained about the ninety-mile-an-hour speed, he would put his Stetson over the speedometer.

Johnson was fond of urinating off the porch of the ranch after everyone else had gone to sleep. Soon after he became President, the Secret Service caught him at it two nights in a row. "The small pleasures of life you have to give up," he groused.

Never very inhibited even in the White House, he once held a meeting and gave his secretary dictation while receiving an enema.

He was a meticulous, expensive dresser and was adamant that his secretaries not wear nylons with runs.

He was a compulsive gift giver. Said son-in-law Patrick Nugent: "Whether it was a pocketknife or a cigarette lighter, and it always had his name on it . . . he'd pull something out of his pocket and say, 'Here, I want you to keep this as a

110

memento of your visit to the Ranch; but for God's sake don't embarrass me by leaving it in a whorehouse someplace.'"

On a 1966 trip to Asia he carried "a planeload" of plastic busts of himself—which an aide handed out from a shopping cart. Later, Johnson gave one to Pope Paul VI as a Christmas present, in exchange for a fourteenth-century painting.

Johnson carried (or kept in his desk for ready reference) a well-fingered personality guide that reminded, "Give spiritual strength to people, and they will give genuine affection to you." (LBJ's emphasis.)

He died of a heart attack on January 22, 1973, at his ranch. "Till the very last," Richard Nixon observed years later, "he thought he could win [over his critics]. I think President Johnson died of a broken heart. I really do."

Uncle Walt

MAX APPLE

SOMEWHERE OVER THE RAINBOW TINKER BELL FLIES. SHE'S TINY AND CUTE AND ETHE-real. She waves a magic wand and from that wand little particles float down to the greasy surface of the earth. We never see the earth, only Tinker Bell levitating near one of the turrets of Fantasyland waving that little wand, endlessly flicking down stardust.

The white dust is not desiccated dreams, it's not even pure cocaine: it's just plain old scouring powder and detergent—Ajax, Comet, Spic 'n' Span, Tide, Rinso, Tinker Bell has them all. She is the cleaning lady of the Magic Kingdom and here cleanliness is godliness.

Since the opening of Disneyland, in 1955, Tinker Bell has been dropping that powder upon the cardsharps and mom-and-pop racketeers who ran the amusement parks that used to sit on the outskirts of our towns the way whores and lepers camped beside the biblical cities. One sight of Tinker Bell, and the amusement parks vanished like evil stepsisters.

Because of her cleansing effects, hordes of Siamese twins are underemployed and bearded ladies have undergone electrolysis. Thousands of milk bottles with weighted bottoms lie unused in trash heaps. Sideshow barkers became used-car salesmen and then drifted into health-studio and home-exercise equipment sales. The strippers long ago became Avon ladies.

Such total obliteration of the local amusement parks was not even Walt Disney's aim. That just happened. Those themeless dirty old places, where all you had was fun, vanished like the silent pictures. They were an incidental loss. When he parked his animated robots and elaborate set designs among the orange groves of Anaheim, Walt Disney's real target was the family vacation.

The amusement park courted you for an hour here and there, an afternoon, an evening . . . an entire day was as unlikely as all day at a ball park. But Walt Disney wanted the day and more. He wanted the weekend and the holiday and, finally, he coveted his neighbor's vacation.

It is said that the monarchs of travel, the Hiltons and Sheratons and Holiday Inns, thought an amusement park was no place for a hotel. They did not understand that Walt Disney was not building a land of cheap thrills and carnival tricks. Everything is honest in Disneyland; there are few games and no hucksters. The middle-class family rules the Magic Kingdom; they have to—they are its stars.

When Disney blew his cartoon and movie sets into life-size environments, he created a new extravaganza starring each participant. At the movies you can only watch. At Disneyland, when it's your turn, you become a part of the action. The theme is not childhood, it's stardom.

On the edge of the land, where the hotel chains turned up their noses at tourism, Walt's buddy Jack Wrather, purveyor of the Lone Ranger and Tonto, built a modest motel. By the millions Americans deserted their seacoasts and mountains. They piled into their cars and headed for Anaheim. Wrather's motel grew to four skyscrapers and their own man-made beach. The metamorphosis of the family vacation had begun. Beginning with Disneyland, the amusement park moved from nickels and dimes into the realm of big business and grand idolatry.

Mickey, a tiny mouse, became a cultural idol and a literal one. He and his fellow rodents, pests, and domestic animals are the central statuary in amusementland. They bestride the fields of pleasure the way soldiers on horseback and carved angels used to guard village cemeteries. Apparently a big smiling mouse or duck suggests a good time. Or maybe the real message from the animal kingdom is patience.

For more than a generation adults and children have been standing in controlled lines, standing between stainless steel bars, awaiting patiently the chance to become part of a simulated jungle, or a pirate town, or a Tahitian island, waiting to ride a river raft with Davy Crockett and pilot a rocket ship over Tomorrowland.

At the end of every line the lifelike idols leer, lights flash, and a droll informative recording turns the adventure into a learning experience that can be captured by a snapshot and encapsulated by a souvenir.

In the Magic Kingdom nothing is wasted and there is no waste. Almost unnoticed among the idols are Disney humans carrying brooms and dustpans, Tinker Bell's little helpers. The mayor of Disneyland says that bubble gum is his worst civic problem.

"Every morning we dispatch a bubble gum brigade armed with six-inch blades."

From the morning sidewalk scraping to each night's grand finale, a march of cartoon characters that straight-faced employees tell you is "an entirely new concept in parades," the Disney experience is clean, orderly, and extravagant. The great marvel of all this splendor is the fact that so many worked so much to accomplish so little.

But Walt Disney, the Kansas City tinkerer, created much more than cartoons and vacuous theme parks. He had the future in his bones. He dreamed the mouse and then the mouse stood up like a man. Mickey planted one foot in California and with the other he tap-danced through the world. Islands dropped from his pockets, new characters sprang from his forehead. The world sank into Depression and war, but three generations on both sides of the Atlantic still grew up with Disney toothbrushes and bedroom slippers. For thirty years we watched *The Wonderful World of Disney* and let Tinker Bell powder our dreams. Those powdered dreams meant a fortune for the Disney corporation, but, alas, Tinker Bell failed the children.

Children know that life is not such a benign game. They know it because they have brothers and sisters, they know it because they have parents, but above all they know it because all the scouring powders in Tink's magic wand cannot cleanse the despair and evil in a child's own thoughts and wishes. Tinker Bell has not replaced Oedipus, though Disney uses myths as if their sole function is titillation.

Disney's dragon is just a fire-breathing big old dog to cartoon Pete, but other heroes do not take dragons as lightly as do Pete and Walt. Siegfried, for one, had to kill the dragon and eat his heart in order to understand the language of birds. And when Siegfried, sickened and stunned, hears the secrets of nature, there is no possible return to naiveté. Not for Siegfried, not for us. The myth grudgingly shows us the bloody price of knowledge.

In the murky depths of the Magic Kingdom there are no secrets, no mythic struggles. Everyone can understand the birds. There is no blood on the hands, no risk of the spirit. The voice of nature talks to everyone. The birds, the squirrels, the chipmunks, the dogs and cats, the leaves on the trees, even the branches and the limbs, talk and sing. All nature babbles, but none of her creatures has anything to say.

In every Disney enterprise the form so continually triumphs over the content that we finally realize what Walt Disney always knew. The nonstop success of the Disney empire for fifty-five years has been based on what Walt recognized in Kansas City: movement is everything. Movement is hypnotic, and movement coupled with electricity and three-dimensional modeling can present the illusion of life without any of the mess.

Disneyland emerged and grew at almost the same time that the Salk vaccine freed the country from the fear of polio. In the summers parents had kept their children from crowds whenever possible, but in post-Salk euphoria, the throngs, in relief, breathed upon one another. The Disney surge in the polio-free late Fifties and Sixties was creating a new kind of infantile paralysis, not a viral paralysis of the body but a paralysis of taste that allowed sentimentality, speedy image, and simple cuteness to hold the reins of art.

The overpraise and overacceptance of Disney creations laid the seeds of yet another generation of sanitized robots. Chip and Dale and Mickey and Minnie are the direct grandparents of R2D2 and E.T. One electronic thoroughbred begets another, just as surely as the new princes of childhood sentimentality, Lucas and Spielberg, are now wallowing in the Oscars and the millions that used to be heaped upon Disney.

E.T., who dies and then returns to life, is the extension of all those Disney swords that draw no blood, all those Bambis and Dumbos and Snow Whites who turn possible tragedy into enormous profit.

Decade after decade of mediocre Disney films triumphed and stroked our sensibilities because the art itself, animation, is such a delight. It has been right from the start. In 1928, when Mickey Mouse as Steamboat Willie joins prototype Minnie to crank up a goat's tail in order to see musical notes leave the beast's mouth and dance to the tune of "Turkey in the Straw," the magic is already in full bloom.

When Dumbo's ears flap and that ungainly mass finally soars, nobody cares where he's going. We love this creature; indeed, we fall for Disney the way we fall in love: what the eye sees is more important than what the mind judges.

Walt Disney knew the secret of speed and the effect of smallness the way a magician knows it, or a cosmetologist. He didn't know much about childhood and human development but he knew everything about the relations, in animated drawings, between proportion, motion, and sound. When he made *Fantasia*, in 1940, the characters, the music, and the movement all meshed in his cartoon ballet. He had his form and he minded it happily ever after.

The form is so pure that it crosses all ideological barriers. When Nikita Khrushchev visited the United States, a scheduling error kept him from seeing Disneyland. Had he made a trek to Disneyland, the old Russian might never have said what he did about burying us. He would have known that nobody has to bury anyone else—things never get that serious.

Yes, we cry for Dumbo and Bambi and Snow White, but not too long and not too hard. Simplicity and clarity are the demigods of the experience, strong emotions are too messy. The cartoon beauties, even when they suffer a little, still overwhelm us with their apparent innocence.

Lucas and Spielberg learned the lesson well, but IBM and Japan perfected the form. For the future that Walt Disney carried in his bones was not just cartoons and amusement parks: he pioneered the precise, clean, insipid, mechanical image. Throw him a kiss every time you get a computer letter. The spelling will be perfect and the margins exact, but the words will babble like Disney's nature.

In a 1964 interview Walt told the Canadian Broadcasting Corporation that he had created a revolutionary new form of entertainment, Audio-Animatronics.

"Our whole forty-some-odd years here," Disney said, "have been in the world of making things move—inanimate things move. Now we're making dimensional human figures move . . . making anything move, through the use of electronics. . . . We're not going to replace the human being—believe me on that. Just for show purposes. . . . We operate [Disneyland] fifteen hours a day and these shows have to go on on the hour." The human figures, he concluded, "don't have to stop for coffee breaks and all that kind of stuff. So that's the whole idea of it."

Walt told the truth. He liked the electronic figures because they were simpler, cleaner, and more dependable than live ones. Dimensional figures don't need coffee breaks or unions or pension funds. They don't even need salaries. Walt Disney was a full generation ahead of the robot pizza parlors and mindless video games. Disneyland and all the Disney experiences provided the basic training for what we are now calling the electronics revolution. The adults who line up for the latest software lined up at Disneyland too, and they probably slept in Mickey Mouse pajamas. The adults and children who sit for hours in front of video games had the myths of their childhood whitewashed by Tinker Bell. Pac-Man and Donkey Kong are electronic dots, as clean and systemic and predictable as Disneyland.

Still, Walt has been dead since 1966; we can't blame him for all the electronic mindlessness, but his shadow spreads, now to Japan, the kingdom of microelectronics where the latest Disneyland may become his ultimate shrine.

Notwithstanding all the triumphs of Disney, there has also been a strong anti-Mickeyness throughout the fifty-five years of success. That anti-Mickey sensibility is most graphically expressed in another pest, a pest created by a comic writer, Franz Kafka of Prague. Only a few years before that golden moment when Walt looked out at his garage in Kansas City and befriended the mouse, Franz Kafka looked into his own soul and found there Gregor Samsa, a serious young man who awakens from uneasy dreams to find himself transformed into a gigantic insect.

If Kafka had not died so young, what a collaboration he and Walt Disney might have achieved. Imagine the Disney version of Kafka's *Metamorphosis*, a man-cockroach happily climbing the walls, dancing, going out to champagne dinners with other roaches. Gregor Samsa, like Mickey Mouse, would have gone out into the world, into a Prague full of roach shops and bars and schools and offices, all administered by a full-fledged roach government. Walt Disney would have known how to put roachness into its proper context, and the context is always company.

The Disney creatures do not live by bread alone. Motion leads to commotion, the inevitable fertile mix is the social world. Once Mickey Mouse moved, like Adam before him, he needed a woman. If she had to be a mouse, so be it. Walt Disney made her a shapely mouse. And in the distance, deep in history beyond the drawings, teeming nature produced all those nephews for Mickey and Donald, not direct descendants who might have offended hygienic Tinker Bell, but family just the same. All those moving, cavorting mice and ducks and chipmunks and elephants and deer, no matter what their dilemma, are lucky.

They always have one another. Nature loves company and animation is even a kind of communal art. Walt had Ub Iwerks at first, and his brother Roy always, and finally hundreds of artists in his Burbank studios.

But young Kafka in Prague couldn't connect even with a wife, and his cockroach never met another cockroach. He lived alone in a room. Kafka's version of Davy Crockett was a professional faster, a man who never found the food he wanted, a creature whose most powerful instinct was doing without.

In their opposite ways Disney and Kafka are the bookends of the century. They have both focused on the smallness of man. Kafka is a total master of the microscopic. Where Disney sees the rodent, Kafka picks out the gnat in the ear. Nothing can be insignificant to a creature like man. Kafka's nightmare of smallness unchecked leads to the milieu of the bureaucrat doing meaningless work in a gigantic office. It leads to the child unnoticed in the thick bustle of his own family. It leads to the overwhelming terror of being small, alone, ugly, and singular, and having no understanding of why this is so and no hope of ever achieving such understanding.

Disney also begins with the premise of an overwhelmingly complicated and threatening world. His most compelling creatures are weak and tiny. They see life passing by through a blade of grass. They hide in the shelter of bushes. The Jiminy Crickets and Donald Ducks are as hopeless and helpless as Kafka's gigantic roach.

But Kafka and the old myths and stories let their characters experience hopelessness. They let them know the terror and the comedy of insignificance. Disney always saves the day. He turns Dumbo's birth defects into fun and profit. He gives individual names and identities to the preconscious Seven Dwarfs and turns them into tiny vignettes of the Protestant ethic. He insists on a fairy godmother, or some other smug adult, to reassure us that it's safe and cute to be little and under siege.

But, Walt, we're not safe. All your cunning and high-technology movement haven't convinced us. The siege starts at birth, and the child needs all the allies he can find. He needs some stuff, Walt, some content, something to grow against. When we were growing up you held our hand, and that was fine, but you used your other hand to cover our eyes. We were young and innocent, Walt, we thought your creatures were as exotic as foreigners, as safe as cigarettes. You were a brilliant capitalist, a creative genius, and a false friend.

WALTER ELIAS DISNEY *was born on December 5, 1901, in Chicago. He spent his boyhood in Kansas City and on a farm outside Marceline, Missouri.*

In his first attempt at art he applied a barrelful of tar to the side of his family's white house. His first remuneration as an artist came when he was ten: in exchange for a drawing a week, a local barber gave him haircuts.

He was a prankster. His mother once met a nicely dressed woman at her front door, began talking with her, then recognized that the visitor was Walt. In high school, Walt would try out jokes on his father, who would listen without a smile, then a few days later say, "You know, I've been thinking about that joke you told me, Walter. It's funny, very funny."

When he first came to Hollywood he worked as a cavalry-charge extra in The Light That Failed.

Living in a one-room apartment, Walt and his brother Roy frequently got on each other's nerves. When they had a fight over Roy's cooking, Roy said he was going to send for his girlfriend and get married. He did, and Walt soon ended up marrying his new sister-in-law's maid of honor.

He conceived of Mickey Mouse on a trip from New York to Kansas City. Initially the character's name was Mortimer Mouse, but Disney's wife, Lillian, liked "Mickey" better. Mickey, Disney once explained, is "a nice fellow who never does anybody any harm."

Disney provided the original voice for Mickey.

Mary Pickford declared that Mickey was her favorite star. Madame Tussaud's London museum enshrined Mickey in wax. Russian director Sergei Eisenstein called Mickey "America's most original contribution to culture."

Many state censorship boards protested against the "grotesque and emotionally expressive" udders that Disney gave his cartoon cows. Disney compromised by adding small, provocative skirts.

Disney stood five feet ten inches tall and was a dapper dresser. He wore bold-colored jackets over gray or blue sweaters. He liked moccasins and hats—Tyroleans, fedoras, Panamas.

He drove a silver Thunderbird convertible, but was never known to put the top down, even in the hottest weather.

He played polo at the Riviera Club with Spencer Tracy, Will Rogers, and Darryl F. Zanuck. However, he always preferred his family to the social life.

His favorite meal was a bowl of chili, a glass of V-8, and soda crackers. He carried crackers and nuts in his pockets to snack on while working. The only type of cake he liked was banana cream. Later in life, as his weight climbed above 185 pounds, he began to diet.

On their early dates Disney would take Lillian to the movies to assess a competitor's cartoons. After they married, he would take her out to dinner, then suggest that they drop by the studio so he could get in a few minutes of work. Lillian would nap on the couch while Walt, working, forgot about the time. Typically, at one in the morning he would remember the clock and wake Lillian up, telling her it was only ten-thirty.

The Disneys lived in Holmby Hills in Los Angeles and, on holidays, at Smoketree Ranch, outside of Palm Springs.

One night when he stayed particularly late at the office, Lillian became extremely annoyed. She recalled, "I think the apology that time was a hatbox tied with a red ribbon. But don't think there was anything as prosaic as a hat in it. It held a chow puppy, with another red ribbon around its neck." Lillian said she could never stay angry at Walt for long.

When he decided he needed a legal adviser, he hired Gunther Lessing, who had advised Pancho Villa. "If he could help Pancho Villa," Disney asserted, "he's just the man we need."

After reprimanding his employees, Disney would apologize: "I was just excited. When I am excited, I get loud. Getting loud when I am excited is just my nature. I just can't help it."

"This damn town," he once swore at New York, "is enough to give anybody the heebie-jeebies."

He was disappointed in 1960 when the Los Angeles police said they could not provide sufficient protection to allow Nikita Khrushchev to visit Disneyland. Disney had wanted to say to the Soviet premier, "Here's my Disneyland submarine fleet; it's the eighth largest in the world."

He died on December 15, 1966, in a Los Angeles hospital, of acute circulatory collapse.

Elvis!

ROY   BLOUNT   JR.

WHEN I WAS IN THE EIGHTH GRADE, 1954, I GOT WIND OF "ANNIE HAD A BABY" ("CAIN' wuck no mo' ") and heard reports of black music shows in Atlanta from fellow adolescents more advanced than I who would wink at each other and repeat the catch phrase "hunchin' and a-jackin'." I don't know what song that was from, but it made more of an impression on me than Elvis Presley did. Of course, when Elvis came, he was on *The Ed Sullivan Show.* You didn't have to be cool to know about Elvis. "We've lost the most popular man that ever walked on this planet since Christ was here himself," said Carl Perkins when Elvis died.

The summer after eighth grade, I went to a party at the house of my Babe Ruth League coach, a wizened and taciturn mill worker whom you would not expect to figure in a pelvic revolution. But the coach's boys had organized the party, and one of Elvis's first singles was playing. My coach's equally wizened but more voluble elder son came up and asked me earnestly, "Do you think Elvis has got it?"

"Yes," I said. Though I was no authority. This was my first rock-criticism conversation—one of the few, in fact, that I have had over the years—and my soundest one. Elvis had managed to make music that hunched and jacked and yet could be heard in one's baseball coach's home. It didn't grab and unsettle me like "Annie Had a Baby," or like Ray Charles or Chuck Berry or Jerry Lee Lewis, and it still doesn't. But it had it. And it made it mellifluous.

There is a wonderful Alice Walker short story, "Nineteen Fifty-Five," about a black blues singer like Big Mama Thornton, who did the first version of "Hound Dog," and a white muddled megarocker like the late Elvis. The Elvis character is guiltily beholden to her, and she says things like, "It don't matter, Son." At the end of the story it comes over the TV that the Elvis character is dead. The Big Mama character doesn't want to watch his fans grieve. "They was crying and crying and didn't know what they was crying for. One day this is going to be a pitiful country, I thought."

And here's what Chuck Berry said when asked after Elvis's death what Elvis would be remembered for: "Oh boop, boop, boop; shake your leg; fabulous teen music; the Fifties; his movies."

But Elvis didn't just siphon off some negritude and slick it up. ("Hound Dog" was written by Leiber and Stoller, who added to the black culture they appropriated and didn't try to appropriate any more than they could carry.) His h-and-j was fired by poor-white disrepressed defiance, and to it he added mooniness, juvenility, niceness, hope, fuzz, hype, and androgyny. Rock 'n' roll.

Whereas Janis Joplin began by trying to sing the blues as unseasoned homely white-girl hysteria, Elvis's sudden rockabilly was fresh and centripetal. He took the guilt out of the blues, says Greil Marcus. That is like taking the grit out of the beach or the smell out of the collards, but Elvis did it. It got people—white people I guess I mostly mean, but aren't white people Americans too?—wiggling. The next thing you knew, there was a Youth Culture, which I think we may assume Elvis did not dream of in 1954. I know I didn't.

The Youth Culture took wiggling for granted, and Mick Jagger's pelvis was to Elvis's as a Cuisinart is to a mortar and pestle. But Elvis was an old redneck boy who loved gospel and drove a truck. He might just about as well have grown up to be Jerry Falwell. For a boy with Elvis's background to move the way he did suddenly proved something, as in 1929 when the *rich* started bailing out. The jump from not shaking that thing at all to shaking it was bigger than the segue from shaking it to undulation. It was Elvis, you could say with some justice, who goosed mainstream America into that jump.

Elvis didn't fit into the Youth Culture. He ballooned—began to wear a girdle, as decent girls did before he came along. He became a martyr: to the new level of profligate absurd glamour-power he established, and to his own abiding adolescence. After his death, when Big Mama Thornton was asked how she felt about having made a hundred dollars or so from "Hound Dog" compared with Elvis's millions, she said, "I'm still here to *spend* my hundred dollars."

Though ever a (naughty) mama's boy, Elvis sprang beyond Big Mama; special effects outjump flesh and blood every time. Even before the Pill, Elvis seemed to obviate the primacy of Jack-hunch-Annie-and-knock-her-up. Boy fans tended to approach him more reservedly than did the girls, to whom he seemed to be saying—*trustworthily*—that he could do you without getting you in trouble, and vice versa.

"Hound Dog" made grim traditional sense as a woman's song about a trifling man. Elvis's version was vaguely raunchy, mostly adorable. How could there be any downside to a man who looked both wholesome and sultry, a man whose sensual lips sang, "Don't be cruel, to a heart that's true"? "Sex is dynamite," generations of American mothers had been telling their daughters, and by *dynamite* they didn't mean fabulous. They meant ruination. Elvis probably would have said, "Yes,'m, I know," to every one of those mothers, and yet he lit that dynamite and went pop. And grinned. Elvis's grin, like FDR's, was historic. It got young people on the road to concluding that they had nothing to feel guilty about but guilt itself, that parents were wrong about sex and probably everything else, that the system (parents), not the heart, was where all the shadows lay.

Over the long haul Elvis was more of a crooner than a rocker. But he was a frontiersman. Ray and Chuck and Jerry Lee remained cut-the-cards, you-*know*-what-I'm-carrying guys, who are never likely to be accused, as Elvis was in a cankered biography by Albert Goldman, of preferring that girls leave their panties on. The other night I watched a tape of Elvis's 1968 comeback concert. He looked like Martin Sheen, Jack Palance, Katy Jurado, Sal Mineo, Ann-Margret (the mouth), and a touch of Grady Sutton. He was pretty, tough, vaunting, shy, dumb, wily, saturnine, and mercurial. Elvis wasn't just heteroerotic: he was close to Norman O. Brown's polymorphous perverse.

Rock 'n' roll evolved in that direction. (I wonder what Elvis made of David Bowie.) And so did American culture until about the time Elvis died. Now there's a different trend. Ronald Reagan, George Shultz, Jesse Helms, George Will, and Frank Sinatra show few traces of the rock revolution. The culture seems to be doubling back, looking for something it dropped. Do you know what my adolescent kids are listening to? Besides Dire Straits's "Industrial Disease"? They are listening to a group called Stray Cats, who play rockabilly.

I have Elvis's last afternoon paper. Or what would have been, if he had lived into the evening of August 16, 1977. I was in Nashville that day. When somebody brought the news into the greasy spoon where I was sitting, the jukebox—I swear—had just finished playing Elvis's latest hit, "Way Down."

ELVIS THE PELVIS, ELVIS LIVES, ELVIS'S EVILS, ELVIS IS VILE, ELVIS'S VEILS (oddly, Elvis disliked Levi's—too close to poverty britches I guess) all seemed to be in the nature of things, but ELVIS DEAD was a jolt. I flew to Memphis. "What's that?" I asked Fred Stoll, Elvis's gatekeeper, at Graceland late that night. "That's Elvis's last *Press-Scimitar*," said Stoll. So I stole it. It still had the rubber band on, until I opened it while writing this piece and the dried-out rubber snapped.

Elvis in his coffin was fat, glowering, and surrounded by similar-looking but vertical heavies who pushed us viewers along. Reportedly Elvis had died "straining at the stool" while reading a book about the discovery of Christ's remains. ELVIS DEAD, all right. But not at peace. He looked like he wanted to make another big leap, but couldn't. He didn't look cool.

Neither did the thousands of people who gathered at the gates of Graceland. People fainted left and right, from the heat, the crowding, and the historical moment. And because if you fainted, you got carried onto the grounds.

"He was really a good man," said a stringy woman wearing off-brand jeans and a halter top revealing a midriff with two moles and a fresh abrasion. "To achieve superstardom at that age and keep his basic Christian qualities. I don't see how he did it. I don't really know."

"He coulda lived another no telling how long," said a fat woman in lemon-lime shorts. "But he just kinda gave himself to the people."

A mother in her late thirties kept edging herself and her little girl, about four, toward the Graceland gate. The girl was crying. An altercation developed in front of them. I don't think anyone could tell what the roots of the disturbance were, but the police moved in and collared a black man. He yelled. He'd been waiting so long. One cop cuffed the man's hands behind his back and thrust a nightstick between the man's legs. Another cop grabbed the other end of the stick and they carried the man away like that, riding him out of Elvis Nation on a rail. The man made a strangled noise. The mother took the occasion to push her daughter, who was screaming now, beyond the barricades and through the gate and into the line, past banks of floral displays (and Styrofoam crosses and artificial roses and gilded plastic cardinals or blue jays), to see the dead man.

You might like Ray and Chuck and Jerry Lee better, and also Little Richard, but I doubt you would fly to see them, God forbid, in their coffins. Whatever else you think about Elvis, he was epochal.

―――――――

ELVIS AARON PRESLEY *had a twin brother, Jesse Garon, who was stillborn on January 8, 1935, in East Tupelo, Mississippi. When Elvis was three, his father, Vernon, served nine months in Parchman Penitentiary for forgery. In 1948 the town authorities alleged that Vernon had been selling moonshine; they gave him two weeks to leave town. The family moved to Memphis.*

On his eleventh birthday Elvis got his first guitar—a $12.75 model his mother bought at the Tupelo Hardware Store. He caused a scene because he had wanted his mother to buy him a shotgun instead.

In the summer of 1953 Elvis, who was driving a truck for an electrical firm, stopped at the Memphis Recording Service, hoping that Sun Records owner Sam Phillips would discover him. Although Phillips was not in, his secretary recorded Elvis; the tapes did not impress him.

By 1954 Elvis had cut his first record for Sun; still, the next year he failed in his audition for The Arthur Godfrey Show.

Phillips sold Elvis to RCA for forty thousand dollars; at his first recording session for his new company he recorded "Heartbreak Hotel," which became number one on Billboard magazine's charts.

Ed Sullivan once said, "I wouldn't have Presley on my show at any time." Eventually Elvis did appear on the show—filmed from the waist up.

Elvis's gyrations upset many people. A clergyman once called him "the twirling dervish of sex." Hedda Hopper condemned Presley as a menace to society and a threat to innocent children. (She later recanted and did the Twist with him at a Hollywood party.)

Senator Estes Kefauver placed a tribute to Presley in the Congressional Record.

In 1956 Elvis dated Natalie Wood, who spent a week with the Presleys in Memphis.

While serving in the Army in Germany, Elvis met his future wife, Priscilla Beaulieu, at a party. She was fourteen. He brought her to Memphis and enrolled her in a Catholic school. He showed his stepmother her picture, saying, "I've been to bed with no less than one thousand women in my life. This is the one, right here." After five years of marriage, Priscilla left Elvis for her karate instructor, Mike Stone.

A Christian churchgoer most of his life, Elvis, for a time, was a follower of Yogi Paramahansa Yogananda.

In 1971 the U.S. Jaycees gave Elvis an award for being one of the "Ten Outstanding Young Men in America." Ron Ziegler was another recipient that year.

He made thirty-one movies and two documentaries. He refused to see his movie Jailhouse Rock after its female lead, Judy Tyler (once Princess Summerfall Winterspring on TV's Howdy Doody Time) was killed in a car accident.

His favorite movie was Lawrence of Arabia. Two of his favorite actors were Tony Curtis and Marlon Brando; he once called James Dean a "genius." He developed a strong aversion to Robert Goulet and once fired a gun at a television screen during a Goulet performance.

He collected badges. Once, carrying a white walking stick and wearing a purple velvet suit and a cape, he came to Washington bent on obtaining a Federal Narcotics Bureau badge. A deputy bureau chief was cordial to Elvis—hoping that he would endorse the agency's campaign against drug abuse—but he firmly refused to give Elvis a badge. A short while afterward the chief received a call instructing him to bring a badge to the Oval Office. Elvis was there waiting for it.

He once flew his entourage a thousand miles for peanutbutter-and-jelly sandwiches.

Toward the end of his life he weighed as much as 230 pounds. At a 1976 New Year's Eve show in Pontiac, Michigan, his trousers split up the middle. Another night, in Memphis, Elvis lost the seat of his pants bending over to kiss one of the girls in front of the stage.

In his last year he dated nineteen-year-old Ginger Alden, Miss Memphis Traffic Safety of 1976. He gave her a Cadillac and an eighty-five-thousand-dollar ring.

He died on August 16, 1977, while sitting on the toilet reading The Scientific Search for the Face of Jesus. *A tissue analysis of his body revealed the presence of depressant drugs Butabarbitol, codeine, morphine, Nembutal, pentobarbital, phenobarbital, Placidyl, Quāālude, Valium, and Valmid. He was buried wearing a diamond ring bearing the inscription* TCB—*short for his motto,* Taking Care of Business. *In his lifetime he had grossed more than a billion dollars.*

After his death women claimed to have made love to his ghost. In 1978 impersonator Dennis Wise underwent facial surgery to improve his resemblance to Elvis.

Jackie, the Prisoner of Celebrity

NORMAN MAILER

JEHOVAH WOULD PERMIT NO GRAVEN IMAGES OF HIMSELF, AND SAVAGES FEEL A PART OF their soul is stolen when a photograph is taken. What do they do when subjected to flashbulbs? The last time I saw Jackie Kennedy Onassis was at a benefit and the cameras were going wild. At one point it was my turn to stand next to the lady, and while I have seen a few such lights, I can testify that my eyes never knew this kind of bombardment before. There is celebrity, and then there is the white heat of celebrity when paparazzi are out, but for sheer impact, for the literal blast of the media at its highest voltage, get your picture taken next to Jackie. It is equal to the blaze of five machine guns turned on you at once.

I remember she stood it with the sad, soldierly dignity of a much-wounded veteran. In the middle of the racket, for the electronic voice of flashes and strobes seems to mount exponentially, I whispered to her—as who does not, since part of the penalty of being Jackie Kennedy Onassis is that everybody wants to offer some bright exchange in her presence?—"Yes," I said to her, "the reason we're all such idiots is these damn lights."

I think it is true of Jackie Kennedy Onassis in social situations—which is the only way I know her—that but a fifth of what you say ever seems to reach her, so deep is her detachment, her star. Yet, of that fifth it could be said that it goes all the way in, and she ponders the portion she accepts. So she nodded and gave her far-off smile. "Yes," she answered, "do you think that is the reason?"

For celebrities are idiots more often than you would expect. Few of one's own remarks should still offer pleasure, but I do like "Fame? Fame is a microphone in your mouth." To celebrities, the wages of success are those flashbulbs in the eye. If one were hit with no more than ten good jabs every day, the brain would soon reflect its damage; the flashbulbs are worse than jabs and sear one's delicacy. They even jar the last remains of your sensibility. So celebrities are surprisingly flat, bland, even disappointing when you talk to them. Their manner has something in common with the dull stuffed-glove feel in the handshake of a professional boxer. His hands are his instrument, so a fighter will guard his hands. Personality is the falling currency of overexposed celebrities, so over the years they know they must offer less and less to strangers. Those flashbulbs cauterize our souls.

Problems of this nature take on, however, another order of magnitude with Jackie Kennedy Onassis. For she is not merely a celebrity, but a legend; not a legend, but a myth—no, more than a myth: she is now a historic archetype, virtually a demiurge. It hardly matters whether in private life she is a good mother or a materialistic woman, generous or greedy, possessed of fine taste or merely well guided by others; indeed, it does not even matter whether she has found more or less happiness, integrity, fulfillment, and all those other words. We will never truly know, and she may not, either.

There are a few people in the world whom the media have projected right out of themselves. They will never again find their identity any more than a space probe sent out to explore beyond the solar system will come back to earth. Of this number, Jackie Kennedy may be the first, since history cast her as the leading lady in what must have been the greatest American drama of them all (at least, if drama has the power to make us all react as one). While we are, on balance, a nation more fortunate than most, and not all that many of us have known tragedy in our personal lives, we are close to tragedy through her. In our history she is the only living symbol of Greek drama. Did the shades of Aeschylus and Sophocles agree for once and say, "Let her now be remarried to a Greek who will be a little like one of our mighty bloodstained kings"?

If so, they did it for the Greeks, not for us. In our national depths (if we still have any) a part of us will never forgive Jackie Kennedy for marrying Onassis. She had no right to do that, Americans will always feel. She was ours. She did not belong to herself. She was twice ours, once as the most beautiful and romantic legend we had ever had in a First Lady; afterward she was ours as the first monumental American widow. We are a country of weeds and frontiers and innovations and hideous designs for mass living, gargantuan corporate structures with all the architectural éclat of a cardboard carton and cancer gulch through all the hours of a universe of day and night TV. We are an overloaded garbage can the size of a universe; we teem, we swarm, we lose ourselves in details and gobble our media like a freak takes pills. But in retrospect we can say that once we had a romantic heroine and she was married to one of the more handsome men in America, and they were President and First Lady, and so our dream life thrived. We dwelt in an iridescent landscape of secret hopes and daring desires; there was a lift of promise in one's work and the prospect of pleasures after the chores. I exaggerate, but then, our dream life lives in the special logic of exaggeration, and so there was something more exciting about America when we had such a heroine, such a beautiful and mysterious lady in such a place. The schizophrenic halves of our nation were bound together. The Hollywood dream life and the superhighways of technology came closer for a little while.

Then the assassinations fell upon us, and the strangest of our American heroines became a Greek heroine. Our nation knew tragedy in the circle of each family as we had not known it since the death of Abraham Lincoln. And we mourned as one nation. We mourned for her as our tragic widow.

Yes, she has lost her identity forever. The shy, still strange, doubtless witty, probably decent, much-harried lady of that second self who would only like to do with her life what each of us would like to do with ours—that is, get a little better, a little wiser, a little classier, a little sweeter, and a little more entitled to love—is lost in isolation. Through no fault of hers, she can never rejoin our high-tech humanly reductive race. She may be lonely within, or mature and become splendid, but we will never know, and she will never reach us. All that is left is to photograph the dignity of her shell. We have dispatched her to the gods, and from those divine fields no legend ever returns.

———————

JACQUELINE BOUVIER KENNEDY ONASSIS *was born on July 28, 1929, in Southampton, Long Island. She was named after her stockbroker father, who derived his nickname, Black Jack, from his swarthy tan.*

When Jackie was four her mother received a phone call from a New York police precinct. "We have a little girl here," said the officer on the line. One of the precinct's men had been patrolling Central Park when Jackie, walking alone, stepped up to him and firmly stated, "My nurse is lost."

She attended Miss Chapin's school, where she was rebellious but bright. She credits her headmistress with being the "first great moral influence" in her life.

When she made her social debut, in 1947, columnist Cholly Knickerbocker named her "Queen Deb of the Year."

That fall she entered Vassar, where she enjoyed Shakespeare and history of religion. She graduated from George Washington University.

Hired as the "Inquiring Camera Girl" on the Washington Times-Herald *in 1952, she interviewed both John F. Kennedy and Richard Nixon. In 1953 she started dating Kennedy. They delayed the announcement of their engagement because the* Saturday Evening Post *was doing a story on Kennedy called "The Senate's Gay Young Bachelor."*

She had difficult pregnancies. She miscarried in 1955; in 1956 a cesarean produced a stillborn child. Caroline, John Jr., and Patrick were also delivered via cesareans; Patrick died thirty-nine hours after birth. Within the Kennedy clan, Jackie was somewhat of a failure at childbirth, and it is said that she felt she had let them down.

Her popularity with the American public began in France. JFK once introduced himself to an audience as "the man who accompanied Jacqueline Kennedy to Paris."

Determined to turn the White House into "the prettiest house in America," she spent $2 million on interior decorating.

"Now I think that I should have known that he was magic all along," she said after Kennedy's assassination. "I did know it—but I should have guessed that it would be too much to ask to grow old with him and see our children grow up. . . . So now he is a legend when he would have preferred to be a man."

After her husband's funeral she stayed on in the White House longer than she should have, because, she said later, she had "no place to go."

When she married Aristotle Onassis, she was thirty-nine and he was sixty-two. The American public did not approve. Even at New York's fashionable Elaine's, one man called to her departing back, "Bye-bye, you silly bitch."

Shortly after they married, Ari gave Jackie $2 million and advised her to invest it in tax-free bonds. Instead she lost most of it playing the stock market. Her husband refused to replace the capital.

Onassis had drooping eyelids, which he taped to his eyebrows to keep his eyes open. The barstools on his yacht were covered with the skins of sperm whales' testicles. The Onassis marriage deteriorated quickly. The couple spent most of the year apart.

Ari left most of his estate to his daughter, Christina; Jackie fought to get more money.

Six months after Onassis's death, she was hired by The Viking Press as a consulting editor, at two hundred dollars a week. She was popular in the office. But when Viking published a book she thought was exploitative of her first husband's assassination, she resigned.

She now works at Doubleday. Her associates say she is personable and pleasant to work with.

She bakes chocolate cakes for special friends.

Her apartment at 1040 Fifth Avenue is decorated in sunny yellows, greens, and golds. She likes to read. She sketches on an easel in front of a living room window overlooking Central Park. She studies pedestrians through a telescope.

She expects her friends to keep quiet about her, especially to the press. Ron Galella, the paparazzo, has taken over four thousand pictures of her. He once made fifteen thousand dollars in one year selling them to national publications. By court order, he must now keep twenty-five feet away from her.

BUILDERS

Architects
of the Enduring

THE BUILDERS DESIGNED NOT JUST BUILDINGS BUT COMPANIES, INSTITUTIONS, policies, and processes. Their materials varied: ideas arranged in exquisite layers, money invested in shrewd patterns, ideals mortared in ways that enabled their structures to withstand obsolescence.

William Paley pieced together a network. He combined a new technology with an overall sense of audience. What he built—CBS— became the model for television, that most powerful expression of mass.

Robert Oppenheimer constructed a weapon. He combined a new technology with a masterful sense of administration. What he built at Los Alamos, working with a newly assembled team of physicists and engineers, shattered a war and altered the course of our future. The accomplishment was profound; so, too, was the moral upheaval that followed.

Thomas Watson Sr. and John L. Lewis built, respectively, a philosophy of management and a philosophy of labor. Watson laid a foundation for IBM that has proved to be as solid as rock: hard work pays off, company loyalty makes the difference. Even today, the IBM management style continues to dominate our fastest-growing, most highly competitive industry. The foundation Lewis laid was no less strong: worker solidarity, the power of organized laborers. With his battalions of miners lined up behind him, Lewis faced down a President. He put into place the cornerstone of establishment unionism.

The Builders' designs were expressions of themselves. Henry Luce's Time Inc. became a towering communications company because it was predicated on its founder's political, social, and moral convictions. Dean Acheson's foreign policy lasted because the statesman who crafted it was so fervently committed to its principle of keeping the Russians from expanding their influence. Both Acheson and Luce held fast to their opinions; nothing could shake their resolve. Their creations have proved immutable.

Intent on changing our destiny, the Builders cast their influence far and wide. Dorothy Day built a tradition of nonviolence indigenous to America. She was a tireless Catholic who worked for peace and pacifism.

The Rockefeller influence on our destiny was more concrete: the heirs to that great fortune built institutions of every kind—political, cultural, and scientific. The buildings they erected are no less imposing—from the glass tower of the United Nations to the stolid cities within a city, Rockefeller and Lincoln centers.

Philip Johnson, too, put up buildings. He shaped the course of American architecture, first by importing the Bauhaus, then by seizing changes in the winds and giving us a skyline of diverse ideas. To corporate America, he emerged the architect of choice.

The Builders built structures that lasted. Such was their mastery.

—L. E.

Thomas Watson's Principles of Modern Management

PETER F. DRUCKER

EVERYBODY KNOWS THAT THOMAS WATSON SR. (1874–1956) BUILT IBM INTO A BIG COM-
puter company and was a business leader. But "everybody" is wrong. Thomas
Watson Sr. did not build the IBM we now know; his son, Tom Watson Jr., did
this after he moved into the company's top management in 1946, only thirty-
two years old (though the father stayed on until 1956 as a very active chairman).
The father's IBM was never more than medium-size; as late as 1938 it had only
$35 million in sales. Of course, it did not make or sell computers; its mainstays
were punch card machines and time clocks.

Instead of being a business leader, Thomas Watson Sr. did not attain personal success and recognition until he was well past sixty. Twice in the Thirties
he personally was on the verge of bankruptcy. What saved him and spurred
IBM sales during the Depression were two New Deal laws: the Social Security
Act in 1935 and the Wage-Hours Act of 1937–38. They mandated records of
wages paid, hours worked, and overtime earned by employees, in a form in
which the employer could not tamper with the records. Overnight they created
markets for the tabulating machines and time clocks that Thomas Watson Sr.
had been trying for long years to sell with only moderate success.

In 1939, when I was working in New York as correspondent for a group of
British papers, I wanted to write a story on Watson and IBM. I had become interested in the company because of the big pavilion it had put up at the New

135

York World's Fair and thought a story on so small a frog behaving like a big shot might be amusing. "Forget it," my editor wrote back. "We are not interested in a story on an unsuccessful company which as far as anyone can tell is never going to amount to much." And Watson was then already sixty-five years old.

But Thomas Watson Sr. was something far more important than a successful businessman who built a big company. He was the seer and, very largely, the maker of what we now call postindustrial society and one of the great social innovators in American history. Fifty years ago he had the vision of "data processing" and of "information." In the midst of the Depression and half broke himself, he financed the research that produced both the theoretical foundations for the computer and the first highly advanced model of it.

Fifty years ago or more he also invented and put into practice what in this country is now known, studied, and imitated as Japanese management— needless to say, he did so without the slightest knowledge of Japan and without owing anything to the then-nonexistent Japanese practices.

In fact, Watson's problem was that he was far ahead of his time, in his vision as well as in his practices.

I first met Watson in the early Thirties. He had been elected president of the American section of the International Chamber of Commerce—a job nobody else had wanted—and I, then a very young reporter, was sent to interview him. But the interview made absolutely no sense to my editor and never appeared. Of course, Watson delivered himself of the platitudes expected from the Chamber of Commerce, about free trade, about international cooperation, and about "the role of the businessman as an ambassador of peace." But then he started to talk of what clearly was his real interest—things he called data and information. But what he meant by those terms—it was not at all what anyone else at the time meant by them—he could not explain. Indeed, newspapers usually put him down as a crank.

I doubt that Watson himself *understood*. He had vision—he *saw*. But unlike most seers, Watson *acted* on his vision.

Some kind of computer would have come without him. There were a good many people at the time working at fast calculating machines, especially under the impetus of World War II, with its need for navigational equipment for fast-moving airplanes, for firing mechanisms for long-range cannon shooting at invisible targets way beyond the horizon, for aerial bombs, and for antiaircraft guns. But without Watson it could have been a very different computer, a "calculating machine" rather than an "information processor." Without Watson and his vision the computer would have emerged as a "tool" rather than as a "technology."

Watson did not invent a single piece of hardware. He had no technical education, indeed little formal education altogether, having gone to work as a salesman of sewing machines, pianos, and organs in his native upstate New York when barely eighteen. He also had no technical talent, nor much grasp of mathematics or theory altogether. He was definitely not an inventor in the mold of Edison or his contemporary Charles Kettering. The computers that he sponsored, financed, and pushed for—one finished in 1943, another four years later, in 1947—contributed little by way of hardware and engineering solutions even to IBM's own early commercial computer in the Fifties.

But Watson saw and understood the computer fifteen years before the term was ever coined. He knew right away that it had to be radically different from a high-speed calculator. And he did not rest until his engineers had built the first operational true "computer." Watson specified very early—in the late Thirties at the latest—what computer people now call the architecture of a computer: capacity to store data; a memory, and random access to it; ability to receive instructions and to change them, to be programmed, and to express logic in a computer language. Watson's 1947 SSEC (Selective Sequence Electronic Calculator) was much more powerful and far more flexible than any machine then in existence or being planned. Its 12,500 vacuum tubes and 21,400 relays could, for instance, solve partial differential equations. It was, above all, the first—and for several years the only—machine to combine electronic computation with stored programs, with its own computer language, and with the capacity to handle its instructions as data—that is, to change, to correct, and to update them on the basis of new information. These are, however, precisely the features that distinguish a computer from a calculator.

When IBM embarked on designing a computer to be sold in large quantities, it applied hardware largely developed by others—mainly university labs at MIT, Princeton, Rochester, and Pennsylvania. But it was all designed to Watson's original specifications. This explains why the 650, IBM's first successful commercial machine, immediately became the industry leader and the industry standard when it was introduced in 1953; why it sold eighteen hundred units during its first five years on the market—twice as many as the best market research had predicted total computer sales worldwide to come to in the entire twentieth century; and why it gave IBM the world leadership in computers the company still holds.

The early *technical* history of the computer is quite murky. And what part Watson and IBM—or anyone else—played in it is remarkably controversial. But there is no doubt at all that Watson played a key role in the *conceptual* history of the computer. There are many others who were important, if not central, in the engineering of the computer. But Watson created the computer age.

The story begins in 1933 when IBM, on Watson's orders, designed a high-speed calculator for Columbia University's scientists and built it out of standard tabulating-machine parts. Four years later, in 1937, Howard Aiken, a Harvard mathematician, suggested that IBM try to link up several existing machines—designed originally for bookkeeping purposes—to create an even faster calculator for the time-consuming and tedious computations needed by astronomers. The work, Aiken estimated, would take a few months and would cost around $100,000. Instead, the work took six years and the cost was well over half a million dollars. For instead of the high-speed calculator Aiken had in mind, Watson went ahead and produced a computer.

First Watson specified an all-electronic machine; all earlier designs, including IBM's own machines, were electromechanical, with levers and gears doing the switching. Of course, *electronic* then meant using vacuum tubes—the transistor was well into the future. And the resulting machines were therefore big and clumsy, tended to overheat, and used a great deal of electricity. Still, no one at the time even knew how to use electronic devices as switches—the key, of course, to computer technology. Even the theoretical work needed had yet to be done. For Watson and IBM to decide to desert the well-known and thoroughly familiar electromechanical technology for the totally unexplored electronics was a leap into the dark; but it was the decision that made the computer possible.

Watson's second specification was equally innovative. His project envisaged what no engineer at the time even dreamed of: a computer memory. Howard Aiken in his research proposal had been concerned with rapid calculation; he wanted a "numbers cruncher." His idea was to build something that would be able to do very quickly what traditional adding machines and slide rules did slowly. IBM added to this the capacity to store data. And this meant that IBM's projected machine would be able to process information. It would have a data bank—a term that, of course, did not exist at the time—and would be able to refer back to it. Thus it could memorize and analyze. It could also—and this is crucial—correct and update its own instructions on the basis of new information.

And this then meant—another one of IBM's then quite visionary specifications—that IBM's machine was going to be capable of being programmed, that is, of being used for any information capable of being expressed in a logical notation. All the designs then being worked on were for single-purpose machines. The best known of these, called ENIAC, constructed at the University of Pennsylvania during the World War II years for Army Ordnance and completed in 1946, was, for instance, designed to do high-speed calculations for fast-firing guns. But it could do little more, as it had neither memory nor programming capacity. IBM, too, had specific applications in mind—especially calculations for astronomical tables. But, perhaps because Watson knew firsthand of the data-processing needs of a host of institutions—public libraries, the Census Bureau, banks, insurance companies, and the like—his specifications called for a machine capable of being programmed for all kinds of data. IBM's machine was a multipurpose machine from the start. This, then, also meant that when IBM finally had a computer that could be manufactured and sold—in the early Fifties—it was both willing and able to supply the users whose demand actually created the computer industry but of whom no one had even thought in the early stages of computer design: business people who wanted computers for such mundane, unscientific purposes as payroll and inventory. Watson's insistence on memory and program thus explains in large measure why there is a computer industry.

Because of Watson's specifications of memory and program, the IBM research project of 1937 helped create computer science. The "analytical machine" that Watson tried to develop needed both computer theory and computer language—again, of course, terms that did not exist then. It needed, of course, first-class engineering, as did all the other calculating machines then designed. But it also created—or at least stimulated—the first computer scientists.

This research produced a prototype in late 1943—called the ASCC (Automatic Sequence Controlled Calculator)—and Howard Aiken did do astronomical calculations on it, in early 1944. But it was far too advanced for the manufacturing technology of its time. In fact, only recently have the materials and the technology become available to manufacture the kind of computer for which Watson organized the research in 1937. Watson then donated the prototype, together with money to run and maintain it, to Harvard and immediately commissioned the work on the next design—the work out of which the SSEC evolved several years later. Its first public demonstration, on January 27, 1948, in New York City—at which it calculated all past, present, and future positions of the moon—ushered in the computer age. Even now, thirty-five years later, the computer that popular cartoons show, with its blinking lights and whirling wheels, is the SSEC as it was displayed at this first public demonstration. And looking at Watson's specifications in retrospect, this is precisely what must have been in his mind's eye all along.

As significant as Watson the computer seer is Watson the social innovator. He was even further ahead in his social vision than he was in his vision of data and information and had perhaps even more of an impact—and was equally (or more) misunderstood by his contemporaries.

Watson became a national figure in 1940, when *Fortune* published a violent, mudslinging attack on him. It insinuated that Watson was the American Führer and tried altogether to make him the symbol of everything repulsive in American capitalism. And it also fixed the popular perception of Thomas Watson as a reactionary and as a paternalist, a perception that still lingers on. But today it is clear that Watson's real offense was to be far ahead of his time.

Rereading the story recently, forty-three years later, I saw right away that what had most irked the *Fortune* writer in 1940 was Watson's ban on liquor in IBM's employee clubs and at IBM parties. He was indeed passionately opposed to alcohol—I once heard that his father or one of his uncles had been an alcoholic. But whatever Watson's reasons, it is perhaps not such a bad idea to keep work and liquor apart.

Then, of course, there was Watson's regimentation of his sales force, that is, his demand that IBM's salesmen wear dark suits and white shirts. But what Watson tried to do, as he had explained to me in my interviews with him a year before the *Fortune* story, was to instill self-respect in salesmen and respect for them among the public. When Watson began, the salesman was a "drummer," disreputable and a smelly crook, who spent his evenings in the small town's whorehouse unless he spent it debauching the farmer's innocent daughter in the hayloft. Watson, who had been a "drummer" himself, had deeply suffered from the contempt for his calling and was determined that his associates have self-respect and be respected. "I want my IBM salesmen," he had said in his 1939 talks with me, "to be people to whom their wives and their children can look up. I don't want their mothers to feel that they have to apologize for them or have to dissimulate when they are being asked what their son is doing" (and there was a clear implication, I thought then, that he was speaking of his own mother).

Watson's heinous crime, however, and the one the *Fortune* writer could not forgive him for, was that he believed in a worker who took responsibility for his job, was proud of it and loved it. He believed in a worker who saw his interests as identical to those of the company. He wanted, above all, a worker who used his own mind and his own experience to improve his own job, the product, the process, and the quality. Watson's crime—and it was indeed seen as a crime in the late Thirties, when a vulgar Marxism infested even fairly conservative members of the intelligentsia—was to make workers enjoy their work and thus accept the system rather than feel exploited and become revolutionary proletarians.

The way Watson did this was, first, to give his employees what we now call lifetime employment. As in Japan today, there was no contractual obligation on the part of Watson's IBM not to lay off people. But there was a moral commitment. In the first Depression years, 1931 and 1932, IBM did indeed lay off a few people, but Watson immediately stopped it. His refusal later, in the darkest Depression years of 1933 and 1934, to lay off workers could have bankrupted IBM. And employment security for workers has been IBM practice for fifty years now.

In the mid-Thirties Watson abolished "foremen." They became "managers," whose job it was to assist workers, to make sure that workers had the tools and the information they needed, and to help them when they found themselves in trouble. Responsibility for the job itself was placed firmly on the work group.

The worker, Watson argued, knew far better than anyone else how to improve productivity and quality. And so around 1935 he invented what we now know as quality circles and credit to the Japanese. The industrial engineer was to be a "resource" to the work group and its "consultant," rather than the "expert" who dictated to it. Watson also laid down that the individual worker should have the biggest job possible rather than the smallest one, and as far back as 1920 he initiated what we now call job enrichment. (And after the old man's death his son, in 1958, put into effect his father's old idea and put *all* employees on a monthly salary, abolishing both the hourly wage and the distinction between blue-collar and white-collar employees.)

Finally, every employee at IBM had the right to go directly to the company's chief executive officer, that is, to Watson, to complain, to suggest improvements, and to be heard—and this is still IBM practice.

Much earlier Watson had invented what the Japanese now call continuous learning. He began in the early Twenties with his salespeople, who were called into headquarters again and again for training sessions to enable them to "do better what they are already doing well." Later Watson extended continuous learning to the blue-collar employees in the plant, and in the Forties he hired Dwayne Orton, a college president from San Francisco, to be the company's director of education.

These practices very largely explain IBM's success. They exorcised the great bugaboo of American business, the employees' alleged resistance to change. They enabled the company in the Fifties and Sixties to grow as fast as any business had ever grown before—and perhaps faster—without much internal turbulence, without horrendous labor turnover, and without industrial strife. And because Watson's salesmen had all along been used to learning new things, middle-aged punch card salesmen without experience in computers or in big-company management could overnight become effective executives in a big high-technology company.

But forty years ago Watson's policies and practices were very strange indeed. They either made Watson look like a crank—which is what most people believed—or they made him into the sinister force the *Fortune* writer saw. Today we realize that Watson was only forty or fifty years ahead of his time. Watson was actually one year older than Alfred Sloan. But whereas Sloan in the Twenties created modern management by building General Motors, and with it the modern "big corporation," Watson ten years later and quite independently created the "plant community" that we know to be the successor to Sloan's "big business enterprise" of the Twenties. He created in the Thirties the social organization and the work community of the postindustrial society.

The first ones to see this, by the way, were the Japanese. Again and again I have been laughed at in Japan when I talk about Japan's management embodying Japanese values. "Don't you realize," my Japanese friends say, "that we are simply adapting what IBM has done all along?" And when I ask how come, they always say, "When we started to rebuild Japan in the Fifties, we looked around for the most successful company we could find—it's IBM, isn't it?"

Watson also anticipated the multinational. And this, too, no one in 1940 could understand. Watson very early established foreign branches of IBM, one in France, one in Japan, and so on. IBM actually had little foreign business at the time and Watson knew perfectly well that he could have handled whatever there was through exporting directly. But he also realized that the IBM he envisaged for the future, the IBM of what we now call data processing and information handling, would have to be a multinational company. And so he created, more than fifty years ago, the structure he knew IBM would have to have and would have to know how to manage were it ever to become the company he dreamed of. He also saw that the central problem of the multinational is to combine autonomy of the local affiliate with unity of direction and purpose of the entire company. This is in large measure the reason why Watson deliberately created what to most people seemed such extreme paternalism—today we would call it the IBM culture. Way back in 1939 he tried to explain it to me. "Foreign affiliates," he said, "must be run by natives of their own country and not by expatriates. They must be accepted as members of their own society. And they must be able to attract the best people their own country produces. Yet they have to have the same objectives, the same values, the same vision of the world as the parent company. And this means that their management people and their professional people share a common view of the company, of the products, and of their own direction and purpose." Most other multinationals still struggle with the problem Watson foresaw—and solved—fifty years ago.

Watson was an autocrat, of course. Visionaries usually are. Because visionaries cannot explain to the rest of us what they see, they have to depend on command.

Watson was a generous person but a demanding boss and not one bit permissive. But he demanded the right things: dedication and performance to high standards. He was irascible, vain, opinionated, a publicity hound, and an incorrigible name-dropper. And as he grew older he became increasingly addicted to being grossly flattered. But he was also intensely loyal and quite willing to admit that he had been wrong and to apologize. The people who worked for him feared him—but almost no one left.

Of course, he did not fit into the intellectual climate of the New York of the late Thirties. He was already sixty-five at that time and his roots were in the small rural towns of the 1880s, with their church socials and their service-club luncheons, with communal singing and pledges of allegiance to the flag—all the things that the "smart set" of the time had learned to sneer at as the marks of the "booboisie." And what was worse and made Watson a menace was that his employees shared Watson's values, rather than those of the intellectuals, and loved to work for him.

Watson was an extraordinarily complex man who fit into no category. He was among the first American businessmen to use modern design and modern graphics for the company logo and company stationery, products, and offices. But he did so mainly because it was the cheapest way to make his company stand out—and he had no advertising money. To get attention for IBM he used the slogan "Think," which he had invented at NCR. His salesmen used THINK notebooks by the thousands—again, it was the only advertising he could afford. And while he himself didn't have much of a sense of humor, he made up a good many of the "Think" jokes and saw to it that they got wide circulation—again, to get attention for his company. Finally he hit upon the brilliant idea of building a huge pavilion at the 1939 New York World's Fair as the one way to make millions of visitors from all over the world aware of his then still small and practically unknown company and, as he told me at the time, "at the lowest cost per thousand viewers anyone ever had to pay."

Watson's popular image is that of the hidebound conservative—and he lent credence to this view by wearing the stiff Herbert Hoover collar long after it had gone out of fashion. But, almost alone among the businessmen of his time, he was an ardent New Dealer and a staunch supporter of Franklin D. Roosevelt. Indeed, FDR offered him major posts in his administration: first Secretary of Commerce, and then ambassador to Great Britain (when Watson said no, the job went to Joseph Kennedy instead). And at the very end of his life Watson urged President Eisenhower to return to New Deal principles and was upset over Ike's insistence on reducing the government's role in economy and society.

Watson had a most unusual personal history, perhaps the most unusual one in the annals of American business. He started out dirt poor as a teenage drummer—not much more than a peddler. He rose to become the star salesman for the then-new National Cash Register Company of Dayton, Ohio—which was the first business-machine company in history. In about fifteen years he had become the company's sales manager. But then the company was indicted for antitrust violations, with which, we now know, Watson had little or nothing to do.

The trial was a sensation, for National Cash had been *the* growth company of the early 1900s. Watson drew a stiff fine and a one-year jail sentence. This conviction was set aside two years later, in 1915, by the Court of Appeals, and the government then dropped the case. But Watson had lost his job; both his career and his reputation were in tatters. It was an experience that marked him for life, an experience that he never forgot.

Already forty, he then had to begin all over again as general manager of a small and until then quite unsuccessful company that owned the punch card patents. It was not until he was past sixty, in the mid-Thirties, that he succeeded in establishing this company, by then renamed IBM, on a firm footing.

Watson—and this, I think, makes the man singularly interesting—was a uniquely American type and one the Establishment has never understood throughout our history. He was possessed of a towering intellect but was totally nonintellectual. He belongs to the same type as Abraham Lincoln, who similarly offended the establishment of his day: the cosmopolitan, polished, learned Bostonians who considered themselves so superior to the yokel President in whose Cabinet they were forced to serve. He was also similar in many ways to America's first great novelist, James Fenimore Cooper, who was also sneered at, despised, and pilloried by the intellectuals and the establishment of his time, such as the New England Transcendentalists. They could not make sense of the powerful, tragic, and prophetic vision in which Cooper foretold the end of the American Dream in such books as *The Pioneers* and *The Prairie*.

This American type is totally native and owes nothing to Europe—which is one reason why the intellectuals of his time do not know what to do with him. Typically the men of this type have a gift for words—and Watson fully shared it. But they are not men of ideas. They are men of vision. What makes them important is that, like Watson, they act on their vision.

That he did so made Watson one of the Americans of his generation who did make a difference.

THOMAS WATSON *was born on February 17, 1874, in Campbell, New York.*

His father, a lumber dealer, wanted him to study law at Cornell but Thomas wanted a job, so they compromised and he went to the Elmira School of Commerce.

After graduation he worked for two years selling pianos, sewing machines, and organs.

After ten days as a salesman for the National Cash Register Company, he hadn't sold one machine. He got a pep talk and went forth "fortified . . . with tried and true homilies." He has been called the world's greatest salesman, but he did not have a flashing smile and a pumping handshake: customers succumbed instead to his bashful reserve.

He became the right-hand man to National Cash Register's chief, John Henry Patterson—who has been described as an amalgam of St. Paul, Poor Richard, and Adolf Hitler. From Patterson, Watson inherited his penchant for starched white shirts and employee regimentation.

At National Cash Register he coined his motto "Think." The slogan later hung in every IBM office alongside Watson's picture. (Other IBM mottoes: Be better than average, Serve and sell, Ever onward.)

In 1914 he joined the Computing-Tabulating-Recording Company, which ten years later, under Watson, changed its name to International Business Machines Corporation.

In 1937 he took a five-month tour of Europe, during which he visited Hitler, Mussolini, and King Leopold of Belgium. His slogan was, World peace through world trade.

Hitler awarded Watson the Order of Merit of the German Eagle for "foreign nationals who have made themselves deserving of the German Reich." Three years later Watson returned the award, because, he said, "the present policies of [the German] government are contrary to the causes for which I have been working."

In 1940 he made $546,294 at IBM, a salary surpassed that year only by that of movie mogul Louis B. Mayer.

He stood six feet tall and dressed conservatively. He shaved twice a day and bathed and changed his shirt at least that often.

He never learned to swim.

His main interest outside of business was art. At age twenty-four he bought his first painting, a Maine farm scene. In 1941 Roosevelt appointed him director of National Art Week. One of Watson's favorite painters was Grandma Moses.

He liked opera, sailing, and horseback riding. "Sports," he said, "are also a great school for thinking."

He had a house in Maine, an estate in Connecticut, and an apartment in Manhattan.

Watson married Jeannette Kittredge when he was thirty-eight and she was thirty. Their marriage lasted forty-four years, until his death. They had four children, Thomas Jr., Jane, Helen, and Arthur.

By the age of five, Thomas Jr. had been to a sales conference; at twelve, he gave a motivational speech on salesmanship. All Watson's sons and sons-in-law joined IBM.

Watson supported the development of eye banks, research on arthritis, the Salvation Army, the United Negro College Fund, the Boy Scouts, and the Girl Scouts. He was a trustee of Columbia University for twenty-three years and helped arrange for Dwight D. Eisenhower to become Columbia's president.

One of IBM's fight songs:

> *Our voices swell in admiration;*
> *Of T. J. Watson proudly sing;*
> *He'll ever be our inspiration;*
> *To him our voices loudly ring.*

He never took a vacation. He worked sixteen hours a day. Although he officially handed over his duties to his sons a month before his death, he never gave up the title of chairman of the board.

On June 19, 1956, at age eighty-two, he died of a heart attack.

Acheson at the Creation

RONALD STEEL

WHEN HE WROTE ABOUT IT ALL YEARS LATER, AFTER THE DRAMA AND THE GLORY HAD passed into memory, he called his book *Present at the Creation*. The title had a touch of arrogance, as befit the man, but also a sardonic quality that was no less characteristic. And it was true that no one had a better right than he to make such a claim. Dean Acheson, as a high State Department official almost continuously from 1941 to 1953 and Secretary of State for the last four of those years, was not only present at the creation of the Cold War world, he orchestrated much of it.

Others, to be sure, left their imprint on American foreign policy during this period: John Foster Dulles, Lyndon Johnson, Richard Nixon, and Henry Kissinger, among the most important. But each followed in the footsteps of his predecessor, innovating, for the most part, within a relatively narrow range of choices. The prints in the forest floor were those made by Dean Acheson. It was he, in the critical years immediately after the Second World War, when America and Russia ceased being allies and became enemies, who formulated the policies and built the institutions that we live by to this day.

Acheson, born in 1893, was of that generation of American leaders scarred by the fascist aggressions of the 1930s and the bitter lesson of the Munich accords. When confronted with Soviet expansionism in Eastern Europe after the war, Acheson saw a repetition of Hitler's ambitions. Believing that the Kremlin

146

was intent on world domination, and rejecting the possibility that it might be driven by fears of insecurity, he sought to galvanize the United States into meeting what he believed to be a global challenge. He did this at a time when the Cold War, as we know it today, was only just taking form, when there were sharp differences of opinion among Americans as to the nature of the Kremlin's ambitions and the extent to which the United States ought to involve itself in the world's disorder.

Acheson had no doubts. He believed that the United States must use its newly acquired power to shape the world according to its vision and its interests. The great imperial nations of Europe had been decimated by the war. The United States, in Acheson's view, had inherited the role once played by Great Britain. It must embrace its power, turn its back irrevocably on the old temptations of isolationism, and enthusiastically assume the mantle of world leadership.

Not everyone shared Acheson's assessment. Walter Lippmann, for example, argued that the Truman administration had exaggerated the Soviet threat; had overemphasized the importance of ideology to the Kremlin; and, by organizing an anti-Soviet coalition in Western Europe, had "furnished the Soviet Union with reasons, with pretexts, for an iron rule behind the iron curtain, and with ground for believing what Russians are conditioned to believe: that a coalition is being organized to destroy them."

Yet it was Acheson who won the day. His was the assessment of Soviet intentions that prevailed, his the policies that were pursued, his the legacy that continues to govern the world we live in. As the architect of the Cold War world, he was either the prime mover or the chief salesman for:

- The Truman Doctrine, which provided the blueprint for global intervention against communism.
- The Marshall Plan, which restored the prosperity of Western Europe.
- The creation of an independent West German state and its militarization.
- The peace treaty and the security alliance with Japan.
- The attempt to achieve international control of atomic energy.
- The decision to build the hydrogen bomb.
- U.S. intervention in the Korean War.
- The defense of Chiang Kai-shek on Taiwan and the decision not to recognize Communist China.
- U.S. military aid to France in Indochina.
- The North Atlantic Treaty Organization.
- NSC-68, the key Cold War document, which called for the global military containment of communism.

To make these policies possible, Acheson effected a Cold War consensus that cut across party lines. Sometimes by the force of his argument, other times by hyperbole, exaggeration, and an appeal to emotion, he persuaded the Republicans to abandon their traditional stance of isolationism and support his policies of global American involvement. Under him foreign policy went bipartisan and everyone became an interventionist.

Acheson was not a great conceptualizer. But he was a brilliant salesman and organizer. He spoke with conviction and authority, understood how to use the bureaucracy rather than be mastered by it, was a forceful and imaginative negotiator, and had the unqualified admiration of the President whose foreign policy he devised. The relationship between Dean Acheson, the suave, acerbic, and urbane diplomat, and Harry Truman, the plain-speaking former haberdasher, seemed an improbable one, but it was based on mutual respect and a similar toughness of spirit.

A Democrat in politics and a bon viveur by temperament, Acheson was an enlightened conservative, a man who radiated duty, tradition, and a sense of noblesse oblige. The impeccably tailored suits, the guardsman's bristling moustache jauntily turned up at the tips, the tall and graceful physique, the imperious Roman nose, the witty phrase that delighted friends and humiliated foes—these were Acheson's trademarks. He had an arrogant self-assurance that irritated many, but also, among friends, a charm that disarmed.

Part of Acheson's charm was his candor. He once told the British that they had "lost an empire and not yet found a role." He described Kennedy as "out of his depth" in the presidency and told an interviewer that he "never thought the UN was worth a damn." It was refreshing to have a public official who spoke with such frankness. Indeed, it is almost unheard of to find one so devoid of cant. That quality added greatly to Acheson's appeal—that and his unquestioned intelligence, wit, and grace under attack.

His elegance of speech, Ivy League accent, and sureness of manner added to his authority. They also made simpler men, like many congressmen, with their rambling thoughts and incomplete sentences, feel ill at ease. He made little effort to cultivate such men, unless he considered them of extreme importance, and displayed toward them an indifference bordering on contempt. This sometimes made him enemies where he would otherwise have had only adversaries and considerably complicated his contentious relations with Congress.

In a country where virtually everyone likes to be considered middle-class and a regular guy, Acheson was set apart. Whereas Nelson Rockefeller, for example, worked indefatigably at the common touch, and indeed seemed genuinely to have it ("Hiya, fella," he used to shout at startled passersby, hand outstretched), Acheson cultivated a patrician style. His education and manner, his wealth and influence, seemed to establish him as a charter member of the American establishment.

Yet his origins were modest enough. His father was a clergyman who emigrated from Ireland to Canada, where he married a whiskey distiller's daughter, and then to Connecticut. Bishop Acheson, who had served in a regiment subduing Indians in western Canada, was a man of action as well as of the cloth. Though young Dean did not inherit his father's faith, the bishop imbued him with a sense of ethics, tradition, and competitiveness.

The position of the clergy is a peculiar one: it is at once dependent on the favors of the rich it serves and somewhat elevated in status above the poor to whom it ministers. It has access to the top, and even a small portal of entry, but must always be on good behavior. Bishop Acheson prepared his son to slip through that portal: first at Groton, the most prestigious and most English of American private schools; then at Yale, for a mixture of scholarship and society; and finally at Harvard law school, for instruction in acquiring money and power.

An indifferent scholar but popular fellow at Yale, where he was invited to join one of the better secret societies, Dean settled down to his studies at Harvard law. There he caught the eye of Felix Frankfurter. The professor, who had a pronounced weakness for all things vaguely English, and for smart young men with good manners and better breeding, recommended him to Supreme Court Justice Louis D. Brandeis. Acheson stayed with Brandeis for two years as his clerk, learning about the law, and even more about politics and how things get done in Washington. In 1921 he joined the law firm now known as Covington and Burling and built a lucrative practice in corporate and international law.

Attaching himself to the conservative wing of the Democratic party, he was rewarded in 1933 by appointment as under secretary of the treasury in Franklin D. Roosevelt's first administration. A few weeks later he was back at the law firm for having had the temerity to challenge FDR's decision to devalue the gold content of the dollar. Though he complained of the President's "arrogant and condescending manner," he retired gracefully, supported FDR for reelection in 1936 and 1940, and in 1941 was brought into the State Department at the intermediate level of assistant secretary.

During the war he worked on the Lend-Lease program, which funneled billions of dollars in American aid to countries resisting Germany and Japan, and on the Bretton Woods accord, which provided the structure for American economic dominance of the postwar world. But it was not until 1945, when the new Secretary of State, James F. Byrnes, promoted him to under secretary, the second-ranking job, that Acheson truly began to shape American foreign policy.

This was a time, one should recall, when the Cold War as we know it today had not yet taken form. The wartime collaboration between Washington and Moscow, and the euphoria of the victory over Germany, persuaded many to believe that the cooperation could continue into the postwar period. Though Moscow's ruthless behavior in Poland and throughout Eastern Europe distressed Americans, the general assumption in 1945 was that the Russians were intent on creating a sphere of influence as a buffer against any future invasion from the West.

Acheson did not share that belief. Remembering well the lesson of Munich in 1938, he applied it to the very different situation of postwar Europe. This persuaded him that any accommodation to Soviet demands in Eastern Europe was tantamount to appeasement and that it was not possible to work out a modus vivendi with Moscow. As second man in the State Department from 1945 to 1947 under chiefs—first Byrnes, then George Marshall—who were abroad much of the time, he was in a position to shape department policy and influence Truman. His was the advice the President followed, his the interpretation of Soviet behavior that determined American policy.

Although many Americans were distressed by Soviet behavior in the months following the end of the war, few saw this as a threat to the United States or as part of a global design that affected American security. The country had just emerged from a long and costly war. It felt secure behind its atomic monopoly, and it wanted to enjoy its deferred consumer pleasures. It had no enthusiasm for the kind of military containment of communism that Acheson envisaged.

It was not until early 1947 that Acheson found the opportunity to turn American policy in a new direction. The arena was Greece. There, the British, facing bankruptcy at home, were no longer able to maintain their sphere of influence. The Greek monarchy, traditionally under British control, was foundering in its struggle against Communist-led insurgents. The British wanted Washington to take over, and Acheson was eager to step into the breach. Though he had few illusions about the democratic nature of the Greek government, he was intent on preventing a rebel victory. He saw a Russian hand behind the insurgent movement, though Moscow was furnishing little direct aid, and believed that Greece was a good place to dramatize the emerging new policy of "containment." Beyond that, he could not help but be stirred by the notion that the United States, now unquestionably the world's greatest power, would assume the glorious mantle of global leadership once worn by the British.

The initial ante was not high: $400 million for Greece, and with Turkey thrown in for good measure. Truman called key congressmen to the White House to make his pitch for this modest aid bill. But neither he nor Secretary of State George Marshall was able to persuade them to use taxpayers' money for such a seemingly quixotic cause. Acheson begged to speak. "This was my crisis," he recalls in his memoirs. "For a week I had nurtured it. These congressmen had no conception of what challenged them; it was my task to bring it home." In this task, the conditions that had inspired the rebellion—the unpopularity of the monarchy, the repressive social conditions—were set aside in favor of the ideological contest. In Acheson's view a rebel victory would mean the spread of communism, and thus of Soviet influence.

"Like apples in a barrel infected by one rotten one, the corruption of Greece would infect Iran and all to the east," he told the startled legislators. The "infection," according to this pestilence metaphor, would spread through Egypt, Africa, and Asia Minor and engulf all of Europe. "The Soviet Union was playing one of the greatest gambles in history at minimal cost." Senate Republican leader Arthur Vandenberg, who had advised Acheson that scare tactics were his best bet, assured him that the administration would get its money.

Three weeks later Harry Truman called a joint session of Congress to dramatize the situation. Using the civil war in Greece as a point of departure, he drew an apocalyptic picture of the struggle "between alternative ways of life." He then went on to give a sweeping definition of America's new foreign policy goals, one that was fashioned by Acheson but became known as the Truman Doctrine: "It must be the policy of the United States," he declared, "to support free peoples who are resisting attempted subjugation by armed minorities or by outside pressures." At first glance it seemed but a restatement of traditional American goals. But its implications were broad, for it put no geographic limit on American involvement, nor did it even limit such involvement to combating overt acts of aggression. To Walter Lippmann it seemed like "the tocsin of an ideological crusade." But its full meaning would not become clear until three years later, with the outbreak of war in Korea.

While Congress was debating the Truman Doctrine Acheson organized the team that put together the ground-breaking American economic aid program to Europe that came to be known as the Marshall Plan. An unparalleled act of enlightened self-interest, it helped stabilize Europe's faltering economies, provide markets for American goods, dampen the appeal of Western European Communist parties, and form an Atlantic trading bloc. Moscow retaliated by pulling Czechoslovakia farther behind the Iron Curtain.

With the Marshall Plan launched in the summer of 1947, Acheson returned to his law practice to recoup his fortune. He had every reason to assume the Truman administration was in its last year. But in one of the most stunning political upsets in American history, Harry Truman won reelection in 1948 and named Acheson as his Secretary of State. It was a triumphant return, but also one that was to make him the focal point of a bitter dispute.

The Republicans had been locked out of the White House since 1932. Some had grown irresponsible, and their loss to Truman in 1948 had made them desperate. They were intent on discrediting the administration by whatever means they could, however ludicrous the accusations. The country by that time had been seized by a fervor of anticommunism, one caused in part by the administration's own methods in overselling the Communist menace in order to get its programs through Congress. With poetic justice, this was now to come home to haunt it.

Acheson became an inviting target for the disgruntled Republicans. They accused him, curiously enough, of being insufficiently anti-Communist. Such a charge could be taken seriously only in the hysterical political climate of the late 1940s and early 1950s. Specifically they attacked Acheson for his altogether honorable refusal to sacrifice innocent State Department officials to McCarthyite inquisitions and for his casual connection with the suspected Russian agent Alger Hiss.

Above all, his critics berated him for being insufficiently enthusiastic about the defeated anti-Communist Chinese leader, Chiang Kai-shek. Despite some $2 billion in American aid, Chiang's corruption-ridden government and ineffectual army had been unable to stem the tide of Mao Tse-tung's Communist forces. Acheson tried to cut American losses in this hopeless cause and in the summer of 1949 issued a thousand-page "white paper" that described the Chiang regime as "corrupt, reactionary and inefficient." It then went on to declare the obvious: that the civil war in China was beyond the control of the

United States and that "nothing that this country did or could have done within the reasonable limits of its capabilities could have changed that result."

It was an unexceptionable observation, but it failed to assuage the administration's critics. Those on the Left wanted to know why the United States had poured so much money into Chiang's coffers if it was a losing cause from the beginning. Those on the Right were infuriated by the administration's evident willingness to wash its hands of Chiang and perhaps even work out a modus vivendi with Mao.

The attack was led by the China lobby, a catchall group of well-heeled American supporters of Chiang with important congressional connections. Among them were Senator Joseph McCarthy, just beginning his rise to fame as a Red-baiter, and an ambitious young congressman from California named Richard Nixon, who captured attention by bemoaning "Dean Acheson's College of Cowardly Communist Containment."

The accusations against Acheson were ironic, to say the least, since few were more militantly anti-Communist and less willing to probe the possibility of a negotiated settlement. "To seek a modus vivendi with Moscow would prove chimerical," he wrote in his memoirs. "Soviet authorities are not moved to agreement by negotiation."

Of Acheson's famous dictum, "negotiation from strength," it was said that the formula meant you should not negotiate when weak, and need not negotiate when strong. He put together the North Atlantic Treaty Organization (NATO), helped persuade Truman to build the H-bomb, and, together with his deputy, Paul Nitze, produced NSC-68, the document that paved the way for quadrupling the defense budget and obliterating the distinction between national and global security. The document's purpose, he later explained, was to "bludgeon the mass mind of 'top government' " so that it would approve a vastly expanded definition of security.

NSC-68 was conceived as an aspiration for the future. But it became a blueprint in June 1950, when Communist North Korea attacked South Korea. At that time the United States had no commitment to South Korea. In fact, Acheson himself had in January 1950 affirmed a decision by the Joint Chiefs of Staff by publicly drawing a U.S. "defense perimeter" excluding that country. Yet when the attack occurred and South Korean resistance collapsed, he urged Truman to intervene with American troops.

He read the attack as a test by the Soviet Union of American resolve. Thus, for him the stakes went far beyond the Korean peninsula. "To back away from this challenge, in view of our capacity for meeting it, would be highly destructive of the power and prestige of the United States," he later explained. "By prestige I mean the shadow cast by power, which is of great deterrent importance." With the Korean War the vague rhetoric of the Truman Doctrine became a reality. The stage was set for the intervention in Vietnam more than a dozen years later.

The decision to send troops to Korea had unforeseen and far-reaching consequences. It involved the United States in a land war on the Asian mainland—an action that even General Douglas MacArthur, commander of U.S. forces in the Pacific, had earlier warned against. Further, it implicated the United States in the Chinese civil war when the administration sent the Seventh Fleet to protect Chiang Kai-shek's defeated army, which had sought refuge on the island of Taiwan. And it was the first crack in what was to become a chasm when Acheson recommended U.S. military support for the French in their colonial struggle against Communist-led rebels in Indochina.

At the beginning the decision to intervene seemed clever. It disarmed the Republicans, who were having a field day accusing Acheson of being "soft on communism." And it galvanized support for the huge military buildup counseled by NSC-68. MacArthur, in a brilliant landing behind enemy lines, sent the North Korean forces reeling back to the 38th parallel, from which they had come. Had it stopped there, the administration would have chalked up a considerable victory at small cost. But Truman and Acheson wanted to show that they could be no less tough against Communists than the Republicans. Instead of stopping MacArthur at the frontier between the two Koreas, they instructed him to pursue the North Korean army. By uniting all Korea under the pro-American government in the South, they would show the Republicans who were the true "liberators" from communism. By adroit diplomacy Acheson pushed through the United Nations a resolution endorsing MacArthur's intervention in the North.

But Truman and Acheson, in their visions of an easy victory, had not counted on the Chinese. They were sure that Peking's warnings to halt the attack were simply a bluff. But as MacArthur's forces approached the frontier of China, a Chinese army surged into battle and pushed the American-led UN army back to the 38th parallel. American losses grew rapidly, and with them disgust with the war and the Truman administration. MacArthur, humiliated by his retreat, wanted to bomb China. But the administration had no intention of opening up a wider war. The fighting in Korea stalled, the casualties mounted, and the public grew increasingly disgusted with a war that the administration could not win and feared to end by a negotiated compromise.

The war was Acheson's undoing. The far Right, always his enemy, had not been appeased; rather, it became more vicious, and the attacks upon him increased. Liberals were dispirited and on the defensive. Virtually no one trusted the administration. Acheson's effectiveness was nearly destroyed. He became an irresistible target for any politician with a grievance, and his appearances before congressional committees took on the air of a Roman circus.

The experience of those last years embittered him. When Dwight Eisenhower replaced Truman in 1953, Acheson returned to his law practice. Occasionally over the years that followed he was brought in as an elder statesman. During the Cuban missile crisis he urged John F. Kennedy to attack the Soviet bases, and he supported the initial intervention in Vietnam. But in 1968, together with Clark Clifford and other "wise men" brought in for advice, he told Lyndon Johnson that it was time to extricate the United States from the Vietnam War. Out of office he seemed to become conservative and rigid. Like most elder statesmen, he missed the excitement of high office. "To leave positions of great responsibility and authority is to die a little," he wrote in his memoirs a few years before his death.

However skilled a negotiator and delightful a companion Acheson might have been, there was a basic part of his nature that served him badly. He had a high disdain for those he considered of lesser intelligence, and he took too much pleasure in the oft-quoted comment that he did not "suffer fools gladly." His definition of a fool, however, was often someone who disagreed with him. There was something too easy and too self-congratulatory in his quick dismissal of opponents. Rather than engage his adversaries in serious argument, he would often choose to ridicule them. "Ninnies" was his word for those who disagreed or would not see. His tart tongue and easy contempt made him enemies he was unwise to have, such as Senator Robert Taft, and caused his last years in office to be more contentious than necessary.

What he accomplished is impressive. He laid the cornerstones of the world we live in. But in some ways he was no less self-righteous and narrow-minded than those whose calumny he had to endure. His attitude toward the public was one of bemusement bordering on contempt. Like many foreign policy managers, he tried to manipulate rather than educate public opinion. Though his mind was wonderfully agile, it was not of the sort that questioned its own assumptions. Of his crucial 1950 decision to aid the French in Indochina, the first step toward the American tragedy in Vietnam, he later said: "I could not then or later think of a better course."

Because his range of self-examination was so narrow, it never occurred to him that the assumptions that governed his Cold War policies might themselves be faulty. He never seriously questioned whether Stalin's ambitions were in fact the same as Hitler's. Nor did he perceive that the policies of military counterforce that he so intently pursued might unfavorably influence Soviet behavior. Whether or not any serious opportunities existed to mitigate the conflict between America and Russia, we cannot be sure, given the perceptions and anxieties of both sides. But it is certain that Acheson was not interested in investigating them.

Though Acheson hardly caused the Cold War, he was instrumental in making the contest seem so ideologically irreconcilable. Confronted with the pragmatic need to persuade the American people to refrain from seeking security in isolation, he chose to frighten rather than to reason with them, to "scare" them, in Senator Vandenberg's approving phrase, rather than to treat them as equals. He sold the Truman Doctrine, the Marshall Plan, NATO, NSC-68, and the Korean War by oversimplifying the reality of the Soviet threat. Because of his low opinion of the public, he made his argument "clearer than truth," to use his own phrase. The result was to help transform a balance-of-power contest, not fundamentally different from those of the past, into an ideological crusade.

In this sense, the two American wars in Asia—Korea and Vietnam—just like the intervention in Central America today, are also part of Acheson's legacy.

By deliberately muddying the distinction between Soviet imperialism and indigenous Marxist revolutions, he added significantly to the confusion between the sweep of American power and the defense of American interests. Thus, to signal his immense influence is also to question the price of his achievement.

DEAN GOODERHAM ACHESON *was born on April 11, 1893, in Middletown, Connecticut. His father, Edward Campion Acheson, was the Episcopal bishop of Connecticut; his mother was the daughter of a wealthy Canadian distiller. Acheson said that with a father who was a minister and a mother who was the daughter of a distiller, he knew good and evil at an early age.*

At the Groton School he was considered "a lone wolf and a rebel." At Yale, a classmate recalled, "Dean moved in a fast circle and seemed to have a great deal more money than he actually had. He was refreshingly bright and intent upon enjoying himself."

He went to Harvard law school, where he roomed with Cole Porter for a short while and studied under Felix Frankfurter. Later, working at the State Department, Acheson walked the mile and a half to work each morning with Justice Frankfurter. "I'll tell you one thing," Frankfurter told a friend. "We never talk about the government or foreign policy. We just talk."

A Georgetown neighbor once remarked of Acheson's guardsman's moustache: "Honestly, some mornings the moustache appears to be a step or two ahead of the Secretary; other mornings it appears to be a step or two behind."

He stood over six feet tall and had blue eyes and a deep voice. He wore a black or gray homburg, a gray or blue pinstripe suit, ties with commanding diagonals, and blue-and-white-striped shirts with stiff white collars. President Truman was said to admire Acheson because he looked the way a Secretary of State ought to look.

When he was assistant secretary of state for congressional relations, Acheson wrote to his daughter, Mary, "This is a low life but a merry one. I was asked to sit at a table with Jessie Sumner of Illinois, the worst of the rabble-rousing isolationists. . . . We got along famously. She is a grand old girl. . . . I often wonder whether I have any principles at all."

He called the Red-baiting Senator Joseph McCarthy "a very cheap, low scoundrel. To denigrate him is to praise him."

He believed that "the best diplomacy is on the personal level." Lord Halifax, Britain's ambassador to the United States during World War II, recalled, "I would be halfway back to the embassy, still chuckling over some remark of his, before I realized that he hadn't told me a single blessed thing." Said Acheson: "I got along with everybody who was housebroken. But I was never very close to the Russians. They were abusive; they were rude. I just didn't like them."

He observed that "some of my worst enemies on [Capitol Hill] were my best friends." In the spirit of bipartisanship he once drafted a speech for a critic of the Bretton Woods bill, which Acheson himself championed. "It was the best attack on the bill ever delivered," he recalled.

"I never thought the UN was worth a damn," he once remarked. "To a lot of people it was a Holy Grail, and those who set store by it had the misfortune to believe their own bunk."

He retreated from Washington to a one-hundred-acre farm, called Harewood, in Sandy Spring, Maryland. Harewood included a run-down 1795 farmhouse, which Acheson renovated. An irrepressible amateur architect, he often said he had missed his calling.

At Harewood, Acheson went horseback riding and chopped wood. He read Mark Twain and Anthony Trollope, his favorite authors. He also gardened: he and his wife, Alice, tended rival flowerpots.

Once, in Washington, the Achesons arrived at a friend's home dressed for a dinner party. When the front door opened, they found that their host, unshaven and wearing a sweat shirt, had been painting his basement. Acheson turned to his wife and hollered, "Goddammit, Alice! You've done it again!"

"To leave positions of great responsibility and authority," he said, "is to die a little." Yet as a private citizen, Acheson counseled Presidents Kennedy, Johnson, and Nixon, and he wrote six books, including Present at the Creation, which won a Pulitzer Prize in 1970.

On October 12, 1971, he was found slumped over a desk in his Harewood study. He had died, at about six P.M., of a heart attack.

Behold the Brothers Rockefeller, Bearing Gifts

ADAM SMITH

TO UNDERSTAND THE PHENOMENON OF THE ROCKEFELLERS, ONE MUST KNOW A BIT about God.

"God," said John D. Rockefeller I, "gave me my money." Such sentiments are not unusual in people of wealth. In the farthest reaches of the Protestant ethic, the money does not even come directly from God; prosperity is a sign of grace, and money is therefore a province in the land of God's grace. Perhaps only God could bestow such a vast wealth of oil; that other oil billionaire, the desert warrior Ibn Sa'ūd, who renamed Arabia after himself, also said that Allah had given him his wealth.

John D. was a Baptist, not a Calvinist; he devoted his Sundays to hymn singing and prayer—his mother's influence. His father was a traveling salesman of cancer cures sold at county fairs; the Rockefeller family was later to say he was "interested in botanic medicine." John D. was a bookkeeper, a man of black ledgers who fined himself twenty-five cents for being late to dinner. He was careful. His father had said, "I cheat my boys every chance I get. Makes 'em sharp." John D. bought a refinery near Cleveland to handle the output of the new Pennsylvania oil fields. He invited his competitors to join him or disappear, and with the collusion of the banks and the railroads they did disappear. By 1880 he controlled more than 90 percent of the favorite and most necessary commodity of the Industrial Revolution, the greatest monopoly since the East

India Company. Newspapers caricatured him as an octopus, a malefactor of great wealth, our first billionaire. Under the urging of a Baptist minister, who warned that the avalanche of wealth would crush him, he began to give his fortune away. Some of it. To get a suitable western Baptist school, for example, he founded the University of Chicago.

John D. begat John D. Jr., who gave away $822 million even as the wealth compounded. Standard Oil was broken into several Standard Oils, which made the family richer; it had a piece of each. The family's Equitable Trust Company was merged into the Chase, and it became the biggest shareholder of the biggest bank. John D. Jr. begat six children, Abby and the five brothers. The Brothers—their generation was known that way—were raised with black ledgers, index cards for Bible sayings, and the notion that large possessions always carry large responsibilities. They had minuscule allowances and were paid for killing flies, but their town house had a gym and an infirmary and their country retreat at Pocantico was ten times the size of Monaco.

The Brothers—John D., Nelson, Laurance, Winthrop, and David—did not always act in concert, but they had a staff and family activities in an office modestly named Room 5600—more a floor than a room—in a spectacular office complex not so modestly named Rockefeller Center.

I have only a peripheral acquaintance with Room 5600. I went there to see Nelson two decades ago, I think about International Basic Economy Corporation, his Latin American venture. My memory is of modern art—enough for a small museum—and mess-jacketed black retainers. Nelson said, "Hiya, fella," and gave me his two-handed greeting: left hand to right elbow, as if to emphasize intimacy, right hand to right hand for the handshake. My memory is of teeth, a large smile, as Teddy Roosevelt is said to have had. I also saw Nelson in his Fifth Avenue apartment. Matisse had painted the wall over the fireplace. It occurred to me that to move the painting, one would have had to take the wall. After the meetings I got a note on stationery that simply said ROOM 5600, signed NELSON. The stationery was so thick it cut my thumb; I bled on the envelope. From time to time Nelson's staff passed me his memos on some cosmic subject; the staff always treated them as if they were written on parchment, or as if they were an early draft of the Magna Charta. Nelson also sent me a book he had written. Years later I found out he had scarcely had time to read it. I never learned who wrote it.

The fifty-sixth floor at 30 Rockefeller Plaza was definitely in the province of God's grace. It was a seat of princely power unmatched by any other family in this country. Social critics looking for interlocking directorates in business missed the point; the Rockefellers did not seek to control American industry. The princely power came from the money the family had given away as much as from the money it was still amassing; it was exercised not merely in business but in the arts, in intellectual life, and in government. In the century of America's imperial power they were the imperial family. There were richer families in Texas, though not many, and the Kennedy family got one richer prize. But the Rockefellers were the establishment. Their influence came not just from money in the bank, but from the bank itself; from an elaborate complex of think tanks and institutes, funded by the Foundation; from relationships that crisscrossed all of American life. Only a President of the United States could mobilize the equivalent talent and brainpower.

Congress waited, in 1974, with a kind of financial prurience. As part of his confirmation hearings as Vice-President of the United States, Nelson was about to reveal the family fortune. Columnists speculated it might be $10 billion. Silver-haired J. Richardson Dilworth, the family's chief operating officer, brought his charts. There was no concentration of economic power, he said; the family was worth only $1.3 billion, and that was spread over so many people. The senators listened deferentially. Nelson's spending—his "loans," since forgiven, to Republican factotums like L. Judson Morhouse, his gifts to former staff members like Henry Kissinger—had already been discussed. Nelson was confirmed. His net worth had been revealed at $218 million, which seemed modest after the Washington rumors. Of course, 1974 was the bottom of the market, so the $218 million undoubtedly rose again. Yet something was missing in the hearings. It was something not quantifiable; the sense of what being a Rockefeller carried, more than wealth. When a Brother went on his honeymoon as a young man, he was a youth out of college, yet he met with prime ministers like a Secretary of State. Wealth alone cannot produce this.

The Chase Bank and the Standard Oil companies required services; great investment banking houses like Lazard Frères and Lehman Brothers Kuhn Loeb served them. Great Wall Street law firms like Debevoise & Plimpton and Milbank, Tweed, Hadley & McCloy also served them. Rockefeller money had helped set up the Council on Foreign Relations to study policy. Rockefeller money had also gone into the Social Science Research Council. The Rockefeller Foundation had created the Institute of Pacific Relations and contributed to the Japan Society; there were also other think tanks and institutes, including the Trilateral Commission. Whenever members of the power elite gathered, there were also one or two representatives from institutions the Rockefellers had created. John McCloy, Douglas Dillon, and the Dulles brothers wielded power longer than the elected officials who appointed them. Policy technocrats like W. W. Rostow, Zbigniew Brzezinski, and Henry Kissinger worked their way up through the institutes.

In legends princes are assigned tasks: slaying dragons, retrieving lost articles of magical properties. The Princes Rockefeller each took an area of society. Nelson was the most visible, a glad-handing extrovert in politics, with Latin America his first interest—the family's Creole Petroleum Company took him to Venezuela. Then he became an assistant secretary of state, then governor of New York, finally Vice-President. Winthrop dropped out of Yale, floundered in the oil business, suffered the family's disapproval for a nonestablishment marriage (to Bobo, a former Miss Lithuania in Chicago), and finally took upon himself a remote fiefdom: Arkansas. He built a model ranch and served two terms as governor. John D. III spent his time on philanthropy; Asia was his particular interest. Laurance was a pioneer venture capitalist stimulated by postwar high-tech, a conservationist who also created luxury resorts. David earned the only Ph.D. in the family (economics, University of Chicago, "Unused Resources and Economic Waste") and went to work for the Chase Bank and became not only its chairman but the untitled chairman of the American establishment, his foreign visits having more panoply than a Cabinet member's. A boyhood collector of beetles, he received them from all over the world as the chairman of Chase and had two named after him by an Arizona research station he subsidized—*armaeodera Rockefelleri* and *cincindela Rockefelleri*.

Princely power can change landscapes. In the urban landscape of Manhattan this is most easily seen: Rockefeller Center, with its open spaces and skating rink, anchors mid-Manhattan. On the East Side is the UN, the site purchased and donated by the Rockefellers; the donation also prevented a possible development that might have rivaled Rockefeller Center. When Wall Street firms were moving to midtown, and the lower end of Manhattan seemed ready to slide into marginal sleaze, like the needle-trades area, David anchored it with a sixty-story skyscraper, the new headquarters of Chase. John D. III was the moving force behind the Lincoln Center for the Performing Arts, on the West Side—more space, more plazas. Uptown were the Morningside Heights institutions, all beneficiaries of Rockefeller philanthropy, even if they did not have the architectural unity provided by leveling blocks and starting anew: Columbia, Barnard, Union Theological Seminary, Riverside Church.

Nor were the Rockefeller monuments limited to Manhattan. Rockefeller investment went into the Embarcadero Center in San Francisco and into Fairington and Interstate North in Atlanta. When the Brothers found an agreeable vacation spot, they sometimes bought it up to preserve its character, donating it to an institution; creating a kind of park; or creating small prestigious resorts, where the upper-middle class could share the original Rockefeller experience, to some degree, at two hundred dollars a day per person. Laurance was the chief proprietor of the RockResorts, and RockResorts are the top of the line, as any travel agent will tell you. Laurance sailed the Caribbean, looking for sites. Little Dix Bay Hotel and Caneel Bay Plantation in the Virgin Islands, and Jenny Lake Lodge, Colter Bay Lodge, and Jackson Lake Lodge in Grand Teton National Park have the highest occupancy rates of any luxury resorts.

Messing with the landscape was not always universally popular with the populace. Nelson's Albany Mall, which was supposed to be a mini-Brasilia, did not meet approving eyes; it was called Instant Stonehenge, and there were references to "edifice complexes" and Mussolini. The billion-dollar Albany Mall was built with state funds, not with Nelson's, and it became a symbol of his open-handed spending, which left New Yorkers some of the most highly taxed citizens of any state. Nor did Californians want the $1 billion landfill project of David and fellow investors in San Francisco Bay; they sidetracked it.

Laurance had this impact on the business landscape: he was a venture capitalist when there was little money elsewhere for venture capital. He did not think of it as venture capital—seed money, a seat on the board, contacts, help with professional management—but it is a style now widespread. He was interested in aviation, so in 1938 he helped Eddie Rickenbacker buy Eastern Airlines from General Motors. He liked the enthusiastic Scotsman J. S. McDonnell and so became an initial investor in McDonnell Aircraft. His postwar ventures range from a metal can company to nuclear power and computers. Prospectuses for a new business going public might list a director from a bank, a director from a law firm, and a director labeled simply "Associate of Laurance S. Rockefeller." For a while that was a Good Housekeeping Seal, the Royal Warrant, Director by Appointment to H. M. the Prince.

The Rockefellers did more than collect art, as the rich do. They brought art to the masses. Abby Aldrich Rockefeller, the mother of the Brothers, had been a great collector and one of the founders of the Museum of Modern Art. Nelson, David, and John D.'s wife, Blanchette, all took turns as president, but Nelson's strong hand was most apparent. More than any other institution, the Museum of Modern Art brought contemporary art to a mass public; once controversial, its collections drew millions through the doors. Nelson also donated the outstanding Museum of Primitive Art to the Metropolitan Museum of Art in New York, in memory of his son, Michael, who was lost in New Guinea.

God's munificence does not always emanate with the same intensity. In the 1970s the establishment came under attack, and the Rockefellers were so much a part of the establishment that they began to lose their mystique as the Princes doing their duty. Winthrop did not take happily, as Nelson did, to the roughhousing of politics; always a boozer, he slurred words in some of his speeches as governor of his adopted province. His second wife left him, and he died of cancer, in spite of his treatment at the Rockefeller-sponsored Sloan-Kettering Institute. John D. III died in an automobile crash, hit head-on by a teenage driver. Laurance had pioneered in venture capital and in conservation, but now there were other venture capitalists and conservationists who did not agree with him. Nelson, elected governor of New York four times, did not finish his fourth term; he resigned to speak on great issues, he said—more specifically, to prepare to be President, but the presidency escaped him. He served as Gerald Ford's Vice-President and died of a heart attack one evening while having wine and cheese with a twenty-five-year-old researcher. David, too, lost the splendor of the mystique. First his Chase Bank was surpassed by Walter Wriston's Citibank, and then it ran into rough times with risky loans to Eastern Europe and Mexico; he resigned with the bank safe but not leading.

"From shirt sleeves to shirt sleeves in three generations," said Andrew Carnegie, and his fellow tycoon J. D. Rockefeller was so fearful of Rockefellers returning to shirt sleeves that he pressed a Protestant sense of duty on his descendants. But, in fact, great fortunes do not disappear. Smaller family businesses may fail and return the family to shirt sleeves, but great fortunes can be totally dissipated only by revolution; otherwise, they are too professionally managed by the establishment of their time. The Depression, which wiped out financiers and farmers alike, only enhanced the fortunes of the Mellons and du Ponts and Rockefellers; so many good opportunities were available so cheap.

As the fortunes are spread through more generations they lose their coherence, and with it the influence of the family. Power and directedness slide into mere comfort, and comfort is commonplace. The present generation of Rockefellers is called the Cousins; there are more than twenty of them. The Cousins have one visible politician, John D. IV, called Jay, who adopted West Virginia as his uncle had adopted Arkansas. It also has at least one Marxist; other Cousins are all over the lot. Some of them have been to psychiatrists; their feelings about being Rockefellers are ambivalent. It is doubtful whether black ledger books and index cards for Bible sayings are omnipresent among their children. Duty, the stern daughter of God, has faded. But Room 5600 continues, serene as a dreadnought on a flat sea; it will last the life of the Republic.

THE BROTHERS ROCKEFELLERS *John Davison Rockefeller was born March 21, 1906, in New York City. Nelson Aldrich Rockefeller was born July 8, 1908, in Bar Harbor, Maine. Laurance Spelman Rockefeller was born May 26, 1910, Winthrop Rockefeller was born May 1, 1912, and David Rockefeller was born June 12, 1915, all in New York City.*

David was the only Rockefeller brother with brown eyes; the others' eyes were blue.

A prominent New York matron forbade her son to play with the Rockefeller boys. "No child of mine will play with the grandchildren of a gangster."

One of the boys' friends, seeing their comparatively small sailboat tied up near an elaborate yacht, said, "How come you guys don't have one like that?" One of the Rockefellers replied, "Who do you think we are, Vanderbilts?"

Their father taught them to keep accounts of the money they earned gardening, shining shoes, swatting flies, and killing copperhead snakes.

They received a five-cent bonus for an accurate ledger and a five-cent fine for unaccounted-for items. John III was most often rewarded; Winthrop most always was in the red. They also raised vegetables, which they sold to the family kitchen at market prices.

Nelson once climbed down a manhole in a New York street because he "wanted to know what was down there."

Each night the young Winthrop went to bed and saw the shadows cast by the bars on the windows. They were meant to protect him from trespassers, but Winthrop thought he was being incarcerated.

Asked why they turned a hose on David while he was shooting his bow and arrow, Nelson and Winthrop replied, "Because he's fat and lazy and we want to keep him moving."

Their father promised them $2,500 each if they did not smoke or drink until they were twenty-one. Only Nelson and David managed to collect.

While at Princeton, John III (called JDR3) was embarrassed when a local shopkeeper hung his check among forgeries he'd received.

At Dartmouth, Nelson wrote his senior thesis defending his grandfather's creation of Standard Oil.

Winthrop decided that Yale was not for him and went to work in the Texas oil fields.

Laurance and JDR3 both stopped midmorning to have a snack of milk and graham crackers, as their grandfather always did.

On his honeymoon trip around the world, Nelson met Gandhi. "He showed no interest in me whatsoever," recalled Nelson.

David's interest in beetles began when he was a boy in the forests of Yellowstone Park. As an adult he would sometimes abruptly stop speaking, reach slowly into his breast pocket for an empty vial, pounce on the beetle specimen he'd seen on the floor, cork and pocket the vial, then resume the conversation as if nothing had happened.

Winthrop—at six feet three inches the largest brother—once won a dance contest with Mary Martin as his partner.

Laurance, someone observed, "seemed most at ease at a cocktail party, drawing on a cigarette while furtively studying the faces in the crowd."

Laurance liked to commute from his Westchester estate to his office at Rockefeller Center in his sixty-five-foot motor cruiser, The Dauntless; it took him fifty minutes whizzing down the Hudson, faster than some commuter trains.

David kept a card file of young politicians and businessmen he met in his travels for Chase Manhattan; at one point his file contained thirty-five thousand names.

JDR3 could often be found in New York at the Japan House—dressed in a kimono, entertaining visiting officials, Kabuki troupes, and No players. He was known as Mr. Asia.

Nelson, who became president of MoMA in 1939, said, "I learned my politics at the Museum of Modern Art." In 1974 Nelson's private art collection contained 3,600 pieces and was appraised at $33,561,325.

Winthrop Rockefeller died of cancer on February 22, 1973, in Palm Springs, California.

John D. Rockefeller III died in an auto accident on July 10, 1978, in Westchester County, New York.

Nelson Rockefeller died of a heart attack on January 26, 1979, in New York City.

Dorothy Day
at the
Barricades

GARRY WILLS

FOR A TEENAGED PACIFIST, SHE DID A LOT OF FIGHTING. SHE QUIT HER FIRST NEWSPA-per job, on the socialist *Call*, after being reprimanded by an editor for slapping an incoherent radical at a public affair. Jailed with suffragists, she bit the notori-ous warden of the Occoquan workhouse and kicked two guards in the shins as they wrestled her down. It was always clear that she would leave her mark on the world; but it must have seemed, in 1917, that the mark she would leave would be a bloody one. No one could have guessed—least of all Dorothy Day herself—that she would become, with Gandhi and Dr. King, one of the princi-pal exponents of nonviolence in our time.

An awesome woman, tall, lantern-jawed, with Modigliani eyes, she began to the left of most leftists. She did not go to jail for women's suffrage—she was too radical to care about liberal measures like the vote. Besides, some of the suffra-gists opposed birth control, and Margaret Sanger had been her first heroine. Dorothy went to jail in order to protest the treatment of *all* political prisoners. She was de facto editor of *The Masses* when it was shut down, in 1917, after most of the staff had been indicted for obstructing the draft. The nominal edi-tor, Max Eastman, was on a lecture tour raising funds for the trial he would have to face. Dorothy testified for him.

Before the end of her twenty-second year, Dorothy had been present (as a child) at the San Francisco earthquake; became a close friend, at the University of Illinois, of Rayna Simons, who died young in Moscow as a kind of female John Reed; interviewed Trotsky in New York; been clubbed by policemen in Baltimore and gone to jail in Washington; edited *The Masses*; held in her arms a friend dying from a heroin overdose; undergone an abortion; and tried to commit suicide.

She had also been involved in an intense but unconsummated affair with Eugene O'Neill. O'Neill's biographers, the Gelbs, think that Nina Leeds in O'Neill's *Strange Interlude* was partly modeled on Dorothy. Dorothy's biographer, William Miller, thinks there is more of her in Josie Hogan of *Moon for the Misbegotten*. When O'Neill's friend Louis Holladay committed suicide with an overdose, it was Dorothy who disposed of the remaining heroin and tidied up the tale of a heart attack for the police. She was a cool-eyed survivor in those boozy days of radical art and politics—prettier than Mabel Dodge, if not as bright; brighter than Louise Bryant, though not as pretty. Moving among people who would be broken or worn out by political and other passions, she was one of life's victors.

And that was her problem. She wanted to be a victim. She was a winner trying hard to join the losers. This was so difficult that her first attempt was degrading, a masochistic love affair with a charming brute named Lionel Moise. Dorothy did not want to submit to others—which seems the reason she had remained a virgin till she met Moise, in 1918. Yet she also wanted someone to conquer her unconquerable will—which led her to crawl back to Moise repeatedly over the next few years.

Moise specialized in getting young women to attempt suicide over him. Dorothy became one of that number, and nursed another, while still a third was taking her turn. Dorothy aborted Moise's child in a vain attempt to please him, then married someone else in order to forget him. On her honeymoon she wrote a novel about the affair, to exorcise Moise. None of it worked. She left her husband and pursued Moise from New York to Chicago.

Moise was a sadist whose very loutishness was the source of his attraction. Hemingway was smitten in his own way by Moise, whom he had known as a fellow newspaperman at the Kansas City *Star*. "He was the fastest man on a typewriter I ever knew," Hemingway said before telling how Moise beat up a woman who had tried to stab him. Carlos Baker, Hemingway's biographer, said Hemingway was stunned by Moise's "facility with words, his prodigious vitality, and his undisciplined talent. Whenever he drank, his active energy overflowed into violence."

Dorothy's autobiographical novel, *The Eleventh Virgin*, is atrocious: "She bit his neck contemplatively." Before her affair, the novel's heroine says, "Oh, I wish I could meet some one who would tempt me very insidiously to give up my virtue, persuading me to wickedness that was lovely just because it was wickedness!"

The result is sometimes like Poe: "I only wish that with every kiss I give you a little of my life would leave me. It would be a lovely way to die, providing I could arrange it with God that my death would coincide with the moment you stopped loving me."

More often it is like Barbara Cartland: "It was delightfully humiliating to be talked to in such a way. It was humiliating but she invited it. As long as he crushed her in his arms meanwhile, he could say anything."

How could so savvy a woman, independent and strong-willed, demean herself this way? Sincere as Dorothy's passion no doubt was, there is a suspicious note of calculation in the affair, as of an experiment. She was exploring one possibility of sacrifice and victimhood. Her novel recorded the results while the experiment was still going forward. Dorothy had broken into journalism as a teenager by seeing how little she could eat, then writing about the experience. Now she was dealing with deeper hungers—she wrote later that she tried "the Baudelairean idea of 'choosing the downward path which leads to salvation.'" Her self-scrutiny in the process suggests that she was using Moise for her own purposes, as she later used a man when she wanted a baby without the entanglements of marriage—or even as she subtly used her spiritual mentor, Peter Maurin, in establishing *The Catholic Worker*. Mel Piehl, the historian of the Catholic Worker movement, has been the subtlest in unraveling that relationship: "It was . . . strategically useful to her as a woman leading a social movement in the sexually conservative Catholic Church, to be able to point to the male cofounder of the movement and to emphasize that she was merely carrying out Maurin's program. There was more than a little dissimulation in this claim, for Day could hardly avoid noticing that Maurin's success depended on her far more than hers depended on Maurin. She was quite sincere in her professions of feminine deference, but she had also ingeniously constructed a situation that allowed her to pay homage to masculine supremacy in theory without being constrained by it in practice."

This calculating side to Dorothy's human relationships would repel us if it were not so clearly subordinated to the mystical quest she had undertaken, in obscure ways, since her childhood. She performed her experiments in order to find God. Even her attraction to O'Neill, drunkenly muttering Francis Thompson's "The Hound of Heaven" in his favorite bar, came from the fact that she saw him as a rebelling believer rather than an unbeliever. God's influence can be read as clearly in those who flee Him as in those who seek Him. Even her masochistic affair with Moise she saw as a pact with God to let her die if love should end. When she survived her own hardest attempt at self-victimization, it became increasingly clear that there was only one will to which she could submit her own.

When her baby daughter was born, Dorothy had her baptized a Catholic. One almost feels that she had the baby in order to baptize it. Another experiment was under way. What would it be like to live a life dedicated to God from birth? It was not her happiest experiment; one cannot live another person's life for her. That, too, would become clearer in time. Dorothy became a Catholic herself in 1927, determined to be an "ordinary" believer. She wrote, now, for the Catholic press. Like Graham Greene, she went to Mexico to observe the sufferings of a persecuted church. She was serenely incapable of seeing any conflict between her conventional theological views, fed by the spiritually satisfying liturgy of her new church, and her radical beliefs. If God is with the victims, with losers, then priests and revolutionaries should be there, too. We all should. It was as simple as that.

In 1932 Peter Maurin, a self-educated French peasant, a radical propagandist of deep Catholic piety, was sent to Dorothy by better-known Catholic journalists who wanted to get rid of him. He was an exasperating dogmatist, but he lived a life with and for the poor. Dorothy, after some initial resistance, was taken by his quirky blend of European learning and practical sense of service to the downtrodden. At his suggestion, she put out the first issue of *The Catholic Worker*, on May Day 1933. The paper—named as a challenge to the Communist *Daily Worker*, edited by Dorothy's old friend and colleague Mike Gold— touched a nerve in the Depression. Maurin's "Christian personalism" was revolutionary but nonviolent. It was concerned less with radical politics than with feeding Christ's forgotten ones. It did not so much oppose the political order as ignore it, trying to forge bonds of community among those ignored by the powerful.

Volunteers flocked to the houses of hospitality in New York, where Peter and Dorothy joined prayer and theological discussion with begging for food and dispensing it to the hungry. Soon there were dozens of houses of hospitality around the country, along with Catholic farms set up to fulfill Maurin's dream of an American peasantry devout and independent. By the end of the Thirties, the Catholic Worker movement was the most vital force in the Catholic Church for change. A Catholic revival, centered largely in the liberal diocese of Chicago, was urged on by men who had been inspired by Dorothy—John Cogley, Ed Marciniak, John Cort, and many others. Seminarians read *The Catholic Worker* and felt called to serve the poor in Peter and Dorothy's way. Many found in the Worker movement a spiritual foundation for Catholic unionism.

During World War II the Worker movement suffered from Dorothy's refusal to abandon her deep-seated pacifism, her opposition to killing in any guise. When their own church ignored or disowned Catholic conscientious objectors, Dorothy cared for them. She was one of the few to criticize in print the government's treatment of Japanese-Americans—one of the things that led J. Edgar Hoover to open what became an extensive file on her. But the dropping of the atomic bombs on Japan gave a new meaning to her calls for peace. When President Truman's glee at the success of the atomic missions was reported, she wrote in her paper: "Mr. Truman was jubilant. True Man. What a strange name, come to think of it." A new generation of true men—peace activists like the Berrigans—responded to her message.

Many have been influenced by her without knowing it. Michael Harrington acquired his concern for the poor while working at a house of hospitality and wrote the book that occasioned the war on poverty. The text of the Second Vatican Council's statement on peace was drafted by a Catholic Worker, James

Douglass—initiating a chain of actions that culminated in the American bishops' recent letter on nuclear war. When Vietnam protests began, Catholics were in the vanguard because of Dorothy. The first draft card burnings were by Catholic Workers. In the Fifties, Dorothy began to go to jail again. She and Ammon Hennacy were arrested annually at civic defense drills—until, in 1961, 2,500 people showed up with them, and the drills were called off. Asked what to do about the Vietnam War, she said, "Fill the jails with our young men." In her seventies she was marching with Cesar Chavez's farm workers.

But her influence cannot be charted in terms of specific political programs or church actions. After her flaming early days she lived most of her life obscurely, not as well known as the Pasionaria types she began with—Mabel Dodge, say, or Louise Bryant. But who lives in a different way now because of Louise Bryant? Yet I know dozens of people whose lives have been altered by Dorothy's words and example—and those dozens know hundreds, and those hundreds know thousands. *The Catholic Worker* lives on, as do the houses of hospitality—and a different kind of "best and brightest" passes through them yearly, along with the poor, the sick, the old. When Dorothy died, in 1980, she was buried in a plain pine box from the church near the Catholic Worker "Maryhouse." A demented bum came up and stared into the coffin—the same kind of company she had been keeping for years; the kind to whom she said, "I know what you are *really* seeking." She had sought the same thing down very weird paths until she found it. And many, to this day, are still seeking because of her.

―――――――――

Dorothy Day *was born on November 8, 1897, in Brooklyn Heights. Her father wrote a racing column called "On and Off the Turf" and later was a partner in Florida's Hialeah racetrack.*

She was a Daughter of the American Revolution but never mentioned it.

While learning Greek in high school, she bought a 150-year-old Greek-language New Testament and set about translating it.

At sixteen she went to the University of Illinois at Urbana; bored, she got only C's and B's. On her own she read labor history, Jack London, Upton Sinclair, Turgenev, Gorky, Dostoevsky, Freud, and Havelock Ellis.

After two years of college, she returned to New York with her family and began to work at the Socialist paper Call. *Her first pieces described her attempts to live on five dollars a week, at that time the average salary of a working woman.* REPORTER . . . EATS FARINA AND CHEESE AND READS WORDSWORTH, *read a headline. Her editor stopped the series. Day later explained, "It is a frightful bore to have to state specifically what you ate . . . [and] how much you paid for it."*

She became engaged to Mike Gold, another reporter at the Call. *She sat with him late at night at Child's restaurant and discussed Freud. When she ate at his mother's home, the mother would break the dishes Day had used. "She used to look at me with great sorrow," Day recalled. "All three of her sons were running around with Gentile girls."*

Her interview with Trotsky was severely cut because Trotsky went on about his opposition to the parliamentarism of the American Socialists.

"For a while," wrote Floyd Dell, "my assistant on The Masses *was Dorothy Day, an awkward and young enthusiast, with beautiful slanting eyes." Day moved into the MacDougal Street apartment Dell shared with two other men on* The Masses *staff. With the apartment to herself in the summer of 1917, Day held an open house attended by John Reed, Max Eastman, and Albert and Charles Boni.*

She hung out in the back room of the Golden Swan saloon with the "Hudson Dusters" gang. "Gangsters admired Dorothy Day," wrote Malcolm Cowley, "because she could drink them under the table. . . ." She once persuaded her friend Eugene O'Neill to read "The Hound of Heaven" to the gang. Day later recalled of her friends at the Golden Swan that "it was a crowd that did a lot of sitting around." Day's rough milieu surprised Agnes Boulton, Eugene O'Neill's second wife: "It was odd because she looked and dressed like a well-bred young college girl. . . . She had a sort of desperate quality beneath her extremely cool manner."

She wrote about Greenwich Village life in her first novel, The Eleventh Virgin, *which she later appraised as a "very bad book."*

When she was twenty-two she married Berkeley Tobey. The marriage lasted less than a year. She lived with and had a child by Forster Batterham. "The man I loved . . . was an anarchist," she said of him. The birth of their child, Tamar Teresa, precipitated Day's turning to Catholicism. When Day was thirty she was baptized. "All my life I have been haunted by God," she said, quoting Kirilov in Dostoevsky's The Possessed.

She wrote a play on the conflict between communism and Christianity. She sold it to Pathé films and spent three months living in Hollywood, getting paid $125 per week. Oblivious to local customs, she drove a secondhand Model T Ford, attended no parties, and lived in the slums of Los Angeles.

She stood five feet nine inches tall and in 1962 weighed 185 pounds. She had blue eyes. Dwight MacDonald wrote that her high cheekbones gave her "a Slavic look, although her ancestry is Scotch-Irish." Judith Gregory, who worked with Day at The Catholic Worker, *described her as "tall, large, stiff, her energy prevailing over an awkward frame."*

Some of her favorite quotations came from Dostoevsky ("The world will be saved by beauty"), from Saint Teresa of Avila (her confession that she had such a grateful nature she could be bribed with a sardine), from Saint Thomas ("Stay in one place until you're pushed out"), and from Paul ("The foolish things of the world hath God chosen, that he may confound the wise").

She loved the sea and collected shells, driftwood, and seaweed. She once lived in a Staten Island fisherman's shack.

She listened to opera. She liked Verdi and Puccini but preferred Wagner, "pagan though he is."

She died in New York City on November 29, 1980, a few days after a heart attack, at the age of eighty-three.

The Ambivalence
of
J. Robert Oppenheimer

MURRAY KEMPTON

THIRTY-NINE YEARS AGO, ROBERT OPPENHEIMER LOOKED ACROSS THE NEW MEXICO sands, took the fireball's measure, and knew that he was the usher who had escorted all the creatures of the earth to the tenebrous dawn of the atomic age. Afterward he would remember—or prefer to believe—that his first conscious thought had been Krishna's:

"I am become death, the shatterer of worlds."

It is unlikely that he himself could say with any assurance whether here was the cry of the stricken sinner or the exultation of the conqueror. His essence was, as always, in the ambiguities of the divided soul and equivocal presence of someone who had come in triumph to a world that would have been safer if he and everyone else who tried had failed.

But then he would himself have been safer if, at the hour that so precipitately discovered him, he had known enough more about the world than it had about him. He had been wrapped at birth in the soft bunting of a well-to-do German Jewish household on Manhattan's Riverside Drive. He came to consciousness in an ambience secure—indeed, smug—about the refinement of the air it breathed but timid about the rough winds beyond. He began his education at the Ethical Culture School, a place of refuge for families that had cast aside the few rags of superstition still adhering to Reform Judaism and swaddled themselves in the credulities of secular humanism. He passed on to Harvard, where Jewish applicants from New York had no large chance of arriving unless they brought with them the promise of departing summa cum laude. He was graduated with honors more than justifying Harvard's confidence and embarked at once for England and Christ's College, Cambridge, and then to Germany and the University of Göttingen. At Cambridge he met Niels Bohr and Paul Dirac, and at Göttingen he studied with Max Born; the great men of theoretical physics had become familiars to him while they were still strangers to the most cultivated of his countrymen.

He carried his German doctorate back to Harvard; he had already begun to robe himself in folds of mystery; Philip Morse, a Princeton graduate student who met him at a Harvard conference on molecular vibrations, had no more vivid recollection of their first encounter than "I didn't know what he was talking about."

His four months at Harvard and five at the California Institute of Technology made the year 1927 the least purposeful he had ever experienced; and it was a relief for him to accept a Rockefeller Foundation grant and escape for twelve months in the European centers of the new physics that were altogether more congenial to him for being so much more aware.

He returned in the summer of 1929 to an assistant professorship at the University of California in Berkeley, where, as he afterward remembered, "I was the only one who knew what this was all about." But even though, or perhaps because, Berkeley had so long been a desert for theoretical physics, he found it most suitable for cultivating a comfortable, if modest, bloom. Its experimentalists never quite found out what he was talking about; but they learned quickly to trust and more and more to depend on the sound and clear assessments of the practicalities of their projects he drew up from his reservoir of the indecipherable.

But for all their affectionate admiration, they never got over the sense that they were in the company of an abstract being, and they were correct in that judgment. His father's textile properties were essentially undamaged by the Depression; and Robert Oppenheimer often recalled that in those days he so seldom glanced at the newspapers that he did not know the stock market had crashed until a long time after it had. The world's coarse rubbings had never chafed his flesh until Hitler shocked him into a political activism that was the more febrile because belated and that so faithfully followed the customary courses of his divorcement from reality as to make him a fellow traveler of the Communists. Those delusions had already grown wispy when the outbreak of the war drew him into research on the potentials of nuclear fission for weaponry.

It was an area of exploration that gave the new physics an authority it had never known before; and Oppenheimer swiftly displayed such unique attributes as bridge between the abstract and the concrete that he was recognized as essential. His earlier leftward excursion was a source of doubts and trepidations, but they yielded to the overpowering necessity for his special qualities, and he was appointed director of the Los Alamos laboratory.

There he showed gifts of command quite beyond any suggested by either his prior history or the highest expectations of his sponsors. He persuaded a hundred scientists to leave the cozy precincts where they were already satisfactorily engaged in military research and to come with him to a closed military outpost in the desert. In the end he was managing a work force of over three thousand.

He was their inspiration, their supervisor, and even their housekeeper, and, collective triumph though theirs was, they all knew that he had done more to build the bomb than anyone else at Los Alamos. Here had been the utmost prodigy of practical achievement; and yet it had been brought about in an isolation sealed off from the run of humanity; there, as always, he had been protected from the routine troubles, discontents, and worries that instruct even while they are cankering ordinary persons, and he was transported to his glittering summit innocent of all the traps that every other man of affairs has grown used to well before he is forty-two years old.

After the war the United States government established an Atomic Energy Commission, and one of its earliest decisions was to approve Robert Oppenheimer as chairman of its General Advisory Committee. One of the commissioners, Lewis Strauss, was also a leading trustee of the Institute for Advanced Study at Princeton. He saw his chance to add to its collection a jewel hardly less precious than Albert Einstein and went down on his knees to persuade Oppenheimer to be director of the institute.

The slow work of Robert Oppenheimer's undoing began in the awe that Strauss brought to their earliest encounters. For it was the awe evoked by a presence whose singular curse was that he was easier to adore than comfortably like. The aura of otherworldly properties is the riskiest of capitals, because the gullible, once disappointed in imagining them divine, are apt to fall into imagining them diabolical. Strauss was one of nature's gullibles, and, having come to worship, he would remain to destroy. There would be others.

As director of Los Alamos's laboratory, he had been all else but the solitary creator of the nuclear weapon; but he had been master of its macabre ceremonies and he could not escape becoming its personification, not just for the public but for a government too quick to assume that since he produced the riddle, he must have brought along its answer. But it did not take long for his country's governors to recognize that Oppenheimer was more riddle than answer.

To their ultimate common despair, he was conscripted as physics tutor to paladins like Under Secretary of State Dean Acheson and Wise-About-Everything John J. McCloy; and he was an automatic choice as scientific member of his country's delegation to the United Nations Conference on International Control of Atomic Energy, the first flight in a search of ever-diminishing expectations.

He complained early in his tenure as chief adviser on international atomic policy that whatever he proposed was uncritically accepted. His wait for relief from that distress was a short one; within a few months his advice was being just as uncritically disregarded.

He first began to sense the limitations of his writ when President Truman asked him, in 1946, to guess when the Russians would develop their own atomic bomb. Oppenheimer replied that he did not know; and Mr. Truman said that he knew the answer and that it was "Never." The misapprehension of Robert Oppenheimer's supernatural qualities had done its worst damage; Mr. Truman could not conceive that the Russians could find the secret because he could not imagine a Soviet Oppenheimer and did not understand that no such ultimately delicate instrument was needed for work rather coarser than he knew.

But even if he had consumed a bit too much of his credit as sage, Oppenheimer's repute as mechanic resided so far beyond doubt that, for the first six years of the AEC's history, it was a matter of course for him to have been the only chairman of its General Advisory Committee.

On November 25, 1947, the young, standing or sitting in the auditorium of the Massachusetts Institute of Technology, listened as if at their devotionals while he recited science's general confession: ". . . in some sort of crude sense, which no vulgarity, no humor, no overstatement can extinguish, the physicists have known sin; and that is a knowledge they cannot lose."

Half a week before, the eight other members of the General Advisory Committee had watched with no less admiration for their chairman's dedication as he led them through the preliminaries of what they had agreed upon— "without debate [but] I suppose not without melancholy"—as their prime task: "To provide atomic weapons and many atomic weapons."

His ambiguities were already traveling into the ambivalence that is the first leg of every journey toward exhaustion.

Long afterward, in his troubles he replied to the charge that he had been less than wholehearted in serving his government's desires, if not its truest interests, by saying: "I did my job, the job I was supposed to do." There was in those words a cold tone stripped of every ideal except the rules of function. It was just that pinnacle of spiritual dispossession that Robert Oppenheimer tried his best to reach, and he would fall short only because he traveled encumbered with too many pieces of baggage he could not quite bear to throw away.

He had crashingly entered the great world without bringing along enough familiarity with the ordinary one. Every famous American physicist before him had been a species of grand tinker more conspicuous for the size of his machines than the breadth of his concepts. Oppenheimer represented instead that first generation of theoretical physicists who had voyaged to Europe and brought it home with them. He thought of science almost as a religious vocation and the higher physics as the sublimest poem in its liturgy.

This susceptibility to abstraction seems the most plausible explanation for his attraction to communism in the years before he fell into practical affairs. Marx's message could never have been as compelling as it was if he had not presumed to call his system "scientific socialism." Oppenheimer would always say that his fear of the Nazis had first brought him close to the Communists; and yet in 1939, when Stalin consummated a treaty of friendship and even a spot of collaboration with Hitler, Oppenheimer's reaction, while by no means uncritical, was somewhat this side of repulsion: Stalin was, after all, a scientific socialist and might know something he didn't.

In July 1945 Edward Teller had solicited Robert Oppenheimer's support for a muster of Los Alamos physicists petitioning Mr. Truman not to drop the bomb on Japan itself.

"He told me in a polite and convincing way," Teller said later, "that he thought it improper for a scientist to use his prestige as a platform for political pronouncements. . . . Our fate was in the hands of the best, the most conscientious men in the nation. And they had information which we did not possess."

Now he had taken upon himself the felt duty of speaking for physics to government and for government to physics. He would be guardian angel over an alliance with too much of the imbalance that obtains when one side is the caterer and the other is the customer and disputes about taste are settled by the palate of the payer.

Oppenheimer maintained this singular legation for five years. He was all but final judge of what could be done and what could not and, consequently, keeper of the gate between the ambitions of others and the official funds that could give them life and force.

The earliest recruits to the army of enemies that eventually overbore Oppenheimer were assembled, not unnaturally, from his oldest friends in the physics department of the University of California, the home where he had grown up and where he had met all of those he had ever consciously harmed and too many of those who would harm him.

He had risen beyond Berkeley and even beyond physics to a grandeur that is at once an affront and a promise, because its object arouses envy and inspires emulation. He had shown the way to an eminence there was no reaching except by a conquest more resounding even than his. He had become a huge shadow between other men and whatever bright particular moon they happened to be baying at.

At Berkeley Oppenheimer had never been more than an honored guest in a house whose master was Ernest Lawrence. Lawrence had earned his Nobel Prize with the great machines he had forced to the outer limits of those laws of physics he insecurely understood and expected someday successfully to defy.

In 1946 Lawrence designed his Materials Testing Accelerator, a piece of hardware too expensively enormous even for his private patrons, his magnificoes. He laid the MTA's conception before the AEC's General Advisory Committee, where he sustained the shock of having it dismissed by Oppenheimer as a vision that, "imaginative" as it was, "cannot do what is expected of it." Lawrence was too powerful for any such summary disposal; he turned, in his wrath, to the Department of Defense and the Joint Congressional Committee on Atomic Energy and so intoxicated them with his promises that the AEC could only give way and buy Lawrence his Materials Testing Accelerator, which swiftly burned itself out.

This demonstration of Oppenheimer's sound judgment increased rather than abated Lawrence's rage at his presumption. For at Berkeley he had taken on the ineffaceable taint of the deserter. He himself had all but ceased to search, whether because he had realized his ambition or because he had shrunk from its consequences. He could be seen as someone who existed only to frustrate the ambitions of others, having lost and perhaps, indeed, deserted the high American confidence that overrides all doubts and compunctions.

Major General Roscoe Wilson was sitting, in January 1951, as the Air Force's representative on an AEC panel on long-range weapon objectives. As always, Oppenheimer was its chairman; and General Wilson went back to headquarters deeply shaken as "a dedicated airman" at having found his country's most authoritative scientific adviser dubious about current prospects for a thermonuclear weapon, pessimistic about any early improvement in devices for detecting atomic explosions, and chilling to notions that anyone present would live long enough to see a nuclear-powered aircraft.

After this cold bath to his dreams, General Wilson felt that he had to "go to the director of [Air Force] intelligence to express my concern over what I felt was a pattern of action not helpful to the national defense."

By the time General Wilson cast his stone at this consecrated object, the odor of incense had already grown faint around it. After September 1949, and the fact of the first successful Soviet nuclear test, Oppenheimer could never again be the symbol, or even personally the sharer, of a national complacency secure in the possession of a weapon beyond any alien's attainment.

Ordinary laymen and officials had taken for granted their country's monopoly of a secret uniquely Robert Oppenheimer's, and they could see no way it could have been lost if it had not been stolen. They kept faith with that misconception well after it had been blown to vapor by executing Julius and Ethel Rosenberg, whose crimes could never have run beyond pilferage too petty to explain the triumph of Soviet research.

Edward Teller knew better than that; he was a theoretical physicist whose attainments and even intuitions were barely less commanding than Oppenheimer's. Teller's contributions at Los Alamos had been smaller than the promise of his talents, because he had spent the war hunting after a thermonuclear weapon quantitatively more dreadful than the bomb delivered upon Hiroshima. His first reaction to the Soviet accomplishment was to recognize in it a public necessity and personal opportunity to renew that pursuit.

He telephoned Oppenheimer to ask what should now be done. "Keep your shirt on," Oppenheimer advised; and that reply left Teller lastingly certain that the chairman of the General Advisory Committee of the Atomic Energy Commission had dropped out of a race it was his duty to run.

There were doses of moral qualm in the mixture of his objections to what Teller zestfully called the Super, but they were rather smaller than his practical doubts. His remedy for the advantage lost to the Soviets was not to aim for the prodigious but to give more attention to the comparatively modest and to concentrate upon smaller nuclear weapons designed for "getting the atom to work on the battlefield as well as the heartland" and to develop a defense system that might diminish Soviet confidence that the United States could be destroyed.

All five of his colleagues on the General Advisory Committee joined him in recommending a low priority for Teller's quest of the absolute. Oppenheimer later professed himself astonished by a unanimity that his enemies could never afterward explain except as the workings of his malicious animal magnetism.

All but one of the AEC's commissioners seem momentarily to have been given pause by the unity in opinion of their scientific advisers; but that one happened to be Lewis Strauss, a minority of undiscourageable militance, who trundled his alarms to the Secretary of Defense and there raised the battalions that would prevail upon Mr. Truman to decree a crash program for the Super.

Oppenheimer's immediate response to this defeat was the suggestion that he yield his General Advisory Committee chairmanship to someone who would bring the necessary enthusiasm to the Super. Secretary of State Acheson responded to this overture by sending back word, "for heck's sake, not to resign or make any public statements to upset the applecart but accept this decision." Oppenheimer stayed on, puzzled, as he afterward said, that anyone could have even transiently mistaken him for the sort of crank who would seek, let alone "find a way to make a public conflict."

He was able to husband a somber hope drawn from his despairs about the Super's feasibility until June 1951, when Teller arrived at a weapons conference in Princeton with the formula that made the hydrogen bomb workable.

Oppenheimer's certainties had eroded and his will was ebbing; but the old intuitive faculty was swift as ever; and he seems to have divined Teller's breakthrough sooner than anyone else there. "Sweet and lovely and beautiful," he is reported to have observed. There was a sudden reglowing of what embers remained from the fires of his earliest conviction that what could be discovered ought to be discovered, wherever it tended. Once more elegance was for him its own absolution.

He set himself thenceforth to do whatever he could to help Teller. But he had lingered too long in the sin of dubiety to earn gratitude or forgiveness from those he had transiently obstructed. A few months after he had speeded Teller on his road, Oppenheimer's term as GAC chairman expired; and neither he nor his masters had any itch to have it renewed. He was sent off with Mr. Truman's warmest thanks ("You have served your country well").

And then President Truman gave way to President Eisenhower, Lewis Strauss became the Atomic Energy Commission's chairman, and Malice put on the robes of Judgment.

Even though Strauss had not quite been tutored up to his pretensions as an amateur of science, he still deserved to be thought of as a professional of sorts, because he had so often profited as a banker alert to the market potential of the by-products of scientific curiosity. In the years when research funds still depended upon private generosity, he had been Enrico Fermi's patron; and now the federal budget had made him a dispenser of benefices so much more opulent that when he retired as AEC chairman, defense agencies were spending five times as much on scientific research as they had in the Second World War.

Strauss did not carry his empire in his eye. His face, with its rosy hue and the blandness of its spectacles, gave no hint of his resentments; and his manner infrequently deviated from an all-but-universal disbursement of deferences. The Strauss who had been obdurate when alone in the Commission's minority would be tyrannical as commander of its new majority.

Extremes in the worship of anything, even reason, inevitably arrive at superstition. Strauss had made of science a cult; and, all the time he was sure of himself as a child of the Enlightenment, his devotions bore him farther and farther back toward those smoking altars where men adored or shuddered before idols they thought either kind or malign but never indifferent.

For Strauss, science had become confused with magic; and since he saw Oppenheimer as the apotheosis of the scientist, he saw him as a species of wizard who would not withhold his powers for good unless he proposed to employ them for evil.

Oppenheimer had abandoned his resistance to the Super as soon as Mr. Truman had approved it; he had been scrupulous, if not quickly enough enthusiastic, about assisting its achievement; and then, having already laid down his arms, he had with no visible complaint yielded his office and withdrawn from the center of affairs.

The very propriety of such conduct was an especial disturbance to Lewis Strauss, whose own disposition so scorned the concept of majority rule that he never thought a question closed until it had been finally settled in his favor.

Insulating the Atomic Energy Commission from Oppenheimer was no problem at all: he was still on call as a consultant, but Strauss had only to abstain from taking the opportunity to consult him.

But in 1953 Strauss and Air Force Secretary Thomas Finletter learned that Oppenheimer had rebounded to a seat on the Office of Defense Mobilization's Scientific Advisory Committee, which had been moldering unnoticed until President Eisenhower suddenly adopted and lodged it in the National Security Council, the most private chamber in his household. This image of their presumed grand antagonist, his radiance rekindled, bearing his potions and reciting his incantations before the President himself, threw the Strategic Air Command and the AEC into the determination that there was no remedy for Robert Oppenheimer's contagions except to get him stripped of the security clearance that was his license.

He had obeyed the state too conscientiously to afford it an easy excuse to find points where he had strayed. He had, of course, been close to the Communists in the lost time when such sympathies were the private citizen's options; but he had candidly confessed his excursions, and even Lewis Strauss had assessed them as trivialities when the AEC reviewed them before approving Oppenheimer's security clearance six years before.

In the interim, to be sure, his security file had grown to a width of four feet and six inches from its birth late in the Thirties, when the FBI recorded him as a new subscriber to the *People's World*, a Communist daily. He himself had contributed little to its engorgement since his enlistment to Los Alamos; and the small scraps of his own giving had all been the consequences of the infrequent times when his official discipline had fleetingly been overcome by private feelings:

1) Late in the Thirties he had been informally betrothed to Jean Tatlock, an on-again, off-again member of the Berkeley unit of the Communist party. After their courses diverged, Jean Tatlock had wandered into those forests of depression that would lead her to suicide in 1944. At one point in the months before the end, she sent word to Oppenheimer that she was anxious to see him. He was too occupied to respond to her appeal until June 1943; but he must have been touched in places he had thought forgotten, because he missed the Los Alamos train to sit with her, talking through the night in her father's house.

Oppenheimer did not yet know that he had embarked upon an existence that did not hold many hours of unobserved privacy. His government's agents had watched them enter the Tatlock home and had remained outside it until the next morning when she drove him to the airport.

2) During his affair with the Left, Oppenheimer's nearest and most mutually ill-fortuned masculine friendship had been with Haakon Chevalier, who taught French at Berkeley. Chevalier's romantic and innocent ardor for the Marxist-Leninist simplicities endured after Oppenheimer's disenchantment with them; but their personal affections survived. One evening, while Oppenheimer was mixing their martinis, Chevalier told him that he had been approached by an industrial chemist on the lookout for physicists who might be willing to use the Soviet consulate as conduit for transmitting information to Russian scientists.

Oppenheimer's only recollected comment was, "That would be a terrible thing to do." But later he had thought it no less than his duty to warn the authorities against the intrusive chemist without identifying Chevalier as his go-between.

This effort to serve both his friend and his nation failed so utterly that the government's agents did not relax their pressure until he surrendered Chevalier's name. He had revealed the weakness that those who thought they knew him best would be the last to impute to him; he was a man who could be bullied.

With this revelation, Chevalier's career commenced a steady decline; and now and then, from promptings livelier in his conscience than his affections, we may suppose, Oppenheimer would make a feeble stab at clearing his name.

3) Communism had attracted—or as the Fifties would prefer to say, infect-

ed—several of his Berkeley graduate students. In 1949 the House Un-American Activities Commitee called him to an inquiry on two or three of them. By now Oppenheimer was thoroughly infused with the developing spirit of his age and in that key he poured out his direct suspicions of Bernard Peters, who had come to California as an exile from Nazi Germany and had gone on to teach physics at the University of Rochester.

Oppenheimer told the Committee that Peters had brought with him to California an abounding fraternal affection for the German Communists, beside whom he had fought Nazi gangs in the Berlin streets before being imprisoned in Dachau, from which he had escaped by guile. To Oppenheimer any such history betrayed a character "not pointing to temperance," an assessment most curiously founded upon little more evidence than the indications of light-mindedness that Peters had shown when he had been so wanting in respect for Hitler's system of justice as to commit the insolence of levanting from one of its concentration camps.

The Committee had listened to Oppenheimer in an executive session and he had been sent away with a warm testimonial from Congressman Richard Nixon for this among so many even larger services to his country. He had felt secure against anyone outside the hearing room ever knowing what he had said about Peters; but he was about to learn how much more careless the government was with his secrets than he could ever be with its.

The Committee's staff provided a Rochester journalist with snippets of Oppenheimer's strictures on Peters; and their publication left the accused jobless and the accuser beset with protests from other physicists. The harm done Peters only too probably distressed him less than the damage he had inflicted upon himself with portions of his old fraternity. He sought to repair both with a letter to a Rochester newspaper, taking note of Peters's denial of affiliation with any Communist party anywhere and hoping that no word of his own would be taken as impugning "the honor and integrity [of] a brilliant student [and] a man of strong moral principles. . . ." That disclaimer seems to have been little meant and was even less effective; after a futile canvass for some haven in an American academy, Peters went off to teach in India.

An unhopeful attempt to comfort a woman the world thought a Communist and he once thought he loved, a failed essay at shielding a friend who may or may not have made a pass at espionage, and a halfhearted try at calling the dogs off someone against whom he himself had raised the scent—those three uneasy passages were the only departures from prescribed discretion that could be found against him by prosecutors whose obsessive curiosity was more than up to discovering any others.

But no more than this was more than enough. His judges needed those dry straws because they dared not engage the whole, awful bale. Oppenheimer's damning offense was the sin of moral qualm; he had contemplated the shadows of the thermonuclear age and shrunk back, however briefly, at a tidal point in what might or might not be man's march toward his own extinction.

This was inarguably a high crime, but it was one for which the spirit of his time forbade any man's condemnation. The Enlightenment is to be distinguished from the Age of Superstition not because it is invariably so much nicer in its treatment of heretics but because it would never burn one without being careful to condemn him for any and all sins except heresy.

Jean Tatlock, Haakon Chevalier, and Bernard Peters were broken fragments from long ago; but their excavation was essential to proceedings whose verdict could not be satisfactory unless it could contrive to define Robert Oppenheimer's departed past as his present. These minor trespasses adumbrated the major crime; his dealings in each case were signs of a piece of Robert Oppenheimer that some might think the redeeming piece: not even his upmost self-rigors could uniformly subsume the private into the public self. The same unruly heart had given itself away in the gesture of Jean Tatlock and the recoil from the specter of the Super.

Oppenheimer was tried before a three-member Personnel Security Board chosen by Lewis Strauss, a prosecutor uniquely blessed with the right to select his jury. The hearings lasted over three weeks and consumed some 990 pages of transcript. Large portions of them were engaged with inconclusive burrowings into the history of the hydrogen decision. Six of the eight prosecution witnesses gave evidence whose main import fell upon the bad advice they felt the accused had given to his masters.

Two of his three trial judges found Oppenheimer guilty. Their names are dust now but they were paladins in their day; and both were obedient to commands of a time never more zealous, with genuflections before the temple of liberty of thought in general, than when it was punishing somebody or other it suspected of liberty of thought in the particular.

Thus, they so wanted it understood that Oppenheimer's hesitations when faced with the Super were no crucial element in their judgment that they felt themselves impelled "to record [the board's] profound and positive view that no man should be tried for his opinions." What they could not forgive was Jean Tatlock, Haakon Chevalier, and Bernard Peters; a man could be tried for his ghosts.

Their findings were sent upward to the Atomic Energy Commission, where honest venom resided. Lewis Strauss himself undertook the composition of the AEC majority opinion that ruled Robert Oppenheimer unfit for future service.

"The work of Military Intelligence, the Federal Bureau of Investigation and the Atomic Energy Commission—all at one time or another have felt the effect of his falsehoods and misrepresentations."

After these savage rites there followed the customary national drill of accommodation. Oppenheimer was allowed to wither with every material comfort. He was still director of the Institute for Advanced Study, and Strauss was still a trustee, and each kept his place.

The motion to retain Oppenheimer was, in fact, tendered to the institute's board by the same man who had, only three months before, officially found him to have "lived far below acceptable standards of reliability and trustworthiness." If Strauss's principles had been the equal of his rancors, he might better have given the board the option of finding either a new director or a new trustee; but he had sounded the temper of his fellow trustees, and he preferred to keep one of his honors at whatever expense to his honor and did not press his vengeance beyond the limits of his convenience.

Whatever outrage any of the physicists felt never extended to troubling anyone above and beyond their own specialized community, and soon stopped troubling even them. Edward Teller was snubbed at the first physics conference he attended after the revelation that he had been a witness for the prosecution at Oppenheimer's trial. But there was no change in the deference of the physicists when they encountered the formidable Strauss; the unassailable immunity is reserved for the man who pays.

Enrico Fermi and I. I. Rabi had joined Oppenheimer in the General Advisory Committee's early remonstrance against the Super; and yet Strauss went on showering them with his blessings and they went on rejoicing in them. Perhaps the distinction between democratic and totalitarian societies is in economy of victimization: totalitarians suppress wholesale and democrats, when a like fit is upon them, manage a decent retail measure of the same effect by pillorying a representative specimen of a class and depending upon his example to cow the rest of its members. It could now be understood that Robert Oppenheimer was the archetype of the physicist not least because he was someone who could be bullied.

In the summer of 1945 he had done what he could to convince a doubting Teller that this country's governors were "the best and most conscientious men . . . who had information that the rest of us did not possess."

He had believed those words, against increasingly intimate access to contrary evidence, all the while his glory blazed; and even now, when it had been extinguished, he seemed somehow to believe them still. Government, not Krishna, and not even science, had turned out to be God for him; as there could be no disrupting a government's decision to immolate Hiroshima, there could be no real disputing its decision to immolate him.

When the curious approached with questions about himself and his life, he would often recommend the closest attention to the transcript of the Hearings of the Atomic Energy Commission in the Matter of J. Robert Oppenheimer. This record of his degradation seemed almost to have become for him the authorized biography; but then, it bore the authority always most requisite for him: it was a government document.

One day, shortly after his disgrace, he sat with a visitor painfully better acquainted with his history than his person.

"What bothers me," Robert Oppenheimer said, "is the complicity."

But where, his visitor wondered, did the complicity lie?

Was it in making the atomic or resisting the hydrogen bomb, in denouncing Bernard Peters or defending Bernard Peters, in leaving Jean Tatlock or returning to her for a few skimpy hours in the night, in hurting Haakon Chevalier or trying to help him, in serving his government too unquestioningly or not questioningly enough—in all the mess we make of life and life makes of us, just where do we locate and house the complicity?

"In all of it," Robert Oppenheimer answered.

The point of him? Who can feel safe in saying? A clutch at a guess might be the sense that it is probably an illusion that any one man much alters history even in the short run, and it is certainly a fact that history crushes every man in the long and that Robert Oppenheimer can touch us still because he was one of the few of those who have lived with both the illusion of being history's conqueror and the fact of being its victim.

But that is a surmise too grand for the almost domestic thoughts that start when we look at his eyes in the old photographs and confront some inexplicable nobility, of stuff so adamant that it can be passed through every variety of the ignoble, do the worst and have the worst done to itself, and somehow shine through all its trash and its trashing.

His death was discreet and his memorial service impeccable. The Juilliard played the Beethoven C-sharp Minor Quartet at the funeral, up through but not beyond the adagio movement. We ought to assume that his was the choice of the C-sharp Minor and that his was the decision to cut it short. Personages of consequence would come to his funeral and bring with them a few troubles of the conscience; and it had never been his way to make uncomfortable the bottoms of his betters.

But all the same, dying as he had living, he had tried to find some means of expressing at once his sense of his own culture and the perfection of his manners.

The C-sharp Minor had been the emblem that Oppenheimer and the aspiring theoretical physicists at his feet in Berkeley had held up to proclaim the difference between their own refinement and the crudities of those stranger cousins, the experimentalists.

Now his votaries were scattered, a few by the main force of public contumely, one chased to India, another to Brazil, and he himself dead, each in his exile.

Young and obscure though they were then, they would have been much too pure to distract themselves from their reveries over the C-sharp Minor to read the program notes and discover that Beethoven had instructed his publisher that "it must be dedicated to Lieutenant General Field Marshal Von Stutterheim." All the while, the portrait of the warrior had hung upon the walls of the little rooms where they dreamed, incarnating the future that would be the unpitying judge of each and all.

NOTE: For many of the facts that sometimes bob up in the above ruminations I have a debt to three works: *Lawrence and Oppenheimer,* by Nuel Pharr Davis (Simon and Schuster, 1968); *The Oppenheimer Case,* by Phillip Stern (Harper & Row, 1969); and Oppenheimer's own preference, the transcript of his ordeal the AEC issued as "In the Matter of J. Robert Oppenheimer" (MIT Press, 1970).

———————

J. ROBERT OPPENHEIMER *was born on April 22, 1904, in New York City. The "J" stood for nothing: his father, a wealthy textile importer, felt that "Robert Oppenheimer" was not distinguished enough.*

At the Ethical Culture School in New York, where he took all the math and science courses available, plus Greek, Latin, French, and German, the young Oppenheimer refused to climb the stairs to the second floor. A note was sent home to his parents: "Please teach your son to walk up stairs; he is holding up class."

As an undergraduate, he once wrote: "It was so hot today the only thing I could do was lie on my bed and read Jeans's Dynamical Theory of Gases."

Oppenheimer graduated from Harvard, summa cum laude, in 1925, then worked at Cambridge University under physicist Ernest Rutherford. He was granted a Ph.D. from the Georgia Augusta University of Göttingen, Germany, in 1927. The professor who administered his Ph.D. orals said, "Phew, I'm glad that's over. He was on the point of questioning me."

Later in his career, many colleagues would comment on his ability to give them an answer before they had formulated the question.

Sometimes Oppenheimer learned a language just to read a work in the original. He learned Italian to read Dante—it took about a month. As a young man, he mastered enough Dutch in six weeks to deliver a technical lecture in the Netherlands. At thirty, he learned Sanskrit and read the Bhagavad-Gita *in the original. He enjoyed passing notes to other savants in that language.*

In speech, he habitually separated his paragraphs with an odd lilting sound, something like nim-nim-nim. *Physicist Wolfgang Pauli called him "the* nim-nim-nim *man."*

Early students called him Opje, a Dutch version of "little Oppenheimer." He was Oppie to his students at Berkeley. His wife, Kitty, attempted to reintroduce "Robert," but eventually she stopped trying.

One night he and a female student went driving and stopped in the Berkeley Hills. Oppenheimer excused himself for a moment to get some fresh air. Walking, he began thinking about a physics problem. He continued thinking and walking— all the way back to Berkeley's faculty club, where, still pondering, he got into bed. An hour or two later, policemen discovered an irate young woman sitting in an abandoned automobile.

He stood six feet tall and never weighed more than 130 pounds. During the years of the atomic bomb project, his weight slipped to 113 pounds.

He moved with an odd gait—a jog of sorts, with much swinging of limbs, head cocked a little to one side, one shoulder higher than the other.

His eyes were a vivid blue.

His hair, which he secretly groomed with a dog's steel comb, was coarse, thick, and curly and was said to form "a halo" around his head. It was dark in 1943, gray by 1954, and white a few years later.

Shortly after the bombing of Hiroshima, he visited President Truman at the White House. "Mr. President," Oppenheimer said slowly, "I feel I have blood on my hands." Truman was stunned for a second; then he reached into his pocket, pulled out a neatly folded handkerchief, and offered it to the scientist. "Would you like to wipe them?" he asked in a hollow voice.

"There are people who say they are not such very bad weapons," Oppenheimer told an audience of scientists after the Hiroshima detonation. "Before the New Mexico test we sometimes said that too. . . . After the test we did not say it anymore."

Though clumsy in most sports, he was an excellent sailor and particularly enjoyed sailing in storms. His twenty-eight-foot sloop was named Trimethy—*a short version of a chemical compound, trimethylene dioxide, for which he had a special affection. In later years he became a superb equestrian.*

His ranch in the New Mexico mountains was named Perro Caliente, or "hot dog," which is what he exclaimed the first time he saw it.

He had a notoriously strange palate. He once made a rancher neighbor a dinner of pepperoni loaf and Limburger cheese. His most famous dish was green chili and scrambled eggs, also known as eggs à la Opje. Yet he often treated friends and graduate students to fancy meals in fancy restaurants. His own appetite was dangerously meager.

The gardenia was his favorite flower. Whenever he went to dinner or a concert with friends, he bought a gardenia for every woman in the party.

He liked to watch Perry Mason *on TV. On Sunday nights he liked to play poker.*

He died of throat cancer on February 18, 1967, in Princeton, New Jersey.

The Life
and Time
of Henry Luce

WILLIAM F. BUCKLEY JR.

IT WAS IN MIDSUMMER 1965 THAT I ARRIVED AT THEIR FIFTH AVENUE APARTMENT TO
have dinner with Clare Luce before undertaking an editorial chore together.
Henry Luce was not there—"He's gone to dinner at the Council on Foreign
Relations," my hostess explained, "but he'll probably be back before you
leave." We ate, although this only after I had been given a class in painting with
acrylics. After dinner, with coffee and liqueurs we entered the small, formal
library with the leather-bound books and the understated austerity: a comfortable room, suited to transact business. The business at hand was to devise a letter to be signed by Clare Boothe Luce. It would go to fifty
luminaries, inviting them to join the committee on which she was serving as
chairman to commemorate the tenth anniversary of *National Review* at a
banquet in November. "We need to phrase it *just* right," she said, putting
on her glasses to look over the draft I had brought in. She fussed with one
word, then another, finally pronounced herself satisfied. At this point Luce
walked in, dressed in black tie, wearing a black fedora. He greeted me, with a
quick nod of the head I came to know as characteristic and with a mumble

186

of sorts, and instantly (he did everything instantly) asked what was it we were up to, and Clare told him.

He had sat down, having poured himself a Scotch and soda and lit a cigarette. "Let me see it," he extended his hand, edging the floor lamp that stood between him and Clare over slightly toward him. He read with concentration while Clare resumed the story she had embarked on before his arrival.

Grunt.

He rose, walked over to the large desk, fished about for a pencil, and started his own editing. This took several minutes, after which he thrust the revised version at me; thought for a moment; retrieved it, and handed it to his wife. "Have a look at that," he said, a trace of the drill sergeant in voice and manner.

Clare did not approve one of his changes, and they wrestled over this for four or five minutes. He contrived a substitute phrase, wrote it down, and then handed the document over to me. I read it. "That is just fine," I commented, as who would not have done under the circumstances.

Ten weeks later I sat at the *National Review* dinner on the dais between Luce and John Dos Passos. During dinner small talk, which was when Henry Robinson Luce could look most bored, I said to him, "Harry"—for a most formal man, he was curiously insistent on being addressed by his Christian name, which he had instructed me to do at our second meeting—"I'm going to hang on to the original letter that brought this gang here. Probably the most expensive editorial attention ever given to 150 words—'edited by Clare Boothe Luce and Henry R. Luce.'" He looked at me, and at first I thought I would need to repeat myself, because he was quite deaf, and when the ambient babbling was loud I had seen him simply give up, internalizing his lively thoughts, rather than struggling to hear badinage he was presumptively uninterested in going to the effort of deciphering. But after a pause he said, "I'm not an editor."

The statement was spoken as arrant aposiopesis. I was required to say, "What do you *mean*, you're not an editor?"

"I'm a promoter."

I remember that Willi Schlamm, who had been very close to Luce for a half dozen years, once told me that Luce's proudest moment had come not when *Life* magazine became, after *Reader's Digest*, the most prosperous magazine venture in America. Not when Dwight Eisenhower was nominated for President and Luce was given primary credit. Not with the publication of the one-hundredth profile of Henry Luce, "The Man Who Reshaped American Journalism." The nearest—said Schlamm—that Luce had ever come to secular elation was when Time Inc. made it into the Fortune 500 top-earning corporations in America. Luce was a businessman trained, by temperament and background, to resist corporate sentimentality as he might a temptress deputized to seduce him from commercial rectitude. I recalled that (through his secretary) he had a year or so earlier accepted a request to bankroll a farewell dinner for a departing Taiwanese diplomat, representative in the United Nations of what they used to call the Government of China. When the bill was sent in by the dinner's impresario, a check came back but for five hundred dollars less. A call to the secretary got only, "Mr. Luce thought the bill too high."

Yet it wasn't penuriousness that made Henry Luce a remarkable business-man. The farewell-party business had been mere reflex, of the kind he occa-sionally shot back with when he suspected exploitation. His special acumen didn't come from knowing how (or caring) to cut corners to effect economies. It came from his confidence that the reading public could be expected to respond to the editorial leadership of a very bright, industrious, and inquisitive man who had a sense of the public appetite. So what, then, was Luce promoting? The marginal subscriber for *Time* magazine?

Yes, in one sense. But in doing so he thought of himself as promoting Amer-ica. Reading *Time* was conceived as a moral, civic, and literary experience of a normative kind. About a special country. For Luce, America was something of a national incarnation; God-led. "What they really couldn't stand in Harry," Clare Luce has said, "was that he believed in God."

A great deal has been written (including much I haven't read) about Henry Luce and his version of the American Proposition. Some of what is written is motivated by ideological hostility, which so readily evolves into personal hostil-ity. Henry Luce made enemies in proportion as he was successful. This was so because his showcase magazine—*Time*—during the late Thirties, the Forties, and Fifties, decided more authoritatively than any other institution this side of the White House what would be the terms of the national debate. And then *Time* had the power, gleefully exercised, to make or break authors, artists, dramatists, and politicians. Luce could sometimes kindle, and always he could fan, movements that would then become national, among them the movement to enter the war against Hitler, the movement to stand by the Christian alterna-tive in China, the desirability of nominating and then electing Eisenhower as President. Luce managed this by conscripting extraordinary literary talents, and by infusing into *Time* an organizing bias that had roots in the Calvinism of the minister's son, the unblushing patriotism of the expatriate boy brought up in China, and the savoir faire of an Ivy League graduate who in college had risen, together with the cofounder of his empire, Briton Hadden, to occupy the two top extra-athletic positions on campus, respectively managing editor and chairman of the *Yale Daily News*, the principal cockpit of power and prestige in those fleeted days of exuberance, high life, and editorial energy (*The New Yorker, Reader's Digest,* and *Time* were founded in the space of three years). For all that the writing style of *Time* was often mannered, it reflected the work of editorial talents from Middle America, so that if his journal sometimes seemed supercilious, the reader was getting the high wit and lusty talent of ut-terly indigenous Americans arguing the conventional virtues. "When we were married, in 1935," Mrs. Luce reminisces, "two thirds of the writers of Time Inc. came from west of the Alleghenies." She meant by that that it was west of the Alleghenies that writers tended to grow who were in more direct touch with the America that invigorated the heart and mind of Henry Luce.

But being American and successful were not enough to cause it to be said that he had "reshaped American journalism." Or to say—as Lord Beaverbrook did—that Henry Luce had reshaped journalism everywhere. How?

To begin with, he had invented the newsmagazine. It was a significant stylistic accomplishment, for one thing, and most people have heard about the dismal prognoses of Luce's friends and friends' parents when approached with the invitation to invest money in a magazine that would report what had happened as long ago as ten days. In order to sustain an interest in the preceding week's news, it became necessary to invest it with meaning, and to enhance its value as entertainment. This Luce knew how to achieve. He knew also to invest the whole of it with an interpretation, which is where his quality as an evangelist became relevant. Tell what happened, tell it well, tell it concisely, but with attention to the belletristic imperative. Relate it to what *should* happen: fuse it into the long morality play that began, really, in the Garden of Eden.

And so it was not only the competitive newsmagazines that learned from Luce, but also the newspapers, which now widened their horizons, paid more attention to style, meaning, moral dimension. And to the challenge of fusing news and opinion.

Dick Clurman, for so long chief of correspondents of Time Inc. and an intimate of the editor in chief, received a telephone call. The end result was an insight into Henry Luce's own thinking, or lack of it, about the nature of his own accomplishments. It appeared he had to lecture that night at Brandeis to four hundred bright students (there being no others at Brandeis) and wished to be coached en route to the airport. He intended, he told Clurman in the limousine, to devote the evening primarily to questions and answers. "What will they ask me?"

"Well, Harry, the first question they will ask you is the obvious one, the one all of us get asked twenty times a week. Which is, How can *Time* call itself a newsmagazine when it is so full of opinion?"

"What shall I answer?"

"You're asking *me* how to answer that?"

"Yes."

So Clurman obliged. It took about ten minutes, and Luce professed himself as satisfied. A few hours later the correspondent of *Time* in Boston, who had accompanied Luce to the lecture, called Clurman to report that the boss had done very well.

"Did they ask him the one about *Time*'s being called a newsmagazine when it is so full of opinion?"

"Uh-huh."

"How'd he handle it?"

"Well, he paused for quite a long while. Then he said, 'I invented the idea, so I guess I can call it anything I like.'"

It worked. With the audience at Brandeis, even as it had worked, still does, with the large audience that subscribes to it, and to its imitators.

The question is reasonably asked whether *Time* magazine resonantly transcribed the idealism of its founder and editor. Certain of his penchants it certainly did. The comprehensive curiosity, for one thing. Luce happens on a little biography of Dante, by Professor Thomas Bergin of Yale—and practically the whole of the book section is given over to it. Political attitudes? *Time* was routinely referred to as "conservative," and this was true in the idiomatic sense of the word—Henry Luce was a registered Republican. But although *Time* would be put to missionary uses, it was never, really, messianic; it never sustained protracted engagements, and that was because Henry Luce, Promoter, had a sense of the limited staying power of the public, whose attention he could engage but only for so long ("I'm tired of anticommunism," he was heard to say in the mid-Fifties). He told a colleague that he owed his success to his ability to stay three weeks ahead of the public. By doing so, he suggested, he could edit a magazine that capitalized on latent curiosity or burgeoning passion. If Henry Luce had had only the editorial intelligence of the common reader, his journal would have sounded flat. If he had had a sibylline editorial intelligence, his journal would have sounded cranky, or avant-garde. His formula—self-confidence, literary flair, apparent omniscience—taxonomized in retrospect, sounds obvious. So does the *Reader's Digest* formula of DeWitt Wallace. But then the formula for the wheel is also obvious, Pizarro thought, marveling that the civilization of the Incas, so advanced in so many ways, had not thought to devise one.

What, one repeats, was Henry Luce promoting, besides the price of Time stock? He was constantly attempting to decoct from the American experience a few social universals. I do not know the story of their personal association, but his attraction to Father John Courtney Murray, the learned and eloquent Jesuit scholar, was overwhelming. And when Father Murray wrote his book, *We Hold These Truths*, which argued the uses of pluralism in the context of a Christian eschatology, suggesting that a remarkable union of the secular and the divine had come together in America, Henry Luce put Father Murray and his book on the cover of *Time*. Did all of this sink home in America? Today Father Murray's book is out of print, the house that published it is defunct, the seminary where Father Murray taught closed. *Time* magazine thrives. America struggles somewhere in between.

In January 1967, my wife and I were houseguests of Barry Goldwater in Phoenix. I was to give a speech to local Republicans, and Mr. and Mrs. Henry Luce had a dinner party for us to which forty or fifty of the city's select were invited. The dinner took a very long time, and although his manners were exemplary, it became obvious that Henry R. Luce wanted to crank up some interesting conversation so that, when later on that night he went to bed, he would not attempt repose in the iniquity of an entire evening heedlessly spent. So the dessert was barely finished when he began clanking his spoon against his water glass and clearing his throat. He announced then what in most households was, in those days, routine; but the thought of excluding Clare Boothe Luce from men's conversation struck me, then as now, as something that could be done only by a Great Promoter promoting suicide. But she went off with the ladies, with injunctions that we were not to spend too long in celibate conversation. And Luce turned to me and said that since I was on my way to Vietnam, I should perhaps let the guests know what were my thoughts on that "protracted encounter."

I decided to run a risk, intending two things: the first to evaluate the performance of Barry Goldwater under the circumstances, the second to judge the reaction of Henry Luce (and Governor Williams of Arizona and others) to that performance. The circumstances were that the meal had taken nearly two and one half hours to serve, and during the whole of that period a waitress, obviously enamored of Senator Goldwater and noticing that the senator took no wine, kept his glass discreetly full of bourbon. Here was the man who, if three years before the voters had gone the other way, would now be living in the White House. How would he perform, during a night of relaxation, under sudden social pressure?

"Harry," I said, "Senator Goldwater has just come back from Vietnam. Why don't we ask *him* for his views?"

I took a deep breath. Senator Goldwater stood, a little shakily. He then proceeded, in ten minutes, to give his reading of the situation in Vietnam, touching on the military, political, geopolitical, and historical picture in a briefing that could not have been done better by Thomas Babington Macaulay. Luce was visibly impressed, both by the analysis and by the forensic performance. Others were then heard from, we joined the ladies, and in due course the guests left. At the door Luce asked if I might drop by the next morning.

He was dressed in a red smoking jacket, in his study, with thirty newspapers and magazines and a pile of correspondence on his desk. "You know," he said, lighting a cigarette, "I've been thinking about the subject we should discuss on your television program in May. Let's scrub the business about the responsibility of magazines. I want to talk about the World Council of Churches."

"What about the World Council of Churches?" I asked.

"You know, I've been involved with those people for a long time, and every year at the annual meeting they first denounce hunger and then denounce capitalism." He permitted himself a tight smile. "I'm going to tell them in Geneva, 'Gentlemen, here are the facts. Now: Denounce either hunger *or* capitalism.'" He smiled, and puffed on his cigarette. "What do you think?"

I said I thought that would be just fine. But a month later he was dead. It wasn't until quite a bit later that I decided that I, and the good old U.S.A., and all those who hold these truths, miss that strange, shy, arrogant, reclusive, gregarious, curious man who, yes, reshaped American journalism.

HENRY LUCE *was born in Tengchow, China, on April 3, 1898, the son of Presbyterian ministers from Scranton, Pennsylvania.*

When he was thirteen, in China, he became obsessed with the Yale entrance exam qualifications. His mother said, "He is the queerest child."

He learned Chinese before he learned English and his Chinese name, Lu-Ssu-i, translates into "one who seeks righteousness." At the Hotchkiss School in Connecticut he was nicknamed Chink.

On his college board Greek exams he scored the highest marks in the country. He was voted "most brilliant" when he graduated from Yale. For his part he found America not "as good as I knew she could be, as I believe she was intended to be."

When he was twenty-four he decided on a name for his magazine after seeing a subway advertisement: "Time to Retire or Time for a Change." (Later, he often left parties abruptly or interrupted conversations by glancing at his watch and saying, "Time to go.")

He wrote, "Not for one sentimental cause shed one small tear." He was a political propagandist and hated communism. In 1928 he advocated fascism as a more orderly form of government for the United States; he thought it could provide national discipline and loyalty.

He stuttered. He was precise, deadly serious, impatient, and loath to engage in small talk. He customarily wore a frown.

His first wife, Lila, tried to slow down her hard-driving husband. She wrote him, "I am going to kidnap you and take you to some leafy solitude . . . to laugh." They divorced after twelve years.

His second wife, journalist and playwright Clare Boothe Luce, became a U.S. congresswoman and U.S. ambassador to Italy. When she first met Luce she found him dull and boorish.

Clare and Henry learned about LSD from a doctor who was researching the drug. Under the doctor's guidance the couple took their first trip together, to "investigate the possibility of a better order in one's living." They found the experience rewarding. Luce, who was tone deaf, said he heard marvelous music. They tripped another half dozen times.

Every morning as Luce rode the elevator to his office on the thirty-sixth floor he prayed to God. No one was allowed to ride in the elevator with him, lest his train of thought be interrupted. Later, Luce, feeling undemocratic, relented and let people ride with him.

He went to Sunday mass regularly and never went to bed without praying on his knees. He knew many religious scholars.

He became a journalist to come as close as possible to "the heart of the world." Of Time *magazine he said, "I am all for titillating trivialities. I am all for the epic touch. I could almost say that everything in* Time *should be either titillating or epic or starkly, super-curtly factual."*

Among the writers who have served time on Luce publications are Archibald

MacLeish, James Agee, John Hersey, Theodore H. White, Dwight MacDonald, and John Kenneth Galbraith.

He said, "We have the H-bomb, and we have Sports Illustrated. These are the two instant symbols of our fears and of our hopes."

He received an annual Time Inc. stock dividend of over $1.25 million. His Calvinist upbringing left him slightly embarrassed about his wealth.

Luce reminded John F. Kennedy of his own father. "I like Luce," said JFK. "He is like a cricket, always chirping away. After all, he made a lot of money through his own individual enterprise so he naturally thinks that individual enterprise can do everything. I don't mind people like that. They have earned the right to talk that way. . . ."

While living in Rome he grew fond of the polar bears in the zoo and often brought them food. When a Time editor came to Rome to discuss setting up a British Time, Luce told him, "The zoo keepers have some sort of cake the bears like better than the stuff I bring, but I'm going to find out what it is."

His nearly bare office was dominated by a wall-size map of the world. His one regret was that he never had an American hometown to use as a reference, a way of explaining his character.

He insisted upon being taken to Haight-Ashbury a few days before his death, to see what the "far-out young" were up to.

On February 27, 1967, he checked into a Phoenix hospital with a slight temperature. At around three A.M. the following morning he got out of bed, went to the bathroom, and shrieked, "Oh, Jesus!" A nurse came running, only to find him dead of a coronary occlusion. He was buried in Mepkin, South Carolina.

John L. Lewis, Union General

VICTOR NAVASKY

WHEN GOVERNOR FRANK MURPHY OF MICHIGAN TOLD JOHN L. LEWIS THAT IF A SIT-down strike at the General Motors plant in Flint wasn't called off he would have to call out the National Guard, Lewis knit his famous eyebrows and gave the governor his answer.

"Tomorrow morning," he thundered (according to his various biographers, Lewis was always thundering), "I shall order the men to disregard your order, to stand fast. I shall then walk up to the largest window in the plant, open it, divest myself of my outer raiment, remove my shirt, and bare my bosom. Then when you order your troops to fire, mine will be the first breast that the bullets will strike."

Then Lewis lowered his voice. "And as my body falls from that window to the ground, you listen to the voice of your grandfather [a member of the IRA who had fought the British troops] as he whispers in your ear, 'Frank, are you sure you are doing the right thing?' " The governor departed, white and shaking, and never issued the order.

Such, at least, is part of the lore and legend surrounding the miner and miner's son who ruled the United Mine Workers of America from 1919 until he was retired, in 1960, and whose bushy eyebrows became as much a part of the national iconography as FDR's cigarette holder. Even though John L. told this story on himself, it has the ring of what he might have called verisimilitude.

The biblical oratory, patronizing rococo style, and violent imagery are all in his inimitable voice, which I would argue is not the least of his legacies. The coal diggers, who worked in inky caverns under the threat of falling roofs, crashing coal cars, recurring explosions, and black lung, took sneaky pride in and not a little courage from the way Lewis presented their case—as he himself once put it, "not in the quavering tones of a mendicant asking alms, but in the thundering voice of the captain of a mighty host, demanding the right to which free men are entitled."

It didn't hurt that in 1933, with the union on the brink of collapse, John L. Lewis provided his own liberal translation of Section 7A of the recently passed National Industrial Recovery Act, which guaranteed workers "the right to organize unions of their own choosing." Under the slogan, The President wants you to join the union!, he risked the entire treasury on an organizing drive. The result: A threefold jump in membership and bituminous-coal code that granted the UMW what it had been struggling for since 1890—such unheard-of items as the eight-hour day and five-day week and the abolition of child labor, scrip, and mandatory trading in the company store and living in company housing. In other words, as Howard Brubaker wrote in *The New Yorker* at the time, Lewis won from the defeated mine owners "all the things the deputy sheriffs usually shoot people for demanding."

But for his men his victories were enhanced by and became indistinguishable from his voice. They knew he was a dictator and they preferred not to ask how many bodies he had buried to win the factional fights that led to his consolidation of control as they basked in the sunshine of his rhetoric, which always seemed to draw new energy from their unspoken yearnings.

That was true even when he resorted to what a later generation would term body language. In 1935, for example, John L. decided it was time to organize "the unorganizable," the unskilled mass production workers, and to do it industry by industry, thereby challenging the jurisdictionally jealous craft unionism of the AFL, of which the UMW was still a member. Those who attended the AFL's 1935 Atlantic City convention still debate whether the punch Lewis landed on the nose of the three-hundred-pound leader of the Carpenters' Union was premeditated or spontaneous. But no one doubts that it had resonance among the increasingly militant rank and file.

This was a time of virtual class warfare. The National Guard was called out more than a dozen times a year; strikes were broken not only by goons and ginks and company finks, in the words of the old labor song, but by tear gas and machine guns. And when a particularly disdainful Chrysler president asked for Lewis's comment in the midst of a negotiation inspired by a spontaneous sitdown at Chrysler, the six-foot-two Lewis stood up and said, "I am ninety-nine percent of a mind to come around the table right now and wipe that damn sneer off your face." Lee Pressman, of the new CIO, later observed, "Lewis's voice at that moment was in every sense the voice of millions of unorganized workers who were exploited by gigantic corporations. He was expressing at that instant their resentment, hostility, and their passionate desire to strike back."

After autos, Lewis and the CIO quickly moved in on rubber, electricity, aluminum. With the UMW providing an estimated 88 percent of the CIO's treasury, what was happening was "a fundamental, almost revolutionary change in the power relationships of American society," in the words of the labor historian Walter Galenson.

He tooled around in a Cadillac, wearing custom-made Sulka underwear, but this did not diminish his capacity to communicate the aspirations of the rank and file. Rather, such accoutrements put him on a negotiating par with those across the table—not to mention such other peers as the President of the United States. When FDR lumped labor with management, declaring his famous "plague on both your houses" (because Little Steel and big John L. were unable to come to terms), Lewis intoned (when he was not thundering, he was intoning): "Labor, like Israel, has many sorrows. Its women weep for their fallen, and they lament for the future of the children of the race. It ill-behooves one who has supped at labor's table and who has been sheltered in labor's house to curse with equal fervor and fine impartiality both labor and its adversaries when they become locked in deadly embrace."

The "sup" to which he had reference was a $500,000 UMW contribution to FDR's 1936 campaign. Lewis was unabashed about demanding his money's worth. "Everybody says I want my pound of flesh, that I gave Roosevelt five hundred thousand dollars for his 1936 campaign, and I want quid pro quo. The United Mine Workers and the CIO have paid cash on the barrel for every piece of legislation that we have gotten. . . . Is anyone fool enough to believe for one instant that we gave this money to Roosevelt because we are spellbound by his voice?"

Lewis opposed FDR for reelection in 1940 and predicted his loss so loudly that when the President won his unprecedented third term, Lewis voluntarily resigned as head of the CIO and went back to full-time duty on behalf of his mine workers. But it never occurred to him to shut up. On the eve of America's entry into World War II, the President of the United States appealed to the patriotism of the president of the United Mine Workers, the only labor leader who had refused to join the wartime no-strike pledge. The uninterrupted production of coal, he wrote, was necessary for the making of steel, "the basic material for our national defense." He asked Lewis to "come to the aid of your country."

Although Lewis was rarely photographed smiling ("That scowl is worth a million dollars," he once confided to a friend), one can see the demon gleam in his eye as he scratched out his answer. "If you want to use the power of state to restrain me, as an agent of labor, then, sir, I submit that you should use the same power to restrain my adversary in this issue, who is an agent of capital. My adversary is a rich man named Morgan, who lives in New York." Signed, in letters which ran two and a half inches tall, "Yours humbly."

On the occasion of the UMW's third walkout in defiance of the War Labor Board directive, *Stars and Stripes* ran a cartoon showing Lewis throwing dirt over the grave of a soldier in Africa. The accompanying editorial said, "Speaking for the American soldier, John L. Lewis, damn your coal black soul." Although his willingness to stand alone won him the hatred of his country, it made Lewis that much more of a hero to his coal miners, and by 1949 he had won them the highest wages of any workers in the fifteen major industries in America.

It was only later—after he retired to preside over the UMW's Welfare and Retirement Fund (a radical innovation in its day, it ministered to the broken bodies of his men) and quieted down—that he came to be regarded as something of a labor statesman.

There was a time when the boys would jump into a cab at Union Station and simply say, "Take me to John L. Lewis." Consider the look of consternation that would cross the cab driver's face if today one of them said, "Take me to Richard L. Trumka."

Trumka, a thirty-three-year-old, quiet miner-lawyer, was elected president in 1982 by a surprising 68 percent of the vote in what was supposed to be a close race against incumbent Samuel Church Jr., also not exactly a household word. Although a Thor-like bust of Lewis confronts visitors on their way to see Trumka, his matter-of-fact style suggests that the miners no longer look for thunderbolts from their leader.

It is tempting to think that the proletarian heroes of yesteryear—and that's what John L. Lewis was, Sulka underwear notwithstanding—have been replaced by invisible reformers and bureaucrats because the victories of Lewis et al. converted blue-collar workers to white-collar life-styles. And it's true that many of today's working coal miners have been to college and to Europe and own their own homes and cars. But the fact is that the UMW is beset with troubles. Forty thousand miners were laid off last year and are paying reduced dues. Lewis, who welcomed automation (he called it mechanization), used to say it was better to have half a million men working in the industry at good wages and high standards of living than it was to have a million in poverty and degradation. But today's active membership is down to 155,000.

Nor is the UMW alone. The decline of basic industries, the rise of high technology, the move to a service sector economy, the emergence of the multinational conglomerate, and the vagaries of global economics have conspired to undermine the American labor movement. Indeed, only a little more than 20 percent of the entire work force is unionized, the major unions are fighting wage decreases rather than winning wage increases, and there are twelve million unemployed.

The workers won their greatest gains in the Thirties only after sit-downs, bloody confrontations, broken court injunctions, and all sorts of good old-fashioned civil disobedience. All of that changed with World War II when the labor movement (*except* for John L.) made its Faustian bargain and, in the name of patriotism, gave up its militancy for security. Then followed the purge of leftists (with all of the energy and organizing skills they represented), and it was not long before the major unions became card-carrying members in the military-industrial complex. Labor had lost its momentum. Even John L. Lewis began to see himself as something of a labor statesman whose job it was to work with the coal industry to anticipate and solve its problems. With his retirement, the passing of A. Philip Randolph of the Brotherhood of Sleeping Car Porters, the airplane-crash death of Walter Reuther, and the mysterious disappearance of Jimmy Hoffa, the voice of labor seems, despite much bluster, rarely to rise above a whisper.

And yet for the unemployed and a majority of the working-but-not-yet-organized, conditions today are reminiscent of nothing so much as 1933, when the conventional wisdom was that the United Mine Workers of America was finished and the mass production workers were unorganizable. Today's dispossessed may be more polite, but it could be a mistake to count them out. A movement can lose touch with its history but can't escape it. The Lewis legacy still reverberates and reminds all who care to listen that government is the servant of the people (which is why he treated all public officials, from the President on down, as his servants); that although they should make damn sure to collect all political debts, trade unions need be beholden to no political party; that sometimes social justice can be purchased only at the price of civic unrest and personal obloquy; and that when rank-and-file discomfort and civil disobedience finds its voice, it is possible to organize even the unorganizable.

JOHN L. LEWIS *was born on February 12, 1880, in the mining town of Cleveland, Iowa.*

A strapping lad with wavy auburn hair, he quit school after the seventh grade and by age fifteen had followed his father into the mines—a world he later described as "a mortician's paradise . . . naked and elemental. Relations are not cushioned by sophistry."

According to one story, a man-killing mule named Spanish Pete once cornered the young Lewis in a mine corridor. Lewis lashed out with his fist and stunned the mule, then grabbed a piece of timber and drove it deep into the animal's brain. Thinking that the mule's death might cost him his job, Lewis filled the gaping wound with clay and reported that Spanish Pete had died of heart failure.

At twenty-seven he married Myrta Bell, a schoolteacher who encouraged him to read Shakespeare, Dickens, and Homer.

He cultivated an image of fierceness, but his scowl often vanished after the cameras had stopped clicking. He rejected suggestions that he stop frowning: "My stock in trade is being the ogre. . . . That scowl is worth a million dollars."

According to another story, Lewis once stepped out of his house just as a bus loaded with tourists passed by. When the tourists watched as the union leader bent over to tie his shoe, Lewis remarked, "Even the posterior of a great man is of interest."

He seldom drank.

He enjoyed reading westerns, mysteries, American Heritage, and accounts of the Napoleonic and Peloponnesian wars.

His mother was a Mormon, but he practiced no formal religion.

He had few close friends.

Although seldom at home, he was intensely loyal to his family. His firstborn child, Mary Margaret, died when she was seven. He was especially protective of his next child, Kathryn, who later in life weighed upward of three hundred pounds, underwent psychoanalysis, practiced yoga, and became devoted to a mystic. He shielded Kathryn from photographers and made her secretary-treasurer of his union's nonmining chapter. He gave union jobs to most of his immediate relatives.

He was susceptible to respiratory ailments. In 1941 he suffered a severe heart attack that put him on the critical list in a Washington hospital. He attempted to keep his illnesses secret.

His desk was usually free of paperwork. He wrote few official policy statements. He preferred to do his business by phone or—especially after he became convinced that the FBI was tapping his calls—over lunch.

Though he rarely had personal contact with rank-and-file miners and seldom invited fellow unionists to his home, he told one biographer, "Think of me as a coal miner."

He was the first labor leader invited regularly to Washington's exclusive Cosmos Club. Society dame Evelyn McLean Walsh invited the Lewises to her parties. His upper-class acquaintances remembered him as being amusing, "the soul of courtesy," and a "brilliant conversationalist."

He sent his son to Princeton and his daughter to Bryn Mawr. He enjoyed riding on a Wyoming dude ranch and deep-sea fishing off Florida. Yet he assured a 1936 convention of miners that his union's officers were "just as poor in this world's goods as any delegate to this convention."

In the 1920s he was a zealous Red-baiter who ousted all union opponents he deemed to be Communists. Later, secure in his power, he commented, "Industry should not complain if we allow Communists in our organization. Industry employs them." He quit the AFL after refusing to take an anti-Communist oath required under the Taft-Hartley Act.

He frequently decried big-business conspiracies, yet he was a business associate of banker Jacob Harriman's. He used UMW dues and pension funds to gain control of the National Bank of Washington. He joined tycoon Cyrus Eaton in an alliance designed to centralize control of coal mines, power companies, and coal-carrying railroads.

"After many years of observation," Franklin Roosevelt wrote a friend, "I have come reluctantly to the conclusion that Lewis' is a psychopathic condition."

American mothers warned their rebellious children that John L. Lewis would get them if they didn't behave.

"When we control the production of coal," he once asserted, "we hold the vitals of our society right in our hands. I can squeeze, twist, and pull until we get the inevitable victory."

In 1960, after serving forty years as UMW president, he withdrew from public view. Nine years later, at eighty-nine, he died of internal bleeding from an undisclosed ailment. Miners walked off the job for a four-day period of mourning.

Philip Johnson: The Man in the Glass House

TOM BUCKLEY

PHILIP JOHNSON PEERED DOWN AT A MODEL OF AN INTERNATIONAL CONFERENCE CENter, then at the drawings that were pinned to the cork wall behind it, and then at the model again.

"Every building has to have a way to get in," Johnson said. "Where do the people come from? Where do they park their cars?" As he spoke the audience stopped whispering. His voice was neutral, even friendly, but his hands darted around the model like lost and irritated visitors.

The young woman whose work it was said, "From here . . . to here . . . and from here to here," as her fingers walked the access routes.

"You mean you have to cross this *highway?*" Johnson asked, his eyebrows rising.

"There's an overpass," she replied, pointing to it.

Johnson pointed to the front of the building. "Who uses the grand entrance? How would you get there by car? I don't see a driveway."

The woman, stammering, said that cars would enter an underground parking area, and their passengers would ascend to the lobby by elevator.

"Ah, I see," he said, but his expression suggested that he found her explanation less than satisfactory.

"Where do the people in the auditorium go during the intermission?"

As the woman showed the siting of the lounges and foyers, Johnson smiled for the first time.

"I've designed a few auditoriums myself and I must say you've handled that part of it quite well," he said. "Thank you."

He returned to his seat, and the other members of the jury of architects and members of the faculty of the School of Architecture of Princeton University took up the inquisition. The young woman was a candidate for a master's degree; the conference center was her graduation thesis. Her project and eight others were each being subjected to the stresses of forty minutes of professional criticism.

Peter Eisenman, a friend and something of a protégé of Johnson's, said, "Important people, distinguished people like Mr. Johnson here, don't want to go into a *parking lot*. They want to come up the grand staircase."

The audience, which included many undergraduates, whose work was not being judged that day, laughed politely. Johnson looked around, smiling and nodding his head in mock-modest agreement.

Eisenman's tone was jocular, but he wasn't exaggerating. Johnson is arguably the most eminent and certainly the best-known architect in the United States, or, for that matter, in the world, with an ego that doesn't wilt in the flash of strobe lights. He has designed scores of notable buildings. At least one of them—the Glass House, his residence in New Canaan, Connecticut—is generally regarded as a masterpiece. In 1978 he received the American Institute of Architects' gold medal, its highest honor. A couple of weeks before his visit to Princeton, he was being congratulated by President Reagan as one of the recipients of a certificate for achievement from the President's Committee on the Arts and the Humanities.

Although he was then only a month from his seventy-seventh birthday, Johnson still had the slim figure and straight back of a cadet. His white hair was sparse and clipped short. Age had worn but not deformed his handsome, strongly modeled face. He wore spectacles with round black frames that, I learned later, were specially made copies of those worn by one of his idols, the French architect Le Corbusier. Architects, like artists, tend to be casual in dress and manner, but Johnson was neither. He wore a beautifully cut gray nailhead worsted suit, a dark blue tie, a white shirt, and polished black oxfords. His speech was dry and precise, his accent unobtrusively upper-class, and his presence quietly self-assured.

At a time of life when most men are either dead or nursing their ailments in retirement, Johnson was at the zenith of his career. He and his partner, John Burgee, had one of the largest practices in the country. They employed sixty architects and were working on seven big projects—costing at least $100 million each—and several smaller ones all over the country. And Johnson was not merely repeating past successes, as even the active elderly are apt to do. Although no one had been more influential in promoting the work of the European masters of modern architecture in the United States in the early 1930s, no one had more quickly lost his enthusiasm for their stark geometric shapes and unadorned exteriors.

As long ago as 1961, in a speech in London, Johnson made his widely quoted comment: "You cannot *not* know history." He went on to tell his audience of architects that they should feel free "to choose from history whatever forms, shapes, or directions you want to . . . using them as you please." In the same way, he was one of the first established architects to praise Robert Venturi's *Complexity and Contradiction in Architecture,* which was published in 1966 and has become the bible of postmodernism, the name that has been given to this new eclecticism.

In attacking modernism, Venturi, a hitherto obscure Philadelphia architect, declared, "I like elements which are hybrid rather than 'pure,' compromising rather than 'clean,' distorted rather than 'straightforward.' . . ." Venturi and his followers were inspired not only by the buildings of the past but also by the garish theatricality of Las Vegas and by the bright, cheap, hectic structures—fast-food outlets, muffler shops, Laundromats, and the like—that most people would say disfigure the nation's secondary highways. Johnson may have led the cheering section for them, but he doesn't design that way himself. His and Burgee's recent buildings have broken the iron laws of modernism, but it has been done discreetly, elegantly, and, their critics might say, superficially. This reticence was a matter of taste—not only theirs but also that of the corporations, public authorities, universities, and speculative builders who decide what major new buildings will look like. After forty years of hearing, in Mies van der Rohe's apothegm, that "less is more," they were not finding it easy to start believing that less is less.

The Johnson-Burgee design for the corporate headquarters of PPG Industries, in Pittsburgh, for example, suggests a Gothic cathedral. Their Republic Bank Center in Houston, with its rising rows of gables, recalls a Dutch town hall of the seventeenth century. A San Francisco office tower recalls the Louvre in having draped female statues on each cornice just below a mansard roof.

The most controversial of their buildings, however, was the new headquarters of the American Telephone & Telegraph Company in New York. When the design was made public in 1978, *Time* put Johnson on its cover, symbolizing the postmodernist revolution.

The 648-foot tower, sheathed in pinkish-gray granite, violates modernism's prohibition against disguising the steel girders that actually support the structure. It has a majestic arched entrance and a domed lobby and public concourse sixty feet high, in which a gilded figure called The Spirit of Communication, taken from the former headquarters on lower Broadway, will be displayed. At the top, instead of the flat roof dictated by modernism, there is an upward-sloping pediment with a deep scoop taken from the center.

That broken pediment, as it is called, has caused more argument than any other empty space twenty feet or so in diameter in the history of architecture. Some critics have hailed it as spirited and imaginative, the crowning touch of another Johnson masterpiece. Paul Goldberger of *The New York Times* wrote, as the building was nearing completion, that his first favorable judgment had been too cautious. AT&T would be, he said, "the finest new skyscraper in New York and perhaps in the nation."

Equally reputable critics damned the building, from its broken pediment on down, as a display of extravagance, arrogance, and perversity. Johnson, they said, was less an architect than an aging couturier desperate to remain in fashion. The largest corporation in the world, as it was before its court-ordered breakup, had spent at least $175 million in the hope of getting a great building. What it had got, they said, was merely one of the most expensive buildings, in terms of square footage, ever constructed, and one that resembled nothing so much as a Chippendale secretary or a grandfather clock.

The first of several long conversations I had with Johnson took place at his office in the Seagram Building in Manhattan, at 375 Park Avenue, a week or so after our brief meeting at Princeton. Johnson served as Mies van der Rohe's assistant in the design of the Seagram Building, which is generally acknowledged to be as good as modern architecture ever got to be, and he has been a tenant since it opened in 1958. Johnson had sole responsibility for the design of the Four Seasons Restaurant, which occupies two levels on the ground floor behind the lobby. It is one of the world's most beautiful restaurants, and Johnson holds court at luncheon there nearly every day that he is in the city.

His office on the thirty-seventh floor, one short of the top, might seem modest to a visitor whose eye wasn't attuned to modernist understatement. There was a Knoll desk of light teak, a Mies van der Rohe desk chair of steel and leather behind it, and four Wegener wood-frame chairs for visitors. A Frank Stella print hung on each wall. There were no architectural drawings or implements to be seen. Johnson does his designing in New Canaan.

As an icebreaker I said that I supposed he enjoyed his campus visits, which kept him in touch with his professional grandchildren.

"Not at all," he replied. "I feel I owe it to the profession, but I do less and less of it. It isn't fair for someone of my experience to judge kids. Their work always looks terrible. Anyhow, the young architects I encourage aren't so young anymore, although they seem young to me. Most of them are at least forty."

Johnson was wearing another of those timelessly fashionable suits, a medium gray chalk stripe. I asked him who his tailor was.

"Bernard Weatherill," he replied. "They've made my suits since I came to New York in 1930."

The question of how a young man happened to be a Weatherill client at a time when most people had only holes in their pockets led to a biographical recitation. Johnson told me that he was born in Cleveland in 1906. His father was a highly successful lawyer. His mother was a graduate of Wellesley. He had two sisters, both living. He attended the Hackley School in Tarrytown, New York, and entered Harvard in 1923, studying philosophy and Greek. Disdaining a dormitory room, he rented a house overlooking the Charles River and hired a cook. However, he said, he was not part of Harvard's high society, which revolved around the Porcellian, Fly, and AD clubs. He had attacks of depression that on two occasions forced him to withdraw from the university, and he did not receive his degree until 1930.

"Except for Lincoln Kirstein, who was the leading intellectual of my class and who is still a close friend, and a couple of others, I didn't know any undergraduates at all," he said. "Almost my only friends were my teachers. One of the reasons for those depressions, I think, was that I had realized that I just didn't have the right sort of mind to do philosophy, which had been my ambition.

"I remember once asking Alfred North Whitehead, who was one of my teachers, how he marked. I said, 'You've giving me a B, and I know I don't know anything.' 'Oh, Philip,' he said, 'I always give an A to those who are acceptable and a B to those who are no good.'"

Johnson had made several summer visits to Europe with his family, but in 1928, during one of his enforced withdrawals, he traveled for the first time to Italy, Greece, and Egypt. As an adolescent he had been profoundly moved by the sight of Chartres Cathedral, but it, and everything else, was blotted out when he saw the Parthenon.

"Epiphanies that move you to tears or leave you feeling exalted for weeks don't translate into words very well, but I had it twice, at Chartres and the Parthenon," he said. "There was a pre-Parthenon Philip Johnson and a post-Parthenon Philip Johnson. Before that I had been rather straightforward, interested in philosophy and rationalism and intellectual things, but without a single devoted passion. After I saw the Parthenon I had a call, as religious people might put it, and I've never changed."

Even so, Johnson thought in terms of architectural history rather than architecture itself. He returned to Europe the next summer to visit the Bauhaus in Dessau, Germany, the fountainhead of the emerging modernist school, and again in 1930. On that trip he was accompanied by Henry-Russell Hitchcock, a young instructor in art history at Wesleyan.

"Modernism interested me because it was reproducible," he told me. "The Parthenon wasn't."

Johnson had become friendly with Alfred Barr, the first director of the newly founded Museum of Modern Art in New York, and on his return he was appointed the first director of its department of architecture. At the same time he and Hitchcock began writing *The International Style,* which was the name they gave to the avant-garde architecture they had seen in Europe. It was published in 1932 and is still in print. In the same year they organized an immensely influential exhibition of modern architecture at the museum, for which the book served, in effect, as a guide. Architects, most of whom hadn't had a chance to design a building since the Crash, became converts by the score. As long as they weren't working, they seemed to be saying, they might as well be not working on something new.

One reason that Johnson had found it easy to get a job at a time when millions of men were eating in soup kitchens was that he did not require a salary. Indeed, he paid the wages of his secretary and of another member of the museum staff, lived quietly and well, wore Weatherill suits, and continued to travel. What made all this possible was the generosity of his father, who had given substantial sums in stock and real estate to Johnson and his sisters. "He wanted us to be able to live our lives as we chose," Johnson said. "He lived to be ninety-six, which makes me feel optimistic. He came east to see the Seagram Building not long before he died. He didn't like it."

Johnson visited Germany again in 1934, but by then Hitler, who had more grandiose ideas about architecture, had shut down the Bauhaus. Even so, Johnson, who had seen the poverty and unrest of the Weimar Republic, was impressed by the rapid economic recovery that Hitler had brought about. Johnson thought it made Franklin Delano Roosevelt's New Deal look lethargic.

In 1934 Johnson and a colleague resigned from the museum to organize a political party along National Socialist lines, an enterprise that lasted, in Johnson's words, "about five days." Aware that Huey Long, the governor of Louisiana, had presidential ambitions and might be headed in the same direction, they went to see him.

"We talked to him twice," Johnson said. "Both times he was in bed in his pajamas. He was smart as hell. He and his people asked us how many votes we could deliver. When we said we couldn't deliver any, they lost interest. They didn't want to bother with a couple of Harvard snots."

After Long's assassination in 1935, Johnson transferred his loyalties to the Union party, a picturesque agglomeration of bereaved Longites, Roosevelt haters, prairie populists, agitators for an old-age pension, and, of course, secret and professed fascists, among them many who put the blame for the world's economic problems on a Jewish conspiracy. Notable among them was Father Charles Coughlin, a Catholic priest whose radio commentaries had made him a national figure. In 1936 the party ran Representative William Lemke of North Dakota for President. Johnson contributed five thousand dollars, a very large sum in those days, but the campaign fell apart almost before it began and was smashed flat in Roosevelt's second-term landslide.

"I ended up voting for Roosevelt myself," Johnson said. "In fact, I voted for him all four times he ran. After that, I lost interest in politics. For the next three years, in fact, I didn't do much of anything. I saw my old friends at the museum occasionally and spent a lot of time at my parents' farm in New London, Ohio. It was another depressing period for me."

In 1939 Johnson was in Zurich, traveling with one of his sisters, when Germany invaded Poland. He got himself accredited as a correspondent of Father Coughlin's *Social Justice*, to which he had years earlier contributed a couple of articles, and hurried to Berlin. On a press junket into occupied Poland he was assigned to share a hotel room for the night with William L. Shirer, the correspondent of the Columbia Broadcasting System. Within a week or so Johnson was on his way back to the United States. The following year he enrolled as an architecture student at Harvard, where Walter Gropius, formerly of the Bauhaus, was teaching.

Soon afterward, Shirer's *Berlin Diary* was published and immediately became a best seller. It contained a passing reference to that fateful night in which he described Johnson as "an American fascist" and went on to say, "None of us can stand the fellow and suspect he is spying on us for the Nazis. . . ."

Johnson's excursion had passed unnoticed until then and his deviant political interests had been pretty well forgotten, but the appearance of the book put him under a cloud that did not lift for many years. Shirer's assumption was not altogether unreasonable, but it was unlikely that there was much that the Gestapo didn't already know about Shirer and his colleagues in the press or that they would have confided in the correspondent of *Social Justice*.

Johnson said that most of his old friends, including Lincoln Kirstein and Edward M. M. Warburg, both of whom were Jewish, stuck by him, but many others cut him dead. He persevered in his studies and in 1943 received his degree. As his senior thesis, instead of a model and drawings, Johnson presented a completed house in Cambridge in the International Style.

Shortly after his graduation, Johnson, who was then thirty-seven, rather old for a soldier, entered the Army. His fluent German and his knowledge of the country might have been useful, but lingering doubts as to his loyalty kept him a private at Fort Belvoir, Virginia, until his discharge.

Even at a distance of forty years and more, Johnson loses his customary insouciance when he discusses that period of his life. His efforts to promote both modern architecture and fascism, he told me, were alike in being idealistic and wrong.

"I am an enthusiast by nature and I thought the International Style was going to change the world," he said. "Architecture, more than any of the arts, actually affects the way people live. I thought that we were helping to popularize a style of architecture that could be universally and inexpensively applied for housing, factories, and everything else and would make the world a better place to live in.

"When it came to politics and economics," he went on, "I knew there was something rotten. The question was what to do about it. Everyone was choosing up sides in those days. I knew that capitalism was completely narrow-minded and self-serving, but I couldn't become a Communist, because it was becoming clearer all the time that it required giving your first loyalty to Russia. I wasn't pro-German or pro-Nazi either. I was pro-American. But I admit that I was very excited about a more authoritarian shortcut to prosperity, which didn't really arrive in the United States, after all, until the war boom.

"I was interested in Huey Long because he presented himself as a kind of socialist. His slogan was, Share-the-Wealth, and I'll never forget how outraged my father's friends at the Union Club in Cleveland were when I drove up in my Packard plastered with SHARE-THE-WEALTH signs. Roosevelt was a sort of socialist, too, and I approved of that part of his program. It's just that progress was so slow in coming and I was very impatient. The Nazi persecution of the Jews, and the artists, and anyone who disagreed with them, was very distasteful to me, but between 1935 and 1939 I had not been in Germany and I didn't grasp their full extent, as I should have. That trip was exceedingly stupid. I was caught up in the excitement of the moment, and off I went. I was a damned fool and I deserved what I got, but the next few years were the worst of my life."

In 1946 Johnson once again became the head of the museum's department of architecture. He was also setting up a practice. It began slowly, in part because he kept failing the New York State licensing examination. One of his first projects, once he had passed, was his own residence, the Glass House, which he sited on a low hill overlooking a man-made pond.

Architectural historians regard it as one of the finest statements of the International Style, superior to a similar house designed by Mies van der Rohe that Johnson acknowledges as his inspiration. ("Mies always said that it was better to be good than original," Johnson told me.) As its name suggests, its walls are built entirely of sheets of quarter-inch glass that are divided horizontally about three feet off the ground and framed by narrow steel pillars painted matte black. It is a single-story structure, only thirty-two by fifty-six feet. There are no interior walls. The only completely private area is the lavatory, which is enclosed, along with other utilities and the fireplace, in a cylinder that rises from the floor through the flat roof. It cost forty thousand dollars, which was a large sum at the time, especially for a house of those modest dimensions that used no wood, lathing, or plaster.

Before beginning the Glass House, Johnson built a guesthouse on the property, which has solid walls and portholes for windows. It provides the heat for the Glass House, which lacks a furnace and air-conditioning. The only ventilation is provided by the glass doors, which do not have screens. Nor are there curtains or blinds. Privacy is provided by the thirty-two-acre tract on which it is built. During the warm months, Johnson keeps the interior lighting dim, while luring the pests away with powerful outdoor lights. Even before the price of oil went through the roof, the Glass House, being uninsulated, cost a sheikh's ransom to heat. When it gets too hot or too cold or too buggy, Johnson retreats to the guesthouse, which has, it might be said, all the comforts of home.

Whatever its practical shortcomings, the Glass House provided a powerful lure for clients. They sipped martinis and watched the sun set, dined exquisitely as the stars winked on, were dazzled by Johnson's charm over the cognac, and hired him before their mosquito bites began to itch. By 1968, when he had phased out that part of his practice, Johnson had designed twenty houses, all of them in the severely modern manner.

In 1953, when Johnson received the commission for the Museum of Modern Art's sculpture gardens, many architects began complaining. They said he had an inside track for museum commissions, but also, in his capacity as head of the architecture department, he was judging their work while competing with them. Frank Lloyd Wright said publicly that Johnson ought to do one thing or the other. Wright was undoubtedly right, but he had no reason to be charitable toward the man who, in his devotion to modernism, had described him, entirely unjustly, as Johnson now admits, as "the greatest American architect of the nineteenth century."

In any event, Johnson resigned from the museum staff in 1954. However, he chose his successor, and his position as the most influential architectural pacemaker in the country was undiminished. In 1957 he was elected to the museum's board of trustees, on which he has continued to serve. In the early 1960s Johnson designed two additions to the museum, which, like the garden, were widely praised. He has, in turn, given to the museum more than 130 paintings, including major works by Stella, Jasper Johns, Robert Rauschenberg, Andy Warhol, and Roy Lichtenstein, worth many millions of dollars, and more than one hundred objects to its architecture and design collection.

Thus, Johnson thought he had been betrayed when, in 1977, Cesar Pelli, the dean of the Yale School of Architecture, was chosen to design a forty-four-story apartment tower above part of the museum. Johnson announced that the museum would get no more works of art from him. However, in 1982 he relented and made a gift of paintings worth $800,000. As a further proof of his goodwill, he bought a small apartment in the tower, although he had to sell a Stella at auction to pay for it. The painting, for which he had paid $3,000, brought $260,000.

Johnson, who ordinarily likes to speak his mind, was circumspect about the affair of the museum tower. The rumor heard most frequently was that, aside from his reputation for going over budget, Johnson, who has a wicked tongue and can be bitchy as well as charming, had at one time or another offended most of his fellow trustees. For example, he publicly described one of them, who is also an architect, as "a sheep in sheep's clothing." "My trouble," Johnson said, "is that when people ask me what I think, and sometimes when they don't, I tell them."

Under the circumstances, the fact that the tower was months behind schedule, far over budget, and embroiled in lawsuits could not have caused Johnson much distress, even though, having sold his former city residence, he had been forced to camp out in a borrowed apartment until the belated completion of his new place.

After 1956 Johnson's practice became largely institutional. It was the sort of work that tends to go to architects who are well off, well born, and well connected. The museum's board is richly stocked with important names, notably Rockefellers. Johnson has received many commissions from them, either directly or indirectly, among them Asia House in New York, the New York State Theater at Lincoln Center, and an art gallery for the late Nelson Rockefeller at his summer home in Seal Harbor, Maine.

Among Johnson's other assignments were the Amon Carter Museum of Western Art in Fort Worth, Texas, and the pre-Columbian art wing of the

Dumbarton Oaks Museum in Washington, D.C. He did buildings at Yale, Harvard, Brown, Sarah Lawrence, and several at New York University's Washington Square campus. He was particularly happy to be asked to design Israel's nuclear research center at Rehovot, which was completed in 1960, because he thought it would finally put to rest any lingering notions that his flirtation with Nazism reflected an anti-Semitic bias.

"Shimon Peres, who is now the head of the Labor party, was always a fan of mine," Johnson said. "He had been to the Glass House, and one night he asked me, 'How come you've never done anything in Israel?' 'Nothing would please me more,' I said. Rehovot was the result. You know, far from being an anti-Semite, I've always been a violent philo-Semite. In fact, right now I think that Israel and Texas are the two greatest countries in the world."

Johnson's projects during that period were not invariably praised, and some of them, notably the Sarah Lawrence dormitories, were execrated. Even so, the critics usually agreed that his buildings were characterized by a lightness and elegance of touch that, even when he was working within the strict rules of the modernist game, gave them an unusual warmth and interest.

However, it was not until 1967, when he joined forces with Burgee, that Johnson stepped up from a kind of boutique architecture and into the big time of tall buildings and proportionate fees. The increased income came none too soon, since he had run through his father's money.

Before teaming up with Burgee, Johnson had generally worked only with assistants. On the few occasions when he had a partner, Johnson got the jobs and did the designing, and the other man took care of everything else. With Burgee, it was different. Although he was only thirty-three at the time, twenty-eight years younger than Johnson, he was already a partner in a major Chicago firm, and he made it clear that he would be a codesigner as well as an administrator.

"All I did in Chicago was to sell jobs and attend building openings," Burgee, a tall, rosy-cheeked man, told me. "I didn't want to be a businessman-architect. I wanted to design buildings. Philip and I had the same objective—to build the best buildings in the world. When he proposed the partnership, he said that I was young enough so that he didn't have to be jealous of me. I had heard that he could be pretty stormy, and I told myself I'd give it a year and see how it worked out. The first time I made a suggestion he said, 'That's the stupidest thing I ever heard,' and I said to myself, 'Oh, oh.' But the next time, he said, 'That's brilliant. Why didn't I think of that?' "

Johnson said, "I don't think I would have had any skyscrapers at all if it hadn't been for John. He's a much better organizer, and he works with people better than I do. I tend to do the beginning sketches, but I wouldn't think of making a line on paper after that without him, because he's a very able designer too. Everybody calls it Johnson's AT&T Building, which annoys the hell out of me. We *both* worked on it, and, in fact, I think it was he who actually came up with the idea of breaking the pediment."

Their first big joint project was the Investors Diversified Services Center in

Minneapolis, which was completed in 1973. It included the first, or one of the first, glass-covered gallerias of shops and restaurants in the country. It received an award from the American Institute of Architects and was acclaimed in the press. Their next was Pennzoil Place in Houston. It comprises a galleria and two thirty-six-story glass towers with sloped tops that are set at an angle to each other so that the closest corners are only ten feet apart.

One of Johnson and Burgee's most unusual projects was the Crystal Cathedral near Anaheim, California. It is a vast structure built entirely of glass, ten thousand panes of it, held in place by a delicate steel framework. The cathedral is the headquarters of the Reverend Dr. Robert H. Schuller, a noted television preacher. Schuller told me that Johnson and Burgee had fully realized his desire for a church "without dark corners." Situated as it is, not far from Disneyland, the Crystal Cathedral attracts as many as five thousand visitors a day.

When I asked Schuller if it weren't expecting too much in the way of divine protection to build a glass cathedral a couple of miles from the San Andreas Fault, he said that Johnson had used a special sort of glass that, instead of breaking into shards, would pulverize into tiny, harmless pellets.

There is an inclination in architecture, as in the other arts, to be distrustful of commercial success. The most successful architects tend to be those who are most adept at not rising above the taste level of their clients. Thus, Johnson's abandonment of modernism was seen by some as merely a matter of convenience.

James Marston Fitch, professor emeritus at Columbia University School of Architecture and the author of many books and articles in the architectural press, spoke with me about Johnson.

"Unfortunately, he is one of the most influential, if not the most influential, architect in the country," Fitch said. "Uniquely among architects, who are not usually communicative outside professional circles, he has a genius for projecting his polemics into the public domain. His work is beautifully detailed and beautifully built, which is by no means common in the profession, but it is fundamentally frivolous. He is candidly an architect for the elite."

He suddenly put on the brakes. "I don't really want to talk about Philip Johnson," he said, quite literally throwing up his hands. "Nothing can be done about him. He is impregnable."

Vincent Scully, the distinguished historian of art and architecture, after saying that he was extremely annoyed at Johnson for misstatements he had made in a recently published interview, added, "But I have to say that the great thing about Philip is that he trusts the young and believes in the new instead of tightening up as he gets older. The AT&T Building makes all other recent skyscrapers look obsolete."

The next time I saw Johnson I told him what I had heard.

"Vincent is absolutely right about the interview," he said. "It was disgraceful—Johnson in his worst enfant terrible pose. As to Jim Fitch, all I can say is that I've always thought of myself more as a populist than as an elitist, not that an elite isn't a necessary part of any society. Architects are pretty much high-class whores. We can turn down some projects the way they can turn down some clients, but finally we've both got to say yes to someone if we want to stay in business.

"Who are the architect's customers? In Russia it's the state. Here it's bourgeois businessmen. My ambition has always been to build cities, or at least city squares or housing projects, but no one ever asked me to. Am I too concerned with style? The same charge could be leveled at anyone who makes changes."

If he had to do it all over again, I asked, would he have promoted modernism?

"Of course not," he replied. "Not when I look up and down Park Avenue and see all those dreadful knock-offs of the Seagram Building and Lever House. But I couldn't have stopped it. No one could, because businessmen found out that that kind of building was cheaper to build."

Johnson, who has never married, is a figure in New York's *haute* bohemia, but his only real interest is architecture. He intends to work for as long as he is able to, although he keeps trying to reduce the amount of work he does. He most admires Mies van der Rohe, Le Corbusier, and Frank Lloyd Wright. As to the quality of his own work, he is modest.

"I think the Glass House will endure," he said, "but it may be that I will be best remembered as a gadfly, an encourager of younger architects, and as an arbiter elegantiarum—the man who introduced the glass box and then, fifty years later, broke it."

Philip Cortelyou Johnson *was born on July 8, 1906, in Cleveland.*

In 1926 his father gave Philip stock in a new company in which he had little confidence. The stock—in the Alcoa company—made Philip, by the time he was twenty-four, wealthier than his father.

Recuperating in Ohio from youthful depression, every day he cried and read two detective stories.

While an undergraduate at Harvard, he never took a single architecture course.

After graduating from architecture school at thirty-six, he repeatedly failed the New York State licensing exam. Even though it was legal at the time to build a private house without an architect's license—outside the city—the police came to Johnson's new office and threatened to padlock it. One policeman told Johnson that he had "enemies in high places."

After abandoning right-wing politics, he helped place architects fleeing Hitler's Germany in key teaching positions in the United States. He designed the Congre-

gation Kneses Tifereth Israel Synagogue in Port Chester, New York, and donated his fee to the temple.

In 1965 he told an interviewer, "What good does it do to believe in good things? It's feudal and futile. I think it's much better to be nihilistic and forget all that."

He has said that, having always wanted to be l'architecte du roi, he would work "for the Devil himself." "Whoever commissions a building buys me," he once said.

He rejected an opportunity to design a skyscraper behind the historic St. Bartholomew's Church on Park Avenue in New York City. He explained that "the texture of the city overruled my natural ambition for making more money."

In 1975 AT&T sent twenty-five of the country's top architectural firms questionnaires asking how each would design the corporation's new Manhattan headquarters. Most of the firms replied immediately. But no reply came from Johnson. After several weeks, AT&T called to see if he had gotten the questionnaire. "It got here," Johnson recalls saying, "but we threw it out. We don't like questionnaires."

In 1979 he received the $100,000 Pritzker Architecture Prize. He gave the money away to libraries, the Museum of Modern Art, and magazines. "I didn't really feel it was my money," he explained.

"When I first went to Egypt and saw Sakkara," architect Kevin Roche once said, "I realized that Philip had been there thirty-five hundred years ago. He was the first person I thought of when I saw those marvelous, sophisticated buildings—they were saying the same things to one that Philip's buildings are saying today. But, you know, I never really think of Philip as an architect. With him, it's always seemed more like an avocation—like being a gentleman farmer. The rest of us are farmers, but Philip is a gentleman farmer."

Though he encourages clients to call him Philip, even long-term associates of his firm call him Mr. Johnson.

He seldom descends from his thirty-seventh-floor office to the thirty-sixth floor, where others in his firm work out the details of his designs.

He asks that the refuse from each work session be thrown out immediately and disdains mementos from past projects.

"The improvement of sex is certainly one of [architecture's] objectives," he once said. "I tried it in my house with domed ceilings and pink reflected light and theatrical dimmers."

He is very social, a crony of the Rockefellers, the Astors, Capote, Warhol, Radziwill.

He has no hobbies: "I don't like sports." In 1979 he designed a Big Sur cottage for himself in the "shingle style" of the 1890s. "I don't know when I'll get there. I hate vacations. If you can build buildings, why sit on the beach?"

In 1975 he had open-heart surgery. Two weeks after the operation he returned to his office.

He professes to no religion and spends every Christmas out of town looking at architecture. "The sins that I've committed . . . ," he has said, "are all against my own integrity as an artist."

TV evangelist Robert Schuller, for whom Johnson designed the Crystal Cathedral in Garden Grove, California, once said: "It's so rare to find a person who's sensitive and sophisticated but who hasn't become emotionally frigid. I think Philip has the same quality that Walt Disney had—the enthusiasm of a boy who's never grown up. Philip and I are just like peas in a pod, I found. Although he says he's not a religious person, I feel that Philip Johnson and I are on a very harmonious wavelength, and one that is transcendent enough to be labeled a spiritual relationship."

What Hath
William Paley
Wrought?

DAVID McCLINTICK

WILLIAM PALEY, THE PATRIARCH OF CBS, THE MAN WHO INVENTED MASS ENTERTAIN-
ment as the world knows it, is dining in his Fifth Avenue apartment with his old
friend Irene Selznick, the renowned theatrical producer, daughter of Louis B.
Mayer, and first wife of David O. Selznick. They are both in good spirits. Paley,
sporting a tan accentuated by his thick silver hair, has just returned from a holiday in Marrakech. As usual, he has been indulging in a rich variety of fine food,
and his modest paunch peeks over his trousers. Selznick, pale and frail by comparison, is relaxing after completing the final manuscript of her long-awaited
memoirs.

Sipping icy Stolichnaya vodka laced with bitters, their food, prepared by
Paley's chef, on trays beside them, they sit opposite each other in easy chairs in
the library, in front of the hearth and French marble mantel, in front of family
photographs, in front of Bill Paley's favorite painting, Matisse's *Odalisque*,
which he has owned since the 1930s, in front of Picasso's *The Pink Lady*, a
more recent acquisition, and in front of dozens of leather-bound books.

This room is Paley's favorite of all the rooms in the three residences he owns
and regularly occupies in Manhattan, Southampton, and the Bahamas. With
soft brown floral chintz covering the walls, it is designed to duplicate a beloved
sitting room in an apartment down the avenue at the St. Regis Hotel, where
Paley lived in decades past. The replication succeeded. Despite the grandeur of

the art, the ambience is warm and informal. Paley is very comfortable here, as is Irene Selznick. The evenings they have spent in this room, as well as in its St. Regis antecedent, are among the most pleasant of the hundreds of times they have been together, occasionally by themselves, more often with other people, since they first met at an opulent Hollywood party, packed with movie stars and given in Bill Paley's honor in the summer of 1929, nearly fifty-four years ago.

No one knows Bill Paley, now eighty-one years old, better than Irene Selznick, who is seventy-five, and they spend most of this January evening reminiscing, mainly about David Selznick, who was one of Paley's most intimate friends from the 1930s until his death in 1965. Perhaps no one has ever amused and stimulated Bill Paley—a restless, energetic man, easily bored—as much as David Selznick did through all of those years. As close as the two men were, however, Irene has never run out of anecdotes about her husband and can still surprise Bill with something he has never heard about David, or has forgotten.

One of the few times in his adult life that Bill Paley wept openly was when he heard a radio report at his St. Regis apartment of Selznick's death in Beverly Hills. It was a severe shock and total surprise to Paley, who had not known that his friend had serious heart disease and could die at any time. Paley has always felt bad that David did not let him know of the illness. Irene, who maintained a close relationship with her ex-husband until his death, tells Paley now: "The point was that he thought the knowledge would be a burden to you, that you would worry about him, and that it would change the climate between you. David loved that climate. He said, why rob himself? Why put a burden on Bill and rob himself of a particular quality of friendship?"

Paley is riveted by this information, which Irene, as is her wont, has hinted at before but never stated so baldly. "When he knew he was going to die," Irene continues, "he said of you, 'I know Bill will miss me terribly.' He didn't want you to miss him in advance."

Paley is moved. "Really," he says softly. "That's very sweet."

The talk of his friend's death does not depress Paley. Mortality—his own and others'—worries him far less in his eighty-second year than it did in his fifties and sixties. Although he misses his many friends who have died, he is able to reminisce happily about them. Indeed, as he and Irene talk late into the evening, it occurs to her that Bill seems freer of care than she has seen him in a long time. Usually he is absorbed by something current—a project, a crusade, a concern, a person—but not tonight. Tonight he seems content. He isn't going on about anything: not about memory lapses, which have troubled him recently; not about loneliness, which has afflicted him since the death of his wife, Babe, in 1978; not about his children and grandchildren, who have brought him considerable worry as well as great pleasure over the years; not about his principal avocations, the Museum of Modern Art and the Museum of Broadcasting, which are both flourishing; and, perhaps most surprising, not about CBS, which he purchased in 1928, when it was a moribund affiliation of sixteen radio stations, and built into a communications colossus that revolutionized the way the world is entertained and informed, and from which he is now struggling to retire gracefully.

"He's in a good phase at the moment," Irene Selznick surmises of Paley a few days after their evening together. "He's finally stepped out of CBS. . . . Some things are settled, like the CBS thing. That's done. . . . I think he's well out of it."

Maybe he is. If anyone would know for sure, it is Irene Selznick. But even Selznick knows that she is guessing and realizes that as long as Bill Paley lives, he might never be "well out of" CBS, out of the world of show business at large, or out of David Selznick's world of Hollywood that Paley reshaped in his own image. It is extraordinarily difficult for a man who made a revolution to withdraw from the vehicle of that revolution. On a psychological plane, it is impossible. Paley himself understands.

"It's like having a child," he says, "I gave birth to it, I'm its founder. . . . It means a lot more to me than it would to somebody coming in to take a high office but who has not been through the experience of starting very low with very little and seeing it progress and grow and become very, very successful. It's pretty hard to jerk yourself away from that entirely, and I won't be doing it entirely. Maybe the kind of resistance I have to apply against myself might be a little awkward for me. I don't know."

The uncertainty and discomfort surrounding Paley's retirement stem in large part from his uniqueness as a revolutionary. Unlike many geniuses and visionaries, Paley at first was no more than incidentally conscious that his life's work had revolutionary ramifications. He did what he did mainly because he enjoyed it immensely, not because he knew that radio and television would change the world, not because he knew that the manner in which people choose to be informed and entertained influences who and what they are. More than most men of his importance, Paley has had fun at his work. For him, in many ways, fun has been the central point of it all.

But the fun—the lack of stereotypical revolutionary zealotry—is deceptive. For there can be no doubt that Paley was and is a genuine revolutionary. Until the 1920s there never had been anything like mass broadcasting—more particularly Paley's brand of broadcasting. Perhaps more than anyone or anything else in the twentieth century, on a level of public taste, sensibility, and emotion, William Paley and the institutions he created have been America. Network radio was one with America from the late 1920s until the early 1950s: the voices of Jack Benny, Amos 'n' Andy, Arthur Godfrey, Bing Crosby, and Edward R. Murrow were as ubiquitous in American life as weather. And network television has been one with America from the 1950s into the 1980s: *I Love Lucy,* Ed Sullivan, *All in the Family, M*A*S*H, The Beverly Hillbillies, Dallas, 60 Minutes,* Walter Cronkite. And movies—countless movies—movies made for theaters and movies made for TV, all seen now mostly on TV by vastly larger audiences than have ever seen them in theaters. These programs, personalities, and films—encompassing brilliance, mediocrity, trash, and worse—defined what America was as it proceeded through the century: what it was concerned about, what it was paying attention to, what it was laughing at, what it was moved by. America was never quite so united as when it listened to Ed Murrow's broadcasts during World War II or watched Walter Cronkite's coverage of the Kennedy assassination and the first moon voyages. Nothing in recent decades has crystallized American passions and focused American minds quite like television coverage of the Vietnam War, the agony of the civil rights movement, the violence of the late 1960s, and the crumbling of the Nixon presidency. No American, according to polls, commanded more public respect in the 1960s, 1970s, and early 1980s than Walter Cronkite.

All of these people and all of these shows (and many of the movies) were on CBS. The other networks had their favorites, too—no one would forget Milton Berle, Johnny Carson, or Huntley and Brinkley. But, decade after decade, America turned most to CBS.

And CBS was the creation, the business, the passion, and the life of one man—William Samuel Paley. He could be forgiven if he found it hard to retire.

In Paley's last full year as CBS board chairman, 1982, the corporation earned revenues of $4.1 billion and profits of $150 million. CBS television and radio were leaders in both entertainment and news, just as they had been throughout much of Paley's tenure. CBS television programs and phonograph records made their way into untold millions of households on every continent, influencing not only audiences but purveyors of entertainment as well. *Dallas*, for example, was seen in eighty-six nations and translated into thirty-two foreign languages. At least one foreign nation—Australia—produced its own replica of *60 Minutes*, using not only the format and style of the U.S. original but the same title and logotype. CBS also was a major force in such diverse businesses as musical instruments (Steinway pianos), publishing (the Holt, Rinehart and Winston book company), toys (Rubik's Cube and Erector sets), and several areas of advanced computer and communications technology.

William Paley's personal net worth probably exceeded $200 million, although he declined to specify. His CBS stock alone was worth about $140 million in the middle of 1983.

When he took control in September 1928, two days before his twenty-seventh birthday, the year-old company was called United Independent Broadcasters and employed about a dozen people quartered in a few offices on one floor of the narrow Paramount tower in Times Square. UIB's only activity was supplying ten hours of programs a week, mostly music, to sixteen radio stations in eleven states. In its first full year of operation, it had taken in $176,737 and paid out $396,803, for a net loss of $220,066. UIB's physical assets—furniture and the like—were worth about $25,000.

Bill Paley paid what seemed like a lot for such a flimsy operation—$500,000 for slightly more than 50 percent of the company and de facto control of the rest—but he was ideally suited for the risk. Already a millionaire, he had graduated from the University of Pennsylvania and worked successfully in his father's cigar business in Philadelphia, proving himself to be an imaginative businessman and a superb salesman. He had also become fascinated by radio and frequently listened to a crystal set late into the night. It seemed inevitable, therefore, that cigars and radio would get together, and they did when Paley's father and uncle, Sam and Jay Paley, were in Europe and young Bill decided to spend fifty dollars advertising La Palina cigars on WCAU in Philadelphia. The elder Paleys reproached Bill for his "extravagance," but it became apparent immediately that radio was a more potent medium for selling cigars than newspapers and magazines were. Sam and Jay relented, and Bill was asked to organize a program for the UIB radio network, whose control then was owned by a friend of the Paley family. When the opportunity arose, Bill decided, with his father's blessing, to purchase the majority interest.

Apart from his wealth, Bill Paley's personality and mode of living were already well established by that time. He was polished, outgoing, and dynamic and had a robust sense of humor. He was a ladies' man and, indeed, a ladykiller. He loved beautiful women—everything about them intrigued him—and he knew they found him attractive. (He read *Vogue* and *Harper's Bazaar* regularly.) He had developed a sophisticated taste for the things that money could buy: fine furnishings and design, travel in Europe, luxurious automobiles, and haute cuisine. In many ways, Bill Paley was the antithesis of David Sarnoff, who by then was rising quickly through the ranks of RCA, owner of the dominant radio network, NBC. While both men were of Russian Jewish extraction, Sarnoff was an up-by-his-bootstraps product of New York poverty—the Lower East Side and Hell's Kitchen. His formal education ended with the eighth grade.

Paley, within two months of taking command at UIB, which he renamed the Columbia Broadcasting System, began introducing fundamental changes that would affect the entire structure and operation of radio in America. Instead of focusing on the phenomenon of radio itself—the mechanics of transmitting sound over the air, which was the principal fascination of Sarnoff—Paley concentrated on the implications of the phenomenon: the massive potential audiences for radio, the substance of the programs that might attract those audiences, and the opportunities for transmitting advertising messages to vastly larger groups of people than could be reached through the print media.

Paley started by changing the basic concept of networking as embodied in the standard contract—then intricate and muddled—between the network and its affiliated stations. He devised a much simpler contract, giving the stations attractive incentives but centralizing at the network virtually all power over the affiliates' broadcasting of network programs. Although the stations' authority was diminished, they liked the Paley plan because it made their own operations much easier. By the beginning of 1929, Paley had tripled the number of CBS affiliates. His formula became standard throughout the industry, and though it was modified over the years, the principle of network dominance of local stations became permanent.

With CBS promising larger and more stable audiences, Bill Paley showed his

prowess as a salesman. In addition to selling time to advertisers, he sold entertainers such as Bing Crosby, Paul Whiteman, Kate Smith, Will Rogers, and
Fats Waller on the notion of appearing on radio, CBS in particular.

"I saw Fats Waller at a private party one night," Paley recalls. "He played and
sang. I thought he was good and called him in for an audition. The people listening said, 'My God, this guy plays a whorehouse piano.' I said, 'Yeah, what's
wrong with that?' He had a special way of singing a song, a special kind of
rhythm. I thought he was terrific."

Once CBS's success seemed assured, the network attracted the attention of
the big motion picture studios. Although decades would pass before movies
and the broadcast media would learn to live together peacefully and profitably,
it was clear to discerning people in both fields that they had much in common.
The first talking picture—*The Jazz Singer*— had been released a little more
than a year earlier. Television was on the way. Bill Paley surmised that he could
learn a lot about show business from the film studios. Early in 1929, just a few
months after Paley had taken command at CBS, Adolph Zukor, the head of
Paramount Pictures, offered Paley $4 million for a 49 percent interest in the
radio network, which by then he controlled in its entirety. Paley held out for $5
million and got it. Thus, he retained control of the company but established its
value at several times what he had paid for it only months before.

The Paramount deal instantly made Bill Paley an important figure in Hollywood. Adolph Zukor escorted Paley to Los Angeles, where he was honored at a
lavish party given by Paramount's production chief Jesse Lasky at his beach
house in Santa Monica. Paley remembers the occasion well:

"For a kid who loved motion picture actresses, and who hadn't been around
anyplace, to suddenly have a party given for *him*, with every great star in the
country there, sort of honoring him and being nice to him, was almost more
than I could stand! Fantastic!" Among the many people Paley met that evening
was Irene Mayer, the twenty-one-year-old daughter of Louis B. Mayer, who
lived next door. Within a few years, Paley and his new wife, Dorothy Hearst,
would become fast friends with Irene Mayer and her new husband, David O.
Selznick. In addition to forming deep friendships with the Selznicks, Paley also
grew very close to Selznick's business partner, John Hay "Jock" Whitney. Paley
would always remember the Atlanta premiere of Selznick's *Gone with the
Wind*, at which he and Dorothy were among Selznick and Whitney's special
guests, as an exceptionally exciting event. Paley formed many other lasting relationships in the movie industry as well (although Paramount, burdened by
the Depression, eventually sold its CBS stock back to CBS).

In addition to inventing a new network structure, bringing new personalities
to radio, and forging important links with Hollywood, Bill Paley shaped the
principles that would govern the broadcasting of news and information. Partly
out of personal conviction and partly out of fear of government interference,
Paley insisted that CBS news broadcasts be "objective," "balanced," and
"fair," and that "commentary" be separated from news reports—all essential
requirements, he felt, for combating demagoguery on the air and establishing

radio as a medium of serious journalism. By hiring an able group of newsmen with backgrounds in print journalism, he proceeded to build a news organization that not only achieved high quality and public acceptance, but was widely copied.

On March 11, 1938, the day Germany invaded Austria, Bill Paley, home in bed with a cold and fever, instructed that a broadcast be assembled presenting live reports of reactions to the invasion from around Europe. "I said, 'Let's do this,'" he recalls, "and was told 'Impossible' by the technicians, and I said, 'Nuts. It can be done. I know it can be done.' And three hours later they found a way of doing it. It sounds like something very casual and very ordinary now. But sitting back that first night and hearing Vienna, Berlin, Paris, London, and Rome, with reports from each of these places giving news of what was happening and what the reactions were to what was happening, was a thrilling thing. It gave radio a whole new dimension. That was a very proud moment in my life. I loved it." The program became the *World News Roundup* and is still a daily staple of the CBS radio network.

By the end of the war, radio had become an integral part of American life. More than fifty-six million radios were in use. Nine out of ten families had radios, more than had cars, telephones, or bathtubs. People spent more time listening to radio than doing anything else except working and sleeping.

At CBS, however, there was a problem: twelve of the fifteen shows with the largest audiences were on NBC. Bill Paley, who had spent the latter part of the war in Europe serving on Eisenhower's staff, had not been as attentive to the business of his company as he would have been otherwise. But he was determined to overtake NBC and marshaled all the powers of his formidable personality to the task. Paley the persuader, Paley the charmer, Paley the dogged negotiator, Paley the master salesman went into action. He wooed Amos 'n' Andy from NBC. Then he went after Jack Benny and, in a complex sequence of maneuvers, persuaded Benny and his sponsor, American Tobacco, to switch networks, too. The next to join CBS was Bing Crosby (who had performed on NBC and ABC after starting with CBS in the 1930s). After Crosby came Red Skelton, Edgar Bergen, Burns and Allen, and Groucho Marx. These personalities, along with others, like Arthur Godfrey, whom CBS developed internally, put CBS in first place. By 1949 it had twelve of the top fifteen shows.

During those years Paley introduced another important change in the modus operandi of network broadcasting. He asserted network control over the content and scheduling of programs that historically had been under the sway of advertisers and ad agencies. Instead of simply selling time to be filled with advertiser-controlled programs, he sold ad time on programs whose content and scheduling were increasingly controlled by CBS. Like his earlier innovations, this change soon was adopted by the rest of the industry.

Moreover, the "Paley Raids," as the defection of entertainers to CBS in the late 1940s was known, signaled a fundamental shift in the balance of power between networks that would affect television as well as radio, and would last for decades. Except for a few brief periods, CBS has been the dominant network for thirty-five years.

William Paley applied the same philosophy to television in its infancy as he had to radio. To him, they were both *mass* media. He said it in the 1940s and he says it now: "What we are doing is satisfying the American public. That's our first job. I always say we have to give most of the people what they want most of the time. That's what they expect from us. It brings 'em entertainment and fun and joy.

"There's nothing wrong with that, either," he adds, anticipating the typical and, by now, tiresome next question: Why is television's "entertainment, fun, and joy" often so superficial, trivial, and worse? In answering the question, Paley first makes the obvious point that not all of TV is junk. He takes pride in the many achievements of CBS News. (In Paley's bedroom is an original Ben Shahn drawing of Ed Murrow, depicted as a knight with a lance on horseback, having just slain Senator Joe McCarthy, whose body lies at the horse's feet.) Paley also points to distinguished dramatic series such as *Playhouse 90* and to more-recent highly acclaimed CBS-TV films like Arthur Miller's adaptation of *Playing for Time*, starring Vanessa Redgrave and Jane Alexander. He loved CBS's cultural cable service too, and his deepest disappointment in years was the company's decision to close it in 1982 because of heavy financial losses.

Paley always has been most intrigued, however, not by the relatively small number of highbrows who can be depended upon to watch cultural fare, but rather by the proclivities of the mass audience, the audience that watches the junk and occasionally will watch a show of higher quality if it is sufficiently enticing.

"We always hear about this word called 'quality,'" he says. "Why is everything so cheap and why do you cater to the lowest common denominator? We don't. But on the other hand, we can't be what a person wants to get out of *The New York Times*. If *The New York Times* had a circulation of forty million, it wouldn't be the same kind of newspaper. It would have to cater to the people it was selling the newspaper to. That's what we do. . . . But to the largest extent possible, we try to raise the standards and try to educate people to like and want better things and enjoy them.

"A perfect strike in this business is getting something that is really high quality and popular at the same time—bring those two things together—that's the thing you're always searching for [examples are *M*A*S*H* and *60 Minutes*]. Sometimes they're successful and sometimes they aren't. We had a thing called *Beacon Hill* once, remember that? [An American *Upstairs, Downstairs*, set in Boston.] That was one of the best things we ever produced, and it was an absolute, total flop. I gave orders that every goddamned costume had to be completely authentic no matter what the cost, no cheating, no cutting corners, this had to be it. And they did it. And it was a very, very expensive production and, I thought, a good production, beautifully cast, the story line was interesting, the direction was good. I could find no fault with it. But the public didn't like it. And that's that. The decision you have to live with, take in your stride. I made a big study of what the hell made it go sour. And the only thing that came out was that this particular show had about, what, ten or twelve servants—remember, they were crowding the kitchen—and the average American just didn't believe that anybody could have ten or twelve servants. . . . Could that have been important enough for the public to turn it off? I don't know. . . . That was a big disappointment.

"Once in a while you get one that goes the other way, and then of course you have a gold mine. . . . Look at *All in the Family*. It was a show that was sort of impossible for most people [including Paley] to think belonged on a television schedule, but it had some strong features. . . . It accommodated people to an issue that they didn't think much about and weren't talking about very much, the bigots who live in this country and how they look and act. I'd never seen anyone else before try to portray them in a very natural way, and [Carroll] O'Connor had the ability to do that. You hated the son of a bitch because he was such a bigot, so highly prejudiced, and then you got to like him a little bit, too, because he was so outspoken, so natural, and so real. So it fit. A very good cast, very good writing. Some of those shows just stick in your memory over the years—they made such a very strong point.

"So you have to lead the audience. I think we have led 'em over a period of years. I think their tastes are better now than they were, say, ten years ago. They're more sophisticated. . . . You sort of hesitate to go too far because the public won't understand it or won't like it. You go a little further hoping they will."

Paley disputes the significance of the networks' recent loss of audience to pay-cable and other forms of television. He cites network surveys indicating that while the networks' percentage of the audience is dropping, they are expected to retain a comfortable majority of the total television audience. That total audience, in turn, is expected to grow enough to leave the networks with a net increase in number of viewers, despite the drop in percentage.

"There's less enthusiasm now for some of the cable services than there was to begin with," Paley points out. "Some of the dreams just haven't come true. You come across a lot of unfortunate endings to things that started out to be so exciting, that looked to be so profitable. The jury's still out on a lot of this stuff."

Paley acknowledges stirrings of discontent in the TV audience. "I think the signals to us are, 'Get better, get better.' "

In addition to dominating broadcasting for five decades, Bill Paley, directly and indirectly, induced fundamental changes in the world's other principal institution of show business—Hollywood—and came to dominate it as well. When Paley and his contemporaries started producing television shows in the late 1940s, only a few thousand people had TV sets, and movie theaters were selling ninety million tickets a week. Movie moguls ridiculed television and predicted its demise. But only a decade later, television was in nearly 90 percent of American homes, weekly movie attendance had dropped to forty million, and the moguls were panicking.

The television networks reacted skillfully. Instead of pressing their advantage to a destructive extreme—a move that might have decimated several film studios—the networks took advantage of the studios' plight in ways that proved profitable for both sides.

First, the networks hired the studios to revive their dormant back lots and make television shows for network viewing—sitcoms, action dramas, and the rest—to the networks' specifications. Having in decades past made a few A pictures and a lot of B pictures, the studios found themselves making a few A pictures and a lot of television shows. Second, the networks made use of Hollywood by supplementing TV program schedules with Hollywood movies made originally for theater viewing. And third, a logical next step in view of audiences' evident enthusiasm for the televising of movies, the networks commissioned the studios to produce movies specifically for television, with no initial theatrical showing.

By the early 1980s, the number of homes with television was approaching 100 percent. Many homes had more than one set. For a monthly fee, one could see Hollywood's A pictures on television without commercial interruption only months after their initial theatrical release. Weekly attendance at theaters had dropped to twenty million, less than a quarter of the audience in the late 1940s. When a studio considered a film project, it asked itself not only "Will it play at the theater box office?" but also "Will it play on television?" If the answer to the second question was no, the movie probably wasn't made. Distinctions between theatrical movies and TV movies blurred. Television and motion pictures, to all intents and purposes, had become a single industry, with television largely in command.

Paley and his colleagues, in effect, had forced the old Hollywood of Paley's friend David Selznick to play by Paley's rules—the rules of television. (Ironically, there was no friction between Paley and Selznick, because they never did business together. As Selznick once told his lawyer, "My preference . . . is NBC, simply *because* of my close friendship with Bill Paley—because dealing with Bill would be akin to dealing with my brother, and I would prefer to deal at arm's length with NBC.")

Perhaps the most visible symbol of the vast changes was in the presidency of the Academy of Motion Picture Arts and Sciences, the old-line movie group that awards the Oscars. The president is a writer-producer, Fay Kanin, whose best—and best-known—film is a movie made specifically for, and shown only on, television: *Friendly Fire.*

Although he became the most influential show business impresario in the world, Bill Paley did not spend every waking moment at the task. Having served in World War II, he returned to the government during the Korean War at the request of President Truman to conduct a study of the nation's natural resources. The study, which took a year and a half, predicted many of the energy shortages the nation is experiencing today. In the late 1960s Paley was active for several years on the board of a corporation formed to help restore Bedford Stuyvesant, a large, poor neighborhood in Brooklyn. Many of the corporation's most crucial meetings were held in Paley's CBS office.

Perhaps his most passionate outside activity has been the Museum of Modern Art. In addition to being an avid art collector himself, Paley has been on the museum's board since 1937, was president from 1968 to 1972, and currently is chairman. He also is chairman of the Museum of Broadcasting, which he founded in 1976 to preserve and exhibit radio and television programs from their beginnings to the present. More recently Paley has started a company to conduct research in genetics, and he is starting another to do research in "artificial intelligence," a field in which scientists are trying to develop computers that can simulate human thinking and reasoning. Paley also has become a partner in Whitcom Investment Company, which was founded by his late friend Jock Whitney. Whitcom's most visible holding is a one-third interest in the *International Herald Tribune,* of which Paley is a cochairman.

Paley travels extensively and has a great deal of fun doing it. Some years ago in France, after watching the filming of a CBS documentary, he and his friend Walter Thayer of Whitcom were spending a couple of days in Deauville before being driven back to Paris. While in Deauville Paley assiduously surveyed local opinions of the best restaurant between Deauville and Paris, so that he and Thayer could have the finest possible lunch en route. Having finally made a choice, they feasted on a multicourse meal featuring lobster and concluding with strawberry tarts. As they were preparing to leave, the chef appeared and said he was sorry they weren't able to try another house specialty, roast duck.

Paley paused for a moment. "How long would it take to prepare?" he asked.

"Twenty minutes, half an hour," the chef replied.

"We'll have it, we'll wait," Paley declared. The duck was served and consumed. Back in Paris a few hours later, Thayer was fast asleep in their two-bedroom suite at the Ritz when he was awakened by Paley knocking on his door.

"It's dinnertime," Paley said. "Where do you want to eat?" A dubious Thayer roused himself, and the two proceeded to a restaurant on the Île de la Cité, where they had another exceptional meal.

Paley says that until he quit smoking seventeen years ago, he could "eat like a horse" without exceeding his "normal" 170 pounds. (He stands about six feet tall.) Since then he has weighed as much as 195 and talks constantly of dieting but never does. He eats pretty much what he wants to, including a lot of rich French, Chinese, and Italian food, and drinks vodka and wine. His main concessions to exercise are two masseurs (one of them a "tough son of a bitch") and a masseuse, each of whom visits his apartment at least once a week.

Paley seems to have the stamina of a man half his age. In January 1981 he and Henry Kissinger were visiting the foreign minister of Oman, who happened to have a billiard room situated down a flight of stairs, beneath his swimming pool. As Kissinger was entering the billiard room he heard a loud

225

crash and a thud. Paley, who had been several steps behind Kissinger chatting with some other people, had fallen down the stairs and struck his head, opening a large cut. Helped to his feet, Paley staggered into the billiard room with "blood pouring out all over the goddamned place." Even though he was stunned, Paley was lucid enough to hear Kissinger say, "No man can survive a fall like that." However, Paley was rushed to a nearby hospital, the cut was stitched and bandaged, he was given a small hat to wear, and he attended a large dinner party that evening. The next day, according to prior schedule, Paley and Kissinger flew several hours to Marrakech, arriving at midnight (four A.M. Oman time). Instead of going straight to bed, Paley insisted on having dinner with their hostess, Marie-Hélène Rothschild, the wife of Baron Guy de Rothschild. Kissinger since has ribbed Paley frequently about the accident. "I've been thinking about that fall of yours. At the time I didn't think you'd survive, but something very odd has happened. Ever since then, you seem brighter and sharper than you used to be. I think you ought to make it an annual event."

Bill Paley loves the parry and thrust of sharp wit—his and others', especially Kissinger's. He is never happier than when he is trading quips with a few close friends over a leisurely dinner at home, at someone else's home, or in a restaurant. That is the way he spends most evenings, rarely going to the theater, concerts, or other public entertainments (although ballet is his favorite performing art). He sees most television and movies on cassettes in private, late at night or on weekends. Except for books on art, most of his reading bears directly on his businesses. He reads only occasionally for pleasure and personal enrichment, and when asked if he has favorite authors, he is unable to name one.

Within and without the constant milieu of fine food and witty friends, women have always played a crucial role in the life of Bill Paley. Despite his age, many younger women find his bluff charm and robust good looks irresistible. And his own ardor for women has not ebbed. "He likes women," declares Irene Selznick. "It doesn't have to be sexual. He likes them . . . it doesn't have to be artistic, it doesn't have to be professional, personal, social, sexual. He likes them." The most important woman was and still is Barbara "Babe" Cushing, his second wife and a hostess and socialite of international renown, to whom he was married for thirty-one years and who died of cancer in 1978. He says he doesn't know whether he will marry again. "Actually, I'm just drifting," he says. "I have friends, I have a good time on the whole."

Several hundred people in formal attire are gathered in the Grand Ballroom of the Waldorf-Astoria to honor Paley, the 1983 recipient of the Business Statesman Award from his alma mater, the University of Pennsylvania's Wharton School of business and finance, from which he graduated in 1922. On the three-tier dais, investment banker Felix Rohatyn is introducing Paley in the way Paley likes to be introduced: with praise, but more important, with humor.

"As a friend," Rohatyn is saying, "his intellect and his taste are a constant joy, both in the quality of his art, in the quality of his intellect, and in the quality of his chef, who is equal to none [laughter]. . . . Bill is a man who is probably the liveliest and most youthful man I know, which is a statement that will probably be attested to by some of the loveliest women in New York City [laughter]. In closing, because I know you want to get to Walter Cronkite [laughter—Paley was to speak before Cronkite], I'd like to give you a little anecdote which I think describes Bill as well as any. My wife at Easter has an Easter egg hunt in our garden. And a couple of years ago we had an Easter egg hunt where she hides a golden egg, and the winner is the man or lady who finds the golden egg. We had a very elegant Easter egg hunt, which included Bill Paley, Henry Kissinger, [union leader] Victor Gotbaum—it was a very ecumenical kind of Easter egg hunt. It must be obvious to you that Bill Paley found the golden egg, but not only did he find the golden egg, he was going to find that golden egg if my whole property was defoliated. And when he found the golden egg, he held it up as if he had just won the marathon. To him it was a terribly important and joyful thing. . . . Bill Paley plays to win, and he wins in great style. . . ."

At his weekend home in Southampton, on a Friday evening in the early spring, Paley decides to watch a movie after dinner. He is critical of movies in general and has walked out of more than he has seen to the end. Years ago, when his children were young, they ran betting pools on precisely how many minutes into a particular film their father would leave the projection room in the family estate on Long Island's North Shore. Occasionally, however, Paley loves a film. He enjoyed *Tootsie*. And recently, on the recommendation of a friend, he located and watched a print of G. W. Pabst's classic *Pandora's Box,* starring Louise Brooks and made in Berlin in 1929. He liked it, too.

This evening in Southampton, accompanied only by his younger daughter, Kate, and a dinner guest, he idles through a list of a dozen or so videocassettes currently in the house that he can play on his Sony Betamax and fifty-inch Mitsubishi television screen. *Papillon. Blow-Up. The French Lieutenant's Woman. North by Northwest.*

There is no surge of interest from anyone.

A clock in the living room strikes nine, and Paley glances at his watch. "*Dallas* is coming on," he says. "You know, the audience is sticking to that show like glue." He doesn't want to watch *Dallas* himself but is simply noting that at this moment millions of other people across America are tuning to it on his network.

Back to the movie list. *Some Like It Hot. Lenny. Top Hat. Bus Stop. The Public Enemy.*

Although Paley predicts he'll fall asleep during the movie, he finally chooses *Some Like It Hot.* He wants to see Marilyn Monroe. And Billy Wilder, the director, is one of his oldest friends in Hollywood.

When the words *Chicago, 1929,* appear on the screen, Paley proclaims, "My birthplace." He chuckles at the entrance of George Raft in the role of the mobster Spats Columbo and at the hilariously grotesque faces of the other mobsters.

"Where do they get those faces?" he asks, laughing.

A third of the way into the movie, during the prolonged slapstick frolic on the train from Chicago to Florida, Paley yawns.

"Had enough?" he asks. "It's sort of boring."

"It *is* pretty dated," someone says.

There is no consensus for turning it off, however, so it stays on, and Paley is delighted when Joe E. Brown enters the film as a wealthy, girl-chasing tycoon. He chuckles frequently the rest of the way, but at the end he yawns again and his only comment is, "It's amazing how chubby Monroe was. I don't remember her being that heavy."

The protracted strain of William Paley's retirement from CBS has not been leavened by the strain's predictability. Paley had his first obvious opportunity to retire in 1966, when he turned sixty-five years old—the company's "mandatory" retirement age. He chose to stay on, to the great disappointment of Frank Stanton, CBS's second-in-command for many years, who felt he had earned the right to succeed Paley. Over the next fourteen years Paley went through four other potential successors: he fired two, demoted a third, the fourth died, and Stanton, too, departed when he reached sixty-five and no exception to the retirement rule was offered.

In 1980 Paley hired Thomas Wyman, the vice-chairman of Pillsbury, as president of CBS, and three years later it appeared that Wyman, a man of exceptional intelligence and personal grace, had progressed much further than any of his predecessors toward genuinely succeeding Paley as the true chief executive.

Is Wyman the right man? Paley says, "I'm giving up a lot based on my strong feeling that he is. He has only been here three years, and there are a lot of indications that he's very well suited for the job. I've said so publicly, and I believe it. God knows, I hope it works."

The retirement is acted out officially on Wednesday, April 20, 1983, at the annual meeting of CBS stockholders, held this year in a cavernous studio at KMOX, the CBS television station in St. Louis, whose sister radio station was one of the original sixteen CBS affiliates. CBS frequently holds its shareholder meetings outside New York, usually at one of its facilities in another major city. Paley has presided at more than fifty such annual meetings as either president or board chairman of the corporation, and this presumably is his last in that role. After today he will hold the less-exalted titles of chairman of the executive committee and consultant, although he will retain his office suite on the thirty-fifth floor of CBS's New York headquarters for life.

Attired, as usual, in a dark suit and dark tie, white shirt, and white pocket handkerchief, his silver hair impeccably coiffed (usually several strands are casually askew), Paley calls the meeting to order precisely at the appointed hour—two P.M.—and delivers a brief farewell address. Not a great orator, not particularly skilled at podium drama or comedy, he simply reads the speech with sincerity, and with evident but understated emotion, in his slightly raspy baritone voice. Only toward the end does his voice begin to break.

"It's difficult to tell you what a jumble of emotions I feel at this time. The memories crowd in. The battles. The victories. The disappointments. The triumphs. And through it all, the people . . . scores, hundreds, thousands, who worked at all levels and in all departments at CBS and who together gave CBS its heart and its mind and its muscle. . . . Wherever CBS goes, my heart will go with it." He gets to the end with misty eyes and a few throat clearings, but without breaking down.

There is an emotional standing ovation. And the meeting itself, because Paley has vetoed fanfare that others had wanted to mount, is something of an anticlimax.

How much has really changed? Tom Wyman has become board chairman as well as president. Paley, however, still owns enough stock for control in most companies. As he has for years, he will meet with Wyman once a week. As he has for years, he will attend most meetings of the management committee and the board of directors. As he has for years, he will confer frequently with the top broadcasting and programming executives on programming details. As long as Paley remains healthy and mentally competent, therefore, the speculation will continue. Suppose he grows disenchanted with Wyman? Does he still have enough power to get rid of him as he did the others? Few insiders will take bets. But few would disagree with Lew Wasserman, the chairman of MCA-Universal, who is something of a show business legend himself and has known Paley well for forty years:

"As long as Bill Paley has breath in his body, he will *be* CBS."

WILLIAM S. PALEY *was born on September 28, 1901, in Chicago. His parents were Russian Jewish immigrants. He says his ambition stems from an early antagonism with his mother. He thought she did not find him attractive. Later he built an art school in Jerusalem in her memory.*

In his youth he was an avid gambler and once owed five thousand dollars, which two loan sharks came to collect. He borrowed the money from his uncle.

When he was eighteen, he decided to be rich before he was thirty-five. Sure enough, before he was thirty he was living in a triplex apartment on Park Avenue with an English butler-valet.

His late party nights prompted him to hire a man to haul him out of bed. Every morning Paley would fire the man for waking him up, then after showering, tell him ". . . just kidding. . . . Come back tomorrow."

He wrote of trips to Paris in the Twenties: "My companions were known as 'the smart set' and followed a routine one spring season after another. There was a right place to have lunch every day, a right place to have dinner; after dinner there was another place, and then began the night life. . . ."

He married Dorothy Hearst on May 11, 1932. They bought an estate on Long Island with eighty-five acres, an indoor tennis court, a swimming pool, greenhouses, guest cottages, and gardens.

He was an early admirer of Picasso and Cézanne and commissioned Matisse to paint his first wife's portrait. After looking at some of Paley's own picture taking, Matisse told him to drop his career and become a photographer.

Having vowed to quit working at thirty-five and become a beachcomber, he worried "like the devil" during his thirty-fifth year over whether to retire. He now feels that he would have had he stayed in his family's cigar business.

In 1943 he made Paul Kesten acting CBS president and went overseas. Working as a civilian for the Office of War Information, he reorganized radio stations in North Africa and reconstructed Italy's radio network. In 1945 he became a colonel and served as deputy chief of General Dwight D. Eisenhower's Psychological Warfare Division.

He was one of the first Americans to reach the Dachau concentration camp at the end of World War II. It gave him a tremendous feeling of dread. Of the war, he wrote: "The indelible impressions of the horrors commingled in my mind with a feeling that life had never been so exciting and immediate and never would be again."

His war service earned him America's Legion of Merit award, France's Croix de Guerre with Palm, and honors from Italy, Poland, Cuba, China, and the Dominican Republic.

In the late Forties he lured away NBC's biggest stars one after another. With them came much of that network's audience. *Variety* named the phenomenon Paley's Comet.

He thinks of Edward R. Murrow as the "most outstanding" man he has ever known. In 1955 he authorized Murrow to offer Winston Churchill $100,000 to do a television interview. Churchill declined.

He takes great pride in his CBS office. His desk is a Parisian *chemin de fer* gaming table. Beautiful objects abound, but he makes sure things are not exactly in place and do not exactly go together.

At one point he started getting sleepy and bored with work at CBS and thought he should change careers. Then he discovered that for months his butler had accidentally been giving him a sleeping pill in the morning instead of a B_{12} vitamin.

He has proposed that each of the three networks agree to give two hours of prime time a week to programs that would appeal to "educated, sophisticated tastes more than to the mass audience."

He is not especially forthcoming with subordinates. He admits there are many CBS people whose skills he admires but never acknowledges.

The happiest years of his life, he has said, were the early years of CBS, when things weren't so complicated.

In thirty-one years of marriage, he and his second wife, "Babe," were not apart *for more than five consecutive nights. He says the pain he felt at her death still strikes him in the early morning.*

He says he could fall in love again but the woman would have to be much younger than him.

VISIONARIES

Taking the
Long, Sharp View

WHILE THEIR CONTEMPORARIES GROPED AT THE PRESENT TO FEEL A PULSE, OR considered the past to discern the course that led to the moment, these nine squinted through the veil of the future. Not that they were mystics. They were much more worldly than that. For most of them, reality was pure and simple; what set them apart was the conviction that a greater reality lay a number of years down the pike.

The Visionaries were determined to seize the future. Ambition flamed in each of them. But whether their ultimate motive was to alter the way we saw or simply to bring home their own bacon, the effect was the same: our destiny was defined by their vision.

To Martin Luther King Jr., the dream was vivid, its outcome inevitable. As he saw it, the way to a brighter morning for all of us was fundamental.

Alfred Barr, another kind of visionary, could draw a straight line from Picasso through Hopper to Warhol. And he had the worldly wisdom to know he would need a fairly big space to house them all. William Levitt, too, knew from housing. He knew that city apartments could never contain the ever-multiplying postwar babies and that, given an alternative, their young parents would give them crabgrass, not asphalt, to play on. Levitt's vision—affordable houses in a more or less bucolic setting—was really no newer than the American Dream itself.

For yet another sort of prophet, Ray Kroc, the future was to sprout on a thousand street corners. Americans were on the move—Kroc saw that through his crystal-clear windshield: selling houses in Michigan one day, buying them in Texas the next; zooming from work to golf course, from high school to mall, with barely enough time to *eat*. The United States was a crazy quilt in search of a stitch. Enter Kroc, who had divined that the fastest route to one nation, under Golden Arches, was through the stomach.

The future didn't shock the Visionaries, it reassured them. Tomorrow held few rude surprises because they saw it coming. Their uncannily correct, long-range forecasts were based on yesterday's conditions, today's cloud formations, and a sure sense of how the fronts moved.

The Visionaries saw through the sublime, and they saw through the prosaic. Whether they concerned themselves with art or science, with mind or spirit, they rode not the breaking wave but the crest. Abraham

VISIONARIES

Maslow, Tennessee Williams, and Reinhold Niebuhr—dissimilar men
who worked on disparate stages—rightly measured their audiences.
They knew we were ready to question our sense of good and evil. John
Ford and Robert Noyce grasped the connection between what was and
what was *to be*—and designed monumental movies and miniature
miracles.

The Visionaries believed fervently what they saw. They went to work.
When they had finished, the rest of us saw.

—L. E.

Martin Luther King, American Preacher

DAVID HALBERSTAM

I BEGIN WITH THE FIRST SCENE IN THE FALL OF 1956, WHEN THE SOUTH WAS STILL AS IT had always been. The Montgomery bus boycott had recently begun; Martin Luther King Jr., was just beginning to come to national prominence, and he had come to Nashville, Tennessee, to speak. I am not sure of the date; in the archives of my memory the scene is still black and white, and in part that is because racial scenes from the South remain clearer that way, but also because color television had not yet come to the country.

In those days I covered some aspects of the civil rights movement for the Nashville *Tennessean,* but when I went out to the black church where King was going to speak, if I recall correctly, I went on my day off. On the *Tennessean* we prided ourselves, with considerable justice, that we were a good paper, willing, unlike most southern dailies, to cover racial stories. But even a good and courageous paper like the *Tennessean* did not necessarily look for trouble, and sending a twenty-two-year-old reporter from the North to cover an outspoken young black minister constituted trouble. Besides, good as we were on basic questions such as integrating schools, we had nonetheless a few idiosyncrasies of our own. Just a few weeks earlier I had done a story on four young black women training at Tennessee State who were going to compete in the forthcoming Olympics and who were, in fact, to excel in the women's events— Wilma Rudolph was among them. In my lead I had referred to "four young coeds" at Tennessee State. The story had been bounced back with orders to rewrite the lead since only whites could rightfully be called coeds. Such were those days, even on a good newspaper.

The black church probably held fifteen hundred people, and perhaps six thousand had turned out. There had been no announcement in the paper or on television, but they *knew*. It was a very orderly and respectful crowd, including those who knew they would not get in. I went around to a side door, sure that the press—in this case it was likely to be only me, the media battalions would come later—could be squeezed in. As I entered I saw a Nashville cop who was a nemesis of mine, a hard-core segregationist for whom being a cop was as much as anything else a means of expressing racial hatred. He nodded and spoke to me; he favored me because I was the only other white face there.

"All this for a nigger preacher," he said.

I nodded at him.

He looked around again, saw the immensity of the crowd, and his face hardened for a moment. "I'll bet he sure can get them going." That seemed to please him, the idea that it would be some updated version of the old revival meeting, a jack-leg preacher holding forth and all kinds of blacks a-whooping and hollering and rolling on the floor. Feeling better, he smiled slightly and waved me in.

That was the first time I heard the Reverend Martin Luther King Jr. Now, more than twenty-five years later, it is remarkably easy to recall his impact. The words have gone, but not the power and the intelligence and the force of the performance. In particular, I remember the special communion in that church between minister and congregation as he and his audience shared with each other. He brought to them his high intelligence, his fierce will, his rare capacity to phrase new truths in old ways, and that strengthened them. And they brought to him their abiding dignity, with which they had suffered through years and years of hardship, and that in turn strengthened him.

Martin Luther King Jr., whose father was a famed preacher and whose grandfather was a famed preacher, was bringing the new social gospel to the old southern black cadence. The gospel cadence was time-honored in those churches; it was a way in which a black preacher allowed his congregation to minister to their wounds and express their emotions without confronting the white ruling class. But Martin King was challenging that, for his ideas were powerful and, if acted upon, they meant that everyone in that church was going to have to confront the white community. In the white vernacular of the time, he was stirring them up. Normally they might have been wary of some almost-unknown young minister from another state asking them to take such great risks. But Martin King was special; he was able to speak those new truths and at the same time remain *of* them, while someone else espousing the same ideas might have seemed desperately alien. What he was saying was simple; it was that the fault for the hardship in their lives lay not with them but with those who mistreated them. That does not seem terribly radical now, but the black pride part of the movement was still years to come and the average southern black was still mired in terrible self-doubt and self-defeat. So King was in effect giving them back a critical part of themselves. His voice seemed to be as much theirs as his. He was destined to be a Nobel laureate, the most important black leader of his generation; but then, when I first heard him, he was all of twenty-seven.

It was his great victory to strip segregation of its moral legitimacy and in so doing, in a society like ours, to prepare it for its legal collapse as well. That he did this without holding office and in a way that a vast majority of white middle-class Americans did not consider threatening is a sign of his immense skill as a moralist-activist. Indeed, he was able to hold up for their inspection the very core of some of their beliefs and do it in a way that required them, rather than him, to pass judgment on themselves. In America today our racial problems are different and infinitely more complicated. Today every American city, be it northern or southern, seems to have a Martin Luther King Boulevard, and old enemies running for office casually invoke his name. But it is important to remember that when the movement that he led began, he could not drink at a southern water fountain, could not ride in most seats on a southern bus, could not eat at a Woolworth's lunch counter, and could not use the men's room in any facility along the highway. Not only could blacks not do these things, they could not do them in a climate that judged them morally and legally unworthy of any such ordinary actions.

In the years before he emerged as a genuine indigenous leader, that is, a native southern son on native southern soil, the leadership of southern blacks was minimal. There were few blacks, no matter how successful they were, whose positions were not in some way or another beholden to the white power structure. The undertakers (business would always be good) and doctors and dentists were successful and relatively free of white pressure, but there was not much leadership there. The old-time preachers, of course, were there and they had their followings, but in the past they had been poorly educated and had served more than anything else as safety valves for their communities' emotions. More often than not they were burdened with the same doubts that weighed on the members of the congregation. Martin King was different; he was a scion of the new black South; throughout the South everyone knew King's daddy and granddaddy, if not personally, at least by reputation. He was well educated and confident; he had been to a great university in the North and received a Ph.D. and in the process had found that white people were no better or smarter or more moral than he. He married a black woman who was equally proud and confident and well-educated. Martin, Jimmy Baldwin once wrote, "never went around fighting with himself like we all did." Nor—as southern whites were now about to find out—was he alone; he was simply the most visible member of a new generation of talented, well-educated, utterly fearless young black ministers surfacing in the South. What distinguished him was the escalating Montgomery, Alabama, bus boycott, of which he became the leader. It gave him first a great regional and eventually a great national platform and audience. The more the segregationists of Montgomery resisted, the more his pulpit grew and the more famous he became.

He did a number of critical things in those brief years. If the first thing was to give ordinary oppressed blacks of the South a sense of their own value, then the second thing was to force the white Christians of the South to confront their own beliefs. This was, after all, probably the most seriously religious section of the country. In the beginning he touched a generation of white ministers, forcing them in turn to confront their own congregations. But he was as much a man of broad politics as he was a man of the church, and his greatest victory was in turning the nation's television networks into his personal pulpit. He and John F. Kennedy were the first great manipulators of modern political television, and Kennedy had several advantages over King: he was overtly in the political arena, he was white, and he was soon President. The years of King's greatest success—from Montgomery in 1956 to the March on Washington in 1963—almost exactly parallel the rise of television in American homes as the prime new political conduit. When he began, we were effectively without true networks; when he had finished his greatest achievements, it was an accepted part of American political life that one campaigned for public opinion, as well as for political office, by means of television.

He did not do this as others did, by stroking journalists' egos, by catering to our personal idiosyncrasies and offering us the small pseudointimacies that we cherish so much. In fact, he was not very good at traditional courting of the press. It was as if he was always a little too stiff, too aloof, too dignified. Instead, he offered reporters two absolutely irresistible things: ongoing confrontations of a high order and almost letter-perfect villains. In that sense he was more than just a master manipulator; he was, in the television age, as great a dramatist of midcentury America as Arthur Miller or Tennessee Williams. He cast his epics well; impoverished blacks would wear white hats and white police officers would wear black ones. He chose his villains carefully; they more often than not proved to be as primitive as their behavior was predictable.

So it was that without holding office he took a powerful existing social order and showed how it really operated and what the human price was. In effect, he took the terrible beast of segregation, which had always been there just beneath the surface, and made it visible. It was not so much that he slew that beast but that, instead, he brought it to the surface, and the beast, forced to reveal its police dogs and cattle prods and water hoses, exposed, died on its own.

It was classic media manipulation, and in subsequent years, as the immense impact of television upon our politics has become a central theme of our time, I have pondered the fairness of what he did. What he did, I am convinced, was more than legitimate, for the other side up to then had manipulated and coerced in its own way. The white power structure that owned all the television stations and newspapers in the South had over many years chosen not to listen to any legitimate black voices and not to hear the growing feeling of black protest. The white press of the South had never reported the thousands of informal meetings or the telephone calls the newspapers had received from mayors and police chiefs and judges and county attorneys and heads of chambers of commerce about what to cover and what not to cover and how best to deal with some local protest—protests that in the past had never become protests because they were never reported. The white manipulation that King was confronting existed in the form of a vast conspiracy of silence in virtually every town and city in the South.

Those early years brought his greatest victories. As he destroyed the moral legitimacy of segregation so too did the legal basis for it begin to come apart. The Civil Rights Act of 1964 was a direct result of King's victories throughout the South. Part of his strength in those early years came from the absolute certainty of his belief. It was as if he believed so strongly in the essential goodness of America on this question that others must see it too, and in time his vision did become true.

Later in his career, as he turned to the North, he came upon harder times, and his leadership and his voice faltered. In the North the task was more complicated. It was no longer a problem of legal or political inequality: blacks had the right to vote. Rather, the problem was of age-old injustices becoming a hardened part of the culture and of the growth of a hard-core underclass. In the North the good old churchgoing blacks who trusted and abided and who had been at the core of his constituency did not exist. Instead, they had become bitter, alienated young blacks who saw the darkness ahead, who knew that the only job they probably had a chance at was as a parking lot attendant. They did not believe that the answer would come through love and goodness and non-violence and Jesus Christ. They were the children of Malcolm, and King knew it.

The last time I saw him was in the spring of 1967. He was already speaking out against the Vietnam War, which cost him powerful allies in Washington and in the more traditional civil rights movements. He was trying to help organize various groups in northern cities without noticeable success. The simple evil of legal segregation, which had bound all blacks together in the South, was gone. The complexity of the problems in the North splintered the black leadership. The problem in the North, he told me one day, was what he called slumism—a bad job was a bad education was a bad home. He still gave the same soaring speeches, but now there was less community with the audience; and as there was less community with the audience, there was, I sensed, a greater interior doubt on his part. There was less resonance to his words. Martin King was, after all, a shrewd tactician and a shrewd politician, and I think he knew that he had come to the end of a certain era and that, from then on, the way of a moderate Christian was going to be much harder in this country.

I was working on a piece about him at the time, and I came home after several weeks on the road to write it. When I was finished, I was satisfied with the piece—except that I did not have *him*. He had remained, as ever, personally elusive, formal, gracious but distant. It was as if any small talk or laughter might detract from the movement and might come at the expense of his own dignity, and thus the dignity of all blacks. (Because of that tendency, the younger black leaders in SNCC had always called him de Lawd.) So I decided to give it one more shot, and I caught a plane to Atlanta; Andy Young took me to be with Martin and his family and many of their friends at someone's swimming pool. He was more relaxed that day than at any time I had seen him before. I have a memory of a young King daughter hurting her knee and Martin going over and comforting her and giving her a piece of fried chicken. "Let's put some chicken on that," he said. "Yes, a little piece of chicken, that's always the best thing for a cut." In the background a photographer from *Ebony* was shooting pictures of the home of the wealthy black contractor whose pool it was. It was quid pro quo; the contractor always helped bail out King and his people when they were arrested; now they were giving the forthcoming spread in *Ebony* a little Nobel laureate class. I have since thought often of that gentle day, of Coretta King teasing Martin about what a poor dancer he was, of little black children running in and out of the pool, of how southern, how middle-class, and, finally, how *American* it all was.

MARTIN LUTHER KING JR. *was born on January 15, 1929, in Atlanta. King had Irish kin on his father's side, Indian on his mother's.*

By the age of thirteen, he had attempted suicide twice, both times by jumping out a second-story window—once when he thought his grandmother had died and then when she actually did die.

"Daddy King" was a Baptist pastor. The Kings were "Negro wealthy," Martin Jr. said later. "We never lived in a rented house and we never rode too long in a car on which payment was due, and I never had to leave school to work."

"He didn't fight much," his brother said of him. "He usually was able to talk any situation to a conclusion."

His father hoped he would become a doctor or a lawyer. But after completing Morehouse College—which he entered at age fifteen—King enrolled at Crozer Theological Seminary. His parents' graduation present, in 1951, was a green Chevrolet. While at Crozer, King avoided anything that smacked of the Negro stereotype. At school picnics he would not eat watermelon.

At Boston University his doctoral thesis was "A Comparison of the Conceptions of God in the Thinking of Paul Tillich and Henry Nelson Wieman."

In Boston he met his wife, Coretta Scott. She found him a good dancer, and

242

earnest, but "somewhat too carefully dressed." During their first phone conversation, he said, "I am like Napoleon at Waterloo before your charms."

In 1957 he traveled some 780,000 miles to deliver 208 speeches.

According to one reporter, he could make the congregation of a country church say "Amen!" to a quotation from Plato.

A student at a sit-in said of King: "He renews my faith in obsession."

"A man who hits the peak at twenty-seven," reflected King, "has a tough job ahead. People will be expecting me to pull rabbits out of the hat for the rest of my life."

He became involved in the 1955 Montgomery bus boycott, which was touched off when seamstress Rosa Parks refused to give up her bus seat to a white person. King said Parks had been "tracked down by Zeitgeist—the spirit of the times." (Parks's own explanation: "I was just tired from shopping. My feet hurt.")

The FBI began tapping his phone in 1957. By 1964 J. Edgar Hoover, obsessed with ruining King's reputation, ordered wiretaps placed on phones in fifteen hotels in which King stayed. Eventually Hoover obtained tapes proving that King had engaged in extramarital sexual activities; he made the tapes available to the press, Congress, and President Lyndon Johnson. He also sent derogatory information to the pope, who ignored it and went ahead with his 1964 meeting with King. Finally he sent excerpts of the hotel tapes to Coretta King, along with an unsigned note to Dr. King saying, "Your end is approaching . . . you are finished. . . . There is but one way out for you. You better take it before your filthy, abnormal, fraudulent self is bared to the nation."

In September 1958, a forty-two-year-old black woman stabbed him with a letter opener while he was signing copies of his book in a Harlem bookstore. (Nelson Rockefeller paid the hospital bill.)

In 1959 he fulfilled his lifelong dream of visiting the country of Mahatma Gandhi. In the hallway of his Atlanta home he hung a large photo of Gandhi.

In 1965, after returning from Norway with the Nobel Peace Prize, he successfully registered at the Hotel Albert, a formerly restricted establishment in Selma, Alabama. While registering he was assaulted by James George Robinson of Birmingham.

He stood five feet seven inches tall and had a thick neck, oval eyes, a baritone voice, broad shoulders, and slim hands.

He enjoyed sports and opera. He often started but never finished the "Moonlight Sonata" on his piano.

Though reluctant to talk about himself, he once admitted, "I'm too courteous. It is one of my weaknesses as a leader."

He received one dollar a year from the Southern Christian Leadership Conference, and six thousand dollars a year from the Ebenezer Baptist Church. He donated the $54,123 awarded to him with the Nobel Peace Prize, to civil rights *activities. Harry Belafonte set aside trust funds for Coretta Scott King and her children.*

He was assassinated in Memphis on April 4, 1968, where he was supporting a sanitation workers' strike. His death set off riots in 125 cities that led to 21,270 arrests and forty-six deaths.

The Last Years of
Tennessee Williams

DOTSON RADER

I FIRST MET TENNESSEE WILLIAMS SHORTLY AFTER HE GOT OUT OF THE MENTAL WARD of what he called Barnacle Hospital, in St. Louis, where he had been confined by his brother, Dakin. Tennessee had flipped out on copious amounts of Doriden, Mellaril, Seconal, Ritalin, Demerol, amphetamine, and too much sorrow in Key West, and Dakin was called when his brother, in a drug-alcohol stupor, fell against a hot stove and badly burned himself. After having Tennessee baptized a Catholic at St. Mary, Star of the Sea Church in Key West—an event lost forever in one of the boozy black holes of his mind—Dakin hauled him to the nuthouse. Soon he was locked in an isolation cell in the violent ward for fighting with other inmates over what they would watch on the communal television set. He liked soaps, and the other loonies wanted to see game shows; a row ensued, and the orderlies dragged him off and shut him away in a padded cell, where he suffered two coronaries and nearly died. For all that and more he never forgave Dakin, and it inculcated in him a terror of going mad that never left him. Years later, near the end of his life, when Tennessee would do something particularly odd—dress in pajamas for a formal party or wander about Key West in a fright wig pretending to be his sister, Miss Rose—I would laugh and try as gently as possible to dissuade him, all the while knowing that when the peculiarity of his actions finally sunk in, he would take it as evidence that his pilot light was about to burn out and Barnacle Hospital lay ahead as the last stop on his trolley line. And days of convincing him once again that he was not going crazy, senile, that one cell too many had not been burned out by booze—all that would follow endlessly.

"I'm happy I never had any children," he told me before he died. "There have been too many instances of extreme eccentricity and even lunacy in my family on all four sides for me to want to have children. I think it's fortunate I never did. Miss Edwina [his mother] went crazy. She thought there was a horse living in her room and when she didn't want to do something, she'd say, 'I can't, Tom. I have to go riding today!' "

The night I met him, I had gone to the opening of an underground movie in Greenwich Village, a porno flick passing as a work of art. The theater was jammed with famous people, writers and painters mainly, which surprised me because I didn't realize then what I know now: common to the people who create our art is a passion for pornography. To the degree that if you bombed five or six skin houses in Manhattan on any given afternoon, you'd probably wipe out half the literary establishment in America. I do not know why that is, nor why so many of our greatest artists—painters, writers, poets, composers—are either gay or Jewish or both. But there you are.

After the movie I went to a party in SoHo, a district of New York that wasn't fashionable then. The party was held in a filthy loft with dim lights, mattresses on the floor, Day-Glo posters, cheap wine, dope, and naked bodies. Among those present were the Warhol gang and Jim Morrison of the Doors, who was given to sexually displaying himself at parties. Also there was the usual assortment of druggies, fetishists, whores, and other popular figures of the day. I suppose in looking back it seems curious that the greatest playwright of our age would be present, but we were in the lees of the Sixties, when you discovered the most famous people in the most improbable places, at Maoist rallies, for example, or in the sex rooms of the Anvil. And Tennessee, who thought himself a radical, a revolutionary, had been physically incapacitated during much of the decade and so had an intense, if belated, curiosity about the social, sexual, and political movements of the period, especially as they touched the young. He liked to slum, in part because he identified with the outcast, the loser, those up against it. And also, in being places where respectable people thought it was unsuitable to be seen, he made a kind of cockeyed solidarity with those who shared with him a hatred of the rich.

"The Sixties were a decade of great vitality," he remembered more than a decade later. "The civil rights movement, the movement against war and imperialism. When I said to Gore Vidal, 'I slept through the Sixties,' I was making a bad joke. I was intensely aware of what was going on. Even in the violent ward I read the newspapers avidly. Then we had brave young people fighting against privilege and injustice. Now we have the de la Rentas. They are the Madame du Barrys of our time! I find them an outrageous symptom of our society, the shallowness and superficiality, the lack and fear of any depth that characterizes this age, this decade. It appalls me."

At the party, Candy Darling, a drag queen and Warhol superstar who would later star in Tennessee's *Small Craft Warnings*, came up to me and said in her breathless way, "Tennessee Williams is here, and he wants to meet you!"

I said, "I thought he was *dead*." I thought that because he had disappeared from public view. In the Sixties people were dropping like flies right and left, and if you didn't hear about somebody for a time you assumed he had succumbed.

Candy Darling brought me over to meet him. I was dressed in a black leather jacket, leather boots, a black cowboy hat, which was the costume I affected then. Tennessee was wearing a gray suit, a multicolored silk scarf, and the most hideous tie I had ever seen—a sort of fluorescent rainbow of clashing colors that Eighth Avenue pimps adore. I was amazed by how tiny he was. (When his body was taken out of the Hotel Elysée in the black plastic bag and lifted into the morgue wagon, I was again reminded in the most terrible way of how little a man he was; so much brilliance came from so small a flame.)

Although he had read one of my books and some of my magazine stuff, he pretended to take me for a hustler. It was the only pass he ever made at me, and in years to come I would realize that if I had consented it would not have worked, because his sexual taste was so specific and so completely delimited by his memory of the body of Frank Merlo that any sexual engagement between us would have been unhappy. For it was through sex that he sought to bridge the distance between himself and his late lover. It was Merlo's death that had shattered him and in the years that remained he tried to overcome the loss, but he never did.

"Frankie [Merlo] was so close to life!" he once told me. "I was never that close, you know. He gave me the connection to day-to-day and night-to-night living. To reality. He tied me down to earth, baby. And I had that for fourteen years, until he died. And that was the happiest period of my adult life."

So the night I met him, Tennessee grinned at me and asked, "How much do you get a night?"

"Two hundred bucks," I replied, playing along.

He paused, rolling his eyes at Candy. "Well, baby, what do you charge to escort an older gentleman to dinner?"

"A hundred bucks."

He feigned shock, felt in his pockets for money, pulled out a few bills. After making a great show of counting his cash, he looked up and asked, "Do you suppose we could settle for *lunch?*"

He was fifty-nine, and I was twenty-six, but to me we both seemed so much older than we were.

The following day I met him for lunch at the Plaza Hotel, where he was staying, and I ended up spending three days with him in his suite until he left for Chicago. Quickly I became used to his routine. He would arise early and make himself a martini, order a pot of coffee, and with a bottle of wine in hand toddle into the living room and sit at his portable typewriter, where he would work until noon. Then we'd lunch and go for a swim. He would swim at the Y, although he had guest privileges at the New York Athletic Club. But he wouldn't go there anymore because the members would make antigay remarks about him and it reminded him too painfully of his father, the shoe salesman, who would cruelly call him "Nancy" in front of his friends. "They're all the same, baby. Shoe salesmen with a bad territory and wives they can't abide. So they take it out on us." But that habit of writing every day and swimming he maintained until he died. It's what kept him alive as long as it could.

And, too, I became used to his falling down, his drug haze, his drinking; hysterical laughter, rage and remorse, the web of self-destructive habits that would undo him. But in some unknown way the spirit that gave the world Blanche DuBois and Stanley, Chance Wayne and Alexandre del Lago, Big Daddy, Amanda Wingfield, Sebastian and Mrs. Venable, One Arm, and more was, by their very creation, so depleted of defense, rendered so exceptionally vulnerable, that it required the "ministrations," as he would say, of drugs and booze to make it through the night. When I met him what I was witness to was the beginning of his irreversible decline, when he could no longer keep his torment under control.

Tennessee told me that artists—by that he meant writers, for he never referred to them by any other term—spend their lives dancing on a high wire without any protective net beneath them, and when they fall it is sudden and final. Only Tennessee's end wasn't sudden. It was protracted and painful, lasting more than a decade during which he saw himself held up to public contempt. One of the few times I saw him cry was when he read a review by John Simon entitled "The Sweet Bird of Senility." Finally, he came to dread every new production, feared the public, and, except for Claudia Cassidy and Clive Barnes, hated the critics. When I first knew him he delighted in being recognized in public. By the end of his life, it mortified him, because he felt like currency debased, like an old ham who had become a caricature of himself.

To again state the obvious: he was our greatest playwright. Only he didn't know it. He was convinced that he was a failure, that his work and life were beyond repair and his plays would not live.

He had begun as a poet, starved as a poet, and because of the very resistance of the world to his poetry, it came to occupy a place of such inordinate importance in purity in his mind that he finally believed that history's judgment on him would rest on his verse. His life as a poet was associated with his early years—the lack of recognition, the poverty and hopelessness of a young poet in this country. His success as a playwright was almost inadvertent, and when it came to him late—he was thirty-five—it was so sudden and massive, so out of proportion to what he had come to expect, that he could never believe it would last. He suspected that his career was a fluke, a series of gimmicks, and sooner or later he'd be found out. From that came his paranoia. "If I didn't have my demons, I wouldn't have my angels."

His demons won the day.

But I didn't know that about him in the days we were first together. All I knew was that I, like every other writer who came after him, was irrevocably affected by his work. You couldn't get away from him because he had changed the way writing was done. With *The Glass Menagerie, A Streetcar Named Desire, Cat on a Hot Tin Roof, The Rose Tattoo, Sweet Bird of Youth, Orpheus Descending, Summer and Smoke,* and other plays, he married poetry to naturalism and opened drama to subject matter never before touched upon in our theater. Incest, homosexuality, cannibalism, impotency, drug addiction, cancer, madness, sexual frenzy, ineffable loss and longing, all redeemed and beatified by poetic gifts for dialogue and scene construction unmatched by any other writer. He ended the puritan sensibility in American theater and liberated it, poetically and thematically, from the moralism and falseness and middlebrow smugness that had held it bound. In so doing, he helped free us all and ushered in an age when, among other things, the opening of a pornographic movie could be a social event. In sum, Tennessee Williams forever changed America's knowledge of herself, opening up to light the darkest corners of her psyche, and thereby forced her to accept truth she did not wish to confront.

Two years ago, on his seventieth birthday, I went to Chicago to be with him for the opening of his last play, *A House Not Meant to Stand.* In a way, being there, he had returned to his beginnings, for it was in Chicago that *The Glass Menagerie* gave him his first success. He was staying in a four-bedroom duplex apartment on top of the Radisson hotel, in an oppressive Twenties-style place that delighted him. He dubbed it the Norma Desmond Suite. He was in high spirits, deeply tanned, and optimistic about the play.

On the morning of his birthday he opened a few gifts and cards and we had champagne. By then, his friendships with the famous who had made their careers on his work—Brando, Taylor, Kazan, Beatty, and others—had fallen away. He felt it.

After swimming that afternoon, we sat drinking in his makeshift study and talking about writing. That, finally, was his life.

I asked him if he had any regrets.

"Oh, God, yes. But I can't think about them now."

He smiled and shook his head. He reached for his wine glass, his hand making an extraordinarily elegant arc as it reached the cold surface; his fingers, one by one, slowly touching it and then lifting it. It was a gesture unique to him, and it brought back such memories to my mind—good times, laughter, pranks, outrageous camping. And the kindliness of his nature. All of those who met him when they were young and came to know him well will tell you what I do: that they never knew anyone kinder. He was the net under the wire for us.

"All my life," Tennessee said, "I've cared about the sufferings of people. There are few acts of volition. I don't believe in individual guilt. I don't think people are responsible for what they do. And yet, knowing that, I believe the moral person must try to avoid evil and cruelty and dishonesty as best he can. That remains to us."

His greatness is that he tried to do that harder and longer than any other artist.

When he died, he was working, naturally, on a new play. He titled it *In Masks Outrageous and Austere,* from a poem by Elinor Wylie. I do not know if he ever finished it, but he talked a lot about it, and I read scenes from it. Or rather I would start to read a scene, and he would grab it from me impatiently and say, "Baby, you don't know how to read!" Then he would sit back, reach for his wine, and, in his deep voice with its Mississippi drawl, read what he had written, cackling with laughter at the most sorrowful passages.

I can hear him reading now as I can hear him padding about the house in the middle of the night and knocking at my door before dawn and asking me to sit awhile with him because he cannot sleep, he is frightened, and will I stay with him until it is light? I can feel myself holding him, listening to him breathe after he's taken yet another Seconal to sleep, listening to make sure the breaths are deep enough and long enough to signal that sleep has come and I can creep away knowing he is safe. He said many times that "death doesn't like crowds. It comes to you when you're alone."

He was right.

> In masks outrageous and austere
> The years go by in single file;
> But none has merited my fear,
> And none has quite escaped my smile.*

TENNESSEE WILLIAMS *was born Thomas Lanier on March 26, 1911, in Columbus, Mississippi, in the rectory of his grandfather's church. He later changed his name to Tennessee because he felt that the imperfection of his early writing had compromised the name Thomas.*

After contracting diphtheria and a kidney ailment, he suffered his first nervous breakdown at age thirteen.

His sister, Rose, was subjected to one of the first prefrontal lobotomies ever performed in the United States.

When he was seventeen, his first published story appeared in Weird Tales, *a pulp. It began: "Hushed were the streets of many-peopled Thebes."*

His first writing prize, twenty-five dollars, was from Smart Set: *third place for an essay addressing the question "Can a Good Wife Be a Good Sport?"*

When his childhood girlfriend, Hazel Kramer, decided to enroll with him at the University of Missouri, his father threatened to withdraw him and succeeded in breaking up Williams's only known romantic relationship with a woman.

During the Depression, Williams left college to work at his father's firm, the In-

---

*© 1932 by Alfred A. Knopf. Renewed 1960 by Edwina C. Rubenstein.

ternational Shoe Company; he dusted shoes for sixty-five dollars a month. Later he said, "I went from shoe biz to show biz."

The year he became eligible to vote he cast his first and last political ballot, for Socialist Norman Thomas.

His agent, Audrey Wood, rescued him from a seventeen-dollar-a-week job as a movie usher and brought him to Hollywood, where MGM offered him $250 a week to write movie dialogue. MGM rejected his screenplay titled The Gentleman Caller—telling him he should draw his paycheck and not bother anyone. He later converted the script to a play, which he called The Glass Menagerie.

Wood described their relationship as love-hate. Williams called her Lady Mandarin and said she was a mother image for her clients—not Whistler's mother, he said, but Brecht's Mother Courage.

He wrote more than twenty-four plays and won two Pulitzer Prizes. The first production of one of his plays was Cairo, Shanghai, Bombay! *in Memphis in 1935. The last production of a new full-length play was* A House Not Meant to Stand, *in Chicago in 1982.*

He was an avid reader of movie magazines. Usually, only bad, sentimental movies could move him to tears.

He had many pets, including a Boston bull terrier named Gigi, a tan tomcat called Gentleman Caller, and an iguana—named Mr. Ava Gardner—who appeared in the film version of Night of the Iguana.

Of Marlon Brando, Williams said he "was always shy with me for some reason. . . . He wanted me to walk up the beach with him and so we did—in silence. And then we walked back—in silence." After Williams's death, Brando said, "I always felt like Tennessee and I were compatriots."

Williams's favorite writers were Chekhov, García Lorca, and Jane Bowles. He called the gazebo outside his Key West home the Jane Bowles Summer House, after her play In the Summer House.

He said, "I've always been blocked as a writer, but I love writing so much that I always break through the block."

He stood five feet six inches tall and had chestnut hair and blue eyes. He had a marvelous, nervous laugh. "The more intense the work became," producer Robert Whitehead recalled, "the more Tennessee would laugh."

He was a monumental hypochondriac. Several times he thought he was losing his sight, and he had four eye operations for cataracts. A heavy user of sedatives and vodka, he constantly thought his heart would stop beating.

"I always feel that I bore people," he remarked, "and that I'm too ugly. I don't like myself. Why should I? I'm quite aware of being mad. I've always been mad."

"Tennessee loved to swim," recalled José Quintero, "and I remember I found him on the steps of the [Chicago] Art Institute, sitting there as if there were no snow, and he said, 'It's a place for art—they will have compassion for the artist. They will have a pool.' That was the Tennessee I loved."

On February 25, 1983, his secretary found him lying next to the bed in his suite at the Hotel Elysée in New York. The previous night he had suffocated on the plastic cap from a medicine bottle.

Williams wrote in his memoirs that his body was to be "sewn up in a clean white sack and dropped overboard, 12 hours north of Havana, so that my bones may rest not too far from those of Hart Crane." But his brother, Dakin, had him buried in St. Louis, a city that he had always despised.

Abraham Maslow and the New Self

GEORGE LEONARD

HE WROTE WITH NONE OF THE DARK GRANDEUR OF A FREUD OR THE LEARNED GRACE of an Erik Erikson or the elegant precision of a B. F. Skinner. He was not a brilliant speaker; in his early years he was so shy he could hardly bring himself to mount the podium. He traveled little; Brooklyn was his home for nearly half his life. The branch of psychology he founded has not achieved a dominant position in the colleges and universities. He died in 1970, but a full-scale biography remains to be written.

And yet, Abraham Maslow has done more to change our view of human nature and human possibilities than has any other American psychologist of the past fifty years. His influence, both direct and indirect, continues to grow, especially in the fields of health, education, and management theory, and in the personal and social lives of millions of Americans.

Maslow confronts us with paradoxes. He started out as a behaviorist, a skilled experimenter, and then went on to demonstrate the crippling limitations of just that kind of psychology in the study of human affairs. He coauthored a textbook on abnormal psychology, a classic in its field, and then went on to investigate, not the pathological, but the exceptionally healthy person. Considering himself a Freudian, he went on to take Freudian psychology out of the basement of warring drives and inevitable frustration, up into the spacious, previously unexplored upper stories of the human personality, where entirely different, non-Freudian rules seemed to prevail.

Working ten to twelve hours a day in the shadow of a heart condition that was to kill him at sixty-two, Maslow produced a rich and varied body of work, one that has altered our way of thinking about human needs and motivations, neurosis and health, experience and values. Some of his theories are still controversial, especially in their particulars, but no one can deny that this dogged and daring explorer has radically revised our picture of the human species and has created a vastly expanded map of human possibilities.

Abraham H. Maslow was born on April 1, 1908, in a Jewish slum in Brooklyn, the first of seven children. His father, a cooper by trade, had come to America from Kiev, then had sent for a hometown cousin to join him as his wife. Young Maslow's childhood was generally miserable. He was alienated from his mother ("a pretty woman, but not a nice one," he later told English writer Colin Wilson) and afraid of his father ("a very vigorous man, who loved whiskey and women and fighting"). His father's business succeeded, and when Abe was nine the family moved out of the slums and into the first of a series of lower-middle-class houses, each slightly more comfortable than the one preceding it. But these moves took the family into Italian and Irish neighborhoods and made Abe the victim of terrifying anti-Semitism. He was not only Jewish but also, by his own account, a peculiar-looking child, so underweight that the family doctor feared he might get tuberculosis. "Have you ever seen anyone uglier than Abe?" his father mused aloud at a family gathering.

Reading was his escape, the library his magic kingdom. And when he chose to go to Brooklyn Borough High School, an hour-and-a-half's journey from his home, Abe got his first taste of success. He became a member of the chess team and of the honor society Arista. He edited the Latin magazine and the physics magazine, for which, in 1923, at the age of fifteen, he wrote an article predicting atom-powered ships and submarines. In terms of sheer, raw intelligence, Maslow was a true prodigy. Tested years later by the psychologist Edward L. Thorndike, he registered an IQ of 195, the second highest Thorndike ever encountered.

At eighteen, Maslow enrolled in New York's City College. It was free and his father wanted Abe to study law. But Maslow found the school impersonal and the required courses dull. He skipped classes, made poor grades, and was put on probation for the second semester.

No matter. Maslow was intoxicated with the rich artistic and intellectual life of New York City in the vintage year of 1927. He discovered the music of Beethoven and the plays of Eugene O'Neill. He went to two concerts a week at Carnegie Hall and sold peanuts to get into the theater. He attended lectures by Will Durant and Bertrand Russell and Reinhold Niebuhr. Like most young American intellectuals of that period, he became a socialist and an atheist.

But if Maslow was in love with the life of the mind, he was even more in love—blissfully, hopefully—with his cousin Bertha. And it was during the year he was nineteen that he experienced two of the great moments of his life, the kinds of moments he was later to call "peak experiences." The first came when he read William Graham Sumner's *Folkways*, a book that introduced him to the idea of cultural evolution, forever disabused him of the assumption that his own society was the "fixed truth from which everything else was a foolish falling away," and triggered a lifelong interest in anthropology. By his own account, he was never again the same.

The second peak experience of that year came when he kissed Bertha. Previously, he had never dared to touch her. His frustration was indeed so painful that it drove him to leave New York City for a semester at Cornell. When he returned, Bertha's sister Anna took matters into her own hands by literally pushing him into Bertha's arms. "I kissed her," Maslow later told Colin Wilson, "and nothing terrible happened—the heavens didn't fall, and Bertha accepted it, and that was the beginning of a new life. . . . I was accepted by a female. I was just deliriously happy with her. It was a tremendous and profound and total love affair."

By now it was clear that Maslow would not become a lawyer, and he went away to the University of Wisconsin to study psychology in earnest. A few lonely, frustrated months later, Abe wired Bertha that they were going to get married. The wedding took place in New York during the December holidays in 1928. Bertha returned to Wisconsin with him and enrolled as a student.

Thus began Abraham Maslow's life as a psychologist. It was a life that would be graced with an extraordinary succession of mentors, distinguished scholars who were somehow drawn to this shy, brilliant young man and wanted him to work with them; they invited him to meals, drove him to meetings, helped get him jobs. One might say that these mentors served an emotional function as surrogate mothers and fathers, but if the Fates had conspired to choose ideal professional influences, they could not have done a better job.

As an undergraduate, Maslow became a lab assistant to William H. Sheldon, who later was to achieve fame with his theory of constitutional types (endomorph, mesomorph, ectomorph). Sheldon and other professors provided a solid grounding in classical laboratory research. Professor Harry Harlow, the noted primate researcher, eventually became Maslow's chief mentor at Wisconsin. In 1932 Harlow shared authorship of a paper on the intelligence of primates with Maslow, and the twenty-four-year-old undergraduate was so inspired by seeing his name in print in the *Journal of Comparative Psychology* that he spent all of his next summer vacation, helped by Bertha, repeating the experiment with every primate in the Bronx Park Zoo.

As a graduate student at Wisconsin, Maslow came up with a truly original line of research. He discovered that the incessant mounting behavior of primates, which involved males mounting males, females mounting females, and females mounting males, as well as the "conventional" mounting of females by males, had more to do with dominance than with sexuality. This activity was, in fact, a means of sorting out the hierarchy of the primate horde. What's more, he learned that the ferocity involved in dominance behavior tends to fade away as one goes up the primate intelligence scale: the monkey uses its dominance position to tyrannize; the chimpanzee, to protect.

Maslow moved from Wisconsin to Columbia University as the eminent behaviorist Edward Thorndike's research associate. And he continued his work on dominance and sexuality, going from simple dominance in animals to dominance-feeling in humans to the relationship between self-esteem and sexuality. In 1936, while still at Columbia, he began doing Kinsey-type interviews with female college students, possibly inspiring Kinsey's own work, which began some two years later. Maslow's interviews showed that highly dominant women, regardless of their sex drives, are more likely to be sexually active and experimental than are less dominant women. But he also found—and this is important in terms of his later work—that "any discussion of dominance must be a discussion of insecure people, that is, of slightly sick people. . . . Study of carefully selected psychologically secure individuals indicates clearly that their sexual lives are little determined by dominance-feeling." Here was a hint, a seed: there seems to exist a state of psychological health that transcends at least one lower drive.

During this period of inspired excitement and feverish work, Maslow continued to collect mentors. One of them was Alfred Adler, an early disciple of Freud who eventually broke with his master.

Maslow also sat at the feet of such eminent psychologists and anthropologists as Erich Fromm, Kurt Goldstein, Karen Horney, and Margaret Mead— some of them refugees from the Nazi terror. It was the late Thirties and New York was both an exciting and a sobering place for a Jewish intellectual.

Of all his mentors, Ruth Benedict, the anthropologist, and Max Wertheimer, the founder of the European Gestalt school of psychology, had the greatest influence on Maslow's life. Both became good friends and often came to dinner with him and Bertha at their modest Brooklyn home. Maslow admired Benedict and Wertheimer inordinately. Not only were they giants in their fields, but they were also, to put it simply, wonderful human beings. He began making notes on these exceptional people. Nothing he had learned in psychology equipped him to understand them. How could they be what they so clearly were in a world of savage, repressed Freudian drives and Nazi horrors? Who was the real human species-type, Hitler or Benedict and Wertheimer?

These questions helped set the stage for the major turning point in Maslow's life, one that was to change psychology and our view of the human personality for all time. The year, as best as it can be reconstructed, was 1942; the place, New York City. By now, though not a great lecturer, Maslow was a beloved teacher, so popular that the college newspaper characterized him as the Frank Sinatra of Brooklyn College. He was working very hard, sometimes teaching nights as well as days for the extra income. He adored his daughters, who were now two and four; their innocence and potential in a darkening world sometimes moved him to tears. And the war was always in the back of his mind. He was too old to be drafted for military service but he wanted to make his contribution in the fight against Hitler. He wanted somehow to enlist himself in the larger enterprise of helping create a world in which there would be no Hitlers, in which "good people" would prevail.

It was in that emotional climate that he happened upon a parade of young American servicemen on their way to combat duty. And he was overcome by the evils of war, the needless suffering and death, the tragic waste of human potential. He began weeping openly. Against the backdrop of those times, the conventional, step-by-step psychology he had been doing was entirely inadequate. He knew he would have to change his life and career. It would have been easy enough to stay on his present course. His research credentials were firmly established. His recently published *Principles of Abnormal Psychology*, coauthored with Bela Mittelmann, was being well received. Maslow was undoubtedly on his way to a successful career in mainstream psychology. But now, tears streaming down his cheeks, he determined to take a more difficult, more uncertain course.

The direction of his exploration was set by a flash of insight that came to him while he was musing over his notes on Ruth Benedict and Max Wertheimer, trying to puzzle out the pattern that made these two people so very different from the neurotic, driven people who are usually the subject of psychological study. As he wrote years later, "I realized in one wonderful moment that their two patterns could be generalized. I was talking about a kind of person, not about two noncomparable individuals. There was a wonderful excitement in that. I tried to see whether this pattern could be found elsewhere, and I did find it elsewhere, in one person after another."

Like many historic breakthroughs, this one, in retrospect, seems obvious, so simple a child might have hit upon it: Up until that time, the field of psychology had by and large concentrated on mental illness, neglecting or entirely ignoring psychological *health*. Symptoms had been relentlessly pursued, abnormalities endlessly analyzed. But the normal personality continued to be viewed primarily as a vague, gray area of little interest or concern. And *positive* psychological health was terra incognita.

From the moment of the turning point at the parade in New York City, Maslow would devote his life and his thought to the exploration of this unknown land, of what he called in his last book "the farther reaches of human nature." In this exploration, he would find it necessary to leave his mentors behind. Though he would go on to form his own network of colleagues and supporters, he would find himself increasingly alone out on the frontiers of human knowledge. He was to become, in his words, "a reconnaissance man, a Daniel Boone," one who enjoys being "first in the wilderness."

Maslow stayed at Brooklyn College until 1951, then went to Brandeis University, in Waltham, Massachusetts, where he became chairman of the psychology department. In 1969 he moved to Menlo Park, California. A special fellowship set up by an industrialist would give him unlimited time for writing. But time was short; he died a year later. Still, in the twenty-seven years after the turning point in his career, he published close to a hundred articles and books that add up to a great synthesis, a bold and original psychological theory.

Maslow's theory is built upon his finding that human needs can be arranged in a hierarchy, beginning with the physiological needs for oxygen, water, food, and the like, then moving up through the needs for safety, belongingness, love, and esteem. Each lower need is, in Maslow's term, "prepotent" to the one above it. A very hungry person, for example, will quickly forget hunger if deprived of oxygen. Generally, each of the lower needs must be met before the one above it emerges. Taken this far, his "hierarchy of needs" is a useful but not particularly shattering formulation. For one thing, it avoids the twists and turns in the Freudian notion that all so-called higher feelings and actions are merely disguised versions of the primary drives of sex and ego-need; tenderness, for example, is seen by Freud as nothing more than "aim-inhibited sexuality." But Maslow goes even further: After all of the "deficiency-needs" listed above are fairly well satisfied, then a need for "self-actualization" emerges. This "being-need" is just as real, just as much a part of human nature as are the deficiency-needs.

The concept of self-actualization crystallized during Maslow's moment of insight about Ruth Benedict and Max Wertheimer, but it evolved and developed through years of studying exceptionally healthy and successful individuals. Self-actualization is, in short, the tendency of every human being—once the basic deficiency-needs are adequately fulfilled—to *make real* his or her full potential, to become everything he or she can be. The self-actualizing person is the true human species-type; a Max Wertheimer is a more accurate representation of the human species than is a Hitler. For Maslow, the self-actualizing person is not a normal person with something added, but a normal person with nothing taken away. In a "synergic" society—the term is Benedict's—what is good for the development and well-being of the individual is also good for the development and well-being of the society. Our type of society is obviously not synergic, which accounts for the rarity of self-actualizing people. Though the physiological needs of most of our citizens are fulfilled, the safety needs are hardly to be taken for granted, what with the prevalence of dog-eat-dog competition and crime. And many lives are lacking in an adequate supply of belongingness, love, and esteem. Maslow sees these lacks, these "holes" in the development of a person, as a prime cause of mental illness. Indeed, for Maslow, neurosis can be viewed largely as a deficiency disease. Thus, the Maslovian thesis cries out against the injustice that deprives so many people of their most basic needs and suggests major reforms in our ways of relating, especially in the family.

For those people who somehow transcend the deficiency-needs, self-actualization becomes a growth process, an unfolding of human nature as it potentially could be. Maslow defines this "true" human nature in terms of the characteristics of self-actualizing people, using not just personal interviews but also the study of such historical figures as Thomas Jefferson, Albert Einstein, Eleanor Roosevelt, Albert Schweitzer, and Jane Addams.

One of the most striking characteristics of these people is that they are strongly focused on problems *outside* of themselves. They generally have a mission in life; they delight in bringing about justice, stopping cruelty and exploita-tion, fighting lies and untruth. They have a clear perception of reality, along with a keen sense of the false, the phony. They are spontaneous and creative, sometimes displaying what might be called a mature childlikeness, a "second naiveté." They are autonomous, not bound tightly to the customs and assump-tions of their particular culture. Their character structure is highly democratic, so that their friendships tend to cut across the dividing lines of class, education, politics, and ethnic background. At the same time, they are marked by a certain detachment and a need for privacy; they generally limit themselves to a rela-tively small circle of close friends. Significantly, they do not lump people or ideas in the usual categories but rather tend to see straight through "the man-made mass of concepts, abstractions, expectations, beliefs and stereotypes that most people confuse with the world."

Self-actualizing people, Maslow discovered, are far more likely than others to have peak experiences—that is, episodes of delight and heightened clarity and even revelation, during which all things seem to flow in perfect harmony. Through numerous interviews and questionnaires, he found that even ordi-nary people take on self-actualizing qualities during peak experiences. He also comes very close to saying that such experiences provide a glimpse into the realm of Being, into ultimate reality itself.

Here is another paradox: Maslow the self-proclaimed atheist insisting upon the importance of a class of human experience that includes the experiences of the greatest religious figures back through the ages. But he himself was always filled to the brim with a religious wonder, with a profound sense of what Rudolf Otto calls *das Heilige*, "the holy"; and he never shrank from presenting the transcendent realm of Being forcefully, even if he did so in a secular, psycho-logical context. At the turn of the century William James had written elo-quently about the mystic experience, but most psychologists ignored this entire aspect of human life or dismissed it as some kind of compensation mech-anism. For Freud, who confessed he had never had such an experience, the "oceanic feeling" is mere infantile regression. Maslow's courage in bringing the peak experience out of the closet has since been validated by several studies and polls showing its universality and value.

When people reach the stage of self-actualization, according to Maslow, many of the assumptions of conventional psychology are overturned. For ex-ample, human motivation prior to Maslow was generally treated in terms of tension reduction, and impulses were considered to be dangerous. But Maslow points out that this is true only in the realm of the lower needs. The "growth-needs" of the self-actualizing person are not mere itches to be relieved by scratching. The higher tensions (problems to be solved, human relations to be deepened) can be pleasurable. Creative impulses, then, are to be welcomed and trusted.

By opening up the previously hidden area of psychological health, Maslow provides a new kind of guidance for the human journey. Self-actualizing peo-ple, he argues, are good choosers. When given an opportunity, they gravitate

259

toward what is good for them and, in his view, good for the human race. "So far as human value theory is concerned," Maslow writes in his 1962 book, *Toward a Psychology of Being*, "no theory will be adequate that rests simply on the statistical description of the choices of unselected human beings. To average the choices of good and bad choosers, of healthy and sick people, is useless. Only the choices and tastes and judgment of healthy human beings will tell us much about what is good for the human species in the long run."

In the 1950s Maslow began to see his work as part of a Third Force in psychology, representing a decisive, positive move beyond standard Freudian psychology, with its sickness-oriented view of humankind, and beyond behaviorism, which tends to treat the individual as a mere point between stimulus and response. With his generous, inclusive spirit, Maslow viewed Third Force psychology as large enough to hold Adlerians, Rankians, Jungians, Rogerians, neo-Freudians, Talmudic psychologists, Gestaltists, and many others. In 1961 his mailing list, which had long been used to circulate papers and ideas, became the basis for the *Journal of Humanistic Psychology*. A year later Maslow was a guiding force in starting the Association for Humanistic Psychology, whose founding members included Charlotte Bühler, Kurt Goldstein, David Riesman, Henry Murray, and Lewis Mumford. Two of the most influential founders were Rollo May, who was instrumental in introducing European existential psychology to the U.S., and Carl Rogers, whose humanistic client-centered approach to psychotherapy and counseling has since spread throughout the world.

The summer of 1962 was to see two events that would play a major role in Maslow's influence on the culture. The first involved his appointment as a visiting fellow to Non-Linear Systems, a high-tech plant in Del Mar, California. Here, Maslow first realized that his theories could be applied to management. He discovered that there were just as many self-actualizing people in industry—perhaps more—than in the universities, and he got the idea that a humane, enlightened management policy devoted to the development of human potential could also be the most effective. He called this concept "eupsychian management," which became the title of his 1965 book on the subject. As it turned out, Maslow's ideas foreshadowed those that are now associated with the best of Japanese management, and it is hard to find a book on management theory today that does not give a prominent place to Abraham Maslow.

The second event of that summer was synchronistic—to use a word coined by Jung to describe coincidences that are more than just that. Abe and Bertha were driving down California's Highway 1 for a holiday, and their progress was slower than anticipated on that spectacular and tortuous coast road. Looking for a place to spend the night, they saw a light and drove off the road down a steep driveway toward what they took to be a motel. They were astonished to find that almost everybody there was reading the recently published *Toward a Psychology of Being* and enthusiastically discussing Maslovian ideas.

The Maslows had stumbled upon what was to become Esalen Institute on the eve of its opening to the public. The institute's cofounder, Michael Murphy, had just bought a dozen copies of the book and given them to the members of his staff. Later, Maslow and Murphy became close friends and Maslow became a major influence on Esalen and on the entire counterculture of the 1960s.

This association was to raise some eyebrows among Maslow's conservative colleagues. The first press reports on the newly minted human-potential movement were, to be as charitable as possible, sensationalized and uninformed, and a less courageous man might have pulled back. But Maslow was not one to flinch under fire. "Esalen's an experiment," he told Bertha. "I'm glad they're trying it." And later, in public symposia, Maslow called Esalen "potentially the most important educational institution in the world."

Maslow's influence on America, transmitted through this lineage, can hardly be overstated. What has happened is that the counterculture of the 1960s has become a major and influential segment of the mainstream culture of the 1980s. This development has been largely ignored by the established journals of opinion but is clearly seen in the surveys of Louis Harris and Daniel Yankelovich, in the sophisticated Trend Reports of John Naisbitt, and in Naisbitt's recent best seller, *Megatrends*.

It is also becoming clear that while the quest for self-actualization might lead some people to a narrow preoccupation with the self, the number who go to this extreme is small, and the "me first" stage is generally temporary, a way station on the journey to social consciousness. This is seen in the Values and Lifestyles (VALS) Program of SRI International, a California-based research and consulting organization, which has adapted Maslow's hierarchy of needs to an analysis of the U.S. population and which numbers some of the nation's most successful corporations among its subscribers. The VALS study shows that the "Inner-Directeds," those who might be said to be on the path toward self-actualization, now make up 21 percent of all Americans and represent the fastest-growing segment of the population. Of this 21 percent, only 3 percent are in the self-centered, narcissistic "I-am-me" category. The Inner-Directeds, for the most part, tend to move inexorably toward social consciousness, service to others, and personal integration—which should come as no surprise to anyone who has given Maslow more than a cursory reading.

Critics argue that Maslow did not adequately deal with the problem of evil, with humanity's darker side, and there is something to this criticism. But Maslow himself was aware that he had much more work to do, "at least two hundred years' worth," he told Bertha shortly before his death. True, Maslow's theory might not be complete, but it never fails to challenge us with a spine-tingling vision of individual potential and health and of a synergic society.

Despair is often comfortable, in some circles even fashionable, and it is easy enough to dismiss or even ridicule Maslow's challenge. After all, nothing is more difficult or painful than to look clearly at your own wasted potential, then start doing something about it. But ever-increasing numbers of Americans are taking the challenge. For example, the fastest-growing movement in health management today involves the field of holistic, health-oriented approaches to the physical that Maslow applied to the psychological. If anything can solve the crisis of medical depersonalization and rising costs, it is this classically Maslovian shift: more and more people working against a pathogenic environment and society while taking personal responsibility for their own positive good health.

In spite of his unorthodox views, Maslow was elected to the presidency of the American Psychological Association in 1967, and now, more than twelve years after his death, his voice is still being heard, even if indirectly, even if by people who barely know his name. Warren Bennis, professor of management at USC, recalls it as "that incredibly soft, shy, tentative, and gentle voice making the most outrageous remarks." Bennis also remembers Maslow for "a childlike spirit of innocence and wonder—always wearing his eyebrows (as Thomas Mann said about Freud) continually raised in a constant expression of awe."

Still, it takes another characteristic to join the shyness, the outrageousness, and the awe into a complete human being, and that is courage, which is the essence of Abraham Maslow's story. Psychologist James F. T. Bugental, who served as the first president of the Association for Humanistic Psychology, lived near Maslow during the last year of his life. "Abe used to go for his walks," Bugental recalls, "and he'd come by our house. We had this myth that one of the cans of beer in the refrigerator was his, and he'd always say, 'Is my beer cold?'

"And he'd drink his beer and get a little sentimental and sometimes show us pictures of his granddaughter and weep because she was so beautiful and innocent and would have to lose her innocence. And sometimes he would talk about the time in his childhood when he'd have to go through a tough Irish neighborhood to get to the library, and about how he would plan his route and sometimes get chased and sometimes get beat up. But he never let that stop him. He went to the library even though he might have to get beat up.

"That's the way I see his life. He never stopped doing what he thought he had to do, even though he might get beat up. He had courage, just plain courage."

———————

ABRAHAM MASLOW *was born on April 1, 1908, in Brooklyn. The eldest of seven children, he remembered "clinging" to his father. "I have no memory," he wrote, "of expecting anything from my mother." He later called his mother a "schizophrenogenic . . . one who makes crazy people. . . . I was awfully curious to find out why I didn't go insane."*

In elementary school he met anti-Semitism and a teacher he later described as a "horrible bitch." Challenging his reputation as the class's best speller, the teacher made Maslow stand up and spell one word after another. When he finally missed one—parallel—the teacher publicly concluded, "I knew you were a fake."

Throughout his adolescence he was intensely shy and, he recalled, "terribly unhappy, lonely, isolated, self-rejecting." A loving uncle, his mother's brother, looked after him. "He may have saved my life, psychically," Maslow said.

He left New York for Cornell University partly because of his strong passion for his cousin Bertha: "I had not yet touched Bertha. . . . And this was getting kind of rough on me—sexually, because I was very powerfully sexed. . . ."

At the University of Wisconsin his professors accepted him as a colleague. Still, he was amazed when, one day in a men's room, a professor stepped up to the urinal next to his. "How did I think that professors urinated?" he later marveled. "Didn't I know they had kidneys?"

At Columbia University he found the initial research he conducted for psychologist E. L. Thorndike boring. He wrote Thorndike a note saying so—even though he stood to lose his job during the Depression. Far from firing Maslow, Thorndike respected his opinion.

For all his popularity with students, Maslow was terrified of public speaking until he was over fifty. In 1925 a paper he wrote never got published because he fled a conference rather than read it. In 1959 he delivered a talk, then for days afterward stayed in bed recovering from it.

He suffered his first heart attack in 1945 and never again was completely healthy. He had an arthritic hip, and though he was always tired, he had trouble sleeping. Only in the year before his death did a doctor discover that Maslow's chronic fatigue was a form of hypoglycemia. For years the ailment had made him crabby, inhibited his work, and stifled his sex life.

Until the age of thirty he considered himself a socialist—"Fabian rather than Marxist." He said he dropped socialism after Franklin Roosevelt put "our whole socialist programme . . . into law" and he didn't see "any great miracles occur."

After his bar mitzvah, at thirteen, he became "a fighting atheist." Yet later in life, when offers came to teach at other universities, he would not leave his teaching job at Brandeis. "Why?" he asked himself. "Partly it's the Jewish business. I have been so proud of the great Jewish university—I didn't realize how much— and I feel like a rat deserting the sinking ship . . . just the way I did when I left Brooklyn and abandoned the poor Jewish students whom nobody loved but me. The guilt of upward mobility."

In 1954 he wrote, "Human nature is not nearly as bad as it has been thought to be. . . . In fact it can be said that the possibilities of human nature have customarily been sold short. . . ."

He enjoyed art museums, shopping, and reading science fiction. He admired J. D. Salinger. (". . . read Franny and Zooey. . . . He says in his way what I've been trying to say. The novelist can be so much more effective.") He also liked Betty Friedan's The Feminine Mystique, which discusses his views on sex and dominance. ("A passionate book—I was swept along unintentionally.")

In 1969 the White House invited him to join a committee to define national goals, but he was too sick to attend. He was miffed by the popular press's indiffer-

ence to his work: "A new image of man . . . a new image of nature, a new philosophy of science, a new economics, a new everything, and they just don't notice it."

Still, at fifty-six he wrote: "With my troubles about insomnia and bad back and conflict over my role in psychology and . . . in a certain sense, needing psychoanalysis, if anyone were to ask me 'Are you a happy man?' I'd say, 'yes, yes!' Am I lucky?. . . The darling of fortune? Sitting as high up as a human being ever has? Yes!"

Five years later, on June 8, 1970, he died of a heart attack. The New York Times *published no obituary.*

Ray Kroc Did It All for You

TOM ROBBINS

IF COWS WATCHED HORROR MOVIES, EVERYBODY KNOWS WHO THEIR FAVORITE MON-ster would be.

Imagine that it's Friday midnight down on the farm and the Guernseys and the Jerseys are gathered around the barnyard TV, spellbound by the rerun of that classic bovine chiller, *Teats Up,* when suddenly the lights flicker, organ music swells, and onto the screen ambles a chesty, cherubic octogenarian in a business suit, swinging a cleaver and flashing a mystic ring with symbolic golden arches on it, and, oh, a terrified moo rises up from the herd and there is much trembling of teat and tail. At that moment, a little bullock in the back is heard to ask, "Mommy, on Halloween can I go as Ray Kroc?"

To cattle, Ray Kroc is the franchise Frankenstein, the Hitler behind a Hereford holocaust, a fiend who has sent about 550,000 of their relatives to the grinder, grinning all the while and encouraging his henchmen with his macabre credo, "Remember, ten patties to the pound!"

It's scant comfort to the cows that Kroc has also doomed fifty million cucumbers to be pickled and chopped, and boiled more than half a billion potatoes in oil. Potatoes and cukes don't mind. They like being processed. It's their idea of freedom.

Some purists might argue that since cucumbers are, in fact, the ovaries of the cucumber plant, they can be fulfilled only through reproduction, but the truth is, many such vegetables are sick and tired of being regarded as sex objects and baby factories; they want to break out of the mold, to travel and meet people and be appreciated for themselves, and Kroc gives them that opportunity. If pickles wore white, Ray Kroc would be Gandhi. But that's another story.

Whether one chooses to mourn with the meats or rejoice with the veggies is a religious decision, and nobody's business but one's own. The point here is not that Kroc has wiped out considerable fauna and flora, nor that he's become thunderously wealthy in the process, but that the manner in which he merchandises his victims' remains has transformed the United States of America.

Kroc, of course, is the man behind McDonald's. He was a middle-aged milkshake-machine salesman out of Chicago when, in 1954, he called on an account in San Bernardino and saw the future. Its name was fast foods.

Curious about how a little California drive-in could keep eight of his Multimixers running continuously, Kroc found a restaurant stripped down to the minimum in service and menu, a precision shop turning out fries, beverages, and fifteen-cent hamburgers on an assembly line. The brainchild of the McDonald boys, Mac and Dick, it combined speed, simplicity, and edibility to a degree that made Kroc giddy, especially when the brothers readily agreed to sell him the rights for national development. It was as if Henry Ford had married Mom's Apple Pie and adopted Ray as their son.

Mac and Dick McDonald, never overly ambitious, were more of a hindrance than a help, but Kroc, an energetic dreamer, built a $7.8 billion empire of 7,400 drive-ins and somewhere along the way named the Big Mac double burger after one of the brothers. (Since these are "family" restaurants, it's easy to understand why it wasn't named for the other one.)

Modern America is dominated—environmentally, culturally, and psychologically—by freeways, and it has been McDonald's and its imitators (hail Burger King! praise Wendy's! sing Jack in the Box!) that have nurtured our freeway consciousness and allowed it to bloom. In the past, hungry motorists could look through their windshields and pick and choose from a glorious ongoing lineup of diners, truck stops, and barbecue pits, but such an array of roadside attractions would defeat the purpose of a freeway, as would the time and trouble involved if a driver had to exit at random and search for the unfamiliar restaurant that might suit his or her schedule, pocketbook, and taste.

Thanks to Kroc, the migrating masses simply aim their stomachs at the landmark arches, sinuous of form and sunny of hue, and by the first belch they're back on the road, fast fed and very nearly serene, which is to say, no entrepreneur has overcharged them; no maître d' has insulted them; no temperamental chef, flirtatious waitress, or intriguing flavor has delayed them; they've neither gagged on a greasy spoon nor tripped over an *x* in a *oie roti aux pruneaux*. With McDonald's they're secure.

That's the fly in the Egg McMuffin. Rather, the fly is that there never *is* a fly in an Egg McMuffin. The human spirit requires surprise, variety, and risk in order to enlarge itself. Imagination feeds on novelty. As imagination emaciates, options diminish; the fewer our options, the more bleak our prospects and the greater our susceptibility to controls. The wedding of high technology and food service has produced a robot cuisine, a Totalitarian Burger, the standardized sustenance of a Brave New World.

McDonald's not only cooks with computers, assuring that every tiny French fry is identical in color, texture, and temperature, but its "specially designed dispensers" see to it that the Big Mac you may scarf today in Seattle has exactly the same amount of "special sauces" on it as the one your cousin gobbled last month near Detroit. If that extreme of uniformity doesn't ring your alarm, you've already half-moved into the B. F. Skinner anthill.

And yet. . . . We still live in a pluralistic society, where there are more than enough French-cooking classes and Serbo-Croatian sushi bars to satisfy the educated palate and the adventurous tongue. Moreover, "gourmet" burger chains, such as the Red Robin and Hamburger Hamlet, are on the rise.

So what if democracy tends to sanctify mediocrity and McDonald's represents mediocrity at its zenith, its most sublime? Fast foods are perfectly suited for America, for a population on the move; a fluid, informal people, unburdened by pretension or tradition; a sweetly vulgar race, undermined by its own naiveté rather than by Asian stoicism or European angst. Today there are McDonald's in Tokyo and Vienna, but they don't blend in and never will. Here, they are at the heart of the matter, reductive kitchens for a classless culture that hasn't time to dally on its way to the next rainbow's end.

When there are dreams to be chased, greener pastures to be grazed, deadlines to be met, tests to be taken, malls to be shopped, Little Leaguers to be feted, sitcoms to be watched, or lonely apartments to be avoided, we refuel in flight. Places such as McDonald's make it easy, if banal.

Columbus discovered America, Jefferson invented it, Lincoln unified it, Goldwyn mythologized it, and Kroc Big Mac'd it. It could have been an omniscient computer that provided this land with its prevailing ambience, it might have been an irresistible new weapons system, a political revolution, an art movement, or some gene-altering drug. How wonderful that it was a hamburger!

For a hamburger is warm and fragrant and juicy. A hamburger is soft and nonthreatening. It personifies the Great Mother herself, who has nourished us from the beginning.

A hamburger is an icon of layered circles, the circle being at once the most spiritual and most sensual of shapes. A hamburger is companionable and faintly erotic. The nipple of the Goddess, the bountiful belly-ball of Eve. You are what you think you eat.

Best of all, a hamburger doesn't take itself seriously. Thus, it embodies that generous sense of humor that persists in America even as our bacon burns and our cookies crumble. McDonald's has served forty-five billion burgers, and every single one of them has had a smile on its face.

So, to Ray Kroc, grant a pardon for his crimes against cows, stay his sentence for having ambushed our individuality at Standardization Gulch. True, he has changed our habits, perhaps for the worse, but a man who can say of himself, as Kroc did, that "it requires a certain kind of mind to see beauty in a hamburger bun" is a man who can cut the mustard.

RAY A. KROC *was born in Chicago, on October 5, 1902, of "frugal, middle-class Bohemian stock." His father, who worked for Western Union, died of a cerebral hemorrhage—having, according to his son's diagnosis, "worried himself to death."*

When he was four, a phrenologist read the bumps on his head. The bump reader predicted that the boy would work in a restaurant.

He attended public school with Ernest Hemingway and, like Hemingway, drove an ambulance in World War I. In Kroc's Army company was a sixteen-year-old boy named Walt Disney.

He dropped out of school to become a jazz pianist.

In his early twenties, as musical director of a small Chicago radio station, he dis-covered the singing comedy team of Sam and Henry. Later they were known as Amos 'n' Andy.

He drove down to Florida in the 1920s to sell real estate. He drove back "stone broke."

In the early days he would fly over a neighborhood and pick out a McDonald's location by counting the schools and church steeples.

He set down rules for his order takers: no long hair or sideburns; no moustaches or goatees; "personnel with bad teeth, severe skin blemishes, or tattoos should not be stationed at service windows."

For many years he refused to hire females, asserting that "they attract the wrong kind of boys."

He donated $250,000 to President Richard Nixon's reelection campaign. He now regards the donation as one of his biggest mistakes.

After six years of paying Mac and Dick McDonald .5 percent of the chain's gross profits, Kroc found that the brothers "were beginning to get on my nerves." In 1961 he bought them out for $2.7 million. They hung on to their original San Bernadino McDonald's, but Kroc opened up his own McDonald's across the street from theirs and drove them out of business.

He has said, "It's dog-eat-dog, and if anyone tries to get me I'll get them first. It's the American way of survival of the fittest."

Worth more than $600 million, he has been cited as one of the five richest Americans.

He owns a 210-acre California ranch, a Versailles-style beach home in Florida, and a six-thousand-square-foot apartment on Chicago's Lake Shore Drive. He sails on a ninety-foot yacht and drives a forty-five-thousand-dollar Rolls-Royce.

He has said, "I have no interest in money."

He made repeated bids to buy the Chicago Cubs. Cubs owner Philip Wrigley turned him down every time.

In 1974, after watching the San Diego Padres play their first home game under his ownership, he raced to the ball park's public-address booth and announced that the Padres were "putting on a lousy show . . . I apologize for it. I'm disgusted with it. This is the most stupid baseball playing I've ever seen!"

His voice becomes higher when he gets excited.

In 1972, to celebrate his seventieth birthday, he gave $7.5 million to various charities and $9 million in stock to McDonald's employees.

He will not give money to any college unless his donation will go toward a trade school. "Educators," he has written, "accuse me of being anti-intellectual. That's not quite right. I'm anti-phony-intellectual. . . . My philosophy about what education should be is best expressed right in McDonald's own Hamburger U. and Hamburger High."

The doorbell of his Fort Lauderdale beach home chimes the jingle, "You deserve a break today. . . ."

He has had the McDonald's golden arches embroidered on the pockets of his blazers and set in jewels on his gold cuff links, tie bars, and rings.

His gall bladder and thyroid gland have been removed and he has had a plastic joint implanted in his arthritic hip. He has diabetes.

In pursuit of his present wife, Joni, he divorced his first and second wives. (Joni turned him down after the first divorce.)

He does not like to spend much time with "society types." He hates "phony sophistication." He frequently entertains business associates at home—performing pop tunes on a grand piano.

[Editor's note: Ray Kroc died on January 14, 1984, after the original publication of this work.]

The Tinkerings of
Robert Noyce

TOM WOLFE

IN 1948 THERE WERE SEVEN THOUSAND PEOPLE IN GRINNELL, IOWA, INCLUDING MORE than one who didn't dare take a drink in his own house without pulling the shades down first. It was against the law to sell liquor in Grinnell, but it was perfectly legal to drink it at home. So it wasn't that. It wasn't even that someone might look in through the window and disapprove. God knew Grinnell had more than its share of White Ribbon teetotalers, but by 1948 alcohol was hardly the mark of Cain it had once been. No, those timid souls with their fingers through the shade loops inside the white frame houses on Main Street and Park Street were thinking of something else altogether.

They happened to live on land originally owned by the Congregational minister who had founded the town in 1854, Josiah Grinnell. Josiah Grinnell had sold off lots with covenants, in perpetuity, stating that anyone who allowed alcohol to be drunk on his property forfeited ownership. *In perpetuity!* In perpetuity was forever, and 1948 was not even a hundred years later. In 1948 there were people walking around Grinnell who had known Josiah Grinnell personally. They were getting old—Grinnell had died in 1891—but they were still walking around. So . . . why take a chance!

The plain truth was, Grinnell had Middle West written all over it. It was squarely in the middle of Iowa's Midland corn belt, where people on the farms said "crawdad" instead of crayfish and "barn lot" instead of barnyard. Grinnell had been one of many Protestant religious communities established in the mid-nineteenth century after Iowa became a state and settlers from the East headed for the farmlands. The streets were lined with white clapboard houses and elm trees, like a New England village. And today, in 1948, the hard-scrubbed Octagon Soap smell of nineteenth-century Protestantism still permeated the houses and Main Street as well. That was no small part of what people in the East thought of when they heard the term "Middle West." For thirty years writers such as Sherwood Anderson, Sinclair Lewis, and Carl Van Vechten had been prompting the most delicious sniggers with their portraits of the churchy, narrow-minded Middle West. The Iowa painter Grant Wood was thinking of farms like the ones around Grinnell when he did his famous painting *American Gothic*. Easterners recognized the grim, juiceless couple in Wood's picture right away. There were John Calvin's and John Knox's rectitude reigning in the sticks.

In the fall of 1948 Harry Truman picked out Grinnell as one of the stops on his whistle-stop campaign tour, one of the hamlets where he could reach out to the little people, the average Americans of the heartland, the people untouched by the sophisticated opinion-makers of New York and Washington. Speaking from the rear platform of his railroad car, Truman said he would never forget Grinnell, because it was Grinnell College, the little Congregational academy over on Park Street, that had given him his first honorary degree. The President's fond recollection didn't cut much ice, as it turned out. The town had voted Republican in every presidential election since the first time Abraham Lincoln ran, in 1860, and wasn't about to change for Harry Truman.

On the face of it, there you had Grinnell, Iowa, in 1948: a piece of mid-nineteenth-century American history frozen solid in the middle of the twentieth. It was one of the last towns in America that people back east would have figured to become the starting point of a bolt into the future that would create the very substructure, the electronic grid, of life in the year 2000 and beyond.

On the other hand, it wouldn't have surprised Josiah Grinnell in the slightest.

It was in the summer of 1948 that Grant Gale, a forty-five-year-old physics professor at Grinnell College, ran across an item in the newspaper concerning a former classmate of his at the University of Wisconsin named John Bardeen. Bardeen's father had been dean of medicine at Wisconsin, and Gale's wife Harriet's father had been dean of the engineering school, and so Bardeen and Harriet had grown up as fellow faculty brats, as the phrase went. Both Gale and Bardeen had majored in electrical engineering. Eventually Bardeen had taught physics at the University of Minnesota and had then left the academic world to work for Bell Laboratories, the telephone company's main research center, in Murray Hill, New Jersey. And now, according to the item, Bardeen and another engineer at Bell, Walter Brattain, had invented a novel little device they called a transistor.

It was only an item, however; the invention of the transistor in 1948 did not create headlines. The transistor apparently performed the same function as the vacuum tube, which was an essential component of telephone relay systems and radios. Like the vacuum tube, the transistor could isolate a specific electrical signal, such as a radio wave, and amplify it. But the transistor did not require glass tubing, a vacuum, a plate, or a cathode. It was nothing more than two minute gold wires leading to a piece of processed germanium less than a sixteenth of an inch long, shaped like a tiny brick. Germanium, an element found in coal, was an insulator, not a conductor. But if the germanium was contaminated with impurities, it became a "semiconductor." A vacuum tube was also a semiconductor; the vacuum itself, like the germanium, was an insulator. But as every owner of a portable radio knew, vacuum tubes drew a lot of current, required a warm-up interval before they would work, and then got very hot. A transistor eliminated all these problems and, on top of that, was about fifty times smaller than a vacuum tube.

So far, however, it was impossible to mass-produce transistors, partly because the gold wires had to be made by hand and attached by hand two thousandths of an inch apart. But that was the telephone company's problem. Grant Gale wasn't interested in any present or future applications of the transistor in terms of products. He hoped the transistor might offer a way to study the flow of electrons through a solid (the germanium), a subject physicists had speculated about for decades. He thought it would be terrific to get some transistors for his physics department at Grinnell. So he wrote to Bardeen at Bell Laboratories. Just to make sure his request didn't get lost in the shuffle, he also wrote to the president of Bell Laboratories, Oliver Buckley. Buckley was from Sloane, Iowa, and happened to be a Grinnell graduate. So by the fall of 1948 Gale had obtained two of the first transistors ever made, and he presented the first academic instruction in solid-state electronics available anywhere in the world, for the benefit of the eighteen students majoring in physics at Grinnell College.

One of Grant Gale's senior physics majors was a local boy named Robert Noyce, whom Gale had known for years. Bob and his brothers, Donald, Gaylord, and Ralph, lived just down Park Street and used to rake leaves, mow the lawn, baby-sit, and do other chores for the Gales. Lately Grant Gale had done more than his share of agonizing over Bob Noyce. Like his brothers, Bob was a bright student, but he had just been thrown out of school for a semester, and it had taken every bit of credit Gale had in the local favor bank, not only with other faculty members but also with the sheriff, to keep the boy from being expelled for good and stigmatized with a felony conviction.

Bob Noyce's father, Ralph Sr., was a Congregational minister. Not only that, both of his grandfathers were Congregational ministers. But that hadn't helped at all. In an odd way, after the thing happened, the boy's clerical lineage had boomeranged on him. People were going around saying, "Well, what do you expect from a preacher's son?" It was as if people in Grinnell unconsciously agreed with Sherwood Anderson that underneath the righteousness the midwestern Protestant preachers urged upon them, and which they themselves professed to uphold, lived demons of weakness, perversion, and hypocrisy that would break loose sooner or later.

No one denied that the Noyce boys were polite and proper in all outward appearances. They were all members of the Boy Scouts. They went to Sunday School and the main Sunday service at the First Congregational Church and were active in the church youth groups. They were pumped full of Congregationalism until it was spilling over. Their father, although a minister, was not the minister of the First Congregational Church. He was the associate superintendent of the Iowa Conference of Congregational Churches, whose headquarters were at the college. The original purpose of the college had been to provide a good academic Congregational education, and many of the graduates became teachers. The Conference was a coordinating council rather than a governing body, since a prime tenet of the Congregational Church, embedded in its name, was that each congregation was autonomous. Congregationalists rejected the very idea of a church hierarchy. A Congregational minister was not supposed to be a father or even a shepherd but, rather, a teacher. Each member of the congregation was supposed to internalize the moral precepts of the church and be his own priest dealing directly with God. So the job of secretary of the Iowa Conference of Congregational Churches was anything but a position of power. It didn't pay much, either.

The Noyces didn't own their own house. They lived in a two-story white clapboard house that was owned by the church at Park Street and Tenth Avenue, at the college. Not having your own house didn't carry the social onus in Grinnell that it did in the East. There was no upper crust in Grinnell. There were no top people who kept the social score in such matters. Congregationalists rejected the idea of a social hierarchy as fiercely as they did the idea of a religious hierarchy. The Congregationalists, like the Presbyterians, Methodists, Baptists, and United Brethren, were Dissenting Protestants. They were direct offshoots of the Separatists, who had split off from the Church of England in the sixteenth and seventeenth centuries and settled New England. At bottom, their doctrine of the autonomous congregation was derived from their hatred of the British system of class and status, with its endless gradations, topped off by the Court and the aristocracy. Even as late as 1948 the typical small town of the Middle West, like Grinnell, had nothing approaching a country club set. There were subtle differences in status in Grinnell, as in any other place, and it was better to be rich than poor, but there were only two obvious social ranks: those who were devout, educated, and hardworking, and those who weren't. Genteel poverty did not doom one socially in Grinnell. Ostentation did. The Noyce boys worked at odd jobs to earn their pocket money. That was socially correct as well as useful. To have devoted the same time to taking tennis lessons or riding lessons would have been a gaffe in Grinnell.

Donald, the oldest of the four boys, had done brilliantly at the college and had just received his Ph.D. in chemistry at Columbia University and was about to join the faculty of the University of California at Berkeley. Gaylord, the second oldest, was teaching school in Turkey. Bob, who was a year younger than

Gaylord, had done so well in science at Grinnell High School that Grant Gale had invited him to take the freshman physics course at the college during his high school senior year. He became one of Gale's star students and most tireless laboratory workers from that time on. Despite his apparent passion for the scientific grind, Bob Noyce turned out to be that much-vaunted creature, the well-rounded student. He was a trim, muscular boy, five feet eight, with thick dark brown hair, a strong jawline, and a long, broad nose that gave him a rugged appearance. He was the star diver on the college swimming team and won the Midwest Conference championship in 1947. He sang in choral groups, played the oboe, and was an actor with the college dramatic society. He also acted in a radio drama workshop at the college, along with his friend Peter Hackes and some others who were interested in broadcasting, and was the leading man in a soap opera that was broadcast over station WOI in Ames, Iowa.

Perhaps Bob Noyce was a bit too well rounded for local tastes. There were people who still remembered the business with the box kite back in 1941, when he was thirteen. It had been harmless, but it could have been a disaster. Bob had come across some plans for the building of a box kite, a kite that could carry a person aloft, in the magazine *Popular Science*. So he and Gaylord made a frame of cross-braced pine and covered it with a bolt of muslin. They tried to get the thing up by running across a field and towing it with a rope, but that didn't work terribly well. Then they hauled it up on the roof of a barn, and Bob sat in the seat and Gaylord ran across the roof, pulling the kite, and Bob was lucky he didn't break his neck when he and the rig hit the ground. So then they tied it to the rear bumper of a neighbor's car. With the neighbor at the wheel, Bob rode the kite and managed to get about twelve feet off the ground and glide for thirty seconds or so and come down without wrecking himself or any citizen's house or livestock.

Livestock . . . yes. Livestock was a major capital asset in Grinnell, and livestock was at the heart of what happened in 1948. In May a group of Bob Noyce's friends in one of the dormitory houses at Grinnell decided to have a luau, and he was in on the planning. The Second World War had popularized the exotic ways of the South Pacific, so that in 1948 the luau was an up-to-the-minute social innovation. The centerpiece of a luau was a whole roasted suckling pig with an apple or a pineapple in its mouth. Bob Noyce, being strong and quick, was one of the two boys assigned to procure the pig. That night they sneaked onto a farm just outside of Grinnell and wrestled a twenty-five-pound suckling out of the pigpen and arrived back at the luau to great applause. Within a few hours the pig was crackling hot and had an apple in its mouth and looked good enough for seconds and thirds, which everybody helped himself to, and there was more applause. The next morning came the moral hangover. The two boys decided to go see the farmer, confess, and pay for the pig. They didn't quite understand how a college luau, starring his pig, would score on the laugh meter with a farmer in midland Iowa. In the state of Iowa, where the vast majority of people depended upon agriculture for a livelihood and upon Protestant morality for their standards, not even stealing a watermelon worth thirty-five cents was likely to be written off as a boyish prank. Stealing a pig was larceny. The farmer got the sheriff and insisted on bringing criminal charges.

There was only so much that Ralph Noyce, the preacher with the preacher's son, could do. Grant Gale, on the other hand, was the calm, well-respected third party. He had two difficult tasks: to keep Bob out of jail and out of court and to keep the college administration from expelling him. There was never any hope at all of a mere slap on the wrist. The compromise Grant Gale helped work out—a one-semester suspension—was the best deal Bob could have hoped for realistically.

The Night of the Luau Pig was quite a little scandal on the Grinnell Richter scale. So Gale was all the more impressed by the way Bob Noyce took it. The local death-ray glowers never broke his confidence. All the Noyce boys had a profound and, to tell the truth, baffling confidence. Bob had a certain way of listening and staring. He would lower his head slightly and look up with a gaze that seemed to be about one hundred amperes. While he looked at you he never blinked and never swallowed. He absorbed everything you said and then answered very levelly in a soft baritone voice and often with a smile that showed off his terrific set of teeth. The stare, the voice, the smile—it was all a bit like the movie persona of the most famous of all Grinnell College's alumni, Gary Cooper. With his strong face, his athlete's build, and the Gary Cooper manner, Bob Noyce projected what psychologists call the halo effect. People with the halo effect seem to know exactly what they're doing and, moreover, make you want to admire them for it. They make you see the halos over their heads.

Years later people would naturally wonder where Bob Noyce got his confidence. Many came to the conclusion it was as much from his mother, Harriet Norton Noyce, as from his father. She was a latter-day version of the sort of strong-willed, intelligent, New England–style woman who had made such a difference during Iowa's pioneer days a hundred years before. His mother and father, with the help of Rowland Cross, who taught mathematics at Grinnell, arranged for Bob to take a job in the actuarial department of Equitable Life in New York City for the summer. He stayed on at the job during the fall semester, then came back to Grinnell at Christmas and rejoined the senior class in January as the second semester began. Gale was impressed by the aplomb with which the prodigal returned. In his first three years Bob had accumulated so many extra credits, it would take him only this final semester to graduate. He resumed college life, including the extracurricular activities, without skipping a beat. But more than that, Gale was gratified by the way Bob became involved with the new experimental device that was absorbing so much of Gale's own time: the transistor.

Bob was not the only physics major interested in the transistor, but he was the one who seemed most curious about where this novel mechanism might lead. He went off to the Massachusetts Institute of Technology, in Cambridge, in the fall to begin his graduate work. When he brought up the subject of the transistor at MIT, even to faculty members, people just looked at him. Even those who had heard of it regarded it merely as a novelty fabricated by the telephone company. There was no course work involving transistors or the theory of solid-state electronics. His dissertation was a "Photoelectric Study of Surface States on Insulators," which was at best merely background for solid-state electronics. In this area MIT was far behind Grinnell College. For a good four years Grant Gale remained one of the few people Bob Noyce could compare notes with in this new field.

Well, it had been a close one! What if Grant Gale hadn't gone to school with John Bardeen, and what if Oliver Buckley hadn't been a Grinnell alumnus? And what if Gale hadn't bothered to get in touch with the two of them after he read the little squib about the transistor in the newspaper? What if he hadn't gone to bat for Bob Noyce after the Night of the Luau Pig and the boy had been thrown out of college and that had been that? After all, if Bob hadn't been able to finish at Grinnell, he probably never would have been introduced to the transistor. He certainly wouldn't have come across it at MIT in 1948. Given what Bob Noyce did over the next twenty years, one couldn't help but wonder about the fortuitous chain of events.

Fortuitous . . . well! How Josiah Grinnell, up on the plains of Heaven, must have laughed over that!

Grant Gale was the first important physicist in Bob Noyce's career. The second was William Shockley. After their ambitions had collided one last time, and they had parted company, Noyce had concluded that he and Shockley were two very different people. But in many ways they were alike.

For a start, they both had an amateur's hambone love of being onstage. At MIT Noyce had sung in choral groups. Early in the summer of 1953, after he had received his Ph.D., he went over to Tufts College to sing and act in a program of musicals presented by the college. The costume director was a girl named Elizabeth Bottomley, from Barrington, Rhode Island, who had just graduated from Tufts, majoring in English. They both enjoyed dramatics. Singing, acting, and skiing had become the pastimes Noyce enjoyed most. He had become almost as expert at skiing as he had been at diving. Noyce and Betty, as he called her, were married that fall.

In 1953 the MIT faculty was just beginning to understand the implications of the transistor. But electronics firms were already eager to have graduate electrical engineers who could do research and development in the new field. Noyce was offered jobs by Bell Laboratories, IBM, RCA, and Philco. He went to work for Philco, in Philadelphia, because Philco was starting from near zero in semiconductor research and chances for rapid advancement seemed good. But Noyce was well aware that the most important work was still being done at Bell Laboratories, thanks in no small part to William Shockley.

Shockley had devised the first theoretical framework for research into solid-state semiconductors as far back as 1939 and was in charge of the Bell Labs team that included John Bardeen and Walter Brattain. Shockley had also originated the "junction transistor," which turned the transistor from an exotic laboratory instrument into a workable item. By 1955 Shockley had left Bell and returned to Palo Alto, California, where he had grown up near Stanford University, to form his own company, Shockley Semiconductor Laboratory, with start-up money provided by Arnold Beckman of Beckman Instruments. Shockley opened up shop in a glorified shed on South San Antonio Road in Mountain View, which was just south of Palo Alto. The building was made of concrete blocks with the rafters showing. Aside from clerical and maintenance personnel, practically all the employees were electrical engineers with doctorates. In a field this experimental there was nobody else worth hiring. Shockley began talking about "my Ph.D. production line."

Meanwhile, Noyce was not finding Philco the golden opportunity he thought it would be. Philco wanted good enough transistors to stay in the game with GE and RCA, but it was not interested in putting money into the sort of avant-garde research Noyce had in mind. In 1956 he resigned from Philco and moved from Pennsylvania to California to join Shockley. The way he went about it was a classic example of the Noyce brand of confidence. By now he and his wife, Betty, had two children: Bill, who was two, and Penny, who was six months old. After a couple of telephone conversations with Shockley, Noyce put himself and Betty on a night flight from Philadelphia to San Francisco. They arrived in Palo Alto at six A.M. By noon Noyce had signed a contract to buy a house. That afternoon he went to Mountain View to see Shockley and ask for a job, projected the halo, and got it.

The first months on Shockley's Ph.D. production line were exhilarating. It wasn't really a production line at all. Everything at this stage was research. Every day a dozen young Ph.D.s came to the shed at eight in the morning and began heating germanium and silicon, another common element, in kilns to temperatures ranging from 1,472 to 2,552 degrees Fahrenheit. They wore white lab coats, goggles, and work gloves. When they opened the kiln doors weird streaks of orange and white light went across their faces, and they put in the germanium or the silicon, along with specks of aluminum, phosphorus, boron, and arsenic. Contaminating the germanium or silicon with the aluminum, phosphorus, boron, and arsenic was called doping. Then they lowered a small mechanical column into the goo so that crystals formed on the bottom of the column, and they pulled the crystal out and tried to get a grip on it with tweezers, and put it under microscopes and cut it with diamond cutters, among other things, into minute slices, wafers, chips—there were no names in electronics for these tiny forms. The kilns cooked and bubbled away, the doors opened, the pale apricot light streaked over the goggles, the tweezers and diamond cutters flashed, the white coats flapped, the Ph.D.s squinted through their microscopes, and Shockley moved between the tables conducting the arcane symphony.

In pensive moments Shockley looked very much the scholar, with his roundish face, his roundish eyeglasses, and his receding hairline—but Shockley was not a man locked in the pensive mode. He was an enthusiast, a raconteur, and a showman. At the outset his very personality was enough to keep everyone swept up in the great adventure. When he lectured, as he often did at colleges and before professional groups, he would walk up to the lectern and thank the master of ceremonies and say that the only more flattering introduction he had ever received was one he gave himself one night when the emcee didn't show up, whereupon—*bango!*—a bouquet of red roses would pop up in his hand. Or he would walk up to the lectern and say that tonight he was getting into a hot subject, whereupon he would open up a book and—*whumpf!*—a puff of smoke would rise up out of the pages.

Shockley was famous for his homely but shrewd examples. One day a student confessed to being puzzled by the concept of amplification, which was one of the prime functions of the transistor. Shockley told him: "If you take a bale of hay and tie it to the tail of a mule and then strike a match and set the bale of hay on fire, and if you then compare the energy expended shortly thereafter by the mule with the energy expended by yourself in the striking of the match, you will understand the concept of amplification."

On November 1, 1956, Shockley arrived at the shed on South San Antonio Road beaming. Early that morning he had received a telephone call informing him that he had won the Nobel Prize for physics for the invention of the transistor; or, rather, that he was co-winner, along with John Bardeen and Walter Brattain. Shockley closed up shop and took everybody to a restaurant called Dinah's Shack over on El Camino Real, the road to San Francisco that had become Palo Alto's commercial strip. He treated his Ph.D. production line and all the other employees to a champagne breakfast. It seemed that Shockley's father was a mining engineer who spent years out on remote durango terrains, in Nevada, Manchuria—all over the world. Shockley's mother was like Noyce's. She was an intelligent woman with a commanding will. The Shockleys were Unitarians, the Unitarian Church being an offshoot of the Congregational. Shockley Sr. was twenty years older than Shockley's mother and died when Shockley was seventeen. Shockley's mother was determined that her son would someday "set the world on fire," as she once put it. And now he had done it. Shockley lifted a glass of champagne in Dinah's Shack, and it was as if it were a toast back across a lot of hard-wrought durango grit Octagon Soap sagebrush Dissenting Protestant years to his father's memory and his mother's determination.

That had been a great day at Shockley Semiconductor Laboratory. There weren't many more. Shockley was magnetic, he was a genius, and he was a great research director—the best, in fact. His forte was breaking a problem down to first principles. With a few words and a few lines on a piece of paper he aimed any experiment in the right direction. When it came to comprehending the young engineers on his Ph.D. production line, however, he was not so terrific.

It never seemed to occur to Shockley that his twelve highly educated elves just might happen to view themselves the same way he had always viewed himself: which is to say, as young geniuses capable of the sort of inventions Nobel Prizes were given for. One day Noyce came to Shockley with some new results he had found in the laboratory. Shockley picked up the telephone and called some former colleagues at Bell Labs to see if they sounded right. Shockley never even realized that Noyce had gone away from his desk seething. Then there was the business of the new management techniques. Now that he was an entrepreneur, Shockley came up with some new ways to run a company. Each one seemed to irritate the elves more than the one before. For a start, Shockley published their salaries. He posted them on a bulletin board. That way there would be no secrets. Then he started having the employees rate one another on a regular basis. These were so-called peer ratings, a device sometimes used in the military and seldom appreciated even there. Everybody regarded peer ratings as nothing more than popularity contests. But the real turning point was the lie detector. Shockley was convinced that someone in the shed was sabotaging the project. The work was running into inexplicable delays, but the money was running out on schedule. So he insisted that one employee roll up his sleeve and bare his chest and let the electrodes be attached and submit to a polygraph examination. No saboteur was ever found.

There were also some technical differences of opinion. Shockley was interested in developing a so-called four-layer diode. Noyce and two of his fellow elves, Gordon Moore and Jean Hoerni, favored transistors. But at bottom it was dissatisfaction with the boss and the lure of entrepreneurship that led to what happened next.

In the summer of 1957 Moore, Hoerni, and five other engineers—but not Noyce—got together and arrived at what became one of the primary business concepts of the young semiconductor industry. In this business, it dawned on them, capital assets in the traditional sense of plant, equipment, and raw materials counted for next to nothing. The only plant you needed was a shed big enough for the worktables. The only equipment you needed was some kilns, goggles, microscopes, tweezers, and diamond cutters. The materials, silicon and germanium, came from dirt and coal. Brainpower was the entire franchise. If the seven of them thought they could do the job better than Shockley, there was nothing to keep them from starting their own company. On that day was born the concept that would make the semiconductor business as wild as show business: defection capital.

The seven defectors went to the Wall Street firm of Hayden Stone in search of start-up money. It was at this point that they realized they had to have someone to serve as administrator. So they turned to Noyce, who was still with Shockley. None of them, including Noyce, had any administrative experience, but they all thought of Noyce as soon as the question came up. They didn't know exactly what they were looking for . . . but Noyce was the one with the halo. He agreed to join them. He would continue to wear a white lab coat and goggles and do research. But he would also be the coordinator. Of the eight of them, he would be the one man who kept track, on a regular basis, of all sides of the operation. He was twenty-nine years old.

Arthur Rock of Hayden Stone approached twenty-two firms before he finally hooked the defectors up with the Fairchild Camera and Instrument Corporation of New York. Fairchild was owned by Sherman Fairchild, a bachelor bon vivant who lived in a futuristic town house on East Sixty-fifth Street in Manhattan. The house was in two sections connected by ramps. The ramps were fifty feet long in some cases, enclosed in glass so that you could go up and down the ramps in all weather and gaze upon the marble courtyard below. The place looked like something from out of the Crystal Palace of Ming in *Flash Gordon*. The ramps were for his Aunt May, who lived with him and was confined to a wheelchair and had even more Fairchild money than he did. The chief executive officer of Fairchild was John Carter, who had just come from the Corning Glass Company. He had been the youngest vice-president in the history of that old-line, family-owned firm. He was thirty-six. Fairchild Camera and Instrument gave the defectors the money to start up the new company, Fairchild Semiconductor, with the understanding that Fairchild Camera and Instrument would have the right to buy Fairchild Semiconductor for $3 million at any time within the next eight years.

Shockley took the defections very hard. He seemed as much hurt as angered, and he was certainly angry enough. A friend of Shockley's said to Noyce's wife, Betty: "You must have known about this for quite some time. How on earth could you not tell me?" That was a baffling remark, unless one regarded Shockley as the father of the transistor and the defectors as the children he had taken beneath his mantle of greatness.

If so, one had a point. Years later, if anyone had drawn up a family tree for the semiconductor industry, practically every important branch would have led straight from Shockley's shed on South San Antonio Road. On the other hand, Noyce had been introduced to the transistor not by Shockley but by John Bardeen, via Grant Gale, and not in California but back in his own hometown, Grinnell, Iowa.

For that matter, Josiah Grinnell had been a defector in his day, too, and there was no record that he had ever lost a night's sleep over it.

Noyce, Gordon Moore, Jean Hoerni, and the other five defectors set up Fairchild Semiconductor in a two-story warehouse building some speculator had built out of tilt-up concrete slabs on Charleston Avenue in Mountain View, about twelve blocks from Shockley's operation. Mountain View was in the northern end of the Santa Clara Valley. In the business world the valley was known mainly for its apricot, pear, and plum orchards. From the work bays of the light-industry sheds that the speculators were beginning to build in the valley you could look out and see the raggedy little apricot trees they had never bothered to bulldoze after they bought the land from the farmers. A few well-known electronics firms were already in the valley: General Electric and IBM, as well as a company that had started up locally, Hewlett-Packard. Stanford University was encouraging engineering concerns to locate near Palo Alto and use the university's research facilities. The man who ran the program was a friend of Shockley's, Frederick E. Terman, whose father had originated the first scientific measurement of human intelligence, the Stanford-Binet IQ test.

IBM had a facility in the valley that was devoted specifically to research rather than production. Both IBM and Hewlett-Packard were trying to develop a highly esoteric and colossally expensive new device, the electronic computer. Shockley had been the first entrepreneur to come to the area to make semiconductors. After the defections his operation never got off the ground. Here in the Santa Clara Valley, that left the field to Noyce and the others at Fairchild.

Fairchild's start-up couldn't have come at a better time. By 1957 there was sufficient demand from manufacturers who merely wanted transistors instead of vacuum tubes, for use in radios and other machines, to justify the new operation. But it was also in 1957 that the Soviet Union launched *Sputnik I.* In the electronics industry the ensuing space race had the effect of coupling two new inventions—the transistor and the computer—and magnifying the importance of both.

The first American electronic computer, known as ENIAC, had been developed by the Army during the Second World War, chiefly as a means of computing artillery and bomb trajectories. The machine was a monster. It was one hundred feet long and ten feet high and required eighteen thousand vacuum tubes. The tubes generated so much heat, the temperature in the room sometimes reached 120 degrees. What the government needed was small computers that could be installed in rockets to provide automatic onboard guidance. Substituting transistors for vacuum tubes was an obvious way to cut down on the size. After *Sputnik I* the glamorous words in the semiconductor business were *computers* and *miniaturization.*

Other than Shockley Semiconductor, Fairchild was the only semiconductor company in the Santa Clara Valley, but Texas Instruments had entered the field in Dallas, as had Motorola in Phoenix and Transitron and Raytheon in the Boston area, where a new electronics industry was starting up as MIT finally began to comprehend the new technology. These firms were all racing to refine the production of transistors to the point where they might command the market. So far refinement had not been anybody's long suit. No tourist dropping by Fairchild, Texas Instruments, Motorola, or Transitron would have had the faintest notion he was looking in on the leading edge of the most advanced of all industries, electronics. The work bays, where the transistors were produced, looked like slightly sunnier versions of the garment sweatshops of San Francisco's Chinatown. Here were rows of women hunched over worktables, squinting through microscopes, doing the most tedious and frustrating sort of manual labor, cutting layers of silicon apart with diamond cutters, picking little rectangles of them up with tweezers, trying to attach wires to them, dropping them, rummaging around on the floor to find them again, swearing, muttering, climbing back up to their chairs, rubbing their eyes, squinting back through the microscopes, and driving themselves crazy some more. Depending on how well the silicon or germanium had been cooked and doped, anywhere from 50 to 90 percent of the transistors would turn out to be defective even after all that, and sometimes the good ones would be the ones that fell on the floor and got ruined.

Even for a machine as simple as a radio the individual transistors had to be wired together, by hand, until you ended up with a little panel that looked like a road map of West Virginia. As for a computer—the wires inside a computer were sheer spaghetti.

Noyce had figured out a solution. But fabricating it was another matter. There was something primitive about cutting individual transistors out of sheets of silicon and then wiring them back together in various series. Why not put them all on a single piece of silicon without wires? The problem was that you would also have to carve, etch, coat, and otherwise fabricate the silicon to perform all the accompanying electrical functions as well, the functions ordinarily performed by insulators, rectifiers, resistors, and capacitors. You would have to create an entire electrical system, an entire circuit, on a little wafer or chip.

Noyce realized that he was not the only engineer thinking along these lines, but he had never even heard of Jack Kilby. Kilby was a thirty-six-year-old engineer working for Texas Instruments in Dallas. In January 1959 Noyce made his first detailed notes about a complete solid-state circuit. A month later Texas Instruments announced that Jack Kilby had invented one. Kilby's integrated circuit, as the invention was called, was made of germanium. Six months later Noyce created a similar integrated circuit made of silicon and using a novel insulating process developed by Jean Hoerni. Noyce's silicon device turned out to be more efficient and more practical to produce than Kilby's and set the standard for the industry. So Noyce became known as the co-inventor of the integrated circuit. Nevertheless, Kilby had unquestionably been first. There was an ironic echo of Shockley here. Strictly speaking, Bardeen and Brattain, not Shockley, had invented the transistor, but Shockley wasn't bashful about being known as the co-inventor. And now, eleven years later, Noyce wasn't turning bashful, either.

Noyce knew exactly what he possessed in this integrated circuit, or microchip, as the press would call it. Noyce knew that he had discovered the road to El Dorado.

El Dorado was the vast, still-virgin terrain of electricity. Electricity was already so familiar a part of everyday life, only a few research engineers understood just how young and unexplored the terrain actually was. It had been only eighty years since Edison invented the light bulb in 1879. It had been less than fifty years since Lee De Forest, an inventor from Council Bluffs, Iowa, had invented the vacuum tube. The vacuum tube was based on the light bulb, but the vacuum tube opened up fields the light bulb did not even suggest: long-distance radio and telephone communication. Over the past ten years, since Bardeen and Brattain invented it in 1948, the transistor had become the modern replacement for the vacuum tube. And now came Kilby's and Noyce's integrated circuit. The integrated circuit was based on the transistor, but the integrated circuit opened up fields the transistor did not even suggest. The integrated circuit made it possible to create miniature computers, to put all the functions of the mighty ENIAC on a panel the size of a playing card. Thereby the integrated circuit opened up every field of engineering imaginable, from voyages to the moon to robots, and many fields that had never been imagined, such as electronic guidance counseling. It opened up so many fields that no one could even come up with a single name to include them all. "The second industrial revolution," "the age of the computer," "the microchip universe," "the electronic grid"—none of them, not even the handy neologism "high tech," could encompass all the implications.

The importance of the integrated circuit was certainly not lost on John Carter and Fairchild Camera back in New York. In 1959 they exercised their option to buy Fairchild Semiconductor for $3 million. The next day Noyce, Moore, Hoerni, and the other five former Shockley elves woke up rich, or richer than they had ever dreamed of being. Each received $250,000 worth of Fairchild stock.

Josiah Grinnell grew livid on the subject of alcohol. But he had nothing against money. He would have approved.

Noyce didn't know what to make of his new wealth. He was thirty-one years old. For the past four years, ever since he had gone to work for Shockley, the semiconductor business had not seemed like a business at all but an esoteric game in which young electrical engineers competed for *attaboys* and the occasional round of applause after delivering a paper before the IEEE, the Institute of Electrical and Electronics Engineers. It was a game supercharged by the fact that it was being played in the real world, to use a term that annoyed scientists in the universities. Someone—Arnold Beckman, Sherman Fairchild, whoever—was betting real money, and other bands of young elves, at Texas Instruments, RCA, Bell, were out there competing with you by the real world's rules, which required that you be practical as well as brilliant. Noyce started working for Fairchild Semiconductor in 1957 for twelve thousand dollars a year. When it came to money, he had assumed that he, like his father, would always be on somebody's payroll. Now, in 1959, when he talked to his father, he told him: "The money doesn't seem real. It's just a way of keeping score."

Noyce took his family to visit his parents fairly often. He and Betty now had three children, Bill, Penny, and Polly, who was a year old. When they visited the folks, they went off to church on Sunday with the folks, as if it were all very much a part of their lives. In fact, Noyce had started drifting away from Congregationalism and the whole matter of churchgoing after he entered MIT. It was not a question of rejecting it. He never rejected anything about his upbringing in Grinnell. It was just that he was heading off somewhere else, down a different road.

In that respect Noyce was like a great many bright young men and women from Dissenting Protestant families in the Middle West after the Second World War. They had been raised as Baptists, Methodists, Congregationalists, Presbyterians, United Brethren, whatever. They had been led through the church door and prodded toward religion, but it had never come alive for them. Sundays made their skulls feel like dried-out husks. So they slowly walked away

from the church and silently, without so much as a growl of rebellion, congratulated themselves on their independence of mind and headed into another way
of life. Only decades later, in most cases, would they discover how, absentmind-
edly, inexplicably, they had brought the old ways along for the journey nonetheless. It was as if . . . through some extraordinary mistake . . . they had been
sewn into the linings of their coats!

Now that he had some money, Bob Noyce bought a bigger house. His and
Betty's fourth child, Margaret, was born in 1960, and they wanted each child to
have a bedroom. But the thought of moving into any of the "best" neighborhoods in the Palo Alto area never even crossed his mind. The best neighborhoods were to be found in Atherton, in Burlingame, which was known as very
social, or in the swell old sections of Palo Alto, near Stanford University. Instead, Noyce bought a California version of a French country house in Los
Altos, a white stucco house with a steeply pitched roof. It was scenic up there
in the hills, and cooler in the summer than it was down in the flatlands near the
bay. The house had plenty of room, and he and Betty would be living a great
deal better than most couples their age, but Los Altos had no social cachet and
the house was not going to make *House & Garden* come banging on the door.
No one could accuse them of being ostentatious.

John Carter appointed Noyce general manager of the entire division, Fairchild Semiconductor, which was suddenly one of the hottest new outfits in the
business world. NASA chose Noyce's integrated circuits for the first computers
that astronauts would use on board their spacecraft (in the Gemini program).
After that, orders poured in. In ten years Fairchild sales rose from a few thousand dollars a year to $130 million, and the number of employees rose from the
original band of elves to twelve thousand. As the general manager, Noyce now
had to deal with a matter Shockley had dealt with clumsily and prematurely,
namely, new management techniques for this new industry.

One day John Carter came to Mountain View for a close look at Noyce's
semiconductor operation. Carter's office in Syosset, Long Island, arranged for
a limousine and chauffeur to be at his disposal while he was in California. So
Carter arrived at the tilt-up concrete building in Mountain View in the back of
a black Cadillac limousine with a driver in the front wearing the complete
chauffeur's uniform—the black suit, the white shirt, the black necktie, and the
black visored cap. That in itself was enough to turn heads at Fairchild Semiconductor. Nobody had ever seen a limousine and a chauffeur out there before.
But that wasn't what fixed the day in everybody's memory. It was the fact that
the driver stayed out there for almost eight hours, *doing nothing.* He stayed out
there in his uniform, with his visored hat on, in the front seat of the limousine,
all day, doing nothing but waiting for a man who was somewhere inside. John
Carter was inside having a terrific chief executive officer's time for himself. He
took a tour of the plant, he held conferences, he looked at figures, he nodded
with satisfaction, he beamed his urbane Fifty-seventh Street Biggie CEO
charm. And the driver sat out there all day engaged in the task of supporting a
visored cap with his head. People started leaving their workbenches and going

to the front windows just to take a look at this phenomenon. It seemed that bizarre. Here was a serf who *did nothing all day* but wait outside a door in order to be at the service of the haunches of his master instantly, whenever those haunches and the paunch and the jowls might decide to reappear. It wasn't merely that this little peek at the New York–style corporate high life was unusual out here in the brown hills of the Santa Clara Valley. It was that it seemed *terribly wrong.*

A certain instinct Noyce had about this new industry and the people who worked in it began to take on the outlines of a concept. Corporations in the East adopted a feudal approach to organization, without even being aware of it. There were kings and lords, and there were vassals, soldiers, yeomen, and serfs, with layers of protocol and perquisites, such as the car and driver, to symbolize superiority and establish the boundary lines. Back east the CEOs had offices with carved paneling, fake fireplaces, escritoires, bergères, leather-bound books, and dressing rooms, like a suite in a baronial manor house. Fairchild Semiconductor needed a strict operating structure, particularly in this period of rapid growth, but it did not need a social structure. In fact, nothing could be worse. Noyce realized how much he detested the eastern corporate system of class and status with its endless gradations, topped off by the CEOs and vice-presidents who conducted their daily lives as if they were a corporate court and aristocracy. He rejected the idea of a social hierarchy at Fairchild.

Not only would there be no limousines and chauffeurs, there would not even be any reserved parking places. Work began at eight A.M. for one and all, and it would be first come, first served, in the parking lot, for Noyce, Gordon Moore, Jean Hoerni, and everybody else. "If you come late," Noyce liked to say, "you just have to park in the back forty." And there would be no baronial office suites. The glorified warehouse on Charleston Road was divided into work bays and a couple of rows of cramped office cubicles. The cubicles were never improved. The decor remained Glorified Warehouse, and the doors were always open. Half the time Noyce, the chief administrator, was out in the laboratory anyway, wearing his white lab coat. Noyce came to work in a coat and tie, but soon the jacket and the tie were off, and that was fine for any other man in the place too. There were no rules of dress at all, except for some unwritten ones. Dress should be modest, modest in the social as well as the moral sense. At Fairchild there were no hard-worsted double-breasted pinstripe suits and shepherd's-check neckties. Sharp, elegant, fashionable, or alluring dress was a social blunder. Shabbiness was not a sin. Ostentation was.

During the start-up phase at Fairchild Semiconductor there had been no sense of bosses and employees. There had been only a common sense of struggle out on a frontier. Everyone had internalized the goals of the venture. They didn't need exhortations from superiors. Besides, everyone had been so young! Noyce, the administrator or chief coordinator or whatever he should be called, had been just about the oldest person on the premises, and he had been barely thirty. And now, in the early 1960s, thanks to his athletic build and his dark brown hair with the Campus Kid hairline, he still looked very young. As

Fairchild expanded, Noyce didn't even bother trying to find "experienced management personnel." Out here in California, in the semiconductor industry, they didn't exist. Instead, he recruited engineers right out of the colleges and graduate schools and gave them major responsibilities right off the bat. There was no "staff," no "top management" other than the eight partners themselves. Major decisions were not bucked up a chain of command. Noyce held weekly meetings of people from all parts of the operation, and whatever had to be worked out was worked out right there in the room. Noyce wanted them all to keep internalizing the company's goals and to provide their own motivations, just as they had during the start-up phase. If they did that, they would have the capacity to make their own decisions.

The young engineers who came to work for Fairchild could scarcely believe how much responsibility was suddenly thrust upon them. Some twenty-four-year-old just out of graduate school would find himself in charge of a major project with no one looking over his shoulder. A problem would come up, and he couldn't stand it, and he would go to Noyce and hyperventilate and ask him what to do. And Noyce would lower his head, turn on his 100-ampere eyes, listen, and say: "Look, here are your guidelines. You've got to consider A, you've got to consider B, and you've got to consider C." Then he would turn on the Gary Cooper smile: "But if you think I'm going to make your decision for you, you're mistaken. Hey . . . it's *your* ass."

Back east, in the conventional corporation, any functionary wishing to make an unusually large purchase had to have the approval of a superior or two or three superiors or even a committee, a procedure that ate up days, weeks, in paperwork. Noyce turned that around. At Fairchild any engineer, even a weenie just out of Cal Tech, could make any purchase he wanted, no matter how enormous, unless someone else objected strongly enough to try to stop it. Noyce called this the Short Circuit Paper Route. There was only one piece of paper involved, the piece of paper the engineer handed somebody in the purchasing department.

The spirit of the start-up phase! My God! Who could forget the exhilaration of the past few years! To be young and free out here on the silicon frontier! Noyce was determined to maintain that spirit during the expansion phase. And for the time being, at least, here in the early 1960s, the notion of a permanent start-up operation didn't seem too farfetched. Fairchild was unable to coast on the tremendous advantage Noyce's invention of the integrated circuit had provided. Competitors were setting up shop in the Santa Clara Valley like gold rushers. And where did they come from? Why, from Fairchild itself! And how could that be? Nothing to it. . . . Defection capital!

Defectors (or redefectors) from Fairchild started up more than fifty companies, all making or supplying microchips. Raytheon Semiconductor, Signetics, General Microelectronics, Intersil, Advanced Micro Devices, Qualidyne—off they spun, each with a sillier pseudotech engineerologism for a name than the one before. Defectors! What a merry game that was. Jean Hoerni and three of the other original eight defectors from Shockley defected from Fairchild to form what would soon become known as Teledyne Semiconductors, and that was only round one. After all, why not make all the money for yourself! The urge to use defection capital was so irresistible that the word *defection*, with its note of betrayal, withered away. Defectors were merely the Fairchildren, as Adam Smith dubbed them. Occasionally defectors from other companies, such as the men from Texas Instruments and Westinghouse who started Siliconix, moved into the Santa Clara Valley to join the free-for-all. But it was the Fairchildren who turned the Santa Clara Valley into the Silicon Valley. Acre by acre the fruit trees were uprooted, and two-story Silicon Modern office buildings and factories went up. The state of California built a new freeway past the area, Route 280. Children heard the phrase "Silicon Valley" so often, they grew up thinking it was the name on the map.

Everywhere the Fairchild émigrés went, they took the Noyce approach with them. It wasn't enough to start up a company; you had to start up a community, a community in which there were no social distinctions, and it was first come, first served, in the parking lot, and everyone was supposed to internalize the common goals. The atmosphere of the new companies was so democratic, it startled businessmen from the East. Some fifty-five-year-old biggie with his jowls swelling up smoothly from out of his F. R. Tripler modified-spread white collar and silk jacquard-print necktie would call up from GE or RCA and say, "This is Harold B. Thatchwaite," and the twenty-three-year-old secretary on the other end of the line, out in the Silicon Valley, would say in one of those sunny blond pale blue-eyed California voices: "Just a minute, Hal, Jack will be right with you." And once he got to California and met this Jack for the first time, there he would be, the CEO himself, all of thirty-three years old, wearing no jacket, no necktie, just a checked shirt, khaki pants, and a pair of moccasins with welted seams the size of jumper cables. Naturally the first sounds out of this Jack's mouth would be: "Hi, Hal."

It was the 1960s, and people in the East were hearing a lot about California surfers, California bikers, hot rodders, car customizers, California hippies, and political protesters, and the picture they got was of young people in jeans and T-shirts who were casual, spontaneous, impulsive, emotional, sensual, undisciplined, and obnoxiously proud of it. So these semiconductor outfits in the Silicon Valley with their CEOs dressed like camp counselors struck them as the business versions of the same thing.

They couldn't have been more wrong. The new breed of the Silicon Valley lived for work. They were disciplined to the point of back spasms. They worked long hours and kept working on weekends. They became absorbed in their companies the way men once had in the palmy days of the automobile industry. In the Silicon Valley a young engineer would go to work at eight in the morning, work right through lunch, leave the plant at six-thirty or seven, drive home, play with the baby for half an hour, have dinner with his wife, get in bed with her, give her a quick toss, then get up and leave her there in the dark and work at his desk for two or three hours on "a coupla things I had to bring home with me."

Or else he would leave the plant and decide, well, maybe he would drop in at the Wagon Wheel for a drink before he went home. Every year there was some place, the Wagon Wheel, Chez Yvonne, Rickey's, the Roundhouse, where members of this esoteric fraternity, the young men and women of the semiconductor industry, would head after work to have a drink and gossip and brag and trade war stories about phase jitters, phantom circuits, bubble memories, pulse trains, bounceless contacts, burst modes, leapfrog tests, p-n junctions, sleeping-sickness modes, slow-death episodes, RAMs, NAKs, MOSes, PCMs, PROMs, PROM blowers, PROM burners, PROM blasters, and teramagnitudes, meaning multiples of a million millions. So then he wouldn't get home until nine, and the baby was asleep, and dinner was cold, and the wife was frosted off, and he would stand there and cup his hands as if making an imaginary snowball and try to explain to her . . . while his mind trailed off to other matters, LSIs, VLSIs, alpha flux, de-rezzing, forward biases, parasitic signals, and that tera-sexy little cookie from Signetics he had met at the Wagon Wheel, who understood such things.

It was not a great way of life for marriages. By the late 1960s the toll of divorces seemed to those in the business to be as great as that of NASA's boomtowns, Cocoa Beach, Florida, and Clear Lake, Texas, where other young engineers were giving themselves over to a new technology as if it were a religious mission. The second time around they tended to "intramarry." They married women who worked for Silicon Valley companies and who could comprehend and even learn to live with their twenty-four-hour obsessions. In the Silicon Valley an engineer was under pressure to reinvent the integrated circuit every six months. In 1959 Noyce's invention had made it possible to put an entire electrical circuit on a chip of silicon the size of a fingernail. By 1964 you had to know how to put ten circuits on a chip that size just to enter the game, and the stakes kept rising. Six years later the figure was one thousand circuits on a single chip; six years after that it would be thirty-two thousand—and everyone was talking about how the real breakthrough would be sixty-four thousand. Noyce himself led the race; by 1968 he had a dozen new integrated-circuit and transistor patents. And what amazing things such miniaturization made possible! In December 1968 NASA sent the first manned flight to the moon, *Apollo 8*. Three astronauts, Frank Borman, James Lovell, and William Anders, flew into earth orbit, then fired a rocket at precisely the right moment in order to break free of the earth's gravitational field and fly through the minute "window" in space that would put them on course to the moon rather than into orbit around the sun, from which there could be no return. They flew to the moon, went into orbit around it, saw the dark side, which no one had ever seen, not even with a telescope, then fired a rocket at precisely the right moment in order to break free of the moon's gravitational pull and go into the proper trajectory for their return to earth. None of it would have been possible without onboard computers. People were beginning to talk about all that the space program was doing for the computer sciences. Noyce knew it was the other way around. Only the existence of a miniature computer two feet long, one foot wide, and six inches thick—exactly three thousand times smaller than the old ENIAC and far faster and more reliable—made the flight of *Apollo* 8 possible. And there would have been no miniature computer without the integrated circuits invented by Noyce and Kilby and refined by Noyce and the young semiconductor zealots of the Silicon Valley, the new breed who were building the road to El Dorado.

Noyce used to go into a slow burn that year, 1968, when the newspapers, the magazines, and the television networks got on the subject of *the youth. The youth* was a favorite topic in 1968. Riots broke out on the campuses as the anti-war movement reached its peak following North Vietnam's Tet offensive. Black youths rioted in the cities. The Yippies, supposedly a coalition of hippies and campus activists, managed to sabotage the Democratic National Convention by setting off some highly televised street riots. The press seemed to enjoy presenting these youths as the avant-garde who were sweeping aside the politics and morals of the past and shaping America's future. The French writer Jean-François Revel toured American campuses and called the radical youth *homo novus,* "the New Man," as if they were the latest, most advanced product of human evolution itself, after the manner of the superchildren in Arthur C. Clarke's *Childhood's End.*

Homo novus? As Noyce saw it, these so-called radical youth movements were shot through with a yearning for a preindustrial Arcadia. They wanted, or thought they wanted, to return to the earth and live on organic vegetables and play folk songs from the sixteenth and seventeenth centuries. They were antitechnology. They looked upon science as an instrument monopolized by the military-industrial complex. They used this phrase, "the military-industrial complex," all the time. If industry or the military underwrote scientific research in the universities—and they underwrote a great deal of it—then that research was evil. The universities were to be pure and above exploitation, except, of course, by ideologues of the Left. The *homo novus* had set up a chain of logic that went as follows: since science equals the military-industrial complex, and the military-industrial complex equals capitalism, and capitalism equals fascism, therefore science equals fascism. And therefore, these much-vaunted radical youths, these shapers of the future, attacked the forward positions of American technology, including the space program and the very idea of the computer. And therefore these creators of the future were what? They were Luddites. They wanted to destroy the new machines. They were the reactionaries of the new age. They were an avant-garde to the rear. They wanted to call off the future. They were stillborn, ossified, prematurely senile.

If you wanted to talk about the creators of the future—well, here they were! Here in the Silicon Valley! Just before *Apollo* 8 circled the moon, Bob Noyce turned forty-one. By age forty-one he had become such a good skier, people were urging him to enter competitions. He had taken up hang gliding and scuba diving. When his daughter Penny was almost fourteen, he asked her what she wanted for her birthday, and she said she wanted to drop from an airplane by parachute. Noyce managed to convince her to settle for glider lessons instead. Then, because it made him restless to just stand around an airfield and watch her soar up above, he took flying lessons, bought an airplane, and began flying the family up through the mountain passes to Aspen, Colorado, for skiing weekends. He had the same lean, powerful build as he had had twenty years before, when he was on the swimming team at Grinnell College. He had the same thick dark brown hair and the same hairline. It looked as if every hair in his head were nailed in. He looked as if he could walk out the door any time he wanted to and win another Midwest Conference diving championship. And he was one of the *oldest* CEOs in the semiconductor business! He was the Edison of the bunch! He was the *father* of the Silicon Valley!

The rest of the hotshots were younger. It was a business dominated by people in their twenties and thirties. In the Silicon Valley there was a phenomenon known as burnout. After five or ten years of obsessive racing for the semiconductor high stakes, five or ten years of lab work, work lunches, workaholic drinks at the Wagon Wheel, and work-battering of the wife and children, an engineer would reach his middle thirties and wake up one day—and he was finished. The game was over. It was called burnout, suggesting mental and physical exhaustion brought about by overwork. But Noyce was convinced it was something else entirely. It was . . . *age*, or age and status. In the semiconductor business, research engineering was like pitching in baseball; it was 60 percent of the game. Semiconductor research was one of those highly mathematical sciences, such as microbiology, in which, for reasons one could only guess at, the great flashes, the critical moments of inspiration, came mainly to those who were young, often to men in their twenties. The thirty-five-year-old burnouts weren't suffering from exhaustion, as Noyce saw it. They were being overwhelmed, outperformed, by the younger talent coming up behind them. It wasn't the central nervous system that was collapsing, it was the ego.

Now here you saw youth in the vanguard, on the leading edge! Here you saw the youths who were, in fact, shaping the future! Here you saw, if you insisted on the term, the *homo novus*!

But why insist? For they were also of the same stripe as Josiah Grinnell, who had founded Grinnell, Iowa, at the age of thirty-three.

It was in 1968 that Noyce pulled off the redefection of all redefections. Fairchild Semiconductor had generated tremendous profits for the parent company back east. It now appeared to Noyce that John Carter and Sherman Fairchild had been diverting too much of that money into new start-up ventures, outside the semiconductor field. As a matter of fact, Noyce disliked many things "back east." He disliked the periodic trips to New York, for which he dressed in gray suits, white shirts, and neckties and reported to the royal corporate court and wasted days trying to bring them up to date on what was happening in California. Fairchild was rather enlightened, for an eastern corporation, but the truth was, there was no one back east who understood how to run a corporation in the United States in the second half of the twentieth century. Back east they had never progressed beyond the year 1940. Consequently, they were still hobbled by all of the primitive stupidities of bureaucratism and labor-management battles. They didn't have the foggiest comprehension of the Silicon Valley idea of a corporate community. The brightest young business-men in the East were trained—most notably at the Harvard business school —to be little Machiavellian princes. Greed and strategy were all that mattered. They were trained for failure.

Noyce and Gordon Moore, two of the three original eight Shockley elves still at Fairchild, decided to form their own company. They went to Arthur Rock, who had helped provide the start-up money for Fairchild Semiconductor when he was at Hayden Stone. Now Rock had his own venture capital operation. Noyce took great pleasure in going through none of the steps in corporate for-mation that the business schools talked about. He and Moore didn't even write up a proposal. They merely told Rock what they wanted to do and put up $500,000 of their own money, $250,000 each. That seemed to impress Rock more than anything they could possibly have written down, and he rounded up $2.5 million of the start-up money. A few months later another $300,000 came, this time from Grinnell College. Noyce had been on the college's board of trustees since 1962, and a board member had asked him to give the college a chance to invest, should the day come when he started his own company. So Grinnell College became one of the gamblers betting on Noyce and Intel—the pseudotech engineerologism Noyce and Moore dreamed up as the corporate name. Josiah Grinnell would have loved it.

The defection of Noyce and Moore from Fairchild was an earthquake even within an industry jaded by the very subject of defections. In the Silicon Valley everybody had looked upon Fairchild as Noyce's company. He was the magnet that held the place together. With Noyce gone, it was obvious that the entire work force would be up for grabs. As one wag put it, "People were practically driving trucks over to Fairchild Semiconductor and loading up with employ-ees." Fairchild responded by pulling off one of the grossest raids in corporate history. One day the troops who were left at Fairchild looked across their parti-tions and saw a platoon of young men with terrific suntans moving into the ex-ecutive office cubicles. They would always remember what terrific suntans they had. They were C. Lester Hogan, chief executive officer of the Motorola semiconductor division in Phoenix, and his top echelon of engineers and ad-ministrators. Or, rather, C. Lester Hogan of Motorola until yesterday. Fairchild had hired the whole bunch away from Motorola and installed them in place of Noyce & Co. like a matched set. There was plenty of sunshine in the Santa Clara Valley, but nobody here had suntans like this bunch from Phoenix. Fairchild had lured the leader of the young sun-gods out of the Arizona desert in the most direct way imaginable. He had offered him an absolute fortune in money and stock. Hogan received so much, the crowd at the Wagon Wheel said, that henceforth wealth in the Silicon Valley would be measured in units called hogans.*

*Dirk Hanson, *The New Alchemists* (Boston: Little, Brown, 1982).

Noyce and Moore, meanwhile, started up Intel in a tilt-up concrete building that Jean Hoerni and his group had built, but no longer used, in Santa Clara, which was near Mountain View. Once again there was an echo of Shockley. They opened up shop with a dozen bright young electrical engineers, plus a few clerical and maintenance people, and bet everything on research and product development. Noyce and Moore, like Shockley, put on the white coats and worked at the laboratory tables. They would not be competing with Fairchild or anyone else in the already established semiconductor markets. They had decided to move into the most backward area of computer technology, which was data storage, or "memory." A computer's memory was stored in ceramic ringlets known as cores. Each ringlet contained one "bit" of information, a "yes" or a "no," in the logic of the binary system of mathematics that computers employ. Within two years Noyce and Moore had developed the 1103 memory chip, a chip of silicon and polysilicon the size of two letters in a line of type. Each chip contained four thousand transistors, did the work of a thousand ceramic ringlets, and did it faster. The production line still consisted of rows of women sitting at tables as in the old shed-and-rafter days, but the work bays now looked like something from out of an intergalactic adventure movie. The women engraved the circuits on the silicon photographically, wearing antiseptic Mars Voyage suits, headgear, and gloves because a single speck of dust could ruin one of the miniature circuits. The circuits were so small that "miniature" no longer sounded small enough. The new word was "microminiature." Everything now took place in an air-conditioned ice cube of vinyl tiles, stainless steel, fluorescent lighting, and backlit plastic.

The 1103 memory chip opened up such a lucrative field that other companies, including Fairchild, fought desperately just to occupy the number-two position, filling the orders Intel couldn't take care of. At the end of Intel's first year in business, which had been devoted almost exclusively to research, sales totaled less than three thousand dollars and the work force numbered forty-two. In 1972, thanks largely to the 1103 chip, sales were $23.4 million and the work force numbered 1,002. In the next year sales almost tripled, to $66 million, and the work force increased two and a half times, to 2,528.

So Noyce had the chance to run a new company from start-up to full production precisely the way he thought Shockley should have run his in Palo Alto back in the late 1950s. From the beginning Noyce gave all the engineers and most of the office workers stock options. He had learned at Fairchild that in a business so dependent upon research, stock options were a more powerful incentive than profit sharing. People sharing profits naturally wanted to concentrate on products that were already profitable rather than plunge into avant-garde research that would not pay off in the short run even if it were successful. But people with stock options lived for research breakthroughs. The news would send a semiconductor company's stock up immediately, regardless of profits.

Noyce's idea was that every employee should feel that he could go as far and as fast in this industry as his talent would take him. He didn't want any employee to look at the structure of Intel and see a complex set of hurdles. It went without saying that there would be no social hierarchy at Intel, no executive suites, no pinstripe set, no reserved parking places, or other symbols of the hierarchy. But Noyce wanted to go further. He had never liked the business of the office cubicles at Fairchild. As miserable as they were, the mere possession of one symbolized superior rank. At Intel executives would not be walled off in offices. Everybody would be in one big room. There would be nothing but low partitions to separate Noyce or anyone else from the lowliest stock boys trundling in the accordion printout paper. The whole place became like a shed. When they first moved into the building, Noyce worked at an old, scratched, secondhand metal desk. As the company expanded, Noyce kept the same desk, and new stenographers, just hired, were given desks that were not only newer but bigger and better than his. Everybody noticed the old beat-up desk, since there was nothing to keep anybody from looking at every inch of Noyce's office space. Noyce enjoyed this subversion of the eastern corporate protocol of small metal desks for underlings and large wooden desks for overlords.

At Intel, Noyce decided to eliminate the notion of levels of management altogether. He and Moore ran the show; that much was clear. But below them there were only the strategic business segments, as they called them. They were comparable to the major departments in an orthodox corporation, but they had far more autonomy. Each was run like a separate corporation. Middle managers at Intel had more responsibility than most vice-presidents back east. They were also much younger and got lower-back pain and migraines earlier. At Intel, if the marketing division had to make a major decision that would affect the engineering division, the problem was not routed up a hierarchy to a layer of executives who oversaw both departments. Instead, "councils," made up of people already working on the line in the divisions that were affected, would meet and work it out themselves. The councils moved horizontally, from problem to problem. They had no vested power. They were not governing bodies but coordinating councils.

Noyce was a great believer in meetings. The people in each department or work unit were encouraged to convene meetings whenever the spirit moved them. There were rooms set aside for meetings at Intel, and they were available on a first come, first served basis, just like the parking spaces. Often meetings were held at lunchtime. That was not a policy; it was merely an example set by Noyce. There were no executive lunches at Intel. Back east, in New York, executives treated lunch as a daily feast of the nobility, a sumptuous celebration of their eminence, in the Lucullan expense-account restaurants of Manhattan. The restaurants in the East and West Fifties of Manhattan were like something from out of a dream. They recruited chefs from all over Europe and the Orient. Pasta primavera, saucisson, sorrel mousse, homard cardinal, terrine de légumes Montesquiou, paillard de pigeon, medallions of beef Chinese Gordon, veal Valdostana, Verbena roast turkey with Hayman sweet potatoes flown in from the eastern shore of Virginia, raspberry soufflé, baked Alaska, zabaglione, pear torte, crème brulée—and the wines! and the brandies! and the port! the

Sambuca! the cigars! and the decor!—walls with lacquered woodwork and winking mirrors and sconces with little pleated peach-colored shades, all of it designed by the very same decorators who walked duchesses to parties for Halston on Eaton Square!—and captains and maître d's who made a fuss over you in movie French in front of your clients and friends and fellow overlords!—it was Mount Olympus in mid-Manhattan every day from twelve-thirty to three P.M., and you emerged into the pearl-gray light of the city with such ambrosia pumping through your veins that even the clotted streets with the garbagemen backing up their grinder trucks and yelling, " 'Mon back, 'mon back, 'mon back, 'mon back," as if talking Urban Chippewa—even this became part of the bliss of one's eminence in the corporate world! There were many chief executive officers who kept their headquarters in New York long after the last rational reason for doing so had vanished . . . because of the ineffable experience of being a CEO and having lunch five days a week in Manhattan!

At Intel lunch had a different look to it. You could tell when it was noon at Intel, because at noon men in white aprons arrived at the front entrance gasping from the weight of the trays they were carrying. The trays were loaded down with deli sandwiches and waxed cups full of drinks with clear plastic tops, with globules of Sprite or Diet Shasta sliding around the tops on the inside. That was your lunch. You ate some sandwiches made of roast beef or chicken sliced into translucent rectangles by a machine in a processing plant and then reassembled on the bread in layers that gave off dank whiffs of hormones and chemicals, and you washed it down with Sprite or Diet Shasta, and you sat amid the particle-board partitions and metal desktops, and you kept your mind on your committee meeting. That was what Noyce did, and that was what everybody else did.

If Noyce called a meeting, then he set the agenda. But after that, everybody was an equal. If you were a young engineer and you had an idea you wanted to get across, you were supposed to speak up and challenge Noyce or anybody else who didn't get it right away. This was a little bit of heaven. You were face to face with the inventor, or the co-inventor, of the very road to El Dorado, and he was only forty-one years old, and *he* was listening to *you*. He had his head down and his eyes beamed up at you, and he was absorbing it all. He wasn't a boss. He was Gary Cooper! He was here to help you be self-reliant and do as much as you could on your own. This wasn't a corporation . . . it was a congregation.

By the same token, there were sermons and homilies. At Intel everyone— Noyce included—was expected to attend sessions on "the Intel Culture." At these sessions the principles by which the company was run were spelled out and discussed. Some of the discussions had to do specifically with matters of marketing or production. Others had to do with the broadest philosophical principles of Intel and were explained via the Socratic method at management seminars by Intel's number-three man, Andrew Grove.

Grove would say, "How would you sum up the Intel approach?"

Many hands would go up, and Grove would choose one, and the eager communicant would say: "At Intel you don't wait for someone else to do it. You take the ball yourself and you run with it."

And Grove would say, "Wrong. At Intel you take the ball yourself and you let the air out and you fold the ball up and put it in your pocket. Then you take another ball and run with it and when you've crossed the goal you take the second ball out of your pocket and reinflate it and score twelve points instead of six."

Grove was the most colorful person at Intel. He was a thin man in his mid-thirties with tight black curls all over his head. The curls ran down into a pair of muttonchops that seemed to run together like goulash with his moustache. Every day he wore either a turtleneck jersey or an open shirt with an ornamental chain twinkling on his chest. He struck outsiders as the epitome of a style of the early 1970s known as California Groovy. In fact, Grove was the epitome of the religious principle that the greater the freedom—for example, the freedom to dress as you pleased—the greater the obligation to exercise discipline. Grove's own groovy outfits were neat and clean. The truth was, he was a bit of a bear on the subject of neatness and cleanliness. He held what he called "Mr. Clean inspections," showing up in various work areas wearing his muttonchops and handlebar moustache and his Harry Belafonte cane cutter's shirt and the gleaming chainwork, inspecting offices for books stacked too high, papers strewn over desktops, everything short of running a white glove over the shelves, as if this were some California Groovy Communal version of Parris Island, while the chain twinkled in his chest hairs. Grove was also the inspiration for such items as the performance ratings and the Late List. Each employee received a report card periodically with a grade based on certain presumably objective standards. The grades were *superior, exceeds requirements, meets requirements, marginally meets requirements,* and *does not meet requirements.* This was the equivalent of A, B, C, D, and F in school. Noyce was all for it. "If you're ambitious and hardworking," he would say, "you *want* to be told how you're doing." In Noyce's view, most of the young hotshots who were coming to work for Intel had never had the benefit of honest grades in their lives. In the late 1960s and early 1970s college faculties had been under pressure to give all students passing marks so they wouldn't have to go off to Vietnam, and they had caved in, until the entire grading system was meaningless. At Intel they would learn what measuring up meant. The Late List was also like something from a strict school. Everyone was expected at work at eight A.M. A record was kept of how many employees arrived after 8:10 A.M. If 7 percent or more were late for three months, then everybody in the section had to start signing in. There was no inevitable penalty for being late, however. It was up to each department head to make of the Late List what he saw fit. If he knew a man was working overtime every night on a certain project, then his presence on the Late List would probably be regarded as nothing more than that, a line on a piece of paper. At bottom—and this was part of the Intel Culture—Noyce and Grove knew that penalties were very nearly useless. Things like report cards and Late Lists worked only if they stimulated self-discipline.

The worst form of discipline at Intel was to be called on the Antron II carpet before Noyce himself. Noyce insisted on ethical behavior in all dealings within the company and between companies. That was the word people used to describe his approach, *ethical*; that and *moral*. Noyce was known as a very aggressive businessman, but he stopped short of cutting throats—and he never talked about revenge. He would not tolerate peccadilloes such as little personal I'll-reimburse-it-on-Monday dips into the petty cash. Noyce's Strong Silent stare, his Gary Cooper approach, could be mortifying as well as inspiring. When he was angry, his baritone voice never rose. He seemed like a powerful creature that only through the greatest self-control was refraining from an attack. He somehow created the impression that if pushed one more inch, he would fight. As a consequence he seldom had to. No one ever trifled with Bob Noyce.

Noyce managed to create an ethical universe within an inherently amoral setting: the American business corporation in the second half of the twentieth century. At Intel there was good and there was evil, and there was freedom and there was discipline, and to an extraordinary degree employees internalized these matters, as if members of Cromwell's army. As the work force grew at Intel, and the profits soared, labor unions, chiefly the International Association of Machinists and Aerospace Workers, the Teamsters, and the Stationary Engineers Union, made several attempts to organize Intel. Noyce made it known, albeit quietly, that he regarded unionization as a death threat to Intel, and to the semiconductor industry generally. Labor-management battles were part of the ancient terrain of the East. If Intel were divided into workers and bosses, with the implication that each side had to squeeze its money out of the hides of the other, the enterprise would be finished. Motivation would no longer be internal; it would be objectified in the deadly form of work rules and grievance procedures. The one time it came down to a vote, the union lost out by the considerable margin of four to one. Intel's employees agreed with Noyce. Unions were part of the dead hand of the past. . . . Noyce and Intel were on the road to El Dorado.

By the early 1970s Noyce and Moore's 1103 memory chip had given this brand-new company an entire corner of the semiconductor market. But that was only the start. Now a thirty-two-year-old Intel engineer named Ted Hoff came up with an invention as important as Noyce's integrated circuit had been a decade earlier: the microprocessor. The microprocessor was known as "the computer on a chip," because it put all the arithmetic and logic functions of a computer on a chip the size of the head of a tack. The possibilities for creating and using small computers now surpassed most people's imagining, even within the industry. One of the more obvious possibilities was placing a small computer in the steering and braking mechanisms of a car that would take over for the driver in case of a skid or excessive speed on a curve.

In Ted Hoff, Noyce was looking at proof enough of his hypothesis that out here on the electrical frontier the great flashes came to the young. Hoff was about the same age Noyce had been when he invented his integrated circuit. The glory was now Hoff's. But Noyce took Hoff's triumph as proof of a second hypothesis. If you created the right type of corporate community, the right type of autonomous congregation, genius would flower. Certainly the corporate numbers were flowering. The news of the microprocessor, on top of the success of the 1103 memory chip, nearly trebled the value of Intel stock from 1971 to 1973. Noyce's own holdings were now worth $18.5 million. He was in roughly the same position as Josiah Grinnell a hundred years before, when Grinnell brought the Rock Island Railroad into Iowa.

Noyce continued to live in the house in the Los Altos hills that he had bought in 1960. He was not reluctant to spend his money; he was merely reluctant to show it. He spent a fortune on landscaping, but you could do that and the world would be none the wiser. Gradually the house disappeared from view behind an enormous wall of trees, tropical bushes, and cockatoo flowers. Noyce had a pond created on the back lawn, a waterscape elaborate enough to put on a bus tour, but nobody other than guests ever saw it. The lawn stretched on for several acres and had a tennis court, a swimming pool, and more walls of boughs and hot-pastel blossoms, and the world saw none of that, either.

Noyce drove a Porsche roadster, and he didn't mind letting it out for a romp. Back east, when men made a great deal of money, they tended to put a higher and higher value on their own hides. Noyce, on the other hand, seemed to enjoy finding new ways to hang his out over the edge. He took up paragliding over the ski slopes at Aspen on a Rogolla wing. He built a Quicksilver hang glider and flew it off cliffs until a friend of his, a champion at the sport, fractured his pelvis and a leg flying a Quicksilver. He also took up scuba diving, and now he had his Porsche. The high-performance foreign sports car became one of the signatures of the successful Silicon Valley entrepreneur. The sports car was perfect. Its richness consisted of something small, dense, and hidden: the engineering beneath the body shell. Not only that, the very luxury of a sports car was the experience of driving it yourself. A sports car didn't even suggest a life with servants. Porsches and Ferraris became the favorites. By 1975 the Ferrari agency in Los Gatos was the second biggest Ferrari agency on the West Coast. Noyce also bought a 1947 Republic Seabee amphibious airplane, so that he could take the family for weekends on the lakes in northern California. He now had two aircraft, but he flew the ships himself.

Noyce was among the richest individuals on the San Francisco Peninsula, as well as the most important figure in the Silicon Valley, but his name seldom appeared in the San Francisco newspapers. When it did, it was in the business section, not on the society page. That, too, became the pattern for the new rich of the Silicon Valley. San Francisco was barely forty-five minutes up the Bayshore Freeway from Los Altos, but psychologically San Francisco was an entire continent away. It was a city whose luminaries kept looking back east, to New York, to see if they were doing things correctly.

In 1974 Noyce wound up in a situation that to some seemed an all-too-typical mid-life in the Silicon Valley story. He and Betty, his wife of twenty-one years, were divorced, and the following year he "intramarried." Noyce, who was forty-seven, married Intel's personnel director, Ann Bowers, who was thirty-seven. The divorce was mentioned in the *San Francisco Chronicle*, but not as a social note. It was a major business story. Under California law, Betty received half the family's assets. When word got out that she was going to sell off $6 million of her Intel stock in the interest of diversifying her fortune, it threw the entire market in Intel stock into a temporary spin. Betty left California and went to live in a village on the coast of Maine. Noyce kept the house in Los Altos.

By this time, the mid-1970s, the Silicon Valley had become the late-twentieth-century-California version of a new city, and Noyce and other entrepreneurs began to indulge in some introspection. For ten years, thanks to racial hostilities and the leftist politics of the antiwar movement, the national press had dwelled on the subject of ethnic backgrounds. This in itself tended to make the engineers and entrepreneurs of the Silicon Valley conscious of how similar most of them were. Most of the major figures, like Noyce himself, had grown up and gone to college in small towns in the Middle West and the West. John Bardeen had grown up in and gone to college in Madison, Wisconsin. Walter Brattain had grown up in and gone to college in Washington. Shockley grew up in Palo Alto at a time when it was a small college town and went to the California Institute of Technology. Jack Kilby was born in Jefferson City, Missouri, and went to college at the University of Illinois. William Hewlett was born in Ann Arbor and went to school at Stanford. David Packard grew up in Pueblo, Colorado, and went to Stanford. Oliver Buckley grew up in Sloane, Iowa, and went to college at Grinnell. Lee DeForest came from Council Bluffs, Iowa (and went to Yale). And Thomas Edison grew up in Port Huron, Michigan, and didn't go to college at all.

Some of them, such as Noyce and Shockley, had gone east to graduate school at MIT, since it was the most prestigious engineering school in the United States. But MIT had proved to be a backwater . . . the sticks . . . when it came to the most advanced form of engineering, solid-state electronics. Grinnell College, with its one thousand students, had been years ahead of MIT. The picture had been the same on the other great frontier of technology in the second half of the twentieth century, namely, the space program. The engineers who fulfilled one of man's most ancient dreams, that of traveling to the moon, came from the same background, the small towns of the Midwest and the West. After the triumph of *Apollo 11*, when Neil Armstrong and "Buzz" Aldrin became the first mortals to walk on the moon, NASA's administrator, Tom Paine, happened to remark in conversation: "This was the triumph of the squares." A reporter overheard him—and did the press ever have a time with that! But Paine had come up with a penetrating insight. As it says in the Book of Matthew, the last shall be first. It was engineers from the supposedly backward and narrow-minded boondocks who had provided not only the genius but also the passion and the daring that won the space race and carried out John F. Kennedy's exhortation, back in 1961, to put a man on the moon "before this decade is out." The passion and the daring of these engineers was as remarkable as their talent. Time after time they had to shake off the meddling hands of timid souls from back east. The contribution of MIT to Project Mercury was minus one. The minus one was Jerome Wiesner of the MIT electronic research lab, who was brought in by Kennedy as a special adviser to straighten out the space program when it seemed to be faltering early in 1961. Wiesner kept flinching when he saw what NASA's boondockers were preparing to do. He tried to persuade Kennedy to forfeit the manned space race to the Soviets and concentrate instead on unmanned scientific missions. The boondockers of Project Mercury, starting with the project's director, Bob Gilruth, an aeronautical engineer from Nashwauk, Minnesota, dodged Wiesner for months, like moonshiners evading a roadblock, until they got astronaut Alan Shepard launched on the first Mercury mission. Who had time to waste on players as behind the times as Jerome Wiesner and the Massachusetts Institute of Technology . . . out here on technology's leading edge?

Just why was it that small-town boys from the Middle West dominated the engineering frontiers? Noyce concluded it was because in a small town you became a technician, a tinker, an engineer, and an inventor, by necessity.

"In a small town," Noyce liked to say, "when something breaks down, you don't wait around for a new part, because it's not coming. You make it yourself."

Yet in Grinnell necessity had been the least of the mothers of invention. There had been something else about Grinnell, something people Noyce's age could feel but couldn't name. It had to do with the fact that Grinnell had once been a religious community; not merely a town with a church but a town that was inseparable from the church. In Josiah Grinnell's day most of the townspeople were devout Congregationalists, and the rest were smart enough to act as if they were. Anyone in Grinnell who aspired to the status of feedstore clerk or better joined the First Congregational Church. By the end of the Second World War educated people in Grinnell, and in all the Grinnells of the Middle West, had begun to drop this side of their history into a lake of amnesia. They gave in to the modern urge to be urbane. They themselves began to enjoy sniggering over Sherwood Anderson's *Winesburg, Ohio,* Sinclair Lewis's *Main Street,* and Grant Wood's *American Gothic.* Once the amnesia set in, all they remembered from the old days were the austere moral codes, which in some cases still hung on. Josiah Grinnell's real estate covenants prohibiting drinking, for example. . . . Just imagine! How absurd it was to see these unburied bones of something that had once been strong and alive.

That something was Dissenting Protestantism itself. Oh, it had once been quite strong and very much alive! The passion—the exhilaration!—of those early days was what no one could any longer recall. To be a believing Protestant in a town such as Grinnell in the middle of the nineteenth century was to experience a spiritual ecstasy greater than any that the readers of *Main Street* or the viewers of *American Gothic* were likely to know in their lifetimes. Josiah Grinnell had gone to Iowa in 1854 to create nothing less than a City of Light. He was a New Englander who had given up on the East. He had founded the first

Congregational church in Washington, D.C., and then defected from it when the congregation, mostly southerners, objected to his antislavery views. He went to New York and met the famous editor of the *New York Herald,* Horace Greeley. It was while talking to Josiah Grinnell, who was then thirty-two and wondering what to do with his life, that Greeley uttered the words for which he would be remembered forever after: "Go west, young man, go west." So Grinnell went to Iowa, and he and three friends bought up five thousand acres of land in order to start up a Congregational community the way he thought it should be done. A City of Light! The first thing he organized was the congregation. The second was the college. Oxford and Cambridge had started banning Dissenting Protestants in the seventeenth century; Dissenters founded their own schools and colleges. Grinnell became a champion of "free schools," and it was largely thanks to him that Iowa had one of the first and best public school systems in the West. To this day Iowa has the highest literacy rate of any state. In the 1940s a bright youngster whose parents were not rich—such as Bob Noyce or his brother Donald—was far more likely to receive a superior education in Iowa than in Massachusetts.

And if he was extremely bright, if he seemed to have the quality known as genius, he was infinitely more likely to go into engineering in Iowa, or Illinois or Wisconsin, than anywhere in the East. Back east engineering was an unfashionable field. The East looked to Europe in matters of intellectual fashion, and in Europe the ancient aristocratic bias against manual labor lived on. Engineering was looked upon as nothing more than manual labor raised to the level of a science. There was "pure" science and there was engineering, which was merely practical. Back east engineers ranked, socially, below lawyers; doctors; Army colonels; Navy captains; English, history, biology, chemistry, and physics professors; and business executives. This piece of European snobbery had never reached Grinnell, Iowa, however.

Neither had the corollary piece of snobbery that said a scientist was lowering himself by going into commerce. Dissenting Protestants looked upon themselves as secular saints, men and women of God who did God's work not as penurious monks and nuns but as successful workers in the everyday world. To be rich and successful was even better, and just as righteous. One of Josiah Grinnell's main projects was to bring the Rock Island Railroad into Iowa. Many in his congregation became successful farmers of the gloriously fertile soil around Grinnell. But there was no sense of rich and poor. All the congregation opened up the virgin land in a common struggle out on the frontier. They had given up the comforts of the East . . . in order to create a City of Light in the name of the Lord. Every sacrifice, every privation, every denial of the pleasures of the flesh, brought them closer to that state of bliss in which the light of God shines forth from the apex of the soul. What were the momentary comforts and aristocratic poses of the East . . . compared to this? Where would the fleshpots back east be on that day when the heavens opened up and a light fell 'round about them and a voice from on high said: "Why mockest thou me?" The light! The light! Who, if he had ever known that glorious light, if he had ever let his soul burst forth into that light, could ever mock these, my very seed, with a *Main Street* or an *American Gothic*! There, in Grinnell, reigned the passion that enabled men and women to settle the West in the nineteenth century against the most astonishing odds and in the face of overbearing hardships.

By the standards of St. Francis of Assisi or St. Jerome, who possessed nothing beyond the cloak of righteousness, Josiah Grinnell was a very secular saint, indeed. And Robert Noyce's life was a great deal more secular than Josiah Grinnell's. Noyce had wandered away from the church itself. He smoked. He took a drink when he felt like it. He had gotten a divorce. Nevertheless, when Noyce went west, he brought Grinnell with him . . . unaccountably sewn into the lining of his coat!

In the last stage of his career Josiah Grinnell had turned from the building of his community to broader matters affecting Iowa and the Middle West. In 1863 he became one of midland Iowa's representatives in Congress. Likewise, in 1974 Noyce turned over the actual running of Intel to Gordon Moore and Andrew Grove and kicked himself upstairs to become chairman of the board. His major role became that of spokesman for the Silicon Valley and the electronic frontier itself. He became chairman of the Semiconductor Industry Association. He led the industry's campaign to deal with the mounting competition from Japan. He was awarded the National Medal of Science in a White House ceremony in 1980. He was appointed to the University of California Board of Regents in 1982 and inducted into the National Inventors Hall of Fame in February 1983. By now Intel's sales had grown from $64 million in 1973 to almost a billion a year. Noyce's own fortune was incalculable. (Grinnell College's $300,000 investment in Intel had multiplied in value more than thirty times, despite some sell-offs, almost doubling the college's endowment.) Noyce was hardly a famous man in the usual sense, however. He was practically unknown to the general public. But among those who followed the semiconductor industry he was a legend. He was certainly famous back east on Wall Street. When a reporter asked James Magid of the underwriting firm of L. F. Rothschild, Unterberg, Towbin about Noyce, he said: "Noyce is a national treasure."

Oh yes! What a treasure, indeed, was the moral capital of the nineteenth century! Noyce happened to grow up in a family in which the long-forgotten light of Dissenting Protestantism still burned brightly. The light!—the light at the apex of every human soul! Ironically, it was that long-forgotten light . . . from out of the churchy, blue-nosed sticks . . . that led the world into the twenty-first century, across the electronic grid and into space.

Surely the moral capital of the nineteenth century is by now all but completely spent. Robert Noyce turns fifty-six this month, and his is the last generation to have grown up in families where the light existed in anything approaching a pure state. And yet out in the Silicon Valley *some* sort of light shines still. People who run even the newest companies in the Valley repeat Noycisms with conviction and with relish. The young CEOs all say: "Datadyne is not a corporation, it's a *cul*ture," or "Cybernetek is not a corporation, it's a *society*," or "Honey Bear's assets"—the latest vogue is for down-home nontech names—"Honey Bear's assets aren't hardware, they're the software of the three thousand souls who work here." They talk about the soul and spiritual vision as if it were the most natural subject in the world for a well-run company to be concerned about.

On June 8, 1983, one of the Valley's new firms, Eagle Computer, Inc., sold its stock to the public for the first time. Investors went for it like the answer to a dream. At the close of trading on the stock market, the company's forty-year-old CEO, Dennis Barnhart, was suddenly worth nine million dollars. Four and a half hours later he and a pal took his Ferrari out for a little romp, hung their hides out over the edge, lost control on a curve in Los Gatos, and went through a guardrail, and Barnhart was killed. Naturally, that night people in the business could talk of very little else. One of the best-known CEOs in the Valley said, "It's the dark side of the Force." He said it without a trace of irony, and his friends nodded in contemplation. They knew exactly what Force he meant.

ROBERT NOYCE *was born on December 12, 1927, in Burlington, Iowa.*

As a boy, he tinkered in his basement workshop. He equipped his bicycle with the engine from a discarded washing machine; he made nitroglycerin. His study of electronics stemmed from his model-airplane hobby: after several of his planes flew away, he grew interested in radio-controlled models. As a youth, he once said, "I was drifting from flower to flower, trying to understand how the universe worked."

In cofounding Fairchild Semiconductor, he said, he discovered a major motivation in "greed," the prospect of "a phenomenal return—if you won, you got several years' salary at once."

Noyce later blamed himself for three mistakes that he felt had held Fairchild back. He confessed to (1) letting work groups get too large, (2) giving too many people the chance to veto an innovation, and (3) tying managers' salaries to the profitability of their current products—thus making them reluctant to try new products.

In 1976, as chairman of the Intel Corporation, Noyce looked out his office window at the cars streaming down the freeway and wondered how soon computers would put an end to commuting: "Ninety-nine percent of the people in those cars are not transporting anything in bulk. If the communications were rich enough, most of them could do their jobs at home."

Noyce holds sixteen patents.

He does his own flying on most trips to his condominium in Aspen, and to Canada and Mexico. He owns a 1947 Republic Seabee—"a show battleship of a plane," he says, "that we use to go to the lake, to go swimming. My wife's a pilot. She flies right seat for me."

For over ten years he sang in a madrigal group. He likes reading adventure stories, sci-fi, Hemingway. He recently finished Abraham Pais's biography of Albert Einstein. (He found it "tough going—every other chapter was about physics.")

An impressive speaker, he has been called "the Mayor of Silicon Valley." He is gregarious, though a psychological test Shockley gave him rated him as an introvert. "I think I am introspective," he says. "I try to find out why I think what I think. At the same time I try to get along with people. I don't believe those two impulses are mutually exclusive."

He has four children by his first marriage. He has "little doubt" that his work contributed to his divorce. "I spent too little time at home. I made the mistake most people make—I thought that by working hard I was providing for my family. But if I had to do it over, I think I'd do it the same way."

He likes working in groups. He thinks about problems throughout the day. "I'll be thinking at a board meeting—and missing most of the meeting—or while I'm driving—and that's dangerous—or in bed—I'll stay awake for hours trying to dope something out."

As a voter, he says, he is a "switch-hitter." "I'll split tickets. I was a registered Democrat up until the last election. I voted for Reagan. I thought the economy was becoming a disaster."

His company has provided integrated circuits for cruise missiles. "But that isn't the same as coming up with a weapon of colossal destruction. If the military wants to buy things we've made, certainly we'll sell them. . . . I think we have to maintain a defense capability, but not to the degree we now have."

He acknowledges that America's scientists often work myopically—without giving much thought to the implications of their work—because of a poor acquaintance with the humanities. "But there is a more severe problem," he affirms, "with humanists who don't understand quantitative thinking. I'd say many engineers and physicists understand history better than historians understand technology."

He doesn't believe Japan will outstrip America in developing new technology. "If you look at any of the Japanese successes, with the possible exception of the tape recorder, you see that they're copies of American ideas." He believes that Japanese culture breeds creative inferiority. "The Japanese climb into a uniform at four years old and stay in uniform until they retire." He warns, nevertheless, that America risks falling behind by failing to invest in new ideas and by overlooking its "enormous shortage of trained manpower. . . . We've got to graduate more engineers and fewer lawyers. We have too many paper entrepreneurs—lawyers and accountants—who don't really produce anything."

He is confident that microelectronics can grow hundreds of times more complex. He adds: "The next question is, Who can use that intelligence? What will you use it for? That's a question technology can't answer."

The House
That Levitt Built

RON ROSENBAUM

I WAS BORN IN MANHATTAN BUT GREW UP IN A SUBURB OUT ON LONG ISLAND. EXCEPT
I'd never say it that way. I'd tell people I was born in Manhattan and grew up in
"a small town out on the South Shore." If pressed further, with great reluctance and deeply shameful feelings, I'd admit the small town was "kind of a
suburb," confess that my childhood home was "sort of a ranch house," but
hastily make sure to qualify these wretched facts by insisting "it wasn't in a *development*, it wasn't like a *Levittown*."

Because of all the burbs in burbdom, none was more scorned and reviled,
none more notoriously, quintessentially burbish, none the target of more ridicule and revulsion than that first, postwar mass-produced middle-class commune called Levittown. Levittown started it all. Once Bill Levitt showed fellow
builders how to mass-produce entire communities, how to do for housing what
Henry Ford did for cars, America went on a nonstop burb-building binge.
Tracts, developments, subdivisions began to grow and multiply all over the in-
terurban map. Levitt and Levittown forever changed the character of the
American landscape. And the landscape of the American character.

Levittown. There had been suburbs before. "The free-standing suburban
villa set in a garden shows up quite early in Egyptian paintings," according to
one authority, and stone tablets boast of the good life in the burbs of ancient
Babylonia. But never in five thousand years of civilization had there been any-

thing like Levittown. Contemporary observers wandering through the mind-stunning maze of curved streets and culs-de-sac with their relentless rhythms of identical blank-faced facades were amazed by the strange dislocation of time and space the cumulative sameness created.

"One gets a curious dreamlike feeling of endlessness and timelessness," said one tripped-out reporter for *Life*. "You could go literally miles in any direction without reaching the end of these impassive rows of little houses."

There was indeed a dreaminess to it, according to the contemporary correspondent from *House Beautiful*, but something darker, more menacing too, something that gave her a sinking feeling and raised the question, "Is this the American Dream or is it a nightmare?"

But before we attempt to answer that question, let's try to locate Levittown a little more precisely in the landscape of the American imagination.

Do you recall the closing lines of *The Great Gatsby*? There's that amazing sad and wonderful passage in which Nick Carraway, Fitzgerald's narrator, surveys the shuttered ruin of Gatsby's dream house and the shattered ruin of his dream and is suddenly seized with a wistful vision. Nick finds himself looking at that glamorous, clamorous stretch of Long Island's north shore Gold Coast and seeing it as it was before the coming of civilization, seeing it through the eyes of the Dutch sailors who discovered it, seeing it in all its undiminished innocence and promise: green and flowering, a blank slate as yet undefaced by the scrawl and sprawl of civilization.

"Man must have held his breath in the presence of this continent," Nick Carraway says, "face to face *for the last time in history* with something commensurate to his capacity for wonder."

Well, not quite the last time, Nick. Because it was here on Long Island just a few miles south of Gatsby's doomed dream house that a guy from Brooklyn named Bill Levitt built quite another sort of dream house. One that would challenge America's capacity for wonder. And horror: the Bill Levitt "Cape Cod."

What you had was a twenty-five-by-thirty-foot wooden box one and a half stories high. Two shuttered windows flanking a front door in the center and a steep pitched roof gave it the generically cute Cape Cod look. Two bedrooms downstairs, an unfinished attic upstairs. And no basement: the place had literally no roots in the landscape it was set upon, just a concrete slab set into a shallow indentation in the earth.

But the wonder—and the horror—of that first Levitt house lay not in any of its particular individual features. No, what made that cute little Levitt Cape Cod so amazing to some, so threatening to others, was its incredible capacity for self-replication. It took root and multiplied almost like a strange, unnatural new life form. Within three years of the completion of the first Cape Cod, some 17,500 Cape Cods, all of them almost exactly alike, had sprouted on what had once been the blank green slate of potato fields.

"The most spectacular buyers' stampede in the history of U.S. housebuilding," said *Architectural Forum.* "A revolution in the housing industry," said a *Time* magazine cover story.

"A social cancer," warned a contemporary sociologist.

Because, while many rhapsodized about Levittown, while thousands of homeless veterans lined up for days and nights for the chance to sign up for a Levittown home—no money down and sixty-five-dollar-a-month payments on a $6,990 full purchase price that included a kitchen full of gleaming gadgets—ecstatic at the chance to own an embodiment of the dream they'd fought a war for, others looked on in growing dismay. They watched one after another Levittown and Levittown-clone community sprouting up on the blank spaces of the interurban map, and they found something unnatural, menacing, even alien, in the bloblike growth of the postwar burbs.

In their newness, their instantaneousness, they were so unlike the prewar river-and-railroad suburbs. Those leisurely tree-shaded nests of urbanity had *evolved* gracefully over decades, not days; they'd developed over the years those characteristic Cheeveresque nooks and crannies of gracefully disintegrating gentility in which lurked appealingly evocative seams of Chekhovian melancholy.

Not the postwar burbs. No nooks, no crannies, no seams in those prepatterned grids pressed into the bare landscape. It was as if they fell to earth instead of growing from it.

Unnatural growths: at first, images of disease dominated dissection of the new burbs by self-appointed social critics. When they weren't calling developments "social cancers," they'd call them "spreading gangrenes." Or "infectious plagues." The attack on the people who lived in the Cape Cod pods was even more vicious—a race of "half men," subhumans, mindless conformists, a mutant breed, alienated, alien.

It's no accident that the locus of the classic horror stories of the postwar era is the burbs. Take *Invasion of the Body Snatchers* (the original version, not the gentrified remake). It was *about* the horror of being in the burbs. About neighbors whose lives had so lost their individual distinctiveness they could be taken over by alien vegetable pods—*and no one would know the difference.* And those evil pods that housed the aliens and stole the souls of the humans: Were they not metaphors, embodiments of the Cape Cod pods of Levittown and the like, whose growth and multiplication came from sucking the individuality out of the humans housed in them?

And then, of course, there is *Dawn of the Dead,* in which cannibalistic zombies risen from the grave roam a vast enclosed suburban shopping mall, and in their dead, blank zomboid trance don't look much different from the suburban shoppers they were when they were alive. The message: The burbs have stolen our souls and turned us into mindless zombies.

But is this true? Are the burbs that bad? If not, what is the source of the near-hysterical horror they've inspired in critics and commentators? Before we try to answer that, let's meet Bill Levitt, godfather of the burbs, the man who's either the Dr. Franklin or the Dr. Frankenstein of the postwar American land-scape.

Trapped. Bill Levitt's limo is trapped in a Manhattan traffic jam and he's fum-ing about the stupidity of cities. Here's the situation: We're sitting in the back seat of Levitt's limo, a space not much smaller than the living room of one of those original Levitt Cape Cods. For almost an hour now Levitt's been trying to make his way through traffic snarls from his Sherry-Netherland apartment on Central Park to a business appointment down in the financial district at One New York Plaza. I'm not sure what the subject of this particular confer-ence is, but I think it may involve the Ayatollah. Levitt's been in protracted ne-gotiations with the Iranian government since the hostage crisis settlement to try to recover some $34 million in assets he's sunk into his unfinished Iranian Levittown, or Levittshahr, as it was called when the ill-fated project began in the mid-Seventies.

But on the other hand, this conference could have something to do with fi-nancing an expansion of the senior citizens' Levittowns he's been building down near Disney World in Florida, the ones he's calling—after his first name—Williamsburg. Or it could be yet another attempt by Levitt to revive his grand master plan for once again remaking the map of America by creating en-tire Levitt-built cities from the ground up on the remaining blank spaces in the landscape. Primary Employment Towns, he calls these proposed projects, and if he gets his way—"it's inevitable; they'll happen," he insists—they could mean the final gutting and dismantling of the conventional urban areas. A fate, you get the feeling, that wouldn't trouble the traffic-snarled Levitt in the slightest. Bill Levitt has just never liked cities. Never understood people who do.

"I can't understand it," he'll tell me later on in the course of our discussions. "I have a friend who goes into rhapsodies over cities and all the joys he gets from them. Well, I don't understand it," Levitt repeats. The man is genuinely puzzled. "I just don't understand it."

Meanwhile, Levitt's limo driver seems not to have understood the route to One New York Plaza and he's gotten us entangled in one dark, shadowy cob-blestoned maze of some of New York's oldest, narrowest streets, the section around Maiden Lane where fifty-story financial powerhouses loom over nar-row, twisted passages no more than fifteen feet wide. These are streets that might have been here since New York was New Amsterdam, streets like those the Dutch sailors from *Gatsby* strode when they finally found Manhattan. And you almost get the sense that these ancient, arthritic American urban alleys *know* exactly who it is they have in their clutches, the man who did more to destroy more cities than Genghis Khan, the man who gave birth to the burbs. It's almost as if they're taking wicked delight in strangling him the way his sub-urbs strangled so many cities.

Finally, we find ourselves stalled completely behind a garbage truck and a hot-dog vendor, utterly becalmed as stock clerks and messenger boys stroll around us and stare through the smoked glass.

And finally, Levitt, dapper and civilized in a dark blue suit, ordinarily a courtly, mild-mannered kind of guy, gives vent to the frustration fuming inside him:

"How can people live this way?" he explodes. "It's ridiculous."

Does Levitt appreciate the karmic resonance of this entangling encounter between himself and the ancient streets of the city? Don't be surprised if he does, because the Levitt family philosophy is deeply imbued with a sense of the fateful reverberations that linked its burb-building destiny to its deep roots in American history.

In fact, while we're trapped here in the back of his limo, he comes up with an absolutely classic illustration of karmic principles that links the seventeenth-century colonization of America with the crucial racial origins of twentieth-century suburbanization.

Levitt's been telling me about his childhood and his father. He was born in 1907 and grew up in Brooklyn on what was then a suburban street, which is now the heart of the notorious Bedford-Stuyvesant ghetto. Levitt's father, Abraham, was an attorney and amateur social thinker who was a passionate believer in the philosophy of a now obscure German thinker named Ernst Haeckel.

"Haeckel wrote a book called *Fate and Free Will*," Levitt tells me, "in which he argued that there is no such thing as free will, that every action has a reaction and every cause has an effect."

I try to get a line on how this cause-and-effect philosophy applies to Levitt's own life work—what were the karmic forces that made it inevitable he should be the one to give birth to the burbs—and damned if he doesn't come up with his account of an incredible and slightly apocryphal concatenation of historical circumstances that leads to a single momentous turning point.

"I could tell you one little thing I've often quoted, but you won't want to use it," he teases me.

"Tell me anyway," I urge him.

"Okay, in the seventeenth century, in 1624 exactly, a man by the name of Captain John Hawkins, an Englishman, brought the first boatload of slaves to Virginia. Up until then there were no black people on this continent. But now the black people were here, they multiplied geometrically until finally a couple of centuries later, as they moved into the north, they moved onto the same street we lived on in Brooklyn. Next to us a black assistant D.A. moved in. Fearing a diminution of values if too many came in, we picked up and moved out. We then got into the suburbs, into building . . ."

"Which started everything, the whole—"

"Exactly."

Even while you read this, whole square miles of identical boxes are spreading like gangrene . . . developments conceived in error, nurtured by greed, corroding everything they touch.

—John Keats,
The Crack in the Picture Window

Little boxes made of ticky-tacky . . .
And they all look just the same.*

—Malvina Reynolds

To the commentators, suburbia . . . is the melancholia of those whose individuality has succumbed to the inexorable pressures of the Organization, bureaucracy, mass culture, uniformity, conformity, monotony.

—Sociologist William Dobriner

So what was the matter with the boobs who moved into the burbs? Didn't they know how tacky it all was? Why couldn't they see with the clarity and sensitivity of the critics of suburbia how superficial their lives were?

To answer these questions you have to understand something about the historical situation that gave birth to the burbs.

The "postwar housing crisis"—it's one of those phrases guaranteed to cause eyes to glaze over with instant and utter apathy. But you have to understand: this was more than some garden-variety *shortage*. This was a time (1945–49) when you had veterans who had got themselves shot up defending Western civilization forced to live in chicken coops.

No exaggeration. This is how a Senate committee described the kind of housing available to the thirteen million veterans who returned home from the war: They were forced to live in "garages, coal sheds, chicken coops, barns, tool sheds, granaries and smokehouses. Such hovels are merely gestures of contempt toward those who are desperate enough to take anything which is offered. . . . Structures with no water available, heating facilities so bad that bottled drinks will freeze in the same room with a large stove, no sanitary toilet facilities, primitive food storage, no sinks, cardboard windowpanes, and paper walls."

Chicken coops. That's what the American system had to offer the people who got shot up fighting for it. Those who wouldn't move in with the hens had the often equally unattractive alternative of moving in with henpecking in-laws and attempting to resume their married life on a cot in the living room.

All of this engendered rising resentments, bitterness, fears of Communist agitation, talk of socialized housing, wailing and despair.

None of which managed to get the arthritic American home-building industry into any useful kind of mobilization. Very little had changed in the way homes had been built since the invention of the nail. *Fortune* called the housing industry "the industry capitalism forgot."

*Copyright © 1962 by Schroder Music Co.

309

That's when Bill Levitt came along, revolutionized the home-building industry, and reshaped the landscape of American life. In the decades before the war, Bill and his brother, Alfred, had been living in the Long Island suburbs and designing individually crafted suburban homes—creating developments like "Strathmore-at-Manhasset"—for the upper-middle-class elite. When the war came, Levitt went to work for the Navy Seabees and began to learn the techniques of fast, mass-built housing, building entire slab-house towns for enlisted men in Norfolk, Virginia.

Coming back to Long Island after the war, he began buying up potato fields; he was itching to take a crack at the housing crisis with a mass-building blitz, but he had to come up with solutions for two problems that were paralyzing the possibility of a private-industry solution to the crisis: the lack of financing and the absence of a workable assembly-line approach to home building.

He tackled the financing first and came up with a solution for the whole country: "I worked very closely with the FHA," Levitt told me. "Got together a little group consisting of four men and we sat down with then-commissioner Abner Ferguson and we explained to him the only way we were going to get a volume of housing was to grant to the veteran, in effect, a one hundred percent mortgage. 'Cause he had no cash."

And so the government agreed to guarantee to banks the entire amount of a veteran's mortgage, making it possible for soldiers to move into a home with no money down.

"Next thing was to build these houses and get them done quickly," Levitt says, "so we evolved a system taking a leaf from the auto industry, but instead of the product going on an assembly line, the product stood still and the mechanics moved. We then broke down the building of the house into twenty-six steps and we made the mechanics specialists in each of these twenty-six steps. The result was that we were building approximately thirty-five houses a day. Nobody apparently had done any of that before. We had a number of imitators, but to the best of my knowledge I don't know anyone who produced that volume in so short a time."

To understand the genius of the Levitt housing revolution you have to imagine what it would be like if cars were still built the way all houses were before Levitt. You'd have to contract with your local garagemen to bring in frame makers, tire installers, braking contractors; your exhaust man and your axle man would be stumbling over each other trying to get their parts to fit together. The time and inefficiency would make it impossible for the average person to own private transportation.

Levitt's solution was as unexpected as it was original. Back then everyone thought the future of mass housing would come from prefabrication—factory manufacture of hollow wall parts with electrical and plumbing conduits already installed, parts then shipped to a site and assembled there. It's one of those ideas that seemed logical but no one had ever made it work on a large-volume basis.

"You end up shipping a lot of air," Levitt explains, dismissively. "Makes it economically impossible."

No, what Levitt invented was not prefabrication but "site fabrication." You don't ship a house from a factory to site, you turn the site into a factory, lay down a thousand slab bases at once, then lay down a thousand "plumbing trees" on the bases, then bring a team through to wire a thousand electrical connections and so on for each of the twenty-six steps until you fold your on-site factory up and leave a thousand completed houses behind.

Still, there was more to the Levitt housing revolution than merely the financing and manufacturing of individual units. Levitt didn't just build houses fast, he created communities.

"The veteran needed a roof over his head and instead of giving him just a roof we gave him certain amenities," Levitt explains. "We divided it into sections and we put down schools, swimming pools, and a village green and necessity shopping centers, athletic fields, Little League diamonds. We wanted community living."

Community living. It was more than that. It was a commune, a mass middle-class baby-boom-breeding incubator commune. Seventy-eight thousand people in Levittown, Long Island. Another seventy-seven thousand in Levittown, New Jersey. Hundreds of thousands in Levittown-like tracts and subdivisions all over the country, all filled with couples of the same age and the same inclination, breeder reactors for the postwar nuclear family. Before long the swelling population of the Long Island Levittown earned it nicknames like "Fertility Valley" and "The Rabbit Hutch."

People living in Levittown thought they were witnessing more than the birth of babies, they were seeing the birth of "a new way of living—and a new kind of person, what might be called the Development Type," as one of them put it.

What was life like for Development Man? By all accounts it was extraordinarily social, a genuine commune.

"Phillips' wife had a birthday last night and what a time we all had," ran one account of a Levittown weekend. *"Hollis brought over his kid and put him in the same bed with Phillips' two kids and then he took out his guitar and played and played and we just sang all night long. I tell ya, the four of us really have it worked out. When the girls go to a garden-club meeting, we boys get together and baby-sit and play pinochle. Or one night we'll all go bowling down at the Village Green. And now we're all taking some of these adult education courses down at the school one night a week. Dick and I are taking a course in 'How to Finish your Attic' and John's learning photography. . . ."*

Levitt himself grew up to be a benign patriarchal father figure for Fertility Valley. Unlike many of his greedy fly-by-night imitators whose subdivision suckers would gladly string them up if they could only find a way to subpoena them, Levitt grew in stature and respect as his homes endured and proved their long-range value over the years. The longer people lived in Levitt homes the more they liked them—and Levitt. The number of Levittown lifers is surprising. I located couples who had not merely moved into original Levitt homes after the war and spent their entire adult lives there; they'd then proceeded to buy and move into Levitt senior-citizen homes down in Florida.

They still gush with pride as they recall Levitt and their total Levitt lives.

"He *was* a father figure," declares Al Ludwig, thirty years in Levittown and now a resident of Levitt's Williamsburg. "He did a great thing for us veterans. He did it well and he could have got a lot more money for it than he did."

"It was like an adventure," Mrs. Ludwig recalls of their first trip out to Levittown to look at a house. "We'd been staying with our folks in the Bronx because no one could find a place after the war; there were no developments. Levittown was like a godsend. My three children will always remember how wonderful it was to grow up there. Each house had other children in it; the blocks were filled with children."

And her neighbors?

"We all got along because we all started with a clean slate, we were all in the same situation. It was a great experience."

But what do they know? They only lived there for thirty years. There were people in America who knew better, people who knew that life in Levittown couldn't have been "an adventure," because it was too spiritually impoverished and lacked the refined influence of experienced interior decorators. These people were the commentators on Levittown who formed the national consensus of contempt for the place.

Levittown drove the commentators *insane*. It's amazing how fierce and unrelenting the assault on Levittown and all it stood for became in the Fifties. It became the symbol of everything intellectuals disliked about that decade. Although little of the onslaught was directed at Levitt personally, the attack on his namesake communities seems to have left some scar tissue. And of all the scars left by the commentators, the wounds, one in particular seems not to have healed at all.

In my very first phone conversation with him, Levitt himself raised the specter of the man who'd been haunting him and taunting him for years.

Lewis Mumford, author of a social history of urban civilization called *The City in History* and other scholarly works, had been among the first sharp critics of Levittown, pronouncing it an instant slum before the paint dried and inveighing against the subsequent new, improved Levittown in Pennsylvania as "socially backward"—"new-fashioned methods to compound old-fashioned mistakes."

"I think by now we've shown that critics like Lewis Mumford were wrong," Levitt announced to me in that first phone conversation. Then he launched into an impassioned attack on Mumford, climaxing it by declaring: "I think that Lewis Mumford has been shown to be a prophet without honor."

At first I thought it was a little odd that Levitt had allowed this one particular writer to get under his skin. But then I put in some time in the historical archives of the Levittown Public Library, immersing myself in the works of

Mumford and the fellow commentators. And I emerged understanding *exactly* why Levitt was so infuriated by this guy he never met.

The Levittown historical archives—it's almost incongruous that a place whose whole essence lay in its ahistorical newness has archives, as incongruous as, say, a Seattle Mariners Hall of Fame—has got just about everything ever written about Levittown. There are the classic attacks, *The Crack in the Picture Window*, ridiculing the suburban couple "John and Mary Drone" for the shallowness of their values, the emptiness of their lives. There's University of Chicago "Lonely Crowd" sociologist David Riesman mourning "The Suburban Sadness" and William H. Whyte ridiculing the status anxiety of the subhuman "Organization Man."

But nothing comes close to the snobbishness of Mumford in *The City in History*. Consider, for instance, Mumford's attack on the automobile culture that was created by the postwar suburbs. Americans don't like cars; they were forced on us unwillingly by poor planning of suburban builders, Mumford argues. How does he know? Well, he knows that "walking still delights the American: *Does he not travel many thousands of miles just to enjoy this privilege in the historic urban cores of Europe?*"

Then there is Mumford on the moral inferiority of those perverted suburban Americans who actually *like* to drive cars: "Speed is the vulgar objective of a life devoid of any more significant kind of esthetic interest." Suburban shopping centers, he tells us, compare unfavorably with the Greek *agora*.

What does he like? What's his idea of a good planned community? "The older colleges at Oxford and Cambridge," he concedes, are fairly well designed.

You get the picture. At the heart of this case against the new suburbia is the typical habit of earlier immigrant groups attempting to support their self-image as an aristocracy by attacking the *stylistic* preferences of later-arriving Americans as *moral* flaws. In Mumford's lockjawed tones we hear once again the frank class and ethnic prejudice of the nineteenth-century WASP deploring the manners and morals of the new urban immigrants.

It wasn't until I finally came upon Mumford's summing-up of his case against suburbia that I underwent the final stage of my conversion experience.

"In the mass movement into suburban areas a new kind of community was produced, which caricatured both the historic city and the archetypal suburban refuge," Mumford writes, "a multitude of uniform, unidentifiable houses, lined up inflexibly at uniform distances, on uniform roads, in a treeless communal waste, inhabited by people of the same class, the same income, the same age group, witnessing the same television performances, eating the same tasteless pre-fabricated foods from the same freezers, conforming in every outward and inward respect to a common mold. . . ."

Reading that, I felt a mixture of rage and shame. Rage at its simplistic stupidity, at the kind of superficial intelligence that judges and condemns the souls of millions because of the surface similarities of their exterior circumstances. These were my friends he was talking about, my family, my high school buddies.

And shame too. Shame at realizing that I had for years internalized this self-disparaging view of my suburban origin, concealing it, apologizing for it, feeling somehow inferior and inauthentic because of it.

"Admitting you grew up in a suburb," one friend of mine says, "is like confessing to a character defect. An unfashionable character defect."

Exactly. To say you're a child of the suburbs is to admit you have no real roots, no authenticity. You lack the funky vitality of an urban upbringing, you lack the charm of farm-bred agrarian virtues, the security of traditional small-town values.

I began to see how myself and other suburban kids had for years been victims of a subtle pervasive cultural prejudice. I began to see myself and my suburban-bred brothers and sisters as, yes, an oppressed minority. Or, come to think of it, an oppressed majority, victimized by a narrow-minded elite who wanted to impose their narrow notions of gentility, their pseudoaristocratic anglophile pretensions to "taste" on those too benighted to have developed it on their own.

I wanted to take Mumford by his starched collar, drag him out of his study, drive him to Levittown, and prove to him that Levittown, far from being a community of conformists, was, in fact, an emblem of the triumph of American individualism.

Levittown a triumph of individualism? I wouldn't have believed it myself but nothing I'd seen or read had prepared me for the bizarre and revealing experience of seeing Levittown today. Although I'd grown up on Long Island and driven all over the place, for some reason I'd never actually driven through Levittown itself. And so all along the only concrete image I'd had in mind of the place came from aerial photographs taken about the time the place was built thirty-odd years ago.

Look at one of those taken from an elevation high enough to capture all 17,500 homes and the place looks like a vast printed circuit or, more contemporarily, an intricately inscribed silicon chip, the individual homes no more than nodes imprinted into a rigidly patterned landscape.

Look at an aerial photograph taken from a lower, copterlike elevation that shows one section of curving roads and culs-de-sac as they were back in 1949 and you can see the facades of the individual houses bare in the glare of their individual plots, but it's still kind of scary.

The two shuttered windows flanking the center door form identical robotic eye-and-nose combos, and so what you see are blank faces set in blank spaces staring blankly across at each other. The empty yards that separate them are utterly unprotected by the few pathetic-looking saplings hardly big enough to give shade to an anthill.

But to drive through the place today is to experience a strange and unexpected transformation. *None* of the houses looks like any other house. Nor like any of the blank faces in the aerial photographs. Almost every single one of them has been added on to, extended, built out, remodeled to the max. The roofs have developed so many dormers it seems like they've grown dormers on dormers. Fronts have sprouted pergolas and porches, roof lines have been raised, pitched, expanded, corniced, and cupolaed. Sides have been carported, breezewayed, broken out, re-covered in redwood, sided in cedar shake, disguised in brick and fieldstone, transformed into ranches, splanches, colonials, and California ramblers. And those once-pathetic saplings have grown and flourished into fifty thousand shade trees spreading and merging, casting cozy coverings of shadows and privacy over the rococo renovations.

Driving through this place at night is like driving through some enchanted gingerbread Swiss village. Occasionally in the moonlight one can get a haunting glimpse amid the additions of the original face of the original Cape Cod shell, the way the innocent face of the child can sometimes be glimpsed in a complex countenance of the adult he's become.

A similar individuating transformation has taken place in the interiors of Levittown homes. In order to inspect some interiors, a woman friend and I posed as a soon-to-be-married couple looking for our first home. The only word to describe the interiors we saw is Dickensian. Like the intricately carved-out, compartmented, cabineted nautical interiors in *Copperfield, Dombey*, and *Drood*, the interiors of Levittown—every square inch of them—have been hollowed out, built in, latched, and sprung; rooms have been divided, opened out, closed off, and redivided, realigned, and redefined. Nothing has remained the same, nor do any two interiors resemble each other or the original.

Just what's been going on here? What's behind this frenzy of remodeling and redefinition? Gomes, the chimney sweep of Levittown, my inside source on the insides of Levittown houses, explained the phenomenon this way:

"You see, a lot of the original owners, they paid off their seven-, eight-, or nine-thousand-dollar purchase price pretty quickly—it's not like they're rich but it left them with a lot of income to dispose of and instead of trading up to some other place where it's gonna be expensive to carry as anything else today, they've been plowing it into the place they've got. They build out, they build in. It's been kind of nonstop."

This nonstop remodeling craze had been a peculiarly Levittown phenomenon from the beginning, and I think there's more to it than a mere mortgage payment calculation going on. I found a clue to the larger implications of rampant remodeling when I came across a 1956 *House Beautiful* article in the Levittown archives.

While the article was ostensibly about the way several Levittown families had redone their homes inside and out, the title provides the key to the meaning of the whole Levittown phenomenon. *House Beautiful* called the piece: "How Individuality Got a Second Chance."

The author, a Levittown resident, rhapsodizes about the remodeling phenomenon as a story of "people who have answered the challenge of conformity by saying 'This is *mine*. This house will look like *me*, this house will sing of *my* spirit.' "

He goes on in this passionate vein to declare that because of the remodeling craze every house in Levittown "*has a signature*. . . . The hunger for individuality is a basic hunger. And the miracle of subdivision suburbia is the miracle of this hunger."

On a more down-to-earth level, he quotes one woman remodeler who explains the phenomenon by saying, "Maybe because they all started out looking so much the same . . . that's why they're trying so hard to be different."

There is a deceptively simple truth in that statement about the nature of individualism. At the heart of individualist ideology is not the idea that all people start out irrevocably different. People are not born "originals." In fact it's the opposite: all men are created equally unformed, equally unoriginal with an equal capacity to grow and remodel themselves into different and original individuals.

Behind this axiom of Jeffersonian individuality is the Socratic theory of consciousness first articulated in Plato's *Theaetetus*—the idea that at birth every individual sensibility is alike in that it's an unmarked wax tablet, what Locke would later call a tabula rasa, a blank slate waiting to be inscribed by experience and remodeled by free will into a uniquely original entity.

And so we can look at the Levittown experience as an exact metaphor for the theory of American individualism. Those identical blank-faced Cape Cod pods all created equal, ready to be inhabited, invigorated, individuated by democratic, undictated-to expressions of free will. We can look at Levittown as an almost perfect laboratory demonstration of the inexorable workings of the American individualist impulse.

How individuality got a second chance. America has always been about starting over with a clean slate. That blank green plain that challenged the Dutch sailors' capacity for wonder was a tabula rasa for those extricated from the carved and pitted plains of Europe. But after two wars and a depression had shaken the confidence of the country in its innocence, American individuality needed a second chance, a belief that it was possible to start over in innocence with the slate wiped clean once again, a chance for Americans to seek out and rediscover the validity of the original individualist impulse. Bill Levitt's Levittown and the blank-slate burbs he gave birth to provided a unique opportunity for the postwar generation to reenact the discovery of America.

Which is not to say that all has been sweetness and light and the rule of reason in Levittown history. The consequences of extreme individualism sometimes can seem extremely bizarre. The Davy Crackpot controversy and the quarter century of school-board wars that followed, culminating in the famous Supreme Court school-book censorship case testify to that.

If you ask most Levittowners the most memorable event in Levittown history, some will point to the opening of the Mid Island Shopping Plaza—one of the first giant malls of its type in America. Some will point to the *enclosing* of the Mid Island Shopping Plaza, making it one of the first giant covered malls of its type in America. But the Davy Crackpot "Lonesome Train" controversy, which began on a summer playground in 1955, has certainly been the event with the most bitter and lasting consequences.

316

Remember the Davy Crockett theme song? "Born on a mountaintop in Tennessee/Greenest state in the Land of the Free."

Remember the refrain? "Davy, Davy Crockett/King of the wild frontier."

Well, in the summer of 1955, a Levittown schoolteacher who was running a summer playground program for ten-year-olds decided to keep the kids occupied by getting them to write parodies of the Davy Crockett theme song. He printed up some of the better ones including one with a refrain that went: "Davy, Davy Crackpot—scared of the wild frontier."

Scared of the wild frontier. For some reason that line touched a nerve. A local housewife began an angry letter-writing campaign attacking the Levittown teacher and the whole school district for promoting Communist party efforts to sully the picture of American heroes. To support her contention that the Crackpot case proved a connection between the schools and the Comintern she dropped another bombshell, which proved to have wider repercussions. She disclosed that Levittown children had been taught to sing a song "written by two communists and used at communistic celebrations."

This subversive song she referred to turned out to be a pop operatic cantata called "Lonesome Train." Its characters were the "common people" who gathered to watch Abe Lincoln's funeral train make its way home to Illinois. Well, it seems that "Lonesome Train" had been singled out as a sinister cat's-paw of the Communist propaganda apparatus in a right-wing article called "Snake in Suburbia's Garden."

Soon half of Levittown was up in arms over this threat, holding mass meetings, calling for expulsion of the song and the school board responsible for tolerating its use. Eventually, after a vicious campaign, they did drive out the school board and established a board of veterans to screen future songs. A counterattack resulted in a protracted and bitter civil war over control of the schools that has not ceased for a quarter of a century. It was one of the later right-wing regimes that started rooting through school libraries, censoring *The Fixer* by Bernard Malamud and other dangerous books, and it took a landmark U.S. Supreme Court decision to put a stop to it.

Have the strenuous efforts of the Levittown school boards to protect their children from parodies of Davy Crockett prevented the children of Levittown from succumbing to the prevailing sins of contemporary suburbia?

Not if you believe Gomes the chimney sweep.

They're turning out the lights in the Mid Island Shopping Plaza as Gomes the chimney sweep stares into the gloom and speaks darkly of the demented progeny of Levittown today.

The big spring chimney-sweeping season is on and Gomes is working part-time in Pannonica, a handicraft store located near one of the outer extremities of the giant cross-shaped covered mall. Gomes, who with his brother owns Pannonica, grumbles about the store's location. And indeed the mall seems to be shrinking into its interior, leaving abandoned and empty stores at the outer extremities like the dying digits of a frostbite victim.

That Levittown *has* a chimney sweep is a testament to the inexorable Dickensian workings of time. But Gomes is the real thing.

"I use genuine English chimney sweep rods," he boasts. And from his unique vantage point Gomes has come to see the sooty heart of darkness of thousands of Levittown homes. According to Gomes, the chimneys of Levittown are holding up better than the children. The chief problem with the chimneys he says are "disintegrating crowns." A lot of Levittown residents found problems with the radiant heating system Levitt installed in those concrete slabs he built their houses on. And so, especially during the recent energy crisis, many of them shifted to oil and coal for heat. Gomes thinks the Levitt chimneys and indeed the Levitt homes are remarkably well built and durable after thirty years, but he foresees the new furnaces causing continuing trouble with disintegrating crowns.

As for the children, however, that's another story. I'd run into Gomes right after leaving the company of a go-getting gold-jacketed Century 21 real estate man who'd been showing me and my "fiancée" an eighty-thousand-dollar Levitt home.

We'd had a curious conversation with the couple who were selling it. They'd been there twenty years, they'd put enormous amounts of work into it. The place had been remodeled inside and out to within an inch of its life—down to a special fold-out display case for the husband's rather intimidating knife collection.

But something struck us as suspicious. The couple were very vague about *why* they wanted to move.

At one point the wife said something cryptic about "kidnapping of children." I think it was something like "we're not moving because of the kidnapping of kids. . . ." And then after hasty glances from her husband and the man in the gold jacket, she amended it to say, "At least that doesn't happen around here. You won't have to worry about that."

When we told Gomes about this exchange, he said he couldn't recall any Levittown child kidnappings. But he added darkly, "The thing you have to worry about here is *getting* kidnapped by the kids. I mean you have kids with guns roaming the streets here."

"Kids with guns?"

"Oh, yeah. You've got kids with guns reeling around, you've got kids keeling over in the classrooms of the schools from drugs. It's gotten pretty bad."

Gomes goes into a whole long rap about the wayward children of Levittown, painting a picture of pandemonium, street gangs, vandalism, drugs, rampant lethargy, and deep sociopathic depression among the flower of Levittown youth.

Well, what is it, what's responsible, we ask Gomes, in the darkening gloom of the mall.

"It's come full circle," he says, cryptically.

"What?" we say. "What's come full circle?"

And then the chimney sweep starts talking about the Levittown version of the "revolution of diminished expectations" that's going on all over America. How the first generation of Levittown children left their parents' dream houses behind to head for the big city, for excitement and adventure elsewhere, looking for something beyond the one-family-house-and-garden life. And didn't quite find it. Came back to Levittown. Scared of the wild frontier, you might say. Moved in with their parents, many of them, waiting for them to die so they could take over their homes because they couldn't afford to build or buy one of their own. Not anymore. That dream, the dream that Levitt created in the dawn of the brand-new-start postwar era, the dream that every family could move into a brand-new home, as new as the American continent once was, create their own history, rather than inhabit someone else's past—that dream is over.

————————

WILLIAM LEVITT *was born on February 11, 1907, in Brooklyn, the first of Abraham and Pauline Levitt's two sons.*

One of his favorite college phrases was "The masses are asses." He dropped out of New York University after his junior year: "I got itchy. I wanted to make a lot of money. I wanted a big car and a lot of clothes."

He stands five feet eight. "His wavy hair and mournful, wide-open eyes," Harper's magazine reported in 1948, "make him look like a tired Marx Brother turned master of ceremonies in a run-down night club."

He has a reputation for being an egotistical know-it-all. (In the 1950s Alfred Levitt left the company, reportedly because he and his brother could not make joint decisions.) Still, when a prospective home buyer once complained that he could find a four-burner stove that would take up no more room than Levittown's present three-burner stoves, Levitt said, "You get it and I'll buy it." The buyer found one, and Levitt canceled his order for one thousand three-burner stoves.

He originally held a competition to decide on a name for his housing project, but he and his brother ended up naming the place after themselves. Several executives urged Levitt to change the project's name, but he nixed the idea. Even before Levittown, New York, was completed, some Levittowners tried to get their post office address changed to that of nearby Hicksville. Residents of Willingboro, New Jersey, having at one time voted to adopt the name Levittown, eventually returned to the name Willingboro. After the Starrett Housing Corporation took over Levitt & Sons, Levitt had to go to court when he wanted to name his new Florida development Levittown. He argued that Levittown *had become a generic term. The judge didn't agree.*

Levitt initially would not sell to blacks. "The Negroes in America," he said, "are trying to do in four hundred years what the Jews in the world have not wholly accomplished in six thousand. As a Jew, I have no room in my mind or heart for racial prejudice. But . . . I have come to know that if we sell one house to a Negro family, then ninety to ninety-five percent of our white customers will not buy into the community. That is their attitude, not ours. . . . As a company, our position is simply this: we can solve a housing problem, or we can try to solve a racial problem. But we cannot combine the two."

In the late 1940s he offered to mass-produce houses in Palestine at cost. A Fortune editor remarked, "That is what I call practical Zionism."

Interviewed in the 1950s, women in Levittown and other mass-produced communities complained of boredom and loneliness. When they were asked whom they missed most, they answered, "My mother." Many, of course, became mothers. Pregnancy became known as the "Levittown look."

"No man who owns his own house and lot," Levitt affirmed, "can be a Communist. He has too much to do."

It was his first wife, Rhoda, who suggested that in building Levittown, New Jersey, Levitt should mix up the house styles—Cape Cod, ranch, colonial. After driving up and down the uniform streets of Levittown, New York, Levitt admitted, "I got lost there myself. . . ."

Yet he maintained that it was "incredibly myopic to focus on the thread of uniformity in housing and fail to see the broad fabric of which it is a part—the mass production culture of America today. . . . This isn't something to grieve over. It's something to glory in—just so long as we keep in mind the difference between material values and those of the mind and spirit. The reason we have it so good in this country is that we can produce lots of things at low prices through mass production. . . . Houses are for people, not critics. We who produce lots of houses do what is possible—no more—and the people for whom we do it think that it's pretty good." In Levittown, he averred, "ninety-nine percent of the people pray for us."

During the building-boom years, Levitt himself didn't own a home. Instead he rented a twelve-room Fifth Avenue apartment in Manhattan and a large Tudor-style mansion in Great Neck, Long Island, as well. A photograph from the period shows a white-jacketed black servant serving the Levitt family drinks by the pool.

Over the years he has built about 140,000 homes in Long Island, Pennsylvania, New Jersey, Puerto Rico, and elsewhere. He has started projects in Nigeria, Venezuela, and Iran.

"I'm not here just to build and sell houses," Levitt once remarked. "To be perfectly frank, I'm looking for a little glory, too. It's only human. I want to build a town to be proud of."

The Political Conscience
of Reinhold Niebuhr

ARTHUR M. SCHLESINGER JR.

WHEN I FIRST BECAME AWARE OF REINHOLD NIEBUHR, HE WAS FORTY-EIGHT YEARS OLD and I was twenty-three. It was the winter of 1940–41. Great Britain was standing alone against Nazi Germany. Our country was consumed in an embittering debate—by far the most angry I have ever witnessed, before or since. The interventionists thought the greatest tragedy that could befall the United States would be the victory of Hitler. The isolationists thought the greatest tragedy would be American involvement in the European war.

I am not a churchgoer, so it took the importunings of friends to get me to Memorial Church in Harvard Yard one snowy Sunday morning. The pews were packed long before the tower bells chimed eleven. A tall man with a massive bald head came to the pulpit. Establishing instant command over the congregation, he spoke, without notes, in a rush of jagged eloquence. His eyes flashed; his voice rose to a roar and sank to a whisper; outstretched arms lent emphasis to his points; but, underneath the passion, the argument was cool, rigorous, and powerful. Man was sinful, he told the hushed but initially dubious audience. Yet even sinful man had the duty of acting against evil in the world. Our sins, real as they were, could not justify our standing apart from the European struggle.

This notion of sinful man was uncomfortable for my generation. We had been brought up to believe in human innocence and virtue. The perfectibility of man was less a liberal illusion than an all-American conviction. Andrew Carnegie had long since expressed the national faith when, after proclaiming the rise of man from the lower to the higher forms, he added, "Nor is there any conceivable end to his march to perfection." But liberals had a particular weakness for the idea that the troubles of the world were due less to human iniquity than to human ignorance and the injustice of social institutions. Enlightened education and reform, we supposed, would remove the obstacles to a better society. The concept of original sin seemed a historical curiosity that had gone out with hard-shell Calvinism.

The memory of that Sunday morning in Harvard Yard lingered, but I did not see Niebuhr again until the war was over and I had come back from service in the European Theater. During the war Niebuhr was chairman of the Union for Democratic Action, an organization of anti-Stalinist liberals, and I encountered him at the meeting in Washington in the fall of 1946 that transmuted the UDA into Americans for Democratic Action. He was as impressive in the corridors as he had been in the pulpit—wise, trenchant, erudite, yet disarmingly open to the views of others and full of humor and humanity. And his interpretation of man and history now came as a vast illumination to young men returning from the war. Nothing in the system of human perfectibility had prepared us for Hitler and Stalin. The holocaust, the concentration camps, the gulags had proven human nature capable of infinite depravity. What had happened to man in his march to perfection?

It seemed a question worthy of further exploration. I began for the first time to read Niebuhr. His life, it developed, helped explain his convictions. Born in Missouri in 1892, he was the son of a Lutheran pastor who had emigrated from Germany after the Civil War. Religion came to young Niebuhr more through Christian nurture than through mystical experience. After the Yale divinity school he went, in 1915, to a parish in Detroit. A pastorate on the urban frontier, immersed in poverty, racial tension, and savage labor-management conflict, awakened his political consciousness and drove him to the Left. By the time he joined the faculty of the Union Theological Seminary, in New York, in 1928, he was an active Socialist.

Yet, as he moved toward heterodoxy in politics, he paradoxically moved toward orthodoxy in theology. Detroit had persuaded him that liberal Christianity, with its sentimental and optimistic view of man, was hopelessly irrelevant to the power realities of industrial capitalism. A more searching conception of human nature was required, and this Niebuhr found in the tragic insights of Augustine and Calvin. His book of 1932, *Moral Man and Immoral Society*, merged Augustine and Marx in arguing that—contrary to the liberal hope—love and reason could not solve the political problem. The law of love might govern relations among individuals (*moral man*), but the law of power governed relations among groups (*immoral society*), and only power could restrain power. For a moment in the dark days of the early Depression, he came very close to Marxism, especially in forebodings about the imminent end of the capitalist era.

He always warned, however, against moral and political absolutism—"a splendid incentive to heroic action," he wrote in *Moral Man*, "but a dangerous guide in immediate and concrete situations." He therefore distrusted Communists from the start; and, as the 1930s wore on, he began to see that Franklin D. Roosevelt's New Deal was in fact an effective way to achieve the equilibrium of power on which human freedom depended. Finding the Socialist party excessively doctrinaire in domestic affairs as well as excessively pacifist and isolationist in foreign policy, he finally resigned in 1940.

While compulsively active in these years as professor, preacher, and publicist, he continued to work out the meaning of Christian faith for the modern world. An invitation to give the Gifford Lectures at Edinburgh in 1939 resulted in *The Nature and Destiny of Man*. In two majestic volumes, he rejected both classical and modern ideas in favor of the biblical conception of man's nature and fate.

He cast his argument in religious terms. Yet even nonreligious readers found two themes especially powerful; or at least I did. One was Niebuhr's presentation of the mixed nature of man. "The plight of the self," he wrote, "is that it cannot do the good that it intends." For man's pretensions to reason and virtue, he argued, are ineradicably tainted by self-interest and self-love. Original sin lies in man's illusion that his inherent finiteness and weakness can be overcome. Overweening self-pride vitiates all human endeavor and brings evil into history.

The second theme was the relationship between history and eternity. The modern illusion, Niebuhr thought, was the idea that redemption is possible within history. But man must understand the incompleteness of all historic good as well as the corruption of all historic achievement. Wisdom, Niebuhr wrote, "is dependent upon a humble recognition of the limits of our knowledge and our power." Understanding that fulfillment lies beyond history, man must understand why all human behavior lies under the inscrutable judgment of God.

"Nothing worth doing is completed in our lifetime," Niebuhr wrote in a later book. "Therefore, we must be saved by hope. . . . Nothing we do, however virtuous, can be accomplished alone; therefore, we are saved by love. No virtuous act is quite as virtuous from the standpoint of our friend or foe as from our standpoint. Therefore, we must be saved by the final form of love which is forgiveness."

Niebuhr's skepticism about human nature made some wonder how he reconciled his political radicalism with his theological conservatism. Throughout history the doctrine of original sin had given despots the pretext to establish governments absolute enough to restrain man's wicked impulses. But Niebuhr had no problem with that. Why should anyone suppose, he asked in *The Children of Light and the Children of Darkness*, that despots are themselves immune to original sin? Quite the contrary: the greater the power, the more certain the corruption. The recognition of the frailty of man requires the diffusion, not the concentration, of authority. Niebuhr summed up his argument in one of the mightiest sentences of our time: "Man's capacity for justice makes democracy possible; but man's inclination to injustice makes democracy necessary."

Nor did recognition of sinfulness enjoin passivity or withdrawal: this was the point I had first heard at Memorial Church. Man is at once free and unfree, creator as well as creature of history; he has the obligation to act or accept the consequences of inaction. His knowledge is fragmentary, his righteousness is illusory, his motives are tainted, but, aware of the precariousness of human striving, he must strive nonetheless. He acts best when he understands his own fallibility and his puniness in the face of eternity. Lincoln was Niebuhr's model of the statesman who combines "moral resoluteness about the immediate issues with a religious awareness of another dimension of meaning or judgment." Humility must temper, not sever, the nerve of action.

If moral man can be led by love of power into behavior that endangers his fellows, immoral society, which lives exclusively by the law of power, is an even more constant danger to humankind. Nothing more terribly menaced the world, Niebuhr thought, than nations intoxicated by delusions about their moral superiority to lesser breeds. The menace was obvious enough in absolutist states like Nazi Germany and Communist Russia. But was it not latent even in democratic states? Niebuhr remained vigorously anti-Communist. Yet, as the Cold War deepened in the early 1950s and John Foster Dulles and Joe McCarthy tried to set the national tone, his worry increased about the mood in his own country. "A frantic anticommunism," he said, "can become so similar in its temper of hatefulness to communism itself."

Were his countrymen forgetting the divine judgment that waits on human pretension? No one, Niebuhr admonished, dare ignore "the depth of evil to which individuals and communities may sink, especially when they try to play the role of God to history." If America perishes, he concluded in his book of 1952, *The Irony of American History*, it will not be because of the unscrupulousness of the Communist foe. It will be because Americans themselves are blind to the hazards of the struggle—a blindness induced "not by some accident of nature or history but by hatred and vainglory."

Niebuhr's compelling reformulation of the Christian theory of man and history helped a distraught generation come to terms with the nightmare of the twentieth century. At the same time, by founding democracy at last on a realistic conception of human nature, his argument strengthened and renewed the democratic faith. Singlehandedly, Niebuhr accomplished a revolution in American liberal thought. His skepticism about fallible man's pretensions to infallibility, his warnings against messianism and utopianism, his ironic portrayal of the gap between righteous purpose and ruthless result, had profound influence after the war on intellectual and (a few) political leaders. George Kennan called him "the father of us all." Ironists in politics like Adlai Stevenson and John F. Kennedy valued not only his philosophical slant but also his practical wisdom. As chairman of Americans for Democratic Action, he expounded the chastened and self-critical but still resolute liberalism that flowed into Kennedy's New Frontier.

His personality reinforced his philosophy. An occasional sadness in life is the discovery that people may be less than the books they write. Niebuhr never disappointed. We had become friends in the 1940s. His wife was the former Ursula Keppel-Compton, a brilliant and lovely Englishwoman who had been at Oxford with Isaiah Berlin and Wystan Auden. Theirs was a welcoming household, whether at their apartment in Morningside Heights or at their summer retreat in the Berkshires.

At the center was Reinie, so overflowing with restless vitality that he could not sit still for long and strode the room to make his points. He was a totally unaffected man, high-minded and generous-hearted, spontaneous in his enthusiasm and in his (occasional) wrath, endlessly curious about ideas and people, never pompous or overbearing. An unforced humility always underlay his polemical vigor. Once denouncing the Christian pacifism of E. Stanley Jones, he suddenly stopped and said, "But who am I to pass judgment on Stanley Jones? He's one of the great Christian saints of our time."

"I doubt," said George Kennan, "that any less sanctimonious man ever wore clerical cloth." Though the truest of believers himself, Niebuhr had unlimited tolerance, at times perhaps even a distinct preference, for unbelievers. The philosopher Morton White said there ought to be an organization called Atheists for Niebuhr. One felt the irony—did he also?—that unbelievers, appropriating so much of his thought, left off when the part that mattered most to Niebuhr—the ineffable mystery and grace of God—came in.

In 1952 Niebuhr suffered the stroke that circumscribed the rest of his life. For a man of boundless energy, partial paralysis was an intolerable exaction. But, after moments of depression, he came to accept his condition. In time he returned to writing and even to occasional preaching. In the 1960s the Vietnam War offered further proof of the susceptibility of the United States to messianic delusions. "Our record as a righteous nation," he wrote in his last article before his death, in 1971, "has proved so filled with error that, obviously, we must stop thanking God we are not like other nations." He was an old Roman in the stoicism with which he observed folly and suffered affliction; in his valor and in his compassion; above all, in the sheer nobility of his mind and heart. One could easily imagine him in a toga.

His influence is all around us. Many Americans who never read a word Reinhold Niebuhr wrote have been altered by his ideas and outlook, just as many who never even heard of him will recognize his most famous prayer. Who can ever forget those now familiar and always luminous words: "O God, give us serenity to accept what cannot be changed, courage to change what should be changed, and wisdom to distinguish the one from the other."

REINHOLD NIEBUHR *was born on June 21, 1892, in Wright City, Missouri; his birth was so uncomplicated that his mother had no distinct memory of it.*

At three, after seeing a dead horse carted away in a wagon, he took pleasure in imitating the horse by lying down on his back and stiffening his limbs. A few years later, however, he could not sleep after hearing his teacher describe how Judas had hanged himself.

At ten he decided to emulate his father and become a minister, because Gustave Niebuhr was, Reinhold thought, "the most interesting man in town."

Three of the four Niebuhr children became theologians. Time magazine would dub them the "Trapp family of theology."

In childhood games, Niebuhr liked to perform "weddings" and "baptisms."

As teenagers he and his two brothers played in a trumpet band in a church basement. The group disbanded because the conductor wouldn't let them play anything except hymns.

The young Niebuhr was blue-eyed and blond. Very early he was bald.

His hands were broad and big-knuckled—"a farmer's hands," an acquaintance said.

At the Yale divinity school he felt like "a mongrel among thoroughbreds and that's what I am."

As a youngster Niebuhr usually spoke German. At Yale he was troubled by his poor command of English.

Not until he had been preaching at Detroit's Bethel Evangelical Church for four years did his congregation decide to conduct services in English instead of German.

His Detroit congregation consisted of eighteen families. He was so poorly paid that for the first five years of his pastorate he could not afford to buy books.

"Now that I have preached about a dozen sermons," he wrote at twenty-three, "I find I am repeating myself. . . . The few ideas that I had worked into sermons at the seminary have all been used, and now what?" Five years passed before he could say, "I am really beginning to like the ministry."

As a young pastor he enjoyed softball, tennis, and basketball. He cracked a china cabinet when he challenged one parishioner to a wrestling match in his dining room.

Niebuhr hated to make pastoral visits. "Usually I walk past a house two or three times before I summon the courage to go in," he wrote in his diary.

He found it difficult to wear a pulpit gown. "I abhor priestliness," he said.

He was famous for waving his arms furiously when he preached. "Reinie doesn't tilt at windmills," said a friend, "he is a windmill."

His face was equally active. Admirers traveled miles to hear him preach because of "his wonderful grimaces."

He had so intense a presence that John Gunther compared interviewing him to tossing paper airplanes into an electric fan.

Members of the Fellowship of Southern Churchmen gave him a nickname—Judgment Day in Britches.

When bombs fell on Edinburgh during his 1939 Gifford Lectures, he didn't even look up.

Abraham Lincoln was his hero. "America's greatest theologian," he called Lincoln.

Niebuhr rarely wrote more than one draft of anything. He was known for his illegible handwriting.

His father had tried to cure him of left-handedness by rapping him across the knuckles one day as he reached for some cheese. The boy thought his father didn't want him to eat so much.

He was delighted by cars. "I love nothing so much in the realm of physical pleasure as the sense of power that comes from 'stepping on the gas,' " he said.

He once was arrested for running a stop sign in Lee, Massachusetts. When he was unable to come up with the bail—fifty dollars—he was jailed. His wife borrowed money to bail him out.

His wife, the former Ursula Mary Keppel-Compton, was the first woman ever to win a First in theology at Oxford. She was described by one of her professors as a "maiden erudite as may be." The couple had two children.

Niebuhr used to tell young couples not to worry if "the first two years of marriage are hell." In 1959 he complained in a sermon that the pope's encyclical on marriage had neglected to say that "marriage is fun."

The Niebuhrs had two big poodles, which the minister walked twice a day. When the couple went out, they'd signal the dogs to be quiet by whispering the word church.

Justice Felix Frankfurter lived near the Niebuhrs' summer home in Massachusetts. After hearing one of Niebuhr's sermons he said, "I liked what you said, Reinie, and I speak as a believing unbeliever." "I'm glad you did," Niebuhr answered, "for I spoke as an unbelieving believer."

Beginning in 1952, Niebuhr suffered a series of strokes. On June 1, 1971, he died quietly in Stockbridge, Massachusetts.

What Alfred Barr Saw

ROBERT HUGHES

THE PERSON WHO DID THE MOST TO CHANGE ART IN AMERICA IN THE LAST HALF CEN-
tury was not Edward Hopper, not Jackson Pollock, and not—God save the
mark—Andy Warhol; neither a critic, Thisberg or Thatberg, nor a dealer. He
was a museum man, Alfred Hamilton Barr. Perhaps "museum man" shades it
wrongly, suggesting a person whose sense of career led him to safe haven in an
existing institution. The point about Barr's institution was that before him neither it nor anything like it existed, in America or out of it. For it was Barr who,
with a lot of help from his friends and colleagues, founded the Museum of Modern Art in New York. It was the Museum of Modern Art—MoMA, for short—
that, between its start in 1929 and the late 1960s, when other museums really
caught up with its programs, played the essential role in converting Americans
to a modernist sensibility in the visual arts. Not just painting and sculpture: all
departments—film, design, photography, and architecture as well. Without
MoMA there would still be a modernist culture in America, for museums do
not create cultures; they reflect and modulate them. (Barr, incidentally, was
strict with himself about this, indignantly rejecting suggestions that he was a
kind of pope, ruling by fiat and creating reputations *ex nihilo*.) But it would not
have the shape we recognize. Its history would be entirely different: different
aesthetic values and historical priorities, different prototypes and "classics."
We take MoMA's and Barr's achievement for granted much as we assume, be-

tween breaths, the continuity of air. MoMA's success as a cultural filter has been so great that we often have difficulty seeing it as a filter; its version of art history has become reality; without MoMA there would still be a painter named Picasso but his name would not *mean* the "Picasso" its syllables now signify in America. Only today, as the art world continues to turn into a system opposed, in most respects, to the idealist community Barr and his colleagues thought it should be—as it becomes less and less distinguishable from show biz, and its Sammy Glicks of both sexes form their dense, clacking colonies from SoHo to Venice, L.A.—do we see what a strenuous effort of imagination and moral will the invention of MoMA required.

Barr was born in Detroit in 1902. It is no surprise that he turned out to be made of evangelical fiber: his father and uncle, and their father before them, had all been Presbyterian ministers. Alfred H. Barr Sr. moved to Baltimore when his son was still a toddler, and there he became professor of homiletics at a theological seminary. Unlike most clergymen in America seventy-five years ago, he was interested—in a refined, amateurish way—in art; and like practically every cultivated American of his time, he saw art in transcendentalist terms, as a means of moral instruction, ennoblement, and spiritual polish, a handmaiden to Religion and Nature. And so he made no fuss when his precocious son, who got into Princeton at sixteen but showed no leaning to the cloth, decided to study art history. Without this background—stable, moralizing, liberal, devoted to reasonable enlightenment—neither Alfred Barr nor the museum he created can really be understood: thanks to it, the son tended always to see art, including modern art, as a tool of social betterment, which people would respond to if only they were allowed to see it. The revolutionary claims made for modernism, its role as an agent of Oedipal revolt and social rebellion, would never impress Barr much. His interest lay in continuities, not fractures. Otherwise, he could never have shaped an institution like MoMA.

He was a solitary at Princeton—not rich, not a jock, ascetic, shy, and a trifle prickly. By 1923, when he had his master's degree, he had decided to spend five years changing jobs and traveling, so as not to be immured within any particular student group. He taught art history at Vassar for a year and earned a reputation as a mild eccentric by hanging an exhibition of Kandinskys and doing amateur theatricals. He had his first European summer in the museums. He taught a year at Harvard, returned to Princeton, and at the end of 1925 was offered an associate professorship at Wellesley. There, he began to develop the first course in modern painting and sculpture ever offered by an American university. It was a tiny affair, with no grades or examinations and only seven students. From this acorn, unimagined oaks would sprout. For in American colleges, as Barr would put it in 1938, "courses in modern art began with Rubens and ended with a few superficial and often hostile remarks about Van Gogh and Matisse . . . the last word in imitation Gothic dormitories had windows with one carefully cracked pane to each picturesque casement. Others of us, in architectural schools, were beginning our courses with gigantic renderings of Doric capitals, or ending them with elaborate projects for Colonial gymnasiums and Romanesque skyscrapers. . . ."

In short, the splendors and miseries of beaux-arts education. It is a common delusion that Barr hated nineteenth-century American culture; he would, for instance, send his students on train rides to look at H. H. Richardson's station buildings along the Boston and Albany line. But he had a wider view than mere ancestor-worship (the slack mind's version of tradition) could satisfy. In 1928 he was teaching an ecumenical course that treated all areas of modernism as products of a general sensibility—music, poetry, and criticism no less than painting and sculpture. "No subject," he wrote to his older friend Paul Sachs, whose museology course at Harvard was training the people who would run almost all the great American museums in the 1930s and 1940s, "deserves a variety of attitudes so much as contemporary." And the stage of the modernist drama—the incomparable theater of hope for cultural renewal—was obviously Europe. In 1927, helped by a gift of four hundred dollars from Sachs, he had gone back across the Atlantic, meaning to research a thesis entitled "The Machine in Modern Art." The subject itself pointed Barr away from Paris, whose grand masters of early modernism (Cézanne, Monet, Seurat) were dead, and whose successors, like Picasso and Matisse, were already middle-aged men. With the exception of Léger and Picabia, few of the great dominators of the Ecole de Paris were interested in machine imagery or the wider aesthetic effects of machine production on culture. But in Russia and Germany, the machine was a cultural obsession of the avant-garde. Its school was the Bauhaus, in Dessau, run by the architect Walter Gropius. The Bauhaus stood for connection without frontiers. In one way or another, every filament of Utopian thought in the visual arts—from Holland to Russia, from the ideals of Mondrian and J. J. P. Oud on one side of Europe to those of Vladimir Tatlin and Eliezer ("El") Lissitzky on the other, from Le Corbusier in France to Klee, Kandinsky, Feininger, Mies van der Rohe, and Gropius in Germany—ran through it and was knotted in it. There is no such school in the world today, largely because the hope of improving morals through design has failed, but partly because the constellation of missionary talent that made the Bauhaus what it was can no longer be assembled: teaching, for most artists and architects, is what you leave behind when you succeed. The Bauhaus was the last effusion of European guild sensibility, but applied to an age of mass production. In the fifty years since the Nazis closed it, it has been both fetishized and lampooned to an absurd degree: it was, after all, neither a gathering of saints nor a convocation of ascetic clowns eating mushed garlic under the sway of an imagined "Silver Prince." But to understand its impact on Barr and other young men who went to see it firsthand, such as the architect Philip Johnson and the architectural historian Henry-Russell Hitchcock, one must remember its program: nothing less than a unity of all the visual arts, which brushed aside the pecking order of beaux-arts education (architecture, painting, and sculpture, then a steep drop to the merely mechanical procedures of engineering and utilitarian design) and asserted that what mattered, the central issue, the key to coherent civilization, was an awareness of design in every field of visual discourse. Outside of Nature, whatever we see is made; whatever is made is designed. The Bauhaus took it as an axiom that it is no easier to design a fine teapot than a fine painting. In doing so it dissolved (or tried to) the social hierarchies that were assumed by the word *fine*. Teapots, posters, photographs, steam engines, carbide lamps, bridges, golf tees, boat propellers, the struts of a Morane-Saulnier biplane: these could embody, and disclose, as much cultural meaning as a Fragonard or a Soutine. They would not, of course, have the same role as images of personal life. But as emblems of collective decision and "rational" social function, they were a rich field of evidence and responsibility.

The logical place to go after Germany was Russia, where, in the wake of the October Revolution, avant-garde art had been granted a kind of official status, for a brief period, and the geniuses of the 1920s—Lissitzky, Tatlin, Eisenstein, Meyerhold, Mayakovsky, among others—had not yet been completely crushed into silence or the gulag by Stalin. The winter of 1927–28 was almost the last time a young American could go to Russia, wander unsupervised among its best artists, and come back with his notes intact. Barr was not sanguine about new Russian architecture; the construction of modern workers' apartments he found "pathetic," "crude," and theory-ridden; but the mounting excitement he felt as he watched Meyerhold's rehearsals and stood in Eisenstein's cutting room while *The General Line* was being edited was not to be duplicated on Broadway or in Hollywood. "We feel as if this were the most important place in the world for us to be," the minister's son jotted in his diary. The knowledge of Russian avant-garde art Barr gleaned on that trip would put him very much ahead of Western museum taste. Not until the late 1960s did Russian Constructivism find its expanding place in the art history books; not until the 1970s would chrome-eyed moguls with swarded potato fields in Easthampton start opening their checkbooks to invest in its frail relics. Even today, it is kept out of view in Russian museums. Along with his notes and memories, Barr brought back from Russia a curious icon in the form of an overcoat (which he had bought for his trip), made of some feltlike material thick enough to serve as a *yurt*, which he wore every winter for fifty years. This garment—which presently acquired the greenish-black patina, and almost the rigidity, of bronze—could be seen a block away when Barr did his gallery rounds, looking like a swaddled thrush.

So his *Wanderjahre* gave Alfred Barr his modernist baptism by total immersion, and when he got back to America a museum precipitated around him. Or so it might seem: in reality, nothing is quite so simple. On the East Coast the desire for some permanent institution devoted to modern art had been growing in several quarters. In Massachusetts, for instance, there was a group of undergraduates called the Harvard Society for Contemporary Art, started by Lincoln Kirstein, a formidably serious undergraduate who would later become the gray eminence of the New York City Ballet, its general director, becoming, in effect, the equivalent of Barr in the realm of dance; the Harvard Society exhibited work by a whole range of modernists, from Braque and Miró to Brancusi and

Calder, and in 1930 it held the first show of Bauhaus design ever mounted in America, anticipating MoMA's by eight years. Before MoMA was formed, the Harvard Society was already running an exhibition program devoted to handicrafts and design as well as the "fine" arts, and it very likely influenced the taste not only of Barr but of the three women who first came up with the idea of a permanent museum of modernism in New York City. These queen bees were Mrs. John D. Rockefeller Jr., Lizzie P. Bliss, and Mrs. Cornelius J. Sullivan. Like Kirstein, like Barr, like any number of intelligent easterners, they were frustrated by the provincialism of American taste and the short shrift that universities had given to art since 1885. Being millionairesses and collectors, they felt they could do something about it. They formed a committee to start a museum. Cunningly, they asked A. Conger Goodyear, a very wealthy man who owned Van Goghs, Gauguins, and Seurats, to be its chairman. Goodyear had just been voted off the board of the Albright Gallery in his native Buffalo, because he had been so wild as to spend five thousand dollars on a Rose Period Picasso; that smarted and he was happy to accept the ladies' exquisitely timed offer. He brought with him some friends, like Frank Crowninshield, editor of the original *Vanity Fair*, and Professor Paul Sachs of Harvard. And when the question arose of who should direct the embryonic museum, whose charter was granted in 1929—just about two weeks after the Wall Street market crash—Sachs wrote to his young friend Alfred Barr at Wellesley. "This is something I could give my life to—unstintedly," Bar replied.

Thirty-one years later, when asked to explain the "cultural explosion" that had brought the 1960 attendance at the Museum of Modern Art to 650,000 —not huge by today's standards but unprecedented then—Barr hazarded that "maybe the education of women has something to do with it. The patronage of arts is largely in the hands of women, just as money is. The feminization of taste is a factor." He was telling less than he knew; without the condensation of leisure, education, and sense of social duty represented by "The Ladies," as Mrs. Rockefeller, Miss Bliss, and Mrs. Sullivan were known by the staff, the museum that bore the fitting acronym of MoMA would not have started. No European museum had ever been started by women. Indeed, none of the great museums of the world, including American ones like the Met or The Art Institute of Chicago, would have tolerated women on their boards. But then, there were quite a few ways in which MoMA differed from its sister institutions. The perky little enterprise that opened to much public hoo-ha on November 9, 1929, in rented office space on the twelfth floor of the Heckscher Building, at Fifth and Fifty-seventh, was unlike any other museum in subject. Its first show was conservative enough—a loan exhibition of Cézanne, Gauguin, Seurat, and Van Gogh, largely drawn (a hint to the New York public) from other museum collections. Nor could its exhibition choices for 1930 —Corot, Daumier, Homer, Ryder, and Eakins among them—have seemed at all *outré*. Nevertheless, the museum was collecting in a field that no museum before had regarded as a fit subject of historical inquiry. A museum in Paris might buy a Maillol or a

Matisse as a gesture toward French art. One in Germany might put together some Klees, Lehmbrucks, and Beckmanns. Some American museums bought the work of some American modernists, and everyone liked Renoir. But the idea of a museum that treated modernism as a wholly international phenomenon and collected it as such: that was new. Before 1929 it was simply assumed that modernism and museum culture were incompatible. "Come on! Set fire to the library shelves! Turn aside the canals to flood the museums!" the Italian futurist Marinetti had trumpeted before the war; such effusions were much publicized, and they stuck in the public mind. They also made established museums chary of letting the work of such "firebrands" into their collections. If anyone had suggested in 1920 that the Cubist still lifes of Georges Braque had far more in common with the tradition of Chardin than with any fantasies of assault on culture, he would have seemed perverse. So the stereotype that MoMA set itself to abolish, as its first project, was the idea of a continuous battle, a basic incompatibility between the old and the new.

But back of that, there was a more basic task—familiarizing the audience with modern art. In 1929 there were still plenty of New Yorkers, never mind Americans west of the Hudson, who thought of Van Gogh as a Dutch nut who chopped off his ear and Picasso as a Spanish nut with a three-eyed mistress and Duchamp as a French nut who painted women on staircases that looked like explosions in a shingle factory. The audience for post-Impressionist painting was tiny and its roster of collectors minuscule—indeed, one might almost say that one consisted of the other. Modernist poets could take a very dim view of their counterparts in painting, too: once in the 1920s, when T. S. Eliot was lecturing at Bryn Mawr College, he was invited to visit the Barnes collection a few miles away: a stupendous array of Cézannes and Matisses, Soutines and pre-Cubist Picassos. "Nuts!" he ungraciously replied; and his *mot de Bastogne* would have been echoed, had they known about it, by most thinking men in America.

Thanks to a few dedicated apostles, like Alfred Stieglitz and his group at the "291" Gallery, some Cubist and later art had been seen in New York; this growing trickle amplified the lessons of the Armory Show of 1913. But the Armory affair had been a confused and confusing event, and the trouble with it—as the late Fairfield Porter, most lyrical of painters and sensible of critics, used to say—was that it left American art more provincial than it had ever been. Painters wanted to imitate new prototypes, like Cubism, but it was no easy thing to make sense of it when so little was permanently on view. The European avant-garde had a thin, spectral but addictive presence in America. Denied full contact, enthusiasts had to make erratic acts of faith in it, like the proverbial blindfolded men trying to deduce an elephant by touch. Thus at the time of the Crash and the birth of MoMA, New York was still a provincial culture, if one defines provincialism in terms of an uneasy, attentuated view of the desired prototype, without the chance to inspect it in depth and context, so that it acquires a fetishistic and remote authority. This state of affairs was what the American Stuart Davis was guying when he mordantly entitled one of his paintings *Colonial Cubism*. The problem hardly existed to the same degree in literature, for books saturate culture through the perfect reproducibility of the text, whereas paintings lose hideously in reproduction and can only be looked at in one place at a time. So it was possible to be sophisticated about Rilke, Joyce, and Kafka and a groping ignoramus on Gris, Kokoschka, and Picasso.

Barr and his colleagues at MoMA proposed to change that, and they did. If America is design-conscious today—and of course it is, to an almost fetishistic degree—the wells of its obsession with look and style were dug by the Museum of Modern Art between the early 1930s and the end of the 1950s. If Americans take photography seriously as an art form, it is largely because MoMA taught them (through three generations of curators whose opinions became policy for every museum in the U.S.) to value it as such. If there is constant argument about the aesthetics of motion pictures—enshrined in the distinction between film and mere "movies"—that argument was first institutionally nurtured by MoMA's Film Library, set up in the old CBS building in 1935. And if the ability to tell a Lichtenstein from a Warhol at fifty paces became as necessary a grace of social survival as the knack of plugging a squirrel in the eye at the same range two hundred years before, that, too, was mainly due to MoMA and its influence. Under Barr's guidance, MoMA set out to change the visual culture of America radically and permanently. It wanted to teach Americans to look at *everything* around them, not only paintings and sculpture (which did not surround them) but auto hubcaps, film, magazine layout, and buildings (which did), and see that such things were the products of a culture and not mere accidents of commerce. They would see that any man-made object from a Van Gogh to the springs of a gondola car could be viewed as design and offer a passage to meaning. All making was speech and no object was mute. Given this ideology, whose sources in the Bauhaus are obvious and whose effect on American education became as pervasive as fluoride, MoMA hoped to chivy and cajole Americans into an actively critical relationship with the world that was being constructed around them: to stop their accepting it as background or as orders from above. But this meant a shift in the image of the museum itself. Barr wanted to move away from the idea of the Museum as Treasure-House (a temple of Utopian stasis, where the immutable gods of art history smiled down: maximal art, minimum labels) to that of the Museum as Educator. A core of work, the collection, steadily expanding, buying and trading, swollen with the funerary endowments of dead trustees and the tax write-offs of live benefactors; around this, a constant orbit of temporary exhibitions, carefully didactic in tone, to widen the art-historical arguments; beyond that, the film programs, design seminars, lectures, and research programs. It was a much more complicated affair than putting some Matisses up and dusting them now and then, and MoMA was the first museum in the world to take on such functions.

In this way, through exhibitions, publishing, lectures, and all the not inconsiderable social pressures a newish museum with a boardful of Rockefellers and the like could muster, MoMA helped show America to itself. It did this by disclosing what was already modern in American culture. Barr, as noted above, was in spirit an internationalist—even though he spoke only a few words of German, less than perfect French, and only a few words of Russian beyond *da* and *nyet*. He shaped MoMA to the same ideals that, among European artists, kept up the search for "art without frontiers"—painting, sculpture, and design that took their stand on systems of imagery that might transcend national schools: the Machine and the Unconscious. Constructivism and Surrealism were the twin pillars of MoMA, one promising an imaginative link to the objective clarities of technology, the other suggesting a tap into man's most secret nature. Barr and his colleagues believed that the images that disclosed modern Europe to the Europeans would also show twentieth-century America to itself—especially since so many of the emblems of modernity that obsessed the European avant-garde had been produced on this side of the Atlantic and were part of the folk culture of new America, unrecognized by museums. For MoMA alone, in the 1930s and 1940s, was interested in the patterns of cultural flow between Europe and the U.S. and saw them—all gaps admitted—as part of a system that needed description.

The point is perhaps too often missed: one still reads cant about MoMA's project of "cultural colonization." Its usual form is the caricature sketched by Tom Wolfe in *From Bauhaus to Our House*. In New York, a booming indigenous architecture of fantasy and joyous Promethean excess, epitomized by the Chrysler Building; in Europe, the dour, flat-roofed austerities of the Bauhaus, the tyrannous glass heart of socialism; enter MoMA and its puritan taste merchants (Barr, Philip Johnson, and Henry-Russell Hitchcock, who named the International Style and showed it at their museum)—and lo, the end of a once-splendid tradition, crockets and fins and spires and all! But, of course, American skyscraper-deco was an import, too (like Renaissance Revival), for architects like William Van Alen and Wallace Harrison deduced it from what they had seen in Paris in the 1920s. Whereas flat-roofed workers' housing had long been conspicuous in America—even William McGonagall, the Sweet Singer of Dundee and the world's best bad poet, observed it when he crossed the Atlantic in 1887, at a time when Mies van der Rohe, being one year old, had exerted only the most limited influence on American building:

> And the tops of the houses are all flat,
> And in the warm weather people gather to chat,
> Besides on the house-tops they dry their clothes,
> And also many people at night on the house-tops repose.

Americans had high-rises long before Le Corbusier dreamed up the fearsome perspectives of *ville radieuse*. The icons of "functionalism" in Europe were common parts of the scene in America—those bridges, factories, silos, and hangars that French and German modernists, from about 1910 on, invoked as emblems of a new age. The Bauhaus derived its obsession with open planning from Frank Lloyd Wright; industrialism was called "Americanism" in prerevolutionary Russia, and the Italian futurists pointed to the American as the man

335

of the future—a creature from outside tradition, with, as Gino Severini put it, "exciting grotesqueries, frightening dynamism, crude jokes, enormous brutalities." The American as Machine Man was as much a fixture of avant-garde fantasy in postwar Europe as the American as Natural Man had been to the French 150 years before. And so no simple model of cultural colonization can describe what was passing between Europe and the U.S. in the years between 1880 and 1940. To depict Alfred Barr as an obsessed missionary thrusting a foreign gospel at a passive circle of rich Americans—a cultural detribalizer, as it were—is to make hash of history.

If the educational faith and sense of Utopian mission that created MoMA were very much of the 1930s, so were the opportunities for collecting.

Compared to now, the field was wide open. It would be as hard for a museum to put together a collection of twentieth-century painting and sculpture that rivaled MoMA's today as it would be to equal the Frick Collection starting from scratch. The works are not on the market, and prices have risen too high. In 1929 there were already some distinguished if unsystematic modernist collectors in America—Quinn, Arensberg, Barnes. But MoMA had little institutional competition and, in almost all art since the death of Cézanne, it was on its own. Barnes, for instance, had no interest in Cubism, let alone Surrealism or Constructivism. In amassing his encyclopedic study collection of modern art, Barr paid prices that would strike collectors today—used as they are to paying tens of thousands of dollars for the merest scrap of well-signed paper—with spasms of disbelief and envy. In 1935 Abby Rockefeller gave Barr some cash to spend in Europe. It was one thousand dollars, a sum that would hardly buy a print by Frank Stella today. With it, he purchased an oil by Max Ernst, three Dada collages, a Kurt Schwitters, two suprematist paintings by Kasimir Malevich, a pastel by André Masson, and a gouache by Yves Tanguy. The museum's great Van Gogh, *The Starry Night*, was priced at thirty thousand dollars in 1936. In 1939, thirty thousand dollars was the asking price of its Douanier Rousseau, *The Sleeping Gypsy*. Frugal millionaires considered such prices very high then and Barr had some difficulty raising the twenty-five thousand dollars needed to buy what must be the most famous picture in the museum's collection, *Les Demoiselles d'Avignon*, by Pablo Picasso. By general consent, this is the painting that provoked Cubism, and its importance as a hinge on which art history turned is not in question. It has become so familiar through exhibition and reproduction as to be a sort of twentieth-century Mona Lisa. But in the late 1930s, three decades after it was made, it still looked alarming, polemical, rebarbative, ugly, and much too big, not to say unfinished. It was offered to Joseph Pulitzer, the St. Louis newspaper magnate who, as a young man, was busy laying the foundations of his personal collection. Pulitzer saw what *Les Demoiselles* was, but he turned it down: "My father," he remarked almost half a century later, "drilled a great taboo into me—*never* liquidate capital to buy luxuries." So he let the painting go, and it went to MoMA. Barr did not have twenty-five thousand dollars, and he had to raise it by selling a small Degas. Today this seems (to put it mildly) a superb art-historical exchange, and not a bad money decision, since *Les Demoiselles* could hardly reach less than $7 million at auction. In 1938 it was not self-evidently so.

Only in the light of such acquisitions do we see how far, on fundamental levels, MoMA shaped our visual taste. If you list the three or four best-known works by almost any leading figure in European art between 1880 and 1940, the odds are that at least one of them will belong to MoMA. Of course, this is to some extent a circle, since MoMA was committed to making its works of art well known: that was the by-product of its educational programs. Nevertheless, who thinks of Van Gogh without *The Starry Night,* Matisse without *Piano Lesson, The Moroccans,* or *The Red Studio,* Léger without *Three Women (Le Grand Déjeuner),* or Mondrian without *Broadway Boogie Woogie?*

But it is not true, as many people have tended to suppose since his death, that Barr's taste was as catholic as it was accurate. His prime allegiance was to European art and he tended to see American painting and sculpture in colonial terms: this was more a shading of taste than an overt policy, but it existed, and it accounts for his mild resistance—*hostility* being rather too strong a word—to the work of the Abstract Expressionists, starting with Jackson Pollock and Willem de Kooning. After twenty years of struggle in bringing European modernism to America, he was not likely to turn around and say that, all of a sudden, the Americans were doing things better. By 1955, however, two things had become clear to the more perceptive members of the art world. The first was that, with all due respect to Ubuesque disrupters like Jean Dubuffet, the generation of French painters that came along after World War II was never going to hold a candle to the aging, dying, or dead monarchs of the Ecole de Paris—Picasso, Braque, Matisse, Bonnard, Brancusi, Miró, Ernst. You could make a lot of noise about painters such as Manessier, with his stained-glass abstractions, or Wols, with his scratchy obsessive drawings, or Fautrier's outraged-looking, sad clods of pigment. You could construct some kind of argument that the heroic years of 1880 to 1930 had their consequence in such art, but the argument always sounded tinny and flat. The truth was that the war and the Occupation had reamed out the cultural life of Paris: literature, thriving on opposition, had survived better than painting. The promotional machinery of the Ecole de Paris—a mechanism that seems clunky and unimposing alongside the large international apparatus that rules the art world today—was running on empty. Picasso, for instance, was not merely an old painter; at seventy-five, with most of his colleagues gone, he was a gray humpy survivor, a fossil god who still painted but whose incalculably numerous, and often quite ungrateful, aesthetic progeny reached back three generations, to Cubism.

So Paris was declining, a fact that would later be erected into a fetish by American cultural nationalists: European entropy and American growth became linked as a tyrannous dogma. But that would not happen just yet. What one had in the present, in 1955, was more suggestive and debatable—the rise of an important *American* group of modernist painters, men (and one woman too, Lee Krasner) who were creating the movement that reversed the flow of influence, backward across the Atlantic. Abstract Expressionism was not a style: the

337

"field" painters, Mark Rothko, Barnett Newman, and Clyfford Still, were working a different vein from the "gestural" artists, Pollock, de Kooning, Robert Motherwell, and Franz Kline. Almost thirty years later we tend to grant Abex a more monolithic presence, a denser aesthetic unity, than it really had. Seeing the work when it was new, Barr was not immune to it by any means—but he was a little slow endorsing it, despite the enthusiasm of some of his colleagues at MoMA, like Dorothy Miller, curator of museum collections. As a result, MoMA missed out on some crucial acquisitions; when Pollock's estate offered to sell one of the late artist's greatest "all-over" drip paintings for twenty-five thousand dollars, Barr was so offended by the price that he is said to have refused to return the call or answer the letters. (Much later, in the early 1970s, a Pollock of equivalent quality, *Blue Poles*, went to Australia for over $2 million.) When Barr wanted to put weight behind a living American artist, he could transform a career: by acquiring not one but three Jasper Johnses from the artist's first show in 1958 for a few hundred dollars apiece, Barr in a sense set the 1960s rolling. But he liked Johns not because of his role as a father of Pop—which in 1958 did not exist—but because he seemed so squarely set in the Dada-Surrealist tradition and was a fine "European" artist with a mellifluous hand.

Yet to say that Barr's taste lost some of its flexibility as his life lengthened is not to say much; every museum man, every critic, is formed by early experience and tends to idealize it. The truly remarkable thing was how open he remained—along with the no-less-striking fact that although Barr, in his increasingly complex and difficult maneuvers with trustees and donors, had to deploy the cunning of a von Clausewitz, he never compromised the integrity of his views for a moment. He did not collect in a big way; he did not deal; he did not moonlight as an "adviser" for the private interests of the millionaire collectors on his board, except when he was dead certain that the work would eventually come to the museum. He was not, in short, a moral postmodernist. Nor was he easy to stampede, since he believed that MoMA, like the Church, had time. For this, and for his championing of European, as distinct from American, art, he duly paid; thus in the mid-1960s, when Marianne Moore, Virgil Thomson, and Glenway Wescott put him up for election to the National Institute of Arts and Letters, its artist members lobbied him off the roster. Long before then, in 1944, Barr had been fired as director of MoMA by its president and chairman of the board, Stephen Clark, who disliked Barr's educational approach and seems, in private, to have resented his maddening intellectual *certezza* in areas of risky taste. For Barr—often without realizing it—could make people who were not fools feel foolish, and when this was added to his legendary impatience with folly, deep jealousies were honed. He did not, of course, leave MoMA. He shifted sideways, with reduced powers, as director of museum collections. His obsessive commitment to art and scholarship remained; although the reins had been cut, he seemed to control the team by mesmerism. (Sometimes his devotion to MoMA's collection could show physical symptoms: in 1958, when the museum caught fire and a huge Monet of water lilies was destroyed, Barr lost seven pounds, about 5 percent of his body weight, in one day.) When he retired in 1967, he was more aged than he should have been and his memory was degenerating tragically: one of his colleagues remembers listening to Barr groping for the name of "that guy—that fellow—the Spaniard . . ." Picasso. He died in 1981 on the one hundredth anniversary of that Spaniard's birth, leaving behind a transformed culture.

ALFRED HAMILTON BARR JR. *was born on January 28, 1902, in Detroit. As a boy he collected plants, butterflies, rocks, and stamps. He thought at one time of becoming a paleontologist.*

Teaching at Vassar, he was regarded as a little far-out. His jackets didn't match his trousers, and he was nicknamed Mr. Mixed-Suits.

He became an instructor at Harvard in 1924, and in the course of one year supplemented his teaching by taking and auditing nine courses in the fine arts, music, and poetry. "I will be buried under my work," he wrote to a friend, "but I shall sing in my sepulcher."

In 1929, when he was mentioned as a possible director of a proposed museum of modern art, Mrs. John D. Rockefeller Jr., one of the originators of the idea, invited him up to Seal Harbor, Maine, to look him over. She wrote, "I liked Mr. Barr and felt that his youth and enthusiasm and knowledge would make up for his not having a more impressive appearance."

The first show put on by the museum, in the Heckscher Building, was so well attended that the regular business tenants of the building complained and the landlord threatened to evict the museum. Despite the crush, Barr met his future wife at the event.

Queried by a reporter about his criteria for awarding prizes at an exhibition, he replied that he had "no beliefs." How, then, another reporter persisted, would he judge the pictures? "By looking at them," he said.

Early on, Metropolitan Museum of Art director Francis Henry Taylor called Barr's museum "that whorehouse on Fifty-third Street." Later, New York Times *critic John Canaday called Barr "the most powerful tastemaker in American art today and probably in the world." Replied Barr: "Reluctant tastemaker."*

Critic John Gruen recalled that when Barr visited a gallery "the temperature of the gallery would mysteriously change" because a nod of approval from him could mean the launching of an artist's career. "Barr, looking oddly taller than he is, would move about the gallery without once altering his expression."

Slender, thin-lipped, horn-rimmed, he could appear absentminded. Once, while giving a lecture, he started to read from a speech by Lenin, fell silent for a long time, and then looked up with a smile of apology and explained, "I'm sorry, I got interested."

Barr came across as "shy, soft-spoken, exquisitely polite," recalled art critic Calvin Tomkins, ". . . and his silences were famous. When asked a question, he would sometimes look out the window for several minutes, formulating his reply, while the questioner nervously wondered whether his presence, to say nothing of the question, had ceased to register."

Coursing with energy, Barr was a chronic worrier and also an insomniac. But his insomnia didn't bother him too much—it gave him more hours to work.

He knew the strategies of three quarters of the world's great battles. He was an avid bird watcher. He hoped for an exhibition of the helmets of man—of Greeks, Romans, pilots, racing drivers.

In 1944, exasperated with Barr's policies and shortcomings as an administrator, the Modern's trustees fired him. Though he could have found a job elsewhere, he stayed put, working on his book on Picasso every day in a tiny office. Staff members constantly sought him out, and in 1947 he was made director of museum collections at the urging of René d'Harnoncourt, who later became museum director. As d'Harnoncourt saw it, his function was "to preserve and nourish the genius of Alfred Barr."

"Of course Alfred would not leave," Barr's wife said. "It was his museum. The Museum was his mistress."

In August 1981 Barr died after an extended illness.

The Cowboy Hero
and the American West
... as Directed by
John Ford

PETER BOGDANOVICH

MR. FORD WAS IN BED, AS HE OFTEN WAS WHEN NOT SHOOTING, WATCHING TV AND half-listening to my attempts at a conversation. Even if the television had not been on, Ford's attitude toward me would have been gruff and lightly sardonic. This was not unexpected, however, since I mainly would talk about his movies, and John Ford never would allow himself to be caught taking any real interest in a discussion of his work or pictures in general. He was seventy-five at the time, 1970, with less than three years to live. I was a thirty-one-year-old director with two movies to my credit, one a documentary called *Directed by John Ford*.

He had been in the film business for over fifty-seven years, fifty-three of them as a director. Only one decade before Jack Ford got into pictures, the film business did not exist, nor the art of movie direction. Ford made 136 pictures, some of which, in the thirty-odd years between 1931 and 1964, earned seventy-two Oscar nominations. They won twenty-three, including six that went to Ford personally. The New York Film Critics voted him Best Director four times. Both achievements still hold the record today. He had been responsible for creating not only the screen personas of several key stars, most prominently John Wayne and Henry Fonda, but an extraordinary number of America's favorite and most enduring pictures, among them *The Informer, Stagecoach, The Grapes of Wrath, How Green Was My Valley, She Wore a Yellow Ribbon,* and *The Quiet Man.*

Every so often, after being consistently edgy and sarcastic, or soon after a particularly cutting remark, Ford would smile at me in an openly affectionate way. This might start me waxing eloquent again on some scene of his, or asking yet another convoluted or weighty question, and pretty soon he would be insulting me again. "Jesus *Christ*, Bogdanovich! Can't you ever end a sentence with anything but a question mark? Haven't you *heard* of the declarative sentence?"

Most people were intimidated by John Ford. His appearance certainly contributed: a grizzled face with one black eyepatch over thick glasses, a short cigar stuck in his mouth, or a portion of a long white handkerchief, which soon turned brown from chewing. His usual expression was either a purposeful, slightly belligerent deadpan or a scowl. Since he always scorned talk of social significance or of art, never discussed his experiences in World War II (in which he had been wounded and decorated), and spoke of himself simply as "hard-nose director" who enjoyed making pictures as "a job of work," it was difficult to find permissible areas to approach. I mentioned, nervously, that John Wayne's birthday was coming up and that I was thinking of giving him a book.

Without turning from the TV, Ford said loudly, "Hmmm?" Whenever he wanted to humiliate, Ford would feign deafness and make you repeat several times the thing you just said. So I repeated about Wayne's birthday and the gift I was planning. For a third time, even louder, Ford said: "Hmmm!!?" I nearly shouted the words *birthday* and *book*. Angrily, Ford said, "A *what*!?" I repeated: "A *book*!" Then, suddenly, Ford's expression changed completely, becoming reasonable and relaxed. "Oh!" he said and turned back to the TV. He grunted and put a corner of the large handkerchief into his mouth. He chewed meditatively for a few moments before looking at me again and, enunciating precisely, said: "He's *got* a book!" When Ford turned back to the TV, there was the hint of a smile beneath his fixed expression.

Ford's remark was a devastating comment on a man he profoundly loved and had, to the greatest degree, helped to create: certainly, without John Ford, there never would have been a John Wayne. I had known Wayne for five years by then, Ford for seven, and the father-son relationship between them was fairly clear: Wayne loved Ford but was still thoroughly intimidated by him. He was privately both critical and frightened of the Coach, as he called him, or Jack—the man after whom Duke Wayne had most patterned himself. Wayne once told me his response to Ford on *Stagecoach*, the 1939 western that had made him a major star: After Wayne had seen the rushes for the first time, Ford asked how he had liked himself. Wayne shrugged and said, "Well, you know what *that* is—I'm just playin' you. . . ."

There was a similarity in many of their mannerisms, especially the graceful way both gestured with their hands and arms. The famous rolling John Wayne walk was Jack Ford's walk. Wayne's brusque screen character was Ford's in real life. But Ford wasn't six feet four, with a strikingly handsome face and ultramanly physique; off-camera, Wayne was gregarious, warm and outgoing, quick to laugh, strangely innocent. Ford, while I knew him, was much like the older characters Wayne had begun to play in *Red River,* the western he did with Howard Hawks in 1947. Hawks would tell me that over the years Ford invariably was complimented for having made *Red River;* Ford always nodded, smiled modestly, and said: "Thank you very much."

Hawks put it succinctly: "I don't see how a person can make a western *without* being influenced by John Ford." And Hawks (who would never make a western without Wayne) was not being generous: he could as easily have extended the influence to most American pictures, because Ford had long ago become as synonymous with the Great American Film as Jean Renoir had with the Great French Film. Before Orson Welles made his first two pictures, *Citizen Kane* and *The Magnificent Ambersons,* he studied one film exclusively; Welles would tell me he had run John Ford's *Stagecoach* forty times. For *Kane,* he also hired one of Ford's favorite cameramen, Gregg Toland; both pictures owe no small amount to Ford's visual influence.

Although Ford was most famous for westerns, he did not make a talking one until ten years after synchronized sound had arrived. Yet his career had begun in the silent era, and during his first three years as a director, Ford made only westerns, thirty of them (nearly all starring Harry Carey). During the Twenties, he made a dozen more, helping to create cowboy stars out of Buck Jones, Hoot Gibson, Tom Mix, and George O'Brien. The first of his pictures to be a runaway success at the box office was a western: *The Iron Horse,* released in the summer of 1924. For his wife Mary's Christmas present two and a half years later, Ford had a new Rolls-Royce delivered to the front door, with a fur coat on the backseat; the note attached read: "This ought to hold you for a while." He meant it, and gave her no other presents for many years.

The vast majority of Ford's films dealt with historical subjects: the American Revolutionary War and Civil War, the Indian wars, the building of the railroads, the taming of the West, the creation of a new civilization. Yet the early westerns he made depicted incidents and lives then barely thirty years past. Ford not only made movies about the famous marshal and gunfighter Wyatt Earp, he had known the man (and others of the epoch) well; they told him how it had been.

During the Thirties, Ford guided Spencer Tracy and Humphrey Bogart through their first feature, and Will Rogers through three (including his last), as well as directed a number of popular, highly regarded films, among them *Arrowsmith, The Lost Patrol, Hurricane,* and *The Informer,* which, for 1935, won Ford his first Academy Award as Best Director and his first New York Film Critics prize. Because he had fought against studio indifference and opposition to get the Irish story done, *The Informer* turned Ford into the hero of the critics and the public. He was already married for fifteen years to Mary McBryde Smith—a magnificent, extraordinarily resilient woman, a direct descendant of Thomas More—and they were the parents of a teenage son and daughter, and Ford's reputation as a family man and artist had never been stronger.

At this moment, his personal life was rocked to its foundation. Ford, now forty, fell profoundly in love with a woman of twenty-six named Katharine

Hepburn, who also fell in love with him. It happened while the two of them were shooting the film version of Maxwell Anderson's historical drama *Mary of Scotland.* Neither Ford nor Hepburn ever spoke of their affair, but of course the families knew. The attraction between them, the explosiveness and independence of both their natures, can be seen reflected in several of the key romantic relationships in Ford's subsequent pictures, notably in the extraordinarily rich emotional interplay between Maureen O'Hara and Walter Pidgeon as the forbidden lovers in *How Green Was My Valley;* between Wayne and O'Hara in *The Quiet Man, Rio Grande,* and *The Wings of Eagles;* and between Clark Gable and Ava Gardner (who was nominated as Best Actress) in *Mogambo.*

Despite their feelings for each other, Ford and Hepburn came to a difficult and painful conclusion. He was an Irish Catholic married to a woman he dearly loved, and with a passionate belief in family. The thirteenth and last child of Irish immigrants (his father was a saloon owner in Maine), Ford was now a famous, wealthy, and respected figure in the world. And Katharine Hepburn was already well on her way to the longest and most influential career of any woman in the movies; she had become a top star and won an Oscar after her first Hollywood season, only two years before meeting Ford, and had been nominated again the same year he won his first. Her reputation for integrity and Yankee strongmindedness matched his. Their first encounters were volatile, but Ford was remarkably gallant and courteous with women, and always pleased with, and refreshed by, a well-phrased and reasoned argument.

Kate Hepburn of Hartford, Connecticut, and Jack Ford of Portland, Maine, were a match made in heaven. But, on the other hand, they both knew how badly their relationship might damage their individual careers and their ability to do what they had evidently been born at precisely the right time to do. They both knew how good they were and how much more they still had to accomplish.

When he and Hepburn decided they could never work together again, they both would have known the degree of happiness they were giving up. The decision, a kind of glorious and idealistic sacrifice, is echoed in most of Ford's subsequent pictures: the burden of duty, tradition, honor, and family is among his central themes.

Eight years later, Hepburn would begin the longest secret love affair in picture history, with another married Irish Catholic father, named Spencer Tracy—a liaison that yielded a handful of memorable costarring vehicles and was not revealed until after Tracy's death. It is difficult not to see a connection between her screen behavior with Tracy and her love not only for him but also for Jack Ford—the truly secret and romantic one.

Ford and Hepburn remained close friends throughout Ford's life; she also had a warm friendship with Mary Ford that continued until Mary died, five years after Jack. In *The Quiet Man,* Ford's single most passionately romantic picture, made in Ireland at age fifty-seven, the Maureen O'Hara character combined the best qualities of the two women who, apart from his mother, Ford most loved; her name in the film was Mary Kate.

Within two years of his and Hepburn's decision, Ford would begin the most expressive, emotionally charged, and poetic series of pictures in American film history. Between 1938 and 1941, while America stayed out of the war, at ages forty-three to forty-six, Ford directed seven profoundly affecting movies. The three release years involved were by far the most productive of quality in Hollywood's entire history; if any one time was the peak for the American screen, it was the years 1939 to 1941, after which the U.S. entry into World War II altered everything. Ford's competition in these years included not only *Gone with the Wind* (which earned thirteen nominations in 1939, against nine for three of Ford's pictures), but a score of other popular and critical milestones, from Capra's *Mr. Smith Goes to Washington* to Lubitsch's *Ninotchka,* from *The Wizard of Oz* to *Citizen Kane.* The Academy nominated Ford each year and he won the last two: the New York Film Critics voted him Best Director all three years. Ford's constant work conveniently managed to prevent him from personally appearing to accept any of his prizes.

This remarkable burst of creativity began, appropriately, with a western; although *Stagecoach* was his ninetieth film, it was not only his first western since the advent of sound, but also his first in thirteen years. Loosely based on a de Maupassant story, *Stagecoach* began the John Wayne myth and established Monument Valley (Arizona/Utah) as Ford's own special country of the West, setting a standard for westerns that only two or three others, including Ford himself, would ever equal or transcend.

His other two films of 1939 starred Henry Fonda: *Drums Along the Mohawk* —Ford's first in color—and *Young Mr. Lincoln.* The director had had to browbeat the actor into accepting the role of Lincoln in their first of seven features together. Fonda recalled Ford demanding: "What do you think you're going to be playing? The Great Emancipator or something?! This is a young jackleg lawyer from Springfield, for God's sake!" The death of Lincoln's early love, Ann Rutledge, and his abiding faith in her spirit reverberate throughout the picture. Ford's other films of this period are *The Grapes of Wrath, Tobacco Road, The Long Voyage Home,* and *How Green Was My Valley.*

In August 1941, four months before Pearl Harbor put America in the war, Ford, age forty-six, went on active duty in the U.S. Navy. With the rank of lieutenant commander (eventually becoming a two-star admiral), he was appointed chief of the Field Photographic Branch, a unit of the OSS, reporting directly to his friend Colonel William ("Wild Bill") Donovan. Though Ford was even more closemouthed about his war activities than he was normally about everything else, he once told a reporter: "Our job was to photograph, both for the records and for intelligence assessment, the work of guerrillas, saboteurs, Resistance outfits. . . . Besides this, there were special assignments." Except for his work on several war documentaries, Ford would not direct a new picture for nearly four years.

Not long after Ford's death, some of his undercover activities for the government became known through his grandson Dan Ford's biography, *Pappy: The Life of John Ford,* and through director Robert Parrish's autobiography, *Growing Up in Hollywood,* which includes the best personal portrait of Ford yet published. Decorated a number of times, Ford was also given the Purple Heart for injuries sustained during the Battle of Midway, which he personally photographed with a hand-held 16mm camera, even after receiving shrapnel fragments in the arm and groin.

The battles they were filming in Hollywood with Duke Wayne were being lived overseas by Jack Ford. Toward the end of the war, the Navy asked Ford to make a picture (with Wayne) in the line of duty; typically, Ford chose America's worst defeat, in the Philippines, as the background to what became the finest and most compassionate of American war films, *They Were Expendable.* A deal was struck with MGM, and Ford demanded from Louis B. Mayer the highest salary ever paid (at the time) to a director, $400,000, and donated all of it to build a recreation center in Los Angeles for veterans of his naval unit.

The first movie Ford directed after the war was a western: shot in Monument Valley, with Henry Fonda playing Wyatt Earp and climaxed by a recreation of the famous gunfight at the OK Corral, *My Darling Clementine* surpassed *Stagecoach* but received almost no special attention. Of the thirty-odd films Ford directed in the last twenty years of his active career, half of them were westerns. Ford had realized that the form he had so greatly influenced, and almost single-handedly perfected into a uniquely American art, could be the equivalent of the myths or legends of the ancient religions and histories of Europe. As the modern, postwar world became increasingly disheartening to Ford—and less and less interested in his work, especially his westerns—he continued nevertheless to explore the themes that profoundly concerned him.

Unquestionably, these westerns were his most mature and resonant achievements: from the towering cavalry/Indian wars trilogy with Wayne, Fonda, O'Hara, and the rest of the Ford family of players—best viewed in this order: *Fort Apache* (1948), *Rio Grande* (1950), *She Wore a Yellow Ribbon* (1949)—to the darkening, increasingly tragic series of frontier stories that began in 1956 with Wayne in *The Searchers* and ended in 1962 with Wayne and Stewart in *The Man Who Shot Liberty Valance,* perhaps the two richest and most complex westerns ever made.

Although Wayne had been a part of Ford's family since 1928 and Ford had not even met Fonda until ten years later, when John Ford went into the war, and after he returned, Fonda clearly was the favorite son. *Stagecoach* had turned Wayne into a box-office attraction virtually overnight, yet all the key male leads in Ford's subsequent pictures had gone to Fonda. After *Fort Apache,* however, Fonda—dissatisfied with most of his other film work—decided to return to the Broadway stage; his first of several huge successes was in the title role of *Mister Roberts,* and he was out of pictures for eight years. In 1954, when Jack Warner hired Ford to direct the film version of *Mister Roberts,* both Marlon Brando and William Holden were proposed for the lead, each of them big names at the time; Fonda was no longer considered a screen draw. Ford said, however, that unless Fonda played Roberts, he would not direct the picture. Fonda was cast. No one told the actor of Ford's intervention.

During the filming, when Ford began to add visual comedy to the script and to beef up the smaller roles, Fonda—having done the play for more than a thousand performances—became indignant, and objected: to him the Broadway text was like Scripture and Ford's additions not only unnecessary but insulting to the integrity of the piece. To patch up the growing rift between star and director, producer Leland Hayward arranged a meeting of the three, he would tell me, "to air their differences." After a few minutes of listening to Fonda's complaints, Ford stood up and socked Fonda on the jaw, sending him to the ground. Fonda would tell me that he had looked up at Ford, age sixty, and realized he could not possibly return the blow. Shortly afterward, Ford suffered a severe gallbladder attack, and Mervyn LeRoy was hired to complete the film. Ford and Fonda did not speak to each other for ten years—not until Ford's daughter, Barbara, told Fonda what her father had done to secure him the Roberts role. The actor called Ford, and though a reconciliation of sorts followed, the two never worked together again.

For Ford's final score of films, John Wayne starred in nearly half, with a range of roles and performances that challenged any Fonda had done. But the shift from Fonda to Wayne had an odd effect on the critical reception of Ford's pictures and on the attitude of the liberal artistic commentary toward Ford himself. Fonda's politics having always been outspokenly Democrat, and Wayne's equally Republican, the assumption was incorrectly made that Ford's political opinions were similar to, even identical with, his favorite star's. Ford, being resolutely "apolitical," as he would say, made no attempt to convince people otherwise. Referring to Wayne, he would tell a reporter, "I love that damn Republican."

Yet director-writers Joseph L. Mankiewicz and Samuel Fuller each would tell me of the same unpublicized Ford incident they had witnessed, one that helped define his true attitudes. In the early Fifties, while Mankiewicz was president of the Screen Directors' Guild, C. B. De Mille launched a major campaign to demand signed loyalty oaths as a prerequisite for remaining a member of the union. Mankiewicz objected. The De Mille faction began to make insinuations about Mankiewicz's "pinko" leanings, and eventually the situation became so heated in the community and in the press that a special membership meeting was called to decide the issue. Mankiewicz flew in from New York for it, he would tell me, knowing that his career was on the line.

In a record turnout, nearly the entire membership attended. A noisy debate between the sizable De Mille group and the Mankiewicz supporters continued for more than four hours. John Ford, by far the most honored and respected member present, sat on an aisle, Fuller said, wearing his baseball cap and untied sneakers, attentive but without comment or change of expression. Finally, after De Mille's own long, impassioned speech, there was a silence and Ford raised his hand. A court stenographer was present and each person who spoke had to give his name and describe his position briefly. Ford stood and said: "My name's Jack Ford—I make westerns." He then went on to praise De Mille's ability to produce pictures that appealed to the public—more so, Ford said, than anyone else in the room; he turned to look across the hall now directly at De Mille: "But I don't like you, C.B.," he said, "and I don't like what you've been saying here tonight. I move that we give Joe a vote of confidence—and let's all go home and get some sleep." Which is what they did.

In his later years, nevertheless, Ford came to be considered close to a reactionary, because throughout the Fifties and into the Sixties, while the chic American cultural fashion became increasingly irresponsible, antimilitarist, antipolice, and antifamily, Ford continued to make pictures with men in uniform, fighting the chivalrous fight, honoring the women and way of life they protected and cherished. The theme to which he returned most often was the glory in defeat. In each of his cavalry films and westerns, the Indian nations had been treated and portrayed with exceptional accuracy and dignity; the cause of their savagery was always placed squarely on the sins of the white invaders and exploiters. When the old Indian chief in *Yellow Ribbon* cries that he and Wayne are "too old" to do anything about the war that is to ensue between their peoples, Wayne's simple response sums up Ford's most essential belief: ". . . but old men should *stop* wars!"

Plagued by several illnesses and increasingly poor vision, Ford would have realized as he entered his sixth decade as a director that each picture he began could very well be his last. Certainly the final two films he made reflected a desire to deal with subjects he felt had not been sufficiently explored in his work: the Indian's tragic history, and woman's. This last movie was originally titled, appropriately, *Chinese Finale,* but eventually released as *7 Women* (1966); it is among his most revealing pictures but unquestionably the most reviled of his career. Ford's American reputation never recovered from the film's poor reviews and worse business. Though his last years were filled with attempts to make a deal on a new movie—two set in World War II, two set in the Revolutionary War, another about a black soldier—the necessary backing never materialized.

One of the greatest mythmakers in our history had been silenced before his time. But then, the America of John Ford was not the America of the Sixties or Seventies, nor of the directionless Eighties. Is any form less honored today or, apparently, less "commercial" than the western? Haven't we turned our backs on the only traditions we have ever honored or respected—the chivalrous code of the West, which glorified women and was pledged to defend the hearth and family?

On March 31, exactly five months before his death from cancer, a frail and emaciated John Ford became the first recipient of the American Film Institute's Life Achievement Award and, in the same televised festivities, the first American filmmaker to receive the nation's highest civilian honor, the Medal of Freedom. President Richard Nixon was on hand, along with the Marine

The Cowboy Hero and the American West . . . as Directed by John Ford

Band, to present the medal. Outside, in front of the building, a protest against Nixon was being led by Jane Fonda.

The irony of the situation was mirrored in one of her father's Ford films: in *Fort Apache* Fonda had played a tyrannical and glory-seeking martinet whose racist miscalculations—a gross underestimation of his Indian opponents—had led to the massacre of most of his men and of himself; yet at the end, Wayne, playing one of the few survivors and a humanist leader the opposite of Fonda's character, nevertheless confirms the false press and public notion of Fonda as a brave and courageous leader. The morale and spirit of the cavalry as a whole was more important, therefore, than the failings and injustices of a single man. Ford would tell me heroes were "good for the country," and yet he would show us the truth behind the fake legends.

Richard Nixon could hardly have been John Ford's favorite President—though President Nixon would tell me that his favorite movie director was John Ford; in 1960 Ford had voted against Nixon, for Jack Kennedy. Nonetheless, Nixon was there that night as President of the United States to pay tribute to an American who had served his country in peace and war under several Presidents; the nation and the nation's history were paying tribute for the first time not only to an artist of films, but to one who had for almost sixty years vividly represented the nation and its history, and the kindred histories of other nations, to the peoples of the world.

The last time I saw Mr. Ford, he was again in bed; it was less than three months before he died. I had come with Howard Hawks, and Ford gave us five minutes, throwing the usual banter at me about my incessant questions: "Howard, does he ask *you* all those damn questions too?" Hawks nodded, grinning. He and Ford and I were pretending that nothing was any different, as though Ford were not pale and weak and ninety-eight pounds and often in excruciating pain. I had entered the room a fraction early and seen Ford assume a casual pose with his cigar. He puffed it nonchalantly until we left. I called him once more from Europe but he couldn't hear me. Kate Hepburn visited him often. The day before his death, Wayne arrived. "Come for the death watch, Duke?" Ford asked. His last words were "May I please have a cigar?" He finished the cigar and, about three hours later, he died.

JOHN FORD *was born on February 1, 1895, in Cape Elizabeth, Maine. Christened Sean Aloysius O'Fienne, he was the last of thirteen children of Irish immigrant parents. The boy was known simply as John Feeney.*

Like his parents, he spoke both Gaelic and English.

As his grandson Dan Ford relates in Pappy, The Life of John Ford, *young*

349

Feeney stood six feet two and weighed 175 pounds. At Portland High School, where he excelled at football, he adopted the name Jack because he thought it sounded as tough as the sport. He was also called Bull Feeney.

Rejected by the U.S. Naval Academy, he went to Hollywood in 1914, after his mother spotted his older brother Francis on the "flicker" screen of Portland's Empire Theater. In Hollywood he took his successful brother's surname of Ford.

Of his craft, John Ford said, "I simply direct pictures, and if I had my way, every morning of my life I'd be behind that camera at nine o'clock waiting for the boys to roll 'em, because that's the only thing I really like to do."

In a career that spanned sixty years, he directed 136 features and documentaries, sixty-three of them silents.

His wife, whom he met on Saint Patrick's Day, 1920, regarded his career as "low Irish." What he needed, she told him, was something "more substantial."

The Fords lived in the same house for thirty-three years.

During the Depression, Ford packed his wife and children off to Manila and then booked himself passage to Hawaii aboard a Norwegian tramp steamer. (His companions were the film star George O'Brien and a Department of Agriculture tropical-insect expert. The skipper was one Captain Earling Crapp.)

He won his first Oscar in 1936, for The Informer. At the movie's preview, a year earlier, Ford had become so upset by the poor reception accorded it that he went to his car directly afterward and vomited.

Oscars followed for The Grapes of Wrath, How Green Was My Valley, and The Quiet Man. Ford prized two other Oscars that were awarded for the wartime documentaries he made for the Navy: The Battle of Midway and December 7th.

During the filming of Hurricane he caught a stagehand impersonating him—complete with pipe, fedora, and New England accent. The man was fired the next day.

When Ford first worked with John Wayne (then Marion Morrison), he challenged Wayne to try to tackle him. The actor (six feet four and two hundred pounds) knocked the director to the ground. Ford got up, dusted himself off, and said, "Come on, let's get back to work. That's enough of this bullshit."

When Ernest Hemingway came to Hollywood in July 1937 to raise money for the Spanish Loyalist cause, Ford met him at the home of Frederic March and was impressed enough to contribute at least one thousand dollars. Later he wrote his nephew, who was fighting in the International Brigade: "I am glad you got some of the good part of the Feeney blood."

Ford and his hard-drinking buddies—including Wayne, Ward Bond, and Johnny Weissmuller—were such regulars at the Hollywood Athletic Club that the management set aside a room for their meetings. The group's name: "The Young Men's Purity Total Abstinence and Yachting Association." Its motto: Jews but no dues. Its elected president: John "Buck" Buchanan, the black steam-room attendant.

In time, their meeting place changed to the Araner, Ford's 110-foot gaff-rigged ketch. The group called itself the Emerald Bay Yacht Club and added another motto: "The yacht club for people who don't like yacht clubs."

He was famous for cheating at golf and as a bridge player was so bellicose and profane that he had trouble finding partners.

He was a notoriously poor dresser. His collars were usually frayed, the seat of his pants usually was shiny, and his socks rarely matched. As often as not, he showed up at work with an old necktie wrapped around his waist for a belt.

When he was appointed lieutenant commander in the Naval Reserve, however, he bought every uniform the Navy had: summer khakis, winter wools, dress whites and blues, watch coats, and greatcoats. Perfectly tailored and perfectly kept.

He was an alcoholic. On at least two occasions, his wife checked him into a hospital after he had been drunk for weeks. In 1954 the filming of Mister Roberts *was held up for days as the company waited for the director to sober up.*

After Ford made The Long Voyage Home, *a film adaptation of some Eugene O'Neill plays, O'Neill told Ford that it was the best film ever made from his work. Moved to the point of tears, Ford said, "If there's any single thing that explains either of us, it's that we're Irish."*

He died of cancer on August 31, 1973, at his home near Palm Desert, California. While he was dying he had a mass celebrated each day in his room.

ADVOCATES

The Strength to Persevere

THEIR CRUSADES WERE WAGED ACROSS LANDSCAPES REAL AND SYMBOLIC. THE Advocates' purpose, one way or another, was to surmount oppression— that which was imposed by outsiders, and that which we imposed on ourselves.

All were master politicians, though their oratorical styles and campaign strategies, their constituencies and oppositions, were as different as possible. Rachel Carson, for instance, was a private soul who used straightforward sentences to fight the destruction of the planet. By contrast, Malcolm X was a firebrand. Malcolm's was the message of the clenched fist. He received his education in prisons and slums, then in turn taught America a lesson in dignity.

In most of the cases that follow, the principal weapons were books. *Silent Spring. The Autobiography of Malcolm X. Unsafe at Any Speed. The Feminine Mystique. All the President's Men. Baby and Child Care.* The numerous titles by Edmund Wilson. Each made a profound difference in how we managed our public and private affairs—and did so in an age when, some say, nobody reads anymore.

Other Advocates used more-modern means. They rode the airwaves. Edward R. Murrow, while staring straight at the camera, drove the stake through Joe McCarthy. John F. Khanlian, along with a multitude for whom he stands here as a particular example, clenched his fist in the face of our war in Vietnam. It was television that unfurled the protester's banner.

The Advocates led their assaults into our collective preserves. And into our most private. Betty Friedan touched the fuse that blew the American housewife out of the kitchen and into the workplace. Within two decades, the national economy was markedly changed. Indeed, so were the intimate whispers between man and woman, alone in a darkened room.

Earl Warren, a surprising crusader, led a nine-man force that defined and defended the inalienable rights of all Americans. He did more to alter law and education than any other individual of our time.

The Advocates changed our ways. How we raised our children. How we worked our gardens. How we drove our cars. How we read our books. How we treated the opposite sex. How we regarded, or disregarded, our leaders on high. How we addressed the people on the far side of the world, how we addressed those next door.

They implored, argued, railed, and reasoned. They hammered home ideas: consumer awareness, environmental protection, school integration, equal opportunity for women, racial pride. What began as so many personal crusades ended in universally accepted, utterly self-evident principles.

The Advocates did more than win their debates. They did more than put points on the scoreboard. The Advocates changed our consciousness.

—L. E.

Edmund Wilson and the Landscape of Literature

JOHN UPDIKE

IN THE LAST FIFTY YEARS, LITERARY CRITICISM, AND FOR THAT MATTER LITERARY CON-sumption, has become increasingly academic. Who would read good books if college students were not compelled to read them? And who would write about them if professors were not obliged, for reasons of career advancement, to publish something from time to time? Yet the leading American critic of this era was a man, Edmund Wilson, who held no more advanced degree than a bachelor of arts from Princeton and whose stints of teaching were brief and few. He once wrote that "after trying to do something with teaching and rather enjoying it at first . . . I've decided that the whole thing, for a writer, is unnatural, embarrassing, disgusting, and that I might better do journalism, after all, when I have to make money." Not that he was against education. Indeed, he seems to have enjoyed and cherished his own more than most. He maintained until the older man's death an affectionate correspondence with Christian Gauss, the favorite of his Princeton professors, and wrote an admiring and grateful memoir of his prep school instructor in Greek: "The thing that glowed for me through Xenophon and Homer in those classrooms of thirty years ago has glowed for me ever since." To Greek and Latin, French and Italian, Wilson added self-taught German, Russian, Hebrew, and Hungarian. One of his complaints about academicians, indeed, was that they were too lazy to read much, and hence elevated the reputations of unprolific writers like T. S. Eliot. Wilson was an immense reader who communicated on almost every one of his thousands of pages of criticism the invigorating pleasure—the brisk winds and salubrious exercise—to be had in the landscape of literature.

There was a musty, walled-in quality about his childhood. He was born in 1895 in Red Bank, New Jersey. His father, Edmund Wilson Sr., was a brilliant and successful lawyer, attorney general for the state of New Jersey under two administrations, yet with something eccentric and delicate about him; he was often, his son tells us in his memoir *A Prelude*, "in eclipse in some sanitorium for what were then called 'neurasthenics.'" The mother of the household, the former Helen Mather Kimball, was hard to get at in another way; she was deaf (she went deaf, in fact, shortly after being told that her husband was mad) and devoted herself to her gardens. Wilson was an only child. His solitude found relief in the array of aunts and uncles that his genteel Presbyterian background provided, and in books. He early pointed himself toward literature. Before he was able to read, he tells us in another memoir, *Upstate*, he suddenly said to himself, "I am a poet," and then corrected this to, "No: I am not quite a poet, but I am something of the kind." By the age of seventeen he was exchanging with his friend Alfred Bellinger precocious literary opinions upon Kipling, Meredith, Shaw, and Pater. At Princeton he fell in with Scott Fitzgerald and John Peale Bishop and remained ever after their enthusiastic, if sometimes chastening, comrade in the pursuit of literary immortality. Though he could be brusque and was invariably frank, loyalty and friendship were among the gifts and appetites the shy boy from Red Bank developed. The Princeton idyll ended in 1916; he got a job as a reporter with the New York *Evening Sun* and extended his collegiate life pleasantly into Manhattan's bohemia. But all pleasantness ended as America entered the war; though he had "never really felt it [his] duty to fight in this war," he enlisted in a hospital unit and served as a stretcher-bearer in France. Like Hemingway, though he made much less of it, Wilson handled the mustard-gas-blinded, the mutilated, and the dead. World War I was the rite of passage for the "lost" generation, from which it emerged wiser than its years and furious to live and to achieve.

Wilson did not set out to be a critic. He settled into New York in 1919 to be a free-lance writer, and some of his projects during the Twenties sound Dadaesque: a letter of 1922 gleefully announces a "tremendous burlesque . . . which will deal with the expedition to capture the glyptodon or plesiosaurus or whatever it is in Patagonia," and in 1924 he traveled to California in hopes (vain) of persuading Charlie Chaplin to take a role in a "great super-ballet" he had written. Wilson composed much poetry, for which he had an indifferent ear, and wrote plays, one of which, *The Crime in the Whistler Room*, was produced in New York by the Provincetown Players. (The leading actress, Mary Blair, became the first of his four wives.) He served as theater critic for *The Dial*, as managing editor for *Vanity Fair*, and as literary editor for *The New Republic*; he wrote reviews for the latter but the three books he published in this decade were all belles lettres: *The Undertaker's Garland* (poems and stories, with John Peale Bishop, 1922); *Discordant Encounters* (plays and dialogues, 1926); and *I Thought of Daisy* (a novel, 1929). The novel, which cost Wilson much Proustian cerebration, now seems a somewhat crabbed valentine to the Greenwich Village of bootleg gin and Edna St. Vincent Millay. Wilson as a fiction writer is far from contemptible: he creates a solid world, has an unforced feel for the macabre and for moral decay, and allows eroticism its centrality in human doings. But aside from the erotic episodes, something leaden and saturnine depresses our attentiveness; Wilson could never skim along the way a story-teller must, simply delighted by surfaces.

The truth may be that the personalities he encountered in life meant less to him than those he met in print. After 1930 his biography becomes largely bibliography. While revising, with much difficulty, *I Thought of Daisy*, Wilson was with relative ease enlarging some essays on Symbolism and its successors into a critical work, *Axel's Castle* (1931): here his indispensable oeuvre begins. Though the individual chapters on Yeats, Valéry, Eliot, Proust, Joyce, Stein, and Rimbaud might be faulted, the sum portrait of modernism was vivid, highly appreciative, historically informed, justly balanced, and unprecedented: authors and writings still little more than rumors or jokes to the general public (and the academic establishment) were, without a trace of popularizing tendency, placed in clear perspective. Wilson was an exemplary animator of authors; his ability to distill out of a mass of reading the shape of a book or the soul of its creator showed a strength of the earth-moving kind and a confidence we might call patrician. A. E. Housman and Henry James would never be the same for those who read the essays on them in *The Triple Thinkers* (1938). The long essays on Dickens and Kipling in *The Wound and the Bow* (1941), which added a phrase to the language, excite us like detective stories as Wilson probes the works for the wounded psyche behind them. He was fearless in judgment; who else in 1938 was praising Henry Miller and panning Louis Bromfield? He would tackle anything; it occurred to him one day "that nobody had ever presented in intelligible human terms the development of Marxism and the other phases of the modern idea of history. . . . I knew that this would put me to the trouble of learning German and Russian and that it would take me far afield . . . but I found myself excited by the challenge." The result was his magnum opus of the Thirties, *To the Finland Station* (1940).

He faithfully and with confessional honesty kept journals, which toward the end of his life he had begun to edit for publication and which Leon Edel is posthumously ushering into print. The third, *The Forties*, was issued in 1983. Wilson's life did seem to fall into decades; he caroused and clowned with the Twenties and brooded over socialism with the Thirties. In the Forties he withdrew from metropolitan life, in 1941 buying a home in Wellfleet, on Cape Cod, and in 1944 finding in *The New Yorker* the ideal sponsor for the physical and mental travels that he loved. In 1946 he published his one best seller, *Memoirs of Hecate County*, and married the last of his four wives, Elena Mumm Thornton. His second wife, Margaret Canby, had died of a fall in Santa Barbara in 1932; his third, Mary McCarthy, recorded her own vision of the early Wellfleet years in her novel *A Charmed Life* and some brilliant short stories. Without forsaking Wellfleet, Elena, or *The New Yorker*, Wilson was drawn in his later decades more and more to the old family summer estate in Talcott-ville, New York, and to reflections upon family history and his own past. His once vivacious interest in contemporary writing settled instead upon such subjects of recondite research as Indian land claims and the Dead Sea Scrolls. But to the end of his life in 1972 he remained a lodestar—an American mind European in its scope and its delight in its own play. One of his late collections is entitled A *Piece of My Mind*—an irreverent friend of mine suggested it should have been called *Kiss My Mind*. Wilson might have appreciated the joke; he tolerated the undignified nickname of "Bunny," wrote limericks in letters to his friends, was an amateur magician who put on shows for children, and to the end of his days showed a cheerful capacity for liquor.

His virtues were old-fashioned American ones: industriousness, enthusiasm, directness, integrity. Among his books is an invaluable anthology, *The Shock of Recognition* (1943), subtitled "The Development of Literature in the United States Recorded by the Men Who Made It." He urged the creation of a definitive series of the classic American literary texts, like the French Pléiade editions—an idea now being handsomely realized by The Library of America. If in Wilson's last decade he soured on the official United States, it was a possessive grandee sourness in the style of Thoreau and Henry Adams. Tax difficulties over his *Hecate County* royalties led to the self-serving fulminations of *The Cold War and the Income Tax* (1963) and the Swiftian preface to the mockingly titled *Patriotic Gore* (1962). Yet *Patriotic Gore* itself is a masterpiece of appreciation of nineteenth-century minds and moral struggle and constitutes a substantial bequest to Wilson's native tradition. In even the quirkiest corner of his production, however, he enriched the American scene as a paragon of intellectual energy and curiosity.

EDMUND WILSON *was born on May 8, 1895, in Red Bank, New Jersey.*

When he was young he was a compulsive list maker. He would list dirty stories, esoteric and vulgar words, and topics suitable for discussion with his deaf mother.

At Princeton he disliked athletics and preferred to read in bed. He wore orange ties and rode an English bicycle. He was voted "worst poet." It was at Princeton that his classmate F. Scott Fitzgerald called him Bunny, as a comment on his shyness.

He enlisted as a private in the Army "to get away from my old life. . . . My life had seemed to me both false and dull; and though I disliked the Army extremely, I got a good deal of satisfaction out of it."

Telling a friend about his new position at The New Republic, *Wilson said, "The magazine has become so dull that the editors themselves say they are unable to read it and the subscribers are dying like flies. . . ."*

In 1924 he tried to persuade Charlie Chaplin to dance in a pantomime ballet he had written. The ballet was designed for "full orchestra, movie machine, typewriters, radio, phonograph, riveter, electromagnet, alarm clock, telephone bells, and jazz band." Chaplin was amused, but he declined.

He suffered a nervous breakdown in the 1930s. He subsequently became concerned, in The Wound and the Bow, *with the relation of neurosis to art.*

He picketed the State Department during the Sacco-Vanzetti trial.

He made a few enemies when he wrote a New Yorker *column asking, "Why Do People Read Detective Stories?" He didn't like mysteries: "One had supposed that the ghost story itself was already an obsolete form; that it had been killed by the electric light. . . . The general run of ghosts needed the darkness. . . ."*

He loved jokes, puppetry, and magic tricks. In one of his favorite tricks he turned a handkerchief into a rabbit. When he accepted the MacDowell Medal, he rolled it between his palms to show he could make it disappear.

He did not teach, give lectures or interviews, make publicity statements, appear on TV, or write books or articles to order. He listed all these policies next to small boxes on a printed postcard; inquirers received a postcard with the appropriate box checked off.

He spent most of his life away from cities. He had a house in Wellfleet, Massachusetts, and in Talcottville, New York.

His outfit for summers at Wellfleet, on Cape Cod, was a stained Panama hat, brown Bermuda shorts, and a long white dress shirt.

He was stout and of medium height, with a big head and patrician features. Zelda Fitzgerald once called him "beautiful and bloodless."

After one meeting he fell deeply in love with poet Edna St. Vincent Millay. He wrote: "Edna ignited for me both my intellectual passion and my unsatisfied desire, which went up together in a blaze of ecstasy that remains for me one of the high points of my life." Her promiscuity hurt him, but he could laugh about her numerous lovers—whom he called the alumni association.

He always fought with waiters about the check. Edith Oliver recalls him saying, "But we didn't eat any bread. You've added it up wrong; it's much less."

Wilson filed no income tax returns from 1946 to 1955 because he felt his income, which averaged two thousand dollars a year from 1947 to 1951, was too small. For this, the government dunned him for $69,000 in penalties and interest.

He never learned to drive a car. Once, however, he did buy a motorcycle: the first time he rode it, he wrecked it and was arrested for driving without a license.

Arthur Mizener wrote of Wilson: "It was his habit to put his head into people's offices in a friendly way and then discover he could think of nothing with which to pass the time of day."

Wilson did not use a typewriter. He said, "I believe that composing on the typewriter has probably done more than anything else for deteriorating English prose."

He once wrote: ". . . as an American, I am more or less in the 18th century—or at any rate, not much later than the early 19th."

He died on June 12, 1972, in Talcottville. On his tombstone is inscribed in Hebrew: "Be strong. Be strong, and let us strengthen one another."

The Case of
Earl Warren v.
Earl Warren

FRANCES FITZGERALD

ASK ANY AMERICAN TO NAME THE GREAT STATESMEN OF THE PAST HALF CENTURY, and the answer will almost invariably begin with the war leaders: Roosevelt and Eisenhower in this country, Churchill and de Gaulle abroad. Press on and ask who are the great American statesmen of the postwar period, and your interlocutor will pause. He or she will bring up the names of American Presidents and secretaries of state and then dismiss each of them with more or less reluctance: if it hadn't been for the assassination . . . for the Vietnam War. Speculation will follow on such questions as: Why do great leaders seem to emerge only in wars or in times of crisis? Why have there been no great leaders in this country for the past forty years? But there is a trick involved. For there was a great American statesman in the postwar period, and he was Earl Warren.

American historians have yet to sort out the postwar history of this country, with the result that most people look upon the Sixties as a period of confusion, most of it still unresolved. But to look quite narrowly at the history of the law in the late Fifties and Sixties is to see a steady and consistent march of reform. In the early Fifties the United States was a legally segregated country—like South Africa in certain respects. Its government, in conflict with totalitarian regimes, developed new security services and new congressional committees with frightening new powers over the lives of its citizens. At the same time, its political fabric remained largely nineteenth century: power resided in the rotten boroughs and in the big-city machines. The Warren Court changed all that, and a good deal else as well. It created much of what we refer to when we speak of civil rights and civil liberties.

Earl Warren was a controversial figure in the Fifties and Sixties. Not only were the Birchers trying to impeach him but liberal law professors were debating whether he had not pushed the Court over the bounds of its authority. At the time of his retirement many legal scholars called him—for better or worse—the most influential Chief Justice since John Marshall. Since then, however, there has been surprisingly little public interest in him. (He looms large only in the minds of those who advocate school prayer.) The author of a recent biography of Warren, Professor G. Edward White of the University of Virginia law school, attributes this to the apparent blandness of the man—to the general perception that he was a relatively simple man of ordinary talents who happened to occupy a highly visible position in an important moment in history. White is correct, but it is also true that the legal revolution carried out by the Warren Court has been so well assimilated as to disappear into history. The philosopher Sir Isaiah Berlin once said that a great man is one who can turn a paradox into a platitude within his lifetime. That is what the Warren Court did. And that is—paradoxically—why it is not given its historical due.

The Warren Court is generally remembered for the school desegregation decision *Brown* v. *Board of Education.* What many forget is the scope of that decision and the multitude of other antisegregation decisions that followed it. The Warren Court struck down the entire legal basis for discrimination—and it did so in the face of an administration largely indifferent to the plight of black Americans. Its impact on other areas of public policy was similarly broad. In a series of decisions on criminal law the Court gave substance to the Fourth, Fifth, and Sixth Amendments. It gave all Americans rights that only some had enjoyed in the past: it gave the poor the right to counsel and the right to appeal a conviction; it also gave effective protection against self-incrimination and illegal search and seizure. With the reapportionment decisions the Court put the principle of "one man, one vote" into practice for the first time in American history. In interpreting the First Amendment the Court significantly enlarged press freedoms, the freedom of citizens to criticize public figures, and the freedom of artists to express themselves in unconventional ways. In the Fifties it was the Warren Court—not the Eisenhower administration—that stood up to the House Un-American Activities Committee and Hoover's FBI, restricting the power of the government to penalize individuals because of their beliefs or associations. Its decisions on the right to political dissent may alone have held the government to its constitutional moorings during the political storms of the Sixties and Seventies.

The Chief Justice did not, of course, make this legal revolution by himself. The very conception of it, as Anthony Lewis has pointed out, owed a great deal to Justice Black, and much of the analytical thinking, particularly in the First Amendment cases, came from Justice Douglas and later Justice Brennan. Still, the great achievements of the Warren Court would have been inconceivable without Warren—without the experience of practical politics he brought to the Court and without his strength of character and leadership. Scholars of the law have criticized him for a lack of philosophical consistency and a lack of analytical finesse, but it may be that even a certain intellectual bluntness contributed to his success. Possibly no one but a man who seemed ordinary, average, and unintellectual could have brought a legal revolution to this country and made it stick.

Warren's career—his life, in fact—presents interesting problems for the biographer. The author of *Brown* was, after all, the same man who took major responsibility for putting the Nisei Japanese into detention camps during World War II. The man who, in the *Miranda* decision, formulated a new criminal justice code had violated most of the rules in that code as district attorney. The Justice who curbed HUAC had once himself pursued "Communistic radicals" and created a loyalty oath for all California state employees. Chief Justice Warren thought the reapportionment decisions the most important of his judicial career—yet as governor of California he had opposed the redistricting of his own state. In his autobiography Warren does not resolve these inconsistencies or explain them away.

The popular view of Warren is that of a big, affable man—a featureless Republican politician who turned into a crusading liberal as a result of his experience on the Court. Eisenhower seems to have had this impression; according to Warren, he once called the appointment of his Chief Justice "the biggest damn fool thing I ever did." But this account of Warren is far from the whole story. In the first place, several extant biographies of him show a gradual political evolution beginning much earlier in his career. In the second place, those who knew Warren describe him as anything but a malleable character. The picture they draw is of a staunch, principled man, self-confident to the point of arrogance—a man who liked to take the lead and who chafed under authority. There is no paradox here. Warren had a strong core of moral and political values but, no political thinker, he reinterpreted these values constantly and almost without self-consciousness. Abstractions meant little to him: he thought himself autonomous and behaved as if he were. The man who most changed the laws and standards of this country was himself most profoundly changed by the times and circumstances in which he lived. Yet he changed his views independently and at his own pace—thus confounding those who explained him reductively with a political label or an account of the political pressures upon him.

Warren grew up in Bakersfield, California, at the beginning of the century, the son of a car repairman and inspector for the Southern Pacific railroad. His parents, both of Scandinavian stock, were frugal, hardworking people who taught their son the value of a dollar and the importance of an education. From the age of fifteen, Warren worked every summer in the rail yards; he saw the building of industrial America and saw the toll it took on families like his own. He went to college and law school at the University of California, Berkeley, and thereafter made northern California his home. After about two years in private practice, he went into the office of the district attorney in Alameda County; the rest of his career was spent in public service. Elected district attorney in 1926, he earned a statewide reputation in the job by doing successful battle against bootlegging, racketeering, graft, and corruption. From Alameda County he organized a state law enforcement association and reformed law enforcement procedures throughout California. In 1938 he was elected attorney general and four years later, governor of California. He served three terms as governor and, reelected with ever-increasing majorities, he became a figure to reckon with in the national Republican party. In 1948 he, rather reluctantly, accepted the nomination for Vice-President on the Dewey ticket and had his only experience of losing an election. At the 1952 Republican convention, as the leader of the California delegation, he threw an important procedural vote to Eisenhower though it closed off his only chance for the nomination. Eisenhower—a man almost immune to political gratitude—found him the logical choice for a vacancy on the Supreme Court in 1953.

When Warren was first elected governor, in 1942, liberal Democrats in the state (including the defeated governor, Culbert Olson, and his housing and immigration commissioner, Carey McWilliams) predicted a period of Republican reaction. As district attorney and attorney general, Warren had been a favorite of what McWilliams called "the Chandler-Hearst-Knowland clique." He had espoused conventional Republican views, championing law and order and the free enterprise system, denouncing Communists, radicals, and aliens. In the famous Point Lobos murder case he had convicted four trade union radicals with the help of a bugging device, coercive interrogation, and prejudicial pretrial publicity (all practices he later outlawed). As attorney general he had blocked the appointment of a liberal Berkeley law professor to the California Supreme Court, charging him with Communist associations. When World War II broke out, he campaigned for a military order to evacuate all persons of Japanese ancestry from the Coast and put them in detention camps. The order was a popular one in California; President Roosevelt signed it, the U.S. Congress endorsed it, and the Supreme Court sustained its constitutionality. But Warren had led the campaign for it, and his public statements about the threat of subversion from "the Japs" showed him as an unreconstructed nativist.

But liberal Democratic predictions to the contrary, Warren's record as governor after ten years was in many ways more liberal than that of Olson himself. Warren fought the oil companies (the companies, with stunning lack of foresight, opposed a gas tax for the construction of highways); he battled the private utilities for public water power projects; and he fought a long and quixotic struggle with the California Medical Association over his plan for a state health insurance system. An able administrator, he staffed important state offices with nonpartisan experts—and with Democrats as well as Republicans. In 1950 he signed into law a loyalty oath for all state employees, but he did so only after a bitter battle with right-wingers in his party over a loyalty oath specifically for the Berkeley faculty. In 1952 right-wingers in the state were calling him a socialist, and Carey McWilliams was calling him an opportunist. A later Democratic governor, Edmund G. "Pat" Brown, called him the best governor the state had ever had.

But Warren was more consistent than his critics understood. The "liberal" and "conservative" labels were merely misleading in his case, for Warren was an old-line Progressive. In college in 1909 he had campaigned for Hiram Johnson, the most powerful and influential of the California Progressives; as district attorney he had seen himself as a professional law enforcement officer and had adopted the Progressive tactic of cross-filing and running in all the primaries. When the Roosevelt landslides wiped out much of the Republican party in the state, Warren survived by maintaining his independence and running on his own record. The Republican press backed him, but the big corporate money did not—and for good reason, since Warren actually believed in free enterprise. His apparently contradictory political attitudes made sense in Progressive terms. White and generally middle-class people, the Progressives wanted clean government, and a government that would serve to defend the interests of the citizen against those of "the special interests": that is, not only the rackets but the political machines and the powerful corporations. As they saw it, the evils of the country came from the great concentrations of wealth and the great concentrations of immigrants. At once populists and nativists, they identified communism and socialism as "alien" ideologies. Thinking of themselves as standing above partisan politics and representing all Americans of goodwill, they saw their role as returning the country to the traditions of the Founding Fathers.

Warren's political views evolved from this Progressive base, but the man remained throughout his life the Progressive ideal type. He lacked vulgar ambition. Austere and even puritanical (the obscenity cases tested his First Amendment scruples to the limit and sometimes beyond), he lived for his work and for his family. He and his wife raised six admirable children and had a tranquil domestic life. He supported his family exclusively on his government salary: he made no outside investments, indeed made no money. His probity was absolute and his integrity unquestionable. For him the ethical questions—what was right, what was fair—always came first. No intellectual, he was an activist and a man who learned by experience. His campaign for a health insurance policy began after he spent a short time in the hospital and realized that many people could not afford hospitalization. He had sympathy, and he had humor, though it was not of the ironic kind. His self-confidence was great enough to permit him to change his mind—and to acknowledge it. Unlike most of the establishment figures involved in the Nisei internment, he later expressed regret about the decision. At all times, however, he had the Progressives' sense of legitimacy in the American tradition—the sense that he represented all Americans of goodwill. This confidence never failed—perhaps in part because the voters almost always seemed to agree.

In his ten years as governor Warren learned a great deal about the world. His horizons expanded—to some extent literally, in the geographic sense. In 1942 he was a provincial: California was then a provincial part of the country, and

Warren had traveled very little outside of it. The 1948 vice-presidential campaign gave him an opportunity to see the rest of the country, and as governor he began to travel abroad. His trip to Japan, and later his trips to Europe, the Soviet Union, and India, changed his perspective: from a nativist superpatriot he became an internationalist and finally a believer in world peace through world law. As district attorney and attorney general, he saw the state through the eyes of a law enforcement officer; as governor, he saw it in many other ways. A patriarchal quality emerged. According to Pat Brown, "He felt the people of the state were in his care, and he cared for them." He saw that the government had affirmative ways of promoting justice and "wholesomeness"—a word he often used. And he began to take classically liberal positions. When the right wing of the Republican party revived in the late Forties and early Fifties, he broke with more and more of the leaders in the state. Richard Nixon became his bête noire. The two men could hardly have been more different, and Warren found Nixon personally offensive. That Nixon was making his reputation on the hunt for Communists in government was enough to make Warren question the whole enterprise of anticommunism. Warren swung around rather slowly on this issue, but after four years on the Court he took a stand in principle against witch-hunting. In a case where a former Communist was indicted for refusing to name former associates *(Watkins v. U.S.)*, he decided that the government could not make such broad-scale intrusions into the lives of citizens. The law owes a lot to Richard Nixon.

President Eisenhower chose Warren for the Supreme Court in 1953 in the conviction that the Californian was a "middle of the road" Republican. The misunderstanding was comical. Eisenhower thought of himself as "middle of the road," but then, so did Warren: the man was incapable of seeing himself as anything else—and thus that was the impression he gave. A few months later Warren surprised the President badly, for the first big case he undertook was *Brown* v. *Board of Education.* From the start he saw *Brown* as a simple matter of justice; he also saw that to overturn the "separate but equal" doctrine was so radical a move as to require a unanimous decision from the Court. As four of the Justices did not see *Brown* as a simple case, he very deliberately set about convincing them that it was. He used diplomacy, shame tactics, and sheer doggedness; finally, in May 1954, the Court handed down a unanimous decision for *Brown* written by him.

Admirers of Justice Frankfurter and of Justice Black make much of the struggle the two men fought for the juridical soul of the new Chief Justice. But Warren's temperament would never have permitted him to agree with Frankfurter on the need for judicial restraint. Warren was an activist, and, particularly with a President who abhorred activity, he felt the Court must assert its responsibility for the fulfillment of constitutional principles. Warren sided fairly consistently with Black after 1957, but his approach to the law was quite different. He did not share Black's concern for literal, textual analysis—and he did not have the theoretical bent of the justices who came from the law schools. He thought in terms of what was fair and what was good for the society, and how in the mid-twentieth century the Constitution might be preserved. What he brought to the Court was experience of the actual workings of the law and sensitivity to the needs of his countrymen. His experience allowed him to write a new code of criminal justice and a new political contract for the nation with the confidence that they would fit and work. He sympathized with the people whose fate he was deciding, and, increasingly, he put himself into the shoes of the poorest and most-despised members of the society. His sophistication lay in the political domain, and it consisted in directing the Court to the major issues of the day and to deciding them in clear statements of principle.

When Warren retired in 1969, the two great questions were whether his legal revolution would take hold and whether he had not permanently altered the historic function of the Court, straining its moral authority to the breaking point. Warren himself worried about the first question, since, as fate would have it, Richard Nixon won the presidential election six months before the Justice decided to retire. Now, just ten years after his death, he might be reassured: a much more conservative Court has kept his legacy of law—partly out of respect for precedent and partly because it acknowledges the legitimacy of the basic principles involved. Looking back, it now appears that rather than having strained the moral authority of the Court, Warren supplied it with the principles it required to carry moral weight into the second half of the twentieth century.

EARL WARREN *was born on March 19, 1891, in Los Angeles. As a boy he was devoted to a burro named Jack. Someone poisoned the burro. "My sorrow at his passing," Warren wrote in his eighties, "remains to this day."*

He was younger than his high school classmates, and too small to try out for any sports teams. His principal heroes became his school's athletic stars.

Once, while serving as a district attorney, he was questioning a police inspector in a murder trial. Sensing that the man was deranged, Warren quickly allowed him to leave the stand. Later, he learned that the man had been carrying a revolver that he intended to use on Warren.

While serving on the Supreme Court, Warren ordered a steel plate placed behind the paneling of the Justices' bench, to provide some protection against gunfire. The Justices took this precaution lightheartedly until the FBI informed them that six Ku Klux Klan members had planned to throw a bomb at the bench.

Although Warren later denied that he had tried to stop Richard Nixon's political career, in 1952 hostility between Nixon and Warren was apparent. At that year's GOP convention, Nixon, pledged as a delegate to presidential candidate Warren, revealed that his real preference was for candidate Dwight D. Eisen-

hower. *In 1962 Warren campaigned vigorously against Nixon when the former Vice-President ran for governor of California. Later, Warren wrote, Nixon worked "against me and the Court over which I presided by conveying the impression that we were a menace to the internal security of the nation."*

While considering the Brown v. Board of Education *desegregation case, he was invited by President Eisenhower to a White House dinner. Warren recalled that after dinner the President took him by the arm and told him that the citizens of the segregating states "are not bad people. All they are concerned about is to see that their sweet little girls are not required to sit in school alongside some big overgrown Negroes."*

In 1957 he informed the American Bar Association that he would refuse an invitation to attend its convention if Vice-President Nixon were also invited. The ABA did not invite Nixon, but at the convention it opened up a discussion of the Supreme Court's Communist party decisions. Surprised and angered by the discussion, Warren resigned from the ABA and never rejoined.

Heading the commission investigating the assassination of President Kennedy, he "could not sleep well for nights" after seeing the coroner's photographs of Kennedy's mutilated skull. He called his ten months on the Warren Commission "the unhappiest time of my life."

He loved football, baseball, fishing, and hunting. A friend once asked Warren if he wanted to shoot quail with some members of the Senate. "All those senators?" Warren asked. "With guns?"

While on the Court he liked to read history and biography, but not fiction. "Novels are too exciting," he explained. Nevertheless, while considering the issue of obscenity during the winter of 1965, his reading matter included Raw Dames, Screaming Flesh, Stud Broad, *and* The Whipping Chorus Girls.

When he was eighty-three, heart failure forced him into Georgetown University Hospital. Justice William Douglas recalled that Warren told him tearfully that President Nixon had denied him admission to Bethesda Naval Hospital, which Warren preferred. Gasping for breath, Warren was moved to comment on the President's refusal to deliver his Watergate tapes: "If Nixon gets away with that, then Nixon makes the law as he goes along."

On July 9, 1974, Warren died. When his casket left the Supreme Court's Great Hall, Justice Douglas saw a flight of pigeons swoop over the procession and imagined his friend's migrating soul: "I like to think that the spirit of Earl Warren is abroad in this land, quickening the conscience of our people."

The Unknown
Nonsoldier

PETER DAVIS

THE 1960S ARE READY FOR ARCHEOLOGISTS. WHO KNOWS WHAT THEY WILL MAKE OF the artifact and shard of rebellion and repression? Sifting through the rubble, they find love beads, roach clips, hand-lettered placards, nightsticks, cattle prods, forehead bandannas, crowd control bullhorns, walkie-talkies, tear-gas canisters. It is the regalia of confrontation. The war in Vietnam, going on forever, longest and least successful war in American history, brought forth its own antidote, the protest movement, which, given time, brought forth *its* own antidote, Richard Nixon, who evoked still more protest, the effect of which was to provide more anger than had been abroad at any time in the national memory, anger that did not subside until both the war and Nixon had at last disappeared.

Protest became a way of life. An astonishing moment arrived in the country during the war, a moment of unprecedented if negative passion, when Americans who knew what they did not want became more important and, in a modest sense, more powerful than Americans who did. Some were leftists sympathetic to socialism. Some were anti-imperialists who did not want America setting up colonies and policing them. Some were pure pacifists. Some were civil rights workers who moved on to the next cause after the Mississippi summer of 1964 gave way to the bombing of North Vietnam in the winter of 1965. All were united in their opposition to the war. Those who recall the antiwar movement fondly say it brought peace and a restoration of dignity; those against it say it gave Russia a domino and America a black eye.

Protesting lasted as long as the war itself. The protesters had many spokesmen, but in the end the movement was distinguished not so much by its leaders as its numbers. American wars had always evoked opposition. The Mexican and Civil wars were unpopular with many people in all sections of the Republic. Pacifists opposed both world wars, and polls showed less support for the government during the Korean conflict, as it was called, than they did even after Tet in Vietnam. But only during Vietnam did so many Americans actually *rise* against an American war. Between 1964 and 1974, according to Louis Harris and Associates, 3 percent of the population attended antiwar demonstrations where arrests were made. That means that 97 percent stayed home, but six to seven million Americans is a lot of disaffection. They marched, spoke, chanted, listened, went on strike, had teach-ins, sit-ins, sometimes had their heads clubbed, sometimes merely stood vigil.

John F. Khanlian's protests took all these forms. In a small way, for a brief moment, his image, if not his name, was recognizable to some, but John Khanlian was not famous then and is not now. He did not lead, nor could he properly be said to have followed. He protested, he said no, and he kept on saying it for a decade, along with a half dozen million others until the war finally stopped.

John Khanlian was a student at Columbia University's School of International Affairs in the spring of 1968, Columbia's spring of crisis. Campus anger erupted from several causes. The university was affiliated with the Institute for Defense Analyses. It had also begun construction of a gymnasium in Morningside Park, a project that had at first been welcomed but by 1968 was being opposed by large segments of Harlem. Student protests against defense contracts and CIA recruiting on campus had brought about disciplinary measures that the Students for a Democratic Society were fighting. After the Tet offensive in Vietnam, which was followed shortly by Lyndon Johnson's abdication and the assassination of Martin Luther King, Jr., protesters at Columbia saw the university as a microcosm of society. Under the campus SDS leader, Mark Rudd, dissent became resistance became revolution.

In late April, SDS mounted its spring offensive. Protesting Columbia's relations with the defense establishment, its plans to build the gymnasium in Harlem, and its intention to discipline several students (including Rudd) for an earlier demonstration, Mark Rudd and three hundred student rebels occupied a university building. The building was Hamilton Hall and it contained the office of the acting dean of the college, who was held prisoner for twenty-four hours. While the university administration tried to figure out what to do, black students decided that the battle over the gym was theirs and they did not want white help. They evicted SDS from Hamilton Hall on the first night of the occupation and released the dean the next afternoon, but Rudd and his colleagues shortly took over—"captured," if one was with the administration; "liberated," if one was against it—four more university buildings.

One of the buildings was Low Memorial Library, a majestic neoclassical structure, location of the offices of Columbia's president, Grayson Kirk, whom SDS saw as the academic equivalent of LBJ. The students held these buildings for a week while official Columbia shuddered, protesters debated hotly, and television viewers around the country were alternatively indignant or filled with admiration. The gymnasium and discipline issues were real, and SDS hoped ultimately to restructure the university, away from serving power interests and toward a participatory democracy; but what fueled the protest, what made it more than just another rump group with its own special crankiness, was the war.

Sympathizing with the rebellion's aims while deploring some of its tactics, John Khanlian was not even a member of SDS. Nor was he one of the original occupiers of any of the Columbia buildings. Halfway through that week he spent several hours one night in one of the five buildings, Fayerweather Hall, which was regarded—in the crisis terminology used by both sides—as held by "moderates." The atmosphere was so charged and language had moved so far to the left that one of the factions that had seized the university buildings could be described as behaving with moderation.

At the end of a week, after threats and negotiations and such a surfeit of ad hocness all around that the semiology of revolt resulted in every little meaning's having a movement all its own, Grayson Kirk finally did call in the police. Kirk had waited so long to do this that the occupation had acquired a legitimacy unanticipated at the start by even the occupiers. But there the Tactical Patrol Force was at last, in the first hours of April 30, 1968, advancing from a nervous city onto the campus of a university founded twenty-two years before the country itself. The force's job was to recapture Columbia's buildings for its administration.

In what they called *Interim Report Prepared by the First Deputy Commissioner of Police for the Commissioner of Police: Arrests Made on the Complaint of Columbia University Administration of Students Trespassing in School Buildings*, a volume whose very title echoes a general's account of Austerlitz, say, or Chickamauga, the police described what happened in meticulously factored prose almost as cleansed of muscle as it is of feeling:

> At approximately 2:30 A.M., the aforementioned police groups, together with the university representatives, approached the buildings that were under siege, and that had been barricaded and locked from the inside by the demonstrators. In front of each of these buildings a group of students and faculty members stood guard, blocking the entrance to the building. At this point, the university representative, using a bullhorn, read a prepared warning to the group requesting them to stop blocking the entrance and to permit the police to enter. This request was refused. The police superior in charge of the detail then read a police warning requesting the people to leave and this request was refused. At this point, the police forced their way through the crowd to the front of the building and opened the door to each building and entered.

John Khanlian's memory is simpler. "When the police were told to clear the campus," he recalls, "I was one of what they had to clear."

That night John Khanlian had gathered with hundreds of students and sympathetic faculty surrounding the occupied buildings, hoping to protect their university from the police, to cordon off the occupiers from attack. There had been such an escalation of both goals and rhetoric as the occupation continued that it had become possible to assemble peaceably on the university campus and believe that what was at stake was not merely the saving of student rebels from the police or the stopping of violence, but the saving of Columbia, the stopping of the Vietnam War, the ultimate if only half-deserved saving of American society.

The protesters were divided on almost everything else but were adamant in their dislike of the war, the single unifying element welding the chain they formed around the occupied buildings. The police and the administration had waited until well after midnight, in the hope that the campus would be quiet by then. Better to hope Times Square would be empty on New Year's Eve or that a condemned man could rest easy. As the Tactical Patrol Force drew near, John Khanlian, a graduate student of international affairs with a presumptive career in the foreign service of the government whose war he was opposing, linked arms with the demonstrators nearest him, stood his ground at the southeast-corner entrance to Low Memorial Library, and watched his future vanish.

After 250,000 of his fellow Armenians were massacred by the Turks around the turn of the century, John Khanlian's grandfather escaped to the United States. Like many emigrants from catastrophe, the family became instantly, passionately American. The next generation of Khanlians, with a single exception, was fervently patriotic, remembering Armenia with anguish, supporting the United States unstintingly in peace and war. The exception was one son of the original greenhorn, the first John Khanlian, who read the lesson of Armenia differently than his relatives. Born in this country in 1909, he grew up wanting nothing to do with war, massacres, revenge, or even Armenia. He wanted peace. The family was not wealthy, but the sons were able to go to college. The first John Khanlian went to Columbia—with its reputation in the 1920s for good football teams and graduates who would do well in the business and cultural establishments—and became a high school history and social studies teacher.

When he married, it was not to an Armenian but to an American woman, six years older than he, of Irish and German lineage. They lived outside New York, in various towns of Westchester County where history teachers were needed, but each Sunday they returned to Riverside Church in the city. Riverside's minister, Harry Emerson Fosdick, was a man John Khanlian admired to the point of reverence. Fosdick had supported the United States in World War I, but in the 1930s, he identified himself strongly with pacifist sentiments and vowed never again to lend his moral authority, or that of his church, to a war. In a famous sermon called "The Unknown Soldier," which John Khanlian had copies of, Reverend Fosdick made a ringing pacifist pledge that later got him into trouble with his congregation during World War II; nevertheless, it was a doctrine he adhered to firmly.

The three sons of John and Helen Khanlian grew up in a household where they felt strongly loved and sternly judged. The two older boys, Richard and Robert, recall their mother as the soft, mollifying influence and their father as the domineering presence whom they could never quite satisfy. "He cared so much," says Robert, who is now a doctor in an urgent-care clinic in Albuquerque, New Mexico, "about each thing we did or wanted to do. He loved us, but he didn't trust us to go around the block. It could get suffocating. Even when he hugged you, all you could remember was that big scratchy face up against yours." John F. Khanlian was the youngest son, born in 1945, the middle initial standing for Fosdick.

"My son didn't like his name," Helen Khanlian recalls. "He wanted to be Jack Frederick Goldberg—he had a friend named Goldberg—until one day, when he was ten, he read Fosdick's sermon on the unknown soldier. He walked into the kitchen with tears streaming down his face and said, 'Mom, I made up my mind. I'll never take part in any war.' "

John F. Khanlian's early years could be the *Boys' Life* story of the young Ben Franklin or Tom Edison. Everything is put to some good use. Like all boys, John has a little club, but what is the first rule? No fighting. When a schoolmate's mother dies of cancer, John and his club sell their old toys to send the proceeds to the American Cancer Society. Even when John plays a prank, a handy lesson is learned. At the age of six he pulls a fire alarm, then runs home and hides under the piano bench. His mother hears the hook and ladder coming around the corner, looks at the cringing John, and takes her contrite son to the Eastchester fire chief, who teaches the boy all about fire control and community responsibility. When he soaps windows on Halloween, his mother tells him some of the elderly neighbors will have trouble washing it off. John springs his club into action and they wash off not only the windows they have soaped, but everyone else's as well. "With Johnny," Helen Khanlian recalls, "sometimes I thought, What is with this boy, he's too good, he's not normal. But then he always left his shoes in the middle of the floor where you fell over them. He still does."

All the boys were tall, but none of them liked to fight. When Robert was beaten up by the neighborhood bully, Richard, the eldest and biggest brother, went over to the bully's house to avenge his brother's honor. He, too, was beaten up, and what he remembers is that he did not really fight once he had taken his stand. When their position had been established, they would follow it up not with physical force but with the testimony, the *argument*, of non-violence.

The Khanlian brothers did not seem characteristic of the men who built America. Neither aggressive, belligerent, nor hostile, they did not resemble Kit Carson, Jay Gould, Henry Ford, or any of the James brothers. No lonesome cowboys, they liked company, liked to act in groups, in concert, cooperatively rather than competitively. Richard and Robert and John Khanlian did not fight, but neither did they run. They always wanted to see what was going on, and to be *seen* to be witnessing, as though their sheer presence was a moral force. When they could, they stopped the fight, and when they could not, they stayed to witness.

But they had the elder John Khanlian to contend with, the loving father so overbearing that all three of his boys were afraid in his presence. The youngest, John, was least afraid; his father had mellowed somewhat by the time John, six years younger than Richard and four years younger than Robert, came along. Robert thinks their father, though he loved his subject and taught it passionately, wanted to be more than a social studies teacher. "We paid for his frustrations," Robert says.

The boys all grew to well over six feet, but they recall allowing themselves to be bullied and intimidated by their father the whole time they lived at home. "We were afraid to confront him directly," says Richard, who now teaches basic math and industrial-safety procedures at the Technical Vocational Institute in Albuquerque, where, coincidentally, the former Columbia SDS leader, Mark Rudd, also teaches. "Yet we were afraid not because he would punish us, but because we didn't feel *he* could take it if we openly rebelled. It was our father, not us, who would be crushed by our rebellion." So the boys did not rebel. They bided their time and simply went their own ways after they grew up. Before settling down, Richard drifted to Paris, Robert worked as a mailman in San Francisco and was an itinerant student at several colleges, and John went west to Earlham, a Quaker college in Richmond, Indiana.

When the Vietnam War began, the draft posed no threat to Richard. He stood six feet eight inches, ineligible for the armed forces, but he wrote his draft board anyway to tell them he would not serve even if they wanted him. Robert simply refused: the draft, the Army, the war. He finally got a letter from a psychiatrist to make his refusal legitimate. John Khanlian, with Fosdick his mentor as well as his middle name, told his draft board he would be a conscientious objector. Their father wrote indignant letters to *The New York Times*. (In the course of his long epistolary career, *the Times* published over forty of them.) "I wash my hands of the whole thing," the elder John Khanlian said of the Vietnam War. "Those protesters ought to go down to the White House and take it apart brick by brick." The sons kept their father's principles and philosophy; it was only his temperament from which they had to distance themselves.

He is six feet four inches tall and large boned, but the overwhelming first impression John F. Khanlian has made on almost everyone he has met since age eighteen—man or woman, teacher or preacher, colleague or client, draft board official or counselor—is of gentleness. He appears to want to help, to please. He appeared that way in the fall of 1963 to Louisa Wright when they were both freshmen at Earlham. The evening they met, Louisa told John she liked people with really large families. John told Louisa that was good because he had nine brothers and sisters. She still liked him after he told her the truth, and their relationship became serious almost immediately. John's other serious involvement during his years at Earlham was his opposition to the war. He and Louisa would break up periodically and then get back together, but he never wavered on Vietnam.

As a Quaker college, Earlham attracts numerous undergraduates possessing a special longing for peace. On a circular grassy space in the center of the campus, known as The Heart, Earlhamites against the Vietnam War held vigils. It was a college tradition not to walk on The Heart, but teachers and students who opposed the war would stand in the space to register their protest. By 1965 they were marching into downtown Richmond, where there were enough rednecks that someone always called the protesters "nigger-loving Commies." In 1966, during the off-year elections in which Vietnam first became a political issue, John Khanlian was involved in a campaign to encourage pledges from congressional candidates that they would negotiate directly with the National Liberation Front to end the war. They got few pledges and elected fewer candidates, but success was never what drove John Khanlian. He kept on protesting because there was a war and he was against it.

Early in 1967 John and some classmates took buses from Earlham to a huge antiwar rally in Central Park. They massed in the Sheep Meadow, enough of them for a small city—activists said 400,000, the police granted 125,000—and they marched to the United Nations, picking up support as they went. John has few heroes, but one of them was present at the UN. "This was the most exciting peace demonstration I ever went to," John remembers, "and the genuine thrill was that Martin Luther King was there. If there is such a thing as a group feeling, with everyone sharing and hoping and even praying for the same thing, I think we had it that day. Stokely Carmichael talked first. He said we were raping Vietnam and when there's a rape going on you don't want negotiations but total withdrawal. I liked that, but King was simply a mountain. He spoke—he *preached*—about the dignity of all men and the need for brotherhood, and he united the struggle for rights at home with that in Vietnam. He said the war in Vietnam stopped us from winning the war on poverty and discrimination in our own country. By the time the day ended, I had the feeling we could actually help bring peace. Yet American involvement in the war lasted six more years, five years longer than King himself did."

A sour note for John was the way the press handled the event. "It always made me resentful that the media focused on the farthest-out element in the crowd, the loudest shouters, those dressed most weirdly, people making statements having nothing to do with the war, like 'Get stoned,' or 'Fuck the pigs.' Anything that provided a quick fifteen seconds of copy, they went for. The overall message of hundreds of thousands of people saying no to the war, petitioning our government to stop the war, was undermined by false media attention to the exotic. The press and TV always look for personalities; they don't seem to understand a collective movement."

By the end of 1967 John had attended other marches and demonstrations, gone to other cities and to Army induction centers, and was counseling draft resisters. One day he stood on the steps of the New York Public Library and read two hours' worth of names of Americans who had died in Vietnam. He had also married Louisa Wright, and they were living near Columbia, where John was studying for his master's degree in international affairs. He had spent a summer in Eastern Europe—in Poland, Hungary, East Germany, and Yugoslavia. "These closed societies didn't offer us a social view we wanted to bring home," John says, "but we did perceive the humanity of our so-called adversaries. That's always dangerous to war making because when you see your enemies as people, you start to realize what a small planet we share." The prospect of a foreign service career, of being able to build bridges between countries as readily as he could befriend individuals, intrigued him. It did not seem impossible at the time for one to be both a pacifist and an official of the U.S. government.

"Louisa must have wondered what she married into," John says. "As soon as the demonstrations began at Columbia, I was hardly ever home. All day I was at the School of International Affairs, at night I'd go to the rallies. We really thought we could stop the war and help change our society."

In time, they were able to accomplish the first of those aims, or at least contribute mightily to the eventual peace. The second goal, however, eluded John Khanlian and his fellow protesters. Although divided on many of their goals, really united only on that of peace itself, they instructed their elders on moral precepts as no recent generation has—perhaps not since the time of the Crusades. They were, indeed, on a kind of crusade: blacks were equal; women were equal; sexuality was good; homosexuals had rights; racial integration was good (until it was bad, at which point it became a plot to destroy black culture); democracy should be participatory, not merely representative. But preeminently, the war was wrong. Variations on the theme said the war was not just wrong but typical of our economic system, not just wrong but an inevitable product of the American political machine, not just wrong but criminal—legally, morally, and constitutionally criminal.

The movement rolled on, unaffected by fear of failure. It was a heady time for those petitioning their leaders, a time of therapeutic intention matched with what felt like a reasonable prospect of success. John Khanlian's hopes were equal to his ideals in the 1960s. No American leadership had ever kindled hopes as the Kennedy and, to an insufficiently recognized degree, Johnson administrations had. It was only after LBJ's declaration of war on poverty and racism that his undeclared war on Vietnam dashed the hope he himself had inspired. The mean little chant, "Hey! Hey! LBJ! How many kids did you kill today?" was not for the frying of Asian babies alone but for the destruction of the illusions of American youth. Thus it was in the United States, as in Vietnam, that a generation of refugees was created, alienated from their traditional society, unable to form a new one of their own.

Louisa Khanlian was a refugee in Morningside Heights. "I opposed the war as much as John," she recalls, "but I was supporting us as editor of a newsletter for the National Council of Churches while he went to class and to demonstrations. I felt inferior to his classmates, who were studying Serbo-Croatian or Chinese, and I guess I felt inferior to John also. I could deal with him alone, but

I didn't feel up to seeing his friends. What was nice was on Sundays we'd take *the Times* to Riverside Park and spend the whole day reading the paper and playing Frisbee with each other. We talked about saving money for the education of our children although we didn't even dream of having any yet." In 1968 Louisa Khanlian was innocent, fearful, idealistic, filled with yearnings for her husband and the future.

Then John Khanlian became a poster.

"With its classified research for the Institute for Defense Analyses that fed the Pentagon and CIA, I didn't like Columbia being the third leg of the military-industrial complex," John Khanlian says. "I was certainly sympathetic to the issues being raised at Columbia, although I was somewhat disillusioned by the cult of personality fostered not only by the media but by some of the leaders themselves. One day Mark Rudd was walking near me on campus and I heard him say, 'I've been talking to some of my people,' and I thought, Oh come off it with the 'my people' stuff. If this is just an ego trip, let me out. But the issues were real. So when the night of the police charge came, and everyone knew the bust was on, I was lined up in front of Low Library to protect the occupiers inside, still hoping for a nonviolent resolution of the crisis, but along with everyone else ready to be pounded or arrested or whatever was going to happen. With our hands and arms locked together, we sang 'We shall overcome,' and then 'We shall not be moved.' After that, while the order to remove us was read, we sang 'The Star-Spangled Banner.' The cops said they would arrest us if we didn't stop blocking the doorway and we said, 'Okay, arrest us,' which we expected them to do peacefully. But then the next order was 'All right, men, clear them out!' and they waded into us with nightsticks and blackjacks."

When the police advanced, John was thinking that he belonged where he was and the Tactical Police Force did not belong where it was. He knew he was exercising his youth and his power, but not with the idea of putting people down in the manner the United States was using to exercise its power. When power and force are translated into violence, then people are not having their humanity respected, John Khanlian thought. In fact, the powers that be are forgetting all about humanity. That was what the United States was doing with its army in Vietnam. That was what the Columbia administration was doing with the New York police at the occupied buildings. John Khanlian was groping toward a new definition of citizenship: it was patriotic to oppose one's government in a bad war. Civil disobedience was not only a right, it was an obligation.

Like the others, John Khanlian did not run when the police charged. He did not want to be hurt, he would not fight back, and he would not run. Since these purposes are not compatible with one another at a mass police bust, he was struck almost immediately. A policeman hit him over the head with a blackjack. John crumpled near the boots of the policeman, who then charged another protester. The pain in his head put John on automatic pilot—a defenseless boxer trying to weather a bad round. He got to his feet slowly and began to walk away. Since it was not raining, he wondered why his face was so wet. "Get out of here," another policeman said to John. "I'm leaving, you can see I'm leaving," John said as he moved off. The policeman swung and caught John squarely in the left eye with his fist. It was a solid connection, like the blackjack to the head, and John actually flew over a hedge, landing facedown on the ground near the Foreign Student Center across from Low. He pulled himself up again and at last was permitted to stagger away. Others around him were falling—cut, kicked, pummeled, bludgeoned.

Seeing blood flow freely, someone yelled, "We need a doctor!"

"Call Dr. Kirk!" an angry protester shouted, referring to Columbia's president.

"Butcher! Butcher! Butcher!" several people cried.

"Let's go, Lions!" yelled a number of student athletes, opposed to the protesters, cheering on the police with Columbia's football slogan.

Several of the angriest protesters shouted their own rallying cry from the sidelines. It was a phrase policemen in Harlem had once used while making arrests, a phrase that had been taken over by black activists and was now appropriated by white radicals: "Up against the wall, motherfucker!"

Moving sixty or seventy yards away to relative safety while remaining on the campus, John Khanlian wiped a hand across his face. Though it was now three o'clock in the morning, the campus was well lighted so the police could go about their business, and John saw his hand come away red. Someone had already taken his picture as he left Low Library, and he decided to stay on campus, where anyone who wanted to could photograph him. "Maybe it would help if people saw what had been done to me," he says. John was no longer content to witness; he now wanted to *be* witnessed as well.

He thought perhaps a picture of him would get into the *Columbia Daily Spectator,* where it might turn more students against the war and the college administration. But his photograph was printed in *The New York Times Magazine, Life* magazine, and many other publications around the country. A few days later, the photograph became a poster. John himself was never identified in any caption or article. He was a poster against the war, an image without a name, like the girl who screamed at Kent State, the bleeding boy with the broken wire-rimmed glasses in Chicago, the insouciant draft resister being carried out of Foley Square by three G-men who all looked like H. R. Haldeman, the napalmed little girl running down Route 1 in Vietnam.

"I was fast asleep, of course," Louisa remembers, "when a woman came pounding on my door. The middle of the night and a complete stranger—a woman, no less—comes to tell me my husband has been hurt but basically he's all right."

"It was almost daylight before I stopped off at home on my way to the hospital," John says. "I told Louisa, 'Don't turn on the light because you're not going to like what you see.' I changed clothes and went down to St. Luke's, where they put eight stitches in my head. The irony was they pounded me the way they did and then didn't even bother to arrest me."

A further irony was that the Tactical Patrol Force had not needed to rush the entrance to Low Library, since another contingent of police had already entered the building through tunnels into the basement. When they had removed protesters from all the occupied buildings, the police made their arrests. The body count for the evening was 711 arrests and 148 injuries, including seventeen policemen. The police came to investigate John Khanlian's complaint that he had been beaten in an unprovoked attack by members of the force. The investigator asked to see the clothes he had worn the evening of the bust. John told him his shirt and jacket were so torn and bloody they had to be thrown away. "They accused us of hiding the evidence," Louisa says.

"The investigator suggested I had smeared my own head and clothes with ketchup and then asked everyone to take my picture," John says. "So they accused me of staging the whole thing for the media."

John did not like being a poster. "A company was marketing me," he says, "like Paul Newman or Jane Fonda, selling my literally bloody face everywhere." In the poster he is holding his right hand up in the V signal Winston Churchill once used to mean victory in war, now adopted by the protesters to mean victory in peace. Wounded, he stares out from the picture amazed, very likely in shock, dead game and—it is impossible not to notice—still gentle. Even with blood all over his face, John Khanlian does not look as if he wants to hurt anyone. Though he did not like being exploited, regardless of how much he believed in the cause, John made a single inquiry to a lawyer about his rights—he had none, it was a news photograph—and let the matter drop.

He went on to take his master's degree at the School of International Affairs, but after the night he was beaten by the police, John knew he would never work for the State Department. "Even if they wanted me, I could not become a mouthpiece for policies I could not in good conscience support," he says. "I struggled for a long time over what to do about the draft board. The best method of resistance may have been to return or burn my draft card and refuse to cooperate in any way. I finally decided to register as a conscientious objector because that's what I felt I really was. The draft board turned me down at first, but I appealed and won. They gave me CO status and I went to teach at the Moorestown Friends School in South Jersey, near Philadelphia." Despite the famous poster, John Khanlian remained, outside of his friends and family, anonymous, an unknown antiwar soldier with a passion for peace.

"No one ever knew who that guy was," a Columbia activist remembers. "Everyone wondered. We just saw the face with all the blood. I wish I knew his name."

A prosperous ex-radical, known to himself and others as a movement heavy, is less curious. "He's an innocent bystander who happened to be walking past when the action occurred," he says. "Someone snapped a picture and the media went for it. Big deal. The guy's a nobody."

In December the trees are sticks in the towns of South Jersey. The towns are almost suburban to Philadelphia, but they are also rural. Signs advertise tractors, loaders, backhoes for rent, but there are no rentals in winter. In winter the men who make their livings on farms work out and bowl, and drink, and wait for the land to come back again. In one such town, Sewell, John Khanlian works, and in another, Mt. Laurel, he lives. He is an educational consultant for the Institute for Political and Legal Education, which is funded primarily by federal grants. Basically, he teaches teachers how to acquaint their high school students with the responsibilities and opportunities of citizenship. How to understand the law and make it operate for them. How to use government effectively and make their voices and opinions heard in politics. It amounts to learning civics in a personal way, making one's citizenship count. "More than anyone else I know," a friend of John Khanlian's says, "John lives his principles." He is now thirty-eight years old.

He jogs, plays basketball once a week, pumps a little iron now and then, and is known to have finished 3,164th in a Philadelphia half-marathon in which there were six thousand starters. He sings in the choir at the Baptist Church, where he is also treasurer. Once every six weeks, he gets up at four A.M. to drive into Philadelphia with a friend who teaches philosophy to buy groceries for their food cooperative. Most of all, John Khanlian has become a dedicated father to his two sons. David, who is nine, goes to Moorestown Friends School, where John spent four years—two of them as a CO—teaching social studies. Jonathan, three, will go to Friends as soon as he is old enough.

Louisa Khanlian takes courses in the computer field, in which she would like to find work. She is her Morningside Heights self plus fifteen years—smart, brave, grim, hopeful. When John brings Jonathan back from a baby-sitter's, he hears hammering coming up from the basement. "What's David doing?" he asks Louisa.

"He's been down there quite a while making something," Louisa says.

"He's really sticking with things now, more than ever before," John says. "I like to see that."

"He's probably angry," Louisa says, "and this is how he's getting it out." She does not speak bitterly but factually. She might have said it's supposed to rain tomorrow. But then John would have said maybe it won't rain and we'll be able to go running.

"Oh, I don't think he's angry," John says. "Probably just involved in whatever he's making. Anger's a little farfetched."

When David emerges from the basement he is carrying a shield he made himself. He wants advice on how to make the sword to go with the shield.

"That saw downstairs is not big enough," John tells him. "The big one's over at my place."

"A sword and a shield," Louisa says when David has returned to the basement. "Do you really think anger is so farfetched?"

"I think he accepts our situation pretty well," John says.

David and Jonathan stay four nights a week with Louisa, three nights with John.

John got a neuromuscular disease in late 1981 and spent six weeks in the hospital, where he decided his life should be more than it was. In the spring of 1982 his father died. As sad as he felt, he also felt liberated. After the funeral his mother sighed and said, "No more fights. I loved him dearly, and I miss him terribly already, but no more fights." John looked forty years down his own road. He did not want to be there. In May he suggested to Louisa that they each take the boys on separate vacations.

"What are you saying?" Louisa asked. "Where would you like to go?"

"Let's each go somewhere different with the boys," John said.

"I don't want to take a year to pull apart," Louisa said. "If we're going to separate, let's separate."

Guilty about his feelings, grateful for Louisa's directness, John found an apartment nearby.

"We had the children we planned for after all," Louisa says, "and we both love them. But even with all those years behind us, together since our freshman year in college, we weren't making each other happy. I don't form friendships easily and he does. For years I didn't get out much. John needs his friends, men and women both, and his causes. I was threatened by that, scared, I guess, and jealous. But he still doesn't know what he wants. He thinks he should get up every day and have the same emotions he did at eighteen. You can't do that."

While John's job has the satisfactions of his principles, he wishes he were more intensely involved in social issues. He feels strongly about the necessity for a nuclear freeze but has not found a way to channel his energies fully. He describes his personal life as being "in disarray except for the boys." The last years of his marriage were tense, unfulfilled; his illness was a kind of cure. "I had sharp leg and back pains while I was in the hospital," John says, "but I realized the pain of our marriage was worse. I wanted it to work out, and so did Louisa, in ways it just wasn't working. I felt unappreciated and so did she. Finally, there was nothing else for us to do."

Right after their first Christmas apart—they still had hung four stockings on what was now only Louisa's mantelpiece, and there had been awkward moments at the gathering of in-laws—John Khanlian took David and Jonathan to Albuquerque for a reunion with his brothers. David was now a big boy on the plane, making friends, giving polite suggestions to the stewardesses. Jonathan alternated between trying to imitate David and curling up in John's lap as his father's baby. The families of the three brothers made a small caravan and drove up to rented cabins in the old railroad junction of Chama, in northern New Mexico, to go cross-country skiing.

Richard and Robert are both divorced; Helen Khanlian, their mother, calls her three sons "the soap-opera boys." On this trip her sons were brothers again, and fathers, and uncles. None of the family's assortment of nine children ever had a chance to feel neglected. One of the brothers was always mending a strap, frying a hamburger, finding a shoe, telling a joke, pushing someone upright onto his skis. The only woman along was a young widow, Kathy

Campbell, who had recently moved west with her two children to live with Richard.

The snow was deep and ready for the Khanlians. In the quiet of the general whiteness surrounding him, John could not imagine anyone in his family downhill skiing. It was expensive and elitist and the long lines at the tows meant you could not feel alone. If you did manage to get off by yourself you would hear the piped music drifting up from some counterfeit chalet. At the end of the day there was all the après stuff that turned an evening into a fashion show at a singles bar.

Cross-country, on the other hand, meant solitude. In the mountains above Chama, at ten thousand feet, the Khanlian brothers took separate trails that crisscrossed each other in a gently sloping meadow. Kathy Campbell was on her own trail and some of the children were pushing their way toward higher ground while others used an old inner tube for a sled.

Except for the hush-hush sound of his own skis, John's silence was expansive, universal. The sun was so bright it was hard to look at the snow; where his brothers had made tracks it was even brighter, pure straight beams of light across the meadow. When they started uphill, snow began to fall, very light and fine, the flakes so tiny that in the brightness they looked like pieces of mica trying to catch the attention of the sun. Soon the sun was blocked and more flakes fell in a kind of snow shower. The ground became shadowed, still white but now ghostly.

His separation pained John as much, almost, as the latter stages of his marriage. But Kathy Campbell, Richard's friend, had gone through worse, was still going through it, in fact, and was enduring. She had known Richard twenty years earlier, in high school, then had moved away when she married. She and her husband, a prominent herpetologist named Duke Campbell, had settled in Florida, where his specialty was alligators. He smoked three packs a day and got cancer. He had it a long time and when he finally died, Kathy was wretched and alone in Florida. Her two children, she said, went right on with their lives, while she was stuck in her grief. She came west after a few months, to combine herself and her children with Richard's family. When she thought of Duke, which she still did all the time, there was at least Richard, strong and gentle like his brothers, with whom she could share her unhappiness. It was not ideal for anyone, but it was working.

The night before, in the cabin in Chama, Kathy had recalled Duke's death, as much for herself as for the Khanlian brothers. "He was in terrible pain all the time," she said, "and he wouldn't take pills because he wanted to go on working and he hated being drugged. The doctors were not much help. They kept holding out hope and were never really straight with either of us. So no one ever relaxed and accepted anything. Something good would happen, something would get us out of this. Duke couldn't face that he was dying. The agony on his last night made him delirious. His final words to me were, 'Kathy, tomorrow you've got to help me find a new hiding place.' That was the end." Kathy was crying when she finished.

Late the next afternoon, John was still skiing when the sun emerged from the snow clouds long enough to set over a mountain, sending a great cylinder of light shooting overhead, and it came to him that more than any conceivable career advancement, more even than the success of the moral causes he enlisted himself in, he wanted to be happily remarried.

In the last light, with the snow becoming gunmetal blue, it was time to quit, but the brothers did not want to. Each of them kicked and glided, kicked and glided on, thrusting forward beyond his own limits. They came to a steep hill, with the frozen trail going straight down, no opportunity for turns. Everyone's muscles were quivering with fatigue. "We'd better turn back," Richard said. "We're at least a mile from the car."

"You have to say that, that's what the oldest brother is supposed to say," Robert said.

"It's a pretty attractive hill," John said.

Dutifully, and because he was the best skier, Richard went first and broke a ski. John went next and not only broke a ski but fell hard on his shoulder, jamming it almost to dislocation. Robert broke no ski but took a header and completed the downhill run on his face. A gash ran the length of his nose. Robert shouldered his skis and walked back up the hill to where John was standing with his own ski-and-a-half. A mist blew over the mountains, enshrouding everything, and the snow took on the tint, at last, of a faded rose. As he approached John, Robert made the V signal from John's famous photograph of fifteen years before. "Looks familiar, doesn't it?" he said, with blood streaming down his nose.

In a café in Chama on their last night in the mountains, John sat against a wall, ringed by his relatives, all around a large table, and compared the Sixties with the Eighties. "People used to long for the certainties of World War II," he said, "but we had our own certainties in the 1960s. Our course was clear—we had to stop that war. I have a certain nostalgia for all we had then. There was a real sense of excitement every day. You never had to pinch yourself to find out if you were alive."

Three men in checked flannel shirts and caps that advertised beer and bulldozers walked in and stood at the bar. The waitress suggested to the Khanlians that they might be more pleased if they moved farther away from the bar to the back of the restaurant. John thanked her but said they were pleased the way they were. The men at the bar played a song on the jukebox about a driver who loved his truck because it always stayed right by his side. The Khanlians' ribs and cheeseburgers arrived. The singer on the jukebox was proud of his truck for being faithful, unlike some other people he could name, and never leaving home without him.

"When I see myself getting comfortable or burned out in my nice job," John went on, "I shudder. We need money, but I'd hate to get hung up on the next dollar. There's too much that needs doing. I know I have to balance my social concerns with my family responsibilities, but the cause is there. Nuclear weaponry is out of anyone's control. Just because the Russians have it is no reason

384

not to work for reductions all around. It's like the revisionists on Vietnam. To-day they're telling us we should have made our longest war even longer, be-cause look how awful life is for the Vietnamese. I react with pain to Vietnam since the war. But the fact that the Vietnamese leaders do not rule their people humanely, and exercise their power in dastardly ways, does not justify Ameri-cans' staying there and destroying their country for them, which is what we were doing. Same with the nukes. I can't drop out and go full-time on the barri-cades, and I don't sing the praises of any totalitarian government, but I can't avoid responsibility for what my government is doing, either." John looked around at his relatives with his old blend of amazement and resolve. "Who's in charge here, anyway?" he asked as if someone present knew the answer and could be made to disclose it.

The explosion from the firecracker thrown by one of the flannel-shirted men at the bar caused the Khanlians' table to shift its ground the way it would if there had been an earthquake. Glasses fell over and a gray dust settled on the salads and what was left of the ribs and cheeseburgers. The firecracker was the size of a hot dog and had landed only a foot from the table. Richard and Robert jumped up and went to the bar. John, pinned behind the table against the wall between a frightened niece and nephew, comforted them and said it was only a bad joke. "Don't worry," he told them. "We'll take care of it."

Richard, at six eight, and Robert, at six three, hovered over the men at the bar. There was nothing like a six-eight frame to cow a bully. "Who did that?" Richard asked, in the same tone John had used when he asked who was in charge.

"I did it," one of the men said, looking toward the ceiling where Richard's head was. "Never mind. I wouldn't do it again." He swiveled his Coors cap back toward his beer mug while his companions huddled closer to him.

"All right, then," Robert said, "no more of that." He and Richard returned to their seats. John had calmed everyone at the table, and a fight, which had loomed over the café a moment before, was now avoided, was almost, in fact, turned into a civics lesson. The Khanlian brothers had not struck back, they had cooled it. In a smug decade that has no use for utopias, smirking even at reform, three brothers were living out their beliefs and getting away with the strategy. "Nonviolence is pretty much the only way I know how to go," John said later.

Musing on what kind of people become heroes in this country, D. H. Law-rence wrote that "the essential American soul is hard, isolate, stoic, and a killer." John Khanlian is gentle, a believer in the group, a revealer of his feel-ings, and he refuses to hurt anyone. What does that make him in terms of American heroism? Perhaps one American archetype was most needed during our national childhood and adolescence, another during our maturity. Differ-ent times called different men to courage, demanded different qualities. John Fosdick Khanlian, with his patience and his sharing and his unthreatening, principled determination, was not the kind of American who built this country, it seemed clear—only the kind who saved it.

JOHN F. KHANLIAN *was born on June 27, 1945, in New Rochelle, New York.*

His father was a stickler for good grammar and for thrift. If one of his sons used a word incorrectly, the father would pretend he hadn't heard him. "We weren't wealthy, and we weren't poor either," John remembers, "yet we'd go into a restaurant and Dad would be stuffing paper napkins into his pocket to take home." When the father's overcoat wore out, he had it made into a snowsuit that each of the boys wore in succession.

As a boy, John was a great fan of Davy Crockett; he memorized all the verses to the Indian fighter's theme song. When he was fourteen he saw On the Beach *and was disturbed by its story of a few people awaiting the effects of an explosion that has destroyed the rest of the world.*

In 1968, when The New York Times *printed the picture of the battered Khanlian (the picture that became a poster), it labeled him "a student militant." Khanlian took offense at the caption and in a letter to the* Times *insisted upon his position of nonviolence. To Khanlian's knowledge, the letter marks the only instance in which he was identified by name as the man in the picture.*

He reads mostly nonfiction. Of late he has particularly admired Michael Arlen's Passage to Ararat—*which taught him about his own Armenian heritage—and Jonathan Schell's* The Fate of the Earth—*which he read twice and quoted from in a talk to his fellow churchgoers at the First Baptist Church of Moorestown.*

He plays Bach, Mozart, Schubert, and Scott Joplin on his piano. He still plays his dozen Beatles albums and records by John Denver. He doesn't smoke, drinks wine and beer on occasion, tries to run three to ten miles a day, drives a 1980 Volkswagen Rabbit diesel.

His job allows him to travel. He recently visited New Orleans. "I like the South. In the Sixties I hadn't been there. I only pictured the rednecks. But you travel and you discover that your stereotypes need to be revised."

He rents a two-bedroom apartment in Mt. Laurel, New Jersey. "A couple of years ago I heard that somebody who owned one of the local apple orchards had sold it off to a developer. I thought it was horrible—*building those apartments. Now I live in one."*

In 1968, the first year he was eligible to vote, he wore a Eugene McCarthy button, then a Dick Gregory button, then voted for Hubert Humphrey. In 1972 he contributed several checks for fifty to one hundred dollars to George McGovern's campaign. In 1976 he voted for Jimmy Carter. In 1980 he voted for John Anderson. He says he would be an avid supporter of Senator Edward Kennedy should he run again for President.

He is rankled by most of the Reagan administration's domestic policies. "But what bothers me the most are Reagan's military stands. The effrontery—the nukespeak—the nerve to call the MX missile 'the peacekeeper'—that really galls me." In support of a nuclear arms freeze, he has written his congressman and joined New Jersey residents in a Capitol Hill lobbying effort. Regarding U.S. intervention in Central America, he says, "I have a clear sense that I don't like what I'm hearing. But I still have to do more reading on the subject. I'm not as informed as I need to be."

He recalls that when he recited his marriage vows in a Quaker ceremony he promised to be a loving husband " 'as long as we both shall live.' I don't think I was ever unloving. But to promise you're going to feel one way the rest of your life—it's scary. We got engaged in college. We each should have had the opportunity to set out and experience the adult world on our own. We tried separating before we had the children. After we had them, we went to six or eight different marriage counselors.

"I've been pleased with how the kids have reacted. Jonathan was only two when we separated, so he has no memories of how it was before. He's always talked about Daddy's home, Mommy's home. Once, he asked why our neighbors had only one house. David was eight when he learned the news. He said he felt a little sad, a little scared. I told him I did too, and he said he understood. I felt like I was talking to a psychiatrist. He listened to me and said, 'Well, you have to get these feelings out.'

"One time I used the word precipitation, and the kids wanted to know what that meant. I said it referred to things that fell from the sky—rain, snow. 'And bombs?' they asked. I've told them about Vietnam, how I felt. But I want them to make up their own minds. Sometimes they talk back and I say, 'Stop mouthing off.' But other times I remember how I was, and I want to say, 'Right on! Tell me off!' "

The Night
Ed Murrow
Struck Back

ARTHUR MILLER

FEAR, LIKE LOVE, IS DIFFICULT TO EXPLAIN AFTER IT HAS SUBSIDED, PROBABLY BE-
cause it draws away the veils of illusion as it disappears. The illusion of an
unstoppable force surrounded Senator Joseph McCarthy of Wisconsin at
the height of his influence, in the years from 1950 to 1954. He had paralyzed
the State Department, cowed President Eisenhower, and mesmerized almost the entire American press, which would in all seriousness report his
most hallucinatory spitballs as hard front-page news. His very name struck
terror not only in the hearts of the several million Americans who in the previous decades of the Forties or Thirties had had a brush with any branch or
leaf of the Left, but also those who had ever expressed themselves with
something less than a violent hatred of the Soviets, Marx, or for that matter
cooperatives—or even certain kinds of poetry. At my own hearing before
the House Un-American Activities Committee, a flank of the McCarthy
movement, a congressman from Cincinnati asked me with wild incredulity,
"You mean you believe that a man has the right to write a poem about *anything*?" When I confirmed this opinion, he turned to his fellow committee-
men and simply threw up his hands.

How this vaudevillelike absurdity could have been taken in dead seriousness
by vast numbers of Americans is hard to explain in retrospect. The Fifties' Red
hunt not only terrified people but drove some few to suicide. It is not easy to

conceive of Harry Truman, ex-artilleryman and quintessential small-town American, being labeled a traitor to his country, yet Senator Joe McCarthy and his fellow Republican leaders blithely went about pronouncing Truman's and Roosevelt's administrations "twenty years of treason." Never was this greeted with scorn or laughter. How to explain it?

Of course, an outrageous mixture of viciousness and naive provincialism is endemic to the political extremes. Stalin awoke one morning and decided that all the Jewish doctors were in a plot to poison the party leadership, and nobody laughed then either. I had known an outlandish tap dancer who in desperation was touring Europe in the Thirties with his little troupe; in Berlin he found himself to his amazement the idol of the newly risen Nazi establishment, and soon of Hitler himself. Tap dancing so delighted Hitler that he spoke of ordaining it the *echt* German dance, which all the *Volk* must begin learning at once—a veritable nation of tap dancers was to spring forth, with my friend to be the head teacher. One morning a uniformed "race expert" showed up at his hotel prepared to measure his cranium, nose, mouth, and the spatial relationships of his face to make sure he was the Aryan type. My friend, a Jew, explained that he had an urgent appointment and took the next train out of the country.

By 1953 it was common talk in Europe that America had at last met her own native dictator in Joe McCarthy; but if a great many Americans agreed, they were in no position to say so safely, especially if they worked in government, or as teachers, or in the larger corporations. Another dreamlike element, moreover, was that McCarthy's Senate Investigating Subcommittee, whose claimed intent was the rooting out of Communists hidden in the government, never seemed to find any actual Reds, let alone one who might be guilty of betraying the United States. To his critics, however, McCarthy would reply, "It isn't the number of Communists that is important; it's the general effect on our government," one of his more candid statements.

He rose like a rocket to his power in a matter of weeks once he had stood on a podium waving a piece of paper and declaring, "I hold in my hand the names of . . ." I have since forgotten whether it was sixty-two or thirty-nine "card-carrying Communists" inside the State Department, but it hardly matters because in subsequent months he himself kept changing the count and of course could never produce one name of an actual person. Yet his fraudulence, which had perhaps seemed so obvious to me because I had uncles like him who shot off their mouths in argument and said anything that came into their heads, was frighteningly persuasive to a lot of Americans, including some important newsmen. One half-understood why the country was still in shock at having "lost" China to Mao, whose revolution had swept into Peking in 1949. How could this mucky peasant horde have won fairly and squarely against a real general like Chiang Kai-shek, whose wife, moreover, was the graduate of an American college and so beautiful besides? It could only be that worming their ways through our State Department were concealed traitors who had "given" the country to the Reds. In the light of Vietnam, we have perhaps come to understand the limits of our power, but in the early Fifties any such concept was unimaginable. Henry Luce, for example, was confidently propagating "the American century," when we would lead the grateful human race into baseball, private enterprise, eight-cylinder Buicks, and, of course, Christianity; and for a fact, the Swiss franc aside, the American dollar was truly the only nonfunny money in the world. Before he had finished, Joe McCarthy would have "named" the revered ex-general of the U.S. Army, George Catlett Marshall, as a Communist.

McCarthy had struck gold with the point of a syllogism; since he was totally and furiously against communism, anyone who opposed him had therefore to be in favor of communism, *if only by that much*. This simply numbed the opposition or backed them into futile defensive postures. For example, when Senator Millard Tydings, having investigated McCarthy's charges that the State Department was full of Reds, reported that they were "a fraud and a hoax perpetrated on the Senate of the United States and on the American people," McCarthy, for revenge, then went into Maryland and, charging Tydings with being "soft" on communism, helped defeat him for reelection! His was a power blessed by Cardinal Spellman, a power that the young John F. Kennedy would not bring himself to oppose any more than did Eisenhower until 1954, near the end of McCarthy's career. For myself, I believed McCarthy might well be on his way to the presidency, and if that happened an awful lot of Americans would literally have to take to the boats.

When it was announced in 1953 that Edward R. Murrow would be devoting the entire half hour of his prestigious weekly TV commentary to an analysis of McCarthy, my own joy was great but it was mixed with some skepticism. Murrow had been the brightest star at CBS for more than a decade and remains to this day the patron saint of anchormen for his judiciousness and devotion to the truth. It was during the London blitz that he had seared our minds with the unique sound of his voice, a gravelly baritone that had rolled out to us across the Atlantic each night from the fog and blast of London under bombardment, his quiet toughness a reassurance that the great beleaguered city was still alive.

But all that anti-Nazi wartime *Gemütlichkeit* was long gone now; indeed, CBS in the past couple of years had cooperated with the unacknowledged blacklisting of radio and TV writers, actors, and directors who had or were accused of having too much enthusiasm for the Left by newly sprouted self-appointed guardians of the airwaves like Red Channels, a broadsheet listing the names of purported subversives. In true private-enterprise style they were always ready to "clear" you for a fee plus your signed anti-Communist declaration, or preferably an ad in *Variety*, which you paid for, with some similarly edifying and spontaneous patriotic locution. Still, it would be fascinating to see how far Murrow and CBS would want to go against the snarling senator from Wisconsin whose totally missing scruples had made him murderously effective as a debater. I was not at all sure it would be far enough.

There was such widespread feeling of helpless paralysis before the McCarthy movement by this time that one questioned whether any mere journalist, whatever his wit and courage, could stay on his feet with him.

In such apocalyptic gloom, very nearly convinced that my days as an American playwright were numbered even as I was generally thought to be a great success, I adapted Ibsen's *An Enemy of the People* with the hope of illuminating what can happen when a righteous mob starts marching. But despite a brilliant performance by Frederic March as Dr. Stockmann, the critics batted the play right back at my feet. For one thing, it was a post-Odets and pre-Brecht time, when things artistic were supposed to deal with sentiments and aspirations, but never with society.

The failure of that production only deepened the sense of a mass mythic shadow dance, a ritualized, endlessly repeated consent to a primitive anticommunism that could end only with demagogues in power over the country. In the Salem witch-hunts of 1692, a story I had known since college, I thought I saw nakedly unveiled something like the immemorial psychic principles of what we were once again living through. There too people had been at odds with a reality that indeed was sawing straight across their conception of themselves and nullifying the omnipotent powers of their society. There too men had been seized with paranoid terrors of dark forces ranged against them. It is hardly accidental that apart from *The Crucible* our theater would mount no other reply to a movement that surely meant to destroy its freedom. So feverish, so angry, so fearful had people become that any mention of the senator's name on a stage, or even an allusion to his antics, would have generated an impacted silence in the majority, and open rage in his partisans.

In *The Crucible* a public hysteria, based upon economic, sexual, and personal frustrations, gathers the folds of the sublime about itself and destroys more than twenty lives in the village of Salem, Massachusetts, in 1692. Between its heroes and villains stands a timeless hunger for mythic solutions to intractable moral and social dilemmas—particularly the myth of a hidden plot by subterranean evil forces to overwhelm the good. But *The Crucible,* too, would fail; either mistrusted as a "false analogy"—there had never been witches but there certainly were Reds, quite as though McCarthy had really uncovered a Soviet plot utilizing highly placed Americans—or regarded as a "cold" play, a charge partially justified by its direction as a disinterred classic. Interestingly, within two years, a new off-Broadway production would succeed, judged hot stuff now by many of the same critics who theorized that I had more warmly revised the script. But the only revision had been the relaxation of society after McCarthy's quick decline and death—which, I suppose, permitted a longer view of the issues raised in the drama.

Shortly before Murrow's broadcast was announced, I had had my own personal little brush with a McCarthyite State Department. The Belgo-American Association, a business group, had invited me to come over to Brussels for the European premiere of *The Crucible* in the National Theatre, and I applied for a renewal of my outdated passport. A new passport was quickly denied me. "Not in the best interests of the United States," they said. So at the end of the opening performance, the audience, believing I was in the house, the papers having reported I had accepted to attend, began calling for the author, who, of course, was still in Brooklyn. The roar of the audience would not cease—to Europeans *The Crucible* at the time was reassurance that fascism had not yet overwhelmed Americans—and the United States ambassador had finally to stand and take my bow for me, a scandal in the papers the next morning when the imposture was revealed. (But who knows if he had stood up in sympathy for me or in silent protest at his department's stupidity in denying me a passport?)

All in all, by the time of Murrow's broadcast, I had only a small capacity left to believe that he would really do more than remonstratively tap McCarthy's shoulder. The broadcast was coming somewhat late in the game, now that an occasional soft murmuring of common sense was being heard in the press—although that, too, was still in danger of being suppressed once the senator got around to blasting its authors. For me, there was little reason anymore to expect a meaningful resistance to McCarthyism when I knew that, myself not altogether excepted, people were learning to keep a politic silence toward idiocies that a few short years before they'd have derided or laughed at.

An unsettling experience at a cocktail party shortly before the broadcast had stayed with me. I had overheard a TV producer assuring a circle of guests that he was free to hire any actor or produce any script he chose to and that no blacklist ever existed. Since I had friends who had not been hired in over a year despite long careers in TV and radio, and two or three who had suffered mental illness as a result, and I knew of at least two suicides attributable to the despair generated by blacklisting, I walked over to the producer and offered him the television rights to *The Crucible*. He laughed, assuring me and his listeners that he would of course be honored but his budget would never stand for what such rights would doubtless cost. So I offered them to him for a dollar. He went on laughing and I went on persisting, growing aware, however, that our little audience, many of them in television and the theater, was turning against me for a display of bad manners.

Leaving that party, I exchanged glances with people who I was certain shared my knowledge and views but who showed nothing in their faces. It was an experience that would be useful to me in future years when writing about the life of the artist in the Soviet Union, China, and Eastern Europe, where what might be called a permanent state of McCarthyism reigns, at times more virulently than others, but always warning artists—who, after all, are the eyes and voices of the society—that their souls ultimately belong to Daddy.

Edward R. Murrow appeared on the screen that night of the much-anticipated broadcast, as usual a picture of classy Bogartian straightforwardness, the cigarette between the fingers with the lethal smoke coiling up around the peaked eyebrows and the straight black hair, unsmiling as ever, his voice nasal and direct. I did not yet own a set, so I was watching this at my poet-friend Leroy's house a couple of blocks from my own in Brooklyn Heights. Leroy believed he was blacklisted in TV and radio, but a few producers occasionally gave him script-writing work because they loved him. People also gave him old but usable cars, trips to Florida, and more or less shared a mystic belief that Leroy must not die of want, with which Leroy agreed. He had once found a new can of anchovies on the sidewalk and a month later, on a different street, the key. Leroy had even graver doubts than I about what Murrow would be able to do.

Murrow could often affect an airy confidence and even sentimentality, rather like Cronkite talking about Vermont farmers, but not tonight; tonight he had his chin tucked in like a boxer and apprehension tightened the corners of his eyes with the knowledge, no doubt, that if some back talk against McCarthy had squeaked up recently in the press, his partisans were still passionate, religiously devoted to him, and numerous. Watching Murrow appear on the tube we were all aware of those millions out there who must hate him now for spoiling their god, or trying to; and even in that poet's snug and remote living room with its in-laws' cast-off furniture, the American violence charged the air. Tina, Leroy's wide-cheekboned blond wife, who usually could never see a TV set switched on without turning away and launching a new topic of conversation, now stared in silence at Murrow's familiar face blossoming on the black and white tube.

To her and Leroy this broadcast was of far more than academic or abstract interest. Two of Leroy's closest relatives had gained some fame as American volunteers fighting for the Spanish loyalists against Franco. This, combined with his having the usual Left views of a Thirties survivor, was enough of a taint on Leroy to damage his right to sign his own name on the occasional radio script he was able to sell. On the slim proceeds of such fitful commerce he pressed on with writing his poems. And Tina pressed on with her winsome complaints that Leroy was stubbornly immune to the American Dream of wealth and fame. Thus she stared at Murrow like a woman in love with a fighter climbing into a ring.

I think it only dawned on us as he started to speak that Murrow was the first man to challenge McCarthy out in public rather than into his sleeve, and I think we were scared for him now, although we were still pretty sure that establishment politesse would gentle his confrontation with the senator. And indeed, Murrow's introduction was not at all belligerent. But this was television, not print, and it quickly became clear what his strategy was going to be—McCarthy was going to hang himself before the whole country by reruns of his own filmed performances. And there now unwound pictures of him hectoring witnesses before his Senate subcommittee, railing against a bespectacled author of an obscure college textbook with the accusation that this man was a member of the American Civil Liberties Union, "listed as a front doing the work of the Communist party." But the stinger was the speech before a mass rally during the recent Eisenhower–Adlai Stevenson contention for the presidency.

A cold and windy day, and McCarthy behind the podium, hatless, a burly and handsome man in a saturnine way, quick to laugh through a clamped jaw—

more of a tight-assed snicker really, as though not to overly warm his icy ironies. Watching him again in these reruns was even scarier than seeing him the first time, in the previous months, for now somehow he was there to be studied and he was indeed villainous, almost laughably so. Now one saw that his great wish was for a high style, his models might well have been Oscar Wilde or Bernard Shaw, epigrammatists of the cutting Irish persuasion who could lay the opponent low with a jibe impossible ever to erase. Oddly, though, it was hardly ten minutes into the program when one knew it was the end of McCarthy, not altogether for reasons of content but more because he was so obviously handling subjects of great moment with mere quips, empty-sounding jibes, lumpy witticisms; it had not seemed quite as flat and ill-acted before.

At one point, as the applause of his audience died down he gave them his little knowing grin and said, "Strangely, Alger . . . I mean Adlai . . ." and a sweep of appreciative roaring laughter sent him into a helpless giggling spell and redoubled his audience's big-decibeled recognition for this association of Adlai Stevenson with Alger Hiss, an accused Communist with whom Stevenson had no connection whatsoever. Now, with the election over and settled and its passions gone, the sheer vileness of this man and his crummy tactic was abstracted from its original moment and there he stood in all his mendacity, appearing joyfully immune to all moral censure or the most minimal claims of decency.

The Murrow broadcast was a deep, if not mortal, wound for McCarthy. At least it seemed so to me at the time. By the end of the half hour all our debt to Murrow came clear and my skepticism toward him had gone. But McCarthy was given his own half-hour rebuttal period three weeks later, and we gathered again to hear what he would have to say. Now live in the studio, a subdued McCarthy seemed to know he had been badly hurt by the Murrow broadcast. A plaintive tenor line lifted his voice into the doubtlessly authentic plaint of a persecuted man. "If there had been no Communists in our government, we would not have given China to the Communists!" This was one of his standards, but under attack now he knew he had to get more specific, and so maps appeared on the screen, showing how the dark stain of communism had spread from Russia over China, engineered by a tiny secret group of schemers, their agents, and their dupes like—yes, like Edward R. Murrow. In his rebuttal, McCarthy, left to himself, undid himself. Unaccustomed to anyone confronting him with his lies, he seemed unable to use elementary caution. Murrow, he blithely said, was a member of the terrorist organization the Industrial Workers of the World; Harold Laski, "the greatest Communist propagandist in England," had dedicated his last book to Murrow. Now snarling, he attempted the ultimate unmasking of Murrow with his by-then familiar horror words: "Edward R. Murrow, the cleverest of the jackal pack which is always found at the throat of anyone who dares to expose individual Communists and traitors; Murrow, who serves the Communist cause as part of the transmission belt from the Russian Secret Police into the American home." McCarthy's desperate appeal ended something like "The Communist party opposes me; Murrow opposes me; Murrow is a transmission belt of Communist propaganda." Such was his counterattack.

But Murrow, unlike others, had a network to allow him the last word. And he had easy pickings: the ACLU had never been "listed" by any agency as a front; Murrow had simply never belonged to the IWW; and Laski, a rather confused on-and-off-again Marxist professor, had dedicated his book to Murrow for his valiant broadcasts from bombed London in the late war. As for the Communists supporting Murrow, this consisted of a notice in the *Daily Worker* that his upcoming McCarthy telecast was a "Best Bet."

Oddly, one lacked the urge to applaud Murrow at the end. He had been so persuasive because he had said what everyone had always known, that Joe McCarthy had merely been the master of the rhetorical style of lawyer-talk, an actor in love with the sound of his voice and his capacity to hold an audience in astonishment.

What ultimately undid McCarthy was hubris, his attacks on the patriotism of the leadership of the Army, on General George Marshall and Eisenhower himself. He may have gone mad with his power and too much booze. But Murrow's broadcast had cut the bag open and it was empty. How could one applaud our having striven so long after wind? Still, there was no doubt that night that Murrow's was the voice of decency, and if he and CBS had not struck at McCarthy until his decline had begun—if it was less a dragon slaying than a coup de grace—it still demonstrated, and would continue for years to come, the persistence of scruple as a living principle, one that had for so long been defied and doubtless would be again, and yet would live.

Murrow, in his summing up, said, "We are not a nation of fearful men," and one knew that there are things that do have to be repeated as fact even when they are only hopes. But for that kind of hope this nation is in Murrow's eternal debt.

Edward Roscoe Murrow *was born on April 25, 1908, in Greensboro, North Carolina. His family of Scotch-Irish Quakers moved to Washington State when he was six. His real name was Egbert; he changed it to Edward while working in a lumber camp.*

His mother was strict and advocated self-restraint and tolerance of others. She wanted him to be a preacher.

His earliest recollections were of trapping rabbits and eating watermelon.

He was a competitive and foolhardy boy. Once he let his brothers tie him to a seatless, pedalless bicycle, which he rode helplessly into a ditch. Another time, when he bet he could duck faster than a friend could fire a BB gun, he caught a pellet between the eyes. Both calamities left him with permanent scars.

Later in life his father, a farmer, would think it funny that Edward was paid so much for his broadcasts—"Especially," he told his son, "since you don't sound any different than you did when you were talkin' and hangin' around the porch years ago."

He was six feet one inch tall and lanky. He had a lopsided, intense face and luminous grin. Some considered him handsome enough to play a war correspondent in the movies.

He greatly admired Marcus Aurelius and Stoicism, and when he started out at CBS, he was considered a stuffed shirt.

He happened to be near Vienna setting up programs for other broadcasters when German troops invaded Austria in 1938. He flew to the spot and delivered his first live broadcast.

He always opened his World War II broadcasts with "This is London," and always closed with "Good night and good luck." A perfectionist, he bled over the copy that one commentator called "metallic poetry." Murrow wrote that the footsteps in nighttime London carried the eerie sound of "ghosts shod in steel-soled shoes." He saw the war as "an orchestrated hell, a terrible symphony of light and flame."

He told his reporters to imagine they were telling their stories to a professor at dinner while the maid's boyfriend, a truck driver, was listening from the kitchen.

Some wondered if he had a death wish. He drove extremely fast—and in an open roadster in the midst of a London air raid. When London became safe, he boarded an American bomber and flew over Berlin.

He sobbed during one harrowing broadcast and said, "The British aren't all heroes; they know the feeling of fear. I've shared it with them."

After the war, CBS chairman William Paley made Murrow vice-president of news and public affairs. Murrow insisted he liked the job, but Paley sensed that he wanted to return to the air. Finally Paley said, "I can tell you're sort of miserable." Murrow countered, "I'll only go back if you order me to." "Okay, Ed," said Paley. "I order you to." A huge smile broke across Murrow's face. "Okay, I'll go back."

Murrow thanked Paley for supporting his program on Senator Joseph McCarthy, saying, "You're the kind of man I'd go hunting with." Albert Einstein appreciatively addressed Murrow at a dinner: "Aha, a fighting man!"

He turned down the New York Democratic nomination for U.S. senator because he hadn't grown up in New York and felt he didn't know the state well enough.

He left CBS in 1961 to become director of the U.S. Information Agency under President John F. Kennedy. His salary dropped from $300,000 to $21,000 a year.

He and his wife, Janet Huntington Brewster, had one son. On their farm near Pawling, New York, Murrow hunted, fished, and played golf.

He had a photographic memory.

He said that lack of work made him miserable, that he was not equipped to have fun.

He was fond of Louis Armstrong, Robert Oppenheimer, Carl Sandburg, and Admiral Hyman Rickover.

"He was a skeptic and a yearner," James Reston once said. "He loved the stir of the world, but at heart he was a lonely critic who hated discipline and authority."

He won many television awards but considered them useless and felt they should be refused. He said television didn't demand enough of its audience. He predicted that future historians would find in his industry evidence of "decadence, escapism, and insulation from the realities of the world in which we live."

In 1965 he died of a brain tumor.

The Flight of Rachel Carson

GEOFFREY NORMAN

YOU DID NOT HAVE TO BE A BIRD WATCHER TO NOTICE, FIFTEEN YEARS AFTER THE END of the Second World War, that something was wrong. Many species were not reappearing in the spring in numbers as large as usual. Some of the larger, most majestic birds seemed on the verge of vanishing altogether. I can remember seeing fewer and fewer ospreys in the places where I had always seen them before and thinking that they were suffering from the same complaint that had eliminated the bald eagle from the rivers and bays and bayous that I prowled. We all knew that eagles did not like to share territory, not with other birds and especially not with man. So I assumed the same was true of the osprey, a raptor like the eagle, colored very much like him, but smaller and more abundant. But they were gone one year. Osprey nests that had been used, spring after spring, sat abandoned in the tall, dead pine trees. Eventually the untended nests crumbled until there were only a few forlorn twigs where they had been.

The absence of the pelicans was even more conspicuous and baffling. All along the coasts of the Gulf and the southern Atlantic, pelicans had been so abundant you felt they were everywhere. If you looked out across a stretch of water and saw a piling without a pelican perched on it, the vista was somehow incomplete. If you sat on a beach for twenty minutes, you would be sure to see a formation of pelicans fly by, pumping their wings in unison, then gliding for a few improbable beats. They looked too heavy for that, and you would never call them graceful. But they were able fliers and very determined, slightly comic and irresistible if you cared about birds.

Not everybody does, of course. And there is nothing wrong with that. But many people who do care about birds care intensely. They care almost as much as John James Audubon cared. Something in the flight and song and color of birds serves for them as a window onto all the wonders and beauty of this world. Such a person was Rachel Carson. And she wrote the book that explained what was killing the birds and why we might be next.

It was the late Fifties when she first took an interest in the slow disappearance and, in some cases, massive die-offs of birds. She was then a best-selling author of a trilogy about the sea, *The Sea Around Us, Under the Sea-Wind,* and *The Edge of the Sea.* Her books were serialized by *The New Yorker* and had earned her a vast following and many correspondents, all of whom she was careful to answer. One of them wrote to ask for her help in stopping the spraying over a private bird sanctuary near Cape Cod. Carson made some inquiries, and as she learned more she became more alarmed. That was the beginning of a labor that was to result in her book *Silent Spring,* which led to action that saved the birds and energized millions to work and campaign and vote for an enduring cause that, for lack of a better name, is called "the environmental movement."

When the book was published, it was an ordinary occurrence for an airplane to fly over a community, trailing a heavy fog that settled slowly to earth and then disappeared like smoke. The fog contained poisons that had been developed during war research and were meant to kill mosquitoes, Japanese beetles, gypsy moths, and other insects lumped together under the category "pests." The poisons were, technically, chlorinated hydrocarbons. The most common was called DDT. The spraying was done in the name of public health.

And it was done enthusiastically, almost messianically. Tourist communities boasted of the number of tons of DDT sprayed over them each year to keep them "insect-free." In their advertising, chemical companies came close to suggesting that their efforts were the last line of defense against famine and plague. The spraying had the uncritical support of the government, especially the Department of Agriculture. Pesticide spraying was public policy from the local courthouse all the way to Washington, D.C. It was profitable, too, for the chemical companies, universities, food packagers, grocery chains, and farmers. But the stakes went beyond profit. People in the pesticide programs *believed* in what they were doing. Their faith was of the same order as the faith of physicists who wanted to split the atom—back before there ever was a bomb. The physicists believed that man was destined first to understand and then to control the universe. The sprayers were more modest. They believed that man was meant to control nature. They did not believe it was necessary, however, to understand it first.

But theirs was a real faith, and it did not react kindly when challenged. Twenty-one years after the publication of *Silent Spring,* against a background of Love Canal, routine alarms over contaminated drinking water, and a scandal at the Environmental Protection Agency, which did not even exist then . . . with those benchmarks to go by, it seems extraordinary today that scientists and intelligent laymen could believe that there was nothing dangerous about dumping tons of poisons on the earth to kill bugs. That the bugs would cooperatively die (rather than build resistance to the poisons) and that nothing else would be harmed. That we could, through chemistry, create an insect-free Eden. But that is exactly what people believed.

Shortly after she had begun her research into the effects of spraying, Rachel Carson was asked to testify at an upcoming trial. A group in Long Island was trying to stop spraying against gypsy moths—spraying that had also killed birds and fish and at least one horse. The group had filed for an injunction and would be getting a hearing. Her testimony could be helpful. She was immediately sympathetic and began researching in preparation.

All her life she had loved birds. She was an Audubon member and, in the days before she became a best-selling author, when she was an anonymous Washington bureaucrat, Audubon outings had been perhaps her greatest source of pleasure. There never was much of it. She'd had to work hard to support her family—mother, father, sisters, and, when one of her sisters died, the small, orphaned children. Though she never married—a fact that her detractors turned into a slur—she supported dependents all of her life, much of the time on a small government salary.

So the outings and the birds must have meant a great deal to her. She loved nature, and had from the time she was a small, solitary girl growing up in Pennsylvania farm country. But more than a lover of birds, she was a scientist. She wrote out of her training. She had read the technical papers about the spraying that questioned both the effectiveness and the safety of the chemicals. She was concerned.

But in the end she was unable to testify at the Long Island trial. She was seriously ill. But she was convinced that the trial was important and could be made to stand for the question of pesticide use worldwide. Somebody, she thought, should attend the trial and write about it. She could not do it herself; she had other projects in mind, among them a book on evolution, and there was the matter of her health. Also, she probably knew that any book she wrote on the subject would become, necessarily, a book on the environment and therefore a large undertaking. An ordeal.

So she wrote E. B. White, whom she knew through *The New Yorker*. He was a writer who cared about the natural world and had the gifts to turn coverage of the trial into something larger than itself. He decided not to write the story but agreed it was important and that somebody should. He urged her to write it. She finally agreed, almost as though she had known all along that she would. But she did not cover the trial, which, as it developed, failed to stop the spraying on Long Island. Instead she started at the very beginning.

The research and writing took four years. During that time she was seriously ill. She had arthritis, developed an ulcer, and came down with staph infections so severe that she could not walk. Her mother was also in poor health. Her niece died and left a very young boy, whom she adopted. Then her mother died. Finally, she was told she had cancer.

The misfortunes did not stop her. Neither did they rush her. Rather, they seemed to deepen her resolve to write the book and make it impregnable. She knew it would be attacked. She wrote letters to her editor, explaining her intentions, and she continued to work.

Her methods were simple enough. She read the available documents and corresponded with experts. Then, she went through several drafts, revising until she was satisfied with the flow of the prose.

The book that her efforts resulted in was about the spraying and what it did to the birds and other creatures. But that does not begin to describe its scope or account for its impact. One might just as well say that Darwin wrote about turtles and the Pacific islands where they were found.

What Carson did in *Silent Spring* was to introduce to the general imagination the concept of ecology: the way the natural world fit together, the pieces so tightly and inextricably bound that you could not isolate cause and effect. The consequences of any action rippled through the whole system, affecting everything and sometimes even changing the system itself. So when we poisoned gypsy moths with massive sprayings of DDT, we were, ultimately, poisoning ourselves.

The book opened with a parable that described a landscape from which the birds and fish had vanished and where people died of mysterious ailments. It is, on rereading, the weakest portion of the book. But you can understand why it was necessary when you recall that in 1962 people needed to be shocked. They thought pesticides were safe, if they thought about them at all.

From that first chapter, she went on to explain that life on the planet had been changing for millions of years, that such change was slow and organic and inevitable. But now there was something different, a new force at work. Man had made it possible to alter the environment suddenly and drastically, with unforeseen and possibly disastrous consequences.

After sounding the alarm and stating her thesis in the first two chapters, she described the poisons that we were encountering—DDT was showing up even in the fatty tissues of Eskimo who lived in areas where the stuff had never been sprayed. She used diagrams to show the molecular structure of the chlorinated hydrocarbons and made the distinctions between these new poisons and the older ones.

The book went on to detail the effects of these poisons on the environment. Not surprisingly, the most affecting chapter was on the birds. The book's title was inspired by some lines in Keats and an imagined spring when no birds returned.

There was information—data on every page. There was nothing half-baked or mystical about the book. More than fifty pages of sources were cited. But the science and information came filtered through her intelligence and shaped by her graceful writing style. On almost every page there was a gem that owed more to her vision than the research of any laboratory scientist. The best passages are, in fact, lyrical.

> Some 10,000 acres of sagelands were sprayed by the [United States Forest] Service, yielding to pressure of cattlemen for more grasslands. The sage was killed, as intended. But so was the green, life-giving ribbon of willows that traced its way across these plains, following the meandering streams. Moose had lived in these willow thickets, for willow is to the moose what sage is to the antelope. Beaver had lived there, too, feeding on the willows, felling them and making a strong dam across the tiny stream. Through the labor of the beavers, a lake backed up. Trout in the mountain streams seldom were more than six inches long; in the lake they thrived so prodigiously that many grew to five pounds. Waterfowl were attracted to the lake, also. Merely because of the presence of the willows and the beavers that depended on them, the region was an attractive recreational area with excellent fishing and hunting.
>
> But with the "improvement" instituted by the Forest Service, the willows went the way of the sagebrush, killed by the same impartial spray. . . . The moose were gone and so were the beaver. Their principal dam had gone out for want of attention by its skilled architects, and the lake had drained away. None of the large trout were left. None could live in the tiny creek that remained, threading its way through a bare, hot land where no shade remained. The living world was shattered.

One of the early readers of the book was William Shawn, editor of *The New Yorker* then and now. He called her one night with his reaction. She later wrote to a friend:

> . . . suddenly I knew from his reaction that my message would get across. After Roger was asleep, I took Jeffie [her cat] into the study and played the Beethoven violin concerto. . . . And suddenly the tension of four years was broken and I let the tears come . . . last night the thoughts of all the birds and other creatures and all the loveliness that is in nature came to me with such a surge of deep happiness, that now I had done what I could—I had been able to complete it—now it had its own life. . . .

Today, Shawn says of the book, "Before *Silent Spring*, nobody talked about the environment and ecology. It was all new to us when she wrote it. There were people who wrote about conservation and there were naturalists. But *Silent Spring* was something new. Rachel Carson was the first one to write things this way."

As she expected, the book was attacked almost as soon as it was serialized in *The New Yorker*. One chemical firm that was not mentioned by name (though its products were) found a lawyer on the staff who was willing to threaten a lawsuit if her publishers actually brought the book out. He was also not above a little Red-baiting. Members of the chemical industry, he wrote in his letter to Houghton Mifflin, had enough trouble with the food faddists already. Now here was a book that would ". . . reduce the use of agricultural chemicals in this country and in the countries of western Europe, so that our supply of food will be reduced to east-curtain parity. Many innocent groups are financed and led into attacks on the chemical industry by these sinister parties." It was later discovered that the lawyer's client was dumping highly toxic chemicals into the Mississippi River. The poisons caused massive fish kills.

Other chemical company spokesmen and officials in the spraying programs worked tirelessly to discredit the book. They attacked it as offering the bad side of an either-or choice, which it did not; Carson said that pesticides had their uses but were dangerous and that we needed to use them with caution. But the forces attacking the book ignored distinctions she was careful to make. She would have us choose birds over people, they said. Her point was that when you kill the birds you are also slowly killing people. M.D.s and heads of university departments of agriculture and presidents of chemical companies attacked the book or merely satisfied themselves with a little ad hominem: ". . . not a scientist," one of them said, "but rather a fanatic defender of the cult of the balance of nature." Another cited her "disregard of the rubrics of evidence, of a nice regard for scientific validity, or any feeling that what she presented should be unbiased." And so on, until it became quite clear that men of science were no more dispassionate now than in the time of Darwin.

Through it all, she kept her silence, letting the book speak for itself. And it held its own very nicely. It was a best seller for almost a year. Translated all over the world. It was the subject of countless stories and editorials in the newspapers, was reviewed favorably and accepted by millions. Still, there was something too unsettling about the book for it to be accepted by such confident voices for the conventional wisdom as *Time* magazine. "Many scientists sympathize with Miss Carson's love of wildlife," *Time* said in its best stodgy fashion, "and even with her mystical attachment to the balance of nature. But they fear that her emotional and inaccurate outburst in *Silent Spring* may do harm by alarming the nontechnical public, while doing no good for the things that she loves."

They need not have worried. Scientists who were willing to use their names—LaMont Cole, Loren Eisley, Julian Huxley, and others—defended and praised the book. Seven years after the book's publication, *Time* introduced a new section in the magazine. It was called The Environment and was accompanied by a photograph of Rachel Carson. The book had prevailed.

Rachel Carson did not live to see DDT banned or to follow the successes and setbacks of the movement her book launched. She died two years after it was published, at her home in Silver Spring, Maryland. She had testified before Congress and appeared on television and been honored widely. She accepted it all with grace and good humor. (Tiring, perhaps, of the nature-loving–foodfaddist charges, she once answered the question "Miss Carson, what do *you* eat?" by saying, "Chlorinated hydrocarbons, just like everyone else.") She left some of her money to the Sierra Club and The Nature Conservancy, and there is a vast wildlife preserve named for her in Maine. A small organization run by a friend continues her work and answers the occasional letter that still comes in addressed to Rachel Carson, usually from someone who has just read the book.

The fight to save the earth from our own destructive excesses will never end. Or, if it does, it will end badly. But since *Silent Spring*, the pelicans and the ospreys have returned. In the morning before I wrote these words, my daughter and I watched from our porch as a pair of ospreys flew along the beach, hunting fish. We admired them together, their graceful, purposeful flight and their heart-catching dives when they spotted prey. They flew on, returning no doubt to their nests and their young, with small fish impaled on their talons. Several large flocks of pelicans also came by, flying in echelon, low to the water, on their way to a rookery. We watched with shared awe, and I recalled some lines Rachel Carson had written a year or two before she began work on *Silent Spring*. Her subject was encouraging awareness in children, and it could serve as a coda:

A child's world is fresh and new and beautiful, full of wonder and excitement. It is our misfortune that for most of us that clear-eyed vision, that true instinct for what is beautiful and awe-inspiring, is dimmed and even lost before we reach adulthood. If I had influence with the good fairy who is supposed to preside over the christening of all children I should ask that her gift to each child in the world be a sense of wonder so indestructible that it would last throughout life, as an unfailing antidote against the boredom and disenchantments of later years, the sterile preoccupation with things that are artificial, the alienation from the sources of our strength.

That sense of wonder never left Rachel Carson. It was her own source of strength and her legacy.

RACHEL CARSON *was born on May 27, 1907, in Springdale, Pennsylvania.*

She grew up on a small farm. Her mother encouraged her to explore the outdoors, and she spent many childhood hours alone in the woods.

She often missed school, perhaps because of her mother's extreme concern for her health.

She loved to read, and from childhood she assumed she would be an author. Her first writing success came at the age of ten, when St. Nicholas *magazine, a children's publication, bought one of her stories. She once said that she doubted "any royalty check of recent years has given me as great joy as the notice of that award."*

Carson had few childhood friends; her teachers paid more attention to her than did her classmates. Next to her high school yearbook photograph was written: "Rachel's like the mid-day sun/Always very bright/Never stops her studying/'Til she gets it right."

In her second year at the Pennsylvania College for Women she took a required course in biology, and by her junior year she had declared a major in zoology. She went on to get an M.A. in genetics at Johns Hopkins, believing that she had abandoned a literary career.

She nonetheless persisted in writing poetry. The Atlantic Monthly *and* The Saturday Evening Post *were among the magazines to reject her work.*

During the 1930s she wrote a series of newspaper articles that served as a trial run for her first book, Under the Sea-Wind, *published in 1941. Typically, she would be paid ten dollars for a short article printed in the Baltimore* Sunday Sun *and titled "Chesapeake Eels Seek the Sargasso Sea."*

Her father died suddenly in 1935; to help support her family and herself, Carson found work with the Bureau of Fisheries in Washington, D.C. She worked as a scriptwriter for a series of broadcasts called Romance Under the Waters.

When her older sister, Marian, died in 1936, Rachel and her mother raised Marian's two children. Needing more money, she took a civil service examination for a job as a "junior aquatic biologist." The only woman to compete for the job, she got the top score. Earning two thousand dollars a year, she worked out of a first-floor office facing an interior court. One day, while trying to glimpse the sky, she remarked, "It's like working in the bottom of a well."

She loved cats, and felt that her three Persians helped her to write. They took turns lying on the manuscripts beside her typewriter.

She hated cooking and left it to her mother. Her mother didn't encourage her to marry, and she never did, prompting some to call Carson "the nun of nature."

Louis J. Halle, the author of Spring in Washington, *met Carson in 1947 and remembered her as "quiet, diffident, neat, proper, and without any affectation. . . . She had dignity; she was serious; and, as with Lear's Cordelia, 'her voice was ever soft, gentle and low.'"*

She did not have much patience for small talk, but her friends credited her with a nice sense of humor.

She was, however, essentially a private person. When, after fifteen years as a relatively obscure government employee, she suddenly found herself famous, she didn't like it. Once, after The Sea Around Us *was published, she was staying with her mother in a motel. Early one morning someone came to the door, pushed her mother aside, and presented two books to Carson for autographing. The author, still in bed, was annoyed.*

She was a perfectionist and wrote slowly—about five hundred words a day. She wrote her first drafts in longhand, revised and revised, then had someone read the passages aloud so she could listen for "passages where disharmonies of sound might distract attention from the thought."

She read other authors frequently. Among her favorites were Thoreau and Melville. She reread Henry Williamson's Tarka the Otter *"more times than I can count."*

Carson felt her theories on nature did not contradict her belief in God. She accepted the theory of evolution; when her mother reminded her once that the Bible says God created the world, Carson replied, "Yes, and General Motors created the Oldsmobile, but how *is the question."*

At the age of fifty-six, at her home in Silver Spring, Maryland, Carson died of cancer.

"I am not afraid of being thought a sentimentalist," she once said, "when I say that I believe natural beauty has a necessary place in the spiritual development of any individual or any society. I believe that whenever we . . . substitute something man-made and artificial for a natural feature of the earth, we have retarded some part of man's spiritual growth. . . ."

Ralph Nader, Public Eye

KEN AULETTA

SNOW PELTED THE LATE-MODEL PLYMOUTH VOLARE AS IT SLID OUT OF THE CITY OF
Oswego, New York, on its way along Route 57 to Syracuse, forty miles south.
Harnessed in the front seat by a three-point seat belt was the guest speaker at
the State University at Oswego that night, accompanied by three undergraduates who had volunteered to drive him to his hotel, near the airport.

The four-door Plymouth barreled along at about thirty-five miles per hour,
lashed by heavy winds that shoved it left and right, pounded by the thickest
snowfall of the year. Suddenly, just after midnight, the car skidded out of control, spinning perpendicular to the highway, its momentum carrying it forward,
slicing through knee-deep drifts, scraping and jumping a wall of ice, and coming to a halt at a forty-five-degree angle at the bottom of a ditch dividing the
four-lane highway.

While the car spun, the passenger in the front seat said nothing. He sat
calmly holding a giant manila accordion file folder containing brochures in his
lap, wrapped in the same black raincoat, gray baggy suit, and blue oxford shirt
he had worn to give five college speeches in thirty hours. While the car spun,
the passengers in the back seat anxiously turned to check that another automobile would not plow into the Plymouth, that the car would not skid to the right,
where a steep plunge menaced. All the while, the passenger in the front seat
fixed his dark, intense eyes on the feet of the driver, never wavering through-

out. When the car finally jolted to a halt, the passenger coolly complimented the student who was driving, Michael Murray of New City, New York, for keeping his foot off the brake. The car might have flipped over had Murray hit the brakes. "That was a classic case of a hydroplane landing," marveled Ralph Nader.

There were no injuries, but the Plymouth was hopelessly mired in the snow. It would take two hours for a tow truck to arrive to yank the car from the ditch, leaving time to contemplate life, and cars, and safety. Ever the evangelist— much like the reverend who asks for witnesses for Christ, Nader's speeches often begin, "How many of you are hungry to become fighters for justice in America?"—Nader pulled from his folder one of the few remaining brochures he had not dispensed in two days, this one illustrating how automobiles equipped with air bags could save lives. Nader was asked how the safety features of this car differed from the first cars he exposed in *Unsafe at Any Speed,* the book that catapulted him to national prominence in 1965.

In rapid order, Nader slapped the dashboard, which is now padded; turned around and gripped the headrest, which now prevents whiplash; touched the steering wheel, which is now padded; rubbed the shift handle, which is no longer "shaped like a dagger"; touched the rearview mirror, which now breaks away on impact, and ran his fingers along the rounded frame, which used to have sharp edges—"That took me five years," he sighed; pulled the safety belt harness, which is now mandatory; pointed to the front window, which is now more shatter-resistant. Stronger door latches, Nader said, now keep doors from flying open during a collision and reinforced steel in the doors affords extra protection.

Although Nader was far from satisfied—"None of these changes was done after 1969, except to reinforce the door"—there is no denying Ralph Nader's legacy. Just eighteen years ago automobile manufacturers claimed that their customers were unconcerned about safety features and should remain free to choose their own interior styles. Nader responded that his copy of the Constitution nowhere asserted a civil liberty "to go through the windshield." Largely through Nader's efforts—with a powerful assist from General Motors, which stupidly assigned a private detective to spy on the young attorney—in 1966 Congress passed the National Traffic and Motor Vehicle Safety Act, establishing a federal agency to set national safety standards and with the power to recall defective cars. Since then, 102.5 million automobiles have been recalled for safety reasons.

Reflecting back on his eighteen years of service as America's foremost consumer advocate, Nader sat recently in his spartan Washington office, surrounded by cartons of printed material generated by the various consumer organizations he has spawned, and softly said, "I think we saved a lot of lives."

Nader's activities have not surprised people who knew the young Ralph Nader. At Princeton University and Harvard law school, classmate Theodore J. Jacobs noted that Nader was different. "I always thought he'd be extraordinary because he didn't have the same value set as everybody," says Jacobs, who had been Nader's administrative right arm until they had a falling-out in 1975. Nader lived alone, and even then he was obsessive. Between their junior and senior years, many Princeton students received scholarships to go abroad. Most treated it like a vacation, including Jacobs, who says, "I went to England to study town planning—and went to Spain on a side trip. Ralph went to Lebanon—and took side trips to Ethiopia and Cyprus." Nader, he remembers, wangled credentials as a stringer for a newspaper and somehow managed to interview Emperor Haile Selassie.

The drive and intensity—the religious fervor—could be seen even earlier, in the boy born in Winsted, Connecticut, in 1934, the youngest of four children of Lebanese-born parents. His parents ran a restaurant and bakery, but they spoke often of injustice. "When they sat around the table growing up it was like the Kennedys," says Mark Green, a friend of Nader's. "Except the subject was not power but justice." His father "is an Old Testament prophet—righteous," says former Federal Trade Commission Chairman Michael Pertschuk, who has visited the family home. When the father thought a store was charging too much, he thundered. When the mother wanted the library to carry a book, she exercised more charm but was no less persistent. At the age of four, Ralph hung around the courthouse listening to lawyers argue cases, and dreamed of becoming a people's lawyer. "I read all the muckraker books before I was fourteen— *America's 60 Families, The Jungle*," says Nader. "Ralph has an inner core that burns," says Jacobs.

After Princeton and Harvard, where he wrote a paper on automobile safety, Nader practiced law in Connecticut. He came to Washington in 1964 and, in his words, "poked around the auto safety issue to see what could be done." He went to work for Assistant Secretary of Labor Daniel Patrick Moynihan, who shared his interest in auto safety.

When Nader's book was published, and after it was revealed that General Motors had spied on him, Nader was transformed into a noble David who bested the giant Goliath. The media feasted on the tall, thin, Jimmy Stewart-type character with the monkish ways who lived in a rooming house; had few possessions; ate only when reminded to, preferring raw vegetables and nuts; took no salary except expenses; and set himself up as a people's lawyer, the consumer's watchdog.

One sees Nader's persistence in his shoes. They are low-cut black Army dress shoes with worn, slanted heels. When he served as a cook in the Army in 1959, Nader says, he purchased twelve pairs of low-cuts for six dollars apiece at the PX. He now wears the eleventh pair, and he says that to buy new heels would cost more than he paid for the shoes. Nader has not purchased a pair of dress shoes since, and he boasts of the one new pair waiting in the closet of his one-room efficiency apartment in Washington, just off Du Pont Circle. Nor has Nader purchased a pair of socks since selecting four dozen calf-length cotton-and-wool socks for thirty-five cents a pair at the PX. "I only regret that I didn't buy two dozen more," he says.

No doubt, a priestly life-style was a key factor in Nader's success. "If he were living in Chevy Chase with a wife and two kids, he never would have gotten the attention he got," says longtime Nader associate Donald Ross. Nader fed the media's hunger for novelty, without allowing success to alter his life-style. Today Nader says he lives on five thousand to six thousand dollars in annual expenses. And he is no less fanatical about what goes in his stomach: in the course of two days on the road recently, Nader accepted a tuna fish sandwich only after quizzing the activist who picked him up at the Boston airport, "Is this today's tuna?"; he grilled two different students about whether the grape punch served at Salem State College was real grape; at Oswego he was thirsty but would not allow the red punch to touch his lips, wondered why the fish served at dinner was fried, and was shocked that anyone would touch the roast beef, saying, "Did you see how red that meat was?" Although Nader can laugh at himself, he says he eats only fourteen pounds of meat a year, can tell you how many teaspoons of sugar are in a can of Coke (nine), and has in the past referred to cigarette smokers as being "weak" in character.

Nader was not the first to advance the issue of consumer rights—one thinks of William Jennings Bryan and nineteenth-century Populists, of the turn-of-the-century muckrakers and Teddy Roosevelt, of the National Recovery Administration's Consumers' Advisory Board during the New Deal, and more recently of former senators Estes Kefauver and Hubert Humphrey. But Nader devoted his full-time energies to this task, recruited staff members at modest salaries and hundreds of volunteers to join his mission to create a Fifth Estate to represent the public against what Nader saw as an unholy alliance between corporations and the government. Under his leadership, they launched studies of corporations and their government regulators. Nader was on the phone to the White House. Nader was testifying on Capitol Hill. Nader was secretly meeting with bureaucratic Deep Throats, unearthing fresh tales of corporate and government perfidy. Nader was huddling late in the night with reporters, parceling out valuable nuggets of news. Nader seemed to be everywhere.

This persistent man left his stamp on more than the auto industry. His well-publicized exposés contributed to a hailstorm of consumer legislation and regulations: meat-packing houses were required to be inspected and to meet minimum standards with passage of the Wholesome Meat Act of 1967; the dangers of working on gas pipelines or in the coal mines were addressed by the Natural Gas Pipeline Safety Act of 1968 and the Federal Coal Mine Health and Safety Act of 1968; revelations about the perils of exposure to unnecessary radiation prompted Congress to pass the Radiation Control for Health and Safety Act of 1968. Additional studies played a role in the passage of the Wholesome Poultry Product Act, the Occupational Safety and Health Act (OSHA), the Safe Water Drinking Act, and the Consumer Product Safety Act. In all, between 1966 and 1973 Congress passed more than twenty-five pieces of consumer, environmental, and regulatory reforms.

Turning from the Congress to the executive branch, Nader aimed the first of what came to be known as "Nader's Raiders" reports at the Federal Trade Commission, an agency created in 1914 to regulate unfair competition and later granted powers to prevent "deceptive acts and practices" of business. This exposé revealed agency mismanagement; worse, it showed the agency was captive to the very industries it was entrusted to police. An embarrassed Nixon administration commissioned its own study, conducted by the American Bar Association, which led to new regulations requiring advertisers to justify the truthfulness of their claims (e.g., "Gets your oven thirty-five percent cleaner").

Another report, "The Chemical Feast," probed the law enforcement efforts of the Food and Drug Administration. Within a year, the three top officials at the agency had resigned and been replaced and the federal government had banished cyclamates from soft drinks and induced manufacturers to cease putting MSG in baby food, two of the report's principal recommendations.

Nader's Raiders struck again and again: evaluations of the government's air and water pollution controls spurred the creation of the Environmental Protection Agency; probes of smoking and sewage dumping led to the creation of no-smoking sections on commercial airlines and to a ban on sewage dumping on railroad tracks; greater public awareness was aroused about the health hazards posed by agricultural pesticides, hormones, additives, and animal antibiotics, and about the cause of brown-lung disease among textile workers.

With a strong push from Nader, Congress passed the Freedom of Information Act in 1974, the only law of its kind in the world. "This law is a hammer you can hold over government," says Donald Ross. Take toxic wastes, for instance. If citizens didn't have access to government records, government might not perform toxic tests and need not worry about releasing the results. "Almost every study we did of a government agency, the records were generated from Freedom of Information requests," says Ross. This "hammer" helped open another avenue to Nader: the courtroom. When Nader couldn't get information from government, he hauled officials into court, pioneering what are now commonly referred to as citizen action suits. Identifying himself as a "consumer of milk," for example, Nader attempted to force the government to rescind a milk-price-support hike granted in 1971. Nader claimed that the milk industry had used "improper and unlawful influences" by donating $422,500 in campaign contributions to Richard Nixon in 1972.

To advance his crusade against unchecked power, Nader went beyond the original muckrakers in that he did more than expose injustice. He helped create new institutional mechanisms. Tapping his writing and lecture fees, he financed the Center for Study of Responsive Law in 1969, which was the guerrilla base of operations for Nader's Raiders. Public Citizen, formed in 1971, became the umbrella organization for a variety of efforts, including the Health Research Group, which, under Dr. Sidney Wolfe and a staff of nine, monitors the federal health regulatory agencies and has been responsible for drawing attention to and prohibiting the use of Red Dye No. 2 and asbestos in spackling and joint compounds. The Litigation Group serves as the legal arm, bringing citizen action suits under the direction of former federal prosecutor Alan Morrison. The lobbying arm is provided by Congress Watch, which also serves as their legislative watchdog. Nader's original Public Interest Research Group

(PIRG), formed in 1970, consists of young consumer and political reform activists and has since inspired PIRG organizations in twenty-six states; in New York State alone PIRG has a budget of over $2 million, twenty-five offices, seventeen campus organizations, and 125 paid workers. These are but several of the organizations hatched by Nader and then spun off on their own, free from his day-to-day direction. "He sends his children out the door," says Alan Morrison, one of many individuals recruited by Nader who now shine on their own.

While Nader keeps in daily contact from his nearby Washington office, or from telephone booths, today he personally supervises just four organizations: the original Center for Study of Responsive Law, the Corporate Accountability Research Group, the Public Interest Research Group, and the Telecommunications Research and Action Center.

Not surprisingly, by 1972 Ralph Nader was a household name, regularly listed among the most-admired Americans. George McGovern, the Democratic nominee for President in 1972, talked of strengthening his faltering candidacy by asking Nader to run as his Vice-President. Four years later President-elect Jimmy Carter invited Nader to Plains, Georgia, to solicit advice. Many former Nader's Raiders were sprinkled throughout the Carter government. And during those next four years Nader played a role in lobbying for the successful deregulation of the airline and trucking industries.

"More than anyone else, Nader made the consumer movement a considerable factor in American economic and political and social life," says former Connecticut senator Abraham Ribicoff, who chaired the first auto safety hearing to call Nadar as a witness. "He was the guardian at the gates." Without Nader's efforts, there would not be a consumer adviser appointed by the President, says Betty Furness, the first to serve in that capacity, under Lyndon B. Johnson. All through her term, says Furness, she was always aware that Nader was watching. In his 1982 book, *Revolt Against Regulation,* former FTC chairman and Senate aide Michael Pertschuk writes of Nader: "For a very broad segment of the U.S. public, his has been the voice and persona of a contemporary Old Testament prophet . . . calling society to account for its drift from its own professed morality. . . . For those already enlisted in the consumer cause, he was the drill sergeant. He roused us from sleep and relaxation and plagued us into the night."

Back in the mid-Sixties, observes Joan Claybrook, president of Public Citizen, consumers rarely complained. They were passive. Today they drag merchants into small-claims court. "Now," she continues, "every county executive or mayor has a department of consumer affairs. Every TV station has a consumer reporter. Every newspaper has consumer reporters." According to the National Association of Consumer Agency Administrators, there are approximately 250 state and local consumer affairs departments; thirty-one states have independent consumer offices, and about forty states have consumer divisions with the state attorney general's office. All of this activity came in Nader's wake.

Even Nader's adversaries acknowledge his legacy. Asserting that Nader probably belongs on any list of the fifty most influential Americans in this century, James Miller, President Reagan's FTC chairman, says, "Nader was more effective than anyone else in dramatizing the need for information. There are market imperfections that need to be addressed." While disapproving of Nader's tactics, Miller says his early efforts led to a "recognition of the need for regulations in some areas. Some of the auto safety aspects, some of the products and drugs—especially in the safety area." Finally, he says, "Nader was one of the important catalysts in the airline and trucking deregulation debates." Boyden Gray, counsel to Vice-President George Bush and the coordinator of Reagan's Task Force on Regulatory Relief, says of Nader, "He raised the consciousness of the consumer as consumer, and my guess is that his legacy will be great."

For almost twenty years, Ralph Nader has been America's premier scold. Although polls suggest he is less popular today than he was, and his bristly righteousness and unwillingness to compromise have alienated many members of Congress, Nader says he still receives between fifteen hundred and two thousand letters a week, many simply addressed, RALPH NADER, WASHINGTON, D.C. Among college students, with whom he spends about a fifth of his time— lecturing, proselytizing, recruiting, hawking brochures—the Reverend Ralph still draws large, enthusiastic audiences. On the trip that ended in a snow-covered ditch outside Oswego, Nader had made five different speeches at five different campuses, surprising audiences with his humor. But while the wit may be newly developed, Nader himself remains remarkably unchanged. And unchanged, too, is the reaction he arouses among many idealistic college students. After listening to him talk at Tufts University, in Massachusetts, Ruth Moscow, a senior from Birmingham, Michigan, exclaimed, "One of the reasons he's important is that he tells me to be idealistic. I'm constantly told, 'Be realistic.' 'Don't be a dreamer.' He tells me that's not true, that I can make a difference. . . . He makes me feel that I have the power to change society." "That notion—that the individual can make a difference—" says Dr. Sidney Wolfe, "is the guts of consumerism."

Nader bridles at being called a scold. People frequently ask why he is so negative. "I say to people, 'Do you say the cop who catches a burglar is negative?' I'm trying to stop corporate criminals. No one in the country is more negative than General Motors. They're forcing you to breathe their noxious and toxic fumes."

This self-appointed-cop image crystallizes the least attractive side of Nader. For Nader represents many of those who came out of the Sixties armed with their Manichaean view of politics, dividing the world into workers versus corporations, white versus dark hats, us versus *them*. While speaking at Tufts, for example, Nader said of elected officials: "What matters are citizens organizing out there because they're *all* opportunists." Imagine if he had said, "*All* Jews or *all* blacks are . . ." Pollution caused by corporations Nader largely blames on "the factor of evil"—not on ignorance, or panic, or cowardice.

Little wonder, then, that members of Congress who vote with Nader on ninety-nine out of one hundred issues are rankled to be denounced as tools of the special interests for a single vote. Even friends of Nader concede he could have gained passage of a Federal Consumer Protection Agency had he been willing to compromise. But Nader is more visionary than pragmatic as a leader. His strengths are his weaknesses. If he had been more flexible, he might have accomplished more. But he would not be the Ralph Nader we know.

Nader piously believes that he can define "the public interest" on most issues, but he often fails to see when legitimate interests collide. What happens when "sainted" workers have a stake in the fortunes of the "evil" auto companies? Or when the interests of employees in protecting their jobs through new trade barriers collide with the interests of consumers, who desire the lower prices of products made in Taiwan? Peter Schuck, a former Nader's Raider, told Larry Leamer, author of *Playing It for Keeps in Washington,* that, like many zealots, Nader was "hostile to politics. They tend to be interested in an antipolitical nirvana where issues are decided on their merits. Part of it is a class thing. People trained at Harvard law school tend to be snobbish. They think they're better than politicians. They forget or refuse to acknowledge what politics is all about. It's a way of getting consent. A politician is mediocre in the way an average citizen is mediocre. A politician's job is to balance the needs of an intense minority with the needs of a large constituency."

Irving Kristol, coeditor of *Public Interest* and a leading conservative theoretician, makes a parallel argument: "The socialist countries regulate less than we do because the socialists take responsibility for running their countries efficiently. Nader takes no responsibility. He only attitudinizes." And the attitude Kristol thinks Nader bequeaths—that politics and government are about greed and corruption—inadvertently fans the very public cynicism Ralph Nader has devoted his adult life to erasing.

This argument about attitude can be taken one step further and leads to a recognition that Nader is more useful as a prod than a prophet, better as a catalyst than a leader. For Nader's concept of an adversarial society, one in which government deals sternly with business, and labor eyes management as an implacable foe, wars with the widespread conviction that America must learn from the Japanese and practice greater conciliation and partnership among government, labor, and business. Cooperation, not confrontation, is the new buzz word of most students of the American economy. In this sense, Ralph Nader is preaching a discredited and perhaps dangerous gospel.

Nader has left another negative legacy, say Kristol and others who view Nader as an emblem for an overregulated society. Vice-President Bush's counsel, Boyden Gray, estimates that the Reagan administration's efforts to reduce many of the regulations inspired by Nader will save "seventy billion dollars' worth of costs to the public over the next decade." Kristol, who serves as a director of Warner Lambert, a pharmaceutical firm, says of Nader and his associates, "They're constantly scaring people by exaggerating the dimensions of real problems. You end up with overregulation." In order to introduce a new product line, he says, drug companies like Warner Lambert must spend tens of millions more to comply with federal regulations, resulting in higher prices to consumers.

Why, asks James Miller, chairman of the FTC, do Americans have to get their cars inspected annually? "There's no evidence car inspections do any good." In his memoir, Michael Pertschuk confesses, "We have learned greater respect for somber, unsentimental analysis of the effects of regulation. . . . We have learned to pay greater heed to the social value of the entrepreneur, to value market incentives as a creative force for productivity and growth. . . . We have learned that we must be accountable for the costs and burdens of regulation."

Nader does not dispute that regulations sometimes go too far. He cites his own support for deregulating the airlines and trucking. But deregulation is not the thrust of Nader's efforts. Naderites see a different part of the same elephant, and thus make different generalizations. They focus on benefits, not costs. They focus on the lives and broken bones and cancer and doctors' bills that are saved. The $70 billion of savings claimed by the Reagan administration "are invented," says Alan Morrison. "They cite savings in reduced CETA regulations. Sure. They abolished the entire CETA public works program! They saved money, and threw people out of work." "If the administration's antigovernment nostrums make such sense," says Nader, "how come it didn't work in the eighteenth or nineteenth century?"

Naderism has been on the wane in recent years. Business political action committees (PACs) have launched an effective counteroffensive; the Reagan administration has succeeded in beating back some of Ralph Nader's cherished advances. But a few defeats do not unmake a revolution. As is true with domestic spending programs, the public is conservative about generalities and liberal about specific programs. Citizens are usually against taxes, but they are for Medicare, for social security, and for those government regulations that cleanse the air we breathe, the water we drink. By filling the government with people from the same industries they now regulate, by emphasizing the "Reagan Revolution" and their desire to liberate corporations from government constraints, Reaganites have managed to scare Americans. As Nader went too far in blaming "the system" and portraying individuals as "victims," so Reagan and his team have seesawed too far the other way, permitting their ideological biases to blind them to corporate greed, incompetence, and pollution. Reagan's FTC chairman, James Miller, reluctantly concedes the Reagan administration he serves may have gone too far in its ideological onslaught against regulation. Sitting in his office, overlooking Constitution Avenue, Miller admits that when he took over the FTC in 1981, "I probably did too much demagoging when I came aboard about the need for change. I wanted to put everyone on notice that I was not going to be captured by the institution." What has happened is that the Reagan administration has put the American people on notice that hard-won consumer gains may be threatened by the crowd now in Washington.

If that is a correct assessment—and recent public opinion surveys suggest it is—then the wheel is already turning. Ralph Nader, the Satchel Paige of the consumer movement, is in no danger of disappearing before he outwears his twelfth and final six-dollar pair of Army shoes.

———

RALPH NADER *was born on February 27, 1934, in Winsted, Connecticut.*

As an adolescent, he read books about Alexander the Great and Genghis Khan and the westerns of Zane Grey.

He no longer reads fiction.

He once wrote: "Every time I see something terrible, it's like I see it at age nineteen. I keep a freshness that way."

He once told a teenage audience to ignore the typical problems of adolescence and "concentrate on what's important. This is not the time to fool around, wasting countless hours watching TV or chit-chatting. Not when the future of civilization is at stake."

"Stripped of its mysticism," author Robert Buckhorn has asserted, "Naderism simply is a plea to Americans not to adjust."

At Princeton, in protest against conformist clothing, Nader refused to wear white bucks and once went to class in a bathrobe. He also tried, unsuccessfully, to stop the university from spraying campus trees with DDT.

He called Harvard law school, his alma mater, a "high-priced tool factory" that prepares its students to practice law only in the service of a bank or corporation.

It was at Harvard law that he owned his last car, a 1949 Studebaker.

From 1961 through 1964 he traveled as a free-lance journalist through Europe, the Soviet Union, Latin America, and Africa.

The president of General Motors apologized to Nader after a Senate subcommittee learned that GM had hired detectives to tail him.

In 1967 the U.S. Junior Chamber of Commerce voted him one of the Ten Outstanding Young Men of the Year.

When a lavish suite was reserved for him at the Hotel Meurice in Paris, he asked for an ordinary room instead. He lives in a rooming house in a low-rent district in northwest Washington and never allows anyone to visit him there.

In the 1960s his one major office expense was a telephone. His operations have expanded, but his own office has remained small, cluttered, dimly lit, and uncomfortable.

In the 1970s the Public Interest Research Groups he had inspired were raising a million dollars a year on college campuses.

In 1971 Americans voted him the sixth most popular public figure—in between Spiro Agnew and Pope Paul.

When a music box given to Mamie Eisenhower on her seventy-fifth birthday failed to work, President Richard Nixon quipped, "Where's Ralph Nader?"

During the last few days before a meat-inspection bill became law, Senator Walter Mondale, the sponsor of the bill, would receive phone calls from Nader at three, four, and five in the morning. After a while, Mondale would just pick up the receiver and say, "Hello, Ralph."

Until 1961 he smoked fifteen cigarettes a day. He no longer smokes, and he drinks only an occasional beer or glass of wine. He doesn't eat ground meat or drink coffee.

He once rode in a convertible without a seat belt.

He eats heartily but won't eat if he's too busy. He gets mad when photographers try to take his picture while he's eating. He lectures waitresses about the evils of Coca-Cola, but it's rumored that he eats candy bars.

One of his proudest moments came when, while in the Army, he made banana bread for two thousand soldiers.

Even busy people must exercise, he says; he advises them to run up the stairs of the buildings they enter.

He refuses dinner invitations from friends who have pets.

He doesn't own a television set. He speaks Arabic and has a working knowledge of Chinese, Portuguese, Spanish, and Russian.

He has virtually no social life but in 1976 he was said to have been seen visiting the house of a young woman who lived on Thirty-fourth Street in northwest Washington. Several mornings the two were seen leaving the rear entrance of the house and getting into a car—which she always drove.

He once said, "My impression of people is that their attention span is about two minutes."

He once theorized, "You've got to keep the opposition off balance. Once you get them tumbling, you can't let up. . . ."

Of his notoriety, Nader once said, "I could have gone to Hollywood and married a starlet and gotten fat and talked about what I used to do."

He once defined his ultimate goal as "nothing less than the qualitative reform of the Industrial Revolution."

My Hero, Malcolm X

DAVID BRADLEY

MARTIN LUTHER KING JR. SHOULD HAVE BEEN MY HERO. I WAS A MIDDLE-CLASS BLACK kid, the son of a preacher, carefully trained in the Ways I Should Go: Christianity, the Protestant Ethic, the social responsibility and respectability prescribed by W. E. B. Du Bois for the Talented Tenth—that cadre of "colored, college-bred men" whose mission, Du Bois wrote, would be to keep the black masses from "brooding over the wrongs of the past and the difficulties of the present, so that all their energies may be bent toward a cheerful striving and cooperation with their white neighbors." I should have been inspired by another middle-class black kid—also the son of a preacher, a product of Atlanta and Atlanta University, the very city and institution that inspired Du Bois's thoughts—who became a white-shirted revolutionary, the most brightly shining example of Christian idealism this nation has ever produced.

But Martin Luther King Jr. left me cold. For me there was something missing in both him and his philosophy. I did not know what. I could only say (as I once did to my father in a moment of ill-advised and quickly withdrawn candor) that King knew more of Christ and Gandhi than he did of white people—at least the ones of my acquaintance.

That insight came to me after I read King's "Letter from Birmingham Jail," in which he expressed a disappointment with the lack of activity of the white moderates. Then, dimly and intuitively, I saw that King's ideas were based on the belief that there existed in American society a moral white majority that would be disgusted by the actions of an immoral white minority against a passive black minority and that would take swift and correct action. Clearly a fallacy.

I could not so quickly analyze King's philosophy when I first read "Letter from Birmingham Jail." But then I came across a wholly irreverent but deadly accurate evaluation of King's adoption of Gandhi's philosophy: "Gandhi was a big dark elephant sitting on a little white mouse. King was a little black mouse sitting on top of a big white elephant." When I read that, I knew not only what I had been trying to say but, in the expression of the thought, there was a mighty intelligence at work. I had found my hero. He was Malcolm Little, aka Detroit Red, Satan, El-Hajj Malik El-Shabazz—Malcolm X.

For someone like me to identify with someone like Malcolm was not as far-fetched as it might sound. In fact, the similarities between Malcolm and King are almost bizarre, given the popular perception that their natures were totally different—that King was a master of cool intellectual protest, while Malcom was a thoughtless firebrand. Both were born in the latter part of the 1920s, Malcolm in 1925, King four years later. Both of their fathers were Georgia Baptist preachers, and both had the early and intense exposure to Christian teaching that such parentage implies. Both had below-standard secondary educations, which forced them to play educational catch-up: Malcolm leaving school in the eighth grade; King, on entering college, having only an eighth-grade reading level. Despite that, both were voracious readers and scholars, primarily of religion and philosophy—both were especially familiar with the writings of Thoreau. Both became ministers as well as scholars, in faiths that emphasized discipline, hard work, abstention from vice, and public service; both were married, with children; both were pilgrims abroad, King having journeyed to Gandhi's India, Malcolm having become, like all good Muslims, a pilgrim to Mecca; both were assassinated when they were just about forty.

Their dissimilarities, however, were crucial. King was a child of relative privilege, his family affluent, fixed, secure, traditionally nuclear. Malcolm grew up in poverty, in a family that moved frequently and was finally broken up after his father's death and his mother's dissolution into insanity. King was a product of the urban South, Malcolm of the North, with experience in rural, suburban, and hard-core urban settings. King's educational handicaps did not interfere with a traditional pattern of study; Malcolm was a dropout. King was a product of black schools until after he received his B.A.; Malcolm knew the dubious benefits of school integration firsthand. In addition to his Baptist training, Malcolm had experience with other religions. His mother, before her breakdown, became a Seventh-Day Adventist, a sect whose practices preadapted him to the laws of Islam. But, perhaps most significantly, unlike King, Malcolm had experience not just with poverty but with the entire underside of American society. A street hustler who graduated from shoeshine boy to dope seller, numbers runner, burglar, drug addict, zoot-suiter, chaser of morally depraved white women, jiver, hipster, and convict, Malcolm knew the welfare system, the criminal justice system, the practical workings of American society that contradicted idealistic theory.

He was also the living embodiment of every negative stereotype popularly associated with the American black. As Carl Rowan, then the head of the United States Information Agency, said in response to foreign eulogizing of Malcolm, "All this about an ex-convict, ex–dope peddler who became a racial fanatic."

What Rowan, and almost all of America, failed to understand was that Malcolm's life was truer than King's, his experience more broad and typical. King was the prototype of the New Negro, Malcolm the stereotype Nigger. King was a saint (a woman tried to stab him through the heart; the surgeon who closed the wound set his sutures in the pattern of a cross), Malcolm a sinner (inspired by his atheism, remarkable even in a prison, his fellow inmates named him "Satan"). King said the good things that middle-class black and white America wanted to hear said; Malcolm said what no one in any establishment wanted said. On subject after subject, Malcolm kicked ass.

On the idea that blacks should develop as immigrant groups had: "Everything that comes out of Europe, every blue-eyed thing, is already an American. And as long as you and I have been over here, we aren't Americans yet. They don't have to pass civil rights legislation to make a Polack an American." On the hypocrisy surrounding the position of blacks in America: "I'm not going to sit at your table and watch you eat, with nothing on my plate, and call myself a diner." On blacks and the American heritage: "We didn't land on Plymouth Rock. It landed on us." On white influence in the civil rights movement: "The white man pays Reverend Martin Luther King, subsidizes Reverend Martin Luther King. . . ." On nonviolence as a way of life: "If they make the Klan nonviolent, I'll be nonviolent." On nonviolence as a universal tactic: ". . . if he only understands the language of a rifle, get a rifle. If he only understands the language of a rope, get a rope. But don't waste time talking the wrong language to a man if you really want to communicate with him." On King's reliance on the promise of protection by federal officials from white southern officials: ". . . asking the fox to protect you from the wolf." In speaking this way, with ideas that sprang from the same works of philosophy and religion as King's ideas, but in an idiom that came from earthier experience, Malcolm spoke in a pungent voice for many blacks, especially those least likely to themselves be articulate, least likely to have access to public attention.

Malcolm certainly was articulate and he certainly got attention, probably contributing to acceptance of King. Malcolm was the horrible alternative. King was aware of this effect and used it, referring to Malcolm repeatedly by warning that a failure to redress black grievances might force blacks into more-violent actions, while acknowledging, at the same time, that business leaders had become "prepared to tolerate change in order to avoid costly chaos."

Malcolm was the spokesman of that chaos. For although the Nation of Islam had been around since the Thirties, it was not until 1959 that it was represented by a regular publication, *Muhammad Speaks*, a creation of Malcolm's. And it was also not until 1959 that the Nation received nationwide media attention. That year CBS aired the documentary *The Hate That Hate Produced.* An inflammatorily edited piece of yellow journalism (even Malcolm described it as being "edited to increase the shock mood" and likened public reaction to "what happened back in the 1930s when Orson Welles frightened America with . . . an invasion by 'men from Mars' "), the CBS program featured Malcolm and thrust him into the public spotlight. In part because Elijah Muhammad had declared him a Muslim spokesman, in part because it was Malcolm who had pushed the Muslim faith into media-conscious urban centers of the East—Boston, Philadelphia, then New York—but mainly because his style of expression brought the kind of provocative drama into a live talk-show studio that King could offer only on taped news broadcasts, by 1963, when King spoke of the positive effect of the violent alternative, Malcolm had become the symbol of that alternative. Although the Nation of Islam, which had come to be called the Black Muslims, was not and never had been violent, and in fact strictly eschewed violence save in self-defense, Malcolm chose to go along with the media representation.

Why he went along was never entirely clear. In his *Autobiography* he claims to have been motivated by a desire to defend the Nation of Islam and Elijah Muhammad from the false image presented in *Life, Look, Time, Newsweek,* and nearly every major media outlet in America. However, it is true that he spoke repeatedly to the white media and was, by design, untempered in speech. And he was as aware of some of his effect on the nonviolent struggle as King was, for he told King's wife while King was jailed in Selma: "If the white people realize what the alternative is, perhaps they will be more willing to hear Dr. King."

Which is not to say that Malcolm's strident pronouncements had no effect on the civil rights movement. For it was at the time of his greatest prominence (greater television presence in 1963 than King) that elements of the movement began to espouse Malcolm-like rhetoric and ideas. The planning of the Mississippi Freedom Summer of 1964 was complicated by the notion that it should be a black struggle carried on without white assistance. Nonviolence was seen as a tactical option rather than a moral imperative; in the wake of the triple killing of civil rights workers near Philadelphia, Mississippi, the field workers of both the Student Nonviolent Coordinating Committee and the Congress of Racial Equality asserted their right to wear guns for self-protection. Later, SNCC also adopted Malcolm's position opposing military service for blacks, coining the slogan "Hell no, we won't go," which became the rallying cry of the antidraft movement, and pushing King to consider and oppose the Vietnam War, as Malcolm had done years before.

Within the Nation of Islam, Malcolm's influence waned, due to jealousy, specifically that of Elijah Muhammad. Yet Malcolm's prominence made the Muslims prominent, bringing in a wave of converts and making the Muslim dreams of economic independence more a reality and the Muslim programs of rehabilitation more effective than ever before. These dreams and programs were models for those of other groups, such as the Republic of New Africa and the Black Panthers, whose leaders found that there was a new acceptance in publishing for words written from prison because of the success of Malcolm's *Autobiography*.

Indeed, Malcolm established the rhetorical style that became the hallmark of the various movements of the late Sixties and Seventies. While the antidraft and antiwar movements drew their strategic and tactical models from the nonviolent civil rights movement, their rhetoric, like that of later black groups, was poured hot from the mold of Malcolm rather than beaten in the shape of King's learned, lofty dissertations. From Malcolm came the sharp turns of phrase, the euphony and rhythm that gave Eldridge Cleaver "If you're not part of the solution, you're part of the problem" and H. Rap Brown "Violence is as American as cherry pie."

At the time of his death, Malcolm's influence was only beginning to be felt. Then he was still popularly seen as a madman, a racist, a man of violence. King, with ironic self-righteousness, considering the circumstances of his own demise, on the occasion of Malcolm's assassination said Malcolm was a victim of the violence that had spawned him.

Precisely what Malcolm was the victim of is hard to say. He himself spoke of the danger from other Muslims. "Any number of former brothers felt they would make heroes of themselves in the Nation of Islam if they killed me. . . . No one would kill you quicker than a Muslim if he felt that's what Allah wanted him to do." But assassinations are not always done quickly. Although the likelihood of international involvement has been widely denied, Malcolm was establishing ties with black leaders in Africa and with Muslim leaders in the Middle East. These connections, especially the Middle Eastern ones, which transcended racial lines and which involved a region in which American foreign policy and economic interests were greatly concerned, surely would have made Malcolm's death a source of some relief to many. We do not know who killed Malcolm. We do know that of the four great political assassinations of the Sixties, Malcolm's was most clearly a conspiracy.

And it was a successful conspiracy. For not only did it result in Malcolm's death but that death obscured what is perhaps the greatest importance of Malcolm as a man, a leader, and an example: that by the time he died, Malcolm had changed.

That change was totally unexpected, in fact virtually impossible, given the racial and social theories of the day. Those theories held that once blacks allowed themselves to leave the high road of moral purity, exemplified by Christian forbearance and *agape* love, once they began to hate their oppressors, they would be lost to hopeless, mindless rage. But Malcolm negated that. "In the past," he said after his pilgrimage to Mecca, "yes, I have made sweeping indictments of *all* white people. I never will be guilty of that again—as I know now that some white people *are* truly sincere, that some truly are capable of being brotherly toward a black man."

Impossible as it supposedly was, such a change might have been acceptable had it been simply extreme (America would have loved to have Malcolm re-cant). But Malcolm insisted on *developing*. He did not give up his hating or his accusation of racism. He simply learned to hate institutions: "Here in America, the seeds of racism are so deeply rooted in the white people collectively, their belief that they are 'superior' in some ways is so deeply rooted, that these things are in the national white subconsciousness. . . . The white man's racism toward the black man here in America is what has got him in such trouble all over this world, with other non-white peoples. . . . That's why you've got all of this trouble in places like Viet Nam."

Malcolm's new ideas were, like many of his ideas, ahead of his time. Fortunately, by means of texts of speeches, interviews, and the tapes from which Alex Haley would create his *Autobiography*, Malcolm spoke beyond his time into an era and to ears, like mine, that were able to understand him and needed to.

For while many of his pronouncements seem silly, overly rhetorical, and extreme, he not only made them and admitted to them but he meant them and moved beyond them. His experience encompassed that of so many of us. He experienced, as every black does, the alienation, isolation, deprivation, elimination, exploitation, and subjugation that is dished out by American society. He saw, as every thinking person must see, the terror of racism, the awesome depth of its roots, the awful subtlety of its poisoned fruit. He felt, as every human people must feel, rage and despair and hatred so powerful as to warp the mind. He acknowledged the damage he had suffered. But he survived. Not just physically. Emotionally. Spiritually. He survived.

To any of us who have at times allowed the pain to defeat us and have wondered, while in the throes of it, if this were the anguish of death, to any of us who have succumbed to the feelings and feared that this was a madness from which we could not recover, to any of us who know we could never, because of our lacking or its lacking, follow a philosophy of saintly forbearance, to any of us who have hated so thoroughly that we have wondered if we could ever love again, Malcolm's example did make and continues to make more than a difference. It gives us hope.

MALCOLM X *was born Malcolm Little on May 19, 1925, in Omaha, Nebraska.*

His mother's father was white. In East Lansing, Michigan, where he grew up, his family raised most of its own food. Malcolm had a small garden and he loved to grow peas. When he was four, white men burned down his family's house.

His father was a Baptist minister who believed in the purity of the black race and in the blacks' destiny to return to Africa to attain true freedom, independence, and self-respect. He was brutally killed by two white men when Malcolm was six.

The family eventually split up, and Malcolm's mother suffered a severe break-down.

In school his favorite subjects were English and history. He was elected seventh-grade class president. He wanted to be a lawyer; he was told he could be a carpenter.

In Boston, where he lived as a hustler, he never missed a lindy hop and had a rich white girlfriend. A friend, he once recalled, took him to "groovy, frantic scenes in different chicks' and cats' pads. . . . Everybody blew gage and juiced back and jumped."

He "conked" (straightened) his hair when he was a teenager. Ingredients: Red Devil lye, two eggs, two potatoes, and Vaseline. He later felt conking was his first step toward self-degradation.

In 1946, after committing many robberies, he was sentenced to prison for ten years. He was not quite twenty-one.

In prison, a self-educated burglar called Bimbi got him interested in correspondence courses in English, Latin, and German. Malcolm studied up to fifteen hours a day. His favorite books included H. G. Wells's Outline of History *and J. A. Rogers's three-volume* Sex and Race. *He belonged to a prison debate society.*

He converted to the Muslim religion while in prison. The Honorable Elijah Muhammad wrote him daily for months. When he was released he went to Detroit and became an assistant minister. In 1954 he became the minister of Temple Seven in Harlem.

In the Black Muslim religion, X suggests mystery and the possibility of power over one's peers and enemies.

He had three daughters and a son with Sister Betty X, whom he married in 1958. They lived on Long Island.

He felt black women should play a subordinate role in the home. He said, "I don't know how many marriage breakups are caused by these movie-and-television-addicted women expecting some bouquets and kissing and hugging . . . then getting mad when a poor, scraggly husband comes in tired and sweaty from working like a dog all day, looking for some food."

He quarreled with Jackie Robinson, who, he said, was used by baseball's "white bosses." He guided Muhammad Ali into the Muslim movement. When Malcolm split with Elijah Muhammad, he counseled the wavering Ali to "find out for [himself]" whether to remain in the movement. Ali stayed and later assailed Malcolm as a "hypocrite."

He trusted people very little or not at all. He once called up Alex Haley in the middle of the night, told him, "I trust you seventy percent," then hung up.

In ordinary conversation he was quiet, pleasant, humorous. He loved gossip, celebrities, and parties. He usually drank only orange juice, coffee, or tea. He could talk for hours about his wife, children, food, religion, and fashion.

He did wicked imitations of national civil rights leaders.

He said Europeans were more humane than Americans. He traveled throughout the Middle East, Africa, and Europe, and thought that a knowledge of nonwhite lands was a requisite for black leaders in America.

424

He was tall, with an impressive stature. A New York Times *reporter wrote, "Malcolm X had the physical bearing and the inner self-confidence of a born aristocrat."*

He described himself as the angriest black man in America.

Martin Luther King Jr. said: "I can't deny it. When he starts talking about all that's been done to us, I get a twinge of hate, or identification with him."

A week before his death, two fire bombs exploded in his Queens house while he and his family were inside. He accused Elijah Muhammad of ordering the bombing. Black Muslim leaders in turn accused Malcolm of setting fire to the house himself "to get publicity." Malcolm once remarked, "I live like a man who's already dead."

On February 21, 1965, ten years after his political life began, he was shot by assassins as he addressed four hundred blacks in a Manhattan ballroom.

Back on the Beat with Woodward and Bernstein

STEVEN BRILL

HAVING TACKLED THE PRESIDENCY AND THE SUPREME COURT, BOB WOODWARD IS NOW completing a book about the life and drug taking and drug death of John Belushi. John Belushi? Besides seeing his new subject as an interesting change of pace that is nonetheless packed with "incredible, important stories about Hollywood," Woodward is drawn to the Belushi story, he says, because of its parallels to the Woodward and Bernstein story.

"About the same time that we had the best-selling paperback [*All the President's Men*], hardback [*The Final Days*], and movie [*All the President's Men*]," he explains, "this guy had the top television show [*Saturday Night Live*], the top record album [*The Blues Brothers*], and the top movie [*Animal House*]. And he was our age. And what did he do with it?"

What did *they* do with it? They didn't speedball themselves away, but they have had their ups and downs, enough downs, in fact, that eleven years after the beginning of their Watergate stardom, Carl Bernstein, thirty-nine, and Bob Woodward, forty, seem and sound wiser than their years. "It's all a matter of how seriously you take it all and whether you begin to believe you're something other than you are," adds Woodward as Bernstein, sitting next to him (at an elegant Washington restaurant where the two still get stares from the kinds of people who are embarrassed to stare), nods in agreement.

What they were, and are, is obscured now by the millions we've seen them

426

make, by the Hollywoodization of their work, and by the jolts the two have suffered (a lost libel trial, two failed attempts to be bigwig news executives, two divorces, and one well-publicized Pulitzer scandal). More than that, the significance
of their work is also obscured by its own success. It seems impossible today that
such household names and words as Donald Segretti, dirty tricks, or Howard Hunt
were once scoops. But they were. And they were Woodward and Bernstein's
scoops, ground out by two plodding reporters, whose original Watergate reporting
in *The Washington Post* in 1972 and 1973 stands today as all it was cracked up to be,
and more, just as their rabidly criticized account of the end of the Nixon presidency, *The Final Days*, towers over other writing about that trauma.

It is not a role they seemed destined for. On the night of the Watergate
break-in in June 1972, Woodward and Bernstein were making a combined salary of less than thirty thousand dollars. Woodward, twenty-nine, had been at
the *Post* for only nine months, having spent five years as a naval officer following college at Yale. A poor writer, he was regarded as one of the lesser lights on
one of the paper's lesser sections, the metropolitan desk. Bernstein, twenty-
eight and the son of a District of Columbia tailor, had dropped out of the University of Maryland to become a reporter at nineteen. Disheveled,
temperamental, and bad on deadlines, he was regarded as a prima donna whose
long feature pieces about local Virginia politics and people were not badly written but probably not good enough to save him from getting fired one day soon
when he rubbed one editor too many the wrong way. In short, these two
weren't world-beaters.

Nor were they a likely team. Despite many highs and lows in their celebrated
relationship, they are now good friends, the kind who as single fathers get together for the weekend and chuckle over how Bernstein's second son has a
crush on Woodward's daughter. But on the morning of the break-in each
viewed the other with contempt. Woodward saw himself being teamed with a
shaggy flower-child journalist; the newsroom-hardened Bernstein saw himself
stuck with a green Yalie.

They quickly found that one thing did bind them: they were real reporters—
not inside-reporters who "cover" the White House for the big dailies and the
newsweeklies and the networks by lapping up leaks from whichever presidential assistant wants to float a trial balloon or embarrass a colleague. So while
most of the rest of the press, including their own paper's White House reporters, reacted to the Watergate break-in with a yawn and a call or two to a top
Nixon aide who assured them that all was kosher, Woodward and Bernstein
were eager to go out and get the story.

They were the first to report that the Watergate burglars were involved with
Howard Hunt and that Hunt was a former CIA operative and was now a White
House "consultant" working for Charles Colson. (There were laughs in the
Post newsroom when Woodward asked an insider-colleague who Colson was.)
How did they find out about Hunt? By getting a copy of the names in an ad-
dress book seized from one of the arrested burglars and noticing "Hunt–W.H."
They then called the White House switchboard and tracked Hunt to Colson's

office and then to a local P.R. firm, whose president volunteered—after what would become the famous Woodward interview method of flattering people by asking their "advice"—that Hunt had worked for the CIA, which they checked with the CIA. (It was after the Hunt story on June 20 that Ziegler, in dismissing the *Post* charge that the burglars were connected to a White House consultant, characterized Watergate as a "third-rate burglary attempt" unworthy of further White House comment.)

And so it went. They made lists, and lists of lists, and hundreds of needle-in-the-haystack phone calls and visits to people's houses and forays into court records. As a result they were the first to link the money paid to the burglars to the Nixon campaign fund, the first to write about Donald Segretti and his "dirty tricks," and the first to report that a secret cash fund at the White House used to pay the burglars and Segretti was controlled by, among others, John Mitchell and H. R. Haldeman. Most important, they came to believe the unbelievable, that the cover-up might be linked to the President himself.

"There came a time," Woodward recalls, "when I said to Carl, 'You know, he could be impeached for this.' And we agreed right then that we could never ever even mention that thought to anyone—not ever, because they'd think we were crazy."

With thoughts like that, spoken or not, they remained outsiders, local reporters covering what had become—*because of their reporting*—a story for the national desk to take over and give to its more experienced, more established reporters. *Post* executive editor Ben Bradlee's decision (primarily at the urging of city editor Barry Sussman) not to take the story away from them insured one legacy of Woodward and Bernstein's work: the lesson, still usually ignored, that reporters who become too close to what they cover—veterans of the White House beat, for example—lose their drive to be the distanced diggers that they're supposed to be.

Federal District Court Judge John Sirica, who presided over the Watergate burglars' guilty pleas, has never been shy about taking credit for the fact that the cover-up was blown open in large part by burglar James McCord's post-guilty-plea letter to Sirica. But even Sirica credits the two reporters. "It was their pressure," he says, "that did it—their stories constantly questioning the White House's version of things that kept the spotlight on the story and encouraged the rest of the press and the prosecutors and then McCord to reveal the truth."

Four months after the June 1972 break-in, Woodward and Bernstein signed a contract for an advance of $27,500 apiece to write a book for Simon and Schuster. They were going to reveal the real story of Watergate. But by mid-1973, with that story rapidly becoming public issue number one, and with all the details of the burglary and cover-up unfolding in the media every day, it seemed they had little to write. It was then, according to both, that Woodward got the idea to write a narrative about how *they* had broken the Watergate story. Once they worked out the structure, they polished off a draft of three fourths of the book in six weeks, with each writing the parts they had been most involved in reporting. Their progress came as a relief to the Simon and

Schuster people, who had begun to worry that despite the fact their authors had won the Pulitzer they were not going to produce a book with anything terribly special in it.

If Woodward and Bernstein's Watergate reporting gave them their place in journalism's hall of fame, it was this account of how they did it—in book and then movie form—that made them true stars, and rich ones. At the time *All the President's Men* was the fastest-selling nonfiction hardback in publishing history. It sold 293,000 copies, and was followed by a paperback, the rights for which were auctioned off at $1,050,000 (another record), and by the movie, starring Robert Redford (Woodward) and Dustin Hoffman (Bernstein), which quickly hit the top of *Variety*'s gross-revenue charts.

Such fame and fortune was not destined to win the once-unknowns a lot of friends among their more established but less rewarded colleagues. And *All the President's Men*, self-serving, if riveting, memoir that it was, was roundly criticized as self-puffery. One of the more notable attacks came from writer Edward Jay Epstein, who opined in *Commentary* that Woodward and Bernstein had done nothing more as "investigative" reporters than report leaks from the law enforcement officials who were doing the real work of bringing the Watergate higher-ups to justice.

Epstein had a good point—generically. Much of what is glorified as scoop investigative reporting is, indeed, little more than the reporting of an ongoing investigation by law enforcement officials. The initial Abscam stories are good examples.

But Woodward and Bernstein did something different. First, they reported much that the investigators had not found and were not about to find because they weren't looking (such as who controlled the secret campaign cash fund). Second, they reported what the investigators had found but had not pursued, such as the Segretti dirty tricks program. In short, the overriding message of their stories was that the investigation was a sham. It was as if Abscam had gone forward but then been shut down prior to indictments because the White House had decided not to indict the people who were caught.

But what about their Deep Throat scam?

There came a time in the summer of 1972 when Woodward and Bernstein put aside all the jealousies and suspicions that had divided them and made a tacit agreement, consummated with an uneasy look from one followed by a grin from the other. An agreement to lie.

One day, Woodward—nagged by his *Post* editors to come up with a second source for everything no matter how convincing the first source—blurted out that his source was Deep Throat, a "government official" he had cited, truthfully, as having provided information for an article a week or two before. Bernstein knew Woodward hadn't consulted Deep Throat for this new story, that, in fact, there was only one source, though an excellent one. Bernstein stared across the editor's office at Woodward, then flashed him a half grin. Hah, he thought to himself. Mr. Straightarrow's lying. Maybe he *is* human. Woodward looked at Bernstein, then looked away, embarrassed at his lie but pleased that it had worked.

And so was born the Deep Throat myth. The duo took to invoking Throat incessantly (always with the same earnest Woodward citing him) as a backup second source or as a composite to take the place of real second sources with less-impressive credentials or whose credentials, if cited, would compromise their anonymity. It turned into a snowballing white lie that helped spice things up when it came time to write a book and screenplay about their Watergate sleuthing.

Sorry. The last few paragraphs are a hoax. But they're believable in large part because Woodward and Bernstein made omniscient, all-innermost-thoughts-revealed, uncheckable-because-it's-unsourced journalism credible, even glamorous.

I don't agree with the guesses of many of Woodward and Bernstein's closest friends that Deep Throat is a nonreal composite. But had I let those few paragraphs stand and simply said in an introduction that my sources were "people involved who spoke only on the condition that their identities not be revealed" and then refused comment after Woodward and Bernstein either denied my story or themselves declined comment, I would probably have been believed by most readers. More important, someone would have published my "account" as journalism.

Ask journalists, and the politicians and businessmen whom journalists write about, what they think Woodward and Bernstein's legacy is and you hear that complaint over and over—that the most excessive of the "post-Watergate" excesses has to do with the new respect and power given to "investigative" reporters with anonymous sources.

Yet whatever these two reporters did by way of creating a climate of opportunity for sourceless frauds (not just *Washington Post* Pulitzer "winner" Janet Cooke, but hundreds of others whose deceptions are not as extreme and/or who haven't been caught), they have more than made up for it by the fact that their own work was the real thing. And in the process of purveying it, they not only brought down a crooked President but also reminded us of what a good idea the Founding Fathers had when they passed the First Amendment. Besides, blaming post-Watergate journalism abuses on Woodward and Bernstein is a bit like saying that Abe Lincoln ruined politics because he was so genuine that he made people trust politicians.

Still, to most reporters Woodward and Bernstein crossed the most permissive boundary of "responsible" journalism in early 1976 with their publication of *The Final Days*. The book caused what in Watergate lingo can only be called a fire storm. Woodward and Bernstein were pilloried by reviewers, mostly fellow reporters, for their omniscient, sourceless narrative of the last days of the Nixon presidency. The clamor grew louder as the book quickly outdistanced *All the President's Men* as the fastest-selling nonfiction hardback ever. In the end, 619,000 hardcover copies were sold, but not before Woodward and Bernstein became such obsessive targets of the press that they agreed to go on *Meet the Press*—as guests—to answer for their scoops. Among the inquisitors on the Sunday talk show was a very angry Jack Nelson. As the *Los Angeles Times* White

House reporter, Nelson, of course, should have been finding out and writing in his paper every day what Woodward and Bernstein wrote in their book.

Nelson began questioning them as follows: "I think that what disturbs a lot of journalists about the book is the methodology you used. . . . What I wonder is, is this the full flowering of the new journalism, and do you think this is healthy for journalism?"

"If there is anything this book is not, it is 'new journalism,' " Bernstein replied. "It is not new journalism; it is not psychohistory. It is very simply reporting, the most basic, empirical type of reporting that you and I do every day. In fact, the real similarity is to be seen in your own stories, and this particular piece of work, which is to say we do use anonymous sources, just as you do in your stories daily about Washington. The difference is in this book we don't use the phrase 'according to informed sources' after every second or third paragraph."

Although it wasn't asked about on the television show, the most criticized portion of *The Final Days* was the passage in which a drunken, semihysterical Nixon and Secretary of State Henry Kissinger are described as praying on a floor in the White House the night before Nixon resigned.

How could the reporters be sure they were right about this poignant, private moment? Well, we now know they were right—because the incident was confirmed by Richard Nixon himself two years after *The Final Days* in his own memoir. And it was reconfirmed by Kissinger in his memoir. (Nixon said he was drinking but does not admit to being drunk or unhinged; Kissinger implies both, but describes the Woodward and Bernstein paragraph as an "unfeeling account.")

Seven years after publication, the rest of *The Final Days* stands similarly undisputed or confirmed by the memoirs and other accounts of Nixon, Kissinger, and others—so much so, in fact, that in reading such memoirs alongside *The Final Days* one gets confused in places as to which is which. With age, the book—which was then read as an un-put-downable narrative of recent events—becomes a classic, vivid portrait of the dynamics of executive power in a three-branch government.

In December 1974, as Woodward and Bernstein were mired in their *Final Days* research, *Time* magazine ran a story entitled "Woodstein's Retreat." It quoted anonymous sources as saying the duo was having so much trouble adjusting to their Watergate fame and fortune that they were both in professional and personal tailspins. (Those involved in preparing the *Time* story maintain today that, for all its Woodstein-like background sources and omniscient reports of what the two were thinking and feeling, it was not a parody.) What would soon be their blockbuster book was described as so impeded by the unwillingness of sources to talk and so behind schedule that the two had "had to hire an outside researcher to help them." (The researcher had, in fact, been on board from the book's inception.) Woodward was portrayed as having gone through "a period of intense disillusionment and self-doubt deepened by a shocking medical report—mistaken as it turned out—that he was dying of leukemia." Of Bernstein it was said, "Friends described him as inhibited by his Watergate-related publicity."

Woodward says the account of his and Bernstein's problems was exaggerated (and that the mistaken medical "report" about him was a doctor's "suspicion" that was ruled out "within twenty-four or thirty-six hours"). But there is no denying that the two had their share of trouble adjusting to superstardom.

Woodward, in fact, remembers a time more than a year after the *Time* article, after *The Final Days* was completed and setting sales records, when, he says, "it all came crashing home to me that we had to take stock. There was a night in early 1976 when Carl and Nora Ephron [then Bernstein's wife] and I were riding in a limousine together to go to a speaking engagement in Baltimore for *The Final Days*. There we were; at that moment we had the number-one hard-cover book, the number-one paperback, and the number-one-grossing movie. We were on top. And I remember Carl saying to me, 'We have to sit down and think about what this could do to us. How we control it. And how we decide what we're going to do next.' Well, he was willing to think about it, but I was just a wall. I couldn't face it. All I wanted to do was retreat. Which I did. I bought a home in Maryland and took my wife there and hid out for a while."

Bernstein, who confirms Woodward's recollection, may have been more willing to talk about the problems they faced, but by most accounts he fared not nearly as well at coping with them. Richard Snyder, who as president of Simon and Schuster made the initial deal for *All the President's Men* in the summer of 1972 and then became close to both authors, remembers a time just before *All the President's Men* was released when, he says, he sat the two down to give them some advice. The movie deal had already been made and it was clear that the book, coming out as it was on the eve of the House impeachment hearing, would be a best seller. "I remember telling them, 'You're going to be very rich and very famous,'" Snyder recalls, in an account confirmed, in its essentials, by Woodward and Bernstein. "'And you've got to prepare for it. . . . You've got to stay who you are and not let all this ruin your lives, your marriages, your careers.'"

Both men, indeed, derailed themselves for a while, but Bernstein did it more flamboyantly and destructively. Woodward kept mostly to himself, socking most of his money away in investments and tax shelters, while Bernstein, who took to the Hamptons and Elaine's, spent much of his fortune. Both went through divorces, but Bernstein made his a semipublic spectacle, in part because he had a notorious affair while his wife was pregnant. And though both saw their careers cool down, Woodward seemed to falter only for a while before gearing up and writing (with *Final Days* researcher and *Post* reporter Scott Armstrong) *The Brethren*—which beat even *The Final Days* in hardback sales velocity and volume.

Published in 1979, *The Brethren* did to Supreme Court reportage what *The Final Days* did to Nixon White House coverage; it made fools of the regular beat reporters covering the Court, and in the process generated the same negative reviews. The book also made the other professionals on the Court beat—law professors—look silly; for the reporters' stories of horse trading and personal conflicts among the justices put the lie to the professors' pontifical speculations on the intellectual underpinnings of all court decisions.

Because Woodward reportedly felt that Bernstein hadn't pulled his weight in the work for *The Final Days,* he hadn't ask him to work on *The Brethren.*

Bernstein says he wouldn't have done the book anyway, because he was tired of print journalism. Distracted may be a better description. For while Woodward was writing *The Brethren* Bernstein was floundering, trying to be what he wasn't. First, he dabbled in a novel about the 1950s. Then he signed with ABC to do interviews. "I was going to be the Oriana Fallaci of the air," he recalls. That, too, came to naught, but it evolved into an offer from ABC to run the Washington news bureau.

"I was awful at it," says Bernstein (an assessment echoed by those who worked with him at ABC). "I'm the most disorganized person in the world and I was supposed to be a manager. . . . Then they hired a deputy for me to manage so I could be free to make assignments. . . . The Washington bureau chief is supposed to have the power to assign the reporters, right? Wrong. I had no power, and I wasn't the type who knew how to play politics to get it."

In 1981 Bernstein accepted a job as a special-assignment reporter for ABC, where he has since done an excellent job on stories ranging from the Falklands war to early presidential campaign jockeying in Iowa. "I started in newspapers [as a part-time copyboy] when I was sixteen," says Bernstein, "so I've done print journalism for a long time. This is the reporting I want to do for now." But he adds, "I know now I want to be a reporter, not a manager."

Woodward, post-*Brethren,* ran into the same kind of snag. Friends say (why can't I use anonymous sources, too?) that, as one puts it, "Bob wanted for a while to be Ben Bradlee—to run the *Post.* But it became clear he couldn't do it. He's a reporter. He's inner-directed. And he's too intense to be the kind of social person and manager, or hand holder, that it takes to run a paper like that. He's not good at supervising people."

In 1979 Woodward, who was by then a favorite not only of Bradlee but of *Post* company chairman Katharine Graham, began assuming a series of editorial jobs, until by 1981 he was the paper's metropolitan editor. It was then that he took to giving his staff speeches about the need to go get "holy shit" stories. (He had whispered "holy shit" to himself when he found out that McCord had once worked for the CIA.) And it was then that a young member of the staff, Janet Cooke, wrote just that kind of story—a horrifying series about a youngster addicted to heroin. Cooke's stories won the *Post* another Pulitzer, except that the prize had to be returned after Cooke's addict was found not to exist.

Cooke was directly supervised by editors working under Woodward, yet he says he takes responsibility for not being more vigilant about making sure her sources were real. He's right. He hardly applied the detached scrutiny to his reporters that he does to his subjects, though in the age of confidential-source journalism so legitimized by Woodward and Bernstein a more skillful Janet Cooke (one, for example, who doesn't fabricate a college degree) would not be caught by any editor who stops short of making himself a full-time detective.

Soon after the Cooke affair, Woodward moved from being metropolitan editor to a new job in charge of a *Post* investigative team, where he reports, writes, and supervises a small staff of other writers. Woodward has scored many scoops in the new spot, including a story that Attorney General William French Smith was involved in highly leveraged (and, therefore, dubious) tax shelters. (Woodward acknowledges that he, too, dabbles in shelters but none with losses that are more than the cash investment; he declines to provide specifics.)

After he had shifted from the metropolitan desk, Woodward was drawn into another imbroglio as celebrated and, for him, as wrenching as the Cooke affair: the libel suit brought by Mobil Oil president William Tavoulareas.

Tavoulareas sued, among others, the *Post*, Woodward, Bradlee, and reporter Patrick Tyler for a story written by Tyler—and supervised by Woodward in his *Post* job as metropolitan editor. Tyler's article, which had been suggested to him by Woodward after Woodward got an anonymous letter tipping him off to the story, charged that Tavoulareas had improperly favored his son in a deal between Mobil and the son's shipping company. In July 1982 Tavoulareas won his case.

Although the verdict has since been overturned by the trial judge, it was at the time the most ignominious libel loss for any respectable publication ever. Except for a few minor mistakes, none of which merited a verdict for Tavoulareas, the article was thoroughly accurate and fair. Yet the headline and the lead paragraph—parts of the story that Woodward as an editor should have supervised but that were handled by other desk editors—were arguably unfair, a point that Woodward now concedes.

But Woodward himself was personally a big hit with the jurors, who were moved by his eloquent exchange with Tavoulareas's lawyer in which he defined the role of journalism as "digging, thinking, and getting the best obtainable versions of the truth."

"Mr. Woodward was impressive," said one juror (who had no idea that Woodward was *the* Woodward of Woodward and Bernstein because the *Post*'s lawyer had mistakenly assumed that all the jurors would know). "He was what a reporter should be. An honest, wonderful young man."

Most who have judged Woodward and Bernstein have always seen Woodward that way. Bernstein is another story. In part, it's a matter of looks, a difference that seemed sharper eleven years after Watergate as the two sat at lunch recently for an interview. Woodward, soft, even boyish, makes his friend and former partner (each doubts they'll team up again) seem craggier, paunchier, and harder looking than he is. It's as if the wrong one has left print for television.

But there's more than looks to the difference between how the two have been accepted. Bernstein is not nearly as liked and respected as Woodward. His stardom is begrudged by many who know them both as much as Woodward's is admired as the real thing. This is probably because Woodward backed up

Watergate with *The Brethren,* while Bernstein is viewed as journalism's Sylvester Stallone, unable to make a non-Nixon killing.

It is, however, an artificial, unfair comparison based on what both consider to be unreal expectations.

"I was in Iowa recently covering John Glenn," says Bernstein. "And we both had the same problem. People came up to him and asked him what it was like being an astronaut. And people came up to me and asked me what it was like breaking Watergate, when all I wanted to do was interview them about the [presidential nominating] caucuses."

The report Bernstein broadcast on Iowa on ABC's *Nightline* was nothing spectacular, just the best, freshest piece of reporting on the early campaign organizing that's been done.

"He was a comedian and we were reporters," says Woodward, coming back to what he sees as his kinship with John Belushi. "And the secret is to get back to seeing what you really are and what you like best and do best. And the reality you have to face when you do that is that you may never be the star you once were. You just may never be up there again."

"That's right," adds Bernstein. "I mean, how many stories are there going to be like Watergate? But that doesn't mean you stop doing what you're good at."

WOODWARD AND BERNSTEIN   *Robert Upshur Woodward was born on March 26, 1943, in Geneva, Illinois. Carl Bernstein was born on February 14, 1944, in Washington, D.C.*

Woodward's father was chief judge of the DuPage County (Illinois) Circuit Court. Bernstein's parents were leaders in the labor movement; during the McCarthy era they were accused of being Communists.

Bernstein admits he was a "terrible student." He preferred reading his father's copy of I. F. Stone's Weekly rather than his class assignments. "The only thing I could do in school was write," he said. "I'd pass the essay exams and flunk the true and false."

In 1967 Woodward was serving as a communications officer aboard a presidential flagship when he received orders moving him to a Vietnam jungle command center. Viewing the assignment as a "death trap," he requested and received a transfer to a guided-missile ship. In 1970 he ended his five years of service and was awarded the Navy Commendation Medal.

Though already accepted at Harvard law school, Woodward applied for a job at The Washington Post—*volunteering to work for two weeks without pay. He performed badly but, luckily, landed a job on a Maryland weekly. The* Post *later rehired him and within nine months he had racked up more front-page by-lines than any other reporter on the sixty-person metropolitan staff.*

Angry that the Post refused to transfer him to the metropolitan desk or to Southeast Asia, Bernstein, just a few weeks before the Watergate break-in, submitted an application to Rolling Stone.

As the Watergate scandal grew more serious, Bernstein began asking himself, "Jesus, are we being fair?" Nevertheless, convinced of Nixon's complicity, he often inserted into his stories what became known in the newsroom as "the-President-is-guilty paragraph" (which the editors routinely excised).

President Richard Nixon resigned a bit more than two years after Woodward and Bernstein started investigating Watergate. When they heard he had resigned, they said they felt numb and, for a time, found it difficult to work.

Reacting to Woodward and Bernstein and The Final Days, Nixon said, "I respect some [press people] but for those who write history as fiction on third-hand knowledge, I have nothing but utter contempt. And I will never forgive them. Never. . . ."

Woodward wrote The Brethren because, he said, the Supreme Court was a "sitting duck." In the book Justice Thurgood Marshall is quoted as greeting Chief Justice Warren Burger by saying, "What's shakin', chiefy baby?" He insists the book did the Court no great damage: "The Court is very resilient. What we found out is that it comes to the right decision and that its votes are not for sale."

Bernstein is generally considered a better writer than Woodward. Woodward is known as a smooth interrogator with a "physician's bedside manner." In researching The Final Days, Bernstein said, there were some sources "who would talk to Woodward that wouldn't tell me the time of day."

Watergate historian J. Anthony Lukas described the pair as "a kind of journalistic centaur with an aristocratic Republican head and runty Jewish hindquarters."

Both married twice; both married reporters.

Bernstein complained that the original script for the movie All the President's Men read like "a Henny Youngman joke book." He rewrote parts of the script, beefing up his screen character as a "swinger." Robert Redford reportedly reminded Bernstein, "Errol Flynn is dead."

Woodward once described himself as "essentially boring." He maintains "it took tremendous guts on Redford's part to play me." He regards his success as "accidental." He says he disdains his fame: "As soon as someone becomes a celebrity, they become less useful to the newspaper. . . . It gives you too much independence from the institution and breaks down the hierarchy."

Bernstein likes to read American history and to listen to his extensive collection of rock and classical music. He seldom discusses his personal life and rarely grants interviews. He denies that he has become smitten with celebrity. He has described his political views as "radical in some ways, anarchistic, perhaps, in others."

"There is no message [in All the President's Men]," Woodward wrote. "It is about two reporters who worked on this story—their methods and legwork. It is also about how newspapers work, who makes the decisions, and what the power structure is."

"We don't perceive ourselves as heroes," Bernstein said. "The book is about human frailties, including our own."

The Emancipation of Betty Friedan

MARILYN FRENCH

BETTY FRIEDAN SEES HER LIFE ALMOST AS A MIRACLE. SHE IS AS SURPRISED AT WHAT she wrought as an explorer who set out to map an island and discovers she has found a continent. Trained as an intellectual, she became a political activist; deeply committed to the warmth, nurturing, and affection of family life, she became the leader of a movement perceived as antagonistic to those qualities; a woman of modest personal goals, she helped to initiate the "second wave" of a movement immodestly dedicated to changing the world. One cannot discuss her without discussing that movement.

Friedan's mother, like so many of our mothers, was unhappy with her life. She had been forced to give up her job on a newspaper when she married, a loss she lamented throughout her later life and which shadowed her pleasure in her family and home. She urged her daughter toward a career in journalism, but young Betty was fascinated by psychology at Smith and Berkeley and did work so outstanding that she was offered a graduate fellowship in that field—an extraordinary event for a woman in the Forties. She was dating a young physicist who resented her opportunity and threatened to break with her. She gave up the fellowship in a paroxysm of guilt and confusion, wanting to pursue her studies, but wanting most of all the love, the home, the children that were supposed to be everywoman's destiny. Like so many women, she wanted above all to avoid her mother's misery, her mother's life, and attempted to do this by renouncing her mother's values. *She* would not spend her life sorrowing over a lost career: she would embrace the man, the home, the children, and live in a bath of felicity. The physicist broke with her anyway.

She went into journalism after all, reporting for the labor press. She found the right man and married him. She was not forced to give up *her* job until she became pregnant with her second child: one maternity leave was deemed sufficient, apparently, and even the newspaper guild refused to support her protest, despite a contract stipulating the right to pregnancy leave. So far had things progressed in a generation.

Friedan continued to write, free-lancing mainly for women's magazines. She was fascinated by women who managed to attain excellence in a discipline—especially the arts—and to raise children at the same time. This was her own dream: a whole life, integration of all talents. She immersed herself in the magazines that were her market, studying them. Over time, she perceived a pattern. Her editors would cut references to her subjects' careers: they claimed a woman painting a crib was interesting to their readers, but a woman painting a picture was not. She had difficulty placing a piece on the natural childbirth of a famous actress: it was too "gory," editors complained. The reality of women's lives—physical, intellectual, emotional—was censored; what appeared was a fantasy, a picture-book image of happy female domesticity that pleased advertisers and presumably tranquilized female readers. Friedan began to analyze the fantasy; she interviewed housewives about the reality of their lives; she thought about the reasons for the promotion of such a false image. She gave the image a name: the Feminine Mystique.

In 1963 she published a book containing her findings, in which she described her personal dilemma and gave accounts of those who shared it. It was an immediate best seller, selling three million copies, and read by millions more. Friedan received thousands of letters from women grateful to her primarily for alleviating their sense of isolation. They had believed they alone felt as they did; they had thought, and many had been told, they were "sick," neurotic because they felt discontent, even desperate, about the vapidity of their lives. Everywhere, people talked about *The Feminine Mystique*; the phrase entered the language.

The women Friedan reached were mainly like herself—middle-class with some education. Most were white, women of the American mainstream, married, mothers; some had prosperous husbands. Inspired and validated by finding their own truth presented as truth, many of them changed their lives, returning to school, entering the work force. But professional and single women, whites and women of color, were also aroused by her book, locating in the feminine mystique the barrier to their advancement; it was their image in men's minds that led men to prevent women from achieving greater effectiveness and scope in their jobs. If Friedan's reputation rested only on this book and the response to it, she would be noteworthy. But she went further: she changed her own life.

Several factors converged at this time. The black civil rights movement had stimulated important legislation, notably the Equal Pay Act of 1963 and the Civil Rights Act of 1964. Discrimination in employment on grounds of race was to be declared illegal. When it was proposed that *sex* be added to those grounds, the House of Representatives dissolved in laughter. Martha Griffiths, then in the House, was humiliated and outraged and threatened that if Congress did not keep "that joke" in the Act, she would force a voice vote on the floor, exposing those who were against women. Margaret Chase Smith leveled the same threat in the Senate. The word *sex* remained in the Act, but no one expected it to change anything.

In 1961 President Kennedy had established a national Commission on the Status of Women, which fully documented the second-class status of American women. Its findings, however, resulted only in the establishment of an advisory council and fifty state commissions: more talk, no action, temporizing. The administration's poverty program had no women in decision-making positions, offered no job training or educational programs to women, had no plans for day-care centers, although the present "feminization of poverty" was already perceptible—women and their children constituted 80 percent of the clientele of urban welfare programs. Even the Equal Employment Opportunities Commission (EEOC), the agency supposed to administer Title VII (forbidding discrimination in employment) of the Civil Rights Act, had no women in decision-making posts except for the presidential appointee, Aileen Hernandez. Indeed, it was discovered that the EEOC was planning to issue a guideline to Title VII that essentially sanctioned continued discrimination against women in employment.

The women who worked in government were outraged but could not act openly; espousal of women's rights was grounds for dismissal, for women or men. Women in media were in a similar position, as were academic and professional women. These women wrote or talked to Betty Friedan. Promoting her book took Friedan across the country and to Europe, and everywhere she spoke to huge audiences of women and listened to their protests. They urged her to "start an NAACP for women"; they insisted that Title VII would never be enforced for women unless they marched on Washington like the blacks. Women in labor unions described how the unions sided with management when women brought complaints, how women were silenced and intimidated at union meetings.

She was fired by the outrage she encountered wherever she went. She herself was astounded at the depth and scope of the problem she had named, at its pervasiveness in American society. Her book had thrust her into a central position, which she accepted with dedication and energy. She went on lecturing; she traveled continually, lived out of a suitcase, spent her nights in drab motel rooms. Ironically, this woman who cherishes the warmth and intimacy of family life had to sacrifice it to a struggle in which she had, accidentally it seemed, become pivotal. She missed her children; her marriage was foundering; but she worked on the euphoria of those who suddenly see a passage to freedom. Under pressure from women in all aspects of life, she finally decided to found a political organization devoted to gaining women's rights, and in 1966, with a small group of women of different races, she founded NOW, the National Organization for Women, the first new feminist organization in nearly fifty years.

For in 1920, after passage of the Nineteenth Amendment granting women the vote, the "first wave" of organized feminism in America essentially collapsed. The women were exhausted; the fight for suffrage had taken seventy years and had drained more than two generations of women. Some stalwarts continued to fight, among them Alice Paul, who in 1923 succeeded in having the Equal Rights Act introduced in Congress. But for the most part, women trusted the vote to provide them with a voice. It did not and could not, in a nation in which both major political parties are controlled by the same forces, forces intent on maintaining a society stratified by economic inequality largely determined by sex and race.

Thus, NOW's Statement of Purpose had to declare, once again, that women are human—an assertion, Friedan says still, that turns the entire culture upside down. Her statement proclaims NOW to be dedicated to equality for women and to political action as a means for achieving it. It declares that black and low-paid women are particular victims of our society; that women are excluded from postgraduate educational institutions and professional associations; that tokenism is unacceptable. It affirms the continuing importance to women of childbearing and child rearing, but rejects the middle-class division of labor, which places the economic burden of the family entirely on men. It locates the arena of its action within the boundaries of American law and outside alignment with any political party.

NOW grew swiftly and was extremely effective, largely because it was a mainstream organization. There has been feminist protest at least since the fifteenth-century writer Christine de Pisan, the first of a series of European intellectuals to protest laws and attitudes based on the idea that women are sub-human, property, and exist for men's sake. Women of all classes thronged to early Christian and, later, early Protestant sects, which offered them at least moral or spiritual equality with men—the opportunity to die with men before the lions or at the stake. Poor women who could no longer feed their families rose up courageously before and during the French Revolution and, in fact, helped to precipitate it. Women composed a heroic segment of early socialist movements, drawn by a vision of equality and social justice.

But it has been exceedingly difficult to unify women. Although they constitute a separate caste, as Simone de Beauvoir has pointed out (caste is conferred at birth and is unchangeable; class is conferred at birth, but can be changed), they are also members of different classes, the classes of their families, to which they feel they owe primary loyalty. Although females are at the bottom of every class and although women in general value felicity more than power, their common cause is obscured by the clashing of classes, races, religious and ethnic categories, and subcultures. Yet without some unity among women as a caste, nothing changes for women, whoever rules the roost.

Friedan's creation of a mainstream women's movement was therefore an extraordinary achievement. It was not performed in a single stroke: after establishing NOW, she and other leaders had to struggle daily to enable NOW to survive and grow, to be heard over the ridicule of the external world, including the media, and to pierce the silence of women's fear. In those years, Friedan was catapulted into international prominence; she became the symbol of the women's movement. She worked tirelessly, literally day and night: she lobbied, she organized, she raised funds. She drew women from across the country into a ferment of activity. If she was often a guest at the White House, she also visited women in labor unions and worked closely with women of color and tried to enlist them in the organization. Her energy seemed limitless: faith and joy buoyed her.

The first battle fought by NOW was to pressure, successfully, the commissioners of the EEOC and the President to rescind the guidelines tolerating sexual discrimination. The immediate consequence of this was that employers, who had recently been forbidden from dividing job advertisements into categories of "colored" and "white," were also prevented from advertising "Help Wanted—Female" or "Help Wanted—Male." Once this had been done, NOW initiated a series of lawsuits against companies that refused to hire women in jobs traditionally reserved for men—as telephone line workers, railroad workers, and others. It fought against "protective" legislation decreeing that women could not lift more than thirty-five pounds. It took up the case of stewardesses who claimed discrimination because they were forced to leave their jobs if they married or when they reached thirty-five. The airlines mounted a tough fight against the EEOC and NOW. So elaborate and expensive was their defense that Friedan came to recognize the economic motive of institutions in maintaining sexist discrimination. By letting women go at thirty-five or before, the airlines saved the costs of pensions and promotions. By keeping women in low economic status, many companies maintained a reliable low-paid marginal labor force who could be hired when needed and fired if an industry had to contract for a time. By hiring young unmarried women, or older women whose children had grown, industry gained the benefit of energy and experience without having to provide raises and advancement.

Maintaining a noncentralized structure offering considerable autonomy to community chapters, NOW in its early years focused action through the establishment of task forces on the treatment of women in the media and textbooks, employment, sports, and marriage and divorce laws. Women came to NOW for help in fighting sex discrimination in their jobs, in establishing standards for day-care centers, in banning segregated living arrangements on college campuses, and more. NOW used political pressure—picketing, marching, lobbying, and media events as well as legal action to fight, one by one, the seemingly unending barriers to women's full citizenship. In 1967, under Friedan's guidance, NOW voted to work for the passage of the Equal Rights Amendment, which had languished in committee since 1923, and for access to legal abortion. These positions led some women to resign from the organization. But once a woman has arrived at a feminist perspective on her life and society, there is no retreat from that realization, and these women formed their own organizations, like the Women's Equity Action League (WEAL), that worked with NOW on issues of shared concern.

In 1969 Friedan joined with Larry Lader and others who supported legal abortion to found what was to become NARAL, the National Abortion Rights Action League. At its inception, the men involved saw it as principally designed to protect doctors who performed abortions; they did not consider abortion a feminist issue and were appalled at the linkage of the two. Friedan rooted access to legal abortion firmly in the basic human right to control one's own body and reproduction. On this ground, abortion became a feminist issue. After the Supreme Court decision of 1973 affirming this right, abortion-related deaths of women dropped by 600 percent.

NOW had many major achievements in those early years. It conveyed to the nation at large the fact that discrimination against women exists; it transformed ridicule of the women's movement by the media and other institutions into serious attention; it was instrumental in the building of a corpus of judgments and laws requiring equity in education and hiring and promotion. It helped to get the ERA passed by the Congress. It also performed two more amorphous but extremely significant functions.

First, it generated many spin-off groups; some, like WEAL, dissociated themselves from NOW because they could not support a particular position (abortion, in this case), yet continued to work on other projects with NOW. Some, like NARAL, were formed because a single issue had grown too complex and demanding to be handled by the parent organization. This was the case also with the NOW Legal Defense and Education Fund, started in 1970 by Friedan and Kay Clarenbach. Although women lawyers invariably worked for and with NOW *pro bono*, the many lawsuits NOW was involved with were still expensive. The Fund was designed to raise and distribute money for such actions. And in 1971 Friedan, with Bella Abzug, Gloria Steinem, Liz Carpenter, Clarenbach, and others, founded NWPC, the National Women's Political Caucus, designed to support candidates for all levels of office and in the judiciary who support the elimination of racism, sexism, institutional violence, and poverty. Each of these organizations has been extremely effective, and remains so.

Second, NOW functioned as a centrist organization, around and against which other groups could align themselves. More-radical women argued that to work for the assimilation of women into a society that was inherently unjust and unworthy was an unworthy act; more-conservative women, fearful of further weakening men's sense of responsibility for their children and the women who raise them, renounced any claim on "rights" that might, they felt, contribute to that process. In the late Sixties various groups tried to take over NOW. Younger women, radicalized by the Vietnam War and by their treatment by men within the antiwar movement, founded formal and informal feminist groups; many also joined NOW. These women represented a wide spectrum of opinion and were intellectually sophisticated. Some were socialists of various "sects"; some believed lesbianism to be the only fully feminist position, and they demanded that NOW affirm this. Since feminists were invariably attacked as "dykes," they should counter this attack by proclaiming, "We are all lesbians," much as King Christian X of Denmark vowed to put on the yellow armband with the Star of David if the Nazis decreed all Danish Jews must wear them.

Friedan's response to these new elements was both personal and political. She was shocked by the idea of a public declaration of lesbianism. She writes, "I am not that far from everywoman" (insofar as everywoman exists), and reminds the reader that she was born in Peoria, Illinois, a symbolic Middletown. But she also felt, with many other NOW leaders, that to take such a position would be a tactical error: she felt lesbianism as a political stance to be antimale, and her own position, from the beginning, had been to gain rights for women without alienating men, but rather seeing them as fellow victims of a divisive, repressive, dehumanized society. A mainstream person, she envisioned social change within capitalism, not through violent revolution or even evolution to a socialist system she considered authoritarian and still unequal.

For several years, these conflicts seethed within NOW, occupying the energies of many women and leaving deep wounds behind—especially the struggle between members of the Young Socialist Alliance (YSA), a branch of the Socialist Workers' Party, and the centrists. But the arguments broadened the thinking and awareness of the entire group and deepened its understanding of the nature of the barriers to the equality of women. In time, NOW reasserted its original mainstream character; dissenters formed other spin-off groups or dropped out of organized feminism (not out of feminism itself) altogether.

The conflict exhausted Friedan, who struggled throughout to prevent NOW from fragmenting into sects. In 1970, divorced and in need of money, she stepped down as president of NOW. Aileen Hernandez, one of the original founders, took over. Friedan's last major act in NOW (although she is still an important member) was to organize the Women's Strike for Equality in 1970. Its centerpiece was to be a march down Fifth Avenue in New York, but Mayor Lindsay had denied the women a permit. Nevertheless, they assembled, nearly fifty thousand women who had for the day abandoned their jobs or their homes to march for equality. When mounted police tried to stop them, Friedan told the women to join hands across the street: "And so we marched, in great swinging long lines, from sidewalk to sidewalk, and the police on their horses got out of the way. And people leaned out of office windows and waved. . . ." The march, the strike, created tremendous awareness nationwide of the women's movement and added to its moral force: it was a huge success.

Friedan returned to writing, teaching, and lecturing; she has been visiting professor at a number of universities in the past fourteen years. In 1976 she published *It Changed My Life*, an account of the early years of NOW. In 1977 she helped to heal the internal split over lesbianism by supporting the proposal for sexual preference at the National Women's Conference in Houston: the hall exploded with cheers and applause.

In 1981 she published *The Second Stage*, an exhortation to women and men to see feminism not as a movement antagonistic to traditional female roles and values, but as a humanizing force in society at large. At present, she is at work on a book on aging, to be called *The Fountain of Age*, searching for ways to see and experience age as a positive part of life. Acute to discrimination, she has discovered that most research on age has been conducted on men, who provide the standard for discussion of the subject, although women in general live longer than men and more of them face extreme old age alone. But both men and women are, Friedan believes, denied personhood after sixty.

If Friedan no longer stands as the spokeswoman for "the" feminist movement, that is partly because there is no single movement, but many, all sharing the same ultimate goal and a few basic principles, yet differing about means and methods. Many feminists diagnose the malaise of the entire Western industrial world as being rooted in sexism. If they are right, the creation of a more humane and just society, which is the goal of feminism, requires change more fundamental than feminists have previously recognized.

Betty Friedan has remained true to her principles, personal and political. She has been and remains a bridge between conservative and radical elements in feminism, and an ardent advocate of harmony and humane values. Her affirmation of the family in *The Second Stage* is a passionate plea for general awareness of the inclusive nature of feminism: its vision of human wholeness; its repudiation of laws and customs that deny men expression of their emotions, sensitivity, and nurturing qualities and deny women expression of assertive intellect, action, and a voice in society. Friedan will stand in history as an initiator of the "second wave" of feminism and as one who has never wavered in fidelity to its larger vision.

BETTY NAOMI FRIEDAN *was born on February 4, 1921, in Peoria, Illinois.*

Of herself in high school, she has said, "I was that girl with all A's and I wanted boys worse than anything."

Being a Jew, she believes, sensitized her to discrimination: "When you're a Jewish girl who grows up on the right side of the tracks in the Midwest, you're marginal. You're in, but you're not, and you grow up an observer."

Although she was a good physics student, she pretended that lab experiments gave her trouble, so that the jocks in the class would help her.

Her father, a jewelry store owner, thought she read too much; he allowed her to take out no more than five library books at a time.

She studied with Gestalt psychologist Kurt Koffka at Smith College and with Erik Erikson at Berkeley.

In 1947 she married Carl Friedan, who went into advertising. Sometimes she made more than he did; to avoid fighting about it, she would purposely lose her purse. Still, their marriage was stormy. Once Carl threw a bowl of sugar at Betty's face, and once she threw a mirror at him, scarring his knuckle. They had three children and were divorced in 1969.

She has said, "I am a woman of self-destruction at times; the culture has built that in."

"I wouldn't be satisfied with a life lived solely on the barricades," she has said. "I reserve my right to be frivolous."

The summer she finished writing The Feminine Mystique, *she dyed her hair blond. She later said she did it "for some strange reason—maybe a last gasp at denying my seriousness." She still condones cosmetics and beauty aids. She has been a regular patron of Vidal Sassoon.*

She once described her life in suburbia as "eight schizophrenic years of trying to be a kind of woman I wasn't, of too many lonesome, boring, wasted hours, too many unnecessary arguments, too many days spent with, but not really seeing, my lovely, exciting children, too much cocktail-party chitchat with the same people, because they were the only people there." Nevertheless, she says she could not have written her first book, "had I not lived those years as a suburban housewife."

One night when she was on a radio talk show in Detroit, the station's switchboard was flooded with phone calls. Housewives were calling, demanding that she be taken off the air.

She visited India when Indira Gandhi became prime minister. She lent the prime minister her black-and-camel Rudi Gernreich cape.

The New York Times *called her "a combination of Hermione Gingold and Bette Davis."*

She gesticulates when she talks and talks almost nonstop. "The Niagara Falls effect of it all!" Senator Charles Percy said, after hearing her testify before the Senate Select Committee on Nutrition and Human Needs. "Some men have the same problem, like Hubert Humphrey. He was Vice-President, but don't forget he never made President."

She has a home in Sag Harbor, Long Island, and a Manhattan duplex filled with Victorian furniture, modern paintings, and books.

She likes to "schlog," a name she has given to her recreational, brisk half-trot.

At a meeting in Kansas City in 1981 a lesbian asked Friedan, ". . . why don't you talk more about gay families?" Friedan replied: "Because it twists the focus to sexual politics. It . . . threatens people who feel sex should be private and are mixed up about it themselves. There has been too much focus on sex in the movement and it's given us a political blind spot on questions like child care. . . . [A lesbian is] not all you are, surely. That's really not the main question, and you shouldn't want it to be. . . ."

Writing in 1981, she affirmed that after the last two decades of feminine protest modern young women can now "say 'no' to superwoman standards . . . because they already feel good enough about themselves as women to trust themselves. . . . They have begun to realize that a little dependence is nothing to be afraid of. . . . I expect my daughter will be a better mother than I was. She won't have my guilts and drivenness, and the self-doubts that kept me from enjoying those years. . . ."

In April 1983 she traveled four thousand miles to Cambridge University to defend the proposition that "feminism is good for men." She asked her debate opponents to forswear their "foppish humor." An opponent, resurrecting Friedan's old phrase, insisted upon his "right to be frivolous." Friedan was dismayed when a tally of undergraduate votes showed her losing the debate 56 to 123. Only the next day did she learn that a clerical error had reversed the tally.

Benjamin Spock's Baby Bible

HARRY STEIN

WHEN *THE COMMON SENSE BOOK OF BABY AND CHILD CARE* APPEARED IN 1946, THE Sunday *New York Times Book Review* accorded it exactly six paragraphs on page 14, above a similarly perfunctory appraisal of something called *The Book of Houses.* The daily *Times* did not report its arrival at all. Neither did the *Chicago Tribune,* nor the *Los Angeles Times,* nor *The Washington Post.* "I guess," observes Dr. Benjamin Spock, "they just didn't take it very seriously." He pauses and offers a wry smile. "Obviously they had other priorities."

Obviously. Though almost instantly the book was in many quarters understood to be a quantum leap forward in its field; though within weeks of its publication it was selling at an astonishing rate, en route to becoming the most successful book ever written in this country; though within a year it was already transforming the daily routine in thousands upon thousands of American households, it was perceived, among those whose perceptions are generally regarded as meaningful, as women's page stuff—*quality* women's page stuff, to be sure, but certainly nowhere near meriting the serious attention of the Italian monarchist movement, or the presidential ambitions of Harold Stassen, or *Wrath in Burma, Burma Surgeon Returns, David the King* ("the sensational best seller about the Bible's most magnificent sinner"), or any of the other volumes featured at length in the book review sections that season. In a society in which significance is almost always a function of power or the bottom line, this child-raising thing, this business of breast-feeding and toilet training, simply didn't seem to *matter* very much.

Thus it was that, ever so quietly—through successive editions of his book and articles in magazines like *American Home, Parents, Ladies' Home Journal,* and *Redbook;* magazines lying around beauty parlors, for Chrissakes—Benjamin Spock, more than any other individual of his time, was able to reshape the process by which human beings are formed in this country.

Though Spock himself has never fully accepted such a characterization, those who eventually saw their world changing in front of them finally came to understand, too late, what the man had been about. In 1968, when Spock was on trial for having counseled resistance to the draft, the government used summary challenges to dismiss every prospective woman juror.

The premise central to Spock's philosophy of child raising is elementary: that babies are human beings, as entitled to understanding, respect, and emotional sustenance as any other representative of the species. Indeed, so obvious does this notion strike the contemporary sensibility that the pre-Spock era seems as utterly remote as the Civil War. But the simple truth is that a mere fifty years ago parents adhered to the other, older set of precepts as routinely, and as enthusiastically, as parents-to-be today troop off to lessons in Lamaze. The tactical aim of parenting in that era, supported by a legion of experts deemed indispensable to the satisfactory completion of the task, was whipping the kid into shape as readily as humanly possible and rendering him, by the standards of the day, "independent." The battle plan for the realization of these aims was as inflexible as any ever devised by von Schlieffen. The child was not to be coddled or excessively catered to. Bad habits were to be broken, *smashed,* and pity be damned. Eating, sleeping, excreting were to proceed on a schedule every bit as rigorous as the *Twentieth Century Limited*'s. Babies, advised Luther Emmett Holt, whose *The Care and Feeding of Children* was a standard in the field for three decades, should be bowel-trained at two months and kept on a liquid diet for a year. "Never, never kiss your child," chastised John B. Watson, author of the best-selling *Psychological Care of Infant and Child* and of the observation that "no one today knows enough to raise a child." "Never hold it on your lap. Never rock its carriage." "If you must," relented the U.S. Children's Bureau's widely circulated pamphlet "Infant Care," "kiss them once on the forehead when they say good night. Shake hands with them in the morning." Even the most benign authorities of the day counseled that thumb-sucking be curbed in the logical fashion—by binding down the troublemaker's arms in his crib.

To be sure, Spock was not the first to challenge the *Mommie Dearest* school of child rearing, or to consider early childhood from a psychoanalytic perspective. By the mid-Thirties, Freud had long since assumed a cult status—already passionate young men of the radical Left were routinely accusing reluctant young women of like politics of being "repressed"—and there were an increasing number of individuals, academics, and the occasional child-care professional making the case for greater flexibility. Articles appeared in psychological journals. Speeches were made. "Those who spank their children," announced one campaigner, Professor Christine Heinig of Columbia University's Child Development Institute, in 1936, "should be spanked themselves"—a suggestion to which even today, if the surveys are to be believed, eight of ten American parents would object in self-protection. A noted Chicago pediatrician, C. Anderson Aldrich, in collaboration with his wife, went so far as twice to question the old ways at book length.

But it took Spock to actually turn the tide.

On the face of it, Benjamin Spock was a most unlikely prospect as a social crusader. Self-contained, a bit of a dandy, this eldest son of upper-middle-class Yankee parents had himself been raised by the book (in his case, Luther Emmett Holt's), and he grew to adulthood the archetypal obedient son. Four months after winning a gold medal in the 1924 Olympic Games as a member of the Yale crew—the same games in which the *Chariots of Fire* gang did their stuff—he found himself striding beside his father toward a New Haven polling place, about to cast his first presidential vote.

"Benny," the father instructed, "Calvin Coolidge is the greatest President the United States ever had."

Spock's reply: "Yes, Father."

It was not until he moved to New York to attend medical school at Columbia that he began to break away, first reassessing his environment—"I was amazed," he says, "absolutely astonished, to find that university-educated people could be Democrats, let alone Socialists"—and then casting his intense gaze upon himself. If, as he would later conclude, his choice of pediatrics as a specialty was largely a result of his mother's influence, so too was his subsequent decision, seemingly a pointless one by the standards of the day, to take a year's residency in psychiatry; at the time, the two disciplines were not seen as being related. "My mother adored infants," he explains, "which had a great deal to do with my attraction to pediatrics. But she was also a very moralistic, opinionated, domineering person. As soon as a child got past the age of one and started showing an inclination toward independence, she would move in to squelch it. That happened to every child in my family. I am sure that as I searched into psychiatry and psychoanalysis I was motivated by the feeling that there must be pleasanter ways to bring up babies than the way I had been brought up."

Indeed, if one buys the notion that Benjamin Spock is the father of modern pediatrics, an odd but persuasive case could surely be made that Mildred Spock, as straitlaced as the subject of any Victorian portrait, was its grandmother, for much of what Spock came to feel about the world was rooted in her motherly ministrations. Though Spock himself regards such an analysis as simplistic, it is difficult not to note how frequently even today, at eighty, he is given to ruminating on his early years, to rifling through the detritus of his childhood for clues to all he has been since. "Yesterday," he noted during a recent interview, "I was looking at a picture of myself at one year, and obviously the world was my oyster. There I was, beaming like a successful captain of industry." He paused. "But all the photographs of me at three, or five, or seven show a wistful and wholly intimidated person."

In fact, Spock says of the most dramatic and dangerous public stance he was to take in his life: "My opposition to the war and my defiance of Lyndon Johnson were, in a sense, a delayed adolescent rebellion. I certainly never rebelled against my parents at home. The fact is, I not only changed my politics during that period, I changed my personality, became a much less tense, anxious person."

Though when provoked, or in the face of incompetence, Spock is apt to show flashes of the old sternness, it is true that he today seems entirely at ease with himself. Once as liberal with his emotions as a French banker, he now laughs easily and often. A former student remembers him as an "odd duck, always, *always* in a three-piece suit." Spock now dresses as casually as everyone in Rogers, Arkansas, which is where he and his second wife, Mary Morgan, have taken to spending a good part of each year. The rest they divide between Maine and the Caribbean; Spock has always been an avid sailor, Morgan has become one. But any suggestion that he is in retirement is inadvertent. He continues to turn out a monthly magazine column, as well as to take on speaking engagements around the country on behalf of the antinuclear movement. Indeed, his vigor is such that Spock can pass for a man two decades younger. "Listen," he says, acknowledging an observation he has heard countless times before, "the fact is I even look younger than I did twenty years ago. Part of that is the beard—it hides a lot—but mainly it's the softening of my character."

Back in 1933, however, when Spock began practicing pediatrics, few mothers on New York's East Side were looking for a baby doctor given to what sounded like abstract theorizing. It was three Depression years before Spock was able to make a semblance of a living, several more before he stopped relying on the offspring of friends, and friends of friends, as patients. Even then, though somewhat known among psychiatric social workers and others of like sophistication, he hardly enjoyed a general reputation worthy of the term.

But this seemingly insurmountable obstacle to commercial and professional distinction—even the obstetricians upon whom other pediatricians relied for referrals were confounded by what Spock was up to—very shortly proved quite the opposite. For those in the publishing business farsighted enough to sense the potential of a very different kind of baby book were obliged, practically by definition, to head for Spock's Park Avenue office. The first of these, a man from Doubleday, he turned down. "I'd only been in practice five years," explains Spock. "I hadn't yet fully worked out this enormous problem of the relationship between psychoanalytic concepts and the little everyday problems that parents present to a pediatrician." But by 1943, when a droll fellow from Pocket Books named Donald Porter Geddes came to him with the same proposition, adding that it did not even have to be a good book—"Don't worry, at twenty-five cents a copy, we can't help but sell a hundred thousand a year"—Spock felt more than ready. "The truth is," he says, "I am a teacherish person. People brought up as strictly as I was usually want to tell other people how to do things."

Thus it was that two years later, with the considerable assistance of his first wife, Jane, he completed a fat manuscript (it would run 507 pages in its original edition, plus eighteen pages of index), beginning, after a brief introduction, with a simple sentence that would prove as memorable as any opening line penned on these shores since Herman Melville's: "You know more than you think you do."

That theme, the insistence that new parents are fully up to the task at hand, that successful parenting is, above all, a matter of relaxing and trusting one's instincts, would alone have been enough to set the book far apart from its grim predecessors; so, too, would the work's extraordinary thoroughness, the fact that it so fully covered the physical and behavioral problems common to small children that it would shortly come to be referred to by numberless readers as "the Bible." But what ultimately assured the book's place, and Spock's, in this country's social history was its preoccupation with the child's emotional development. Though simply written, at times even chatty, *Baby and Child Care* preached, as fervently as any religious tract, a specific set of precepts: that babies are born to be reasonable; that excessive coercion not only tends to be counterproductive but is often destructive of the spirit; that if punishment is a matter of routine, something is terribly wrong. "Can you spoil a baby?" he asks in a famous passage that would, in time, help to inspire a thousand guides to sensitive mothering, fathering, grandparenting. "You can if you work at it actively, but it doesn't come from feeding him when he's hungry, comforting him when he's miserable, being sociable with him in an easygoing way."

If so innovative—indeed, revolutionary—a doctrine seemed likely to generate heat, the truth is, the book was met only with warmth, a circumstance Spock ascribes principally to its friendliness. "It's very hard," he says, "for a doctor to write a book for the laity without being at least condescending and probably scolding—the 'Look out, stupid, if you don't do *exactly* as I say you'll kill your child' kind of thing. Doctors are trained to believe they're God and to *tell* 'em they're God. Well, of course, my orientation was to reassure parents."

But there was a great deal more to it than that. Quite simply, the book's timing was a coincidence unprecedented in American publishing, for it appeared at the precise historical moment when, as neatly as a page flipping in a ledger, this country was leaving behind its past. So distinct was that moment that, like the aftermath of the First World War twenty-five years earlier, it is reducible to a handful of powerful images; only this time the mental newsreel features not flappers or flagpole sitters or bathtubs of gin, but young men in uniform streaming off troopships into waiting arms, and a smiling Harry Truman signing the GI Bill, and row upon row of new tract houses; not a society losing its bearings, but one teeming with youngish men and women desperate to make up for lost time. The couples that touched off the baby boom were, many of them, twentieth-century pioneers, putting hundreds, thousands of miles between themselves and their families. To these, perhaps even more than to the rest, Spock was a kind of salvation, a parental voice readily available between soft covers. With, of course, the pointed distinction that his counsel was altogether different from what they'd likely have picked up at home. But Spock's call to flexibility was precisely what so many in this new generation of parents, war-weary and in the process of freeing *themselves* from the old constraints, ached on some unconscious level to hear. That they followed it so readily, and in such numbers, seemed at the time as natural as a Democrat in the White House.

By the mid-Fifties, the pendulum had swung so violently in the new direction that, to Spock's consternation, it had become clear that a large number of parents were getting into trouble by failing to exercise any leadership at all; that, for example, some children, refusing to be put to bed, were actually staying up all night. "The trouble," says one father thus buffaloed, thirty-five years later, "is that Spock was such a reaction to what had gone on before that the feeling in the air was to let the child have his head. You just erred in that direction."

Consequently, in his 1957 revision of the book, Spock restated at greater length and with more force a position he had held all along: that a child not only needs guidance but is usually miserable if he doesn't get it; that respecting a child does not mean parents must forfeit their self-respect.

Spock did not, however, find himself subject to personal attack on the "permissiveness" issue for another decade—until, to be precise, the day in 1968, shortly after his indictment on the antidraft charges, that the Reverend Norman Vincent Peale denounced him from the pulpit as being responsible for "the most undisciplined age in history."

Spock, who is a stickler for precision, still bristles at the charge—"He claimed I had urged 'instant gratification,'" he says, "which proves the man hadn't even read my book"—but, having been taken up with gusto, first by proadministration publications across the country and then, with even greater impact, by Spiro Agnew in the 1970 congressional campaign, the canard has pursued him ever since.

The particular irony in this is that Spock, personally conservative in dress and manner, was himself an austere father. Both of his sons have raked him over the coals for what they feel was a yawning emotional void in their childhoods, his failure to show them physical affection; the older, born prior to the full development of Spock's child-raising philosophy, has acknowledged publicly that as a boy he never kissed his father. Even into the late Sixties, as he made his way from campus to campus as a counterculture hero, part of Spock remained as doggedly proper as his own father had been. "I frequently had to resist the temptation," he reports now, with a laugh, "to ask some of these unkempt young men I'd meet why they didn't take a few minutes to clean themselves up."

Although sales of the book have remained steady—at about a million a year worldwide—it is beyond question that the campaign of distortion waged against him has had a profound effect on the way Spock is viewed in this country, so much so that the true nature of his impact upon those raised by his book has been largely obscured. Spock himself has tended to minimize his influence—"I never thought of myself as changing society," he says. "I was not a sculptor, looking to make the ideal person of the future"—but that, too, is begging the issue. The truth, if so categorical a term can be applied to so complex an equation, would seem to be that in helping to shift the focus of the American parent to the child's emotional health, in highlighting the benefits of growth by will rather than by rote, he *has* contributed to the making of a generation of adults less subject to regimentation than any that has come before; but, too, the pervasive misapplication of the new theories has resulted not only in literal millions of tyrannical infants and chronically unpleasant eight-year-olds and abusive teenagers, but, inevitably, in an extraordinary number of young men and women who *are* primarily concerned with their own gratification; people who, if the divorce statistics and the level of cocaine use and the number of self-help manuals crowding the best-seller lists are any indication, have contributed to an era of egocentrism unprecedented in this country's history.

Spock himself has appeared to acknowledge this, not only in his increasingly urgent call to parents to assert themselves, but even more pointedly in the addition to his book, beginning with the third edition in 1968, of what he refers to as the "world view." "You can see that psychological concepts don't help unless they are backed up by a sense of what's right and proper," he writes. "I think that more of our children would grow up happier and more stable if they were acquiring a conviction, all through childhood, that the most fulfilling thing that human beings can do is to serve humanity in some fashion and to live by their ideals."

That is a view that, if taken to heart by a sufficient number of Spock's readers, would be far greater cause for alarm among those who direct this society than mere agitation against the draft. To a remarkable degree, ours is a culture in which the drive to succeed obscures more-humane impulses; a culture in which the notions of achieving significant personal success and of remaining fully attentive to spouses, children, and friends are very nearly mutually exclusive. Were the inconceivable to occur—were our values as a people abruptly to shift dramatically in the direction suggested by Spock—one can only imagine the sense of panic, of dislocation, in boardrooms and government offices around the country.

But, as Spock himself observes, "People don't read the book for its political content, they use it for when the kid has colic."

Spock's brand of idealism has, of course, more than occasionally been taken for utopianism of the most farfetched kind. Even some of his ideological allies look upon him with bemusement. "Well, we'll have to talk to Spock," one antiwarrior told a reporter when the search was on for an alternative presidential candidate for 1968. "He'll do anything."

"I'm willing to run for anything, including dogcatcher," replied Spock when the remark was repeated to him, "for peace."

And four years later, in 1972, he did run, bearing the standard of the People's party—this, despite the presence of George McGovern on the Democratic line.

But upon even cursory examination, Spock's political sensibility is consistent with all the rest, reflecting the same belief in the human capacity for self-improvement and—one of his pet phrases—common sense that has always marked his work in pediatrics. Not unremarkably, positions he once took wearing his baby-doctor's hat can now be read as explicitly political. More than two decades before feminism was perceived as an issue, let alone given a name, Spock, in publications aimed at housewives, was urging the creation of public day-care centers, professionally staffed, "where mothers of young children could drop in without appointment or enrollment"; recommending high school courses in baby care for young men; and, over and over, observing that those males who denigrate women and have little time for their children are, in fact, the ones most terribly unsure of themselves.

"The majority of men," he elaborates today, "keep themselves out of touch. Even good fathers say, 'I'll get interested when he becomes a human being'— which, I suppose, means when he's able to discuss politics. Or football."

It is, indeed, one of the odder quirks of recent social history that in the early Seventies this agitator for a more compassionate America, this fifth columnist in the nursery, found himself under savage attack from militant feminists for the alleged pro-male bias of his famous book. Though in the latest revision, published in 1976, Spock is responsive to the outcry—the generic baby is no longer referred to as "he"—and though he continues to be ardently profeminist, he readily observes that "it is interesting to note how few of those doing the attacking actually had anything to do with babies themselves."

However, there is seemingly no bitterness in this. Spock has been around long enough to understand the curious way in which this society tends to evolve; to know, far better than most, that a period of overreaction is all but inevitable when old modes begin to give way to new. Quite startlingly, in fact, he expresses the view that through such persistent challenges, it is not inconceivable that this country might yet become as humane a place as any on the planet, "a heaven on earth."

When this assertion meets with vigorous challenge, when it is argued that the set of circumstances necessary to bring about such an outcome are roughly as likely as those that would have a czar back in the Kremlin, Spock sits back for a long moment and considers. Yes, he finally concedes, he always has been an optimist. He smiles. "That comes from being extremely well loved and well fed during my first year."

BENJAMIN SPOCK *was born on May 2, 1903, in New Haven, Connecticut. His father, Benjamin Ives Spock, was a corporation lawyer. The family is descended from Dutch immigrants named Spaak who changed their name after settling in the Hudson River valley.*

Whereas Spock's father was serene, his mother was an impulsive and violent disciplinarian whose behavior bordered on cruelty. She beat her children with a rawhide whip and locked them in closets. To make them hardy, she had them sleep, year round, in an unheated tent on the roof of the front porch.

When Spock was a child he was scared of many things: fire engines, lions that he thought inhabited the thicket near his house, a dinosaur that his friend Mansfield said lived at the bottom of his cellar stairs, and the fat Italian lady who came down the street in the spring, digging dandelions. He was afraid to go to school by the most direct route, because it would take him past a barking dog and a bully.

He took his time learning to talk. When he did speak, it was with maddening slowness. Once, when his mother and his sister Betty were driving up a hill, Betty tumbled out of the car. Spock murmured: "Betty's . . . gone." Mrs. Spock failed to hear him even when he repeated himself. Only when they reached the top of the hill did she realize that Betty, kicking and screaming, was lying back in the middle of the road.

He always loved dancing and girls. But he was shy. For four years he was smitten with Peggy Ramsey, a beautiful, quiet girl whose father had died. It was not until he underwent psychoanalysis, at age thirty, that he realized that the third girl he adored—whom he eventually married—was also fatherless. He interpreted this pattern as indicating an unusually deep fear of competing with his own father.

He met his future wife, silk heiress Jane Cheney, during his junior year at Yale. He asked her to marry him on their first weekend together. She said no.

As a young man he copied his father's Republican conservatism. In the 1930s FDR's New Deal converted him to liberalism. In the 1950s he accepted American foreign policy, viewing the Korean War as a "necessary repelling of aggression."

By 1967 he had retired as supervising pediatrician of Western Reserve University's Family Clinic, in order to devote all of his time to the campaign against the war in Vietnam. He was found guilty in 1968 of "conspiracy" to foment draft resistance. The conviction was overturned in 1969.

Joining the peace movement in 1962, he found demonstrating "excruciatingly embarrassing, like one of those bad dreams where suddenly you are downtown without any clothes on." His militancy grew, however, and at his 1968 trial he asked, "What is the use of physicians like myself trying to help parents to bring up children healthy and happy, to have them killed in such numbers for a cause that is ignoble?"

He has been arrested for civil disobedience about a dozen times. Once he and several incarcerated clerics stayed up singing hymns until three in the morning. "The acoustics in a jail are marvelous," Spock said.

In the 1972 presidential election he won 78,801 votes. He came in fourth—behind the right-wing American party candidate and ahead of the Socialist Workers party candidate.

He likes to figure-skate, and at fifty-four he learned to dance on skates. People used to dine at the rinkside restaurant at the Cleveland Skating Club to watch the famous doctor dance.

He stands six feet four inches tall. His large-boned frame makes him difficult to *fit, so he has his suits custom made. He is partial to a three-piece suit with a watch chain that has no watch but that children love to play with.*

Besides an assortment of toys, he had in his office a construction that allowed children to climb up a small flight of stairs and through a trapdoor to reach his examining table. He once said that one of his faults as a pediatrician was that he "whooped it up too much with children."

After forty-eight years of marriage he and his wife, Jane, were divorced. "If I had had a career from the beginning and kept it up," Jane Spock said, "Ben and I would still be married." In the 1976 edition of Baby and Child Care *Spock encouraged wives to pursue careers and, in a page-long dedication, thanked Jane for her contributions to his work. His ex-wife said the dedication was a case of too little, too late.*

In 1976 Spock married Mary Morgan Councille, a businesswoman. She was in her thirties, he was seventy-three. She had not read Baby and Child Care.

Eighty years old, he rows eight miles a day.

At least once a month he sends letters supporting nuclear disarmament to his two senators, his congressman, and the President.

"I'm very disappointed," he said recently, "that so few young people are interested in politics. They seem to keep their noses to the grindstone, interested only in getting good grades and getting a good job."

456

CHAMPIONS

Setting
the Standards

THEY WERE THE MEASURE BY WHICH OTHERS WOULD BE JUDGED. THEY WERE A class apart. The Champions established bench marks.

Franklin Delano Roosevelt was the thirty-second President of the United States but the George Washington of modern America. He was the founding father of the past half century. He gained his office when we needed the force of new ideas, when any good idea was better than business as usual. FDR had a slew of them: his first hundred days are a case study of how an individual can not only move a mountain but turn it upside down. If there was a philosophy behind the action, it was his commitment to action itself. His efforts put us on the road to recovery.

If Franklin Roosevelt embodied hope, Eleanor Roosevelt embodied faith and charity. Whether beside him or off on her own trail, she set our standard of humanitarianism, not just in America but worldwide. As First Lady she was the champion of the children, the hungry, the poor. Her travels, first as the President's wife, later as a true world citizen, and later still as our voice at the UN, made her this country's most conspicuous saint. There has been no one to match her ever since.

Jackson Pollock championed Abstract Expressionism, the school that dominated painting from the end of World War II to the early Sixties. Along with the works of de Kooning, Rothko, and Reinhardt, Pollock's revolutionary canvases changed the course of modern painting. His chaotic swirls and splashes liberated the new artist from the grip of the Surrealists. And when his oils dried, America was no longer a colony of the art world, it *was* the art world. New York had replaced Paris as its capital.

Popular culture, too, had its Champions. Duke Ellington is the epitome of jazz not because of his composing, his arranging, or his playing but because of all three. Versatility and imagination—there was no mistaking the Ellington band, fine-tuned and consistently impeccable under the guiding hand of the man at the piano. Likewise, at the movies, there was no mistaking Katharine Hepburn: elegant, proud, purely original. She was an American beauty who got by on character, purpose, and brains. These were her uncompromising standards.

General Dwight D. Eisenhower was our military champion in chief. With Patton, Bradley, and MacArthur he led U.S. troops into far-flung and difficult battles. He was our first truly modern general: an able administrator, a loyal warrior, a statesman.

Finally, there were the literary Champions: Ernest Hemingway, William Faulkner, F. Scott Fitzgerald. However different they were as men and as writers, they set the standard that all American writers since have dared to achieve. They were, and they remain, the heavyweights.

The Champions still reign. They are the summit of our aspirations.

—L. E.

In the Days of
Mr. Roosevelt

SAUL BELLOW

IT WAS IN CHICAGO THAT ROOSEVELT WAS NOMINATED IN 1932, WHEN I WAS SEVEN-teen years of age, just getting out of high school. When he defeated Hoover in November of that year, he didn't become President, merely. He became *the* President, presiding over us for so long that in a movie of the early Forties Billie Burke—Silly Billie—said to a fat, flummoxed senator that she had just been to Washington to see the Coronation.

Early in the Depression, my algebra teacher, an elderly lady whose white hair was piled in a cumulous formation over her square face and her blue-tinted square glasses, allowed herself a show of feeling and sang "Happy Days Are Here Again." Our astonishment was great. As a rule, Miss Scherbarth was all business. Teachers seldom sounded off on topics of the day. It's true that when Lindbergh flew to Paris Mrs. Davis told the class, "I do hope, from my heart, that he is as good a young man as he is brave, and will never disappoint us." A revelation to the sixth grade. But that Miss Scherbarth should interrupt her equations to sing out for FDR showed that the country had indeed been shaken to its foundations. It wasn't until later that I understood that city hall was busted and that Miss Scherbarth wasn't being paid. In the winter of '33, when I was a freshman at Crane College, the whole faculty went to the Loop to demonstrate at city hall. Shopkeepers were taking their scrip (municipal funny

461

money) at a discount. My English teacher, Miss Ferguson, said to us afterward, "We forced our way into the mayor's office and chased him round his desk."

Miss Ferguson, a splendid, somewhat distorted but vigorous old thing, believed in giving full particulars. To chant the rules of composition was part of her teaching method. She would dance before the blackboard and sing out, "Be! Specific!" to the tune of Handel's "Hallelujah Chorus." A charming woman, she had overlapping front teeth, like the new First Lady. As she flourished her arms while singing her messages it was not difficult to imagine her in the crowd that burst through the mayor's doors. They cried, "Pay us!"

In 1931 Chicago had elected its first foreign-born mayor. He was a Bohemian—Anton Cermak—and a formidable politician, one of the builders of the Democratic Machine, soon to be taken over by the Irish. Cermak, who had tried to block Roosevelt's nomination, went down to Florida to make peace with the President-elect. According to Len O'Connor, one of the most knowledgeable historians of Chicago, Pushcart Tony was urged by alderman Paddy Bauler, who bossed the German vote, to come to terms with FDR. "Cermak," Bauler later recalled, "said he didn't like the sonofabitch. I sez, 'Listen, for Cry sakes, you ain't got any money for the Chicago schoolteachers and this Roosevelt is the only one who can get it for you. You better get over there and kiss his ass or whatever you got to do. Only you better get the goddamn money for them teachers, or we ain't goin' to have a city that's worth runnin'.' So he goes over and, Christ Almighty, next thing I hear on the radio is that Cermak's got shot."

The assassin, Zangara, had supposedly aimed at Roosevelt, although there were those in Chicago who asserted that Cermak was his real target. Lots of people were in a position to benefit from Cermak's death. As he was rushed to the hospital Cermak supposedly whispered to Roosevelt, "I'm glad it was me instead of you." This legend was the invention of a Hearst reporter, John Dienhart, who was a drinking pal of the mayor, as well as his public relations man. Dienhart's last word on this subject, as quoted in O'Connor's *Clout*, was, "I couldn't very well have put out a story that Tony would have wanted it the other way around."

Years later, the *Chicago Tribune* reported that in a letter of thanks to Mrs. W. F. Cross, the Florida woman who had struck away Zangara's arm as he was pulling the trigger, the White House had written, "By your quick thinking a far greater tragedy was averted." Colonel McCormick's files collected anti-Roosevelt facts as Atlantic beaches gather stones. The Colonel's heart never softened toward the Roosevelts. But the writer of the White House letter, perhaps Roosevelt himself, had it right. Alas for Pushcart Tony Cermak, the tragedy *would* have been far greater.

The Roosevelt era began, therefore, with the unwilling martyrdom of a commonplace Chicago politician who had gone to make a deal—an old deal—with the new guy, an eastern swell, old money from an estate on the Hudson, snooty people, governor of New York (so what!), a President with pince-nez and a long cigarette holder. How was Pushcart Tony to know that he had been killed by a bullet aimed at the very greatest of American politicians? Jefferson (himself no mean manipulator) and Madison had had eighteenth-century class. Jackson had had fire. Lincoln was our great-souled man. Wilson was the best America had to show in the way of professorial Waspdom. But FDR was a genius in politics. He was not an intellectual. He browsed in books of naval history, preferring those that were handsomely illustrated, and he pored over his stamp albums like many another patrician. Great politicians are seldom readers or scholars. When he needed brainy men, he sent to Columbia University for them. Following the traditions of monarchy, he created a privy council of brain trusters, who had more influence, more money to spend than the members of his Cabinet. Experts now tell us that Roosevelt was an ignoramus in economic matters, and the experts are probably right. But it wasn't the brain trusters who saved the U.S.A. from disintegration; it was—oddity of oddities—a country squire from Dutchess County, a man described by a shrewd foreign observer as the Clubman Caesar and by the witty if dangerous Huey Long as Franklin De La No. The unemployed masses, working stiffs, mechanics, laid-off streetcar conductors, file clerks, shoe salesmen, pants pressers, egg candlers, truck drivers, the residents of huge, drab neighborhoods of "furriners," the greenhorns today described as ethnics—all these swore by him. They trusted only Roosevelt, a Groton boy, a Social Register snob, a rich gentleman from Harvard and Hyde Park. They did not call for a proletarian President.

There were many for whom it was bliss then to be alive. For older citizens it was a grim time, for the educated and professional classes the Depression was grievously humiliating, but for the young this faltering of order and authority made possible an escape from family and routine. As a friend of mine observed during the complacent Eisenhower period, "The cost of being poor has gone so high. You have to have a couple of hundred bucks a month. Back in the Thirties we were doing it on peanuts." He was dead right. Weekly rent in a rooming house was seldom more than three dollars. Breakfast at a drugstore counter cost fifteen cents. The blue-plate-special dinner of, say, fried liver and onions, shoestring potatoes, and coleslaw, with a dessert of Kosto pudding, appeared on the hectographed menu for thirty-five cents. Young hustlers could get by on something like eight or ten dollars a week, with a bit of scrounging. The National Youth Administration paid you a few bucks for nominal assistance to a teacher, you picked up a few more at Goldblatt's department store as a stockroom boy, you wore hand-me-downs, and you nevertheless had plenty of time to read the files of the old *Dial* at the Crerar Library or in the public library among harmless old men who took shelter from the cold in the reading room. At the Newberry you became acquainted also with Anarchist-Wobbly theoreticians and other self-made intellectuals who lectured from soapboxes in Bughouse Square, weather permitting.

Between the Twenties and the Thirties a change occurred in the country that was as much imaginative as it was economic. In the Twenties America's stability was guaranteed by big business, by industrialists and statesmen whose Anglo-Saxon names were as sound as the gold standard. On March 4, 1929, when Herbert Hoover was inaugurated, I was out of school with a sore throat and had the new Majestic radio in its absurd large cabinet all to myself. I turned the switch—and there was the new Chief Executive taking the oath of office before a great crowd. From the papers, I knew what he looked like. His hair was parted down the middle, he wore a high collar and a top hat, and looked like Mr. Tomato on the College Inn juice bottle. Full and sedate, he was one of those balanced and solid engineering-and-money types who would maintain the secure Republican reign of Silent Cal, the successor of the unhappy Harding. Big Bill Thompson, Chicago's Republican mayor, was a crook—all the local politicians were grafters and boodlers but nobody actually felt injured by them. Great men like Samuel Insull or General Dawes were very sharp, certainly, but on the whole they were probably okay. The gangsters, who did as they liked, murdered one another, seldom harming ordinary citizens. Chicago, a sprawling network of immigrant villages smelling of sauerkraut and home-brewed beer, of meat processing and soap manufacture, was at peace—a stale and queasy peace, the philistine repose apparently anticipated by the Federalists. The founders had foreseen that all would be well, life would be orderly; no great excesses, no sublimity.

The sun shone as well as it could through a haze of prosperous gases, the river moved slowly under a chemical iridescence, the streetcars rocked across the level and endless miles of the huge Chicago grid. The city greeter, Mr. Gaw, who manufactured envelopes, met all prominent visitors at the railroad stations with old-style pizzazz and comical bombast. Chicago belonged to the Boosters, to the real estate men and the utilities magnates, to William Randolph Hearst and Bertie McCormick, to Al Capone and Big Bill Thompson, and in the leafy back streets where we lived all was well.

A seven-cent streetcar fare took us to the Loop. On Randolph Street we found free entertainment at Bensinger's billiard salon and at Trafton's gymnasium, where boxers sparred. The street was filled with jazz musicians and city-hall types. My boyhood friend Fish, who was allowed to help himself to a quarter from the cash register in his father's poolroom, occasionally treated me to a hot dog and a stein of Hires root beer on Randolph Street. When we overspent, we came back from the Loop on foot—some five miles of freight yards and factories; joints that manufactured garden statuary, like gnomes, trolls, and undines; Klee brothers, where you got a baseball bat with the purchase of a two-pants suit; Polish sausage shops; the Crown theater at Division and Ashland, with its posters of Lon Chaney or Renée Adorée, its popcorn machine crackling; then the United Cigar Store; then Brown and Koppel's restaurant, with the nonstop poker game upstairs. It was a good dullness, this Hoover dullness. Higher activities were not prohibited, but you had to find them for yourself. If you subscribed to the *Literary Digest*, you might get the complete works of Flaubert as a bonus. Not that anybody read those red buckram-bound books.

Fish matured before the rest of us. At fourteen he was being shaved by the barber, paying grandly with two bits from his papa's cash register. His virile Oriental face was massaged with witch hazel, his chin was powdered, he came on boldly with the girls. He spent money also on books, pamphlets, and magazines. What he wanted from them was no more than a few quick impressions—he was no scholar—and after he had read a few pages he passed the magazines and pamphlets on to me. Through him I became familiar with Karl Marx and V. I. Lenin; also with Marie Stopes, Havelock Ellis, V. F. Calverton, Max Eastman, and Edmund Wilson. The beginning of the Great Depression was also the beginning of my mental life. But suddenly the comedy of comfort stopped, the good-natured absurdities of the painted flivver, Pikes Peak or Bust, the Babbitt capers. There were no more quarters in the till.

The tale of America as told in the Twenties by America's leaders was that this country had scored one of the most brilliant successes in history. Hoover boasted in a 1928 campaign speech that the conquest of poverty in the United States was a palpable reality. "The poorhouse is vanishing from among us . . . our industrial output has increased as never before, and our wages have grown steadily in buying power. Our workers, with their average weekly wages, can today buy two and often three times more bread and butter than any wage earner of Europe. At one time we demanded for our workers a full dinner pail. We have now gone far beyond that conception. Today we demand larger comfort and greater participation in life and leisure."

How bitterly Hoover must have regretted the full dinner pail. He had, after all, meant well. To postwar Europe he had been a benefactor. But now the big businessmen who boasted of the bread and butter they were stuffing us with (Silvercup, not European bread) became once more what Eleanor Roosevelt's Uncle Teddy had called "malefactors of great wealth." Their factories closed and their banks failed.

Private misery could not be confined; it quickly overflowed into the streets. Foreclosures, evictions, Hooverville shanties, soup lines—old Dr. Townsend of Long Beach, California, was inspired with his plan for the aged when he saw elderly women rooting for food in garbage cans. Maggoty meat for Americans? Were Chicago and Los Angeles to become Oriental cities like Shanghai or Calcutta?

The great engineer had botched his job. What would his successor do? Reputable analysts, taking Roosevelt's measure, were not encouraged by their findings. Walter Lippmann wrote in 1932 that FDR was "an amiable man with many philanthropic impulses" but accused him of "carrying water on both shoulders," of hanging on to both right-wing and left-wing supporters, a politician lavish with "two-faced platitudes." Roosevelt was no crusader, no enemy of entrenched privilege, "no tribune of the people," and Lippmann saw in him no more than "a pleasant man who, without any important qualifications for the office, would like very much to be President."

But Lippmann had examined the wrong musician, studied a different score, for when Roosevelt sat down to play, he stormed over the executive keyboard, producing music no one had ever heard before. He was dazzling. And the secret of his political genius was that he knew exactly what the public needed to hear. It amounted to that, a personal declaration by the President that took into account the feelings of the people, and especially their fears. In his first inaugural address he told the great crowd before the Capitol, "This is preeminently the time to speak the truth, the whole truth, frankly and boldly. This great Nation will endure as it has endured, will revive and will prosper." And then, "We do not distrust the future of essential democracy. The people of the United States . . . have asked for discipline and direction under leadership. They have made me the present instrument of their wishes."

With this powerful statement the tale of the Twenties concluded, and a new tale began. Against the boastfulness of the Coolidge-and-Hoover decade were set the humiliations and defeats of the Depression. It was generally agreed that the Depression was to be viewed as what insurance companies term an act of God, a natural disaster. Peter F. Drucker puts the matter correctly in his memoirs: "As after an earthquake, a flood, a hurricane, the community closed ranks and came to each other's rescue . . . the commitment to mutual help and the willingness to take chances on a person were peculiar to Depression America." Professor Drucker adds that there was nothing like this on the other side, in Europe, "where the Depression evoked only suspicion, surliness, fear, and envy." In the opinion of Europeans the only choice was between communism and facism. Among world leaders, Roosevelt alone spoke with assurance about "essential democracy." It is not too much to say that another America was imaginatively formed under his influence. Recovery programs were introduced with public noise and flourishes during his first hundred days, and although huge sums were spent, it presently became apparent that there would be no recovery. That he was nevertheless elected repeatedly proves that what the voters wanted was to live in a Rooseveltian America, which turned the square old U.S.A. of the Hoovers topsy-turvy. I can remember an autumnal Chicago street very early one morning when I heard clinking and ringing noises. The source of these sounds was hidden in a cloud, and when I entered the sphere of fog just beginning to be lighted by the sun, I saw a crowd of men with hammers chipping mortar from old paving bricks—fifty or sixty of the unemployed pretending to do a job, "picking them up and laying 'em down again," as people then were saying. Every day Colonel McCormick's *Tribune* denounced these boondoggles. In the center of the front page there was always a cartoon of moronic professors with donkey tails hanging from their academic mortarboards. They were killing little pigs, plowing under crops, and centupling the national debt while genial FDR, presiding at the Mad Hatter's tea party, lightheartedly poured out money. The brick chippers, however, were grateful to him. These jobless bookkeepers, civil engineers, or tool-and-die makers were glad to work on the streets for some twenty dollars a week. The national debt, which enraged the Colonel, that dotty patriot, meant nothing to them. They desperately needed the small wages the government paid them. The drama of professional dignity sacrificed also appealed to many of them.

Memorable days. In 1934 I took to the road with a pal. With three dollars between us, enough to keep us in cheese and crackers, we bummed the freights. We joined the multitude of men and boys that covered the boxcars like flocks of birds. In South Bend, Indiana, we passed the Studebaker plant and a crowd of sit-in strikers yelling and cheering from the rooftop and the open windows. We shouted and joked with them, rolling at about five miles an hour in summer warmth through the fresh June weeds, the Nickel Plate locomotive pulling us toward a horizon of white clouds. It now occurs to me that I didn't know how hard I was grieving for my mother, who had died just before Roosevelt was inaugurated. With her death and the remarriage of my father the children scattered. I was turned loose—freed, in a sense: free, but also stunned, like someone who survives an explosion but hasn't yet grasped what has happened. I didn't know anything. At the age of eighteen I didn't even know that I was an adolescent. Words like that came later, in the Forties and Fifties.

Of course I sympathized with the strikers. Thanks to Fish's pamphlets I was able to call myself a socialist, and the socialist line was that FDR's attempted reforms were saving the country for capitalism, only the capitalists were too stupid to understand this. Radical orthodoxy in the Thirties held that parliamentary European reformism had failed and that the real choice, on a world scale, was between the hateful dictatorships of the Right and the temporary and therefore enlightened dictatorships of the Left. American democracy would not in the long run prove an exception. So said the radicals. One of them, Edmund Wilson, had written in 1931 that if American radicals wished to accomplish something valuable, "they must take communism away from the communists and take it without ambiguities or reservations, asserting emphatically that their ultimate goal is the ownership of the means of production by the government." And in a weird panegyric of Lenin written after his pilgrimage to the tomb on Red Square, Wilson told his readers that in the Soviet Union you felt that you were "at the moral top of the world where the light never really goes out." He spoke of Lenin as one of the very highest products of humanity—"the superior man who has burst out of the classes and claimed all that man has done which is superior for the refinement of mankind as a whole."

I was an early reader of Edmund Wilson's *Axel's Castle*. By 1936, I had also read his *Travels in Two Democracies*. Wilson had opened my eyes to the high culture of modern Europe and on that account I was in his debt. Besides, I had met him in Chicago when he was hauling a heavy gladstone bag on Fifty-seventh Street near the University, hot and almost angry, shining with sweat and bristling at his ears and nostrils with red hairs. A representative of all that was highest and best on the streets of Hyde Park—imagine that! His voice was hoarse and his manner huffy, but he was kindly and invited me to visit him. He was the greatest literary man I had ever met and I was willing to agree with all his views, whether the subject was Dickens or Lenin. But despite my great admiration for him and my weakness for inspired utterances, I was not carried away by his Lenin worship. Perhaps because my parents were Russian Jews, I was as distrustful of Lenin and Stalin as Wilson was of American politicians. I didn't *believe* in Roosevelt as Wilson apparently believed in Lenin. I seem to have sensed, however, that Roosevelt was holding the country together, and in

467

my obstinate heart I resisted the Wilsonian program for American radicals. I couldn't believe, anyway, that liberal graduates of Harvard and Princeton were going to abduct Marxism from the Marxists and save the U.S.A. by taking charge of the dictatorship of the American proletariat. I secretly believed that America *would* in the end prove an exception. America and I, *both* exceptional, would together elude prediction and defy determinism.

You didn't have to approve Roosevelt's policies to be a Rooseveltian. Myself, I liked his policies less and less as time went by. I can recall the marks I gave him (in my helplessness). For recognizing Hitler as a great evildoer he rated an A. His support of England moved me deeply (high marks). In his judgment of the Russians he fell to a D. With Joe Kennedy in London and Joseph Davies in Moscow, one of the most disgraceful appointments in diplomatic history, he flunked out. For opinions on his dealings with Stalin I refer the reader to the Poles, the Czechs, the Romanians, etc. He did nothing to prevent the murder of millions in Hitler's death factories, but of that we were then ignorant.

His most dazzling successes were domestic and psychological. For millions of Americans the crisis of the old order was a release, a godsend. A great gap opened, and a fresh impulse of the imagination rushed in. The multitudes were more mobile, diverse, psychologically flexible; they manifested new moods and colors; they were more urbane under FDR's influence. What was most important, for those who had the capacity for it, was the emotional catharsis of making a new start, of falling and rising again. The Thirties were more sociable, more accepting of weakness, less rigid, less idolatrous, and less snobbish.

The Roosevelt influence was especially gratifying to the foreign-born. Millions of them passionately hoped to be *included*, to be counted at last as true Americans. Certain of the immigrants were parochial. Poles and Ukrainians, for instance, preferred to keep to their own communities and customs. Others, catching the American fever, changed their names, made up new personalities, and, energized by these distortions, threw themselves into the life of the country. Who knows how many people became somebody else, turned themselves into jazz singers, blackface comedians, sportsmen, tycoons, antebellum southern ladies, Presbyterian vestrymen, Texas ranchers, Ivy Leaguers, high government officials. It is not too much to say that these self-created people, people with false credentials, actors invisibly consumed by guilt and fear of exposure, were often empire builders. There's nothing like a shameful secret to fire a man up. If Hawthorne had not understood this, *The Scarlet Letter* would never have been written.

For these fertile and productive impostors, it was bliss to hear FDR say that in this country we were all of us aliens. An actor himself, he put on the most successful act of all. He even had a secret: he could not walk. Behind this secret much deeper secrets were concealed.

Consider briefly, for the purpose of contrast, the career of Fitzgerald's Jay Gatsby, a pretender who could not forgive himself. Born James Gatz, he was remade (should we say twice born?). Boy Scout motives of self-improvement and naive love-idealism kept him pure in heart and gullible. What Americans learned from Roosevelt's example was that amour propre (vanity, secrecy, ambition, pride) need not give anyone a bad conscience. You could, as Yeats suggested, "measure the lot, forgive myself the lot." Roosevelt, who, with his democratic charm, his gaiety, the dramatic nobility of his head, *looked* the great man, sent Americans the message that beyond pretending and theatricality there was a further range in which one's deeper nature could continue to live, its truth undamaged. We may pretend, he seemed to be saying, as long as we are not taken in by our own pretenses. That way schizophrenia lies. From memoirs written by members of his inner circle we have learned that he loved spoofing, he was a gifted comedian who made fun of himself, a practical joker. He was well acquainted with Lear's *Nonsense Rhymes* and with *The Hunting of the Snark*. The irrational has its legitimate place by the side of the rational. Okay. Life is real and earnest, but it is also decidedly goofy. With Roosevelt this was always clear. Others were more nebulous and more difficult. Compare, for instance, Roosevelt's Fala with the little dog of Richard Nixon in his "sincere" Checkers speech.

In domestic politics FDR's victorious intuition was that a President must discuss crises with the public in the plainest terms. Democracy cannot thrive if leaders are unable to teach or to console. A certain amount of deception is inevitable, of course. So many of society's institutions stand upon a foundation of fraud that you cannot expect a President to "tell all." Telling all is the function of intellectuals, supposedly. For Roosevelt it was sufficient to attack big business and expose malefactors of great wealth. He was not a philosopher. For his relations with the public he might, however, have taken his text from Isaiah: "Comfort ye." Among his successors in the White House, only Truman in his different, "give 'em hell" style took a personal line with the voters. Some of our recent Presidents, sophisticated technicians, instinctively resisted the personal line with the public. To Johnson and to Nixon this was an abomination. They were not leaders, they were professional behind-the-scenes operators. The very thought of taking the public into their confidence was horrifying to them. Forced to make a show of candor and an appeal for confidence, they averted their faces, their eyes filmed, their voices flattened. Frightful for a man like LBJ, stuffed with powers and with secrets, to abase himself before the cameras. He was not a Coriolanus but a democratic technician. Under such technicians decay was inevitable.

A civilized man, FDR gave the U.S.A. a civilized government. I suppose that he was what Alexander Hamilton would have called an "elective king," and if he was in some respects a demagogue, he was a demagogue without ideological violence. He was not a führer but a statesman. Hitler and he came to power in the same year. Both made superb use of the radio. Those of us who heard Hitler's broadcasts will never forget the raucous sounds of menace, the great crowds howling as he made his death threats. Roosevelt's chats with his "Fellow Americans" are memorable for other reasons. As an undergraduate I was fully armored in skepticism, for Roosevelt was very smooth and one couldn't be careful enough. But under the armor I was nonetheless vulnerable. I can recall

469

walking eastward to the Chicago Midway on a summer evening. The light held long after nine o'clock and the ground was covered with clover, more than a mile of green between Cottage Grove and Stoney Island. The blight hadn't yet carried off the elms, and under them drivers had pulled over, parking bumper to bumper, and turned on their radios to hear Roosevelt. They had rolled down the windows and opened the car doors. Everywhere the same voice, its odd eastern accent, which in anyone else would have irritated midwesterners. You could follow without missing a single word as you strolled by. You felt joined to these unknown drivers, men and women smoking their cigarettes in silence, not so much considering the President's words as affirming the rightness of his tone and taking assurance from it. You had some sense of the weight of troubles that made them so attentive, and of the ponderable fact, the one common element (Roosevelt), on which so many unknowns could agree. Just as memorable to me, perhaps, was to learn how long clover flowers could hold their color in the dusk.

———

FRANKLIN DELANO ROOSEVELT *was born on January 30, 1882, in Hyde Park, New York. Between the Delanos and the Roosevelts he claimed twelve Mayflower ancestors. He once began a speech to the Daughters of the American Revolution, "Fellow immigrants!"*

He was an only child. Until age five, he wore dresses and had blond curls. He called his doting parents "Sallie" and "Popsie."

He earned C's at Harvard but became president of The Harvard Crimson. *He was passed over for membership in the college's elite Porcellian club—a snub that Eleanor Roosevelt believed gave her husband an inferiority complex.*

At Columbia law school he discovered "how unimportant the law really is." Bored, he flunked two courses and dropped out before graduation. He still passed his bar examination.

His devotion to his mother—who set up house with her son and his wife— eventually reduced Eleanor to tears. It also rankled a New York politician who early on sought to recruit Roosevelt for the state assembly. FDR was eager to run. "But," he said, "I'd like to talk to my mother about it first." "Frank," said the politician sternly, "there are men back in Poughkeepsie waiting for your answer. They won't like to hear you had to ask your mother." Roosevelt replied, "I'll do it."

Before he was paralyzed he walked in his sleep. Afterward, he feared dying in a fire and practiced crawling across the floor as an escape measure. He could always joke about his handicap; when ending a conversation, he would say, "Goodbye. I've got to run."

While recovering from polio, he wrote a movie script based on the history of the ship Old Ironsides, *but Hollywood didn't bite. He also invested in several business schemes, started an intercity dirigible freight line, and had plans to market Argentinian herb tea.*

He stood six feet two inches tall and weighed about 190 pounds. Woodrow Wilson once called him "the handsomest young giant I have ever seen." In overcoming polio, he built up his arms and chest. "Maybe my legs aren't so good," he said, "but look at those shoulders! Jack Dempsey would be green with envy."

He was a talker and usually dominated White House dinner conversations. Winston Churchill—whom he once called "horribly" garrulous—said, "Meeting him is like opening a bottle of champagne."

He was flirtatious. His daughter Anna said, "If Father became friendly with a princess or a secretary, he'd reach out and give a pat to her fanny and laugh like hell and was probably telling a funny story at the same time, whereas to Mother that was terrible."

He had a hearty sex drive, but in 1916, after six children, his wife said, "No more." During the remaining twenty-nine years of their marriage, they slept apart. In 1918 FDR agreed to end his two-year affair with Eleanor's social secretary, Lucy Mercer. But Elliot Roosevelt has asserted that around 1923 his father began a twenty-year affair with Missy LeHand, FDR's private secretary, and that Eleanor condoned the relationship, allowing the two to occupy adjoining bedrooms in the White House.

He sometimes referred to himself as "Pappa." He liked to think of himself as father to many people other than his own children. On one of his cross-country tours an old woman in Marietta, Ohio, knelt down and patted the dust where he had left a footprint.

He liked going on trips, and he liked trees, politicians, and donkeys. He liked the word pipelines.

He called each person on the White House staff by his or her first name. The chief doorkeeper, who had been in the White House for thirty years, nearly fainted when the President addressed him as "Pat."

His son James once said, "Of what was inside him, of what really drove him, father talked with no one."

He was known to cry only once—after the death of his mother, when he discovered the memorabilia of his life that she had collected.

Late in life he grew interested in Kierkegaard and his emphasis on the natural sinfulness of man. "I want to go back to Hyde Park," he said in 1939. "I want to take care of my trees. I want to make the farm pay. I want to finish my little house on the hill."

On the morning of April 12, 1945, he was posing for a portrait at his cottage in Warm Springs, Georgia. Suddenly he raised a hand to his forehead and said softly, "I have a terrific headache." He slumped into his chair, unconscious. Three hours later he was dead, of a cerebral hemorrhage.

471

Eleanor the Good

JOHN KENNETH GALBRAITH

ONE DAY IN THE AUTUMN OF 1940, WITH AMERICAN ENTRY INTO THE WAR IN THE MIDdle distance, I was giving thought to a task with which I had recently been charged. It was to guide a substantial number of the ordnance and munitions plants then being planned—some sixty in all—into the southern and south central states. There they would employ white and maybe black workers lost in those days to rural poverty; a yet greater industrial concentration in the East and Northeast would be avoided. I was chairman of a civilian committee dedicated to this end, and we were making no appreciable progress in persuading the War Department, as it then was, to our design.

I turned for help to individuals knowledgeable in the folkways of the Roosevelt administration and in particular to Donald Comer, a Birmingham textile manufacturer, the liberal son of an Alabama governor, a power in southern politics and a man well experienced in making his way around Washington. Could he get us to the President on the issue? Comer said it was far more important to get to Mrs. Roosevelt. And so we did. We made an appointment, boarded the train to New York, and went to her Washington Square apartment, where she was staying at the moment. The rooms were of modest size; my memory is of beige slipcovers and upholstery, all a trifle on the rusty side. There were three of us in the delegation; our third man was a Washington functionary who had joined us only to share in the Roosevelt darshan. He said nothing, and after the

472

meeting we never saw him again. Comer and I, in contrast, were eloquent, even impassioned. After assuring herself as to our motives, Mrs. Roosevelt promised to help. In subsequent weeks we found we had the support of the President. A fair number of plants went south; in ensuing years they doubtless had an effect on the economic development of the region. It was the kind of difference that all who were around at the time will tell you that Eleanor Roosevelt made.

I assume that she did, indeed, speak to the President; in any case, her effect on his policies is not in doubt. But Eleanor Roosevelt's true influence was not by way of her husband; it was directly on the people of the United States and the world at large. There is proof in the fact that it continued undiminished for nearly two decades after the death of Franklin Roosevelt. Had she been confined to the role of a wife, however brilliant and effective, she would have been forgotten long since.

The difference Eleanor Roosevelt made in her own right was threefold. There was, first, her advocacy of civil equality in the Republic. Franklin D. Roosevelt had many things on his side; a commitment to black and minority rights was not one of them. His coalition—white, mainly rural southerners by whom white supremacy was assumed and northern urban political machines and proletarians—would not have survived an affirmative stand on civil rights for more than a week. But Eleanor was not deterred; she dared the awful scorn reserved for those who associated politically with southern blacks; she even in those perilous days had her picture taken shaking hands with them. Being willing to risk this, she both paved the way for others and showed that some, perhaps much, of the resulting reaction was quite harmless hot air. Her interest was not less in the old, the jobless, the young, and the poor. These concerns continued and expanded after the President's death.

Her second achievement was in showing, more than any other person of her time, that an American could truly be a world citizen. This was manifest in her incessant and concerned travels, her early and enduring commitment to the United Nations; it was deeply evident in her speeches and writing, and in her pioneering support for human rights. In this day and age it is pleasant, if somewhat surprising, to recall that there was a time when American leaders were not feared but loved. So it was with Eleanor Roosevelt. I was in India when word came of her death. I had the flag at the embassy lowered to half-staff not as the kind of self-gratifying gesture in which I am deeply experienced; it was what the Indians expected. Our loss was equally theirs.

Finally, more than anyone else in her time, Eleanor Roosevelt showed that a woman could have an independent—and powerful—position in political life. This, in turn, is her claim to being one of the pioneer figures in the modern women's movement. The notion that politics was somehow a male monopoly never crossed her mind. Nor that she was entitled to any deference because she was a woman. She assumed a position of full equality with men as a matter of course; more than that, she never hesitated to show the superiority associated with an incisive mind, wide-ranging information, a superbly accurate assessment of political motives, and a devastating re~~onse to political idiocy and pretense.

This last brings me to a most important point. Women did not get anywhere in political or other public life because they were admired or loved. Nor do they now. They began to make progress only when they were feared. This was the lesson of Eleanor Roosevelt. I saw her on various occasions. I never did so without a certain sense of trepidation. When she gave you her views, including what she thought of your ideas or plans, you were not left in any doubt. Certainly not if you were inadequate or foolish or she thought so. That sense of anxiety, tension, is the feeling anyone exercising power must induce. This she did. The women who led the feminist movement in the years following her death had a similar capacity to command respect, which is another way of saying that men were a little afraid of them. Eleanor Roosevelt, in major measure, was their model.

ELEANOR ROOSEVELT *was born on October 11, 1884, in New York City. She was the niece of President Theodore Roosevelt and the fifth cousin once removed of her future husband, Franklin.*

She was raised by her grandmother. When she was eight her mother died. When she was ten she lost her father, who had been exiled from the family because of his addiction to drugs and alcohol.

As a young woman she was painfully shy yet energetic. Summering on the Hudson, she rose before dawn with one of her aunts, rowed five miles to fetch the mail, then returned before breakfast.

Before they married, she and FDR never kissed. He wrote her poems, and he proposed during a walk. Eleanor's uncle, President Theodore Roosevelt, gave her away at the wedding. Asked by reporters what he made of two cousins getting married, the President replied, "It is a good thing to keep the name in the family."

On the honeymoon FDR had a startling dream in which he saw a beam spinning dangerously above her head. When she woke him, he asked, "Don't you see it?"

She believed in fresh air and once rigged a window with a wire contraption in which to cradle her daughter Anna. Neighbors threatened to report her to the Society for the Prevention of Cruelty to Children.

She told Anna that sex was an ordeal to be borne. Her son Elliot remembered her as being straitlaced and squeamish.

After thirteen years of marriage, she discovered that her husband was having an affair with Lucy Mercer, her social secretary. She offered a divorce, but they de-

cided to stay together. He agreed to stop seeing Mercer. Yet when he died at Warm Springs, Georgia, Mercer was present. Eleanor was not.

She was bent on self-improvement. One summer she tried to teach herself Spanish; she failed. She enrolled in a business school to learn typing and shorthand. She found a housewife to teach her to cook.

In the Twenties she wrote an article for Redbook *magazine titled "Women Must Learn to Play the Game as Men Do." In an early composition she wrote, "It may seem strange, but no matter how plain a woman may be if truth and loyalty are stamped upon her face all will be attracted to her, and she will do good to all who come near her."*

She never forgave her mother for calling her "Granny" as a child. Yet even as a woman she had difficulty disagreeing with her mother's opinion that she was plain, ugly. When the nation's designers voted her the best-dressed woman of 1934, she was ecstatic and considered it one of her life's greatest honors.

FDR called her his "eyes and ears" and would often undo department heads by saying, "Yes, but my missus tells me . . ."

Her son James recalled the scene when she told FDR that her brother Hall had died: "Father struggled to her side and put his arm around her. 'Sit down,' he said, so tenderly I can still hear it. And he sank down beside her and hugged her and kissed her and held her head to his chest. . . ."

When she heard that an assassin had tried to kill FDR, she said, "These things have to be expected."

She wrote a daily newspaper column on her household events as First Lady. Believing that people would like to know that accidents befall even those in the White House, she reported when a butler dropped a tray.

When the House Committee on Un-American Activities called in some young members of the radical Left, she advised them as to what to say and later invited six of them to the White House for dinner.

She resigned from the Daughters of the American Revolution in 1936 because it excluded blacks.

At a White House tea she might shake hands with five hundred to a thousand people in an afternoon. Yet her life as First Lady came to seem very impersonal. She later wrote of her White House years: "[I] was lost somewhere deep down inside myself."

She developed a close friendship with Associated Press reporter Lorena Hickok, who lived in the White House for four years. Eleanor wrote her more than 2,300 letters, a few of them passionate. "Hick darling . . ." she wrote. "Oh, I want to put my arms around you. I ache to hold you close. Your ring is a great comfort. I look at it and think she does love me. . . ." The First Lady acknowledged, ". . . so you think they gossip about us. . . . I am always so much more optimistic than you are—I suppose because I care so little what 'they' say."

She died on November 7, 1962, of bone marrow tuberculosis.

Jack the Dripper

KURT VONNEGUT JR.

JACKSON POLLOCK (1912–1956) WAS A PAINTER WHO, DURING HIS MOST ADMIRED PE-riod, beginning in 1947, would spread a canvas on his studio floor and drib-ble or spatter or pour paint on it—and sometimes get up on a stepladder to look down at what he'd done. He was born in Cody, Wyoming, which is named in honor of a legendary creator of dead animals, "Buffalo Bill" Cody. Buffalo Bill died of old age. Jackson Pollock came east to the state of New York, where he died violently at the age of forty-four, having, as the fore-most adventurer in the art movement now known as Abstract Expression-ism, done more than any other human being to make his nation, and especially New York City, the unchallenged center of innovative painting in all this world.

Until his time, Americans were admirable for their leadership in only one art form, which was jazz. Like all great jazz musicians, Pollock made himself a champion and connoisseur of the appealing accidents that more-formal artists worked hard to exclude from their performances.

Three years before Pollock killed himself and a young woman he had just met, by driving his car into an embankment on a quiet country road, he had begun to move away in his work from being what one critic called "Jack the Dripper." He was laying on much of the paint with a brush—again. He had started out with a brush, and as an enemy of accidents. Let it be known far and wide, and especially among the philistines, that this man was capable of depicting in photographic detail the crossing of the Delaware by the Father of our Country, if such a tableau had been demanded by the passions of himself and his century. He had been meticulously trained in his craft by, among others, that most exacting American master of representational art, a genius of antimodernism, Thomas Hart Benton.

Pollock was a civilian throughout the Second World War, although in the prime of life. He was rejected for military service, possibly because of his alcoholism, which he would conquer from time to time. He went without a drink, for example, from 1948 through 1950.

He continued to paint and teach and study during the war, when the careers of so many of his American colleagues were disrupted, and when painters his own age in Europe had been forbidden by dictators to paint as they pleased and were used as fodder for cannons and crematoria and so on.

So—while Pollock is notorious for having broken with the past, he was one of the few young artists who during the war pondered art history uninterruptedly, and speculated in peace as to what the future of art might be.

He should be astonishing even to people who do not care about painting—for this reason: he surrendered his will to his unconscious as he went about his job. He wrote this in 1947, eight years after the death of Sigmund Freud: "When I am *in* my painting, I am not aware of what I'm doing."

It might be said that he painted religious themes during a time of enthusiasm in the Occident for peace and harmony to be found, supposedly, in a state that was neither sleep nor wakefulness, to be achieved through meditation.

He was unique among founders of important art movements in that his colleagues and followers did not lay on paint as he did. French Impressionists painted a lot alike, and Cubists painted a lot alike, and were supposed to, since the revolutions in which they took part were, for all their spiritual implications, quite narrowly technical.

But Pollock did not animate a school of dribblers. He was the only one. The artists who felt themselves at least somewhat in his debt made pictures as madly various as the wildlife of Africa—Mark Rothko and Willem de Kooning and James Brooks and Franz Kline and Robert Motherwell and Ad Reinhardt and Barnett Newman, and on and on. Those named, by the way, were personal friends of Pollock. All vigorous schools of art, it would seem, start with artificial extended families.

What bonded Pollock's particular family was not agreement as to what, generally, a picture should look like, but whence inspiration for pictures should come, hey presto—the unconscious, the part of the mind that was lively, but which caught no likenesses, which might not even have suspected that there was a world outside the cranium.

Who can count, poring over yellowing journals and manifestos, all the art movements that have given themselves fanfares during this most volatile of all centuries? Almost all of them have died as quickly as do lightning bugs. A few have lived as long as dogs and horses. Abstract Expressionism is exciting more painters than ever, twenty-seven years after Jack the Dripper's death, and, because it celebrates what a part of the brain can do rather than what pictures should look like it promises to outlast elephants and whales, and perhaps even tortoises.

James Brooks, at seventy-seven a dean of the movement, describes in conversation the ideal set of mind for a painter who wishes to link his or her hands to the unconscious, as Pollock did: "I must lay on the first stroke of paint. After that, I insist that the canvas do at least half the work." The canvas, which is to say the unconscious, considers that first stroke, and then it tells the painter's hand how to respond to it—with a shape of a certain color and texture at that point there. And then, if all is going well, the canvas ponders this addition and comes up with further recommendations. The canvas becomes a Ouija board.

Was there ever a more cunning experiment designed to make the unconscious reveal itself? Has any psychological experiment yielded a more delightful suggestion than this one: that there is a part of the mind without ambition or information, which nonetheless is expert on what is beautiful?

Has any theory of artistic inspiration ever urged painters so vehemently, while they worked, to ignore life itself—to ignore life utterly? In the Abstract Expressionist paintings in museums and on the walls of art lovers, and in the vaults of speculators, there is very little to suggest a hand or a face, say, or a table or a bowl of oranges, or a sun or a moon—or a glass of wine.

And could any moralist have called for a more apt reaction by painters to World War II, to the death camps and Hiroshima and all the rest of it, than pictures without persons or artifacts, without even allusions to the blessings of Nature? A full moon, after all, had come to be known as "a bomber's moon." Even an orange could suggest a diseased planet, a disgraced humanity, if someone remembered, as many did, that the commandant of Auschwitz and his wife and children, under the greasy smoke from the ovens, often had had fresh fruit for breakfast.

An appropriately visceral and soul-deep reaction by painters to Auschwitz and Hiroshima and all the rest of it was going to take place within the borders of this rich and sheltered nation when a young and, by most reports, profoundly unhappy genius from, of all places, Cody, Wyoming, began to treat each canvas as a Ouija board. It had seemed impossible that any real artist could honorably create harmonious pictures for a European and North American civilization whose principal industry had become the manufacture of ruins and cripples and corpses.

But then Jackson Pollock found a way.

PAUL JACKSON POLLOCK *was born on January 28, 1912, on a sheep ranch in Cody, Wyoming. He preferred "Jack" to "Paul," so he dropped the latter completely when he moved to New York City.*

By the time he was fourteen, he was milking a dozen cows twice a day.

He had four brothers: three of them became painters and one became a writer.

The Pollocks later moved from Wyoming to Los Angeles, where Jackson enrolled in Manual Arts High School. His art teacher there introduced him to Buddhism and the teachings of Jiddu Krishnamurti. Manual Arts expelled Pollock twice: once for distributing his Journal of Liberty, *attacking the school faculty, and once for giving two girls money to help them run away from home.*

In New York he studied at the Art Students League under Thomas Hart Benton. Benton gave him the only formal instruction he ever had, introduced him to Renaissance art, and got him a job in the League cafeteria. Of Benton, Pollock said: "He drove his kind of realism at me so hard I bounced right into nonobjective painting."

He later came under the influence of Mexican muralist José Clemente Orozco. During the 1930s Pollock made twelve sketching trips across America—driving an old Ford and riding on freight trains.

In New York he lived with his brother Sandy at 76 West Houston Street and worked as a school janitor for ten dollars a week. Under the Federal Art Project, he painted two murals for Greenwich House. Under the Emergency Relief Administration, he cleaned the statue of Peter Cooper in Cooper Square.

In 1944 Pollock was virtually unknown. By August 1949 his paintings hung in five U.S. museums and forty private collections, and he had had a one-man show in Paris.

On being a celebrity, Pollock said, "I feel like a clam without a shell." Ad Reinhardt said, "Pollock wanted to become a celebrity and he did. He got kicked out of the "21" Club many times."

If anyone "discovered" Pollock, it was John Graham, who organized a show in 1940 with works by Pollock, Willem de Kooning, and Arshile Gorky. However, art patron Peggy Guggenheim said, "Pollock was the new genius I just discovered." She also said of Pollock, "To me, he was like a trapped animal who should never have left Wyoming."

Pollock married Lee Krasner, an artist, and they moved to a big white clapboard house in the Springs, in the Hamptons, on Long Island.

He always slept late; whether he'd been drinking or not, he often slept twelve to fourteen hours.

He made great spaghetti sauce and he loved to bake bread and pies. He contributed apple pies for auction at the annual village benefits.

He had a love for jazz and for music in general. But he had trouble carrying a tune and was an awkward dancer.

He was six feet tall, blond, prematurely balding, and had hazel eyes. He wore high boots, blue jeans, and a neckerchief.

He had a pet crow, Caw-Caw, whom he trained to talk and to come when he called. He had two dogs, Gyp and Ahab.

Pollock's grocer in the Springs, Dan Miller, bought a Pollock that he identified to mystified viewers as an aerial view of Siberia.

If a lifelike image appeared in a painting, Pollock rubbed it out; every picture, he said, must retain "a life of its own." He also stopped titling his paintings and simply numbered them, because he felt numbers were neutral: "They make people look at a picture for what it is—pure painting."

"My painting does not come from the easel," he said. "I prefer to tack the unstretched canvas to the hard wall or the floor. . . . On the floor I am more at ease. I . . . can . . . literally be in the painting. This is akin to the method of the Indian sand painters of the West."

When fellow artist Hans Hoffmann asked about the importance of nature in Pollock's work, Pollock said, "I am nature."

Betty Parsons, who represented him during his most prolific years, said, "I loved his looks. There was a vitality, an enormous physical presence. . . . You could not forget his face. . . . He was always sad. He made you feel sad; even when he was happy, he made you feel like crying."

On the day of Pollock's death, he said to Conrad Marca-Relli, "Life is beautiful, the trees are beautiful. The sky is beautiful, but I have only the image of death."

He died in a car crash on August 11, 1956, in Southampton. Pollock was driving toward his home in a green 1950 Oldsmobile convertible, for which he'd traded two black-and-white paintings.

The Grand Duke of Jazz

ALISTAIR COOKE

IN CLAIMING DUKE ELLINGTON AS THE SUPREME JAZZ TALENT OF THE PAST FIFTY years, it has become necessary to say what he was not. For, nine years after his death, his music is being recycled as an Ellington industry, which was launched with deafening electronic blare in the Broadway production of something called *Sophisticated Ladies*. This travesty presented Ellington as a great American songwriter (which he was not) and as the leader of the lushest and noisiest of the big bands.

Was he not a songwriter? He wrote four or five haunting songs and a string of slack, sentimental ditties, nearly all of which were crooned, in a strangulated semirock fashion, in the aforesaid circus. Yet, surely, Ellington's was a big band? Certainly, it was rarely, if ever, anything else. But it was the Duke's distinction, springing from his great gifts as a creator of essentially unsung jazz compositions, to scorn throughout his life the big band clichés—the pumping brass, the two-bar or four-bar mechanical riffs, the set harmonies, the predictable final ensembles. It was his first great achievement to rise to a peak in the Forties—refining and transcending the big band mush in the moment of its vast popularity.

To pick Ellington, or for that matter any other single talent, from the wealth of jazz originals—Jelly Roll Morton, Armstrong, Beiderbecke, Hines, Parker, Thelonious Monk—not to mention their offshoots and disciples, is to invite one of those tedious quarrels that have nagged at jazz criticism ever since M. Hughes Panassié with his cloak swept into New York in 1938 and proclaimed a descending order of jazz royalty at odds with the accepted hierarchy of Charles Edward Smith, Otis Ferguson, and one or two other pioneer American jazz critics. A preference for Ellington over scores of remarkable talents is simply like picking Bach over the lesser composers and no doubt greatly gifted instrumentalists of his day. There probably would have been another Bix or Hines or Parker by another name, single great talents developing out of what had gone before. There were far better songwriters than Ellington, and he was the first to admit that his piano playing, considered as a solo turn if not as an inspirational cue to his instrumentalists, was modest at best. But no one else, in the eighty- or ninety-year history of jazz, created so personal an orchestral sound and so continuously expanded the jazz idiom.

Before elaborating on the uniqueness of this achievement, a thumbnail biography is in order. He was born Edward Kennedy Ellington in Washington, D.C., in 1899, the son of a White House butler. For want of deeper psychological probing, we must believe that this privileged status insulated him from the common lot of his race and kept him noticeably aloof from the strains of its coming turmoil. Or, since he had a presence of unassailable dignity, you could say that he was a natural aristocrat, with the aristocrat's social ease, lacking utterly the self-awareness of the whiskey ad's "man of distinction" or the thundering poise of the international jet set.

Like many another son of a devout black family—like Hines, like Waller—he was given piano lessons in the hope that he would graduate to the local church organ. But Ellington took as eagerly to sketching and plotted a career as an artist. This dilemma was solved for a time by doing sign painting by day and running a small band by night. After a short, rough period of treading water on the ocean of a pseudo-symphonic jazz orchestra in New York, he returned disheartened to Washington but was enticed back to Manhattan by Fats Waller. Pretty soon, egged on by Ada "Bricktop" Smith, he landed his first big job, at the old Hollywood nightclub on Broadway, with a band that soon added Bubber Miley, Joe Nanton, and Harry Carney to his original Washington sidemen: Otto Hardwick, Arthur Whetsol, and Sonny Greer. They became and remained—some of them for twenty, thirty more years—the nucleus of his incomparable band. In 1932 a young English jazz critic, James Wiltshire, marveled that while such as Morton and his Red Hot Peppers, the Five Pennies, McKinney's Cotton Pickers, had come and gone, "the Duke goes on forever." Forever meant for five unflagging years. Only after Ellington's death, at seventy-five, could we appreciate the astounding fact that this unique and always developing music had lasted with few lapses for forty-seven years!

The very first recordings, in the late Twenties ("East St. Louis Toodle-Oo," "When a Black Man's Blue," "Rockin' in Rhythm"), introduced to jazz a harmonic texture that owed a little to Morton and more to Don Redman, the first consequential arranger-composer, but was already so weird and original as to leave no agreeable impression on the dance-band public outside Harlem. Indeed, for most of Ellington's life, and except as he managed an occasional popular hit ("Mood Indigo" was the first), his music was always a minority cult. Certainly, to the generations that looked on Fred Waring and Leo Reisman and, later, Tommy Dorsey and Glenn Miller as jazz bands, Ellington's most characteristic music would have been as unpleasant as early Stravinsky to the couples who danced to Strauss waltzes.

The essence of this music is that of an orchestral composer of themes of growing complexity, from the simplest blues chords and early Dixieland, through the swing era, on into bop and the antiphonies and plotted discords of the moderns, and at the end into his sacred music of the late Sixties. At the very end, in his last recorded solo, he managed a historic irony by playing a blues—"The Blues Is Waitin' "—of a piercing and beautiful simplicity. He moved with all the influences of his time and transmuted them, both in the moment of adapting them and in the act of performance, so that they could not, and cannot, be reproduced by other orchestras from even the most scrupulously annotated score. Ellington did not write for trombone, trumpet, clarinet, and alto sax. He wrote for Lawrence Brown's trombone or for Nanton's; for Cootie Williams's trumpet (the superb "Concerto for Cootie"); for Johnny Hodges's sensuous, scooped pitch; for Bigard's melting clarinet ("Clarinet Lament"). The true business of composing began in the studio, with pages of scribbled themes and tentative bridge passages, which were then tried out on different fusions of instruments, an obbligato transferred from this man to that, the Duke halting, shouting, talking all the time. An hour or two later, what had started as a taste in Ellington's head came out as a rich, harmonious meal.

Somebody said of Sir Thomas Beecham that when he conducted Mozart, the whole orchestra was hypnotized into becoming exclusively Mozart players. The Ellington men were equally melded into nothing but the Ellington sound. In a sentence, the experience of sitting in with him at rehearsal was not to follow the polishing of a finished score but to be present at the Creation.

EDWARD KENNEDY ELLINGTON *was born on April 29, 1899, in Washington, D.C. His father, James Edward, was a blueprint maker and, on occasion, a butler at the White House during the McKinley and Theodore Roosevelt presidencies.*

Young Edward was a mama's boy; by his own admission he was "spoiled rotten" by all the women in his family. His mother, Daisy, used to follow him to school from a discreet distance. He spied her nonetheless.

He loved baseball. But after he was hit on the head with a bat, Daisy decided that piano lessons would be safer.

He called his piano teacher Mrs. Clinkscales. He was her poorest pupil. At her annual recital, he was the only student to forget his part.

By the age of twelve he had read all of Sherlock Holmes.

It was a social-climbing childhood acquaintance named Edgar McEntree who gave him the nickname Duke—because he thought Edward needed a title to be his friend.

When it was discovered that Ellington had a talent for drawing and painting, his music lessons dwindled. Still he continued to play the piano at parties—only because, he said, "I learned that when you were playing piano there was always a pretty girl standing down at the bass clef."

He first began to take piano seriously while hanging around Washington's foremost poolroom. His first professional job was playing for a traveling magician.

At one point, while providing Music-for-All-Occasions, he operated a sign-painting business. He recalled that "when customers came for posters to advertise a dance, I would ask them what they were doing about their music. When they wanted to hire a band, I would ask them who's painting their signs."

His first band was much more successful in Washington than in New York, where Ellington struggled for recognition. Once, in one night, he wrote a show called Chocolate Kiddies *for five hundred dollars. The promoter pawned his wife's engagement ring to come up with Ellington's fee, then took the show to Berlin, where it played for two years. The promoter returned a millionaire.*

Daisy Ellington died in 1935, and her son said he never fully recovered. Later, when asked why he favored the color blue, he said that his mother had always dressed him in blue on Sundays.

He didn't like green. It reminded him of grass. He thought grass unnatural; it reminded him of graves. He also warned people about "fresh air poisoning." He said it once took him weeks to recover from a bout of fresh air in Virginia Beach.

He bought a new suit every week. Sometimes he wore eight in one day.

During World War II Ellington played cupid when, in relinquishing a taxi to a soldier on furlough, he asked, "Won't you and your wife take this taxi? I always think servicemen come first." The soldier and the woman beside him didn't know each other, but they took the taxi, became acquainted, and were married before the furlough was over.

He was a ladies' man and dropped remarks like, "You make that dress look so beautiful" and "Does your contract stipulate that you must be this pretty?" According to his son, Mercer, Ellington "never seemed to be interested in the perfect woman. If she had a scar, or was slightly misproportioned—big-busted, big-hipped, or a little off-balance—than he was more interested."

In 1950, while working in Stockholm, he refused to sign an antibomb petition. Later he learned that the Communist Daily Worker *claimed he had signed. He was incensed and wrote in* The New Leader, *"I never sign petitions, not even petitions circulated by bona fide Negro organizations. I've never been interested in politics. The only 'communism' I know of is that of Jesus Christ."*

In 1951 the NAACP, as part of a general boycott in Richmond, Virginia, boy-

cotted one of his concerts. Ellington was upset; the NAACP made it up to him by giving him three awards.

He ate oddly. He liked to eat his dessert first: pie, whipped cream, a little syrup, and a few maraschino cherries. He said it made a meal set better.

In 1965 the Pulitzer Prize music jury, while recommending that no prize be given for music that year, unanimously recommended that Ellington be given a special citation. When the Pulitzer committee rejected the recommendation Ellington said, "Fate is being kind to me. Fate doesn't want me to be famous too young." He was then sixty-six years old.

He died nine years later, of cancer, in New York City.

Ike
and the
Generals

JAMES SALTER

HE POSSESSED, LIKE HIS BOSS, AN INVINCIBLE SMILE. THE ERA HAD TWO OF THEM. Roosevelt's was the hail of a champion. Ike's, they say, was worth twenty divisions.

Generals never smile. That was only one of the rules he broke. MacArthur didn't smile. Bradley either, it wasn't his nature—besides, his teeth were false. Ike smiled all the way, and his smile was instant and true. Even de Gaulle, a man not easily taken in, was impressed by him and sensed both generosity and warmth.

He never really commanded like Napoleon or Grant. "He let his generals in the field fight the war for him," MacArthur commented disdainfully, while "he drank tea with kings and queens." In an even more acidic mood, he described him as the "best clerk I ever had."

We see the grand MacArthur striding through the surf onto the shore of the Philippines, fulfilling his pledge, trouser legs soaked, weathered hat on his head, the legendary figure who fought back from stunning defeat across a battlefield that was an ocean so vast that men's perceptions could barely cross it and who even after victory did not return home but chose to remain in Tokyo as proconsul and govern the shattered Japanese. He did it magnificently and with remarkable discernment, knowing it would be the capstone of a great career. While poor Eisenhower, whose dream of the future was merely a quiet

486

cottage, had to oversee the demobilization, accepted the presidency of Columbia, for which he was ill-suited, recovered his poise to some extent in command of NATO, and finally lifting his head to the shouts was swept to the presidency by an adoring public. Thus the farm boy and the last of the aristocrats.

He was born in obscurity in northern Texas, one of seven children, all boys, in a family that always had to struggle and soon moved back to Kansas. From his mother Eisenhower inherited his chin, high forehead, and steady gaze. She was a hardworking, honest, no-nonsense woman, a pacifist who eventually became a Jehovah's Witness. "He that conquereth his own soul is greater than he who taketh a city," she told her son.

It was 1890, bread cost three cents a loaf. The plains were still crude and raw, the railroad the sole connection with the rest of the world. He was born into a home where the Bible was read daily, into a town that still lived by the frontier ethic, and into a world where man's temporal role could be summed up in one word: *work*. As a boy he grew vegetables behind the house and sold them. He worked in the Belle Springs Creamery, where his father was also employed, after school. Together with his brother he tried to earn enough money so that one of them could go to college, the other to follow afterward. Years later he was asked by someone if he was really a conservative. "Any of you fellows ever grow up working on a farm?" he asked.

At the urging of a friend, he took the exam for Annapolis and for West Point too while he was at it. It turned out he was too old for the naval academy, but the first man for West Point failed the physical and Eisenhower got the appointment. He arrived in June 1911. He had come mainly for a free education. Here he is, making his first, brief appearance as a running back for Army: sandy hair, five feet eleven inches, stocky, called Ike by his classmates. As a measure of his indistinguishability, there were four other "Ikes" in the class. There were also nicknames like Nigger, Jew, Dago, and Chink. It was the class of 1915, the class they later said "the stars fell on." In what could pass for a gentleman's world, a backwater world as was the army it fed into, they rode horses, studied geology, engineering, natural philosophy, and hygiene, and pitched tents for the summer at the far end of the Plain. It was a closed world that held a certain comradeship and mystery.

He did not seem destined for greatness. Academically he was only average. He was not one of the cadet pantheon; neither was Bradley. He was well enough liked, confident, breezy. He preferred poker to dancing, and his classmates noted that he was fond of shooting the bull.

Caught up in the rising swell of the First World War, he was given training assignments and rose to become a lieutenant colonel on his twenty-eighth birthday, but the war ended and he had suffered the classic grief of young officers—he had not seen action. The Army quickly shrank. Everyone was demoted. He reverted to the rank of captain and together with Mamie vanished down the dusty roads that led to routine and remote posts—Leavenworth, Camp Meade, Fort Benning—while Jimmy Walker, Lindbergh, and Babe Ruth strode the stage. Lingering behind him, like a faint epitaph, was the opinion of one of his instructors at West Point who, like the others, had found him unremarkable: "We saw in Eisenhower a not uncommon type, a man who would thoroughly enjoy his army life. . ." But not much besides.

The most important group in the United States Army of the Twenties and Thirties was Pershing's men, the officers who had found his favor either before or during the war. George Marshall, who had been in his headquarters in France, was one. Douglas MacArthur, though he had performed brilliantly as a troop commander, a dashing and gallant figure right out of *Journey's End* rising to become the youngest brigadier general in the army, was not. He was too vivid, too pushy, too iconoclastic. He and Marshall never liked each other. They had much in common—both were aloof, puritanical, driven. Marshall, however, had hardly a single watt of military glory. It was the "loftiness and beauty of his character" that stood out, as Dean Acheson noted. MacArthur was not without character, but the thing that shone so unmistakably from him was ambition.

Another of Pershing's favorites was George Patton, who had gone to France as the old man's aide and wangled his way into the front lines, commanding the first tanks near the end of the war. Eisenhower met him in 1919 at Camp Meade. Patton was a temporary colonel, tall, glamorous, every inch a soldier. He was rich and so was his wife—he would always be known as the wealthiest man in the Army. He owned a yacht, played polo, and taught ladies' riding classes. He was five years older than Eisenhower, with a high, squeaky voice and a foul mouth with which he loved to shock social gatherings, but he also had shrewdness and an intense love of his profession. It was at Patton's house one night that Eisenhower met and made an impression on a general named Conner, who a few months later invited him to come to Panama as his executive officer. He was the first of the two important sponsors Eisenhower was to have during his career.

Fox Conner was a Mississippian with the common touch who'd been Pershing's operations officer in France and had a reputation in the Army as a brain. He was always quoted as saying that if we ever had another war he hoped to God we wouldn't have allies. In Panama he took Eisenhower under his wing, encouraging him to read and discussing with him strategy, commanders, and the fate of nations.

"Someplace along the line there Ike got serious—there isn't any question about that," one of his classmates remembered. It's uncertain exactly when or how this happened. It may have been due in part to the settling effect of marriage or to the death of his young son from scarlet fever a year before Panama. The change may have been something that was coming all along. What we do know is that when Conner arranged for him to get into Command and General Staff, the most important of the Army schools, Eisenhower went, determined to do well. Those admitted were already an elect, and graduation high in the class was said to mark a man for future advancement. At the end of the year Eisenhower was number one.

George Marshall always kept a file of officers who impressed him and it's probable that Eisenhower's name first came to his attention at this time.

Known for years mainly as a coach of post football teams, Eisenhower was now viewed differently. The Army didn't exactly stand on its head for him, but in a few years he found himself in Washington working for the assistant secretary of war and then for the chief of staff, a man of dizzying ego, phenomenal memory, and comprehensive knowledge who liked to refer to himself in the third person—in short, MacArthur. They had adjoining offices with only a slatted door between them. When MacArthur accepted the post of military adviser to the Philippines, he took Eisenhower with him for what MacArthur said would be a year or so.

They arrived in Manila in September 1935. Already balding, wearing a white suit and straw hat as did MacArthur, Ike is in many ways fully formed—the man who, unknown to himself, will command the war. He stands dutiful and frowning in the tropical sun as his renowned chief poses. He was twenty years into his profession now and still a major. Years later a woman asked him if he knew the celebrated MacArthur. Yes, he knew him, Eisenhower said, he'd studied dramatics under him for seven years.

In the Philippines they worked to create a defense force. There was little money or equipment, and as the hundreds of ordinary days drifted behind there began to appear, drawing closer and closer, the storm they all knew was coming. Everybody felt it. One evening on an antiquated radio Eisenhower heard Neville Chamberlain declaring war. The first flicker of lightning. In far-off Europe catastrophe had arrived.

Eisenhower went to MacArthur and requested to return to the States, feeling he would be needed more there. He left at the end of 1939 and began a series of assignments as what he had always been, a staff officer, first at regimental, then division and corps level. He bumped into Marshall at some maneuvers soon after getting back. Duty in the Far East, everyone knew, was duty with houseboys, servants, amahs. Even privates got spoiled. With the barest of smiles Marshall inquired, "Well, Eisenhower, have you learned to tie your shoes again?" It was only the second time they had met.

In the fall of 1941 in huge maneuvers held in Louisiana, Eisenhower stood out as chief of staff of the victorious Third Army. He got his promotion to brigadier general just as the dust of the maneuvers was settling. It was late September. Two months later, all negotiations at an impasse, a powerful Japanese strike force left port and slipped into the fog of the Northern Pacific under sealed orders that when opened read "Pearl Harbor."

It is easy to see in retrospect the confusion and fears, the long ordeal the end of which no one could foresee, the great wave that swept over the nation and half the world, the greatest event of the century: the Second World War.

Summoned abruptly from San Antonio to Washington a few days after the bombing of Pearl Harbor to fill a need in plans for someone who knew the Far East, Eisenhower went directly from the train station to Marshall's office. He was to face an immediate test. For twenty minutes Marshall outlined the grave situation in the Pacific with its nearly insoluble equations. Then he looked at Eisenhower and said only, "What should be our general line of action?"

Eisenhower had just arrived, he was unfamiliar with the latest plans, he had no staff. He hesitated for a moment and then said, "Give me a few hours."

Sitting in an empty office, he thought at some length and then, with one finger, began to type out his recommendations. He went back to Marshall. The Philippines, with their weak forces, would probably fall, Eisenhower said. Nevertheless, everything possible should be done to help them hold out. This was important. All the peoples of Asia would be watching the coming battle there— they would accept defeat but not abandonment. Meanwhile, Australia was the key—it had to be built up as a base of operations and the long line of communications to it kept open at any cost. "In this last we dare not fail."

When he had finished, Marshall said just four words: "I agree with you."

Now began desperate days, during which they tried to find men, aircraft, equipment, and, above all, ships to carry them to distant garrisons. The news was worse and worse—naval disasters, staggering Japanese triumphs. The days were eighteen hours long and Eisenhower came home exhausted to his brother Milton's house in Falls Church for a sandwich at midnight. In three relentless months, however, he had Marshall's confidence and was wearing a second star.

Allied strategy was, Europe first—the defeat of Germany before anything else. The Americans favored a direct, cross-Channel invasion of the Continent to which the British agreed in principle but with deeply ingrained reservations. For a nation that had known Gallipoli and would soon know Dieppe, the idea of a seaborne assault against a strongly defended mainland was not something to be viewed with enthusiasm. Ike had been responsible for drawing up plans for the invasion force to be built up in Britain and he offered Marshall a profile of the sort of officer who should be sent to command it, someone who was flexible, whom Marshall trusted completely, and who might further serve as Marshall's deputy when the former was named to lead the invasion (which was expected). A month later, an officer "then almost unknown," as Churchill called him, arrived in England and was welcomed at Chequers for the first time by the prime minister, who was wearing a siren suit and carpet slippers. That officer was Eisenhower.

They were to become very close, and it was always Ike's good fortune to have a supporter on one side as staunch as on the other. For his own part, he had come with the determination to get along with the British. You could call a British officer a bastard, the word was, but you could not call him a British bastard. He became a champion of Allied cooperation. It was not merely a question of the British agreeing to call lorries trucks and the Americans in exchange to call gasoline petrol, it was the task of hammering out an acceptable common strategy and bending difficult and proud commanders to fight side by side. The war was not waged in a spirit of pure harmony. Generals have ambitions. Nations have their goals.

Eisenhower was a major general when he came to England, almost a lowly rank. He was nearly fifty-two years old, he had never commanded troops, never seen a battle. In a matter of a few months, the invasion put aside for the time being, he found himself, quickly promoted, in a damp tunnel in Gibraltar waiting uneasily while fourteen convoys from both sides of the Atlantic, all bearing forces under his command, converged for simultaneous landings at Casablanca, Oran, and Algiers.

The invasion of North Africa had been hastily decided upon and planned, with Eisenhower as the logical commander since it was to appear as an American initiative. Actual military command, however, was in the hands of three experienced deputies, all British, for land, sea, and air.

There were problems with the colonial Vichy French, battles with the French fleet, and the usual early disgraces that go with poor officers and green troops. Americans dropped their weapons, abandoned equipment, and fled at Kasserine Pass. Eisenhower had neither the tactical nor strategic experience required, the chief of the British Imperial Staff, Alan Brooke, decided. He was putty in British hands, said Patton, who was also making his first appearance in the war; "I would rather be commanded by an Arab," Patton wrote in his diary. "I think less than nothing of Arabs." A depressed Eisenhower kept repeating, "Anybody who wants the job of Allied commander in chief can have it." Nevertheless, he took full responsibility for the confusion and first defeats, and by spring, the supply situation better, the bad weather past, his reorganized forces had battled through Tunisia to meet Montgomery coming the other way. In the sudden, final collapse in May 1943, almost 250,000 Germans and Italians, many of them driving their own trucks in search of POW compounds, were taken prisoner. These were veterans, and with them went the Mediterranean.

Sicily was next, a less than brilliant campaign. The plan of invasion was uninspired—the Germans never could comprehend why the Strait of Messina had not been immediately seized to cut them off. The fighting was in the heat of summer, fierce and bloody. Patton, now an army commander, revealed some of his dash here and also his impulsiveness. Bradley, more temperate, would rise above him. Neither of them liked Montgomery: "pompous, abrasive, demanding, and almost insufferably vain," Bradley described him.

The campaign in Italy was more of the same—bad strategy, landings in the wrong places, lost opportunities. As Mediterranean Theater commander, Eisenhower was far from the center of things. Italy was a mere sideshow compared to the immense scale of the Russian front, where literally hundreds of divisions were engaged, and in the course of a battle the opposing armies might lose a division a day. Though assured there would be a second front in the spring, Stalin shrewdly demanded to know who its commander would be. That he would be American was understood, since the bulk of the forces were to be American. That it would probably be Marshall was also understood. But at the last moment Roosevelt decided otherwise. The principal figures had been in their roles too long to change. A deeply disappointed Marshall had the grace to send Eisenhower as a memento the handwritten note that named him supreme commander.

Generals who do not fail, succeed. From the middle of the pack, past Clark, who was left mired in Italy, past Bradley, who had gotten a star first but was late getting to Europe, past the brash Patton, through all of it, gathering strength, experience, the feel of battles, learning to predominate in conference, perfecting the structure, prodding, cajoling, slowly becoming unchallengeable, Ike made his way.

When he arrived back in London to take charge of the enormous planning, D-day was set for May 1, 1944, a mere three and a half months away.

The Germans knew it was coming. There were fifty-eight German divisions in France, all that could be taken from the east for what Hitler had told his generals would be the decisive battle of the war. If the Allies were defeated, they would never invade again, he pledged—the losses and the blow to morale would be devastating. The Germans could then transfer their entire strength to the grinding eastern front "to revolutionize the situation there." The waters off the French coast were dense with steel piles, stakes armed with mines, iron barriers. There were over four million land mines laid along the beaches, wire, concrete gun emplacements. At Dieppe, at Tarawa, these defenses had proved murderous.

To England convoy after convoy had brought the heaviest of all things: armies, with their vehicles, tanks, mountains of munitions, guns. D-day had finally been set for the fifth of June. On that morning tides, moon, everything would be right. But not, as it turned out, the weather. At the last moment the initial eight-division assault had to be postponed, and the following day, with only an uncertain pause in the winds and storm and the immense force leaning forward, as it were, Ike turned it over in his mind, pondered on destiny, and said at last, "Okay, we'll go."

He stood at an airfield in the darkness saluting each paratroop plane as it took off. In his pocket was a folded message on which he had scribbled a brief statement to be used in the event of disaster: the landings had failed and the troops, having done all that bravery and devotion could do, had been withdrawn. "If there is any blame or fault attached to the attempt, it is mine alone." These were the words, as historian John Keegan says, of a great soldier and a great man.

In France, dogs were barking in the windy darkness. Beneath the low clouds and the usual steady sound of aircraft crossing, the Germans were asleep, expecting a quiet night, when, at about two in the morning, into the country behind the beaches twenty-four thousand armed men came floating down. It was the airborne overture. The ships came at dawn, appearing out of the mist in numbers so great they could not be counted.

On the American beaches alone there were eight thousand casualties. Utah was not too bad, but Omaha was a bloodbath. The outcome was in doubt there for half the day. By that night, however, 150,000 Allied troops had gotten ashore. "Their road will be long and hard," Roosevelt broadcast to the nation that night, leading it in prayer. "Give us faith in Thee, faith in our sons, faith in each other. . . ."

The campaign that began that day lasted for eleven months and became the greatest Allied victory of the war. Eisenhower held big cards and he played them correctly. His armies and his generals by that time were battle-hardened, but there was also considerable finesse. He deceived the Germans by keeping Patton, whom they feared, in England for a long time in command of a phantom army. When the battle of Normandy was over, Rommel was writing to his wife, "We're finished . . ."—even if the German High Command did not admit it, even though the life and death struggle went on. The Allies had more matériel, better intelligence, and, above all, command of the air, but the Germans were incomparable soldiers and for them there was no way out. Generals committed suicide and men by the tens of thousands died along the road.

That December saw the last great German offensive of the war. Massed in absolute secrecy, under the cover of bad weather, three German armies fell on the four weak divisions that were stretched out to cover eighty-five miles of front in the Ardennes. It was an attack that Hitler personally had conceived and von Runstedt commanded. Almost simultaneously the first V-2s began to fall on England.

It was just before Christmas. Ike had only that day received his fifth star and was celebrating by drinking champagne and playing bridge when the word came of what would become the Battle of the Bulge. At first neither he nor Bradley could believe what was happening, but soon the scope of the breakthrough became apparent. "Calamity," Alan Brooke admitted, "acted on Eisenhower like a restorative and brought out all the greatness in his character." There were black headlines in the newspapers and grave meetings, but Ike had come of age. He committed his strategic reserves to hold the critical area around Bastogne at all costs, which they did. At the end of a week the weather broke and fighter-bombers swarmed over the front. From this time on, Bradley noted, Montgomery or not, Ike ran the war.

On May 7, 1945, with Eisenhower refusing to see the German emissaries who had come to sign the surrender as he had refused to meet captured generals throughout the war, the road at last came to an end. The thrust into Europe, the crusade, as he called it, was over. There had been 586,628 American casualties during the campaign.

Perhaps he was not a great general. He was not a heroic one. He cannot be imagined crying to his troops, "Forty centuries look down upon you!" or "God for Harry! England and Saint George!" He was a new invention, the military manager, and the Army was made over in his image. Those who think of him only as President, an old crock with a putter, fail to see the man as he really was. He was tough, resilient, wise. In a sense, the war used him up. For years he gave it every hour, every thought, every breath. It discovered him, and he is entombed in it, together with our greatest victory. The rest is epilogue.

He died on March 28, 1969, twenty-four years after the surrender. He was in Walter Reed Hospital, an invalid, ruined by heart attacks. His last words were, "I want to go. God take me."

DWIGHT DAVID EISENHOWER was born on October 14, 1890, in Denison, Texas. His parents belonged to the Protestant River Brethren sect. Their name came from the German for iron-hewer—*one who forges shields and swords.*

Growing up on a three-acre farm in Abilene, Kansas, he preferred reading to agriculture. His mother locked his history books in a closet, but Ike opened the closet with a piece of wire. He especially enjoyed reading about Hannibal; he memorized the Carthaginian general's battle moves.

Out of the 165 cadets in the West Point class of 1915, he ranked 61st academically and 125th in conduct.

He played left halfback on West Point's football team and once wrenched his knee tackling Jim Thorpe.

At twenty-five he married Mamie Doud, the vivacious daughter of a Denver meatpacker. Mamie said she was fed up with "lounge lizards with patent leather hair." At the wedding reception, Eisenhower refused to sit down for fear he'd ruin the crease in his pants.

One month after the wedding, Eisenhower embraced his wife and said, "Mamie, there's one thing you must understand. My country comes first and always will. You come second." Nevertheless, Ike assisted his bride in housekeeping, about which she knew little. He did the cooking and cleaning and, to stretch his Army pay, hemmed Mamie's dresses.

During the war he acquired a black scotty, Telek. "I want someone to talk to," Eisenhower said of the pooch, "and I want someone who can't ask questions about war and can't repeat what I say if I say anything."

Separation for over two years from Mamie provoked some acrid correspondence. "Please try to see me in something besides a despicable light," Ike wrote; ". . . you don't really think of me as such a black-hearted creature as your language implies."

Before the D-day invasion he haggled for seven hours with Winston Churchill over battle strategy. After Eisenhower's invasion plans were adopted, Churchill wrote, "Historians will consider and describe it as a great military movement, but I must tell you, my dear general, it was the fourth-best possibility."

"One thing I like about you," General Douglas MacArthur said to Eisenhower, "[is that] you have a short fuse—a magnificent temper."

Eisenhower wrote to General George C. Marshall, asking to be relieved of duty so he could divorce Mamie and marry Kay Summersby, the young Irish woman who served as his staff driver. Marshall sent a fuming reply promising, if Eisenhower went ahead with his plans, to "bust" him out of the Army and make his life miserable. Harry Truman destroyed the Marshall-Eisenhower correspondence, lest it prove embarrassing in Eisenhower's bid for the presidency.

At the 1945 Potsdam conference, Truman said to Ike, "There is nothing that you may want that I won't try to help you get. That definitely includes the presidency in 1948."

"The trouble with Eisenhower," Truman also said, "is he's just a coward. He hasn't got any backbone at all."

"I can think of nothing more boring, for the American people," Eisenhower said, "than to have to sit in their living rooms for a whole half an hour looking at my face on their television screens."

Walter Lippmann appraised Eisenhower's popularity, saying: "But for the Twenty-second Amendment [restricting the President to two terms] Ike could be reelected even if dead. All you need do would be to prop him up in the rear seat of an open car and parade down Broadway."

At the White House, he and Mamie slept in a king-size, pink-ruffled bed. He tolerated the pink bed even though he had once moved out of a London hotel suite because the bedroom was "whorehouse pink."

He had a two-hole, chip-and-putt golf course laid out on the White House lawn. When squirrels disturbed his golfing concentration, he had them box-trapped and removed.

When he was president of Columbia University he introduced Russian language courses to the curriculum—in spite of criticism that he was thereby being soft on communism.

He loved fried-egg sandwiches, bridge, poker, trout fishing, Oriental rugs, flying, Mark Twain, playing golf with Bob Hope, getting up early. His favorite dessert was prune whip.

He was once described as "the average American raised to the nth power."

He died on March 28, 1969, at Walter Reed Hospital, following his seventh heart attack.

Hepburn
in Autumn

TRUMAN CAPOTE

At one time I lived within a three-block radius of three interesting la-dies—or artists, if you will. I admired them all: Katharine Hepburn, Tallulah Bankhead, and Dorothy Parker.

Katharine Hepburn still lives in her elegant (but not too elegant—God for-bid!) town house a few blocks away. My first encounter with her was when I was about fourteen years old. We were seated in the same theater row; her companion was the deep-voiced English actress Constance Collier; we were watching Helen Hayes in *Twelfth Night*—her usual case-of-the-cutes per-formance.

Suddenly I had to take a leak, which required my passing Hepburn's seat. She hissed: "Damn you! Don't you step on my foot!" I was so startled—I glanced down and saw she had a foot costumed in bandages. And I *did* trounce it. Why? Well, there are occasions when one accidentally does what one is warned not to. "Damn you! I told you not to . . ." But by this time I had es-caped to the lobby and out into the street, stunned that my favorite young ac-tress should turn out to be such a rowdy, but grateful to be free of Helen Hayes's schoolgirl-caliber meanderings.

Years passed. I became a writer, and one day I interviewed Constance Col-lier. Shortly after, I was walking along the street in Turtle Bay where Hepburn lives. I think she would scream if she knew how familiar I am with that private dwelling, the furniture and objects. But once she lent it to an Englishman who was directing a play of mine and so I visited there often. It was tasteful but tiresome. All chintz and expensive Americana, with a shielded, secretive little garden on the ground floor.

Now on this particular day when I was strolling through Turtle Bay the streets were yellow and crimson with late-autumn leaves. A tall, trousered, angular, skinny, but rather tomboyish, butch-looking lady was raking the leaves off her sidewalk: Hepburn. Another lady, handsome, elderly, amply clothed, squatted on the stoop: Collier. They looked like wholesome country women accomplishing rural work somewhere in Connecticut. Hepburn's cheeks had the glow of October apples; her rolled-up sleeves exposed freckled arms; her straying hair was the color of the reddish leaves scattering the sidewalk.

Miss Collier, recognizing me, introduced me to the redheaded raker.

Without glancing at me, she said: "Is this the brat from *The New Yorker?*" A reference to my place of employment.

Miss Collier said: "Kate! Really!"

I said: "Miss Hepburn! Really!" And danced off laughing and scuttling the pavement leaves.

KATHARINE HEPBURN *was born on November 8, 1909, in Hartford, Connecticut. Her father was a leading urologist and her mother was a suffragette and an early advocate of birth control.*

The second of six children, she recalled that her father "had no patience for self-pity. When any of us would start mooning about, bidding for attention with 'I'm not feeling very well,' he'd say, 'Take an aspirin, go to your room, and lie down. Don't inflict the way you feel on the rest of us.' Naturally our recoveries were miraculous."

As a child she called herself Jimmy, idolized cowboy star William S. Hart, shaved her head during the summer, and put on plays to raise money for the Navajos (who in turn bought themselves a phonograph).

In 1928, within months after graduating from Bryn Mawr, she toured in Death Takes a Holiday. *She recalled that before long, however, the producers "said they'd give me the privilege of resigning from the cast and I said, 'Well, I'm not taking that privilege so if you want to fire me, go ahead, but get out of here because you'll be lucky if I don't kill you.' "*

In 1933, having gained stardom with her first film, A Bill of Divorcement, *she returned to Broadway in* The Lake. *Her miserable performance provoked Dorothy Parker to observe that Hepburn "ran the gamut of emotions from A to B."*

Despite her success in Bringing up Baby *and* Holiday, *a leading exhibitor*

497

labeled her "box office poison," prompting Hepburn to stomp out of Hollywood. She was rejected for the part of Scarlett O'Hara in Gone with the Wind. (David O. Selznick explained, "I just can't imagine Clark Gable chasing you ten years.") Finally she agreed to play the lead on Broadway in The Philadelphia Story. Having bought the play's movie rights, she returned to Hollywood, sold the rights to MGM for a handsome profit, and starred in the film version, which broke Radio City attendance records.

She was the first woman to win three Oscars as best actress (for Morning Glory, Guess Who's Coming to Dinner, and The Lion in Winter). She won another for On Golden Pond in 1982. She has won eight other Oscar nominations (for Alice Adams, The Philadelphia Story, Woman of the Year, The African Queen, Summertime, The Rainmaker, Suddenly Last Summer, and Long Day's Journey into Night).

From 1928 to 1934 she was married to Ludlow Ogden Smith, a socialite Philadelphia stockbroker. Convinced that "marriage is not a natural institution," she never remarried. Howard Hughes followed her around the country and taught her to fly. But eventually she ended their romance, explaining to a friend that Hughes bored her. "Sometimes I wonder if men and women really suit each other," she once remarked. "Perhaps they should live next door and just visit now and then."

She made nine films with Spencer Tracy, and for twenty-seven years the two maintained a romance that was an open secret. In 1965 she alternated with Louise Tracy, the actor's wife since 1928, in keeping vigil at his bedside.

She stands around five feet six inches and weighs about 110 pounds. She never wears makeup; but she did have cosmetic surgery performed on her eyelids, because, she said, they "were looking like a possum's." "My family thought I was nice looking," she once commented, "but I never thought so. Freckled people are funny looking, I think. They're rather sweet. They're like a sort of spotted dog. They're sort of pathetic."

She takes several cold showers a day. "I try to look clean. I think that's the best that can be said of me: that Kate Hepburn looked clean."

She never eats in restaurants. ("Can't bear to pay the prices. Can't bear to see anybody be dumb enough to pay the prices.") A big eater, she likes Viennese chocolate, red meat and vegetables, and the second joint of a chicken leg.

She thanks her parents for an "all right brain," but confesses, "I don't think I've used my intelligence as much as I could have. I think I could have amounted to something. . . . I'd much rather have been a painter or a writer."

She says she will never retire and will never write any memoirs.

"I put on pants fifty years ago," she said at seventy-two. "I have not lived as a woman. I have lived as a man. I've just done what I damn well wanted to and I've made enough money to support myself and I ain't afraid of being alone."

The Three Kings:
Hemingway, Faulkner,
and Fitzgerald

RICHARD FORD

SOME BOYS, ALAS, DO NOT COME TO SERIOUS READING, NOR GOD KNOWS TO SERIOUS writing, precisely like hounds to round steak. Though, then again, special boys sometimes do.

I remember a few years ago reading in *Exile's Return*, Malcolm Cowley's wonderful book on the Twenties, the teenage correspondence between Cowley and Kenneth Burke. It is pretentious, chin-pulling stuff sent from Burke's parents' apartment in Weehawken to Cowley's house in Pittsburgh, dwelling chiefly on whatever were the palmy literary aspirations just then dawning on those two little booksniffs. It was 1915. Cowley was just leaving for Harvard, having already, he boasted, banged through Kipling, Congreve, and Conrad, plus a dozen other of the greats. Burke—poet and teacher to be—was contemplating his first grand tour of France, rhapsodizing about how much he loved the moon and all those things that didn't fit him out for literature, while advertising himself as "somewhat of an authority on unpresentable French novels" and the lesser Chopin—altogether things that they must both blush at now. But still, I thought: What smart boys they were! And what remarkable letters! They had already read more, I realized, digested it better, gotten it down for quicker recall, and were putting it to fancier uses at seventeen than all I'd read, understood, remembered, or could hope to make use of to that very moment. Or maybe ever. And my hat was, and continues to be, off to them.

Until I entered college at Michigan State, where I'd come from Mississippi in 1962 to learn to be a hotel manager, my own reading had been chiefly of the casual drugstore and cereal box type. Whatever came easy. And what *I* was doing when I wasn't reading Congreve or Kipling or Faulkner, Hemingway, or Fitzgerald at an early and seasoning age was whirling crazy around Mississippi in a horrible flat-black '57 Ford Fairlane my grandparents had bought me; fecklessly swiping hubcaps and occasionally cars, going bird hunting on posted land with my buddy-pals, snarfling schoolgirls, sneaking into drive-ins, drinking, fighting, and generally entertaining myself fatherlessly in the standard American ways—ways Cowley and Burke never write about that I've seen, and so probably knew little about firsthand.

Though, in truth, my "preparation" strikes me as the more usual American one, starting off from that broad middle ground between knowing nothing and knowing a little *about* something. Conceivably it is the very plane Faulkner and Fitzgerald and Hemingway themselves started out from at my age, or a couple of years younger—not particularly proud of their ignorance, but not sufficiently daunted by it to keep them (and me) from barging off toward appealing and unfamiliar terrains. They were novelists, after all, not experts in literature. And what they wrote about was people living ordinary lives for which history had not quite readied them. And it is, I think, a large part of why we like them so much when we read them. They were like us. And what they wrote about reminded us of ourselves and sanctioned our lives.

Reading was, in truth, my very problem in Mississippi. While I always read faster and with more "comprehension" than my school grade was supposed to (I used to pride myself, in the tenth grade, that I could read as well as any Ole Miss freshman), I was still slow, slow. Slow as Christmas. And I am still slow, though more practiced now. I have thought that had I been evaluated by today's standards, I'd have been deemed a special student and held back. Whereas in Mississippi, 1960, I was decidedly college prep.

I have also realized, since then, that I may well and only have changed from hotel management to the study of literature in college not so much because I loved literature—what did I know?—but because it was a discipline for the slow (i.e., careful). And I'll admit as well that at Michigan State knowing about Faulkner, Hemingway, and Fitzgerald, which I began to do that first year, was a novelty to set one comfortably and creditably apart from one's fraternity brothers from Menomonie and Ishpeming, who by that time were already sunk greedy-deep into packaging engineering, retailing theory, and hotel management—all those necessary arts and sciences for which Michigan State has become justly famous.

I remember very distinctly the first time I read anything by F. Scott Fitzgerald. I read the story "Absolution," in my first English literature class at MSU. It was 1962. And I remember it distinctly because it was the first story assigned for class, and because I didn't understand anything that happened in it.

"Absolution" was written by Fitzgerald in 1924, when he was twenty-seven, hardly older than I was when I read it. In it, a fantasizing little Minnesota schoolboy lies in Holy Confession, then gets mistakenly forced to take Communion with an impure soul. Later, and in a state of baleful terror, the boy—Rudolph Miller—confesses what he's done to the same priest, who absolves him peevishly, only then promptly and in Rudolph's presence suffers his own spiritual crack-up, giving up his senses to a giddy rhapsody about glimmering merry-go-rounds and shining, dazzling strangers—all, we suppose, because he'd done nothing more venturesome than be a priest all his life. Little Rudolph sits by horrified. But in his wretchedness he has figured out already that private acts of pride and comfort matter more than public ones of abstraction and pretense. And while the priest writhes on the floor, howling like a lunatic, Rudolph slips away, having acknowledged something mysterious and consequential that will last him all his life.

End of story.

It is one of Fitzgerald's very best; youthful innocence brought into the alembic of a tawdry, usurping experience. A genuine rite of passage. Real drama.

I did not understand it because even though my mother had been a convent girl in Ft. Smith, still occasionally sat in on masses, and, I believe, wished all her life and secretly that she could be a Catholic instead of a married-over Presbyterian, I did not know what absolution meant.

That is, I did not know what the word meant, and indeed what all the trouble was about. A considerable impediment.

Nor was I about to look it up. I was not big on looking things up then. It could've been that I had heard of F. Scott Fitzgerald before. Though I don't know why I would have. He was not from Mississippi. But you could argue that Americans up to a certain age, and at that particular time, were simply born knowing who F. Scott Fitzgerald was. Ernest Hemingway and William Faulkner, too. It's possible they were just in the American air. And once we breathed that air, we knew something.

It is also true that if I knew *about* F. Scott Fitzgerald—likewise Hemingway and Faulkner—before I knew them hands-on, through direct purchase of their published work, say for instance, as I had read hungrily through some Mississippi dowager's private stacks, opened to the bookless boy who craved to read and to learn (the way it happens in French biographies, though not in mine), it is because by that time, 1961–62, all three were already fully apotheosized; brought up to a plane of importance important Americans always seem to end up on: as celebrities, estranged from the rare accomplishments that first earned them notice.

What I didn't know, though, was what absolution meant, nor anything much of what that story was about. If I had, it might've changed my life, might've signaled me how to get along better with my own devious prides and festerings. But I was just too neck-up then in my own rites of passage to acknowledge anybody else's. And while I may even have known what that expression meant, I couldn't fathom the one Fitzgerald was writing about.

So my first experience with him gave me this: Puzzlement. Backed up by a vague, free-floating self-loathing, I was, after all, not very studious then, and I balanced that habit with a vast ignorance I was not aware of. I was pledging Sigma Chi at the same time.

I know I knew who William Faulkner was by at least 1961. He *was* from Mississippi. Though I had not read a word he'd written about it. When I got to Michigan State, though, he immediately became part of the important territory I was staking out for myself. He, and Ross Barnett, and a kind of complex, swinish liberalness I affected to keep black guys from stomping on me on general principle.

I *had* laid eyes on William Faulkner. At the Alumni House at Ole Miss in the fall of 1961. Or at least I remember thinking I had. And in any case I certainly told people at Michigan State I had—tightening my grip on things rightly mine. But I know I had never read anything of his, or even of Eudora Welty's— who lived only a few blocks from me and whom I used to see buying her lunch at the steam table at the Jitney Jungle grocery, where our families shopped, but never bothered to inquire about, though her niece, Elizabeth, was in my class.

I had, by the time I left high school, strangely enough, read Geoffrey Chaucer. He was unavoidable in senior English. I could (and still can) recite from memory the first fourteen lines of the Prologue to *The Canterbury Tales*, in Middle English, without giving one thought to what any of it signifies.

I had also "written" a term paper on Thomas Wolfe by then, though I hadn't read a word he'd written either. I had been given Andrew Turnbull's biography of Wolfe and had boosted most of my text straight from there, verbatim and unconsidered. I got a B.

I do remember, somewhere in this period, noticing that a friend of mine, Frank Newell, had a copy of *The Wild Palms*. It was on his bookshelf at home, in the old green-tinted and lurid Random House dust jacket with the pastel wild palms on it. I thought that Frank Newell's family were literary people because of that. And I thought *The Wild Palms* was probably a novel about Florida. In a year I would read my first Faulkner, in the same English class in college: "A Rose for Emily." And I liked it immensely. But I was surprised to know Faulkner wrote some scary stories. Somehow I had expected something different from a man who'd won the Nobel Prize.

As for Hemingway, I remember that best of all. I knew who he was by at least 1960, when I was sixteen, because my mother liked him. That is, she liked *him*.

I, of course, had not read a word, and I can't be absolutely certain my mother had, though she was a reader. Books like *The Egg and I* and *Lydia Bailey* went around our house in Mississippi, and we both had put in a lot of time in the Jackson Public Library, where it was either cool or warm at the right times of the year and where I would browse in comfort through the *National Geographics*.

What she liked about Hemingway was, I think, the way he looked. His picture had been in *Life* or *Look* in the Fifties, looking about like the Karsh photo that's still sometimes seen in magazines. A rough yet sensitive guy. A straight-talking man of letters in a fisherman's sweater. The right look.

She also liked something he'd said in public about dying, about how dying wasn't so bad but living with death till it indignified you was poison, and how he would take his own life when that happened to him, which I guess he did. That my mother liked, too. She kept the quotation on a three-by-five card, written in her own hand, stuck inside the phone book, where I would occasionally see it and feel craven embarrassment. She admired resolution and certainty about first principles. And so, I suppose, did I, though not with enough interest to hunt up a novel of Hemingway's and see what else there was to it. This was about the time my father died of a heart attack, at home, in my arms and in her presence. And we—she and I—became susceptible to certain kinds of rigor as stanches against grief and varieties of bad luck. For a while during this period she kept company with a big, burly-bluff guy named Matt, who was married and drove a powerful car and carried a .45 caliber pistol strapped to the steering column (I liked him very much) and who growled when he talked and who might've seemed like Hemingway to someone who knew absolutely nothing about him, but who had a notion.

In any case, though, my mother, who was born in northwest Arkansas, in a dirt-floor cabin near the Oklahoma line and the Osage Strip, and who has now died, was, importantly, the first person I knew of who was truly Hemingwayesque. And that included Ernest Hemingway himself.

These, then, were the first writers' names to be chalked, if obscurely, onto my remarkably clean slate, a fact vouched true to me by my ability to remember when I knew of them and by my dead reckoning that before that time I knew of no writers at all—except Geoffrey Chaucer and a part of Andrew Turnbull that I stole. I arrived at 1962, the year I would first read William Faulkner, Scott Fitzgerald, and Ernest Hemingway, remarkably ignorant for a boy of eighteen; as unlettered, in fact, as a porch monkey, and without much more sense than that idle creature of what literature was good for, or to what uses it might be put in my life. Not at all a writer. And not one bit the seasoned, reasonable, apprentice bookman customary to someone who before long would want to be a novelist.

For these three kings, then, a kingdom was vacant.

And so I read them, badly. At least at first.

It was in the dog days of the New Criticism that I read *The Sun Also Rises*, *Absalom, Absalom!*, and *The Great Gatsby*. We were being instructed to detect literature's most intrinsic worth by holding its texts aloof from life and history, and explicating and analyzing its parts to pieces. Close reading, this was known as. And my professors—one, a bemused, ex-second-string football player from Oregon; and the other, a gentle, strange-suited, bespectacled man with the picturesque, Hemingway name of Sam Baskett—put us through our formalist/objectivist paces like dreary drill sergeants. Point of view. Dramatic structure. Image. Theme. Hemingway and Faulkner were still alive at that time, and Fitzgerald managed somehow to retain his contemporariness. And there was, among us students, a fine, low-grade brio that here we were reading new work. Probably my teachers admired these men's writing. Generationally they were much more under the thumb of their influence than I could ever be, and possibly they had wanted to be writers themselves once. (One told me that people who wanted to be writers should take jobs as fire watchers and live alone in towers.) But they still chose to teach literature to satisfy a weary system, and in any case it was in these dry classroom anatomies that I first learned exactly what meaning meant.

Symbols, I remember, were very much on my teachers' minds then, and so on mine. I was not yet *reading like a writer.* Indeed, I was just learning to read like a reader—still slowly—so that I never really got onto the symbol business as straight as I might've. But we Jessie Westoned the daylights out of poor Hemingway and Fitzgerald; unearthed wastelands, identified penises, fish, and fisher kings all over everywhere. From my sad underlinings and margin notes of that time, I can see that Dr. T. J. Eckleburg, the brooding, signboard optometrist, was very important to my reading of *The Great Gatsby.* He meant God, fate, decadence, evil and impotence, and was overlord of the wasteland—all qualities and identities I could not make fit together, since they seemed like different things, and since my sense of meaning dictated that assignments only be made one to one.

Jake Barnes's mystery war wound likewise supplied me no end of industry. For a time everyone in that book was wounded, or at least alienated very badly. Many things are marked "Ironic." Many things are marked "Imp." And everywhere I could I underlined *rod, bull, bandillera, worm,* and noted "Symb."

Of course, I paid no special attention to the lovely, lyrical celebration of comradeship among Jake and Bill and the Englishman, Harris, there on the Irati—a passage I now think of as the most sweetly moving and meaningful in the novel. Nor to the passage in *Gatsby* where Nick tries to say how Gatsby must've felt at the sad end of things, when he had "paid a high price for living too long with a single dream." I suppose I was just too young for all that, too busy making things harder, getting my ducks set in a straight row.

This, as I've said, was around the time I read "Absolution," and was completely puzzled by it. I was not, however, puzzled by Faulkner, whose gravity and general profusion so daunted the Michiganders I sat beside in class, since he resisted our New Critical shakedown like a demon. There was really just too much of everything in *Absalom, Absalom!* Life, in words, geysering and eddying over each other, so that just being sure what was what and who was who became challenge enough to make you beg off choosing among what things might formally *mean*—a valuable enough lesson, certainly for anyone who wants to learn about anything, ever.

Faulkner dazzled me, of course, as his writing inevitably will. But being from where he was from, I was already acquainted with the way the white man's peculiar experience in that particular locale over time begot the need to tell; to rehearse, explain, twist, revise, and alibi life clear out of its own weirdness and paradox and eventually into a kind of fulgent, cumulative, and acceptable sense. Begot, in fact, so much larruping and fabricating that language somehow became paramount for its own sake (a fresh idea to me) and in turn begot its own irony, its own humors, and genealogy and provenance.

That, I came to understand, was meaning, too.

For me, reading Faulkner was like coming upon a great iridescent glacier that I had dreamed about. I may have been daunted by the largeness and gravity and variety of what he told. But he never puzzled me so as to make me feel ignorant, as I had been before I read him, or when I read "Absolution." To the contrary. When I read *Absalom! Absalom!* those years ago, everything came *in* to me. I got something. Somehow the literal sense of all I did and didn't understand, lay in the caress of those words—all of it, absolutely commensurate with life—suddenly seemed a pleasure, not a task. And I loved it.

Before, I don't believe I'd known what made literature necessary; neither what quality of life required that it be represented, nor what quality in literature made such abstractings a good idea. In other words, the singular value of written words, and their benefit to lived life, had not been impressed on me. That is, until I read *Absalom! Absalom!*, which, among other things, sets out to testify by act to the efficacy of telling, and to recommend language for its powers of consolation against whatever's ailing you.

I point this out now because if anything I read influenced me to take a try at being a writer—even on a midget scale—it was this pleasure I got from reading Faulkner. I wrote my first story about this time, a moody, inconclusive, not especially Faulkner-like domestic minidrama called "Saturday," which I liked. And putting those events together makes me understand now how much the wish to trade in language as a writer traces to a pleasure gotten from its use as a reader.

Not that it has to be that way. For some writers I'm sure ideas come first. For others, pictures. For others, probably symbols and Vico. But for me it was telling, in words. I don't think I ever read the same way after that but began to read, in my own way, like a writer. Not to satisfy a system, but to take whatever pleasure there was from language, no matter what I understood or could parse. And that, I am satisfied now, is the way one should always read. At least to start.

In the spring of 1964, my wife and I—barely not children and certainly not yet married—drove in an old Chrysler north from East Lansing up into the lake counties where most of Hemingway's Michigan stories are set—Charlevoix, Emmet, Mackinac. The two of us hiked around sunny days through East Jordan and Petoskey, picnicked on beaches where the rich Chicagoans used to come summers, boated on Walloon Lake, staying in a little matchstick motel across the straits in St. Ignace just to say we'd been there and seen the bridge that wasn't there when Hemingway wrote about the country.

Though I was there to get a closer, more personal lowdown on those stories; stories I had been reading that spring, had loved on instinct, felt intensely, but that had also sparked my first honest act of literary criticism: namely, that I felt they never *ever* quite said enough. They forbore too much, skimped on language, made too much of silences. As if things were said only for the gods, and the gods didn't tolerate that much. And I was there, I suppose, curious and nervous about silences, to tune in on things with some experience of my own. It seems romantic now. And it probably *was* silly. But it was my way of taking things seriously and to heart. My way of reading.

What I didn't understand, of course, and certainly didn't learn marching around those woods fifty years too late, was that these were a young man's stories. And their severe economies—I think of "Indian Camp," because it was my special favorite—were the economies and silences of a still limited experience, an intelligence that wasn't finished yet, though certainly also a talent masterful at mining feeling with words, or at least at the nervy business of stripping words in such a pattern as to strand the feelings nicely inside the limits of the story.

It was a young man's aesthetic, and ideal for impressing another young man.

But I wanted badly to know why that Indian had killed himself! And I did not understand why Nick's father wouldn't just come out, while they were heading home in the boat, and say it. Tell us. Telling was what writing did, I thought. And I wasn't savvy enough myself *not* to be told. Faulkner would've told it. He'd have had Judge Benbow or Rosa Coldfield spill it out. Fitzgerald would've had somebody try to explain later on, in another city in the Middle West.

Hemingway, though, was after something he thought was purer. Later, I read in *Death in the Afternoon* that he aimed for the "sequence of motion and fact which made the emotion." Whereas, if you said a thing—explained it—you could lose it, which is what Jake Barnes says. And indeed what you lost was the feeling of the thing, the feeling of awe, terror, loss. Think of "Hills Like White Elephants," a story I admire and that students love because it seems so modern. No one says abortion in it. Yet the feeling of abortion—loss, puzzlement, abstraction—informs every slender, stylized gesture and line, and the story has a wonderful effect.

But the embryo writer in me, even then, wanted more. More language spent. More told so that I could know more of what went on there and feel it in the plush of the words. A man had died. And I wanted the risk the other way, risking the "blur" Hemingway so distrusted—an effect caused by a writer who has not seen something "clearly," yet who still needs to get at a truth by telling it. The world, for me, even back in 1964, seemed too various, too full, and literature too resourceful to draw such rigid lines about life just to preserve a feeling.

To me, Hemingway kept secrets rather than discovered them. He held the overcomplex world too much at arm's length either because he wouldn't on principle or couldn't say more. And for that reason I distrusted him. He valued accuracy and precision over truth, and for that reason, despite his effects, he seemed a specialist in what he himself called "minor passions." Even today, when I am always surprised at how much broader a writer he is than I remember, he still seems like a high school team captain with codes, a man who peaked too early and never went on to greater, harder feats.

Not, of course, that I didn't take with me something valuable from Hemingway, namely a deference for genuine mystery. I may now know what absolution means and why the Indian kills himself—too many doctors, too much pain and indignity. I may know beyond much doubt what was Jake Barnes's wound. But I also learned that for anyone, at any time, some things that matter can't be told, either because they're too important or too hard to bring to words, and these things can be the subject of stories. I think I learned that first and best reading Hemingway, learned the manners and protocols and codes a story observes when it comes round something it thinks is a consequential mystery. I may still prefer that mystery, once broached, be an inducement, not a restraint, to language, a signal to imagination to begin saying whatever can be said. But to have learned of that mystery at an early age is no small thing. And my debt for it is absolute.

From this highly reactive time, my memories of Fitzgerald are, at best, indistinct. I made my way through *The Great Gatsby*, exclusively settling matters of point of view and Dr. Eckleburg's significations. Then I simply left off, my memory retaining only the faraway beacon light on Daisy Buchanan's boat dock (it was "Imp."), and Gatsby floating dead in his swimming pool, a memory I soon confused with the beginning of the movie *Sunset Boulevard*, in which the corpse played by William Holden, not Nick Carraway, tells the story.

What I *was* attentive to, though, in my bird dog's way, were the subliterate runs and drumbeats of words, their physical and auditory manifestations, the extremes of utterance and cadence, what Sartre called the outside of language. It is undoubtedly one reason I liked Faulkner best, since he offers so much to the poorly educated but overly sensitized.

And my belief was that these etherish matters were matters of literary style. And like all novices, I became preoccupied with that.

What followed, then, was a partitioning up of literature into Faulkneresque and Hemingwayesque, leaving a kind of stylistic no-man's-land for all the other people. To me, Fitzgerald, by having the softest drumbeats, the fewest linguistic extremes and quirks, the rarest ethers, didn't really seem to have much of a style, or if he did he had a poor, thin one.

It seems feasible that one could think that putting Fitzgerald midway between the great putter-inner and the great taker-outer casts a kind of convenient cosmos map of the male soul and its choices. Though what I was doing twenty years ago, when I was almost twenty, was just confusing style with idiosyncrasy and making myself its champion.

Not that it was entirely my fault.

My ex-quarterback of a professor (we'd heard he'd played behind Terry Baker, and so had had plenty of time for reading) had assigned us all to write a paragraph in either "the style of Hemingway" or "the style of Faulkner"—a miserable, treacherous task to assign any student, but particularly to one who had begun to write. (Though I now understand it was designed chiefly to kill class time.)

But we all wrote. And when we read our paragraphs aloud, mine produced the profoundest response from my instructor. He stopped me three sentences in and complained to all that my Hemingway sounded like everybody else's Faulkner, and that I clearly was not much good for this kind of thing.

I was badly stung. I liked style, whatever it was. And I believed I could be its master. Only I saw I needed to study it harder—Hemingway and Faulkner in particular, and what was so odd about them that I couldn't imitate them separately.

Nobody, though, was asking me to write a paragraph in the style of Fitzgerald at this time. *Fitzgeraldian* was not a word. And so for this reason he fell even more completely below my notice.

It is notable to me that somewhere in this period someone placed in my hands, for reasons I do not remember, a copy of Arthur Mizener's gossipy, pseudo-scholarly biography of Fitzgerald, *The Far Side of Paradise*, the edition with the Van Vechten photo on the front, a smiling, wide-faced Fitzgerald practically unrecognizable from the Princetonian–Arrow shirt profile on the Scribner's books.

Reading Mizener was a big mistake for me. His biographer's interest was the archly antinew critical one of mutually corroborating art and life. And since Fitzgerald, at least for a time, had lived a very, very *rich* life, there set on for me a long period in which I could not distinguish accurately all he'd done from all that he'd written: the profligacy, the madness, the high style and helling around, ruinous wives, prep schools, the Plaza, Princeton, New York, Paris, Minnesota, Hollywood. I read the other novels, the stories and notebooks. And though I didn't exactly forget them, they just fell to his life. *He* seemed smart and too clever and poignant and overweening. But the books almost always faded back into Fitzgerald myth, into imputation, half-fact, lie, remembrance, and confession—annals where even now for me they have their truest resonance.

Today, I still believe it's as much his failure as mine that I remember as much about him as I do, but can sort out so little of his work. And that his life— vulnerable, exemplary, short writer's life—save for a brilliant novel and a few excellent short pieces, makes a better story. It is tempting to think that, like Dick Diver and Amory Blaine and Anthony Patch, he represents some promising but spoilable part of our American self-conception. And since that is not exactly tragic, it is maybe more appealing and exemplary to us as biography than illusion.

Recently I read *The Great Gatsby* again, for possibly the fourth time (I know people who brag they read it every year). Fitzgerald wrote it before he was thirty, and as I get older it only gets better. I believe it is one of the maturest, more sophisticated and seamless books I have read, and I don't fault myself for not getting it back in 1964, since it has, I think, more to teach an older man than a young one.

And I have found its style: its elegant economies and proportionings, the sleek trajectory of its complex little story, the strategy of withholding Gatsby until his place is set, Fitzgerald's certain eye for the visual detail and, once observed, for that detail's suitability as host for his wonderful, clear judgment about Americans and American life—a judgment, Wilson said, "saturated with twentieth-century America."

The essence of Fitzgerald's style finally was that he itched to say something smart on the page, and made his novels accommodate that. It is why as a young man he was always better in shorter, manageable forms, and why a savvy young man might've learned plenty from him without ever having to mimic. And it is why I had such a hard time at first, my own ear then being chiefly to the ground.

Faulkner, of course, was the best of all three, and the very best of any American writing fiction in this century. It is not even discredit to Hemingway and Fitzgerald to say so. Liking Faulkner or not liking him is akin to liking or not liking the climate in some great territorial expanse. It seems like tautology. Whereas Hemingway and Fitzgerald, I sense, come to our affections more like the weather does, passingly.

No writer, including Henry James, minted more robust characters freshly and indelibly into our American literary memory. All those Snopeses, Temple Drake, Thomas Sutpen, Benjy Compson, Dilsey. A bear. No writer has exceeded his own natural regionalism (that dark American literary peril), or survived the codification of his style, or confessed apparently less of his personal life as grandly as Faulkner has. No one braves as much in a sentence. No one is as consistently or boisterously funny as Faulkner while remaining serious and dramatic. And, of course, no American writer this century has been so influential—impressive is the best word—both in the restraining effects of his work on other writers, and in the most generous ways as well: his work always urges all of us if not to be more hopeful, at least to be more various, to include more, see more, say more that is hopeful and surprising and humorous and that is true.

I loved Faulkner when I read him first. He stumped the symbolizers, the mythologizers, the taxonomists, the *pov* guys dead in the brackets in East Lansing. He would not reduce so as to mean more. And that I liked.

Though it seemed to me, then, as it did ten years later when I was writing a novel set in Mississippi—my home too—that that was because he'd appropriated everything there was. It was even possible to want to write like Faulkner without knowing you did; to want to put down some sense of a life there without realizing it existed first in his sentences. Until the end of the Fifties —1963—I am convinced, a large part of *everybody's* idea of the South came from William Faulkner, whether they'd read him or not. He was in the American air, as I said before. And that went for the air southerners breathed too, since we could see how right he'd gotten it, and since, of course, he was ours.

How can I measure what it was worth to read Hemingway, Fitzgerald, and Faulkner back then in the Sixties? Influence on a writer is a hard business to assess, and I'm not sure I would tell the truth if I could, since real influence means being affected by the weather in another writer's sentences, sometimes so much that you can't even imagine writing except in that weather. And no one who's any good ever wants to write like anyone else.

One truth is that my generation of writers—born mostly in the Forties—has not lived "the same life, the generic one" that Lowell speaks about in his elegy for his friend John Berryman. We have not all prized or even read the same books. We have not all had or aspired to teaching jobs. We do not all know one another. Lowell, of course, was probably wrong about his generation, since, from what I can tell of his thinking, it included only about fifteen people. But of my own, I am sure we are too many, too spread out and differently inclined ever to have been influenced similarly by another generation's writers.

Another truth is that I don't remember a lot of those books anymore. And I never read them all to start with. A fellow I met recently, who had spent time in a North Vietnamese prison, asked me if I thought Francis Macomber's wife shot him on purpose. And I had no idea. In my mind I had confused that story with *The Snows of Kilimanjaro,* and when I went back to figure out the answer, I was surprised. (Of course, Hemingway being Hemingway, I'm still not 100 percent sure what happened.)

Likewise, when I began to think on this essay, I chose a Faulkner novel just to graze over for atmosphere, one I thought I hadn't read—*Sanctuary*—but knew to be easy because of what Faulkner had written about it. Only now that I've finished it, I really can't be certain if I'd read it years ago or not. Odd. But there you are.

Still, as a little group, they seem to have traversed the Sixties and Seventies intact, despite the fact of a unique and intense war's being on then, and of immediate life's altering so rapidly and irrevocably. To me, they seem far away, their writing become *literature* finally. But that is only because I don't read them so much, and when I do it is usually to teach readers who were being born just when Hemingway and Faulkner were dying.

Though *their* pleasure seems certain.

I have always assigned classes to read "Babylon Revisited," Fitzgerald's bitter, touching story about Charlie Wales, the man who comes to Paris to reclaim his daughter, lost to him by the calamities of the Twenties, and the Crash, and by his own bad luck and improvidence. It is one of my favorite stories. And there is always a sentiment among students that it keeps its currency because of the Thirties' similarities—at least in my students' minds—to those years since the Sixties were over.

Faulkner still seems to excite the awe and affection he excited in me, though no one—correctly—wants to write like him. Only Hemingway, I detect, can occasionally exert a genuine and direct influence on young writers' "style." His old, dour, at-war-with-words correctness seems to ride the waves of austerity, ascending in tough, Republican times, and declining when life seems abler to support grand illusions.

As writers whose work taught me serviceable lessons about writing at a formative age, all three get high marks for mentorship—a role Hemingway cared much to fill, and that Faulkner, if we take to heart the sarcasm of his Nobel address, probably thought was ridiculous.

By 1968, when I had started graduate school in California, people were still talking about Faulkner, Hemingway, and Fitzgerald, though primarily just as Dutch uncles to our own newborn artistic credos. We were all tiny savages then, trying on big boys' clothes. Though it was still good to be able to quote a particular novel—*As I Lay Dying* was popular—or to own something specific one of them had reportedly said and be able to unsheathe it fast. *The Crack-Up* was highly prized as a *vade mecum*, along with the *Paris Review* interviews and *A Moveable Feast*.

Anyone who actually *wrote* like Faulkner or Hemingway was, of course, thought to be washed up from the start. But with their books, others' faults could be neatly exposed, crow and humble pie served to order. We were being read to by Richard Brautigan, taught by E. L. Doctorow, and imitating Donald Barthelme. But we were still interested in how those older men got along in the world where there were no grants or teaching jobs, and how they acted out their parts. One fellow in my class actually asked us all to call him Papa. And when I remember that, I need no better proof that they were in our lives, still behind us all, like Mount Rushmore in the Santa Ana Hills.

Speaking selectively, I know I learned from the economies of *The Great Gatsby* how to get on with things narrative; how to get people in and out of scenes and doors and sections of the country by seizing some showy detail and then going along to whatever was next.

From Hemingway I learned just how little narrative "instrusion" (we talked that way) was actually necessary to keep the action going, and I also learned to value the names of things, and to try to know how things worked as a way of dominating life and perfecting its illusion. There was, as well, the old workshop rapier that said Hemingway's famous dialogue, when actually spoken aloud, sounded like nothing more than an angry robot on Valium, and not like real talk. Yet locked within is the greater lesson that the page is officially different from the life, and that in creating life's illusion, the page need not exactly mimic—need not nearly mimic, really—and, moreover, that this very discrepancy is what sets art free.

From Faulkner I'm sure I learned that in "serious" fiction it is possible to be funny at the expense of nothing—a lesson also discernible in Shakespeare; that it is sometimes profitable to take risks with syntax and diction, and bring together words that ordinarily do not seem to belong together—the world being not completely foregone—and in this small way reinvent the language and cause pleasure. And finally, from Faulkner, that in representing life one needs to remember that many, many things do not stand to reason.

They were all three dead, of course, before I had written a word. Already kings. But still, I and my generation might have learned from them just what time in life our words could start to mean something to someone else—nervy business, when you think of it. They all wrote brilliant books in their twenties. We might also have learned that great literature can sometimes be written by amateurs who are either smart enough or sufficiently miscast to need to take their personal selves very seriously. In this way we might've learned some part of what talent is.

And last, we might've learned from them that the only real *place* for a writer in this country is at the top of the heap. That the only really satisfactory sanction available, the one our parents could appreciate as happily as the occupations they wanted for us—the law and banking—is success and the personal price for success is sometimes very high, and is almost always worth it.

What I remember of them, though, is something else again, different from what they taught me. Though by saying what I actually remember, or some of it, I may say best why for me and possibly for people like me, they are three kings.

I remember, for instance, what Nick Carraway said about all our personalities, and Gatsby's in particular: that they are only "an unbroken series of successful gestures."

I remember that Hemingway gave up his first good wife, and never forgave himself for it, and that Fitzgerald kept his until she helped ruin him. (On the eve of my marriage I remember asking my soon-to-be-wife to please read *The Beautiful and the Damned*, and to promise not to ruin me in that particular way.)

I remember Hemingway saying, "It is certainly valuable to a trained writer to crash in an airplane that burns."

I remember Darl Bundren in *As I Lay Dying*, describing his sister Dewey Dell's breasts as "mammalian ludicrosities which are the horizons and valleys of the earth."

I remember Horace Benbow saying to a man already doomed, "You're not being tried by common sense. . . . You're being tried by a jury."

I remember where I learned what a bota bag was and how it was used—important gear for a fraternity man.

I remember where I learned what it meant to have *repose*—*Tender Is the Night*—and that I didn't have it.

I remember that dead Indian very distinctly.

I remember what Fitzgerald said—sounding more like Hemingway than our version of Fitzgerald, but really speaking for all three writers—that "Life was something you dominated, if you were any good."

And last, I remember what Fitzgerald wrote in his notebook about Dick Diver: "He looked like me."

This is the important stuff of my memory: objects, snapshots, odd despairs, jokes, instructions, codes. Plain life charted through its middle grounds. Literature put to its best uses. The very thing I didn't know when I started.

These men were literalists, though they could be ironic. They were writers of reference. They were intuitors and observers of small things for larger purposes. They were not zealots, nor politicians. Not researchers nor experts nor experimenters. They seemed to come to us one to one. And though Faulkner could seem difficult, really he was not if you relented as I did.

Their work, in other words, seemed like *real* work, and we gave up disbelief without difficulty and said willingly, "This is our writing." They wrote to bring the news. And they were wondrous at that task. They wrote a serious, American literature that a boy who had read nothing could read to profit, and then read for the rest of his life.

"You've got to sell your heart," Fitzgerald said, and write "so that people can read it blind like braille." And in a sense, with their work they sold their hearts for us, and that inspires awe and fear and even pity. Reverence suitable for kings.

———

HEMINGWAY, FAULKNER, AND FITZGERALD *Ernest Miller Hemingway was born on July 21, 1899, in Oak Park, Illinois. William Cuthbert Faulkner (originally Falkner) was born on September 25, 1897, in New Albany, Mississippi. Francis Scott Key Fitzgerald was born on September 24, 1896, in St. Paul, Minnesota.*

Hemingway stood six feet tall, and though he usually weighed around 210, he once ballooned to 260. He had brown eyes, dimples in both cheeks, a slight speech impediment, and straight, dark hair that he once dyed bright copper, using his wife's hair color. He hated wearing ties, and his clothes, an editor recalled, resembled "items left over from a rummage sale."

Faulkner stood five feet five inches and weighed about 140 pounds. He had a soft voice, small hands and feet, dark brown eyes, and a beaked nose. He stained his dental bridgework—his "Sears-Roebuckers"—by constantly smoking a pipe. Meeting him in the 1930s, a Hollywood producer saw his tailored tweeds and gleaming oxfords and felt sure that he "traveled with a valet." (Faulkner at the time was dirt poor.)

Fitzgerald stood about five feet seven inches and weighed about 140 pounds. At Princeton he was so tender, so fresh and blond, that someone said he looked like a jonquil. Throughout his life he was partial to natty, collegiate clothes. But it was in women's attire that he made his biggest splash—dressing up as a chorus girl for a college play.

The son, grandson, and husband of alcoholics, Faulkner was himself an alcoholic. While working in Hollywood he hired a weekend male nurse to carry his bourbon in a black bag and to make sure he arrived at the studio on Monday morning.

Hemingway was a vat for gallons of wine, Scotch, rye, and rum. In 1956 his wife, Mary, lamented, "How can you stand by silently while someone you love is destroying himself?"

Fitzgerald passed out the first time he met and drank with Hemingway. Two martinis and some dinner wine could knock Fitzgerald out; but he could also down thirty-two bottles of beer in a day, and took Nembutal at bedtime and Benzedrine with breakfast. "I was drunk for many years," he wrote in his notebook, "and then I died."

Hemingway was married four times. "I know wimmins," he once said, "and wimmins is difficult." He considered his first divorce a "sin" that could never be absolved.

Faulkner's marriage was unhappy throughout—on the honeymoon his wife apparently tried to drown herself. But he never divorced. In Hollywood he did have an ardent affair with Howard Hawks's secretary, Meta Carpenter.

After Zelda Fitzgerald told her husband that he could never satisfy her because of a "matter of measurements," Hemingway assured his friend that the Fitzgerald penis was perfectly adequate. Hemingway insisted Zelda was jealous of her husband's work. Zelda called Hemingway a "phony he-man." She charged that Scott and Ernest were lovers, claiming to have heard Scott mutter in his sleep, after meeting Hemingway, "No more, baby."

In 1924 Fitzgerald read some of Hemingway's first work and wrote editor Max Perkins: "I'd look him up right away. He's the real thing." In 1951 Hemingway wrote to Malcolm Cowley: "As you know Scott was one of the worst writers who ever wrote prose. . . . Scott caught the surface and the people that he knew or met with a fine brightness . . . But . . . how could he ever know people except on the surface. . . ."

Fitzgerald admired Faulkner's work, and said that it "abundantly demonstrated" a "grotesquely pictorial country," the South. In 1936, after a bout of drinking, Hemingway told James T. Farrell that Faulkner was a better writer than either of them. In 1947, pressed to name America's best writers, Faulkner ranked Hemingway behind two others, because, he said, Hemingway lacked "the courage to get out on a limb . . . to risk bad taste, overwriting, dullness. . . ." Angry, Hemingway had a brigadier-general friend fire off a long letter to Faulkner attesting to Hemingway's gutsiness in World War II. Faulkner later apologized for his remark, and on several occasions complimented Hemingway in print. But Hemingway held a grudge; he declared that Faulkner, "a no-good son of a bitch," could keep his "Anomatopoeio County"—that any county was too small for Hemingway; that his world was the Gulf Stream.

Hemingway died in Ketchum, Idaho, on July 2, 1961, after shooting himself. Faulkner died in Oxford, Mississippi, on July 6, 1962, of coronary thrombosis. Fitzgerald died in Hollywood on December 21, 1940, of a heart attack.

EPILOGUES

The Nameless,
the Faceless,
the Millions

The Common Man

IRWIN SHAW

IN AN ADDRESS ON THE PRICE OF FREE-WORLD VICTORY DELIVERED BY HENRY AGARD Wallace on May 8, 1942, during World War II, the Vice-President coined a phrase—"The century on which we are entering can be and must be the century of the common man." The two words—*common man*—go back at least as far as the Greeks and probably earlier than that, but Mr. Wallace bravely enclosed them in a time frame, not unknown as a politician's signal to the electorate that in the orderly progress of his period in office he will improve the lot of the majority of his constituents, in this case Democrats, who had had a particularly unhappy passage between 1930 and 1941. Although many of us have good reason to believe that we all descend from a common single cell and a common tribe of apes and through the ages men have been deployed in common tasks and formations such as centurions, phalanxes, rifle platoons, and assembly lines, the phrase struck, at least for a moment for Americans, a meaningful chord. Outside the plush precincts of the rich and the privileged, who must have received the news impolitely, it probably meant to the workingman and the lowly soldier that once the war was over, power and prosperity would pass with serene and evenhanded justice to the man at the plow and the lathe, the stenographer at the desk, the brakeman on the railroad, the child graduating from elementary school.

• • •

My own attitude was one of cautious skepticism. Growing up in the Depression had fortified an inborn inclination toward pessimism. By the time Mr. Wallace made his speech I had already grown wary of large pronouncements on high, and since then I believe I have written about the so-called common man only once and that once with an ulterior motive and ironically subversive intent. It was in Cairo during the war and I was a private working on the Army newspaper *Stars and Stripes—Middle East* and spending a good deal of my waking hours in a small, cool bar run by a Russian named George who claimed to have invented the Bloody Mary. The bar was popular and crowded with troops of all nationalities—American, British, South African, New Zealand, Polish, and French, among others. Most of the good bars in Cairo were off limits to other ranks, as the British so deftly put it, but George's was a home away from home for those members of the lower class with a few piasters in their pockets and no bars or pips on their shoulders. Once in a while an officer or two would come in, have a quiet drink, and, to avoid contamination, get out as inconspicuously as possible. But the word about the bar must have gotten around among the brass, and one sad afternoon George had to put up the sign forbidding entrance to enlisted men.

With the smeary pages of *Stars and Stripes* open to me, I wrote an icy article reminding our readers of our Vice-President's brave words about this being the century of the common man, relating the pious abstraction to the blunt reality that kept privates, corporals, and sergeants away from their chosen watering-holes. The pen in this case, I am happy to say, proved mightier than the sword, and in two days the offending sign was removed and we were all lined up at the bar as before.

I took the whole affair as an omen that the British empire was sinking into the fathomless depths of history and that the Colonel Blimps would retire grumbling to their clubs, never to be heard from again, and that other ranks, a group to which I instinctively and forever belonged, would, from then on, in war and peace, drink wherever they damned well pleased.

Mr. Wallace was never my favorite politician, and by siphoning off Democratic votes to a benighted third party, he nearly presented us with Mr. Dewey as President of the United States, but I salute him belatedly for his speech in May 1942.

Fifty years ago the common man, if we continue to use the phrase, was selling apples for a nickel apiece on the street corners and lining up for soup kitchens. Fifty years later apples were too expensive to be sold charitably on street corners, but soup kitchens have again sprung up. A few glances through the history of the last fifty years may, with luck, immunize us against false hopes and desperate apples the next time we are exposed to lofty rhetoric about the century in which we live.

The word *common* is an explosive one, loaded with concealed megatons of meaning. A flick of the pages of the Oxford English Dictionary reveals that there are many uses of the word that are thoroughly unobjectionable: for example, "the common good" has a neighborly and reasonable sound; "commonwealth" is an optimistic and almost utopian synonym for a state; "common cause" might conceivably raise a tingle of patriotism in even the flintiest heart; a liberal dose of common sense has contributed largely to making America as great as we believe it to be today; a common tongue, aside from endowing our literature with its rampant anglophilia, reassures us that despite the differences in race and religion there is an almost mystic tie of words that binds us, even though the deadliest war in our history was fought between men who spoke the same language and with our growing Spanish-speaking population we are faced with the looming divisiveness of bilingualism.

These are surface matters—underneath there are minefields of abuse in the two syllables: "a common prostitute" is no one's idea of a compliment; nobody is happy to invite the common hangman to dinner. While for something to be prevalent is not necessarily a mark against it, unless it be an epidemic, to be marked as vulgar or ordinary can be the stimulus to violence. When a man says that a woman has rather a common look, he is not seeking a wife in that place, and when Byron described an acquaintance as being of the commonest clay, he was risking a duel.

For a writer of fiction the words are uneasy ones. It is his business, like God's, to distinguish one human being from every other human being in the world. If he is not so inclined, let him go to business school and become a statistician. In Europe, with its stratified classes through the centuries, there might be some sort of case for the statisticians: as recently as Hitler, the Germans allowed themselves to be treated as obedient sacrificial numbers, and in the Soviet Union the masses wheel as directed, although in both countries there were and have been the inevitable flare-ups of talent, ingenuity, and fortune, the unpredictable luck of the human race playing the odds and from time to time throwing sevens and elevens.

But in the wild and extravagantly open society of America, its rules set down by the educated and mostly liberal aristocrats of the Age of Reason, the flare-ups have become, if I may use the word in another sense, commonplace. Lincoln from his log cabin, Grant from his failing businesses in Missouri, Truman from his haberdashery, Eisenhower from Abilene somehow getting into West Point, Johnson from his dusty plains, Richard Nixon from his father's general store, Ronald Reagan from his college reporter's desk, to name only a few of our leaders, good or ill, have all come from what we might call the common stock, if not the common heritage.

Let us not, however, overpraise common men. In the 1930s, when *Esquire* was just born, it was the common man who did not listen to the President, who knew that Hitler was preparing for war and what had to be done to forestall it, only to be prevented by the common men of voting age from doing so. I can say this without arrogance, because I was with them in their denial. That we made it up later, paying the price in blood, is a cause for relief but not for self-congratulation.

• • •

It is not difficult to describe or at least recognize the uncommon man. This issue of *Esquire,* for one, is replete with examples. The common man, *Homo americanus,* however, is harder to classify. One is forced to resort to generalizations. Perhaps the closest we can get to a rule is that what is best for the greatest number is fair democratic policy and might be applicable here. If we accept this as true, or at least pragmatically useful, we might be inclined to say that the common man in 1983 is better off than his predecessor in 1933. For one thing, if we believe in the absolute value of life, as I do, he lives longer than he did then. Diseases that carried off populations fifty years ago have been conquered, starvation and unemployment are not considered to be the inevitable punishment of inherent sin and lack of ambition, and the state is committed to the alleviation, however grouchy, of economic and social misfortune. The forests of television masts all over our country testify to the fact that Americans are more richly entertained in one week than a royal favorite of the king at the court of Louis XIV in a given year. The news from all corners of the world is available in a manner that was inconceivable half a century ago, and the traffic jams on our highways prove that we are free by the tens of millions to move from place to place at a moment's whim. Working days are shorter and, theoretically, at least, are spent by the greater part of the labor force in more-agreeable surroundings, and the arrangement of our leisure hours has become a gigantic industry. Despite glaring inequities, no politician today could say that one third of our population is ill-housed and ill-fed, and with all their well-justified complaints our black citizens and our wives and sisters are politically more powerful and socially and economically freer than they were in the beginning of the Roosevelt era.

On the cultural front we find that there is a greater percentage of our young people, most of whose parents never went further than high school, who are now college graduates than in the good old days, although there is a persistent rumor that they neither read nor write as well as the Class of '33. Freedom of the press has now reached the point where even the commonest of men can stroll down to his corner drugstore and pick up a magazine or a book whose writers or publishers would have been locked up summarily in 1933 for moral offenses. No writer today has to invent a word like *fug,* as Norman Mailer did in 1948, and if this is not a victory for the common man, it at least is a tribute to his actual vocabulary.

The amassing of treasure by the government that makes it possible for us to send men to walk on the moon and photograph the rings of Saturn from up close is surely a sign that the taxpayer (soul brother and Doppelgänger of the common man) who foots the bill is in better shape than his counterpart was fifty years ago, and the sums spent on diet books and systems of exercise suggest that a great number of common men and women these days are eating well, if not as wisely as they might.

The gifts lavished by science on Americans, common and uncommon, rich and poor alike, are without precedent. Two hundred million of us can watch a football game at the same time. The silicon chip has abolished the need to be able to add, subtract, multiply, or, even in a great many cases, make any mental effort whatever. Where in 1933 it took five days by fastest ocean liner to get from New York to London, we now can make the voyage in less than four hours. An objection can be sensed here—we are discussing the common man and he is not likely to have over two thousand dollars in his pocket to pay the fare. But I have made the trip and can assure the reader that by even the narrowest of standards one can find passengers in the cabin of the Concorde who fully deserve the title.

Up to now we have looked at the bright side of the coin. It is time to see if there is a dark side. And of course there is.

First and foremost, the air we breathed in 1933 was not designed to poison us, and the food we ate, when we could afford it, was, as far as we knew, not radioactive or apt to cause mutation of our genes. Here and there, it is true, there were towns, usually ones set in valleys or at the confluence of rivers, where steel was manufactured or coal mined that had occasional atmospheric conditions that made it hard for old folk to breathe or dangerous for people with bronchial ailments to go out of doors. Today we are as surprised and joyous as children whose school has been unexpectedly shut down for the day when we look up and see a blue sky above the spires of our cities. No matter how gloomy the ordinary man's surroundings might have been, it was never necessary for the government to buy out a town because it was eternally tainted with chemical wastes and resettle the town's citizens elsewhere at the public expense.

While we knew that the war to end all wars, of 1914 to 1918, was not the end of the tournament, but rather a kind of quarterfinals, and we felt in our bones that the era of armed conflict was not over, in 1933 no one, aside from some weird scientists in obscure laboratories, believed that after the next unpleasantness nothing could be expected to be left alive on the planet.

It is time to try to arrive at some definitions. Who is the common man? Is he the jolly fellow in the beer advertisements storming with his comrades into a saloon after an honest day's physical labor? Is he the man who fixes your television set and overcharges you? Is he the bank clerk who after seeing you at his window once a week for five years suspiciously goes over to look up your account each time you try to cash a fifty-dollar check? Is he the man who collects your garbage or shingles your roof or tries to sell you a used car? Is he the ward heeler fawning at your door collecting votes or the smart young lawyer who can use the votes to his own advantage? Is he your freshman economics instructor fascinated by the works of Adam Smith or the air traffic controller put out of work by President Reagan? Is he the ex-grunt still brooding about the way his fellow citizens have treated him after Vietnam? Is he or she on welfare? If he is a she, does she recognize the fact that the term "common man" includes her, since the term "common person" is abusive? Is he or she out of work and if so, does that include the son of the President, who collected unemployment insurance during the weeks his ballet company did not perform? If a bank president is dropped from his job and becomes unemployed, does he then become a common man? A movie star? A ferocious pitcher in the big leagues whose arm has gone dead and is now trying to sell real estate? Is he the liberal plumber who advocates busing or his carpenter neighbor who pickets against it? Is he the citizen who votes or the citizen who says it makes no difference who's in there? Is he the weary commuter who watches three football games on Sunday or the equally weary commuter who enjoys listening to Stravinsky in his free time? Is he the gay schoolteacher or the impoverished minister? Is he the black who curses himself for not having completed high school or his brother who went to Harvard and has it made as the first vice-president of an advertising concern?

Is he Muhammad Ali, who was born a descendant of slaves and at whose birth there were probably very few signs that one day he would be a cult figure and pay millions of dollars yearly to the federal government in taxes? Did the parents of Herschel Walker know as he was being delivered that their new son's photograph would some twenty years later adorn the pages of newspapers all over the country because he decided not to finish his senior year in college or did they merely congratulate themselves on having a nice new healthy addition to their family and the human race? Did the parents of Jonas Salk hope merely that their newborn infant would turn out to be a normal, fairly contented man or were they secretly aware that their offspring was in the course of time going to make a discovery that would eradicate a crippling and fatal plague?

Is he a merchant seaman? Eugene O'Neill served in the fo'c'sle. Does he repair bicycles? Remember Henry Ford. Is he a football player? "Whizzer" White ran like a frightened antelope through the National Football League before becoming a justice of the Supreme Court of the United States. Does he work as a singing waiter in a Bowery saloon? Irving Berlin collected his tips nightly at just such a job. Is he a shoe salesman? Tennessee Williams earned his living bringing down size 9E's in St. Louis before striking out for Broadway. Does he sell insurance? Charles Ives, who wrote some of the greatest music of our time, worked at the trade. Was she an immigrant woman who taught elementary school classes in Milwaukee and then became the prime minister of a foreign state? Read the obituary notices of Golda Meir in *The Jerusalem Post*.

Does our definition of the common man include the true believer who campaigns against abortion as a sin that leads to eternal damnation and the newly liberated woman who announces that her body is hers to do with as she wishes and that it is her right to decide whether or not she will ever bear children? Do we claim as a common man the profane and shifty redneck from the bayous of Louisiana who might have toppled our government if he had lived? Consider Huey Long. What about the professional soldier? Think of James Jones sweating out his hitch in Hawaii before Pearl Harbor. Does our man work as a general practitioner in a New Jersey slum? William Carlos Williams carried his little black bag faithfully for more than forty years, writing the marvelous poems in his spare time. Was he a Jewish boy from Brooklyn who made a buck fighting bulls? Sidney Franklin was carried on the shoulders of aficionados from the great arenas of Spain. Was he a young hick who jumped from airplanes at country fairs for nickels and dimes? Charles Lindbergh did just that.

Was he a funny little fat man who grew up on Army posts where is father led the regimental band? Fiorello LaGuardia became the best mayor New York City ever had.

Common stock, ladies and gentlemen, common stock.

God, the saying goes, must love the poor—He made so many of them. Substitute *common man* for the word *poor* and the adage is as true or false as ever. But God—or Nature—avoids redundancy. No snowflake is geometrically the same as any other snowflake, no man's fingerprint matches any other's, no set of genes is assembled in the exact order of any other arrangement of genes. *Change, difference, chance, surprise* are the words by which we live. In the yeasty ferment of the American experiment definition is as untrustworthy as prediction. Fifty years from now will we, common men all, survive in our institutions, in our children and grandchildren, in any form that the man in 1933 or the man of 1983 would find as recognizable and familiar?

The jury, dear reader, is still out.

Other ranks, front and center. The bar is open.

The War Hero

THOMAS B. MORGAN

FOR MANY REASONS, INCLUDING AMERICA'S UTTER DEFEAT IN VIETNAM, A CRISIS OF belief in heroics of all kinds, and a certain failure of memory, the glorification of military heroes is at a low ebb today, especially among the young. It may even be lower than in the early Thirties. In *those* days, few hearts leaped as General Douglas MacArthur, who had won seven Silver Stars for bravery in World War I, and his troops were employed to break up a demonstration of job-less war veterans demanding their bonuses. Still, there had been no My Lai to disgrace, no final lift-off from the roof of our embassy in Saigon to humiliate. I don't think this disenchanted state is such a bad thing, considering the tend-ency of certain hawkish politicians to confuse a healthy respect for human courage and the military virtues with tolerance for the use of war as an instru-ment of some misbegotten diplomatic policy other than true self-defense. And remembering the way our mood changed from the Thirties to the post–Pearl Harbor Forties, I don't think it is going to last forever, either. But for now, among other things, it means that veterans of our recent dirty wars, and of World War II as well, are getting far less consideration than they deserve in rhetoric as well as rights. They answered when called. They risked greatly and sacrificed much. There were real heroes among them. Can it hurt the younger generation to be reminded of this, even to hear it from me, an ex-Army private of World War II who neither fired nor was fired upon in anger from January 11, 1945, the day at age eighteen I entered basic training, to the war's end?

Fortunately, as we have needed men to serve, we have found them in abundance—men willing to take unthinkable chances for their country's good intentions, surviving or not, as luck would have it, not with the recklessness of the elite nor the strange joy of the professional, but with the wry fatalism of civilians become soldiers. This contemporary model of the American war hero was created for us in World War I, perhaps most of all by the glorification of Sergeant Alvin York, a hillbilly pacifist who reluctantly joined the Army, won the Congressional Medal of Honor for prodigious feats in the trenches of France, and returned home to national acclaim. A generation later, Gary Cooper portrayed him in *Sergeant York,* a celebrated movie (twelve Academy Award nominations, a Best Actor award for the star) released shortly before the Japanese attack on Pearl Harbor. Cooper's York not only argued for the primacy of civic responsibility over private conviction, but also reinforced and reflected the glory of the American war hero as a common man for an audience of millions. He was a white European, of course, a product of democracy, jealous of his freedom, outside the regular Army and any military tradition other than that of "civilian control," slow to anger, mighty in wrath, valiant in the face of death, and modest in victory. He made soldiering an act of public virtue.

Once World War II was under way, the outcome of battles on land, sea, and air came to depend more and more on machines and war matériel than manpower. But the heroic model endured. On the one hand, a new style of war reporting emerged to fill our need on the home front to believe that every American serviceman was, in some way, necessary; the dispatches of Ernie Pyle and the Willie and Joe cartoons of Bill Mauldin simply said: Every man is some kind of hero. On the other hand, as the inability of most men to make a difference became more apparent, the glorification of those who could became more intense. Hero worship became the solace for the reality of automated war. It also became the screen behind which the true cost of war could be hidden as well as the full extent of man's pain, even if he was a hero. A case in point is that of Audie Leon Murphy, whom I met briefly in the Sixties, four years before he died. He was, I think, the quintessential war hero of our time, perhaps of future time as well.

In the almost forty-six years of his life, Murphy served barely three years on active duty in the United States Army. He spent most of that period during World War II in Europe with Company B, 15th Regiment, Third Division. When he returned to civilian life, he was still not old enough to vote. Yet he had been through a half dozen field promotions from private to first lieutenant and commander of his company and arguably had won more decorations than any other American soldier who fought in that war, or any single U.S. war—a record that still stands. The Defense Department's final tabulation of Murphy's decorations lists twenty-four, including the Congressional Medal of Honor and one or more awards of every medal for bravery that this nation bestows, a special citation for personally having killed 240 Germans in combat in Sicily, Italy, and France, and a number of foreign commendations. He might have won more. But in the spring of 1945, the Army excused Murphy from further combat in the hope of keeping him alive until his nomination for the Medal of Honor could be processed, affidavits collected, and the medal itself draped on his chest. Years later, Murphy acknowledged that he had been nineteen years old at the end of his combat career, not twenty as the Army records showed. At age seventeen, in 1942, he had lied about his age, enlisting one year before he should have been eligible for service. The U.S. Army thereby had gained a one-year advantage over the German Wehrmacht, and Murphy had a head start on his career as a war hero.

He seemed to have a genius for combat, unimaginable pluck and good fortune, and reflexes that read like barely repressed suicidal instincts, as in his citation for the Congressional Medal of Honor:

> Near Holtzwihr, France, 26 January 1945 . . . Second Lieutenant Murphy commanded Company B, which was attacked by six tanks and waves of infantry . . . ordered his men to withdraw . . . while he remained forward at his command post and continued to give fire directions to the artillery by telephone. Behind him, to his right, one of our tank destroyers received a direct hit and began to burn. Its crew withdrew. . . . With the enemy tanks abreast of his position, [he] climbed on the burning tank destroyer, which was in danger of blowing up at any moment, and employed its .50 caliber machine gun against the enemy. He was alone and exposed to German fire from three sides, but his deadly fire killed dozens of Germans and caused their infantry attack to waiver. . . . For an hour, the Germans tried every available weapon to eliminate [him], but he continued to hold his position and wiped out a squad which was trying to creep up unnoticed on his right flank. Germans reached as close as ten yards, only to be mowed down by his fire. He received a leg wound, but ignored it and continued the single-handed fight until his ammunition was exhausted. He then made his way to his company, refused medical attention, and organized the company in a counterattack which forced the Germans to withdraw. . . .

A friend of Murphy's named David McClure, who helped Murphy write his 1949 best-selling war memoir, *To Hell and Back,* and in the following years sought to clarify narratives of Murphy's exploits, has determined that Murphy was not wounded during his famous stand but was limping and bleeding from a wound received in action the day before for which he had refused medical attention—and was also considerably handicapped by the aftereffects of gangrene in an earlier hip wound, which would plague him for the rest of his life!

At the end of the fighting in Europe, the Army made national news out of Murphy's many decorations. The first accounting verified just fourteen medals, but one better than the thirteen won by runner-up Captain Maurice Britt, a former pro football player for the Detroit Lions. Britt was nominated for the Congressional Medal of Honor after a battle at Mount Rotondo in Italy and lost his arm three months later at Anzio even before his medal was confirmed. It was enough to make Murphy the best-known soldier of that time and create of him an inescapable public image. A twenty-five-year career in Hollywood as a movie actor, plus sidelines as a real estate promoter, horse breeder, volunteer crime fighter, and gambling man, would never seriously challenge it. No subsequent triumph or failure in Murphy's life came close to changing it. From then on the phrase "most decorated soldier of World War II" followed his name. It was as though some force of nature had decided that Murphy would always be prey to irony. We would idolize him for his war record, but let him keep the horror of his deeds and whatever the experience of those horrors might cost him, like Captain Britt's right arm, out of sight.

The tension between man and image would be a permanent fact of Murphy's life. When sour investments bankrupted him in 1968, it was news because he was the most decorated soldier of World War II. Otherwise, it was not news at all. Two years later, when he and a bartender friend allegedly beat up a dog trainer at the end of an absurd argument over pet care (they were tried and acquitted of assault with intent to murder), the bewildered and bewildering Murphy again aroused the media—he was still the most decorated soldier of World War II. And when, on a wet morning at the end of May 1971, the crack-up of a small chartered plane took his life and that of the pilot and four other passengers, the lead on *The New York Times*'s front-page story, of course, read, "Audie Murphy, the nation's most-decorated hero of World War II, and five other men were found dead today . . . near the summit of a craggy, heavily wooded mountain twelve miles northwest of here [Roanoke, Virginia.]" It was as though he had never lived except as our war hero.

And the curse of the image continued at the graveside. Murphy, a few days before his forty-sixth birthday, was buried under two oak trees in Arlington National Cemetery. A eulogy issued at the White House hailed the war hero who "not only won the admiration of millions for his own brave exploits, he also came to epitomize the gallantry in action of America's fighting men." Not that one would expect more than that from the Commander in Chief in the depths of the Vietnam War, but why not a word about Murphy's four Purple Hearts? Why not a word about how he had endured the death or displacement of all but one member of the original 235-man Company B with which he first went to war? And why not a word about what it might have meant to him to kill 240 Germans? In Sicily, for example, on his second day in combat, as described in *To Hell and Back*, Murphy killed for the first time. He shot dead two Italian officers mounted on white horses. "Now I have shed my first blood," he wrote. "I feel no qualms; no pride; no remorse. There is only a weary indifference that will follow me throughout the war." Once he had killed, Murphy's spirit seemed to fade. He fell into a kind of existential void, the sense of which permeates his extraordinary memoir.

But no one mentioned the price of glory at Murphy's funeral. We dispatched

Murphy from the American scene as he had arrived on it, and as he remains, insofar as memory of him persists (for example, a portrait of him hung in the state capitol at Austin; the veterans hospital named for him in San Antonio; the annual Audie Murphy Patriotism Award of Decatur, Alabama; memorabilia displayed in the Audie Murphy Room, W. Walworth Harrison Library, Greenville, Texas); to us, he is *the boy hero who won more medals than anyone else.*

As foretold, it seems, by an issue of *Life* dated July 16, 1945, Murphy's feat was his fate.

Life was a weekly in those days, one of several magazines with the popularity that television has now and the image-making power to name a hero if not actually give him birth. Especially during the war, *Life* was our Homer. That week, it gave us Lieutenant Murphy on the cover in black and white. He looked positively mythical. His freckled, unlined, cherub-cheeked face smiled out from under an uptilted officer's cap, radiant over three discrete rows of campaign ribbons representing his fourteen medals and headlined MOST DECORATED SOLDIER all in caps. Murphy's face really was a thing to behold, a most Americanly innocent face, a small-town Texas boy's face, the face of a young Ulysses coming home unscathed, unstressed, nonneurotic. And inside good old *Life*, more of the same in text and photographs: "Life Visits Audie Murphy: Most decorated soldier comes home to Farmersville, Texas." Murphy, a combat infantryman with seven campaign stars, and not a mark on him! It was a blessing! And great for morale on the home front (we still had Japs to go, you see)! Once viewed on *Life*'s eleven-by-fourteen glossy sheets, *Life*'s Murphy was the only Murphy. (The cover story so impressed James Cagney that he called Murphy on the phone, subsequently brought him to Hollywood, and helped him build his movie career.) How, indeed, could another humanly suffering Audie Murphy exist behind such bright, brave eyes?

There was even a nice coincidence that happened on the very date of the Murphy issue of *Life* that would further define the hero's image: at Alamogordo, New Mexico, on July 16, 1945, the world's first atomic bomb exploded. That successful test (although we did not hear about it right away) rendered crazy and probably obsolete the great nations' strategy (out of Von Clausewitz) of engagements between massive armies of men spread across vast battlefields—the kind from which Murphy had emerged so gloriously.

To be a great hero, one needs a great war. And inasmuch as no future war is likely to achieve greatness—that is, the rightness—of Murphy's war, no comparable hero is likely to emerge either. After a thermonuclear exchange, there will be no heroes at all; and in the next nasty, twilight Third World guerrilla wars, how will any American soldier achieve the stature of a Murphy at Holtzwihr? Who now, for example, remembers Sergeant Joe R. Hooper, most decorated soldier of the Vietnam War? Hooper killed an estimated 115 Vietcong and North Vietnamese in combat to Murphy's 240 Germans. Hooper won the Congressional Medal of Honor (his citation reads like a scene from *The Dirty Dozen*), two Silver Stars, and one Bronze Star (as Murphy did). Hooper did not receive either the Distinguished Service Cross or the Legion of Merit (as Murphy did), but he had *seven* Purple Hearts, three more than Murphy. The amazing Joe Hooper, from Zillah, Washington, possessed the right record for national recognition, but from the wrong war. (Hooper died in 1979 of natural causes.) It was Audie Leon Murphy's destiny to be not only "most decorated," but also, perhaps, the last of the great war heroes.

I still remember Murphy as he was the time I met him.

It was in the late spring of 1967. He was at home in North Hollywood with a couple of days to kill before leaving town to make his fortieth movie, a low-budget adventure picture in Algeria. Notwithstanding a singularly wooden acting style, the lasting dignity of Murphy the war hero had, over the years, sustained the credibility of Murphy the movie actor in one hackneyed role after another that called, sooner or later, for the killer of 240 Germans to shoot somebody. He was most believable to me in the 1955 movie version of *To Hell and Back*, his own story. He was also competent-to-good in two movies directed by John Huston, as the young soldier in *The Red Badge of Courage* (1951) and as a mean cowboy in *The Unforgiven* (1960). The Huston films bracketed Murphy's peak years as a movie actor with a future. Still, in the mid-Sixties, he could count on one or two low-budget Westerns or adventure stories annually at about $100,000 per, provided he was willing to perform in such cost-saving places as Algeria. As a property for himself, Murphy was hanging on. So, one morning, while working on another Hollywood assignment, I got in touch with him through a friend and he invited me to stop by at his home that evening after dinner.

I found Murphy's two-story brick-and-shingle house at the dead end of Toluca Road, which took its name from nearby Toluca Lake in the San Fernando Valley. The place had good defensive position. The rear was guarded by the Los Angeles River, the right flank by the Lakeside Golf Club fairway, the left flank by a long carport, and the front by a white iron grillwork fence. There were avocado, lemon, orange, and tangerine trees in the yard; a rose garden, growing long-stemmed "Audie Murphy" roses; and a flagpole. It was after dark and the flag was down. A separate backyard fence enclosed a small swimming pool and protected visitors from a big, scary police dog named Eric. In the carport, there were a Camaro sports car and a Toronado sedan, both popular among motor fans at the time. I learned later that Murphy had recently owned an expensive Lincoln Continental "kustomized" by George Barris, a specialist in restyling production cars. Murphy's Barris creation had one-way-vision back windows, special sound and temperature insulation, a half dozen stereo speakers, and compartments for guns and other weapons. But Murphy had sold the car a while back and, by Hollywood standards, though he was living well enough, he was not living really well.

Not Audie Murphy, but an athletic-looking friend of his named Jerry opened the front door after I'd rung the chimes. Jerry said that Mrs. Murphy had gone out to her evening Bible class at the Methodist church, the Murphy boys (Terry, fifteen, and James, thirteen) were in their rooms, and Murphy himself was at the pool table in the game room concentrating on a combination shot with four dollars at stake. Jerry led me into a small room toward the sound of clinking pool balls beyond a closed door. On a table in one corner was a small, unkempt glass case containing about a dozen of Murphy's medals. Jerry said that Murphy didn't want his medals. He had given some to local kids, friends, and a relative or two; some he had lost. In fact, Jerry said, Murphy had taken some pains over the years to de-emphasize "the whole deal." He belonged to no veterans' organizations, stayed away from parades, and avoided ceremonies that might require a show of ribbons. In 1963 he had refused to attend President John F. Kennedy's White House party for all living winners of the Medal of Honor. As for the actual medals themselves, Murphy would often say, Jerry told me, "I feel they belong to a lot of people and not just me," and then give them away. Murphy's wife, Pamela, had finally gathered up a selection and put them in a glass case to preserve them for the boys. I saw that the Medal of Honor was awry and looking tacky. Murphy's premier Purple Heart had slipped down to the bottom of the case and turned over on its face.

I went ahead of Jerry into a white-shuttered room next to the Murphys' kitchen; a regulation pool table fit the space but snugly at one end. Beside the table, resting his cheek on his cue, stood Murphy, taller than I'd expected. He was about five feet ten, heavier, and older. He wore a white shirt with silver-and-turquoise cuff links in the shape of horseshoes, no tie, and gray slacks. He had an undeniable and undisguised paunch. His face was full, threatening to become round. He combed his red-brown hair up and back with a kind of kid-next-door flourish. His teeth were his own and very white. He had a petite quality despite his heft, so that he really didn't look forty-two, except at the corners of his moody blue eyes. He was still boyish, but a much older boy.

Murphy stuck out a small freckled hand and gripped my hand inconclusively. He said it would only take a minute to finish his game with Jerry. His voice was Texas-nasal, but long since had been invaded by the even, upper-register tones of anxious southern California.

Through several turns at the table, Murphy and his friend Jerry played even. But then Murphy accidentally sank the eight ball. Jerry happily scooped four dollar bills out of a corner pocket. Murphy lost quietly.

"I got a passion for this game," Murphy said. "We sacrificed this room—the dining room—for it. Now we eat all our meals in the kitchen and don't miss the dining room. We don't entertain very often, that's for sure. Tell you the truth, I've never gotten along with *Hollywood* Hollywood people and they don't get along with me."

Jerry racked the balls for a new game and handed me his cue. He was off on a date.

"I've got four extra dollars to spend," Jerry said, chortling.

"Tell about the time I won five thousand dollars from you," Murphy said.

"Yes, you did," Jerry said. "Then I won it all back."

After Jerry left, Murphy asked me if I'd like to play. I told him to go ahead and break. Murphy sank the four ball on the break.

"It's true about the five thousand dollars," he said. "I won it off Jerry, and then I lost it right back. I've just told you the story of my life."

Murphy missed an easy shot on the one ball. He was no pool shark. He knew the game, but his bridge was weak. I was no shark, either, but I beat him in about ten minutes.

"I'd have played better," Murphy said, "if we'd had a bet on it."

With a slightly rolling gait, favoring his old hip wound, Murphy walked ahead of me into another room off the dining-pool room. It was a big, cheerful space in brick and wood with big Hollywood lamps, soft furniture, and a thick carpet. It was a living room that did not feel lived in; it was an expensive room for company in a house where not much company had come. In the far wall, an open door led to another room that should have been the garage. I could see a bed and a desk with another big lamp.

"Garage," Murphy said. "I remodeled the garage to make a room where I could be by myself."

I must have seemed ready to ask why.

"It was necessary," he said cryptically.

Murphy waved me to the couch and seated himself in a high-backed easy chair. He tossed one leg over the arm and heaved a deep and prolonged sigh.

For a moment he seemed so weary, I thought he might be falling asleep. But then he perked up and smiled. "Well," he said, "if I hadn't been in the movies, I might have been a farmer. Ha-ha. A happy farmer. But don't get me wrong. I'm grateful to the movie business. The only trouble is the typecasting. You make a success in Westerns, they milk it dry—until you're dry. That's why Hollywood has just about dried up for somebody like me. I did very well on *To Hell and Back*. Maybe a half million before taxes. But that was 1955. You get older, it shows up on the screen. That's the truth—age is the worst thing of all. Time is what's chasing you. Anyway, I've made three movies in the past two years. Not much. I get a piece of the action, is the only hope. There hasn't been much action. My last picture was a terrible experience. Went all the way to Israel to make it, bring it in under budget. I had to do all the stunts myself. I had to do everything except pack my own lunch. Things were different when I was working on *The Red Badge of Courage*. Now, that was 1950. I had the best time on that picture. And it was such a flop! That Huston! He's made so many flops and he is such a big failure that no one here can believe it, so he goes on and on. Me, Murphy, I'm a middle-sized failure, so people believe *that*. That's why I'm off to Algeria."

In the driveway headlights flashed, and moments later Pamela Murphy came in carrying church literature. She and Audie had married in 1951, four days after his divorce from Wanda Hendrix, who was an up-and-coming starlet of the moment. That marriage had lasted fifteen months. This one was in its sixteenth year, despite some earlier separations. Pamela Murphy was from Oklahoma and part Cherokee, a dark, trim, good-looking woman with fine cheekbones and a softly harassed manner. She brought in the teenage Murphy boys, who were dark like their mother and shy. I shook hands with the boys. They scurried out, followed by their mother. She paused at the door.

"You want to know about me?" she asked. "I'm a coward and I admire courage." Then she went out.

Murphy laughed, weary again. I told him I had been at Carlsbad Army Air Base in New Mexico when I first saw his picture on the cover of *Life*. I said I'd always wondered why he hadn't stayed in the Army.

"Wasn't my decision," he said. "West Point turned me down because too much of my right hip was gone. I can't swim because of it. I've got other ailments, besides. Fifty percent disability—shrapnel in my legs, a nervous stomach, regular headaches. So listen, I didn't want to be an actor. It was simply the best offer that came along.

"But you've got to understand me. You see, with me—" Murphy paused, as though deciding whether to go ahead with his thought "—with me, it's been a fight for a long, long time to keep from being bored to death. *That's what two years of combat did to me!*" Murphy's voice had risen and he had brought both feet down on the floor. He looked at me wide-eyed and frowning.

"Let me tell you something," he said. "Beginning eight years ago—up to last year—I had seven years of insomnia. *Seven years!* Outside of cancer, I don't know anything that can be as bad as that. It was just all of a sudden, I could not sleep. I'd be half dazed. The furniture in my room would take on odd shapes.

"Then there was my nightmare, a recurrent nightmare. A feeling of exasperation. I would dream I am on a hill and all these faceless people are charging up at me. I am holding a M-1 Garand rifle, the kind of rifle I used to take apart blindfolded. And in the dream, every time I shoot one of these people, a piece of the rifle flies off until all I have left is the trigger guard! The trigger guard!

"Then I would wake up. So, that's why I began sleeping in the garage with the lights on all night so that when I woke up from the dream, I'd know where I was. After a while, a doctor put me on a synthetic tranquilizer. You know, pills. I could sleep three or four hours, taking one pill each night. But then I had to take more. I built up on that stuff until I was half-asleep all the time, day and night. I lost twenty-two pounds. I was so tranquilized, I didn't care about anything. I was a zombie. I dissipated all my money. I gave it away. I was not interested in anything. If a bus got in my way while I was driving on the freeway, I'd just force it to the side of the road. I sold off my airplane, my boat, my car, over eight hundred acres of land, my ranch, all my horses—everything!"

Murphy paused, heaving that weary sigh again.

"I'm sorry I can't offer you a drink," he said. "I rarely drink and never smoked."

Murphy looked down at his hands as though he were surprised to see them.

"Well, it was sure interesting how my friends reacted," he said. "It was like going on patrol and some damn machine gun opens up on you and you look around and all the green troops are gone and only the seasoned troops are left. I sure found out who were the seasoned troops among my friends, and not very damn many, either.

"So—there was another thing, too—it was the *noise*. Noise! In combat, you see, your hearing gets so acute you can interpret any noise. But now, there were all kinds of noises that I couldn't interpret. Strange noises. I couldn't sleep without a weapon by my bed. A pistol. Because the least little noise bothered me. That's why I had the garage made into a bedroom, to be away from the noise. The least little noise—there was a time when a cannon wouldn't wake me. And now I could barely survive in the garage. . . .

"Anyway, I would up looking for something to do. I mean, I'd sold everything and here I was, in the dullest town in the world. So I started betting on horses. I love horses, but this gambling went way beyond that. I got so that four hundred dollars was a minimum bet. Even that was boring. I didn't care whether I won or lost. It was as if I wanted to destroy everything I had built up. I got irritable. I hated everything and everybody. The last two or three years of it, I was just sleepwalking.

"Finally, last year in Florida, I realized that I'd become addicted to tranquilizers. Once I did, I knew what I had to do. I locked myself in a hotel room and threw away the pills. I stayed in there for five days, having withdrawal pains just like a junkie. I had convulsions. But I quit. I stopped the pills, and I quit gambling. This past year, I feel like I've been starting my life all over again. I've been sleeping lately—most nights, anyway. But I won't take any more pills. Not one."

Murphy tapped his fingertips together.

"You know," he said, ruefully, "there are only two of us left from the old outfit and we're both half dead."

Abruptly, he stood up, quite agitated.

"Listen," he said, "I'm going to make you a coffee. You look like you need a coffee."

"Okay," I said, "coffee's fine."

We went into the kitchen. Murphy put on a pot and took down a jar of instant coffee. I sat down at the kitchen table. Murphy set out one cup, milk, and a box of Oreos. He nibbled on a cookie. He seemed calmer.

"I guess people don't understand about war," he said. "I go back in my mind twenty-five years. I remember thinking it was going to be a great adventure. I remember we came under artillery fire my very first day in action. That was in Sicily. And I saw a couple of guys I knew get blown up. I was very serious after that. Very serious. I wanted to take what toll of the enemy I could. The only time I didn't like to shoot was when the Germans pushed up the poor Italians, who didn't want to fight in front, to bear the brunt of our attack. A lot of Italians were needlessly shot. The fact is, in a war, a lot of people are needlessly shot.

"Mostly, though, your thoughts are elsewhere. I mean, the training—the brainwashing—makes you go ahead and you react against the enemy even though you have so much fear. You become an effective soldier when you get over this fear and you use your training and you try to think ahead. It's a game of chance for a while, but after two or three fire fights, you begin to improve your odds by taking advantage of the terrain and your weapons. You get more polished. Your attitude changes. You get a more professional outlook.

"The way I remember it, the first shock of combat numbs your senses. That's a good thing, because numbness keeps you from running away. The shock of combat is a little like the shock after a wound. You don't feel the pain right away. Then, after another little while, you sit down and appraise the situation. You realize you are going to do what you have to do. Once you accept the fact that you are going to get it if you are going to get it, your mind clears up. You become decisive. That's important, because indecision kills people in war more often than anything else."

Murphy smiled.

"I'm forgetting your coffee," he said. He put the jar on the table, told me to help myself, and then poured the water.

"I've always wondered," I said, "how I would've made out."

"Everybody does," he said kindly. "Let me tell you, the enemy is very impersonal. The enemy is just a number of people out there in uniform trying to kill you. So all you can do is develop the mental attitude of an executioner and get on with the job. The trouble is, as I've been trying to tell you, it is very hard to overcome this attitude later. Now, a couple of times, I felt real anger in combat—felt something personal.

"Once was when my friend Tipton got shot. We were near St. Tropez and these seven Germans waved a white flag. But when Tipton jumped out of our hole to capture them, they shot him through the heart. I was angry then. I threw some grenades and then I got a machine gun. I went up after them and settled their cases.

"The other time, there was a sniper who'd killed two of our people. I don't know what it was about sniping, but I had a vendetta feeling about it that I didn't have when we were just two groups of men fighting each other. I got permission to go after this sniper alone. I put socks on over my boots and took off everything that might rattle or make any kind of noise. Then I went out to find him. I saw him first, *sensed* him before he saw me. He raised his rifle, but I had a bead on him and, of course, I shot him. I remember that he had papers on him showing he'd won extra furloughs for being such an effective sniper."

The telephone rang. Murphy looked startled. Then, as he took a step across the kitchen to answer it, he said, "I probably won't sleep tonight."

I gathered that the call was from someone involved in his Algerian movie deal. Murphy talked for several minutes. Then he said "Yup" several times and hung up.

"Like all calls in Hollywood," he said, "that was about money. But still, if I'm going to get out of acting, I've got to learn producing."

He didn't seem too sure of himself.

"I guess you learn it," he said, "like you learn anything else. Same as you learn about combat. You learn that war is a struggle of group against group, each trying to figure out how to destroy the other as quickly as possible with the least loss to their own. The point is that losses are inevitable. So you learn not to get too friendly with anybody. Combat is not like the movies or what you read in books, even my book. Every action is new people. One way or another, people come and go. Your side is just like the other side—people in uniform trained to do what they have to do. There are only fleeting moments of the kind where a unit has the drama of a war movie. Battlefields are empty places. You don't remember guys' names. You remember that one-one-zero-eight-seven-eight-three is the number of your rifle, but names are too personal. That's really how it is.

"But there's this to say for combat. It brings out the best in men. It's gory and it's unfortunate, but most people in combat stand a little taller."

Murphy's voice had become insistent and, I thought, a little defensive. Once in Italy, he had testified for the prosecution in a desertion case against a rifleman of Company B. The man had not been where he was supposed to be during a coordinated attack and the adjutant had brought him up on charges. The man was court-martialed and jailed. "You have a comradeship," he said, "a rapport that you'll never have again, not in our society, anyway. I suppose it comes from having nothing to gain except the end of the war. There's no competitiveness, no money values. You trust the man on your left and on your right with your life, while, as a civilian, you might not trust either one of them with ten cents."

Murphy folded his arms across his chest. He was suddenly as shy as his own two boys, as though he might have seemed too proud. I said I thought it was time for me to go. He said how about lunch tomorrow and I said fine. Then he walked me to the door. He shook hands warmly and pointed at the notebook I carried.

"I guess what all that says is that I really identified with soldiering," he said. "That's my problem, I'll admit. To become an executioner, somebody cold and analytical to be trained to kill, and then to come back into civilian life and be alone in the crowd—it takes an awful long time to get over it. Fear and depression come over you. It's been twenty-odd years already." Murphy shrugged. "Did you know that doctors say the effect of all this on my generation won't reach its peak until 1970? So, I guess I got three years to go."

Next day about noon, Murphy picked me up in his Camaro and we drove to a restaurant in the Valley. It was a gloomy place smelling of dead cigars and air conditioning. Murphy ordered a small steak and a big salad soaked in cheese dressing. When the food came, Murphy ate rapidly. He was wearing a gray jacket with black piping, which he kept zipped up to his throat. He looked cold, as though he had been up all night. I asked him whether he'd slept and he assured me he'd had a good night. I thought he was lying.

Lunch over, it seemed Murphy had nothing to do until late afternoon, when he was to meet his boys and spend some private time with them before the Algeria trip the next day. We drove in the Camaro to Barris's Kustom City, where his late Lincoln Continental had been restyled. Murphy said he liked to hang around Barris's garage-and-showroom when he couldn't think of anything better to do. "It's a way to beat the boredom," he said. The place had the feel, if not the charm, of a toy shop. There were a half-dozen cars on display, each tailored like a teenager's dream of superpower with enormous hoods, jazzed-up interiors, and phallic tail fins. A mechanic, "kustomizing" a new Cadillac, waved to him. He said: "Hiya, Murph." Murphy got into the Cadillac, tried the wheel, punched some buttons, climbed out again. "Nice," he said. Murphy stood around watching the mechanic for about twenty minutes. Then he asked me if I was bored. I said no. About ten minutes later, Murphy said he thought he could use a steam bath and a rubdown over at a gym in West Los Angeles run by a friend of his named Terry Hunt. The gym was forty minutes away.

"Well, it's what you have to do," Murphy said, "in a dull town, you want to kill an afternoon and you don't play golf."

In traffic, squinting slightly at the bright sunlight, Murphy drove carefully and calmly with one hand on the wheel and told me about his early life.

His birthplace was a farm near Kingston, Texas, a little town in a poor farming area not far from Dallas. "The land is like gumbo," he said, "all black." His father was a sharecropper, farming under a landlord and giving up part of his profits in exchange for seed, equipment, and the land itself. "It was a type of slavery," Murphy said. The family was Irish Protestant with nine children. Audie was in the middle, born in June 1925, he told me. His mother used to work alongside his father and the older children with her youngest baby swinging from a jumper hung on a tree at the edge of their field. They were always poor. The Depression made things worse. In the Thirties, when Audie was twelve, his father disappeared. "He just ran off," Murphy said. "I was always ashamed of how he left us, but now I'm not so critical. I heard from him after the war. He'd had real troubles, moving from farm to farm, from Celeste, Texas, to Floyd, Texas, trying to make ends meet for himself. No one can know how harsh it was who hasn't lived through it. You'd hear your brothers and sisters crying hunger at night. And you'd make dang sure you learned how to shoot straight with your twenty-two, because if you missed the rabbit, there'd be no meat for dinner." Murphy had to leave school in the eighth grade to work full-time to support the family. He did odd jobs, pumped gas, and wrestled groceries in Greenville, Texas. His biggest paycheck was sixteen dollars for a week's work.

When he was sixteen, his mother died of cancer. "She was a broken woman," Murphy said, "brokenhearted and broken in body." Texas authorities placed his younger brothers and sisters in an orphanage. They stayed there until after the war, when Murphy used the first money he made to get them out.

Orphaned and alone, Murphy was working in a radio repair shop in Greenville, Texas, when the Japanese bombed Pearl Harbor. He decided to enlist. The Marine Corps pointed out that he was underage and underweight (at five feet six, Murphy weighed 120 pounds) and rejected him. The Army took him on his seventeenth birthday, believing he was eighteen. "I though I'd like the service," Murphy said. "And besides, it was a way to escape sharecropping." He fainted during his first attempt at close order drill under the summer sun at Camp Wolters, outside Mineral Wells, Texas. He had a series of bloody noses because he was too light to control the Army's standard bolt action .03 rifle. "It kept kicking me in the face," he said, "and I barely qualified with it." And he sagged dangerously under his regulation sixty-pound pack, until he learned to stuff it with toilet paper instead of the usual gear. "I was so little," he said, "but I made it all the way with Company B. And wouldn't you know? Soon as I got out of the Army, I started to grow. It was that dern helmet holding me down all the time!"

About three that afternoon, Murphy pulled up at one of the taller buildings in West Los Angeles. Terry Hunt's health club was on the top floor. Hunt had befriended Murphy during his early days in Hollywood and Murphy had named his eldest son after him. He was now a paternal, pink-faced man in his late fifties. "Terry is like a father to me," Murphy said.

We went to the locker room, where Murphy peeled off the gray jacket. I saw then that Murphy carried a .45 automatic pistol stuck in his belt. Murphy lifted the pistol, weighed it in his hand, checked the safety, and passed it to Hunt for safekeeping.

"I carry it for protection and therapy," Murphy said to me.

Murphy could tell the gun made me uneasy. He said he liked to help out some friends of his in the police department, rode with them on an occasional drug bust, things like that. I nodded.

"Well, just forget about the gun," he said.

Murphy finished undressing, took a steam, and let the masseur rub him for half an hour or so. Shaved, dressed, and re-armed, he looked cheerier than I had seen him. He seemed to feel he had accomplished something. He tried to pay for the services of the gym, but Hunt refused his money. It was part of their ritual. Murphy explained to me that this gym was his sanctuary, the one place you could always go.

"Terry's always been here for me," Murphy said. "That's why I think it's not so bad to go up and down the ladder in life a couple of times. Even when you're a loser, you're a winner, because you find out who your real friends are."

Beaming, Terry Hunt embraced Murphy and wished him well in Algeria.

It was nearly five when Murphy pulled up in front of my hotel. He kept the motor on to run the air conditioning. He tried the radio, found some news, listened for a minute, turned it off. There had been a big demonstration in New York against the war in Vietnam. Murphy shook his head sadly.

"Gee," he said, "I'd hate their guts if they had any."

"I think we should get out of Vietnam," I said.

"No, you can't leave Vietnam unless you win the war."

"I don't think the Vietnamese want us over there."

"Listen, when you feel you are morally right, you just have to act and let people catch up later. That's the way it is in war."

"I'm not saying I know about war."

"You never know about any war until you're in the situation.'

"I'm sure you're right about that."

"It'll take one million troops! But I say—we go in, we do the job. Then we get out! There's no other way!"

A look of terrible weariness came over Murphy's face, then the trace of a smile. He stuck out his hand and we shook hands.

"Well," he said, "thanks for being so nice."

I never saw Murphy again or the movie he made in Algeria. Back in New York, I filed my notes on our conversations. As it happened, Murphy's luck went from bad to worse. Neither film producing nor real estate nor oil prospecting paid off for him. He declared bankruptcy the next year; then came the assault case; then, death on the business trip. But at least I had learned that he was more than the most decorated soldier of World War II, more than the war hero of our time. He was also a casualty—so much of his spirit, in fact, had been killed in action.

Should the national mood toward military glory change again, I hope Murphy will be remembered, but truly this time, as much for his suffering as for his deeds. Then, if he really is the last of the great war heroes, those who remember him will know what that meant.

The Emigré

ELIZABETH HARDWICK

OUR COUNTRY, FROM THE FIRST A VAST TRANSCENDENTAL DIASPORA UNDER THE CE-
lestial protection of two oceans, in the Thirties fell heir to, by way of unprecedented disasters, a radiance of genius. The émigrés were of such lofty achievement
and possibility that the mere listing of the names is a sort of embarrassment because it seems to reduce the irreducible. Or it seems to try by order and condensation to contain the disorderly solitary eminence of the bearers of the names.
Emigrés, exiles, refugees from Germany and Austria, Hungary, Russia, Spain,
Poland, Italy—and elsewhere, elsewhere. The density of the arts and sciences and
the very luggage of civilization these persons carried with them surpass understanding. In the last fifty years they were among us in such multiplication it
seemed as if they were some natural transcontinental cargo rather than an astonishment delivered by tragic history. The national psyche accommodated the savants, when it knew of them, with extraordinary and respectful generosity—and
some amused and puzzled wonder. In any case, it was clear that there wasn't
enough laurel in the Rockies to adorn this large, polyglot pantheon of the uprooted
and the overrun. Some arrived with their Nobel Prizes and more gained them
while here. Some appear in encyclopedias as Americans: American theoretical
physicist, b. Ulm, Germany. Albert Einstein.

In 1904 Henry James wrote of the "effect of the infusion," the infusion being
the swarm of foreign-born persons he found buzzing about and sometimes

stinging his sensibilities when he returned to New York after a gap of twenty-one years. It appeared to him the Italians on the Lower East Side were not Italians at all. They seemed to have rid themselves, in a moment, as it were, of the peasantlike hierarchical courtesies, the attractive ancient colorations that made them so agreeable when they were tending the vines of Italy. They were not discourteous; they were simply a transplant transmogrified—a new, mysterious being. Wandering in the downtown ghetto, the New Jerusalem, he wondered, "Who can ever tell, moreover, in any conditions and in presence of any apparent anomaly, what the genius of Israel may, or may not, really be 'up to'?"

To wonder what the later elite Jewish intelligentsia of Europe was "up to" could scarcely enter our minds in a colloquial phrase since it would require not a lovely, drifting social imagination of the kind James shows in *The American Scene* but, instead, immense imagination and information in the higher reaches of mathematics, physics, biology, art history, music, and on and on.

The émigrés from Nazism and fascism and also Russian communism were survivors of every sort and every condition. The Jews were united in their pain and grief, something not transferable to the American scene except perhaps to their fellow Jews of no matter how long a local citizenship. However, for the extraordinary talents simple assimilation into American culture for practical reasons was not a demand, since it was their fate to be exceptions without boundaries, even though they had suffered from the boundaries of their circumstance in a time of catastrophe.

Our institutions and a wide, if sometimes imperfect, hospitality asked of these gifted émigrés only that they continue to be themselves or continue to complete the self achieved with such spectacular promise in the past. This was a benign and unusual condition, something the earlier groups fleeing from pogroms or gross poverty could not have understood. The unusual welcoming was in many cases chilled by difficulties in language and by what might be called "medium" or obscure previous celebrity. And so there were learned art historians, critics, essayists, political theorists, wandering about New York with the merely respectable anonymity of some NYU doctorate.

Nabokov spoke of his European Humbert Humbert, that outrageous disturbance in *Lolita* who swept in his libidinous travels across the continent like a dust storm, as a "salad" of mixed genes. That is, he was French, Austrian, English, with a "dash of the Danube." And to some extent the "salad" defines most of the distinguished exiles. They were German or Hungarian or Russian, but they were also very much European and had moved about from country to country for education and inspiration. Einstein himself lived as a youth in Munich and Milan and was graduated from the Polytechnic Academy in Zurich, where he became a Swiss citizen. He was a professor also in Prague, and when his fame was established he accepted the directorship of the Kaiser Wilhelm Institute in Berlin. Had he not then resumed his German citizenship he could not, as a Jew, have been deprived of it and his property in 1933.

As we know, this European arrived at the Institute for Advanced Study in Princeton and became for America the iconographical "genius," the abstruse incarnate, and also the liberal and tormented spirit about nuclear weapons and civic affairs.

Nabokov, Stravinsky, and Balanchine, Europeans from St. Petersburg by way of the Russian Revolution, do not quite create in our minds the sense of some tremendous and unique burden borne through life. They were not Jewish—Nabokov's wife was Jewish—and they maintained their "Russian-ness," which had about it an ineffable charm not often granted to "German-ness." Of course, the Russians' memories were of loss of countryside, of language, and like all refugees, they came from a cemetery.

The Firebird was performed in Paris in 1910 and Stravinsky came to America later as a supreme example and influence in world music. Nabokov, who had continued to write in Russian in Germany and France, began here to write in English and to put Humbert Humbert and Professor Pnin into a fantastical American landscape. Where there is an overwhelming invention of style and conception, as with Schoenberg in California, citizenship and placement are simply existence honored and not matters of creative additions. With Balanchine a perfect reciprocity was accomplished—the wedding of imperial Russian technique with American dancers and, when he wished it, the compli-cated tonalities of a kind of American aura.

Henry Kissinger, so extraordinarily visible and palpable, has never quite dis-engaged his Germanness, his boyhood in Fürth, but that is surely merely his inextinguishable accent and little else. This curious émigré, or rather this most curious one among the émigrés, has an innate American flair. He alone, among the figures who come to mind, seems to express the old will to exploit the conti-nent, build the railroads, get the copper out of the ground. Still, a Continental sophistication and a Mitteleuropa skill at diplomatic maneuver somehow in-form his American endeavors. His "image" announces that he is both the Old World and *us* in a high-flown, canny admixture.

If for Kissinger the United States was still the frontier, the country acted in a custodial mode for many of the others. At the Institute in Princeton the custo-dial gesture was elaborate, courtly, and rather daunting. Gödel and Von Neumann and Einstein under the trees and spires at the end of the ride through the industrial wasteland of New Jersey. And Panofsky and Auerbach and Thomas Mann and Hermann Broch: one does not like to line them up like a very large cast in *Playbill.*

The New School for Social Research was, by comparison, a modest practical-ity, utilitarian and saving for many contentious thinkers, among them the phi-losophers Hannah Arendt and Leo Strauss, and the political historians Hans Kohn and Hans Morgenthau. Nevertheless, no institution in America was a convent, a retreat. Instead, the refugee world was a battlefield—they fought among themselves, about ideas, and often they struggled with the new country itself. They were ambitious, often arrogant, often rivalrous. The quarrels and differences among them are very interestingly described in Anthony Heilbut's *Exiled in Paradise.*

And they came into the postwar world of the H-bomb, McCarthyism, and the Cold War. Thomas Mann returned to Europe in disillusionment. Edward Teller, Hans Bethe, Einstein, and Leo Szilard, preeminent figures of the nuclear age, disagreed painfully and in ways that were important for themselves and for the country. Hannah Arendt's *Eichmann in Jerusalem* aroused ferocious controversy.

Many of the émigrés became teachers, and perhaps it is not amiss to think of them as exercising a certain imperial, if uncoercive, role among our young artists and thinkers. The Bauhaus architects dominated the skyline and the professional schools in an almost military fashion. They left a vast and often beautiful permanency of steel and concrete even the most aggressive postmodernism cannot undo, for such is the nature of buildings. Tom Wolfe expressed his native's chagrin at the imposition of "foreign forms," but his advocacy of a sort of containment of idea in architecture, and painting as well, implies that the America the refugee professionals entered was a sort of Maginot Line, self-important but easily outflanked. And of course this was not true. As a part of the civilized community we were already knowledgeable about theorems, physics, the unconscious, atonalism, Cubism, European fiction and poetry, and the general ideas in circulation. No one ever knows just why certain notions prevail in historical periods except that they serve the creative impulses at large.

Still, there was a need for buildings and there was the money to build them with, and the triumph of the Bauhaus group was indeed noticeable. Psychiatry also seemed to find here a peculiar local demand, as if it were some happy interest-bearing note. "So. Now vee may perhaps to begin," Philip Roth's Dr. Spielvogel says. Bruno Bettelheim, Erik Erikson, Karen Horney, and the manic futurist Wilhelm Reich—in combination a fantastical therapeutic spread—achieved what one might call a reinforced definition. And not to speak of those emblematic practitioners in their intense occupation of New York's Central Park West and Park Avenue.

"Stone by stone we shall remove the Alhambra, the Kremlin and the Louvre and build them anew on the banks of the Hudson."—Benjamin de Casseres, 1925. De Casseres spoke of "things," treasures of antiquity and every period following, bought and displayed and *owned.* He could not know that the Hudson Valley was to be the collector and connoisseur of the actual bodies of creative Europe. France and England and Switzerland had been the custodians for centuries—Herzen and Turgenev, Marx.

> *Between the enormous fluted Ionic columns*
> *There seeps from heavily jowled or hawk-like foreign faces*
> *The guttural sorrow of the refugees.*
>
> —Louis MacNeice,
"The British Museum Reading Room"

New York, Manhattan—a fanatical urbanism, a spectacle, a metaphorical landing place. So if you are banished from Frankfurt, Berlin, St. Petersburg, or

Warsaw, there is left no possibility except the twentieth-century capital. The city of the future, peculiar, uncomfortable, an orphan brilliant indeed, and no matter the lack of a family album of monuments, cathedrals, old squares, and palaces. Manhattan itself, with those early pictorial towers that seem to end in a medicating hypodermic needle, is one of the "characters" of the last fifty years. Its purpose is to be exploited, whereas the purpose of the Old World cities is to exist as a slowly accreting density and storehouse of the national history. New Amsterdam: Mondrian's *Broadway Boogie Woogie* and the austere Dutchman himself in his studio on the East Side.

"What Piranesi invented the ornamental rites of your Roxy Theatre? And what Gustave Moreau apoplectic with Prometheus lighted the venomous colors that flutter at the summit of the Chrysler Building?"—Dali in New York. (This quotation and the preceding one from de Casseres are found in a work of almost frenzied brilliance and originality: *Delirious New York*, 1978, by the young Dutch architect Rem Koolhaas.)

In America we are not a Folk in the manner of the Germans, French, English, and even the Russians. We are too self-created, vagrant, of too random and unpredictable congruence for that. The claim to insist upon a folk by the negation "un-American" is a bullying and unhistorical folly. The elite émigrés met here not only the greath wealth of the country and the Bill of Rights but a rich and porous ground. For the general dissemination of ideas a physical presence is not necessary. The exception is the A-bomb and the H-bomb, the most spectacular achievements of émigré science and perhaps of any science in that the terms of everything were altered forever. In this case the American presence of Fermi and Leo Szilard at Columbia, Hans Bethe and Edward Teller at Los Alamos was of an overwhelming significance, spanning the limits of science, politics, the direction—still unknown—of human history.

The aggressiveness of American mass culture was a challenge many of the refugees seemed unprepared for, even if they were not dilatory in abstracting principles from it. Their complicated intrusions and failures in Hollywood have their own formidably detailed history. Nothing could soften the final fact that this elite was unlike any other. They had been the objects of the worst and most powerfully organized evil intentions the world had ever known. Whatever Weimar or Viennese café-pride they exhibited was only a manner, a style. It was painful to learn to write in English, or to remain, like Isaac Bashevis Singer, a writer in Yiddish slowly finding his audience in the fiercely competitive glut of American fiction.

Surely the only happy exile is based upon caprice and personal taste—French food, sunlight all the year, cheap villas, servants, old cultures, and sometimes merely the escape from a too dear and watchful family and village. Finding Oxford and Cambridge too "down-home" seemed to have spurred the transition of Auden, Isherwood, and Huxley. In the end the most striking thing about the exiles' great influence on our times is that it was marked by a certain equity. What we offered to them and what we received in return was accomplished with rare historical and human balance.

Notes on the Contributors

MAX APPLE   Max Apple was born and raised in Grand Rapids. His father earned a living as a scrap dealer. As a youngster Apple would ride with his father on their short-wheelbase Dodge carrying discarded machinery and other refuse found at factories—"anything that could . . . be melted down to a more pristine condition." From those earliest days Apple planned to be a writer. "My grandmother told me stories, and I liked to listen to stories. You know Gorky says, 'It all depends on who your grandmother is.' "

At the University of Michigan he wrote his dissertation on Robert Burton's *The Anatomy of Melancholy*, which, Apple reminds us, was a best seller in the seventeenth century. In his first collection of stories, *The Oranging of America* (1976), he set off everyday cultural references against pop fantasy and, according to one admirer, translated "the most battered of our cultural clichés into glistening artifacts." The quick wit and runaway imagination that sparked that book lit up his novel *Zip* (1978), the tale of a nice Jewish boy, a junkyard dealer from Detroit, on the make in the 1960s. Apple now teaches at Rice University in Houston. A new collection of stories, *Free Agents*, was published in 1984.

KEN AULETTA   Ken Auletta's last book, *The Underclass*, published in 1982, was a closeup look at the hard-core unemployed. To write the book, Auletta spent thirty weeks with a "life-skills" class in Manhattan; and for two and a half years he traveled from Appalachia to Oakland, talking with longtime welfare recipients, street criminals, addicts—all to report the varied concerns of the nation's poor.

Auletta grew up in Coney Island and was educated at the State University of New York and Syracuse University. He began his journalistic career writing for *New York* magazine and *The Village Voice*, for whom he covered New York City fiscal crises as well as the presidential campaign of Jimmy Carter. As a contributing editor of *Esquire* in the late 1970s, he wrote about Roy Cohn and the media. His book *The Streets Were Paved with Gold* was published in 1979, and a second book, *Hard Feelings*, appeared in 1980. Today Auletta divides his life between a once-a-week column in the New York *Daily News* and his writing for *The New Yorker*. A new book, *The Art of Corporate Success*, a look at the Schlumberger multinational company, portions of which have appeared in *The New Yorker*, was published in 1984.

SAUL BELLOW   When the Swedish Academy awarded Saul Bellow the Nobel Prize for Literature in 1976, it honored a man believed by many to be the most accomplished homegrown writer at work in America today. His fiction, a mingling of intellectual speculation and gritty vernacular, reflects roots in both the Old and New Worlds. Born the son of Russian Jews, he spent his early years in Montreal—years in which he was immersed in Old Testament studies and spoke English, Hebrew, Yiddish, and French. Eventually the family settled in Chicago. The writer achieved fame in his thirties with the publication of *The Adventures of Augie March* (1953), a sprawling narrative about Chicago and a young man's struggle to find himself. It brought Bellow the first of three National Book Awards.

In the next thirty years, Bellow delivered work of extraordinary range and virtuosity: *Seize the Day, Henderson the Rain King, Herzog* (the novel with which he is most closely identified—a reporter once addressed the writer as Mr. Herzog), *Mr. Sammler's Planet, Humboldt's Gift* (for which he was awarded the Pulitzer Prize), and *The Dean's December*. A new collection of stories, *Him with His Foot in His Mouth*, was published in 1984.

ROY BLOUNT JR.   Roy Blount (rhymes with punt) has one of the quirkiest minds at work today. Nowhere is he funnier than in *Crackers* (1980), his masterpiece of ethnic ambivalence. In it, he wrestles with his mixed feelings about being from Georgia, and having a Georgian as President. Moreover, it is a lament for the unrealized "Crackro-American Camelot."

His cracker voice notwithstanding, Blount himself is not a cracker. He graduated from Vanderbilt, Phi Beta Kappa; then, thinking he might like to write or teach, he studied English literature at Harvard. For a time he wrote a column for *The Atlanta Journal*, which often contained his own limericks. He took a job at *Sports Illustrated* and wrote his first book, *About Three Bricks Shy of a Load* (1974), after spending a year with the Pittsburgh Steelers. (Blount, it seems safe to say, was the inspiration for country lyricist Elroy Blunt in Dan Jenkins's *Semi-Tough*.) In the late 1970s, he did a sports column for *Esquire* and later reviewed music for the magazine. He lives in Massachusetts now, "on the outskirts of Mill River . . . a short-skirted town." *One Fell Soup,* a collection of essays, appeared in 1983. A new collection of his writing, *What Men Don't Tell Women,* was published in 1984.

PETER BOGDANOVICH   "I was born and then I liked movies," Peter Bogdanovich once said. At twelve, the youngster began keeping a card file on every picture he saw, noting his original and, later, his revised opinions; at twenty-six, after years of writing articles and monographs on his favorite directors, he went to Hollywood, soon to become the first noted American director who was also a critic and film scholar. For a while in the early 1970s he wrote a Hollywood column for *Esquire.*

Bogdanovich first attracted critical attention as a director in 1968 with *Targets,* a thriller he also wrote, produced, and starred in. Then, in 1971, the New York Film Festival became something of a Bogdanovich festival with the unveiling of *Directed by John Ford,* his documentary on the legendary director's half-century career, and *The Last Picture Show,* his brilliant re-creation of life in a small Texas town in the early 1950s. The film was nominated for eight Academy Awards. He went on to make *What's Up, Doc?, Paper Moon, Nickelodeon, Saint Jack,* and *They All Laughed.* Much of his time the last three years has been devoted to writing *The Killing of the Unicorn,* a memoir of actress Dorothy Stratten, out in 1984.

DAVID BRADLEY   David Bradley was raised in Bedford, Pennsylvania, in farm country, "perilously close to the Mason-Dixon line." His father, a minister and historian, encouraged his interest in writing; and at nine, young Bradley wrote his first work, *Martian Thanksgiving,* a play performed by his Scout troop. "For a Cub Scout it was very sophisticated," he recalls. "It even had flashbacks." By the time Bradley entered the University of Pennsylvania in 1968, he had settled on a writing career; he wrote his first novel, *South Street,* as an undergraduate.

For his second novel, *The Chaneysville Incident,* Bradley drew upon legends he had heard as a child—of thirteen runaway slaves, who, when intercepted near Chaneysville in their flight to freedom, asked to be killed rather than sent back into slavery. When Bradley's mother, doing research on blacks in Bedford, came upon thirteen unmarked graves, the story "which all along had the power of myth, took on the force of fact." The book was nearly ten years in the writing, and Bradley was honored with the PEN/Faulkner Award for the best fiction of 1981. Today he teaches creative writing at Temple University. He has just completed a screenplay and is working, always, on his next novel.

STEVEN BRILL   Steven Brill is the founder and editor of *The American Lawyer,* a maverick legal monthly "about lawyers, not about the law." Anything but dull, the magazine is filled with inside stories, lively columns like Bar Talk, Big Deals, and Courtly Manners (which evaluates the performances of lawyers before the Supreme Court), and first-rate investigative journalism, some of the best written by Brill himself. For all the complaints by lawyers about the brashness of the magazine, some 175,000 of them read it every month. And the publication has been sued only three times—unsuccessfully.

Brill was born in New York and began his journalistic career two years prior to graduating from Yale law school in 1975 (he likes to point out that he never took the bar exam). Earlier, he had served as an assistant to New York mayor John Lindsay and had worked as a consultant to the Police Foundation in Washington. In the late 1970s he was a contributing editor of *Esquire* and wrote a column on legal affairs for the magazine. His book, *The Teamsters* (1978), was an ambitious effort to clarify the operation of a powerful and controversial union. A new book is now in the works, though Brill won't testify as to its contents.

TOM BUCKLEY   Tom Buckley was born in Chatham, New York. He never considered any career but journalism, and after graduating from Columbia University and spending two years in the Army, he went to work for *The New York Times.* By the time he resigned in 1982, he had spent twenty-nine years at the paper. He was an office boy, a copy editor, a critic, a columnist, a Vietnam correspondent, and, finally, a *Times Magazine* staff member. He has, he says, "earned the right to wear a trench coat."

Buckley wrote his first article for *Esquire* in 1965; it was about a coal mine cave-in ("the longest piece I ever wrote," he recalls). He did other stories for the magazine, on topics as diverse as transsexuals, ballistic submarines, Texas oilman H. L. Hunt, and a Vietnam fighter ace. Now he has written a book called *Violent Neighbors;* it's about Central America and the United States's traditional role there. Based primarily on a series of trips Buckley took to the region in 1981 and 1982, the book was published in 1984. Buckley lives in New York, and, he notes, "My idea of a skyscraper is still the Empire State Building, the Chrysler Building, the RCA Building—they haven't improved on those."

WILLIAM BUCKLEY JR.   When William Buckley was eight, he fired off a letter to the king of England demanding that Great Britain repay its war debt. The future "scourge of American liberalism" was born with a fierce determination. No sooner had he left college in 1950 than he wrote *God and Man at Yale,* enraging faculty and alumni with his indictment of liberal education. He spent a year in Mexico as a CIA agent, working under operative E. Howard Hunt. Then, in 1955, determined to "revitalize the conservative position," he launched the *National Review,* which he edits still.

Buckley is a founder of the New York Conservative party and ran for mayor on that ticket in 1965. (He got 13.4 percent of the vote.) His column, On the Right, runs today in some three hundred newspapers. And since 1966 he has hosted *Firing Line,* where his hypnotically facile vocabulary and unrelenting interrogation have made him a media celebrity. Lately he has channeled his literary energies into a series of spy thrillers, featuring Blackford Oakes, handsome Ivy Leaguer who battles international communism ("I don't like creepy protagonists," the author says). The newest Oakes adventure, *The Story of Henri Tod,* appeared in 1984. He is currently at work on another novel.

TRUMAN CAPOTE   Since 1948 and the appearance of *Other Voices, Other Rooms,* Truman Capote has been impossible to ignore: on the book's jacket was that notorious picture of the author reclining on a Victorian couch, his eyes leveled provocatively at the camera. He was twenty-three, a New Orleans country boy who came to the big city and seduced it with his precocious mastery. For more than a decade he delighted readers with elegantly fashioned tales that drew upon his own, at times eccentric, imagination—*The Grass Harp, Breakfast at Tiffany's, A Tree of Night, A Christmas Memory*—as well as essays (*Local Color, The Muses Are Heard*) and film scripts (*Beat the Devil, The Innocents*).

Then, combining his skills as novelist *and* journalist, he distilled a new literary genre—a kind of reporting that revealed reality to be more compelling than fiction. And in 1966, *In Cold Blood,* his mercilessly detailed account of a Kansas mass murder, established him as a major force in American writing. In the mid-1970s, chapters of his long-awaited *Answered Prayers,* thinly disguised tales of the socially elite, caused a sensation when they appeared in *Esquire.* He continues to work on any number of pieces, long and short, which will likely be incorporated in the still-awaited volume.

ALISTAIR COOKE   Fifty-one years ago, British-born Alistair Cooke came to this country to study theater. Once here, he traveled the length and breadth of the country and began, he says, "to take up what I felt was the real drama . . . America itself." In 1938 he commenced commenting on American affairs for the BBC. In time, through his broadcasts and, later, his newspaper dispatches, he became perhaps the premier journalistic liaison between the two countries—a presence once described as "a sort of kindly stepfather, who is intensely interested in his adopted offspring but is not about to nag."

In 1952 the vast American television audience came to know Cooke as host of the prestigious Sunday-night program *Omnibus,* which won five Emmys during its eight-year run. Twenty years later, his impressionistic and "unabashedly subjective" series *America* was awarded four Emmys. The book based on the series, *Alistair Cooke's America* (1973), was a best seller. Many a TV viewer knows him today as the urbane and witty host of PBS's *Masterpiece Theatre.* Cooke lives in New York, and there he records his fifteen-minute talk for the BBC, *Letter from America,* just as he has since 1946.

SARA DAVIDSON   Sara Davidson grew up in Los Angeles, in a world of surfboards, bongos, and trampolines. Until she was seventeen, she scarcely knew the rest of the world was any different. Studying at Berkeley, she watched the school change from a sleepy campus to the turbulent community where the first student uprisings of the 1960s took place. Later, as the New York correspondent for *The Boston Globe,* she covered stories as diverse as the shooting of Robert Kennedy and the inner workings of the Playboy Club. For *Esquire* she wrote about the foremothers of the women's liberation movement and about Ozzie Nelson and family. For other magazines, she covered counterculture, communes, radical activists, and rock groups.

Her first book, *Loose Change* (1977), a social history of the 1960s, was based on her own experiences and those of two women she had known at Berkeley. In *Real Property,* published three years later, the title story recounted life in Venice, California, on the brink of the 1980s. In the late 1970s she traveled widely in the Middle East and has drawn upon her experiences there, and in California, for her first novel, *Friends of the Opposite Sex,* which was published by Doubleday in 1984.

PETER DAVIS   At one time Peter Davis was best known for *Hearts and Minds,* his controversial feature-length film about Vietnam. What began with his research into the "Pentagon Papers" case soon outgrew the politics of the moment. "The film," Davis says, "is how I feel about the war." It won an Academy Award for best documentary in 1975. Movies were, in fact, part of the Davis birthright. He grew up in Hollywood in a screen-writing family. He studied at Harvard and made a name in New York as a writer and television producer. He co-authored the acclaimed television documentary *Hunger in America* and wrote and produced *The Selling of the Pentagon,* which, despite the wrath of Spiro Agnew, won numerous awards, including an Emmy in 1971.

When Davis, a full-time writer now, began *Hometown* (1982), he asked the Census Bureau where to go "to combine . . . social research with techniques of storytelling." The Bureau suggested Hamilton, Ohio. So, in much the same manner as anthropologists Robert and Helen Lynd researched *Middletown,* he lived on and off in Hamilton, taking down stories of ordinary people for a book that revealed the diverse drama of our daily lives. A new book is in the works.

PETER DRUCKER   Author of seventeen books on management and business—among the best known are *Practice of Management,* published in 1954 and still in print today; *Management: Tasks, Practices, Responsibilities* (1974); and *Managing in Turbulent Times* (1980)—Peter Drucker is widely regarded as America's (possibly the world's) foremost authority in his field. His work has been translated into as many as twenty languages and has sold millions of copies. From his earliest days as a financial editor in Germany (from which he emigrated in 1933) to the present, in his editorial writing for *The Wall Street Journal,* he has always been an outspoken master of management philosophy.

Today Drucker lives in southern California, where he is a professor of social science and management at Claremont Graduate School as well as a professor of Oriental art at the Claremont Colleges. In 1982 he set about speaking to an audience well beyond the business community with the publication of his first novel, *The Last of All Possible Worlds.* A second novel, *The Temptation to Do Good,* appeared in 1984. He is also at work on yet another book about management, this one called *The Problem of Success.*

STANLEY ELKIN   To readers of *Boswell; Criers and Kibitzers, Kibitzers and Criers; A Bad Man; The Dick Gibson Show; Searches and Seizures; The Franchiser; The Living End;* and, most recently, *George Mills,* Stanley Elkin is at once a bright satirist and a bleak absurdist. Few serious funny writers can match his brisk and busy imagination. So inspired are his improvisations on the English language that he was once asked to write dialogue for the computer that was to inseminate Julie Christie in the movie *Demon Seed.*

Elkin was raised in Chicago. His father traveled to the Midwest selling costume jewelry. (Elkin wears his father's twenty-five-year Coro jewelry company pin on a gold chain around his neck.) He was educated at the University of Illinois and joined the faculty of Washington University in St. Louis in 1960; he holds the Merle Kling Professorship in Modern Letters there today. Elkin has a bit of trouble getting around: some twenty years ago he suffered the first symptom of multiple sclerosis. "It's a dumb disease," he says. "It kills you by inches but you suffer by yards." His writing, nonetheless, goes on; he's at work on a new novel called *The Magic Kingdom.*

FRANCES FITZGERALD   With her first book, *Fire in the Lake,* a study of the devastating effects of American involvement in Vietnam, Frances FitzGerald won the Pulitzer Prize in 1973, a National Book Award, and the Bancroft Award for history. These achievements, as well as her reporting on Iran and on North Vietnam and Cuba and Jamaica, led *The New Yorker's* William Shawn to call her "one of the best nonfiction reporters of her generation." She likes to think of her work as that of an "amateur historian."

Growing up in New York, FitzGerald was initiated early into the world of politics and power: her mother, Marietta Tree, was a onetime United Nations ambassador; her father, a deputy director of the CIA. At Radcliffe she studied Middle Eastern history and flirted with the idea of being a novelist. In 1966 she went to Southeast Asia. There, she never fancied herself a war correspondent; but through prodigious research, she documented a cultural and historical background against which the war could be assessed. In her second book, *America Revised* (1979), she critiqued American history textbooks. In her recent writings she has focused on new forms of community in the United States—all of which will likely take shape as a book.

RICHARD FORD   Richard Ford was born in Jackson, Mississippi. His father was a traveling salesman, and his grandfather owned a hotel. Ford grew up in a demimonde of hotels, cafés, and train stations. His experiences there as well as later odd jobs and travels form much of the material of his fiction—a kind of "dirty realism" in which perplexed, restless characters on society's fringe often figure. Graduating from high school in 1962, the same year James Meredith entered Ole Miss, he decided, like many of his generation, to leave the South. At Washington University law school, he discovered he might make a good lawyer but "would never be a Supreme Court justice." When his law books were stolen, he took the theft as a sign and dropped out.

Since then Ford has lived in many places—California, Chicago, New Orleans, and in southern Mexico near Oaxaca, where he wrote much of *The Ultimate Good Luck.* In 1976 "In Desert Waters," an excerpt from *A Piece of My Heart,* ran in *Esquire* and marked his first appearance in a national magazine. Ford divides his time now between Montana, New York, and a house near Clarksdale in the Mississippi Delta. A new novel, *The Sportswriter,* is due to be published in 1985.

MARILYN FRENCH   The Women's Room, Marilyn French's enormously popular feminist novel of 1977, sold some three million copies in paperback and over three hundred thousand in hardcover. Three years later, the paperback rights to her second novel, *The Bleeding Heart,* were sold for nearly $2 million. For all this, however, she is a writer who moves easily from fiction to the history of ideas and back again. Her doctoral thesis at Harvard was a dissertation on Joyce, published in 1976; she also wrote a book on Shakespeare, in which she analyzed his perception of the differences in men's and women's experiences.

Her own life has included marriage and a son and a daughter, now adults. She has taught at Hofstra, Harvard, and Holy Cross, but with the success of her books, she concentrates now on her writing, dividing her time between homes in New York City and Florida. She has completed another book, *On Women, Men, and Morals*, about the historic limitations on the roles of both women and men, slated for publication in 1985; and, sure enough, she has written the first draft of a new novel, one that explores relationships between mothers and daughters.

JOHN KENNETH GALBRAITH   At Harvard, where John Kenneth Galbraith taught for over a quarter of a century, his lectures were often delivered to standing-room-only audiences. And his polished and witty books—among them, *The Affluent Society* (1958), *The New Industrial State* (1967), and *Economics and the Public Purpose* (1973)—are some of the most widely read analyses of the American economy. (He once explained his method: he writes four drafts, then on the fifth he "puts in that note of spontaneity everybody likes.")

Raised on a small farm in Ontario, he studied animal husbandry in Canada before going on to earn degrees from Berkeley. In the war years he administered the system of price controls; then in 1949, he returned to Harvard, where he had taught before the war. Galbraith had been involved in Democratic party politics for many years when, in 1961, President Kennedy named him ambassador to India, where he served during a couple of tense years. Reportedly, Kennedy regarded Galbraith as his best ambassadorial appointment. Out of that tour of duty came *Ambassador's Journal* (1969). His lively memoir, *A Life in Our Times*, appeared in 1981. His last book, *The Anatomy of Power*, arrived in October 1983.

BOB GREENE   Each month Bob Greene chronicles the times in his American Beat column in *Esquire*. Based in Chicago, he also writes a column for the *Tribune*, which is syndicated in some 150 newspapers. And he is seen as a contributing correspondent on ABC News' *Nightline*. Born in Ohio and educated at Northwestern, Greene was writing a newspaper column by the age of twenty-three. Three collections of his writings have been published; the last, *American Beat*, a miscellany of *Esquire* and *Tribune* columns, appeared in 1983. He is also the author of *Billion Dollar Baby* (1974), for which he had gone on a nationwide tour as a performing member of the Alice Cooper band.

The birth of a daughter in 1982 was the occasion for Greene's next book. Preparing for the birth of a child, he read all the right books, only to find that none had really prepared him for the experience of fatherhood. For Greene, it was an irresistible story. Without telling anyone, he sat down each night and kept an account of Amanda Sue's progress. The book, *Good Morning, Merry Sunshine: A Father's Journal of His Child's First Year*, was published in 1984.

DAVID HALBERSTAM   David Halberstam made his name at *The New York Times*, where, in 1964, his controversial coverage of the Vietnam War won the Pulitzer Prize. His career as a newspaperman began at Harvard, where he was managing editor of *The Crimson*. After graduation he went on to work in West Point, Mississippi, on the *Daily Times Leader* (circulation 4,000) a year after the Supreme Court decision to desegregate schools. Then, in 1960, he was hired by the Washington bureau of the *Times*.

Halberstam joined *Harper's* in 1967, and two profiles he did for the magazine—on Robert McNamara and McGeorge Bundy—led to his epic volume *The Best and the Brightest,* a best seller in 1972. He had already written two novels and *The Making of a Quagmire, The Unfinished Odyssey of Robert Kennedy,* and *Ho.* In *The Powers That Be* (1979) he told how the media have changed politics and society, a theme he traced in his histories of four press giants: *Time,* CBS, *The Washington Post,* and *The Los Angeles Times.* For *The Breaks of the Game* (1981), Halberstam, who loves basketball, spent a season with the Portland Trail Blazers. He is currently working on a new book on the automobile industry.

ELIZABETH HARDWICK   Elizabeth Hardwick is one of our most versatile and demanding literary voices. Cofounder and advisory editor of *The New York Review of Books,* winner of the George Jean Nathan Award for dramatic criticism, astute political reporter—she has imposed her high standards upon a wide range of literature. And yet, her main subject, the one to which she has returned again and again, for more than thirty-five years, is the "difference" of being a woman. It colored both of her early novels, *The Ghostly Lover* in 1945 and *The Simple Truth* in 1955, as well as many of her essays collected in *A View of My Own* (1962) and *Seduction and Betrayal: Women and Literature* (1974), which was nominated for a National Book Award.

Hardwick came to New York in 1939, soon after graduating from the University of Kentucky. Her aim, she has said, "was to be a New York Jewish intellectual." For a while she studied at Columbia but left to concentrate on her fiction. In 1949 she married poet Robert Lowell. Her novelistic memoir, *Sleepless Nights,* was published in 1979. Today she is a professor at the Columbia Graduate School of the Arts. Her last collection of essays, *Bartleby in Manhattan,* was published in 1983.

ROBERT HUGHES   Robert Hughes is the longtime art critic for *Time.* In 1980 he caused a stir in the art world with his audacious book *The Shock of the New,* in which he undertook nothing less than a reconsideration of modern art from 1880 to 1980. In it, and in the BBC series he wrote and narrated, he analyzed both the flowering and decline of modernism over the hundred-year span.

The sardonic Hughes comes from Sydney, Australia, where his father was a lawyer in a family firm. (The father was also a World War I fighter pilot who kept pieces of an aircraft in the garage.) Hughes studied architecture and dabbled in painting. When an exhibition of his paintings netted some seven thousand dollars, he left for London. There, he cheerfully concedes, he ran through his money like a man who had inherited a fortune and expected more to come. In 1966 he published a book on Australian art and in 1969 wrote another, *Heaven and Hell in Western Art.* After *Time* reviewed the book, an offer came from New York to become the magazine's art critic. Hughes, then a poorly paid free-lancer, took off at once. He is now completing *Chains,* a study of Australia's colonization by the British. A television series entitled *American Visions,* about American art and society, started production in 1984.

MURRAY KEMPTON   For more than thirty years, Murray Kempton has covered labor leaders, mobsters, politicians, Communists, Freedom Riders, and a dozen other subjects with a style and skill rare in daily journalism. Born and raised in Baltimore, he graduated from Johns Hopkins in 1939. In 1942 he signed on as a labor reporter at the *New York Post*, a leftist paper then. In the McCarthy era, he was one of the few journalists to defend the civil liberties of American Communists—"internal exiles," he called them. His first book, *Part of Our Time* (1955), was a study of the leftists of the 1930s. And when he covered the emerging civil rights struggle of the 1950s, he sent back dispatches of such economy and elegance that they were very nearly short stories. *America Comes of Middle Age* (1963) was a collection of columns from that time.

In 1963 Kempton moved to Washington to work at *The New Republic*, but he returned to New York and the daily press a year later. In 1973 he won a National Book Award for *The Briar Patch*, an examination of the "Panther 21" trial and the quality of American justice. He's still plying his trade, now for the Long Island paper *Newsday*, where his column appears four days a week.

KEN KESEY   In the summer of 1964 Ken Kesey drove from San Francisco to the New York World's Fair with his band of Merry Pranksters in a converted 1939 school bus painted to look like a Jackson Pollock canvas. Along the way they created "happenings" for startled passersby. In flaunting his cross-country antics, Kesey emerged as a leading voice in the discourse of the 1960s. He was born on a farm in Colorado, studied at the University of Oregon, and spent a year in a writing program at Stanford. In 1959 he volunteered—for seventy-five bucks a day—as a subject for experiments with hallucinogens at Veterans Hospital in Menlo Park. Afterward, he stayed on at the hospital and worked as a ward attendant. The hospital experience became the grist for his celebrated novel *One Flew Over the Cuckoo's Nest* (1962). *Sometimes a Great Notion*, a sprawling saga of a Northwest lumber dynasty, followed in 1964.

The Pranksters dispersed in 1969, and Kesey settled down on a farm in Pleasant Hill, Oregon. There he and his family raise cattle and sheep, and when the chores are done, he writes. A new novel, *Sailor's Song*, about a fishing village overrun by a Hollywood film company, is due out in 1985.

GEORGE LEONARD   In his writing George Leonard has dealt boldly and imaginatively with the changing aspects of modern life. In such books as *The Decline of the American Male* (1958), *Education and Ecstasy* (1968), *The Transformation* (1972), *The Ultimate Athlete* (1975), *The Silent Pulse* (1978), and *The End of Sex* (1983), he has examined the shifting relationships between men and women, people and sports—and "humankind" in general. For seventeen years Leonard served as an editor of *Look* magazine, and in that position he documented many of the social changes taking place in America. And not only did he report them, but as a vice-president of the Association for Humanistic Psychology, he frequently participated in them as well.

Today Leonard lives what he calls "a protean life" in Mill Valley, California: he writes and lectures, and two days a week he gives classes in aikido, the most demanding of the martial arts. And, inspired by aikido, he has written a manual with Dr. Joel Kirsch for teaching Leonard Energy Training (LET), an alternative way of dealing with everyday conflict and stress. In time, says Leonard, his LET courses will be offered all across the country.

Notes on the Contributors

DAVID McCLINTICK   *Indecent Exposure,* David McClintick's account of the crimes of David Begelman and the corporate battle for control of Columbia Pictu res, was the hottest property in Hollywood in the summer of 1982. Long before its pub lication, scores of pirated galley proofs circulated through the film and business communities. More than a riveting book of revelations, though, it was a sobering dist illation of the boardroom politics behind the making of motion pictures.

McClintick broke the Begelman story in 1977 in *The Wall Street Journal,* for which he worked for eleven years, most of them as a broad-gauge investigative rep orter. He was born in Kansas, educated at Harvard, and spent four years in Army Intel ligence. His previous book, *Stealing from the Rich,* was highly acclaimed, and he's now at work on a book about the Chase Manhattan Bank and the wielding of worldwide econ omic power. Interestingly, the writer is also the possessor of a Grammy award. Three years ago, McClintick, a longtime student of the Frank Sinatra phenomenon, contribu ted some five thousand words of liner notes for a new Sinatra album, *Trilo gy.* The album, it turned out, was nominated for six Grammys. It won one: Best Album Notes of 1980.

NORMAN MAILER   Author of twenty-seven bo oks; winner, twice, of the Pulitzer Prize, for *Armies of the Night* and *The Executioner's Song,* and of the National Book Award, for *Armies of the Night;* sometime actor (*Ragtime*); candidate for mayor of New York City (on a secessionist ticket); and veteran of countless controversies—Norm an Mailer has styled himself, with abundant good humor, as a legend. He started writin g at Harvard, where he took a degree in engineering in 1943. He served in the Philippi nes as an infantryman, and back in New York, he took fifteen months to finish his famou s work, *The Naked and the Dead.*

After an unhappy stint in Hollywood, Mailer settled in Greenwich Villa ge and helped found *The Village Voice,* for which he wrote columns expoun ding his philosophy of "Hip." *The Deer Park,* his pansexual novel set in Hollywo od, appeared in 1955. Out of the 1960s and 1970s came volumes of highly personalized reporting, on Vi etnam, on politics. For *Esquire* he reported on the 1960 Democratic c onvention, and in 1965, under the pressure of monthly deadlines, he wrote *An American Dream* in serial form for the magazine. His last novel, *Ancient Evenings,* is part of a trilogy of sorts he is planning for the future.

CHARLES L. MEE JR.   Charles Mee's book, *The Ohio Gang* (1981), was a breezy run through the presidency of Warren G. Harding, a subject that appealed to the writer because, he says, he saw in Harding a resemblance to the present officehol der. Mee calls himself "a writer with a strong interest in politics" rather than a historian, but he is best known for such popular histories as *Meeting at Potsdam* (19 75), a vivid account of the two weeks in 1945 when Truman, Churchill, and Stalin gathered to recons truct the world out of the ruins of the war. The book was later turned into a tele vision production. Among his other works are *White Robe, Black Robe* (1972), *Seizure* (1978), and *The End of Order: Versailles 1919* (1980). And scattered among the histori es are a number of children's books.

Mee grew up outside Chicago and was educated at Harvard. He came to New York in the 1960s, when some of his plays were produced off-Broadway. He joined the staff of

554

American Heritage, and in 1967 he was made editor of that company's *Horizon* magazine, where he stayed until 1975. In 1984 his latest book, *The Marshall Plan,* was published and his play *The Investigation of the Murder in El Salvador* was produced at the Mark Taper Forum in Los Angeles. He is currently at work on a narrative history of the Constitutional Convention of 1787.

ARTHUR MILLER   Arthur Miller grew up in Harlem and Brooklyn. As a young man in the early 1930s he worked in an auto-parts warehouse. Eventually, he went off to the University of Michigan, from which he emerged with a socialist fervor. In the war years Miller wrote radio dramas while working as a truck driver and steam fitter in the Brooklyn Navy Yard. Then, in 1947, his play *All My Sons* opened on Broadway to resounding acclaim.

Miller took only six weeks to write the enduring, Pulitzer Prize–winning *Death of a Salesman,* which many consider *the* great American play. His subsequent works *The Crucible* (1953) and *A View from the Bridge* (1955) also endure as modern classics. In 1956 he was cited by the House Un-American Activities Committee for refusing to "name names" of leftist associates. Further disquieting publicity accompanied his five-year marriage to Marilyn Monroe, and in those years he wrote only the screenplay *The Misfits.* His next play was the introspective *After the Fall* in 1964. He went on to write *Incident at Vichy, The Price,* and *The Creation of the World and Other Business.* In 1983 he directed a Chinese production of *Death of a Salesman* in China, and *Salesman in Beijing,* about that production, was published in 1984.

THOMAS B. MORGAN   For as far back as he can remember, Tom Morgan wanted to be a writer. More than thirty years ago, fresh out of Carleton College in Minnesota, he wrote letters to fifteen editors in New York; the only one who responded was Fred Birmingham, the managing editor of *Esquire.* Hired as an assistant editor, Morgan read "slush" (unsolicited short stories) and wrote captions and, later that year, saw his first story published in the magazine. Over the next years he wrote for numerous magazines and, since 1949, some forty articles and short stories for *Esquire.* Among them were pieces on Gary Cooper, John Wayne, Nelson Rockefeller, and Alf Landon. In May 1983 the magazine published "The Latinization of America" and in July 1984 his piece about what has happened to the journalists who covered the Vietnam War.

In 1969 Morgan became press secretary to New York mayor John Lindsay, and for a time in the mid-1970s he was editor of *The Village Voice.* He has published four books, including a novel, *This Blessed Shore.* He also founded *Politicks,* a provocative journal of political opinion, which he edited until it ceased publication in 1978. That year marked Morgan's return to writing and the start of a new novel, called *Snyder's Walk,* about journalism in the 60s.

VICTOR NAVASKY   Victor Navasky has often been in the thick of things as a political journalist, sometime campaign manager, and now editor of *The Nation.* He grew up in New York City and was educated at Swarthmore and Yale law school. At Yale, he was a founder of *Monocle,* a celebrated magazine of political satire. He went on to an editorial job at *The New York Times Magazine* and for a while wrote a column on publishing, In

Cold Print, for the *Times Sunday* Book Review section. In 1974 he served as campaign manager for Ramsey Clark when the former Attorney General made his initial run for the Senate.

Navasky's first book, *Kennedy Justice* (1971), an examination of the ways Robert Kennedy used his power as Attorney General, was nominated for a National Book Award. While writing that book he became interested in the role of informers in government cases, and as he warmed to his research he began to investigate the Hollywood informers of the 1950s. His work led to *Naming Names* (1980), a study of the Hollywood blacklist period. His latest book, written with Christopher Cerf, was published in 1984. Entitled *The Experts Speak: A Definitive Compendium of Authoritative Misinformation*, it is, according to Navasky, "a collection of false expertise in politics, science, the arts, economics, and philosophy."

GEOFFREY NORMAN Geoffrey Norman is a regular columnist for *Esquire*, and before that, he was an editor at the magazine. "I liked the magazine but was never much good at living in New York," he explains. "The only thing for it was to move to the country and write about it for the magazine. They bought it—and so far we've both been happy with the arrangement." Norman's column, formerly called Outdoors, is now The Environment. Of the change, he says, "It's more fun to fish for trout and write about it than to study water pollution and write about *that*, but I suppose if you care about the one, then you have an obligation to do the other. When you look into it a little, you discover that conservation is a lasting American theme going back to Thoreau and maybe further."

Norman grew up in the South, on the Gulf Coast of Florida and Alabama, where he still spends several months a year. He has a home in Vermont as well. His first novel, *Midnight Water*, was published in 1983. His *Esquire* story, "Armed and Dangerous," won an Edgar Award as the best mystery short story in 1979. He is currently working on another novel and planning a nonfiction book about the intracoastal waterway.

GEORGE PLIMPTON George Plimpton grew up in New York City, the son of a lawyer and diplomat. Looking for something to do upon graduation from Harvard and King's College, Cambridge, he became editor, in 1953, of *The Paris Review*, a newly launched literary quarterly. He is still editor of the magazine, which for thirty years has published fine fiction and developed the literary interview to its highest state of refinement.

Plimpton is probably best known for *Paper Lion* (1966), a funny, sometimes painful, account of his playing pro football with the Detroit Lions. The notion of challenging the champions—both for the fun of it and to reveal the psychology of the sport—actually began in 1959, when he went three rounds with Archie Moore. He proceeded to lose a set of tennis to Pancho Gonzalez and a rubber of bridge to Oswald Jacoby. And after an afternoon's pitching against the All Stars at Yankee Stadium, he wrote *Out of My League*, an account Hemingway called "the dark side of the moon of Walter Mitty." He is now at work on a book about his experiences playing hockey with the Boston Bruins. With Jean Stein he has edited *American Journey: The Times of Robert Kennedy* and *Edie: An American Biography*. He had two books out in 1984: one called *Fireworks*, about his great passion, and the other an oral biography he edited about Diana Vreeland called *D.V.*

DOTSON RADER   Dotson Rader was born in Evanston, Illinois, and grew up as an evangelist's son, on a holy roll around the country. He attended a Minnesota military school, then went on to Columbia University, in time to demonstrate against the war in Vietnam. Although the university expelled him for campus dissent in 1968, it had, by 1980, acquired his papers for its library. ("A great irony," observes Rader, who recalls lunching with Columbia president Michael Sovern and having "a good laugh about it.")

Rader is the author of *I Ain't Marchin' Anymore!*; *Government Inspected Meat*; *The Dream's on Me*; *Miracle*; and *Beau Monde.* He is now writing two books: one on Tennessee Williams and another on runaway children. (His highly acclaimed *Parade* series on runaways brought him before Congress to testify on their behalf.) In 1982 Rader converted to Catholicism. "The doctors thought I had a fatal disease," he explains, "and I started taking God very seriously. I had an inexplicable recovery. When you're about to check into the big hotel in the sky, you try to get on better terms with the management."

RICHARD REEVES   It has been suggested that Richard Reeves picked up his pessimism about politicos from the "fetid municipal air of Jersey City," where he grew up and where his father was a county judge. For a time he avoided politics altogether, studying at Hoboken's Stevens Institute of Technology and later working days as an engineer and nights as an editor of a local weekly. What he liked, he found, was newspapering; he became a reporter for the Newark *Evening News* and eventually landed at *The New York Times.* By the time he left in 1971, he had become chief political correspondent and along the way had won several awards for investigative journalism.

In his first book, *A Ford, Not a Lincoln* (1975), he recounted the first hundred days of the Ford administration. For *American Journey: Traveling with Tocqueville in Search of American Democracy* (1982), Reeves revisited America, asking questions and eliciting remarkable candor from modern Americans posted along the pathways the Frenchman had traveled. In 1984 his book about Pakistan was published. In the late 1970s he covered politics and media as an *Esquire* columnist; in 1980 he won an Emmy for *Lights, Cameras, Politics,* an ABC documentary. Today his syndicated newspaper column appears twice weekly.

TOM ROBBINS   Tom Robbins is one of the most articulate voices of the literate underground. His novels, crammed with metaphors, hyperboles, and puns, are notable for their wildly imaginative style and bizarre, meandering plots. Born in Blowing Rock, North Carolina, Robbins dropped out of more than one university and knocked about on several newspapers before launching his literary career in 1971 with *Another Roadside Attraction* (which details the clamor that ensues when the mummified body of Jesus Christ is discovered gracing a roadside zoo and hot-dog stand). Sales were scant, and Robbins's career might well have died aborning had not the book taken off when it appeared in paperback. Before long, the unsung writer had a huge cult following.

The fine madness continued in 1976 with *Even Cowgirls Get the Blues* and in 1980 with *Still Life with Woodpecker.* An excerpt from his last book was an *Esquire* cover story. Through it all, Robbins maintains that "for all my playfulness, I feel that I'm a philosophical writer. I believe in fun, but I'm very serious about the issues I deal with." He lives now in a coastal village north of Seattle and is working on what he describes as his "James Michener epic."

RON ROSENBAUM   Ron Rosenbaum grew up in what he's now proud to call a suburb—Bay Shore, Long Island—and once manned a doughnut-making machine at the local mall. Although he graduated from Yale, Phi Beta Kappa, with highest honors in English literature, he is best remembered there for composing a still-popular, obscene football cheer. Abandoning a Carnegie Fellowship, he became a staff writer for *The Village Voice* in time to get tear-gassed at mass antiwar demonstrations. He went on to cover presidential politics and the Nixon impeachment hearings as the *Voice*'s White House correspondent.

Rosenbaum began writing for *Esquire* in 1971 with pieces on a shadowy undercover agent known as "Tommy the Traveler" and on the "phone phreak" underground. He specialized in what he calls "strange deaths and unsolved mysteries," among them the tales of Sarah Miles, Burt Reynolds, a dead body in Gila Bend, Arizona, and the shocking double suicide of identical-twin gynecologists in New York City. For a time, he edited *More,* the journalism review, and based on this experience wrote a satirical novel, *Murder at Elaine's.* He is now at work on a second novel about what he cryptically calls "the most perplexing psychological mystery of the century."

JAMES SALTER   James Salter grew up in New York City. His father was a graduate of the U.S. Military Academy—first in his class. He resigned his commission "but not his glory," recalls Salter, who followed in his father's footsteps and enrolled at West Point. For ten years he served in the Air Force. He wrote when and how he could. And in 1957, when his first book, *The Hunter,* was accepted for publication, Salter left the service. A second novel, *The Arm of Flesh,* appeared and "vanished without a trace." When *A Sport and a Pastime* was published in 1967—"one of the most murmurously erotic novels ever written," reported James Wolcott in *Esquire*—it was, the writer says, "the real beginning of my career."

In the late 1960s Salter lived in France and wrote several movie scripts—among them, *Downhill Racer.* In 1975 the sensuous, memorable *Light Years* appeared, and in 1979 another novel, *Solo Faces,* was published. Today Salter lives in Bridgehampton, Long Island. He continues to write film scripts, and his stories are seen in various magazines, including *Esquire,* where the haunting "Foreign Shores" ran in September 1983. A collection of his stories is due to be published in 1985.

ARTHUR M. SCHLESINGER JR.   Arthur Schlesinger is the son and grandson of distinguished historians. No sooner had young Schlesinger left Harvard, where his father taught, than he began his own historical study, *The Age of Jackson,* for which he would win the Pulitzer Prize in 1946. That year he became an associate professor in Harvard's history department, a considerable plum for a twenty-nine-year-old scholar. In 1947 he helped found Americans for Democratic Action, and with the publication, in 1949, of *The Vital Center,* he emerged as a leading exponent of Democratic liberalism.

In the 1950s Schlesinger completed three volumes of *The Age of Roosevelt* and acted as adviser to several presidential aspirants. Then, in 1961, tired of "being upstairs writing the speeches while the political decisions were being taken elsewhere," he joined the White House circle as a special assistant. A *Thousand Days,* his memoir of the Kennedy tenure, won for Schlesinger a second Pulitzer Prize, as well as a National Book Award. *The Imperial Presidency* followed in 1973, and *Robert Kennedy and His Times* in 1978. Today he teaches at the City University of New York, as he has since 1966, and has resumed work on the fourth volume of *The Age of Roosevelt.*

IRWIN SHAW   Irwin Shaw wrote five years ago in introducing his book, *Irwin Shaw Short Stories: Five Decades,* that he had "written stories in Brooklyn . . . Connecticut, Cario, Algiers, London, Paris, Rome, the Basque country, on ships, in the Alps, in the Mojave Desert, and bits and pieces on transcontinental trains." In nearly a half century of writing, he created, prodigally, a crowded gallery of memorable characters. Among the books, many of them filmed, are *The Young Lions; Two Weeks in Another Town; Voices of a Summer Day; Rich Man, Poor Man; Evening in Byzantium; Beggarman, Thief;* and *Acceptable Losses.*

Writing professionally from the time he left Brooklyn College, Shaw came to public attention in 1935 with a play, *Bury the Dead,* which had a successful run on Broadway. Over a dozen of his stories were published in *Esquire,* beginning in 1939. One of them, "The Eighty Yard Run," endures as a classic. His 1969 *Esquire* piece, "Muhammad Ali and the Little People," in which he championed the boxer's cause, is credited to many with helping Ali get back into the ring. Shaw lived in Europe since 1951, but he often visited the United States, where he summered in Southampton. He died in 1984, five months after the original publication of this work.

WILFRID SHEED   Wilfrid Sheed was born in London, the son of writers Frank Sheed and Maisie Ward, founders of the avant-garde Catholic publishing house, Sheed & Ward. When he was nine, the family moved to Torresdale, Pennsylvania. There young Sheed became "perhaps the outstanding solitary baseball player" of his generation, until, at fourteen, an attack of polio cut short that unpromising career. Eventually, he took a degree in history at Oxford and settled in Greenwich Village to write and, in time, turn out some of the most urbane and polished prose on either side of the Atlantic. Twice nominated for the National Book Award, for *Office Politics* and *People Will Always Be Kind,* he has also written A *Middle Class Education, Max Jamison,* and *Transatlantic Blues.*

His fiction aside, Sheed is that rare critic and observer who has the ability to write with equal authority on serious art and popular culture. Collections of his essays and reviews were published as *The Morning After* and *The Good Word and Other Words.* In the late 1960s his film column ran in *Esquire.* His last book, in 1982, was a biography of Clare Boothe Luce. Today Sheed lives in Sag Harbor, New York, and is at work on a memoir of his parents to be published in 1985.

Notes on the Contributors

ADAM SMITH   It has been said of Adam Smith that he writes about money as if it were love or art or religion—not business. Indeed, his excursions through the financial thicket—*The Money Game* in 1968, *Supermoney* in 1972, and *Paper Money* in 1981—have met with extraordinary success. And when he turned from money to the human psyche in *Powers of Mind* (1975), he led readers into the shady realms of consciousness expansion with the same authority.

"Adam Smith" is in fact George J. W. Goodman, the national affairs editor of *Esquire*. He was born in St. Louis, and studied at Harvard and Oxford. When he was told that the Ph.D. thesis he planned on political economy was "too contemporary for Oxford," he wrote a novel instead. Later, he wrote three more novels, then went to work on Wall Street as a securities analyst and fund manager. Among second-graders, he is known as the author of *Bascombe, the Fastest Hound Alive*. He began using his pseudonym at *New York* magazine in 1966 when he was writing about the workings of Wall Street and wished to ensure his continued welcome in the financial district. Today he sits on corporate boards, and in his Unconventional Wisdom column in *Esquire* he illuminates the world's worries with clarity and wit.

RONALD STEEL   In his last book, *Walter Lippmann and the American Century* (1980), Ronald Steel traced the career of one of America's most influential twentieth-century journalists. The book, some ten years in preparation, was a prodigy of research. Steel had access to Lippmann's huge collection of private papers, and from the author's careful presentation of material came a book rich in personal, political, and historical detail.

Even before he wrote the Lippmann biography, Steel was well known as a scholar of American politics and foreign policy. An earlier work, *Pax Americana* (1967), was extolled by Henry Steele Commager as "the most ardent and, to my mind, the most persuasive critique of American foreign policy over the last twenty years. . . ." Born in Illinois, he graduated from Northwestern and studied political economy at Harvard. He spent some time in the foreign service but then dropped out. (He was, very briefly, our vice-consul in Cyprus.) While living in London in the mid-1960s, he was contributing skillful pieces to *Commonweal*, *The New Leader*, *Commentary*, and *The New York Review of Books*. He has since taught at the University of Texas, Rutgers, Wellesley, Yale, UCLA, Dartmouth, and most recently at Princeton.

HARRY STEIN   When Harry Stein resigned in 1982 as *Esquire*'s Ethics columnist, a group of fans designed a T-shirt that read: BUT WHAT WOULD HARRY STEIN DO? There are, he discovered in doing the column, a lot of "closet ethical people." Stein grew up in New Rochelle, New York. His father was a writer, so writing always seemed a reasonable pursuit. At Pomona College, Stein, a "lettered troublemaker," and some fellow students took over a near-defunct school paper and turned it into a radical tabloid. They achieved a certain notoriety when, in the interest of free speech, they invited the Communist party to recruit on campus. (They were relieved of the paper.)

Stein went on to the Columbia school of journalism and later wrote for several publications. A memorable piece on Tiny Tim for *New Times*, where for a time he was an editor, led to a book on the performer. For *Esquire* he wrote about Harry Ritz, Mason Reese, Reggie Jackson. In 1976, in Paris, he helped found an English-language paper called *The Paris Metro*. It was a considerable succès d'estime during the two and a half years it was published, and Stein himself contributed a humor column. In Paris he also began a novel, *Hoopla*, which was published in 1983. He is now at work on another novel.

WILLIAM STYRON   William Styron was brought up in Virginia's Tidewater region at "almost the last moment when it was possible to get, firsthand, a sense of . . . old-fashioned Southern life. . . ." His grandmother used to tell him stories about the slaves she had owned. Styron started to write at Duke University, where he took classes as a Marine and received a degree in 1947. At twenty-six, he finished *Lie Down in Darkness*, hailed as "one of the finest first novels of its generation." It was followed by *The Long March* and, later, *Set This House on Fire*. Styron then retreated into literary silence, brooding over a subject that had haunted him since childhood: the 1831 slave revolt led by Nat Turner.

Working with transcripts of testimony given by Turner and encouraged by James Baldwin, who came to live with the Styrons for a time, the writer completed his famous "meditation on history." *The Confessions of Nat Turner* won the Pulitzer Prize in 1968—but not without a storm of controversy over the literary, historical, and social implications of a white man speaking in a black man's voice. Styron wrote about human suffering in a more contemporary setting—post–World War II Brooklyn—in *Sophie's Choice*. A new work of fiction is in the offing.

LEWIS THOMAS   Dr. Lewis Thomas's first batch of essays, *The Lives of a Cell*, was an amazing and unlikely success: a biology book that became a best seller. The book won a National Book Award in 1975—but not in the category of science; it was honored as a contribution in arts and letters. And it seduced thousands of nonscientists into reading about bacteria, mitochondria, and life itself. *The Medusa and the Snail*, his second collection, appeared five years later, followed by *The Youngest Science* and *Late Night Thoughts on Listening to Mahler's Ninth Symphony* in 1983.

The author was, and still is, a biologist and a researcher; he is also a former president of New York City's Memorial Sloan-Kettering Cancer Center. Some of the doctor's earliest memories are of house calls with his father in the family Franklin. At Princeton, he was temporarily deflected from medicine to poetry—Thomas is also a published poet—but he went on to Harvard medical school. During years spent as an "academic tramp" he moved away from the practice of medicine toward research and teaching, rising through the various posts to become dean of New York University and then of the Yale medical schools. In 1973 he took charge of the Sloan-Kettering complex. In 1981 he became chancellor and this year was appointed president emeritus. Today Dr. Thomas writes a regular column for *Discover* magazine.

JOHN UPDIKE   John Updike left his rural home in Shillington, Pennsylvania, for Harvard, Oxford, and *The New Yorker*, where he went to work at twenty-three and where his verbal dexterity caused a sensation. In 1957 he left *The New Yorker* and New York and moved to New England; but hardly an issue has come out since without an essay, poem, or story by this gifted and versatile writer. A prolific and dedicated craftsman, Updike is best known for his subtle and highly detailed novels, particularly *The Centaur*, which won a National Book Award in 1964, and the "Rabbit" books: *Rabbit, Run*; *Rabbit Redux*; and *Rabbit Is Rich,* which won the Pulitzer Prize in 1982.

He has given us swatches of many other lives as well: in *Couples* he examined the consequences of sin in a post-Fall Eden; in *Bech: A Book* and *Bech Is Back* he projected his own literary concerns; and in *The Coup* he expanded his fictional territory to include a beleaguered black dictator in the imaginary land of Kush. The writing continues in Beverly Farms, Massachusetts, in a huge white house overlooking the Atlantic. *Hugging the Shore,* a collection of essays, literary criticism, and miscellanea, won the National Book Critics Circle Award for criticism in 1983. *The Witches of Eastwick,* a novel, was published in 1984; it is his twenty-eighth volume.

GORE VIDAL   Gore Vidal was born in West Point, New York, at the U.S. Military Academy, where his father was an instructor of aeronautics. (The youngster, it is said, could pilot a plane, unassisted, at ten.) After his parents divorced, he spent a good deal of time with his grandfather, the blind Senator Gore of Oklahoma, whom he guided around Washington and read to from the *Congressional Record.* Vidal first attracted public attention in 1946, at the age of twenty, with his precocious first novel, *Williwaw.* He then went on to write a handful of promising novels, a number of first-rate television plays, two stage hits—*Visit to a Small Planet* (1957) and *The Best Man* (1960)—and a good many controversial literary essays.

In 1960 Vidal ran for Congress as a Democrat-Liberal in a conservative New York district. Although defeated, he gave the Republican incumbent a much closer race than expected. In the early 1960s he wrote political columns for *Esquire,* and a collection of his political journalism was published as *Rocking the Boat. Julian,* his first novel in ten years, appeared in 1964, followed by the darkly humorous *Myra Breckenridge,* then *Burr, Myron, 1876, Kalki, Creation, Duluth,* and most recently, *Lincoln,* published in 1984.

KURT VONNEGUT JR.   Readers of *Player Piano; The Sirens of Titan; Mother Night; Cat's Cradle; God Bless You, Mr. Rosewater; Slaughterhouse-Five; Breakfast of Champions; Slapstick; Jailbird;* or *Deadeye Dick* know that Kurt Vonnegut's great gift is the ability to translate the most-absurd human follies into madly comic fiction. A pacifist long before it was fashionable, he was a cult figure in the 1950s—at a time when he was dismissed by "serious" critics as a slick writer of science fiction. Not until the 1963 publication of *Cat's Cradle* did he move into the realm of critical acceptance.

Vonnegut traces his "youth-minded notions" to his midwestern parents and his scientific bent to his father, who insisted that young Kurt learn "something useful," which turned out to be biochemistry. He was inducted into the Army in 1942, then returned to college after the war, only to leave for a stint as a P.R. man for General Electric; his first book, *Player Piano* (1952), was a savage satire on his experience there. In the war he was captured by the Germans and survived the fire bombing of Dresden quartered in a underground meat locker; the surrealist *Slaughterhouse-Five* (1969) was an exorcism of that haunting memory. It has been his most popular work.

TOM WICKER   Twice a week Tom Wicker writes the In the Nation column in *The New York Times* and has done so since 1965. Wicker was born in Hamlet, North Carolina, and attended the University of North Carolina. He learned his trade working at a number of papers in his home state. Then, in 1957, the *Winston-Salem Journal* sent him to cover the nation's capital. He moved on to *The Tennessean* in Nashville, and in 1960 he signed on at the *Times*. There his by-line soon became familiar as he covered the White House, Congress, and the national political scene. In 1964 he became the *Times's* Washington bureau chief.

Wicker's best-known book is *A Time to Die* (1975), an unforgettable account of the 1971 Attica prison rebellion. A remarkable story in itself, it was all the more remarkable because Wicker was a mediator in the uprising and as a result was forced to confront the slaughter there. An excerpt from the book, "The Men in D Yard," was an *Esquire* cover story. Wicker is also the author of *Kennedy Without Tears* (1964), *JFK & LBJ* (1968), and *On Press* (1978), as well as seven novels. His eighth novel, on the American Civil War, *Unto This Hour*, was published in 1984.

GARRY WILLS   By his own account, Garry Wills led a sheltered life until 1967, when he was denied tenure at Johns Hopkins because his writing for the *National Review* and the *National Catholic Reporter* was thought to be an "unseemly diversion of academic energy." Then he was offered a job as a contributing editor of *Esquire*. With that, he went from being a classicist who wanted to write journalism to a journalist moonlighting in the classics. To each job he brings a gift for lucidity and wit and an education that includes five years in Jesuit seminaries and a classics Ph.D. from Yale.

Much of what Wills wrote for *Esquire* in those years—on Jack Ruby, on race relations in America, on the Catholic Church—went into *Jack Ruby, The Second Civil War*, and *Bare Ruined Choirs*. But he is best known for his incisive political commentaries, especially as they appear in *Nixon Agonistes* (1970); *Inventing America* (1978), his revisionist study of Jefferson and the Declaration of Independence, which won a National Book Critics Circle Award; and *The Kennedy Imprisonment* (1982), a demystification of the Camelot legend. He is now a professor at Northwestern. A new book, *Cincinnatus*, on George Washington, was published in 1984.

TOM WOLFE   Tom Wolfe grew up in Richmond, Virginia. His father was an agronomist and editor of *The Southern Planter*, a farm journal of the time. When Wolfe was twenty-one, he tried out as a pitcher for the New York Giants; failing, he settled instead for a Ph.D. in American studies at Yale. At *The Washington Post* and then at the *New York Herald Tribune*, he began to display the hyperbolic style and sheer irreverence that would make him one of our foremost and wittiest contemporary journalists.

In 1963 Wolfe went to California to write about customized cars for *Esquire*. Months later he returned with plenty of notes but no idea how to pull the story together. "Okay, just type out your notes and send them over," managing editor Byron Dobell told him; the rough memo ran as it was ("The Kandy-Kolored Tangerine-Flake Streamline Baby"). In the next years he poured out a mixed-media word-show of articles, dissecting pop movements and summing up entire eras and phenomena with catchphrases—radical chic, the me decade, the right stuff—that are now a part of the language. The writing goes on: *The Painted Word, From Bauhaus to Our House*. And a new book about New York is in the works, called, for now, *The City of Ambition*.